Oxford Primary Thesaurus

Chief Editor: Susan Rennie

OXFORD
UNIVERSITY PRESS

OXFORD
UNIVERSITY PRESS

Great Clarendon Street, Oxford, OX2 6DP
Oxford University Press is a department of the University of Oxford.
It furthers the University's objective of excellence in research,
scholarship, and education by publishing worldwide. Oxford is a
registered trade mark of Oxford University Press in the UK and in
certain other countries

First published 1993
Second edition 1998
Revised second edition 2002
Third edition 2005
Fourth edition 2007
Fifth illustrated edition 2012
Sixth edition 2018
Based on *Oxford Primary Thesaurus* 2024 edition

British Library Cataloguing in Publication Data

Data available

ISBN: 978-1-38-205157-6

10 9 8 7 6 5 4 3 2 1

Printed in China

MIX
Paper | Supporting
responsible forestry
FSC
www.fsc.org
FSC™ C110497

Oxford Corpus

You can trust this book
to be up to date, relevant
and engaging because
it is powered by the
Oxford Corpus, a unique
living database of children's
and adults' language.

For school: Discover eBooks,
inspirational resources,
advice and support.

For home: Helping your
child's learning with free eBooks,
essential tips and fun activities.

www.oxfordowl.co.uk

Contents

Preface

The **Oxford Primary Thesaurus** has been specially written for primary school children aged 8+. It is designed to address school and curriculum needs and has been checked by teachers. It is also designed to complement the **Oxford Primary Dictionary** which is aimed at the same age range.

A special feature of this edition are the literary quotations that show how words in the thesaurus have been used by children's authors. There is also a special **Become a Word Explorer** section at the back of the thesaurus. This includes advice on using synonyms and other types of language, and tips on how to make writing more varied and colourful through the use of a thesaurus. It also contains content on punctuation and grammar.

How to use your thesaurus

word class
tells you what type of word it is, for example *NOUN*, *VERB*, *ADJECTIVE* or *ADVERB*

guide words
show the first and last word on a page

headword
is big and bold; it is the word you look up and is in alphabetical order

numbered sense
if a word has more than one meaning, they are numbered

example sentence
shows you how you might use a word; each meaning of a word has a separate example

label
tells you that certain synonyms are only for *informal* or *formal* use

synonyms
words that mean the same, or nearly the same, as the headword

OPPOSITE
words that are opposite in meaning to the headword; they are also called antonyms

---

level to lift

A B C D E F G H I J K L M N O P Q R S T U V W X Y Z

level VERB
❶ *Dad levelled the garden to make a lawn.*
• even out, flatten, smooth
❷ *A serious earthquake levelled the town.*
• knock down, demolish, destroy, devastate

level NOUN
❶ *The water had reached a high level.*
• height
❷ *The lift takes you up to the sixth level.*
• floor, storey, tier
❸ *What level have you reached in judo?*
• grade, standard, stage, rank, degree

lever VERB
Slowly, I levered open the lid of the chest.
• prise, wrench, force

liable ADJECTIVE
❶ *You're liable to make mistakes when you're tired.*
• likely, inclined, disposed, prone, ready
OPPOSITE unlikely
❷ *If you break anything, you'll be liable for the cost.*
• responsible, answerable, accountable

liberal ADJECTIVE
❶ *We each got a liberal helping of ice cream.*
• generous, ample, plentiful, lavish, abundant, copious, bountiful
OPPOSITES meagre, miserly
❷ *She has a liberal attitude towards most things.*
• broad-minded, easy-going, lenient, tolerant, permissive
OPPOSITE strict

liberate VERB
The prisoners were liberated at the end of the war.
• free, release, set free, emancipate, discharge, let go, set loose
OPPOSITE imprison

liberty NOUN
❶ *The animals have liberty to wander around the park.*
• freedom, independence
❷ *The king granted the prisoners their liberty.*
• liberation, release, emancipation

licence NOUN
He has a licence to practise as a doctor.
• permit, certificate, authorization, warrant

license VERB
Are you licensed to drive this vehicle?
• permit, allow, authorize, entitle

lid NOUN
Can you help me get the lid off this jar?
• cap, cover, covering, top

lie VERB lies, lying, lay, lain
❶ *Jamal was lying on his bed, reading.*
• recline, stretch out, lounge, sprawl, rest
To lie face down is to be **prone**.
To lie face upwards is to be **supine**.
❷ *The castle lies in a valley.*
• be sited, be situated, be located, be found

lie VERB lies, lying, lied
I don't trust them—I think they're lying.
• deceive someone, bluff
(informal) fib

lie NOUN
He accused the newspaper of printing lies.
• deceit, falsehood, dishonesty
(informal) fib
OPPOSITE truth

life NOUN
❶ *My hamster, Fluffy, leads a very easy life.*
• existence, being, way of life
❷ *Our lives depended on finding water.*
• survival
❸ *You seem to be full of life today!*
• energy, liveliness, vigour, vitality, spirit, sprightliness, animation
❹ *I'm reading a life of Elvis Presley.*
• life story, autobiography, biography

lift VERB
❶ *The removal team lifted the piano carefully.*
• pick up, raise, elevate, pull up, hoist
❷ *The plane lifted off the ground.*
• rise, ascend, soar

lift NOUN
Take the lift to the top floor.
*A North American word is **elevator**.*

special synonyms
words that are similar in meaning to the headword, but can only be used in special cases

Word web
gives words that are related to the headword and are useful for project work and story writing

phrase
a small arrow (➤) marks phrases and idioms, take a look at some entries and see if you can spot them

light to like

alphabet
on every page to help you find your way around the thesaurus easily

light *NOUN*

WORD WEB
SOME KINDS OF NATURAL LIGHT:
- daylight, moonlight, starlight, sunlight, twilight

SOURCES OF ARTIFICIAL LIGHT:
- bulb, candle, chandelier, floodlight, fluorescent lamp, headlamp or headlight, lamp, lantern, laser, neon light, searchlight, spotlight, street light, torch

VARIOUS FORMS OF LIGHT:
- beam, flash, flicker, glow, halo, lustre, radiance, ray, reflection, shaft

WRITING TIPS
You can use these words to describe light.

TO DESCRIBE HOW LIGHT APPEARS:
- bright, brilliant, harsh, luminous, lustrous, strong, diffused, dim, muted, soft, warm

LIGHT MAY:
- beam, blaze, dazzle, flash, flicker, glare, gleam, glimmer, glint, glisten, glitter, glow, shimmer, shine, sparkle, twinkle
In the still woods, the only movements were bars of sunlight glinting like green glass through the leafy canopy.—PAX, Sara Pennypacker

light *ADJECTIVE*
❶ The artist worked in a **light** and airy studio.
- bright, well-lit, illuminated
OPPOSITES dim, gloomy
❷ She was wearing **light** blue jeans.
- pale
OPPOSITE dark
❸ The parcel looks big, but it is quite **light**.
- lightweight, portable, weightless, slight
A common simile is as **light** as a feather.
OPPOSITE heavy

❹ A **light** wind rippled the surface of the water.
- gentle, faint, slight
OPPOSITE strong
❺ We had a **light** meal before we went out.
- small, modest, simple, insubstantial
OPPOSITES heavy, substantial
❻ I brought a book for some **light** reading.
- undemanding, entertaining, lightweight
OPPOSITE serious

light *VERB* lights, lighting, lit or lighted
❶ We lit the candles on my birthday cake.
- ignite, kindle, set alight, set fire to, switch on
OPPOSITE extinguish
❷ The fireworks lit the sky.
- light up, brighten, illuminate, shed light on, shine on
OPPOSITE darken

like *VERB*

OVERUSED WORD
Try to vary the words you use for like. Here are some other words you could use.

TO LIKE A PERSON OR ANIMAL:
- be fond of, be attached to, care for, love, adore, cherish, esteem, admire, hold dear *(informal)* have a soft spot for
Lauren is very attached to her new puppy.

TO LIKE SOMETHING OR LIKE DOING SOMETHING:
- be keen on, be partial to, be interested in, delight in, enjoy, appreciate, prefer, relish
I'm not very keen on broccoli.
What sort of films do you enjoy?
OPPOSITE dislike

like *PREPOSITION*
The witch's hand looked **like** a knobbly tree.
- similar to, the same as, resembling, identical to
OPPOSITE unlike

243

a b c d e f g h i j k **l** m n o p q r s t u v w x y z

Writing tips help you write creatively by suggesting ways to describe how things look, move or sound

highlighted letter shows you which letter you are on

Overused word offers more interesting alternatives for common words such as big, bit, happy, nice and sad

cross reference points you to another headword where you will find even more words, look for see or see also at the end of some entries

literary quotation shows you how an author has used a word in a story or poem

WHICH WORD?
notes words that are easily confusable with the headwords, try looking for them in your thesaurus

Introduction

What is a thesaurus for?

Here are three good reasons to use your thesaurus:

- **to find a more interesting word**
  What words can you use besides *kick* for striking a football?
  Look up **kick** and **ball** to find some other verbs to describe footwork.

- **to find the right word**
  What do you call the home of a fox? Is a young otter known as a *cub*
  or a *pup*? Look up **animal** to find the answers.

- **to give you ideas for writing**
  Imagine you are describing a giant's castle. Look up **castle** for ideas for
  the setting, then **big** to find adjectives to describe how *colossal* and
  mammoth everything is in a giant's world.

What is the difference between a thesaurus and a dictionary?

A **dictionary** tells you what a word means, whereas a **thesaurus** tells you
what other words have the same meaning, or are related to the word
in some way. A dictionary gives you a *definition* of a word; a **thesaurus**
gives you *synonyms* of a word.

For example, if you look up **clothes** in a dictionary, it will tell you that
clothes are things that you wear. But a thesaurus will give you some
other words for clothes (**garments, dress, attire**) and will list particular
types of clothes (**jeans, kilt, pyjamas**).

You often use a dictionary to check the meaning of something you have
read or heard. You use a thesaurus to find ways to write or say something
yourself.

Language notes

Special notes at the end of some entries highlight points about language.

OPPOSITE and **OPPOSITES** notes list
words that mean the opposite.

WHICH WORD? notes explain the
difference between similar words that
can be easily confused with each other.

Special panels

Throughout this thesaurus, you will see special tinted boxes which give extra help on finding and using words. There are three types of panel, each marked by a special symbol:

Overused words   Writing tips   Word webs

 ## OVERUSED WORD

The **Overused word** panels offer more interesting alternatives for common words like **big**, **happy**, **nice** and **sad**. If you use these words too often, your writing will seem dull and boring.

Here is a complete list of all the **overused word panels** in this thesaurus:

bad	good	look	sad
beautiful	happy	lovely	say
big	hard	move	small
bit	like	nice	strong
eat	little	old	walk

 ## WRITING TIPS

Writing tips can help you to create more colourful descriptions by suggesting ways to describe how people, things or animals look, move or sound. Other **writing tips** offer suggestions for creating dialogue or for using idioms. Here is a list of all the **writing tips** in this thesaurus:

afraid	building	hair	sound
angry	clothes	light	surprised
animal	colour	nose	tooth
ball	exclamation	planet	un–
bell	eye	river	voice
bird	face	sea	water
boat	feel	sky	weather
body	food	smell	writing

WORD WEBS

As well as exploring *alternative* words, you can explore *related* words. The **Word web** panels give lists of words related to a topic word, such as **animal** or **castle**. These can be useful for both project work and for story writing.

accommodation	chess	fabric
aircraft	church	fairy
alien	clothes	family
amphibian	coin	farm
animal	colour	fighter
anniversary	communication	figure of speech
armed forces	competition	fish
armour	computer	flower
art	cook	food
artist	cricket	football
astronaut	criminal	fossil
athletics	crockery	fruit
bear	cutlery	furniture
bee	dance	game
bicycle	day	ghost
bird	desert	glasses
blue	detective	green
boat	dinosaur	group
body	disaster	hair
bone	dog	hat
book	dragon	herb
brown	drawing	horse
building	drink	hospital
car	drum	house
card	education	ice
castle	entertainer	illness
cat	explorer	injury
cave	expression	insect
cheese	eye	island

jewel	planet	song
jewellery	plant	sound
job	poem	space
jungle	polar	spice
kitchen	politics	sport
knife	pottery	spy
knight	poultry	story
light	prehistoric	superhero
magic	punctuation	sweet
mathematics	pyramid	swim
meal	railway	sword
measurement	red	tennis
meat	religion	tent
medicine	reptile	theatre
metal	restaurant	time
moon	road	tool
mountain	robot	tooth
museum	rock	toy
music	room	transport
myth	royalty	travel
needlework	ruler	tree
nut	school	vegetable
ocean	science	vehicle
paint	sea	water
paper	seashore	weapon
park	seaside	weather
party	shape	wedding
pasta	shellfish	white
pattern	shoe	wood
pet	shop	writing
photograph	sing	yellow
pirate	snake	zodiac

Aa

abandon VERB
❶ The robbers **abandoned** the stolen car.
• leave, desert, forsake, leave behind, strand
(informal) dump, ditch
❷ We **abandoned** our picnic because of
the rain.
• cancel, give up, scrap, drop, abort, discard

abduct VERB
The pirates **abducted** two members of
the crew.
• kidnap

ability NOUN
Skin has a natural **ability** to heal itself.
• capability, competence, aptitude, talent,
expertise, skill

able ADJECTIVE
❶ Will you be **able** to come to my party?
• allowed, permitted, free, willing
OPPOSITE unable
❷ Penguins are very **able** swimmers.
• competent, capable, accomplished, expert,
skilful, proficient, talented, gifted
OPPOSITE incompetent

abnormal ADJECTIVE
It's **abnormal** to have snow in June.
• unusual, exceptional, extraordinary, peculiar,
odd, strange, weird, bizarre, unnatural, freak
OPPOSITE normal

abolish VERB
I wish someone would **abolish** homework!
• get rid of, do away with, put an end to,
eliminate
OPPOSITE create

about PREPOSITION
There are **about** two hundred pupils in the school.
• approximately, roughly, close to, around

➤ **to be about something**
The film is **about** a dog called Scruff.
• concern, deal with, involve

above PREPOSITION
The drone flew **above** the houses.
• over, higher than

abroad ADVERB
We're planning to go **abroad** next summer.
• overseas, to a foreign country

abrupt ADJECTIVE
❶ The book came to a very **abrupt** end.
• sudden, hurried, hasty, quick, unexpected
OPPOSITE gradual
❷ The sales assistant had a very **abrupt**
manner.
• blunt, curt, sharp, rude, gruff, impolite,
tactless, unfriendly
OPPOSITE polite

absence NOUN
There's an **absence** of salt in the soup.
• lack, want, need, deficit
OPPOSITE presence

absent ADJECTIVE
Why were you **absent** from school yesterday?
• away, missing
To be absent from school without a good
reason is to **play truant**.
OPPOSITE present

absent-minded ADJECTIVE
The **absent-minded** professor had forgotten
his papers.
• forgetful, careless, inattentive, vague
OPPOSITE alert

absolute ADJECTIVE
The hypnotist asked for **absolute** silence.
• complete, total, utter, perfect

absolutely ADVERB
This floor is **absolutely** filthy!
• completely, thoroughly, totally, utterly,
wholly, entirely

a
b
c
d
e
f
g
h
i
j
k
l
m
n
o
p
q
r
s
t
u
v
w
x
y
z

A
B
C
D
E
F
G
H
I
J
K
L
M
N
O
P
Q
R
S
T
U
V
W
X
Y
Z

absorb VERB
A sponge absorbs water.
• soak up, suck up, take in, fill up with, hold, retain

absorbed ADJECTIVE
➤ to be absorbed in something
I was so absorbed in my book that I forgot the time.
• be engrossed in, be interested in, be preoccupied with, concentrate on, think about

absorbing ADJECTIVE
'101 Dalmatians' is an absorbing book.
• interesting, fascinating, intriguing, gripping, enthralling, engrossing, captivating

absurd ADJECTIVE
The idea that little green men live on Mars is absurd.
• ridiculous, silly, ludicrous, preposterous, foolish, laughable, nonsensical, idiotic, senseless, stupid, unreasonable, illogical
(informal) daft
OPPOSITES sensible, reasonable

abundant ADJECTIVE
Birds have an abundant supply of food in the summer.
• ample, plentiful, generous, profuse, lavish, liberal
OPPOSITES meagre, scarce

abuse VERB
❶ *The rescued dog had been abused by its owners.*
• mistreat, maltreat, hurt, injure, damage, harm, misuse
❷ *The Prime Minister was abused by the protesters in the crowd.*
• be rude to, insult, swear at
(informal) call someone names

abuse NOUN
❶ *They campaigned against the abuse of animals.*
• mistreatment, misuse, damage, harm, injury

❷ *A spectator yelled abuse at the referee.*
• insults, name-calling, swear words

accelerate VERB
The bus accelerated when it reached the motorway.
• go faster, speed up, pick up speed
OPPOSITE slow down

accent NOUN
❶ *My mum speaks English with a Jamaican accent.*
• pronunciation, intonation, tone
❷ *Play the first note of each bar with a strong accent.*
• beat, stress, emphasis, rhythm, pulse

accept VERB
❶ *I accepted the offer of a lift to the station.*
• take, receive, welcome
OPPOSITE reject
❷ *The club accepted my application for membership.*
• approve, agree to, consent to
OPPOSITE reject
❸ *Do you accept responsibility for the damage?*
• admit, acknowledge, recognize, face up to
OPPOSITE deny
❹ *They had to accept the umpire's decision.*
• agree to, go along with, tolerate, put up with, resign yourself to

acceptable ADJECTIVE
❶ *Would a pound be acceptable as a tip?*
• welcome, agreeable, appreciated, pleasant, pleasing, worthwhile
❷ *The teacher said my handwriting was not acceptable.*
• satisfactory, adequate, appropriate, permissible, suitable, tolerable, passable
OPPOSITE unacceptable

access NOUN
The access to the lighthouse is over those rocks.
• entrance, way in, approach

access *VERB*
Can I access my email on this computer?
• get at, obtain, reach, make use of

accident *NOUN*
❶ *There has been an accident at a fireworks display.*
• misfortune, mishap, disaster, calamity, catastrophe
A person who is always having accidents is accident-prone.
❷ *A motorway accident is causing traffic delays.*
• collision, crash, smash
An accident involving a lot of vehicles is a pile-up.
A railway accident may involve a derailment.
❸ *It was pure accident that led us to the secret passage.*
• chance, luck, a fluke
➤ **by accident**
I found the piece of paper by accident.
• by chance, accidentally, coincidentally, unintentionally

accidental *ADJECTIVE*
❶ *The damage to the building was accidental.*
• unintentional, unfortunate, unlucky
❷ *The professor made an accidental discovery.*
• unexpected, unforeseen, unplanned, fortunate, lucky, chance
OPPOSITE deliberate

accommodate *VERB*
❶ *The hotel can accommodate thirty guests.*
• house, shelter, lodge, provide for, cater for, put up, take in, hold
❷ *If you need anything, we'll try to accommodate you.*
• serve, assist, help, aid, oblige, supply, please

accommodation *NOUN*
Have you booked your holiday accommodation yet?
• housing, lodgings, quarters, premises, shelter, rooms

WORD WEB

PLACES WHERE PEOPLE NORMALLY LIVE:

• bedsit, flat, house

KINDS OF HOLIDAY ACCOMMODATION:

• apartment, bed and breakfast, boarding house, chalet, guest house, hotel, motel, self-catering, timeshare, youth hostel
Accommodation for students is in a **hall of residence** or *(informal)* **digs**.
Accommodation for the armed services is in **barracks** or a **billet**.
see also **building, house**

accompany *VERB*
A guide accompanied us through the museum.
• escort, go with, follow, attend, travel with, tag along with

accomplish *VERB*
She accomplished her goal of sailing round the world.
• achieve, finish, complete, carry out, perform, succeed in, fulfil

account *NOUN*
❶ *I wrote an account of our camping trip in my diary.*
• report, record, description, history, narrative, story, chronicle, log
(informal) write-up
❷ *Money was of no account to him.*
• importance, significance, consequence, interest, value
➤ **to account for**
Can you account for your strange behaviour?
• explain, give reasons for, justify, make excuses for

accumulate *VERB*
❶ *Our family has accumulated a lot of rubbish.*
• collect, gather, amass, assemble, heap up, pile up, hoard
OPPOSITE scatter

a
b
c
d
e
f
g
h
i
j
k
l
m
n
o
p
q
r
s
t
u
v
w
x
y
z

A

❷ *Dust had accumulated on the mantelpiece.*
• build up, grow, increase, multiply
(OPPOSITE) decrease

B

C

accurate *ADJECTIVE*
❶ *The detective took accurate measurements of the room.*
• careful, correct, exact, meticulous, minute, precise
(OPPOSITES) inexact, rough
❷ *Is this an accurate account of what happened?*
• faithful, true, reliable, truthful, factual
(OPPOSITES) inaccurate, false

D

E

F

G

H

accuse *VERB*
➤ **accuse of**
We accused our opponents of cheating.
• charge with, blame for, condemn for, denounce for
(OPPOSITE) defend

I

J

K

L

accustomed *ADJECTIVE*
➤ **accustomed to**
Desert plants are not accustomed to rain.
• acclimatized to, familiar with, used to

M

N

O

ache *NOUN*
The ache in my tooth is getting worse.
• pain, soreness, throbbing, discomfort, pang, twinge, pain

P

Q

ache *VERB*
My legs ached from the long walk.
• hurt, be painful, be sore, throb, pound, smart

R

S

T

achieve *VERB*
❶ *He achieved his ambition to play rugby for Wales.*
• accomplish, attain, succeed in, carry out, fulfil
❷ *The singer achieved success with her first album.*
• acquire, win, gain, earn, get, score

U

V

W

X

achievement *NOUN*
To climb Mount Everest would be an achievement.
• accomplishment, attainment, success, feat, triumph

Y

Z

acknowledge *VERB*
❶ *The queen did not acknowledge her cousin's claim to the throne.*
• admit, accept, concede, grant, recognize
(OPPOSITE) deny
❷ *Please acknowledge my email.*
• answer, reply to, respond to

acquire *VERB*
Where can I acquire a copy of this book?
• get, get hold of, obtain
To acquire something by paying for it is to **buy** or **purchase** it.

across *PREPOSITION*
We could see their camp across the river.
• on the other side of, over, beyond

act *NOUN*
❶ *Rescuing the boy from the river was a brave act.*
• action, deed, feat, exploit, operation
❷ *The best act at the circus involved three clowns.*
• performance, sketch, item, turn

act *VERB*
❶ *We must act as soon as we hear the signal.*
• do something, take action
❷ *Give the medicine time to act.*
• work, take effect, have an effect, function
❸ *Stop acting like a baby!*
• behave, carry on
❹ *I acted the part of a pirate in the play.*
• perform, play, portray, represent, appear as

action *NOUN*
❶ *The driver's action prevented an accident.*
• act, deed, effort, measure, feat
❷ *The fruit ripens through the action of the sun.*
• working, effect, mechanism
❸ *The film was packed with action.*
• drama, excitement, activity, liveliness, energy, vigour, vitality
❹ *He was killed in action in the Second World War.*
• battle, fighting

active ADJECTIVE
❶ We lead a very **active** life.
• energetic, lively, dynamic, vigorous, busy
❷ My friend is an **active** member of the football club.
• enthusiastic, devoted, committed, dedicated, hard-working
OPPOSITE inactive

activity NOUN
❶ The town centre was full of **activity**.
• action, life, busyness, liveliness, excitement, movement, animation
❷ My mum's favourite **activity** is gardening.
• hobby, interest, pastime, pursuit, job, occupation, task

actor or actress NOUN
A company of **actors** performed a play in the school hall.
• performer, player
The most important actor in a play or film is the **lead** or the **star**.
The other actors are the **supporting actors**.
All the actors in a play or film are the **cast** or the **company**.

actual ADJECTIVE
Did you see the **actual** crime?
• real, true, genuine, authentic
OPPOSITES imaginary, supposed

actually ADVERB
What did the teacher **actually** say to you?
• really, truly, definitely, certainly, genuinely, in fact

acute ADJECTIVE
❶ She felt an **acute** pain in her knee.
• intense, severe, sharp, piercing, sudden, violent
OPPOSITES mild, slight
❷ There is an **acute** shortage of food.
• serious, urgent, crucial, important, vital
OPPOSITE unimportant
❸ Clearly the aliens had an **acute** intelligence.
• keen, quick, sharp, clever, intelligent, shrewd, smart, alert
OPPOSITE stupid

adapt VERB
❶ I'll **adapt** the goggles so that they fit you.
• alter, change, modify, convert, reorganize, transform
❷ Our family **adapted** quickly to life in the country.
• become accustomed, adjust, acclimatize

add VERB
The poet **added** an extra line in the last verse.
• join on, attach, append, insert
➤ to add to
The herbs **add to** the flavour of the stew.
• improve, enhance, increase
➤ to add up
❶ Can you **add up** these figures for me?
• count up, find the sum of, find the total of
(informal) tot up
❷ The story just doesn't **add up**.
• be convincing, make sense

additional ADJECTIVE
There are **additional** toilets downstairs.
• extra, further, more, supplementary

address VERB
The head **addressed** us in assembly.
• speak to, talk to, make a speech to, lecture to

adequate ADJECTIVE
❶ A sandwich will be **adequate**, thank you.
• enough, sufficient, ample
❷ Your work is **adequate**, but I'm sure you can do better.
• satisfactory, acceptable, tolerable, competent, passable, respectable
OPPOSITE inadequate

adjust VERB
❶ You need to **adjust** the TV picture.
• correct, modify, put right, improve, tune
❷ She **adjusted** the central heating thermostat.
• alter, change, set, vary, regulate

A
B
C
D
E
F
G
H
I
J
K
L
M
N
O
P
Q
R
S
T
U
V
W
X
Y
Z

➤ **to adjust to**
I found it hard to adjust to my new school at first.
• adapt to, get used to, get accustomed to, become acclimatized to, settle in to

admiration NOUN
I'm full of admiration for her work.
• praise, respect, approval
OPPOSITE contempt

admire VERB
❶ *I admire his skill with words.*
• think highly of, look up to, value, have a high opinion of, respect, applaud, approve of, esteem
OPPOSITE despise
❷ *The travellers stopped to admire the view.*
• enjoy, appreciate, be delighted by

admission NOUN
❶ *We were surprised by the admission of guilt.*
• confession, declaration, acknowledgement, acceptance
OPPOSITE denial
❷ *Admission to the castle is by ticket only.*
• entrance, entry, access, admittance

admit VERB
❶ *The hospital admitted all the victims of the accident.*
• receive, take in, accept, allow in, let in
OPPOSITE exclude
❷ *Did he admit that he told a lie?*
• acknowledge, agree, accept, confess, grant, own up
OPPOSITE deny

adopt VERB
❶ *Our school has adopted a healthy eating policy.*
• take up, accept, choose, follow, embrace
❷ *We have adopted a stray kitten.*
• foster, take in

adore VERB
❶ *Rosie adores her big sister.*
• love, worship, idolize, dote on
❷ *(informal) I adore chocolate milkshakes!*
• love, like, enjoy
OPPOSITES hate, detest

adult ADJECTIVE
An adult zebra can run at 70km an hour.
• grown-up, mature, full-size, fully grown
OPPOSITES young, immature

adult NOUN
Adults are not allowed in our club.
• grown-up
OPPOSITES young person, child

advance NOUN
❶ *You can't stop the advance of science.*
• progress, development, growth, evolution
❷ *This computer is a great advance on our old one.*
• improvement

advance VERB
❶ *As the army advanced, the enemy fled.*
• move forward, go forward, proceed, approach, come near, press on, progress, forge ahead, gain ground, make headway, make progress
OPPOSITE retreat
❷ *Mobile phones have advanced in the last few years.*
• develop, grow, improve, evolve, progress

advantage NOUN
We had the advantage of the wind behind us.
• assistance, benefit, help, aid, asset
OPPOSITES disadvantage, drawback

adventure NOUN
❶ *He told us about his latest adventure.*
• enterprise, exploit, venture, escapade
❷ *They travelled the world in search of adventure.*
• excitement, danger, risk, thrills

adventurous ADJECTIVE
❶ *I dreamed of being an adventurous explorer.*
• bold, daring, heroic, enterprising, intrepid

❷ *She has led a very **adventurous** life.*
• exciting, eventful, dangerous, challenging, risky
OPPOSITE unadventurous

advertise *VERB*
*We made a poster to **advertise** the cake sale.*
• publicize, promote, announce, make known
(informal) plug

advice *NOUN*
*The website gives **advice** on building a bird table.*
• guidance, help, directions, recommendations, suggestions, tips, pointers

advise *VERB*
❶ *What did the doctor **advise**?*
• recommend, suggest, advocate, prescribe
❷ *He **advised** me to rest.*
• counsel, encourage, urge

aeroplane *NOUN*
see **aircraft**

affair *NOUN*
The theft of the jewels was a mysterious affair.
• event, happening, incident, occurrence, occasion, thing
➤ affairs
*I don't discuss my private **affairs** on the phone.*
• business, matters, concerns, questions, subjects, topics

affect *VERB*
❶ *Global warming will **affect** our climate.*
• have an effect or impact on, influence, change, modify, alter
❷ *The bad news **affected** us deeply.*
• disturb, upset, concern, trouble, worry

affectionate *ADJECTIVE*
*She gave me an **affectionate** kiss.*
• loving, tender, caring, fond, friendly, devoted
OPPOSITE unfriendly

afford *VERB*
*I can't **afford** a new bike just now.*
• have enough money for, pay for, manage, spare

afraid *ADJECTIVE*
❶ *We felt **afraid** as we approached the haunted house.*
• frightened, scared, terrified, petrified, alarmed, fearful, anxious, apprehensive
OPPOSITE brave
❷ *Don't be **afraid** to ask questions.*
• hesitant, reluctant, shy
➤ to be afraid of
*Luke was **afraid of** large hairy spiders.*
• be frightened of, be scared of, fear, dread

😊 WRITING TIPS

SOMEONE WHO FEELS AFRAID MIGHT:

• blanch, go or turn pale, have goose pimples or goosebumps, quake in their boots, shudder, stand frozen or rooted to the spot, tremble like a leaf

SOMETHING WHICH MAKES YOU AFRAID MIGHT:

• give you goose pimples or goosebumps, make your hair stand on end, make your knees tremble, strike fear into you or your heart
The hairs stood up stiff with terror in the nape of Slightly's neck.—PETER PAN, J. M. Barrie

---

again *ADVERB*
*Would you like to come round **again** next week?*
• another time, once more, once again

against *PREPOSITION*
*I signed a petition **against** cruelty to animals.*
• in opposition to, opposed to, hostile to

age *NOUN*
*The book is set in the **age** of the Vikings.*
• period, time, era, epoch, days

age VERB
❶ *The man had **aged** since we last saw him.*
• become older, look older
❷ *The wine is left to **age** in the cellar.*
• mature, develop

agent NOUN
for secret agents see **spy**

aggressive ADJECTIVE
*Bats are not **aggressive** creatures.*
• hostile, violent, provocative, quarrelsome, bullying, warlike
OPPOSITE friendly

agile ADJECTIVE
*Mountain goats are extremely **agile**.*
• nimble, graceful, sure-footed, sprightly, acrobatic, supple, swift
OPPOSITES clumsy, stiff

agitated ADJECTIVE
*I felt **agitated** before my music exam.*
• nervous, anxious, edgy, restless, fidgety, flustered, ruffled, disturbed, upset, unsettled
OPPOSITE calm, cool

agony NOUN
*He screamed in **agony** when he broke his leg.*
• pain, suffering, torture, torment, anguish, distress

agree VERB
❶ *I'm glad that we **agree**.*
• be united, think the same, concur
OPPOSITE disagree
❷ *I **agree** that you are right.*
• accept, acknowledge, admit, grant, allow
OPPOSITE disagree
❸ *I **agree** to pay my share.*
• consent, promise, be willing, undertake
OPPOSITE refuse
➤ **to agree on**
*We **agreed on** a price.*
• decide, fix, settle, choose, establish

➤ **to agree with**
❶ *I don't **agree with** animal testing.*
• support, advocate, argue for, defend
❷ *Onions don't **agree with** me.*
• suit

agreement NOUN
❶ *There was **agreement** on the need for longer holidays.*
• consensus, unanimity, unity, consent, harmony, sympathy, conformity
OPPOSITE disagreement
❷ *The two sides signed an **agreement**.*
• alliance, treaty
An agreement to end fighting is an **armistice** or **truce**.
A business agreement is a **bargain**, **contract** or **deal**.

ahead ADVERB
❶ *They sent a messenger **ahead** with the news.*
• in advance, in front, before
❷ *I stared **ahead**, trying to see through the mist.*
• forwards, to the front

aid NOUN
❶ *We can climb out with the **aid** of this rope.*
• help, support, assistance, backing, cooperation
❷ *They agreed to send more **aid** to the poorer countries.*
• donations, subsidies, contributions

aid VERB
*The local people **aided** the police in their investigation.*
• help, assist, support, back, collaborate with, cooperate with, contribute to, lend a hand to, further, promote, subsidize

aim NOUN
*What was the **aim** of the experiment?*
• ambition, desire, dream, goal, hope, intention, objective, purpose, target, wish

aim VERB
❶ *He **aims** to be a professional dancer.*
• intend, mean, plan, propose, want, wish, seek

A B C D E F G H I J K L M N O P Q R S T U V W X Y Z

❷ *She aimed her bow and arrow at the target.*
• point, direct, take aim with, line up, level, train, focus

air NOUN
❶ *We shouldn't pollute the air we breathe.*
• atmosphere
❷ *This room needs some air.*
• fresh air, ventilation
❸ *They were singing a traditional air.*
• song, tune, melody
❹ *There was an air of mystery about the place.*
• feeling, mood, look, appearance, sense

air VERB
❶ *He opened the window to air the room.*
• freshen, refresh, ventilate
❷ *I have a right to air my opinions.*
• express, make known, make public, reveal, voice

aircraft NOUN

WORD WEB

SOME TYPES OF AIRCRAFT:

• aeroplane, airliner, airship, biplane, bomber, drone, fighter, glider, helicopter, hot-air balloon, jet, jumbo jet, seaplane

PARTS OF AIRCRAFT:

• cabin, cargo hold, cockpit, engine, fin, flap, flight deck, fuselage, joystick, passenger cabin, propeller, rotor, rudder, tail, tailplane, undercarriage, wing

PLACES WHERE AIRCRAFT TAKE OFF AND LAND:

• aerodrome, airfield, airport, airstrip, helipad, heliport, landing strip, runway

PEOPLE WHO FLY IN AIRCRAFT:

• pilot, aviator, balloonist; co-pilot, cabin crew, flight attendant; passengers

air force NOUN
see **armed forces**

airy ADJECTIVE
Our hotel room was pleasantly light and airy.
• fresh, breezy, ventilated
OPPOSITES stuffy, close

alarm VERB
The barking dog alarmed the sheep.
• frighten, startle, scare, panic, agitate, distress, shock, surprise, upset, worry
OPPOSITE reassure

alarm NOUN
❶ *Did you hear the alarm?*
• signal, alert, warning, siren
❷ *The sudden noise filled me with alarm.*
• fright, fear, panic, anxiety, apprehension, distress, nervousness, terror, uneasiness

alarming ADJECTIVE
We have received some alarming news.
• frightening, scary, terrifying, shocking, startling

alert ADJECTIVE
The guards were told to stay alert at all times.
• vigilant, watchful, sharp, observant, attentive, awake, careful, on the alert, on the lookout, ready, wary, wide awake
A phrase meaning 'to stay alert' is to keep your eyes peeled.
OPPOSITE inattentive

alert VERB
We alerted them to the danger.
• make aware, warn, notify, inform, signal, tip off

alien ADJECTIVE
❶ *The desert landscape looked alien to us.*
• strange, foreign, unfamiliar, different, exotic
OPPOSITE familiar
❷ *Could those be the lights of an alien spacecraft?*
• extraterrestrial

alien NOUN
I wrote a story about aliens from another galaxy.
• extraterrestrial, alien life-form

WORD WEB

AN ALIEN FROM ANOTHER PLANET MIGHT BE:

• humanoid, insect-like, lizard-like, reptilian, intelligent, primitive, super-intelligent, telepathic

BODY PARTS AN ALIEN MIGHT HAVE:

• antenna, blotches, scales, slime, sucker, tentacle, webbing

TRANSPORT AN ALIEN MIGHT USE:

• alien vessel, flying saucer, mothership, pod, spacecraft, spaceship, starship, time machine, transporter beam
An alien might call someone from Earth an **Earthling**.
see also **planet, space**

alight *ADJECTIVE*
The bonfire was still *alight*.
• burning, lit, on fire, ignited

alike *ADJECTIVE*
All the houses in the street looked *alike*.
• similar, the same, identical, indistinguishable, comparable, uniform

alive *ADJECTIVE*
Fortunately, my goldfish was still *alive*.
• living, live, existing, in existence, surviving, breathing, flourishing
OPPOSITE dead

alliance *NOUN*
The two countries formed an *alliance*.
• partnership, union, association, federation, league
An alliance between political parties is a coalition.

allocate *VERB*
I *allocated* some pocket money for buying presents.
• allot, assign, set aside, reserve, earmark

allow *VERB*
❶ They don't *allow* skateboards in the playground.
• permit, let, authorize, approve of, agree to, consent to, give permission for, license, put up with, stand, support, tolerate
OPPOSITE forbid
❷ Have you *allowed* enough time for the journey?
• allocate, set aside, assign, grant, earmark

all right *ADJECTIVE*
❶ The survivors appeared to be *all right*.
• well, unhurt, unharmed, uninjured, safe
❷ The food in the hotel was *all right*.
• satisfactory, acceptable, adequate, reasonable, passable
❸ Is it *all right* to play music in here?
• acceptable, permissible

ally *NOUN*
The two countries work together as *allies*.
• friend, partner
OPPOSITE enemy

almost *ADVERB*
❶ I have *almost* finished the crossword.
• nearly, practically, just about, virtually, all but, as good as, not quite
❷ *Almost* a hundred people came to the concert.
• about, approximately, around

alone *ADJECTIVE, ADVERB*
❶ Did you go to the party *alone*?
• on your own, by yourself, unaccompanied
❷ Zoe felt very *alone*.
• lonely, friendless, isolated, solitary, lonesome, desolate

also *ADVERB*
We need some bread, and *also* more butter.
• in addition, besides, additionally, too, furthermore, moreover

alter *VERB*
They have *altered* the route for the cycle race.
• change, adjust, adapt, modify, transform, amend, make different, revise, vary

A B C D E F G H I J K L M N O P Q R S T U V W X Y Z

alternative *NOUN*
I lost my bus money and had no **alternative** but to walk.
• choice, option

altogether *ADVERB*
❶ I'm not **altogether** satisfied.
• completely, entirely, absolutely, quite, totally, utterly, wholly, fully, perfectly, thoroughly
❷ Our house has five rooms **altogether**.
• in all, in total, all told

always *ADVERB*
❶ The sea is **always** in motion.
• constantly, continuously, endlessly, eternally, for ever, perpetually, unceasingly
❷ This bus is **always** late.
• consistently, continually, invariably, persistently, regularly, repeatedly

amateur *NOUN*
All the players in this team are unpaid **amateurs**.
OPPOSITE professional

amaze *VERB*
It **amazes** me to think that the Earth is billions of years old.
• astonish, astound, startle, surprise, stun, shock, stagger, dumbfound
(informal) flabbergast

amazed *ADJECTIVE*
I was **amazed** by the number of messages we had received.
• astonished, astounded, stunned, surprised, dumbfounded, speechless, staggered
(informal) flabbergasted

amazing *ADJECTIVE*
The Northern Lights are an **amazing** sight.
• astonishing, astounding, staggering, remarkable, surprising, extraordinary, incredible, breathtaking, phenomenal, sensational, stupendous, tremendous, wonderful, mind-boggling

ambition *NOUN*
❶ She has always had great **ambition**.
• drive, enthusiasm, enterprise, push, zeal
❷ My **ambition** is to play tennis at Wimbledon.
• goal, aim, intention, objective, target, desire, dream, wish, hope, aspiration

ambitious *ADJECTIVE*
❶ If you're **ambitious**, you will probably succeed.
• enterprising, enthusiastic, committed, go-ahead, keen
OPPOSITE unambitious
❷ I think your plan is too **ambitious**.
• grand, big, large-scale

amend *VERB*
I **amended** the letter to make it clearer.
• change, alter, adjust, modify, revise

among *PREPOSITION*
We played hide-and-seek **among** the bushes.
• between, amid, in, in the middle of, surrounded by

amount *NOUN*
❶ Mum wrote a cheque for the correct **amount**.
• sum, total, whole
❷ There's a large **amount** of paper in the cupboard.
• quantity, measure, supply, volume, mass, bulk

amount *VERB*
➤ **to amount to**
What does the bill **amount to**?
• add up to, come to, total, equal, make

amphibian *NOUN*

WORD WEB

SOME ANIMALS WHICH ARE AMPHIBIANS:

• bullfrog, frog, newt, salamander, toad, tree frog
for other animals see **animal**

a
b
c
d
e
f
g
h
i
j
k
l
m
n
o
p
q
r
s
t
u
v
w
x
y
z

A B C D E F G H I J K L M N O P Q R S T U V W X Y Z

ample *ADJECTIVE*
❶ *The car has an ample boot.*
• big, large, spacious, roomy
OPPOSITE small
❷ *We had an ample supply of food.*
• abundant, plentiful, generous, substantial, considerable, profuse, lavish, liberal
OPPOSITE meagre
❸ *No more juice, thanks—that's ample.*
• plenty, sufficient, lots, more than enough
(informal) heaps, masses, loads, stacks
OPPOSITE insufficient

amuse *VERB*
I think this joke will amuse you.
• make you laugh, entertain, cheer up, divert
(informal) tickle

amusement *NOUN*
❶ *What's your favourite amusement?*
• pastime, recreation, entertainment, diversion, game, hobby, interest, leisure activity, sport
❷ *We tried not to show our amusement.*
• merriment, hilarity, laughter, mirth

amusing *ADJECTIVE*
I didn't find his jokes very amusing.
• funny, witty, humorous, comic, comical, hilarious, diverting, entertaining
OPPOSITES unamusing, serious

analyse *VERB*
We analysed the results of our experiment.
• examine, study, investigate, scrutinize

ancestor *NOUN*
Our family's ancestors came from Chile.
• forebear, forefather, predecessor
OPPOSITE descendant

ancestry *NOUN*
She was proud of her African ancestry.
• origins, descent, heredity, heritage, blood, extraction, pedigree, stock

ancient *ADJECTIVE*
❶ *Does that ancient camera still work?*
• old, old-fashioned, antiquated, out of date, obsolete
❷ *In ancient times, our ancestors were hunters.*
• early, primitive, prehistoric, remote, long past, olden
The times before written records were kept are **prehistoric** times.
The ancient Greeks and Romans lived in **classical** times.
OPPOSITES modern, contemporary
see also **museum, pyramid**

anger *NOUN*
I was filled with anger when I read the letter.
• rage, fury, indignation, ire
(old use) wrath
An outburst of anger is a **tantrum** or a **fit of temper**.
anger *VERB*
Cruelty towards animals angers me.
• enrage, infuriate, incense, madden, annoy, irritate, exasperate, antagonize, provoke
(informal) make your blood boil, make you see red
OPPOSITE pacify

angle *NOUN*
❶ *He wore a top hat set at a slight angle.*
• slope, slant, tilt
❷ *Let's look at the problem from a different angle.*
• viewpoint, point of view, perspective

angry *ADJECTIVE*
Something in the message had made him angry.
• cross, furious, enraged, infuriated, irate, livid, annoyed, incensed, exasperated, fuming, indignant, raging, seething
(informal) mad
(old use) wrathful
To become angry and lose control is to **lose your temper**.
OPPOSITE calm

angry ADJECTIVE

animal NOUN

*Wild **animals** roam freely in the safari park.*

• creature, beast, brute

WORD WEB

A word for wild animals in general is **wildlife**. A scientific word for animals is **fauna**.

VARIOUS KINDS OF ANIMAL:

• amphibian, arachnid, bird, fish, insect, invertebrate, mammal, marsupial, mollusc, reptile, rodent, vertebrate

An animal that eats meat is a **carnivore**. An animal that eats plants is a **herbivore**. An animal that eats meat and plants is an **omnivore**. Animals that sleep most of the winter are **hibernating** animals. Animals that are active at night are **nocturnal** animals.

SOME ANIMALS THAT LIVE ON LAND:

• aardvark, anteater, antelope, ape, armadillo, baboon, badger, bat, bear, beaver, bison, boar, buffalo, camel, cheetah, chimpanzee, chinchilla, chipmunk, deer, dormouse, echidna, elephant, elk, fox, gazelle, gibbon, giraffe, gnu, gorilla, grizzly bear, hare, hedgehog, hippopotamus or *(informal)* hippo, hyena, jackal, jaguar, kangaroo, koala, lemming, lemur, leopard, lion, llama, lynx, meerkat, mongoose, monkey, moose, mouse, ocelot, opossum, orangutan, otter, panda, pangolin, panther, platypus, polar bear, porcupine, rabbit, rat, reindeer, rhinoceros or *(informal)* rhino, skunk, snow leopard, squirrel, stoat, tapir, tiger, vole, wallaby, warthog, weasel, wildebeest, wolf, wolverine, wombat, yak, zebra

for animals commonly kept as pets
see **pet, amphibian, bird, fish, insect, reptile**

SOME ANIMALS THAT LIVE IN THE SEA:

• dolphin, killer whale or orca, manatee or sea cow, narwhal, porpoise, seal, sea lion, walrus, whale

SOME EXTINCT ANIMALS:

• dinosaur, dodo, mammoth, quagga, sabre-toothed cat or smilodon
see also **dinosaur**

PARTS OF AN ANIMAL'S BODY:

• antler, claw, fang, foreleg, hind leg, hoof, horn, jaws, mane, muzzle, paw, snout, tail, trotter, tusk, whisker, fur, coat, fleece, hide, pelt

MALE AND FEMALE ANIMALS:

A male elephant or whale is a **bull** and a female is a **cow**.
A male fox is a **dog** and a female is a **vixen**.
A male goat is a **billy goat** and a female is a **nanny goat**.
A male hare or rabbit is a **buck** and a female is a **doe**.
A male horse is a **stallion** and a female is a **mare**.
A female lion is a **lioness**.
A male pig is a **boar** and a female is a **sow**.
A male sheep is a **ram** and a female is a **ewe**.
A female tiger is a **tigress**.
A male wolf is a **dog** and a female is a **bitch**.
see also **cat, cattle, deer, dog**

a
b
c
d
e
f
g
h
i
j
k
l
m
n
o
p
q
r
s
t
u
v
w
x
y
z

YOUNG ANIMALS:

A young beaver is a **kit**.
A young bear, fox or lion is a **cub**.
A young goat is a **kid**.
A young hare is a **leveret**.
A young horse is a **foal**, **colt** (male) or **filly** (female).
A young pig is a **piglet**.
A young otter or seal is a **pup**.
A young sheep is a **lamb**.
see also **cat, cattle, deer, dog**

HOMES OF SOME BRITISH WILD ANIMALS:

• **den, lair**
A badger lives in a **sett**.
A beaver lives in a **lodge**.
A fox lives in an **earth**.
An otter lives in a **holt**.
A rabbit lives in a **burrow** or **warren**.
A squirrel lives in a **drey**.

SOUNDS MADE BY ANIMALS:

• **bark, bay, bellow, buzz, gnash, growl, grunt, hiss, howl, jabber, oink, purr, roar, snap, snarl, snort, snuffle, squeak, trumpet, whimper, whine, woof, yap, yelp, yowl**
A sheep **bleats**.
A donkey **brays**.
A frog **croaks**.
Cattle **low** or **moo**.
A cat **mews** or **miaows**.
A horse **neighs** or **whinnies**.
for groups of animals see **group**

WRITING TIPS

You can use these words to describe an animal:

TO DESCRIBE HOW AN ANIMAL MOVES:

• **bound, creep, crouch, dart, gallop, gambol, leap, lumber, nuzzle, pad, paw, pounce, roam, scuttle, skip, slink, slither, spring, stamp, stampede, trot, waddle**
The hounds started to spread out in a circle around him. They were growling and snapping, looking for a chance to pounce.
—HERE BE MONSTERS, Alan Snow

TO DESCRIBE AN ANIMAL'S BODY:

• **agile, nimble, sinewy, wiry; lumbering, majestic, mighty, muscular, powerful**
*The cheetah stretched its long, **sinewy** body.*

TO DESCRIBE AN ANIMAL'S SKIN OR COAT:

• **coarse, fluffy, furry, glistening, glossy, hairy, leathery, matted, prickly, scaly, shaggy, shiny, silky, sleek, slimy, slippery, smooth, spiky, thick, thorny, tough, wiry, woolly; dappled, mottled, piebald, spotted, striped**
She was a strong, well-made animal, of a bright dun colour, beautifully dappled, and with a dark-brown mane and tail.—BLACK BEAUTY, Anna Sewell

anniversary *NOUN*

WORD WEB

The anniversary of the day you were born is your **birthday**.
The anniversary of the day someone was married is their **wedding anniversary**.

SPECIAL ANNIVERSARIES:

• **centenary** (100 years), **sesquicentenary** (150 years), **bicentenary** (200 years), **tercentenary** (300 years), **quatercentenary** (400 years), **quincentenary** (500 years), **millenary** (1000 years)

SPECIAL WEDDING ANNIVERSARIES:

• **silver wedding** (25 years), **ruby wedding** (40 years), **golden wedding** (50 years), **diamond wedding** (60 years)

announce *VERB*

❶ *The head **announced** that sports day was cancelled.*
• **declare, state, proclaim, report**
❷ *The DJ **announced** the next record.*
• **present, introduce, lead into**

announcement NOUN
❶ The head reads the **announcements** in assembly.
• notice
❷ The prime minister issued an **announcement**.
• statement, declaration, proclamation, pronouncement
❸ I heard the **announcement** on TV.
• report, bulletin, newsflash

annoy VERB
❶ I was **annoyed** that I missed the bus.
• irritate, bother, displease, exasperate, anger, upset, vex, trouble, worry
OPPOSITE please
❷ Please don't **annoy** me while I'm working.
• pester, bother, harass, badger, nag, plague, trouble, try
(informal) bug

annoyance NOUN
❶ Mrs Garcia's face showed her **annoyance**.
• irritation, anger, exasperation, vexation
❷ Is the dog an **annoyance** to you?
• nuisance, bother, trouble, worry

annoying ADJECTIVE
My cousin has a lot of **annoying** habits.
• irritating, exasperating, maddening, provoking, tiresome, trying, vexing, troublesome

anonymous ADJECTIVE
❶ An **anonymous** donor gave the school some money.
• unnamed, nameless, unidentified, unknown
❷ I received an **anonymous** letter.
• unsigned

answer NOUN
❶ Did you get an **answer** to your letter?
• reply, response, acknowledgement, reaction
A quick or angry answer is a **retort**
❷ The **answers** to the quiz are on the next page.
• solution, explanation

answer VERB
❶ You haven't **answered** my question.
• give an answer to, reply to, respond to, react to, acknowledge

❷ 'I'm quite well,' I **answered**.
• reply, respond, return
To answer quickly or angrily is to **retort**.
➤ to answer back
She doesn't like it when I **answer back**.
• argue, protest, object

anthology NOUN
see **collection**

anticipate VERB
I **anticipate** that the result will be a draw.
• expect, predict, forecast, foretell

antique ADJECTIVE
The palace was full of **antique** furniture.
• old, old-fashioned
Antique cars are **veteran** or **vintage** cars.

anxiety NOUN
❶ We waited for news with a growing sense of **anxiety**.
• apprehension, concern, worry, fear, nervousness, dread, tension, strain, stress, uncertainty, doubt
OPPOSITES calmness, calm
❷ In his **anxiety** to win, he started before the gun went off.
• eagerness, keenness, desire, impatience, enthusiasm

anxious ADJECTIVE
❶ Are you **anxious** about your exams?
• nervous, worried, apprehensive, concerned, uneasy, fearful, edgy, fraught, tense, troubled
(informal) uptight, jittery
OPPOSITE calm
❷ I'm **anxious** to do my best.
• eager, keen, impatient, enthusiastic, willing

apologetic ADJECTIVE
The shopkeeper was **apologetic** about his mistake.
• sorry, repentant, remorseful, regretful, penitent, contrite
OPPOSITE unrepentant

a
b
c
d
e
f
g
h
i
j
k
l
m
n
o
p
q
r
s
t
u
v
w
x
y
z

apologize VERB
The ogre apologized for being rude.
• make an apology, say sorry, express regret, repent, be penitent

appal VERB
They were appalled by conditions in the prison.
• disgust, revolt, shock, sicken, horrify, distress

appalling ADJECTIVE
❶ *He suffered appalling injuries in the accident.*
• distressing, dreadful, frightful, gruesome, horrible, horrific, horrifying, shocking, sickening, revolting
❷ *This handwriting is appalling—I can barely read it.*
• bad, awful, terrible, deplorable, disgraceful, unsatisfactory, atrocious
(informal) abysmal

apparent ADJECTIVE
There was no apparent reason for the crash.
• obvious, evident, clear, noticeable, detectable, perceptible, recognizable, conspicuous, visible
OPPOSITES concealed, unclear

appeal VERB
➤ to appeal for
The prisoners appealed for our help.
• request, beg for, plead for, cry out for, entreat, ask earnestly for, pray for
➤ to appeal to
That kind of music doesn't appeal to me.
• attract, interest, fascinate, tempt

appeal NOUN
❶ *Did you hear their appeal for help?*
• request, call, cry, entreaty
An appeal signed by a lot of people is a petition.
❷ *Baby animals always have great appeal.*
• attractiveness, interest, charm, fascination

appear VERB
❶ *Snowdrops appear in the spring.*
• come out, emerge, become visible, come into view, develop, occur, show, crop up, spring up, surface
❷ *Our visitors didn't appear until midnight.*
• arrive, come, turn up
(informal) show up
❸ *It appears that the baby is asleep.*
• seem, look
❹ *I once appeared in a musical.*
• act, perform, take part, feature

appearance NOUN
❶ *They were startled by the appearance of the ghost.*
• approach, arrival, entrance, entry
❷ *Mrs Traore had a grim appearance.*
• air, aspect, bearing, look

appetizing ADJECTIVE
The appetizing smell of baking filled the house.
• delicious, tasty, tempting, mouthwatering food

appetite NOUN
❶ *When I was ill, I completely lost my appetite.*
• desire to eat, hunger
❷ *Explorers have a great appetite for adventure.*
• hunger, desire, eagerness, enthusiasm, passion, keenness, wish, urge, taste, thirst, longing, yearning, craving, lust, zest

applaud VERB
The audience laughed and applauded.
• clap, cheer
OPPOSITE boo

application NOUN
❶ *Have you sent in our application for a refund?*
• request, claim
❷ *The job needs a lot of patience and application.*
• effort, commitment, dedication, perseverance, persistence, devotion

apply VERB
❶ *The nurse told me to apply the ointment generously.*
• administer, put on, lay on, spread

❷ *My brother has **applied** for a new job.*
• make an application for, ask for, request
❸ *The rules **apply** to all our members.*
• be relevant, relate, refer
❹ *The vet **applied** all her skill to save the animal's life.*
• use, employ, exercise, utilize

appoint *VERB*
❶ *The school governors **appointed** a new teacher.*
• choose, select, elect, vote for, settle on
❷ *We **appointed** a time for our meeting.*
• arrange, decide on, fix, settle, determine

appointment *NOUN*
❶ *I have an **appointment** to meet the bank manager.*
• arrangement, engagement, date
❷ *The team are waiting for the **appointment** of a new captain.*
• naming, selection, choice, choosing, election
❸ *My aunt got a new **appointment** overseas.*
• job, post, position, situation

appreciate *VERB*
❶ *He **appreciates** good music.*
• enjoy, like, love
❷ *I **appreciate** her good qualities.*
• admire, respect, regard highly, approve of, value, esteem
OPPOSITE despise
❸ *I **appreciate** that you can't afford much.*
• realize, recognize, understand, comprehend, know, see
❹ *Mum hopes that the value of our house will **appreciate**.*
• grow, increase, go up, mount, rise

apprehensive *ADJECTIVE*
*Are you **apprehensive** about your exams?*
• worried, anxious, nervous, tense, edgy, uneasy, troubled, frightened, fearful

approach *VERB*
❶ *The lioness **approached** her prey.*
• draw near to, move towards, come near to, advance on

❷ *I **approached** the head to ask if we could have a party.*
• speak to, contact, go to
❸ *The volunteers **approached** their work cheerfully.*
• begin, undertake, embark on, set about

approach *NOUN*
❶ *We could hear the **approach** of heavy footsteps.*
• arrival, advance, coming
❷ *They made an **approach** to the bank manager for a loan.*
• application, appeal, proposal
❸ *I like her positive **approach**.*
• attitude, manner, style, way
❹ *The easiest **approach** to the castle is from the west.*
• access, entry, entrance, way in

appropriate *ADJECTIVE*
*It's not **appropriate** to wear jeans to a wedding.*
• suitable, proper, fitting, apt, right, tactful, tasteful, well-judged
OPPOSITE inappropriate

approval *NOUN*
❶ *We cheered to show our **approval**.*
• appreciation, admiration, praise, high regard, acclaim, respect, support
OPPOSITE disapproval
❷ *Our boss gave her **approval** to our plan.*
• agreement, consent, authorization, assent, go-ahead, permission, support, blessing
OPPOSITE refusal

approve *VERB*
*The head **approved** my request for a day off school.*
• agree to, consent to, authorize, allow, accept, pass, permit, support, back
OPPOSITE refuse
➤ **to approve of**
*Her family did not **approve of** her marriage.*
• like, favour, welcome, appreciate, admire, value, praise, commend, applaud, respect, esteem
OPPOSITE condemn

a b c d e f g h i j k l m n o p q r s t u v w x y z

A B C D E F G H I J K L M N O P Q R S T U V W X Y Z

approximate ADJECTIVE
What is the approximate length of the journey?
• estimated, rough, inexact, near
OPPOSITE exact

approximately ADVERB
The film will finish at approximately five o'clock.
• roughly, about, around, round about, close to, nearly, more or less

apt ADJECTIVE
❶ *He is apt to be careless with money.*
• likely, liable, inclined, prone
❷ *Your comments on my essay were very apt.*
• appropriate, suitable, proper, fitting, right, well-judged, pertinent
(informal) spot on

aptitude NOUN
She has a remarkable aptitude for music.
• talent, gift, ability, skill, expertise, potential, bent

arch VERB
The cat arched its back.
• curve, bend, bow

arch NOUN
They saw the arch of a rainbow in the sky.
• curve, arc, bend, bow

archer NOUN
see **arrow**

Arctic ADJECTIVE
see **polar**

area NOUN
❶ *From the plane we saw a big area of desert.*
• expanse, stretch, tract
A small area is a **patch**.
An area of water or ice is a **sheet**.
❷ *I live in an urban area.*
• district, locality, neighbourhood, region, zone, vicinity

arena NOUN
for places where sport takes place see **sport**

argue VERB
❶ *You two are always arguing over something.*
• quarrel, disagree, differ, fall out, fight, have an argument, squabble, wrangle, bicker
OPPOSITE agree
❷ *We argued over the price of the book.*
• bargain, haggle
OPPOSITE agree
❸ *He argued that it was my turn to walk the dog.*
• claim, assert, try to prove, maintain, reason, suggest
➤ **to argue about something**
We could argue for hours about football.
• debate, discuss

argument NOUN
❶ *They had an argument over who should pay.*
• disagreement, quarrel, dispute, row, clash, controversy, debate, difference, fight, squabble, altercation
❷ *Did you follow the argument of the book?*
• line of reasoning, theme, outline, gist

arid ADJECTIVE
No plants could grow in the arid soil.
• dry, parched, barren, waterless, lifeless, infertile, sterile, unproductive

arise VERB
❶ *We can phone for help if the need arises.*
• occur, emerge, develop, ensue, appear, come into existence, come up, crop up, happen
❷ *(old use) 'Arise, Sir Lancelot!' said the King.*
• stand up, get up

arm NOUN
The skeleton held out a bony arm.
for parts of your body see **body**

arm VERB
The children armed themselves with sticks.
• equip, supply, provide

18

armed forces *PLURAL NOUN*

WORD WEB

THE PRINCIPAL ARMED FORCES ARE:

• air force, army, navy
Men and women in the armed forces are
troops.
A new member of the armed forces is
a **recruit**.
A young person training to be in the armed
forces is a **cadet**.

VARIOUS GROUPS IN THE ARMED FORCES:

• battalion, brigade, company, corps, fleet,
garrison, legion, patrol, platoon, regiment,
squad, squadron

MEMBERS OF THE ARMED FORCES INCLUDE:

• aircraftman, aircraftwoman, commando,
marine, paratrooper, serviceman,
servicewoman, sailor, soldier
see also **soldier**

armour *NOUN*

WORD WEB

PARTS OF A MEDIEVAL KNIGHT'S ARMOUR:

• breastplate, gauntlet, greave (shin
guard), **habergeon** (sleeveless coat),
helmet, visor
Armour made of linked rings is **chain mail**.
An outfit of armour is a **suit of armour**.
see also **knight**

arms *PLURAL NOUN*
The bandits were equipped with arms.
• weapons, guns, firearms, ammunition

army *NOUN*
see **armed forces**

aroma *NOUN*
The aroma of lavender filled the air.
• smell, scent, odour, fragrance, perfume

around *PREPOSITION*
❶ *The mermaid wore a coral necklace around
her neck.*
• about, round, encircling, surrounding
❷ *There were around a hundred people in the
audience.*
• about, approximately, roughly,
more or less

arouse *VERB*
*The plan to build a supermarket aroused
strong feelings.*
• cause, generate, evoke, stir up, excite,
stimulate, incite, provoke, lead to, produce,
set off, whip up
OPPOSITES calm, quell

arrange *VERB*
❶ *The books are arranged in alphabetical
order.*
• sort, order, put in order, group, organize,
categorize, classify, collate, display, sort out,
set out, lay out, line up
❷ *Do you need any help arranging
the party?*
• plan, organize, prepare, set up, see to

arrangement *NOUN*
❶ *They have improved the arrangement of
the garden.*
• layout, organization, design, planning
❷ *Did you change the arrangement of
my files?*
• order, grouping, display, distribution,
spacing
❸ *We have an arrangement to use the
swimming pool.*
• agreement, deal, bargain, contract,
scheme

arrest *VERB*
❶ *The police arrested the suspects.*
• seize, capture, detain, apprehend, hold,
take prisoner, take into custody, catch
(informal) nick
❷ *Doctors are trying to arrest the spread of
the disease.*
• stop, prevent, halt, hinder, check, delay

arrive *VERB*
When is the train due to arrive?
• appear, come, turn up, show up, get in
When a plane arrives, it **lands** or **touches down.**
➤ **to arrive at**
We arrived at the castle before midnight.
• get to, reach

arrogant *ADJECTIVE*
Their arrogant manner annoys me.
• boastful, conceited, proud, haughty, self-important, bumptious, pompous, snobbish, superior, vain
(informal) cocky, snooty, stuck-up
OPPOSITE modest

arrow *NOUN*
The spine of an arrow is the **shaft.**
The point of an arrow is the **arrowhead.**
Arrows are shot using a **bow.**
A holder for several arrows is a **quiver.**
The sport of shooting arrows at a target is **archery.**
Someone who practises archery is an **archer.**

art *NOUN*
❶ *The art of writing letters is disappearing fast.*
• skill, craft, technique, talent, knack, trick
❷ *She took a course in art and design.*
• artwork, fine art

WORD WEB

SOME TYPES OF ART, CRAFT AND DESIGN:

• animation, applique, baking, basketry, batik, beadwork, carpentry, ceramics, collage, crochet, cross stitch, decoupage, digital art, drawing, embroidery, enamelling, engraving, fine art, graphics, illustration, jewellery, knitting, landscaping, macrame, metalwork, modelling, mosaics, needlework, origami, painting, patchwork, photography, pottery, printing, quilting, screen printing, sculpture, sewing, sketching, spinning, stained glass, stamping, stencilling, textiles, watercolour, weaving, woodwork
for people who work in arts and design see **artist**

article *NOUN*
❶ *Have you any articles for the jumble sale?*
• item, object, thing
❷ *Did you read my article in the magazine?*
• essay, report, piece of writing

artificial *ADJECTIVE*
❶ *Organic gardeners don't use artificial fertilizers.*
• man-made, synthetic, unnatural, manufactured
OPPOSITE natural
❷ *She had an artificial flower in her buttonhole.*
• fake, false, imitation, unreal, bogus, counterfeit
OPPOSITES genuine, real
❸ *Captain Hook gave us an artificial smile.*
• pretend, sham, affected, simulated
(informal) put on
OPPOSITES genuine, natural

artist *NOUN*

WORD WEB

SOME ARTISTS AND CRAFTSPEOPLE:

• animator, baker, blacksmith, carpenter, cartoonist, designer, embroiderer, engraver, goldsmith, graphic designer, illustrator, jeweller, knitter, mason, painter, photographer, potter, printer, quilter, sculptor, seamstress, silversmith, tailor, tattoo artist, textile designer, weaver
for performing artists see **entertainer**

artistic *ADJECTIVE*
Mum's flower arrangements are very artistic.
• creative, imaginative, aesthetic, attractive, beautiful, tasteful
OPPOSITE ugly

ascend VERB
❶ *It took the rescuers a long time to ascend the mountain.*
• climb, go up, mount, move up, scale
❷ *The plane began to ascend.*
• lift off, take off
❸ *The eagle ascended into the air.*
• fly up, rise, soar
OPPOSITE descend

ascent NOUN
The bus moved slowly up the steep ascent.
• climb, rise, slope, hill, gradient, incline, ramp
OPPOSITE descent

ashamed ADJECTIVE
He was ashamed because of what he had done.
• sorry, remorseful, repentant, embarrassed, shamefaced, abashed, mortified, apologetic, penitent
(informal) red-faced
OPPOSITES unashamed, unrepentant

ashes PLURAL NOUN
Next morning, the ashes of the bonfire were still glowing.
• embers, cinders

ask VERB
❶ *I asked them to be careful with the parcel.*
• beg, entreat, appeal to, implore, plead with
❷ *'Are you ready?' I asked.*
• demand, enquire, inquire, query, question
❸ *I'm going to ask you to my party.*
• invite
(formal) request the pleasure of your company

asleep ADJECTIVE
I didn't hear the phone because I was asleep.
• sleeping, dozing, having a nap, napping
(old use) slumbering
A patient asleep for an operation is **anaesthetized** or **under sedation.**
An animal asleep for the winter is **hibernating.**
OPPOSITE awake

➤ to fall asleep
We waited until the giant fell asleep.
• drop off, doze, nod off
To fall asleep quickly is **to go out like a light.**

aspect NOUN
❶ *The book describes some aspects of life in ancient Rome.*
• part, feature, element, angle, detail, side, facet
❷ *The ruined tower had an unfriendly aspect.*
• appearance, look, manner, air, expression, face, countenance
❸ *The front room has a southern aspect.*
• outlook, view, prospect

assault NOUN
The old man was the victim of a serious assault.
• attack, mugging
assault VERB
It's a serious crime to assault a policeman.
• attack, strike, hit, beat up, mug

assemble VERB
❶ *A crowd assembled to watch the rescue.*
• gather, come together, converge, accumulate, crowd together, flock together, meet, convene
OPPOSITE disperse
❷ *We assembled our luggage at the front door.*
• collect, gather, bring together, pile up, put together
❸ *The general assembled his troops.*
• round up, rally, muster

assembly NOUN
There was a large assembly of people in the market square.
• gathering, meeting, crowd, throng
An assembly for worship is a **service.**
A large assembly to show support for something, often out of doors, is a **rally.**
An assembly to discuss political matters is a **council** or **parliament.**

a
b
c
d
e
f
g
h
i
j
k
l
m
n
o
p
q
r
s
t
u
v
w
x
y
z

A
B
C
D
E
F
G
H
I
J
K
L
M
N
O
P
Q
R
S
T
U
V
W
X
Y
Z

An assembly to discuss and learn about a particular topic is a **conference** or **congress**.

assent NOUN
The pirates gave their assent to the plan.
• agreement, approval, consent, go-ahead, permission
OPPOSITE refusal

assert VERB
The prisoner asserted that she was innocent.
• state, claim, contend, declare, argue, insist, maintain, proclaim, insist, protest, swear, testify

assess VERB
The test will assess your knowledge of French.
• evaluate, determine, judge, estimate, measure, gauge, value, weigh up

asset NOUN
Good health is a great asset.
• advantage, benefit, help, blessing

assign VERB
He assigned the difficult jobs to the older children.
• allocate, allot, give, consign, hand over, distribute, share out

assignment NOUN
The spy was given a tough assignment.
• job, task, piece of work, mission, project, duty, responsibility

assist VERB
We were asked to assist the gardener with the weeding.
• help, aid, support, cooperate with, collaborate with
OPPOSITE hinder

assistance NOUN
❶ *Do you need assistance with your luggage?*
• help, aid, support, encouragement
❷ *We bought new sports equipment with the assistance of a local firm.*
• backing, collaboration, cooperation, sponsorship, subsidy, support

assistant NOUN
The magician was training a new assistant.
• helper, partner, colleague, associate, supporter

associate VERB
➤ **to associate one thing with another**
I associate Christmas with holly and snow.
• connect with, identify with, link with, relate to
➤ **to associate with someone**
I don't think you should associate with those people!
• be friends with, go about with, mix with

association NOUN
❶ *We have started a junior tennis association.*
• club, society, group, league, fellowship, partnership, union, alliance
A political association is a **party**.
A business association is a **company** or organization.
❷ *The association between the two men lasted many years.*
• friendship, relationship, link, partnership, closeness

assorted ADJECTIVE
I bought a bag of sweets with assorted flavours.
• various, different, mixed, diverse, miscellaneous, several

assortment NOUN
There was an assortment of sandwiches to choose from.
• variety, mixture, selection, array, choice, collection, diversity

assume VERB
❶ *I assume you'd like some chocolate.*
• suppose, presume, imagine, believe, guess, expect, gather, suspect, think
❷ *The bandit assumed a disguise.*
• put on, adopt, dress up in, wear

assure *VERB*
I assure you that I will take care of your dog.
• promise, give your word to

astonish *VERB*
It astonished us to learn that the house was haunted.
• amaze, astound, surprise, stagger, shock, dumbfound, leave speechless, startle, stun, take aback, take by surprise
(informal) flabbergast, take your breath away

astonishing *ADJECTIVE*
The volcano was an astonishing sight.
• amazing, astounding, staggering, remarkable, surprising, extraordinary, incredible, breathtaking, phenomenal, sensational, stupendous, tremendous, wonderful

astound *VERB*
see **astonish**

astounding *ADJECTIVE*
see **astonishing**

astronaut *NOUN*
The astronauts climbed aboard the spacecraft.
• spaceman or spacewoman

WORD WEB
THINGS AN ASTRONAUT MIGHT USE OR WEAR:

• jet pack, oxygen tank, moon boots or space boots, space helmet, spacesuit, visor

PLACES AN ASTRONAUT MIGHT VISIT:

• alien planet, moon base, space lab, space station, star base
see also **moon, planet, space**

astronomy *NOUN*
for words used in astronomy see **space**

ate *past tense see* **eat**

athlete *NOUN*
for events in which athletes take part
see **athletics**

athletic *ADJECTIVE*
You need to be athletic to run in a marathon.
• fit, active, energetic, strong, muscular, powerful, robust, sturdy, vigorous, well-built
(informal) sporty
OPPOSITES feeble, puny

athletics *PLURAL NOUN*

WORD WEB
SOME ATHLETIC EVENTS:

• cross-country, decathlon, discus, heptathlon, high jump, hurdles, javelin, long jump, marathon, pentathlon, pole vault, relay race, running, shot-put, sprinting, steeplechase, triathlon, triple jump
for other sports see **sport**

atmosphere *NOUN*
❶ *The atmosphere on Mars is unbreathable.*
• air, sky
❷ *There was a happy atmosphere at the party.*
• feeling, mood, spirit

atrocious *ADJECTIVE*
Everyone was shocked by the atrocious crime.
• wicked, terrible, dreadful, abominable, brutal, savage, barbaric, bloodthirsty, callous, cruel, diabolical, evil, fiendish, horrifying, merciless, outrageous, sadistic, terrible, vicious, villainous

attach *VERB*
Attach this label to the parcel.
• fasten, fix, join, tie, bind, secure, connect, link, couple, stick, affix, add, append
OPPOSITE detach

a
b
c
d
e
f
g
h
i
j
k
l
m
n
o
p
q
r
s
t
u
v
w
x
y
z

A B C D E F G H I J K L M N O P Q R S T U V W X Y Z

attached *ADJECTIVE*
➤ **attached to**
The twins are very attached to each other.
• fond of, close to, dear to, devoted to, loyal to, affectionate towards, friendly towards, loving towards
OPPOSITE not close to

attack *NOUN*
❶ *The pirates' attack took us by surprise.*
• assault, strike, charge, rush, raid, ambush, invasion, onslaught
An attack with big guns or bombs is a **blitz** or **bombardment.**
An attack by planes is an **air raid.**
❷ *The newspaper published an attack on his character.*
• criticism, outburst, abuse, tirade
❸ *I had a sneezing attack in assembly.*
• bout, fit, spasm
(informal) turn

attack *VERB*
❶ *The travellers were attacked by highwaymen.*
• assault, beat up, mug, set on, assail
To attack someone else's territory is to **invade** or **raid** it.
To attack someone from a hidden place is to **ambush** them.
To attack the enemy with bombs or heavy guns is to **bombard** them.
To attack by rushing at the enemy is to **charge.**
To attack a place suddenly is to **storm** it.
If an animal attacks you, it might **savage** you.
❷ *They attacked the minister's reputation.*
• abuse, criticize, denounce
OPPOSITE defend

attain *VERB*
The team attained a total of twelve gold medals.
• get, obtain, reach, achieve, accomplish, gain

attempt *VERB*
They will attempt to reconstruct a Viking ship.
• try, endeavour, strive, seek, aim, make an effort

attempt *NOUN*
The pole-vaulter cleared the bar at the first attempt.
• try, effort
(informal) shot, go

attend *VERB*
Are you going to attend the end-of-term concert?
• go to, appear at, be present at
➤ **to attend to**
❶ *Please attend carefully to my instructions.*
• listen to, pay attention to, follow carefully, heed, mark, mind, note, notice, observe, think about
❷ *Who will attend to the washing up?*
• deal with, see to
❸ *The nurses attended to the wounded.*
• take care of, care for, look after, help, mind, tend

attention *NOUN*
❶ *Please give your full attention to the teacher.*
• concentration, consideration, thought, observation, awareness, heed, concern
❷ *The survivors need urgent medical attention.*
• treatment, care

attentive *ADJECTIVE*
Drivers should be attentive at all times.
• alert, paying attention, watchful, vigilant, observant, careful, listening, on the alert, on the lookout, sharp-eyed, wary, wide awake

attitude *NOUN*
I'm trying to take a more positive attitude to life.
• outlook, approach, behaviour, stance, frame of mind, disposition, view, position, manner, mood

attract *VERB*
❶ *Do you think our exhibition will attract people?*
• interest, appeal to, fascinate, tempt, entice
❷ *Baby animals attract big crowds at the zoo.*
• draw, pull in
OPPOSITE repel

attractive *ADJECTIVE*
❶ *He was a very attractive young man.*
• beautiful, pretty, good-looking, handsome, gorgeous, glamorous, striking, fetching, charming, lovely, delightful, pleasing, fascinating, captivating, enchanting
see also **beautiful**
OPPOSITES unattractive, repulsive
❷ *There are some attractive bargains in the sale.*
• appealing, agreeable, interesting, desirable, tempting, irresistible

audible *ADJECTIVE*
see **hear**

audience *NOUN*
The audience were enthralled by the jugglers.
• crowd, spectators
The audience for a TV programme is the **viewers**.
The audience for a radio programme is the **listeners**.

authentic *ADJECTIVE*
❶ *That is an authentic painting by Picasso.*
• genuine, real, actual
OPPOSITE counterfeit
❷ *The book is an authentic account of life at sea.*
• accurate, truthful, reliable, true, honest, dependable, factual
OPPOSITE false

author *NOUN*
see **writer**

authority *NOUN*
❶ *I have the head's authority to go home early.*
• permission, consent, approval
❷ *The king had the authority to execute the prisoners.*
• power, right, influence
❸ *My friend is an authority on steam trains.*
• expert, specialist

automatic *ADJECTIVE*
❶ *We took our car through the automatic car wash.*
• automated, mechanical, programmed, computerized

❷ *My sneezing was an automatic response to the pepper.*
• instinctive, involuntary, impulsive, spontaneous, reflex, natural, unconscious, unthinking

available *ADJECTIVE*
❶ *There are no more seats available.*
• obtainable, free
❷ *Is there a phone available in the library?*
• accessible, ready, usable, at hand, handy, within reach, convenient
OPPOSITE unavailable

average *ADJECTIVE*
It was an average kind of day at school.
• everyday, ordinary, normal, typical, usual, regular, commonplace, familiar
OPPOSITES unusual, extraordinary

avid *ADJECTIVE*
My sister is an avid reader.
• keen, eager, enthusiastic, passionate, ardent, fervent, zealous

avoid *VERB*
❶ *The driver tried hard to avoid the collision.*
• get out of the way of, avert, dodge, keep clear of, steer clear of, fend off, shun
❷ *The outlaws avoided capture for months.*
• elude, evade, run away from, escape from
❸ *How did you manage to avoid the washing up?*
• get out of, dodge, shirk

await *VERB*
I await your reply to my letter.
• wait for, look out for, be ready for, expect, hope for

awake *ADJECTIVE*
Hester lay awake all night worrying.
• wide awake, restless, sleepless, conscious, astir
Insomnia is a condition where someone is unable to sleep.
OPPOSITE asleep

a
b
c
d
e
f
g
h
i
j
k
l
m
n
o
p
q
r
s
t
u
v
w
x
y
z

awaken VERB
❶ *Mum awakened us at seven.*
• wake, waken, rouse, arouse, call, alert
❷ *The dragon will awaken at dawn.*
• wake up, become conscious, stir

award NOUN
Kirsty got a national award for gymnastics.
• prize, trophy, medal

award VERB
My friend was awarded first prize in the competition.
• give, present, grant

aware ADJECTIVE
➤ **aware of**
The spy was aware of the dangers of the mission.
• acquainted with, conscious of, familiar with, informed about
OPPOSITE ignorant of

awful ADJECTIVE
❶ *The weather was awful last weekend.*
• bad, dreadful, terrible, appalling, dire, abysmal
(informal) rubbish, lousy
❷ *The teacher complained about our awful behaviour.*
• disgraceful, shameful, disobedient, naughty
❸ *The team captain was an awful bully.*
• unpleasant, disagreeable, nasty, horrid, detestable, unkind, unfriendly
❹ *The country was shocked by the awful crime.*
• horrifying, shocking, atrocious, abominable, outrageous
❺ *I feel awful about forgetting your birthday.*
• sorry, ashamed, embarrassed, guilty, remorseful
for other ways to describe something bad see **bad**

awkward ADJECTIVE
❶ *The parcel was an awkward shape.*
• bulky, inconvenient, unmanageable, unwieldy
OPPOSITE convenient

❷ *The giant was very awkward with his knife and fork.*
• clumsy, unskilful, bungling
OPPOSITE skilful
❸ *We found ourselves in a very awkward situation.*
• difficult, troublesome, trying, perplexing, tough
OPPOSITES straightforward, easy
❹ *Are you trying to be awkward?*
• obstinate, stubborn, uncooperative, unhelpful, exasperating
OPPOSITE cooperative
❺ *I felt awkward as I didn't know anyone at the party.*
• embarrassed, uncomfortable, uneasy, out of place
OPPOSITES comfortable, at ease

Bb

baby NOUN
• infant, child
A baby who has just been born is a **newborn**.
A baby just learning to walk is a **toddler**.
The time when someone is a baby is their **babyhood**.
for names of baby animals see **animal**

babyish ADJECTIVE
I think that game is babyish.
• childish, immature, infantile
OPPOSITES grown-up, mature

back NOUN
We always sit at the back of the bus.
• end, rear, tail end
The back of a ship is the **stern**.
The back of a piece of paper is the **reverse**.

The back of an animal is the **hindquarters, rear** or **rump.**
A fin or spine on the back of an animal is a **dorsal fin** or **spine.**
OPPOSITE front

back ADJECTIVE
The back door of the cabin was locked.
• end, rear, tail
The back legs of an animal are its **hind** legs.
OPPOSITE front

back VERB
❶ *A big lorry was backing into our driveway.*
• go backwards, reverse
❷ *I'm backing the blue team to win the race.*
• bet on, put money on
❸ *The council is backing the plan to build a skate park.*
• support, sponsor, endorse
➤ **to back away**
When the dog growled, the robber backed away.
• back off, retreat, give way, retire, recoil
OPPOSITE approach
➤ **to back out of something**
The injured player may have to back out of the final.
• drop out of, withdraw from
➤ **to back someone up**
Will you back me up if I need help?
• support, second

background NOUN
❶ *I drew a mermaid with the sea in the background.*
OPPOSITE foreground
❷ *The first chapter deals with the background to the war.*
• circumstances (of), history (of), lead-up (to)
❸ *My mother's family has a Swedish background.*
• tradition, upbringing, ancestry

bad ADJECTIVE
This has been a bad week for all of us.
• awful, horrible, terrible
OPPOSITES good, fine, excellent

OVERUSED WORD

Try to vary the words you use for **bad**. Here are some other words you could use.

FOR A BAD PERSON OR BAD CREATURE:

• wicked, evil, cruel, malevolent, malicious, vicious, villainous, mean, nasty, beastly, monstrous, corrupt, deplorable, detestable, immoral, infamous, shameful, sinful, notorious
Beedle the Bard... rather liked Muggles, whom he regarded as ignorant rather than malevolent.—THE TALES OF BEEDLE THE BARD, J. K. Rowling
A bad person is a **scoundrel, rogue** or **rascal.**
A bad character in a story or film is a **villain** or *(informal)* **baddy.**
OPPOSITES good, virtuous

FOR A BAD ACCIDENT OR BAD ILLNESS:

• serious, severe, grave, distressing, acute
Ingrid has a severe case of chickenpox.
OPPOSITE minor

FOR BAD BEHAVIOUR:

• naughty, mischievous, disobedient, disgraceful, wrong
That mischievous kitten drank my milk!
OPPOSITES exemplary, angelic

FOR A BAD EXPERIENCE OR BAD NEWS:

• unpleasant, unwelcome, disagreeable, horrible, awful, terrible, dreadful, horrific, appalling, shocking, hideous, disastrous, ghastly, frightful, abominable, diabolical
The letter contained disagreeable news.
Another word for a bad experience is an **ordeal.**
OPPOSITES good, excellent

FOR A BAD HABIT OR SOMETHING THAT IS BAD FOR YOU:

• harmful, damaging, dangerous, undesirable, detrimental, injurious
Fizzy drinks can be harmful to your teeth.

a b c d e f g h i j k l m n o p q r s t u v w x y z

A
B
C
D
E
F
G
H
I
J
K
L
M
N
O
P
Q
R
S
T
U
V
W
X
Y
Z

FOR A BAD PERFORMANCE OR BAD WORK:

• poor, inferior, weak, unsatisfactory, inadequate, incompetent, awful, hopeless, terrible, useless, worthless, abysmal, shoddy
(informal) rubbish
The worst part of the film is the incompetent acting.

FOR A BAD SMELL OR BAD TASTE:

• disgusting, revolting, repulsive, sickening, nauseating, repugnant, foul, loathsome, offensive, vile
A nauseating smell wafted from the kitchen.
OPPOSITES pleasant, appetizing

FOR BAD TIMING:

• inconvenient, unsuitable, unfortunate, inappropriate
You've caught me at an inconvenient moment.
OPPOSITES convenient, opportune

FOR BAD WEATHER:

• harsh, hostile, unfavourable, adverse, miserable
(informal) lousy
Penguins face hostile weather in the Antarctic.
OPPOSITES fine, favourable

FOR FOOD THAT HAS GONE BAD:

• mouldy, rotten, off, decayed, sour, spoiled, rancid
The strawberries have started to go mouldy.
OPPOSITE fresh

TO FEEL BAD ABOUT SOMETHING:

• guilty, ashamed, sorry, remorseful, repentant
Scrooge feels repentant by the end of the story.
OPPOSITES unashamed, unrepentant

bad-tempered *ADJECTIVE*
Trolls are always bad-tempered before breakfast.
• cross, grumpy, irritable, moody, quarrelsome, fractious, ill-tempered, short-tempered, cantankerous, crotchety, snappy, testy, sullen
OPPOSITES good-tempered, cheerful

bag *NOUN*
I put my wet clothes in a plastic bag.
• sack, carrier, holdall, satchel, handbag, shoulder bag
A bag you carry on your back is a **backpack** or **rucksack**.

baggage *NOUN*
We loaded our baggage on to a trolley.
• luggage, bags, cases, suitcases, belongings, things
(informal) gear, stuff

baggy *ADJECTIVE*
The clown wore a pair of baggy trousers.
• loose, loose-fitting, roomy

bake *VERB*
for ways to cook things see **cook**

balance *NOUN*
➤ **to lose your balance**
Rick lost his balance and fell off the branch.
• totter, wobble

bald *ADJECTIVE*
The ogre had a bald patch on the top of his head.
• bare, hairless
OPPOSITE hairy

ball *NOUN*
❶ *Wind the string into a ball.*
• sphere, globe, orb
A small ball of something is a **pellet** or **globule**.
❷ *We kicked a ball about in the playground.*
for games played with a ball see **sport**

ban *VERB*
*Rollerblades are **banned** from the playground.*
• forbid, prohibit, bar, exclude, outlaw
OPPOSITES allow, permit

band *NOUN*
❶ *The king was surrounded by a **band** of
courtiers.*
• company, group, gang, party, troop, crew
❷ *I play piano in the junior jazz **band**.*
• group, ensemble, orchestra
❸ *His hair was tied with a **band** of elastic.*
• strip, stripe, ring, line, belt, hoop

bandage *NOUN*
*You need a **bandage** on that knee.*
• dressing, plaster, gauze, lint

bandit *NOUN*
Bandits used to live in these mountains.
• robber, brigand, thief, outlaw, desperado,
highwayman, pirate, buccaneer

bang *NOUN*
❶ *There was a loud **bang** as the balloon burst.*
• blast, boom, crash, thud, thump, pop,
explosion, report
for other types of noise see **sound**
❷ *He got a **bang** on the head from the
low ceiling.*
• bump, blow, hit, knock, thump, punch,
smack, whack, clout
(informal) wallop

bang *VERB*
*The taxi driver **banged** on the door.*
• hit, thump, strike, bash, slam, wham

banish *VERB*
*The king's brother was **banished** forever.*
• exile, expel, deport, send away, eject

bank *NOUN*
❶ *The temple was built on the **banks** of the
River Nile.*
• edge, side, shore, margin, brink
❷ *We rolled our Easter eggs down a
grassy **bank**.*
• slope, mound, ridge, embankment

banner *NOUN*
*The turrets were decorated with colourful
banners.*
• flag, standard, streamer, pennant

banquet *NOUN*
*There was a **banquet** on the queen's birthday.*
• dinner, feast

bar *NOUN*
❶ *Did you eat the whole **bar** of chocolate?*
• block, slab, chunk, wedge
A bar of gold or silver is an **ingot**.
A bar of soap is a **cake**.
❷ *The window had iron **bars** across it.*
• rod, pole, rail, stake, beam, girder

bar *VERB*
❶ *Two athletes were **barred** from competing in
the race.*
• ban, prohibit, exclude, keep out
❷ *A fallen tree **barred** our way.*
• block, hinder, impede, obstruct,
stop, check

bare *ADJECTIVE*
❶ *I put suncream on my **bare** arms and legs.*
• naked, nude, exposed, uncovered,
unclothed, undressed
❷ *The wolf had a **bare** patch on its back.*
• bald, hairless

a b c d e f g h i j k l m n o p q r s t u v w x y z

A ❸ *We slept outside on the bare mountain.*
- barren, bleak, treeless
B ❹ *Inside, the dungeon was cold and bare.*
- empty, unfurnished, vacant
C ❺ *There wasn't a bare patch of wall left.*
- blank, plain, clear, empty
D ❻ *There is only room to pack the bare essentials.*
- basic, minimum
E

barely ADVERB
F *We barely had time to get dressed.*
- hardly, scarcely, only just
G

bargain NOUN
H ❶ *We made a bargain with the captain to take us ashore.*
I - deal, agreement, promise, pact
❷ *That camera you bought was a bargain.*
J - good buy, special offer
(informal) snip, steal
K
bargain VERB
L *He refused to bargain with the pirates for his life.*
M - argue, do a deal, haggle, negotiate

N **barge** VERB
➤ **to barge into**
O ❶ *People were running around and barging into each other.*
P - bump into, collide with, veer into
❷ *A messenger barged breathlessly into the room.*
Q - push into, rush into, storm into
R

S **bark** VERB
The guard dog began to bark fiercely.
T - woof, yap, yelp, growl
for other animal noises see **animal**
U

V **barrel** NOUN
The smugglers carried barrels of gunpowder.
W - cask, drum, tub, keg, butt

X **barren** ADJECTIVE
Pictures show the surface of Mars as a barren
Y *landscape.*
Z

- dry, dried-up, arid, bare, waste, lifeless, infertile, sterile
OPPOSITES fertile, lush

barrier NOUN
❶ *Spectators were asked to stay behind the barrier.*
- wall, fence, railing, barricade
A barrier across a road is a **roadblock**.
❷ *His shyness was a barrier to making friends.*
- obstacle, hurdle, drawback, handicap, hindrance, stumbling block

base NOUN
❶ *The footprints stop at the base of the pyramid.*
- bottom, foot
❷ *The doll's house comes with a wooden base.*
- foundation, support
A base under a statue is a **pedestal** or **plinth**.
❸ *The mountaineers returned to their base.*
- headquarters, camp, depot

basement NOUN
- cellar, vault
A room underneath a church is a **crypt**.
An underground cell in a castle is a **dungeon**.
for other parts of a building see **building**

basic ADJECTIVE
❶ *These are the basic moves in ice-skating.*
- main, chief, principal, key, central, essential, fundamental, crucial
❷ *My knowledge of Chinese is very basic.*
- elementary, simple
OPPOSITE advanced

basically ADVERB
Basically, I think you're right.
- essentially, in essence, at heart, fundamentally

basin NOUN
Fill a basin with soapy water.
- sink, bowl, dish

basis NOUN
What is the basis of your argument?
- base, core, foundation

basket *NOUN*
A basket of food is a **hamper**.
A basket on a bicycle is a **pannier**.
A small basket of strawberries is a **punnet**.

bat *NOUN*
*A **bat** is used to hit the ball in cricket and baseball.*
In golf, you hit the ball with a **club**.
In snooker, you hit it with a **cue**.
In tennis, you hit it with a **racket**.
In hockey, you hit it with a **stick**.

batch *NOUN*
*Ellis made a fresh **batch** of pancakes.*
• lot, bunch, amount, quantity

bathe *VERB*
❶ *It was too cold to **bathe** in the sea.*
• swim, go swimming, splash about, take a dip
To walk about in shallow water is to **paddle**.
To walk through deep water is to **wade**.
❷ *The nurse gently **bathed** the wound.*
• clean, cleanse, wash, rinse

batter *VERB*
*The prisoner **battered** his fists against the door.*
• beat, pound, thump, pummel

battle *NOUN*
*The **battle** raged for many months.*
• fight, clash, conflict, action, engagement, hostilities, struggle

bay *NOUN*
*Dolphins were swimming in the **bay**.*
• cove, inlet, gulf, harbour, sound

be *VERB* am, are, is; was, were; being, been
❶ *I'll **be** at home all morning.*
• stay, continue, remain
❷ *The concert will **be** in March.*
• take place, happen, come about, occur
❸ *She wants to **be** a barrister.*
• become, develop into

beach *NOUN*
*We found these shells on the **beach**.*
• sands, seashore, seaside, shore
*for things you might see or do on a beach see also **seashore, seaside***

bead *NOUN*
❶ *Zaire wore a string of coral **beads**.*
*for items of jewellery see **jewel***
❷ *The explorer wiped **beads** of sweat from his brow.*
• blob, drop, droplet, drip, pearl

beam *NOUN*
❶ *Wooden **beams** ran across the ceiling.*
• bar, timber, joist, plank, post, rafter, spar, strut, support
❷ *A **beam** of sunlight entered the cave.*
• ray, shaft, stream, gleam
A strong narrow beam of light used in various devices is a **laser**.

beam *VERB*
❶ *In the photo, we are all **beaming** at the camera.*
• smile, grin
(OPPOSITES) frown, scowl
❷ *The satellite will **beam** a signal back to Earth.*
• transmit, send out, broadcast, emit

bean *NOUN*
see **vegetable**

bear *NOUN*

WORD WEB

SOME TYPES OF BEAR:

• black bear, brown bear, grizzly bear, polar bear
A young bear is a **cub**.
A bear lives in a **den** and **hibernates** in winter.
Animals rather like bears are the **koala** and **giant panda**.
A toy bear is a **teddy bear**.
*for other animals see **animal***

bear *VERB* bears, bearing, bore, born
or **borne**
❶ *The rope won't bear my weight.*
• carry, support, hold, take
❷ *The messenger bore a letter from
the king.*
• bring, carry, convey, transport, take,
transfer
❸ *The gravestone bears an old inscription.*
• display, show, have
❹ *The stench in the cave was too much
to bear.*
• put up with, cope with, stand, suffer,
tolerate, endure, abide
❺ *The lioness has borne three cubs.*
• give birth to

bearable *ADJECTIVE*
*The temperature at midday is high, but
bearable.*
• tolerable, endurable, acceptable
OPPOSITE unbearable

beast *NOUN*
In the darkness, they heard a wild beast howl.
• animal, creature
You might call a large or frightening beast a
brute or **monster**.
for mythological beasts see **myth**

beat *VERB* beats, beating, beat, beaten
❶ *It's cruel to beat an animal with
a stick.*
• hit, strike, thrash, batter, whip, lash, flog
(informal) whack, wallop
for other ways of hitting see **hit**
❷ *I beat my brother at chess for the first time.*
• defeat, conquer, vanquish, win against, get
the better of, overcome, overwhelm, rout,
thrash, trounce
(informal) hammer
❸ *Beat the eggs, milk and sugar together.*
• whisk, whip, blend, mix, stir
❹ *Can you feel your heart beating?*
• pound, thump, palpitate
➤ **to beat someone up**
The bully threatened to beat me up.
• assault, attack

beat *NOUN*
❶ *Can you feel the beat of your heart?*
• pulse, throb
❷ *Reggae music has a strong beat.*
• rhythm, accent, stress

beautiful *ADJECTIVE*

OVERUSED WORD

Try to vary the words you use for
beautiful. Here are some other words you
could use.

FOR A BEAUTIFUL PERSON:

• attractive, good-looking, handsome,
pretty, gorgeous, glamorous, radiant,
elegant, enchanting, dazzling, stunning,
magnificent, resplendent
*This balcony belonged to an attractive
middle-aged lady called Mrs Silver … And
although she didn't know it, it was she who
was the object of Mr Hoppy's secret love.*
—ESIO TROT, Roald Dahl
OPPOSITES ugly, unattractive

**FOR A BEAUTIFUL DAY OR BEAUTIFUL
WEATHER:**

• fine, excellent, glorious, marvellous,
sunny, superb, splendid, wonderful
It was a glorious day for a bicycle trip.
OPPOSITES dull, gloomy, drab

FOR A BEAUTIFUL SIGHT:

• charming, delightful, glorious,
magnificent, splendid, spectacular,
picturesque, scenic
*The Northern Lights are a spectacular
sight.*

FOR A BEAUTIFUL SOUND:

• harmonious, melodious, mellifluous,
sweet-sounding
The nightingale has a sweet-sounding song.
OPPOSITE grating

beauty NOUN
Elves are famous for their beauty.
• attractiveness, prettiness, loveliness, charm, allure, magnificence, radiance, splendour
OPPOSITE ugliness

beckon VERB
The guard was beckoning me to approach.
• signal, gesture, motion, gesticulate

become VERB becomes, becoming, became, become
❶ *I soon became frustrated with the video game.*
• begin to be, turn, get
❷ *Eventually, the tadpoles will become frogs.*
• grow into, change into, develop into, turn into
❸ *That style of hat becomes you.*
• look good on, suit, flatter

bed NOUN
❶ *The children slept on hard, wooden beds.*
• bunk, mattress
A bed for a baby is a **cot**, **cradle** or **crib**.
Two single beds one above the other are **bunk beds**.
A bed on a ship or train is a **berth**.
A bed made of net or cloth hung up above the ground is a **hammock**.
❷ *We planted daffodils in the flower beds.*
• plot, patch, border
❸ *These creatures feed on the bed of the ocean.*
• bottom, floor
OPPOSITE surface

bedraggled ADJECTIVE
After its swim, the puppy was wet and bedraggled.
• messy, scruffy, untidy, dishevelled, dirty, wet
OPPOSITES smart, spruced up

bee NOUN

WORD WEB

SOME TYPES OF BEE:
• bumblebee, drone, honeybee, worker, queen
A young bee after it hatches is a **larva**.
A group of bees is a **swarm** or a **colony**.
A place where bees live is a **hive**.
A person who owns bees and collects their honey is a **beekeeper**.
for other insects see **insect**

before ADVERB
❶ *Have you used a camera before?*
• previously, in the past, earlier, sooner
OPPOSITE later
❷ *Those people were before us in the queue.*
• in front of, ahead of, in advance of
OPPOSITE after

beg VERB
He begged me not to let go of the rope.
• ask, plead with, entreat, implore, beseech

begin VERB begins, beginning, began, begun
❶ *The hunters began their search at dawn.*
• start, commence, embark on, set about
OPPOSITES end, finish, conclude
❷ *When did the trouble begin?*
• start, commence, arise, emerge, appear, originate, spring up
OPPOSITES end, stop, cease

beginner NOUN
This swimming class is for beginners.
• learner, starter, novice
A beginner in a trade or a job is an **apprentice** or **trainee**.
A beginner in the police or armed services is a **cadet** or **recruit**.

beginning NOUN
The house was built at the beginning of the last century.

a
b
c
d
e
f
g
h
i
j
k
l
m
n
o
p
q
r
s
t
u
v
w
x
y
z

A
B
C
D
E
F
G
H
I
J
K
L
M
N
O
P
Q
R
S
T
U
V
W
X
Y
Z

• start, opening, commencement, introduction, establishment, foundation, initiation, launch, dawn
The beginning of the day is **dawn** or **daybreak**.
The beginning of a journey is the **starting point**.
The beginning of a stream or river is the **origin** or **source**.
A piece of writing at the beginning of a book is an **introduction**, **preface** or **prologue**.
A piece of music at the beginning of a musical or opera is a **prelude** or **overture**.
OPPOSITES end, conclusion

behave *VERB*
*Our neighbour is **behaving** very strangely.*
• act, react
➤ **to behave yourself**
*We promised to **behave** ourselves in the car.*
• be good, be on your best behaviour

behaviour *NOUN*
*I give my puppy treats for good **behaviour**.*
• actions, conduct, manners, attitude

being *NOUN*
*They looked like **beings** from another planet.*
• creature, individual, person, entity

belch *VERB*
*The chimney **belched** clouds of black smoke.*
• discharge, emit, send out, gush, spew

belief *NOUN*
❶ *She was a woman of strong religious **beliefs**.*
• faith, principle, creed, doctrine
❷ *It is my **belief** that he stole the money.*
• opinion, view, conviction, feeling, notion, theory

believable *ADJECTIVE*
*None of the characters in the book is **believable**.*
• credible, plausible
OPPOSITES unbelievable, implausible

believe *VERB*
❶ *I don't **believe** anything he says.*
• accept, have faith in, rely on, trust
OPPOSITES disbelieve, doubt
❷ *I **believe** they used to live in Colombia.*
• think, assume, feel, presume, reckon, suppose

bell *NOUN*

WRITING TIPS

You can use these words to describe how a bell sounds:
• chime, clang, jangle, jingle, peal, ring, tinkle, toll
The front-door bell clanged loudly, and the Rat, who was very greasy with buttered toast, sent Billy, the smaller hedgehog, to see who it might be.—THE WIND IN THE WILLOWS, Kenneth Grahame

belong *VERB*
❶ *This ring **belonged** to my grandmother.*
• be owned by
❷ *Do you **belong** to the sports club?*
• be a member of, be connected with

belongings *PLURAL NOUN*
*Don't leave any **belongings** on the bus.*
• possessions, property, goods, things

below *PREPOSITION*
❶ *We saw goldfish swimming **below** the surface.*
• under, underneath, beneath
❷ *The temperature never fell **below** 20 degrees.*
• less than, lower than
OPPOSITE above

belt *NOUN*
❶ *The prince wore a **belt** of pure gold.*
• girdle, sash, strap, band
❷ *We walked through a **belt** of woodland.*
• strip, band, line, stretch

bench *NOUN*
We sat on a bench in the park.
• seat, form
A long seat in a church is a **pew**.
for other types of seat see **seat**

bend *VERB*
This drinking straw bends in the middle.
• curve, turn, twist, curl, coil, loop, arch,
warp, wind
A word to describe things which bend easily is
flexible or *(informal)* **bendy**.
OPPOSITE straighten
➤ **to bend down**
I bent down to tie my shoelaces.
• stoop, bow *(rhymes with cow)*, crouch,
duck, kneel

bend *NOUN*
Watch out for the sharp bend in the road.
• curve, turn, angle, corner, twist, zigzag

beneath *PREPOSITION*
The tunnel ran beneath the castle.
• under, underneath, below
OPPOSITES above, over

beneficial *ADJECTIVE*
Drinking water is beneficial to your health.
• favourable, useful, advantageous,
salutary
OPPOSITES harmful, detrimental

benefit *NOUN*
What are the benefits of regular exercise?
• advantage, reward, gain, good point
OPPOSITES disadvantage, drawback

benefit *VERB*
The rainy weather will benefit gardeners.
• help, aid, assist, be good for, profit
OPPOSITES hinder, harm

benevolent *ADJECTIVE*
*The lady greeted us with a benevolent
smile.*
• friendly, kind, warm-hearted, sympathetic,
generous, charitable, benign
OPPOSITE malevolent

bent *ADJECTIVE*
❶ *After the crash, the car was a mass of
bent metal.*
• curved, twisted, coiled, looped, buckled,
crooked, arched, folded, warped
(informal) wonky
❷ *The witch had a bent back and walked with
a stick.*
• crooked, hunched, curved, arched,
bowed *(rhymes with loud)*
OPPOSITE straight

beside *PREPOSITION*
You can sit beside me if you like.
• next to, alongside, by, close to, near
➤ **beside the point**
The fact that you're ill is beside the point.
• irrelevant, neither here nor there,
unimportant

besides *ADVERB*
❶ *No-one knows the secret, besides you
and me.*
• as well as, in addition to, apart from,
other than
❷ *It's too cold to go out. Besides, it's
dark now.*
• also, in addition, additionally, furthermore,
moreover

besiege *VERB*
❶ *The Greeks besieged Troy for 10 long years.*
• blockade, cut off, isolate
❷ *The film star was besieged by reporters.*
• surround, mob, plague, harass

best *ADJECTIVE*
❶ *She is our best goalkeeper.*
• top, leading, finest, foremost, supreme, star,
outstanding, unequalled, unrivalled
OPPOSITE worst
❷ *We did what we thought was best.*
• most suitable, most appropriate

bet *NOUN*
I had a bet that our team would win.
• gamble, wager
(informal) flutter

a b c d e f g h i j k l m n o p q r s t u v w x y z

A
B
C
D
E
F
G
H
I
J
K
L
M
N
O
P
Q
R
S
T
U
V
W
X
Y
Z

bet *VERB* bets, betting, bet or betted
❶ *I bet you 50 pence that it will snow tomorrow.*
• gamble, wager, stake, risk
❷ *I bet my brother forgets my birthday.*
• feel sure, be certain, expect

betray *VERB*
❶ *He betrayed us by telling the enemy our plan.*
• be disloyal to, be a traitor to, cheat, conspire against, double-cross
Someone who betrays you is a **traitor**.
To betray your country is to commit **treason**.
❷ *The look in her eyes betrayed her true feelings.*
• reveal, show, indicate, disclose, divulge, expose, tell

better *ADJECTIVE*
❶ *Which of these songs do you think is better?*
• superior, finer, preferable
❷ *I had a cold, but I'm better now.*
• recovered, cured, healed, improved, well

between *PREPOSITION*
Let's divide the chocolate between us.
• among, amongst

beware *VERB*
Beware! There are thieves about.
• be careful, watch out, look out, take care, be on your guard
➤ **beware of**
Beware of the bull.
• watch out for, avoid, mind, heed, keep clear of

bewilder *VERB*
We were bewildered by the directions on the map.
• confuse, puzzle, baffle, bemuse, mystify, perplex, fox
(informal) flummox

beyond *PREPOSITION*
The village lies just beyond those hills.
• after, past, the other side of

biased *ADJECTIVE*
A referee should not make a biased decision.
• prejudiced, partial, one-sided, partisan, unfair
OPPOSITE impartial

bicycle *NOUN*
(informal) bike, push bike

WORD WEB

A person who rides a bicycle is a **cyclist**. An indoor arena for bicycle racing is a **velodrome**.

SOME TYPES OF BICYCLE:

• mountain bike, racing bike, reclining or recumbent bike, road bike, tandem, trailer bike
A cycle with one wheel is a **unicycle**.
A cycle with three wheels is a **tricycle** or *(informal)* **trike**.
A cycle without pedals is a **scooter**.
A type of bicycle used in the past was a **penny-farthing**.

THE MAIN PARTS OF A BICYCLE ARE:

• brakes, brake lever, chain, crossbar, gear shift, handlebars, pedals, saddle

bid *NOUN*
❶ *There were several bids for the painting at the auction.*
• offer, price, tender
❷ *Our bid to beat the world record failed.*
• attempt, effort, try, go

big ADJECTIVE

OVERUSED WORD

Try to vary the words you use for **big**. Here are some other words you could use.

FOR SOMETHING BIG IN SIZE OR WEIGHT:

• large, huge, enormous, massive, great, gigantic, colossal, mammoth, overgrown
(informal) whopping, ginormous, mega
OPPOSITES small, little, tiny
The Dragon Stoorworm ... was absolutely ginormous and almost completely covered Scotland, from the top to the bottom, and all the way across from side to side.—THE DRAGON STOORWORM, Theresa Breslin

FOR A BIG PERSON OR BIG CREATURE:

• giant, hefty, hulking, burly, mighty, monstrous, towering
The Trunchbull, this mighty female giant, stood there in her green breeches, quivering like a blancmange.—MATILDA, Road Dahl

FOR A BIG DISTANCE OR BIG AREA:

• immense, vast, infinite
A vast stretch of ocean lay before them.

FOR SOMETHING BIG INSIDE:

• roomy, spacious, sizeable
Inside, the spaceship was surprisingly roomy.
OPPOSITE cramped

FOR A BIG AMOUNT OR BIG HELPING:

• ample, considerable, substantial
We each got an ample helping of porridge.
OPPOSITES meagre, paltry

FOR A BIG DECISION OR BIG MOMENT:

• important, significant, serious, grave
Yesterday was the most significant day in my short life.
OPPOSITES unimportant, minor

bill NOUN
My granny offered to pay the bill.
• account, invoice, statement, charges

billow VERB
❶ *Smoke billowed from the mouth of the cave.*
• pour, swirl, spiral
❷ *The sheets on the washing line billowed in the wind.*
• swell, bulge, puff, balloon

bind VERB binds, binding, bound
We bound the sticks together with some rope.
• attach, fasten, tie, secure, join, connect, lash, rope

bird NOUN

WORD WEB

A female bird is a **hen**.
A male bird is a **cock**.
A young bird is a **chick**, **fledgling** or **nestling**.
A family of chicks is a **brood**.
A group of birds is a **colony** or **flock**.
A group of flying birds is a **flight** or skein.
A person who studies birds is an **ornithologist**.

SOME COMMON BRITISH BIRDS:

• blackbird, blue tit, bullfinch, bunting, chaffinch, crow, cuckoo, dove, greenfinch, jackdaw, jay, lark, linnet, magpie, martin, nightingale, pigeon, raven, robin, rook, skylark, sparrow, starling, swallow, swift, thrush, tit, wagtail, waxwing, woodpecker, wren, yellowhammer

BRITISH BIRDS OF PREY:

• buzzard, eagle, falcon, hawk, kestrel, kite, merlin, osprey, owl, sparrowhawk, vulture

BRITISH FARM AND GAME BIRDS:

• chicken, duck, goose, grouse, partridge, pheasant, quail, turkey
Birds kept by farmers are called **poultry**.

a b c d e f g h i j k l m n o p q r s t u v w x y z

SOME SEA AND WATER BIRDS:

• albatross, auk, bittern, coot, cormorant, crane, curlew, duck, gannet, goose, guillemot, gull, heron, kingfisher, kittiwake, lapwing, mallard, moorhen, oystercatcher, peewit, pelican, penguin, puffin, seagull, snipe, stork, swan, teal

BIRDS FROM OTHER COUNTRIES:

• bird of paradise, budgerigar, canary, cockatoo, flamingo, hummingbird, ibis, kookaburra, macaw, mynah bird, parakeet, parrot, toucan

BIRDS WHICH CANNOT FLY:

• emu, kiwi, ostrich, peacock, penguin

PARTS OF A BIRD'S BODY:

• beak, bill, claw, talon, breast, crown, throat, crest, feather, down, plumage, plume, wing
see also **feather**

SOME TYPES OF BIRD HOME:

• nest, nesting box, aviary, coop, roost

SOUNDS MADE BY BIRDS:

• cackle, caw, cheep, chirp, chirrup, cluck, coo, crow, gabble, honk, peep, pipe, quack, screech, squawk, trill, tweet, twitter, warble
A turkey **gobbles**.
An owl **hoots**.

SPECIAL NAMES:

A female peacock is a **peahen**.
A young duck is a **duckling**.
A young goose is a **gosling**.
A young puffin is a **puffling**.
A young swan is a **cygnet**.
An eagle's nest is an **eyrie**.
A place where rooks nest is a **rookery**.
for groups of birds see **group**

WRITING TIPS

You can use these words to describe a **bird**:

TO DESCRIBE HOW A BIRD MOVES:

• circle, dart, flit, flutter, fly, glide, hop, hover, peck, perch, preen, skim, soar, swoop, waddle, wheel
The post owls arrived, swooping down through rain-flecked windows, scattering everyone with droplets of water.–HARRY POTTER AND THE HALF-BLOOD PRINCE, J. K. Rowling

TO DESCRIBE A BIRD'S FEATHERS:

• bedraggled, downy, drab, fluffy, gleaming, iridescent, ruffled, smooth, speckled
*The peacock displayed its **iridescent** tail.*

bit *NOUN*

❶ *Jose divided the cake into eight bits.*
• piece, portion, part, section, segment, share, slice
❷ *These jeans are a bit long for me.*
• a little, slightly, rather, fairly, somewhat, quite

OVERUSED WORD

Try to vary the words you use for **bit**. Here are some other words you could use.

FOR A LARGE BIT OF SOMETHING:

• chunk, lump, hunk, wedge, slab
And they all went over to the tunnel entrance and began scooping out great chunks of juicy, golden-coloured peach flesh.–JAMES AND THE GIANT PEACH, Road Dahl

FOR A SMALL BIT OF SOMETHING:

• fragment, scrap, chip, particle, speck, sliver, pinch, touch, dab, atom, iota
(informal) smidgen
*The map was drawn on a **scrap** of old paper.*

a
b
c
d
e
f
g
h
i
j
k
l
m
n
o
p
q
r
s
t
u
v
w
x
y
z

FOR A BIT OF FOOD:

• morsel, crumb, bite, nibble, taste, mouthful
*Please try a **morsel** of chocolate mousse.*

FOR A BIT OF LIQUID:

• drop, dash, dribble, splash, spot
*Add a **splash** of vinegar to the sauce.*

bite *VERB* bites, biting, bit, bitten
❶ *I **bit** a chunk out of my apple.*
• munch, nibble, chew, crunch, gnaw
(informal) chomp
for other ways to eat see **eat**
❷ *Take care. These animals can **bite**.*
• nip, pinch, pierce, wound
When an animal tries to bite you it **snaps** at you.
When an insect bites you it **stings** you.
A fierce animal **mauls** or **savages** its prey.

bitter *ADJECTIVE*
❶ *The medicine had a **bitter** taste.*
• sour, sharp, acid, acrid, tart
(OPPOSITE) sweet
❷ *His brother was still **bitter** about the quarrel.*
• resentful, embittered, disgruntled, aggrieved
(OPPOSITE) contented
❸ *The wind blowing in from the sea was **bitter**.*
• biting, cold, freezing, icy, piercing, raw, wintry
(informal) perishing
(OPPOSITE) mild

bizarre *ADJECTIVE*
*'Whiskers' is a **bizarre** name for a goldfish!*
• odd, strange, peculiar, weird, extraordinary, outlandish
(OPPOSITE) ordinary

black *ADJECTIVE, NOUN*
*The pony had a shiny **black** coat.*
• coal-black, jet-black, pitch-black, ebony, raven

You can also describe a black night as **pitch-dark**.
Common similes are **as black as coal** and **as black as night**.

blame *VERB*
*Don't **blame** me if you miss the bus.*
• accuse, criticize, condemn, reproach, scold

bland *ADJECTIVE*
*This cheese has a really **bland** taste.*
• mild, dull, weak, insipid
(OPPOSITES) strong, pungent

blank *ADJECTIVE*
❶ *There are no **blank** pages left in my school notebook.*
• empty, bare, clean, plain, unmarked, unused
❷ *The old woman gave us a **blank** look.*
• expressionless, faceless, vacant
blank *NOUN*
*Fill in the **blanks** to complete the sentence.*
• space, break, gap

blanket *NOUN*
❶ *The baby was wrapped in a woollen blanket.*
• cover, sheet, quilt, rug, throw
❷ *A **blanket** of snow covered the lawn.*
• covering, layer, film, sheet, mantle

blast *NOUN*
❶ *A **blast** of cold air came through the open door.*
• gust, rush, draught, burst
❷ *They heard the **blast** of a trumpet.*
• blare, noise, roar
❸ *Many people were injured in the **blast**.*
• explosion, shock

blatant *ADJECTIVE*
*Do you expect me to believe such a **blatant** lie?*
• barefaced, flagrant, obvious, shameless, brazen, unabashed

blaze *NOUN*
*Firefighters fought the **blaze** for hours.*
• fire, flames, inferno

blaze *VERB*
Within a few minutes the campfire was blazing.
• burn brightly, flare up

bleak *ADJECTIVE*
❶ *The countryside was bleak and barren.*
• bare, barren, desolate, empty, exposed, stark
❷ *The future looks bleak for the club.*
• gloomy, hopeless, depressing, dismal, grim, miserable
OPPOSITE promising

blemish *NOUN*
This peach has a blemish on the skin.
• fault, flaw, defect, imperfection, mark, spot, stain

blend *VERB*
❶ *Blend the flour with a tablespoon of water.*
• beat together, mix, stir together, whip, whisk
❷ *The paint colours blend well with each other.*
• go together, match, fit, harmonize
OPPOSITE clash

blessing *NOUN*
❶ *The author gave the film her blessing.*
• approval, backing, support, consent, permission
OPPOSITE disapproval
❷ *A warm hat is a blessing in cold weather.*
• benefit, advantage, gift, asset, comfort
OPPOSITES curse, evil

blew *past tense see* **blow**

blight *NOUN*
The tower block is a blight on the landscape.
• menace, nuisance, affliction, curse, evil, plague

blind *ADJECTIVE*
Polar bear cubs are born blind.
• sightless, unsighted, unseeing
A common simile is as blind as a bat.
OPPOSITES sighted, seeing

➤ **blind to**
The captain was blind to his own faults.
• ignorant of, unaware of, oblivious to
OPPOSITE aware of

bliss *NOUN*
Having a whole day off school was sheer bliss.
• joy, delight, pleasure, happiness, heaven, ecstasy
OPPOSITE misery

blob *NOUN*
The alien left blobs of green slime on the carpet.
• drop, lump, spot, dollop, daub, globule

block *NOUN*
❶ *A block of ice fell from the glacier.*
• chunk, hunk, lump, piece
❷ *There must be a block in the drainpipe.*
• blockage, jam, obstacle, obstruction
block *VERB*
❶ *A tall hedge blocked our view of the house.*
• obstruct, hamper, hinder, interfere with
❷ *A mass of leaves had blocked the drain.*
• clog, choke, jam, plug, stop up, congest *(informal)* bung up

blockage *NOUN*
We spent ages clearing the blockage in the drain.
• block, obstacle, obstruction, jam

bloodshed *NOUN*
In ancient times, this was a scene of bloodshed.
• killing, massacre, slaughter, butchery, carnage

bloodthirsty *ADJECTIVE*
The bloodthirsty pirates rattled their swords.
• brutal, cruel, barbaric, murderous, inhuman, pitiless, ruthless, savage, vicious

bloom *NOUN*
The pear tree was covered in white blooms.
• flower, blossom, bud
WHICH WORD? Note that a **bloom** is a single flower. A mass of flowers is **blossom**.

bloom *VERB*
The daffodils bloomed early this year.
• blossom, flower, open
OPPOSITE fade

blossom *NOUN*
I love to see the cherry blossom in spring.
• blooms, buds, flowers
WHICH WORD? Note that blossom usually
means a mass of flowers. A single flower is
a bloom.

blot *NOUN*
The old map was covered with ink blots.
• spot, blotch, mark, blob, splodge, smudge,
smear, stain

blot *VERB*
➤ **to blot something out**
The new tower block blots out the view.
• conceal, hide, mask, obliterate, obscure

blotch *NOUN*
*The dragon had green skin with purple
blotches.*
• patch, blot, spot, mark, blob, splodge,
splash, stain

blow *NOUN*
❶ *He was knocked out by a blow on the head.*
• knock, bang, bash, hit, punch, clout, slap,
smack, swipe, thump
(informal) wallop, whack
❷ *Losing the hockey match was a
terrible blow.*
• shock, upset, setback, disappointment,
catastrophe, misfortune, disaster,
calamity
blow *VERB* blows, blowing, blew, blown
The wind was blowing from the east.
• blast, gust, puff, fan
To make a shrill sound by blowing is
to whistle.
➤ **to blow out**
I blew out the candles on my birthday cake.
• extinguish
➤ **to blow up**
❶ *I need to blow up the tyres on my bike.*
• inflate, pump up, swell, fill out

❷ *The soldiers tried to blow up the enemy
hideout.*
• blast, bomb, destroy
❸ *Do you think they could blow up this
photograph?*
• enlarge

blue *ADJECTIVE, NOUN*

WORD WEB

SOME SHADES OF BLUE:

• azure, cobalt, indigo, navy blue,
sapphire, sky-blue, turquoise

blunder *NOUN*
*Forgetting her birthday was a terrible
blunder.*
• mistake, error, fault, slip, slip-up, gaffe
(informal) howler

blunt *ADJECTIVE*
❶ *This pencil is blunt.*
• dull, worn, unsharpened
OPPOSITES sharp, pointed
❷ *Her reply to my question was very blunt.*
• abrupt, frank, direct, outspoken, plain,
tactless
OPPOSITE tactful

blur *VERB*
❶ *The steamy windows blurred the view.*
• cloud, darken, obscure, smear
❷ *The accident blurred her memory.*
• confuse, muddle

blurred *ADJECTIVE*
*The background of the photograph is all
blurred.*
• indistinct, vague, blurry, fuzzy, hazy,
out of focus
OPPOSITES clear, distinct

blush *VERB*
The actor blushed with embarrassment.
• flush, go red, colour

a
b
c
d
e
f
g
h
i
j
k
l
m
n
o
p
q
r
s
t
u
v
w
x
y
z

A
B
C
D
E
F
G
H
I
J
K
L
M
N
O
P
Q
R
S
T
U
V
W
X
Y
Z

blustery *ADJECTIVE*
It was a typical, blustery day in autumn.
• gusty, windy, blowy, squally
OPPOSITE calm

board *NOUN*
The tabletop was made from a wooden board.
• plank, panel, beam, timber
for board games see **game**

board *VERB*
We boarded the plane for Morocco.
• get on, enter, embark

boast *VERB*
They were always boasting about how rich they were.
• brag, show off, crow, gloat, swagger
(informal) blow your own trumpet

boastful *ADJECTIVE*
Giants are boastful creatures and brag about everything.
• arrogant, big-headed, conceited, vain, bumptious
(informal) cocky, swanky
OPPOSITES modest, humble

boat *NOUN*
Several fishing boats were moored in the harbour.
• ship, craft, vessel

WORD WEB

SOME TYPES OF BOAT OR SHIP:

• barge, canoe, catamaran, cruise liner, dhow, dinghy, dugout, ferry, freighter, gondola, hovercraft, hydrofoil, junk, kayak, launch, lifeboat, motorboat, oil tanker, punt, raft, rowing boat, schooner, skiff, speedboat, steamship, tanker, trawler, tug, yacht

MILITARY BOATS OR SHIPS:

• aircraft carrier, battleship, destroyer, frigate, gunboat, minesweeper, submarine, warship

SOME BOATS USED IN THE PAST:

• brigantine, clipper, coracle, cutter, galleon, galley, longship, man-of-war, paddle steamer, schooner, trireme, windjammer

WORDS FOR PARTS OF A BOAT OR SHIP:

• boom, bridge, bulwark, cabin, crow's nest, deck, engine room, funnel, galley, helm, hull, keel, mast, poop, porthole, propeller, quarterdeck, rigging, rudder, sail, tiller

SPECIAL NAMES:

The front part of a boat is the **bow** or **prow**.
The back part of a boat is the **stern**.
The part below deck where the crew live is called the **fo'c'sle**.
The left-hand side of a boat is called **port**.
The right-hand side of a boat is called **starboard**.
A shed where boats are stored is a **boathouse**.

WRITING TIPS

You can use these words to describe **how a boat moves:**
• cut through the waves or water, drift, float, glide, lurch, pitch, roll, sail, steam, tack
So the boat was left to drift down the stream as it would, till it glided gently in among the waving rushes.–ALICE THROUGH THE LOOKING-GLASS, Lewis Carroll

bob *VERB*
A plastic duck bobbed up and down in the water.
• bounce, dance, toss, wobble

body *NOUN*

WORD WEB

The study of the human body is **anatomy**.
The main part of your body except your head, arms and legs is your **trunk** or **torso**.
The shape of your body is your **build**, **figure** or **physique**.
The dead body of a person is a **corpse**.
The dead body of an animal is a **carcass**.

OUTER PARTS OF THE HUMAN BODY:

• abdomen, ankle, arm, armpit, breast, buttocks, calf, cheek, chest, chin, ear, elbow, eye, finger, foot, forehead, genitals, groin, hand, head, heel, hip, instep, jaw, knee, kneecap, knuckle, leg, lip, mouth, navel, neck, nipple, nose, pores, shin, shoulder, skin, stomach, temple, thigh, throat, waist, wrist

INNER PARTS OF THE HUMAN BODY:

• arteries, bladder, bowels, brain, eardrum, glands, gullet, gums, guts, heart, intestines, kidneys, larynx, liver, lung, muscles, nerves, ovaries, pancreas, prostate, sinews, stomach, tendons, tongue, tonsil, tooth, uterus, veins, windpipe, womb
for bones in your body see **bone**
for parts of animal bodies see **animal**

WRITING TIPS

You can use these words to describe a person's **body:**

TO DESCRIBE A LARGE, HEAVY OR STRONG BODY:

• athletic, beefy, brawny, burly, dumpy, fat, hefty, hulking, muscular, sinewy, squat, stocky, stout, thickset, flabby, plump, rotund, well-rounded
Aunt Agatha was a stout woman, and Stella thought the outfit made her look rather like a giant violet frog.—THE POLAR BEAR EXPLORERS' CLUB, Alex Bell

TO DESCRIBE A SMALL OR WEAK BODY:

• petite, short, slender, slight, slim, svelte, thin, bony, gangly, gaunt, lanky, tall, puny, scraggy, scrawny, skinny, spindly, wiry
Hiccup was just absolutely average, the kind of unremarkable, skinny, freckled boy who was easy to overlook in a crowd.—HOW TO BE A PIRATE, Cressida Cowell

---

bog NOUN
We felt our boots sinking into the bog.
• swamp, quagmire, quicksand, fen

boil VERB
❶ *Would you like your egg boiled or fried?*
for ways to cook food see **cook**
❷ *The water must be boiling before you add the pasta.*
• bubble, seethe, steam

bold ADJECTIVE
❶ *It was a bold move to attack the fortress.*
• brave, courageous, daring, adventurous, audacious, confident, enterprising, fearless, heroic, valiant, intrepid, plucky
OPPOSITE cowardly
❷ *The poster uses large letters in bold colours.*
• striking, strong, bright, loud, showy, conspicuous, eye-catching, noticeable, prominent
OPPOSITES inconspicuous, subtle

bolt VERB
❶ *Did you remember to bolt the door?*
• fasten, latch, lock, secure, bar
❷ *The horses bolted when they heard the thunder.*
• dash away, dart, flee, sprint, run away, rush off
❸ *Don't bolt your food.*
• gobble, gulp, guzzle, wolf down
for other ways to eat see **eat**

bond NOUN
❶ *The prisoner tried to escape from his bonds.*
• chains, fetters, ropes, handcuffs, manacles, shackles, restraints
❷ *There was a special bond between the twins.*
• attachment, connection, tie, link, relationship

bone NOUN

WORD WEB

The bones of your body are your **skeleton.**

SOME BONES IN THE HUMAN BODY:

• backbone or spine, collarbone, cranium or skull, pelvis, ribs, shoulder blade, vertebrae

a
b
c
d
e
f
g
h
i
j
k
l
m
n
o
p
q
r
s
t
u
v
w
x
y
z

A
B
C
D
E
F
G
H
I
J
K
L
M
N
O
P
Q
R
S
T
U
V
W
X
Y
Z

bonus *NOUN*
I got a **bonus** on top of my pocket money last week.
• extra, supplement, reward, tip, handout

book *NOUN*

WORD WEB

A book with hard covers is a **hardback**.
A book with soft covers is a **paperback**.
A book which is typed or handwritten but not printed is a **manuscript**.
A thin book in paper covers is a **booklet**, **leaflet** or **pamphlet**.
A book which is part of a set is a **volume**.
A large heavy book is a **tome**.
The person who writes a book is the **author**.
A book which sells a lot of copies is a **bestseller**.

SOME TYPES OF BOOK:

• album, annual, anthology, atlas, audiobook, comic book, dictionary, e-book, encyclopedia, graphic novel, guidebook, manual, novel, picture book, reading book, reference book, story book, textbook, thesaurus

BOOKS YOU CAN WRITE OR DRAW IN:

• diary, exercise book, jotter, journal, notebook, scrapbook, sketchbook

SOME PARTS OF A BOOK:

• appendix, bibliography, blurb, chapters, contents page, cover, foreword, illustrations, index, introduction, preface, prologue, title page
for ways to describe a book or story see **writing**

book *VERB*
Have you **booked** a seat on the train?
• order, reserve, engage

boom *VERB*
❶ The teacher's voice **boomed** along the corridor.
• shout, roar, bellow, blast, thunder, resound, reverberate
❷ Business was **booming** in the Riverbank Cafe.
• be successful, do well, expand, flourish, grow, prosper, thrive

boost *VERB*
Winning the cup really **boosted** the team's morale.
• raise, uplift, improve, increase, bolster, help, encourage, enhance
OPPOSITES lower, dampen

boot *NOUN*
for types of shoe or boot see **shoe**

border *NOUN*
❶ The town is on the **border** between France and Germany.
• boundary, frontier
❷ I drew a thin line around the **border** of the picture.
• edge, margin, perimeter
A decorative border round the top of a wall is a **frieze**.
A border round the bottom of a skirt is a **hem**.
A decorative border on fabric is a **frill**, **fringe** or **trimming**.

bore *past tense see* **bear**

bore *VERB*
They **bored** a hole right through the outer wall.
• drill, pierce, sink, tunnel

boring *ADJECTIVE*
The film was so **boring** I fell asleep.
• dull, dreary, tedious, tiresome, unexciting, uninteresting, dry, monotonous, uninspiring, insipid, unimaginative, uneventful, humdrum
OPPOSITES interesting, exciting

borrow *VERB*
Can I **borrow** your pencil?
• use, take, obtain, acquire
(informal) cadge, scrounge
OPPOSITE lend

44

boss *NOUN*
There is a new **boss** at the football club.
• head, chief, manager, leader, director
(informal) gaffer

bossy *ADJECTIVE*
Stop being so **bossy** towards your sister.
• domineering, bullying, dictatorial, officious,
tyrannical
An informal name for a bossy person is
bossy boots.

bother *VERB*
❶ Would it **bother** you if I played
some music?
• disturb, trouble, upset, annoy, irritate,
pester, worry, vex, exasperate
(informal) bug, hassle
❷ Don't **bother** to phone tonight.
• make an effort, take the trouble,
concern yourself, care, mind

bother *NOUN*
It's such a **bother** to remember the password.
• nuisance, annoyance, irritation,
inconvenience, pest, trouble, difficulty,
problem
(informal) hassle

bottle *NOUN*
Bring a **bottle** of water with you.
• flask, flagon, jar, pitcher
A bottle for serving water or wine is a **carafe**
or **decanter**.
A small bottle for perfume or medicine is
a **phial**.

bottle *VERB*
➤ **to bottle something up**
It's not healthy to **bottle up** your anger.
• hold in, cover up, conceal, suppress
`OPPOSITES` show, express

bottom *NOUN*
❶ We camped at the **bottom** of the mountain.
• foot, base
`OPPOSITES` top, peak
❷ The wreck sank to the **bottom** of the sea.
• bed, floor
`OPPOSITE` surface

❸ A wasp stung me on the **bottom**.
• backside, behind, buttocks, rear, rump, seat
(informal) bum

bottom *ADJECTIVE*
I got the **bottom** mark in the maths test.
• least, lowest
`OPPOSITE` top

bough *NOUN*
The robin perched on a **bough** of the tree.
• branch, limb

bought *past tense see* **buy**

bounce *VERB*
The ball **bounced** twice before it reached
the net.
• rebound, ricochet, spring, leap

bound *past tense see* **bind**

bound *ADJECTIVE*
❶ It's **bound** to rain at the weekend.
• certain, sure
❷ I felt **bound** to invite my cousin to the party.
• obliged, duty-bound, committed, compelled,
forced, required
❸ The accident was **bound** to happen.
• destined, doomed, fated
➤ **bound for**
The space rocket was **bound for** Mars.
• going to, heading for, making for,
travelling towards, off to

bound *VERB*
The puppies **bounded** across the lawn.
• leap, bounce, jump, spring, skip, gambol,
caper, frisk

boundary *NOUN*
The lamp post marks the **boundary** of Narnia.
• border, frontier, edge, end, limit, perimeter,
dividing line

bout *NOUN*
❶ She's recovering from a **bout** of flu.
• attack, fit, period, spell
(informal) turn

a
b
c
d
e
f
g
h
i
j
k
l
m
n
o
p
q
r
s
t
u
v
w
x
y
z

❷ *A judo* **bout** *is between two contestants.*
• contest, match, round, fight, battle, combat

bow NOUN *(rhymes with* **go***)*
The archer raised his **bow** *and arrow.*
for words to do with archery see **arrow**

bow NOUN *(rhymes with* **cow***)*
The captain stood at the **bow** *of the ship.*
• front, prow
for other parts of a boat or ship see **boat**

bow VERB *(rhymes with* **cow***)*
❶ *The prisoner* **bowed** *his head in shame.*
• lower, bend, duck
❷ *The servant knelt and* **bowed** *in front of the king.*
The corresponding movement of a woman is to **curtsy.**

bowl NOUN
There was a **bowl** *of fresh fruit on the table.*
• basin, dish, vessel
A large bowl for serving soup is a **tureen.**

bowl VERB
Can you **bowl** *a faster ball next time?*
• throw, pitch, fling, hurl, toss
for other ways to throw a ball see **ball**

box NOUN
• case, chest, crate, carton, packet
A small box for jewellery or treasure is a **casket.**
A large box for luggage is a **trunk.**

boy NOUN
• lad, youngster, youth
(informal) kid

brag VERB
Ashanti is still **bragging** *about her swimming medal.*
• show off, boast, gloat, crow
(informal) blow your own trumpet
A person who is always bragging is a **braggart.**

brain NOUN
You'll need to use your **brain** *to solve this riddle.*

• intelligence, intellect, mind, reason, sense, wit

branch NOUN
❶ *A robin perched on a* **branch** *of the tree.*
• bough, limb
❷ *I've joined the local* **branch** *of the Kennel Club.*
• section, division, department, wing

branch VERB
Follow the track until it **branches** *into two.*
• divide, fork

brand NOUN
Which **brand** *of ice cream do you like?*
• make, kind, sort, type, variety, label
The sign of a particular brand of goods is a **trademark.**

brandish VERB
Captain Hook **brandished** *his cutlass at the crew.*
• flourish, wield, flaunt, wave

brave ADJECTIVE
It was **brave** *of you to save the cat from drowning.*
• courageous, heroic, valiant, fearless, daring, gallant, intrepid, plucky
A common simile is **as brave as a lion.**
OPPOSITE cowardly

bravery NOUN
The police dog was awarded a medal for **bravery.**
• courage, heroism, valour, fearlessness, daring, nerve, gallantry, grit, pluck
(informal) guts, bottle
OPPOSITE cowardice

brawl NOUN
We could hear a **brawl** *on the street outside.*
• fight, quarrel, scuffle, tussle
(informal) scrap

breach NOUN
❶ *Handling the ball is a* **breach** *of the rules.*
• breaking, violation

You can also talk about an **offence** against the rules.
❷ *The storm caused a **breach** in the sea wall.*
• break, split, crack, gap, hole, opening, fracture, rupture, fissure

break NOUN
❶ *Can you see any **breaks** in the chain?*
• breach, crack, hole, gap, opening, split, rift, puncture, rupture, fracture, fissure
❷ *Let's take a **break** for coffee.*
• interval, pause, rest, lull, timeout
(informal) breather

break VERB breaks, breaking, broke, broken
❶ *The vase fell off the shelf and **broke**.*
• smash, shatter, fracture, chip, crack, split, snap, splinter
(informal) bust
❷ *The burglar was arrested for **breaking** the law.*
• disobey, disregard, violate, flout
❸ *In her last race, she **broke** the world record.*
• beat, better, exceed, surpass, outdo
➤ **to break down**
*Our car **broke down** on the motorway.*
• fail, go wrong, stop working
(informal) pack in, conk out
➤ **to break off**
*We'll **break off** for lunch at one o'clock.*
• have a rest, pause, stop
➤ **to break out**
*A flu epidemic **broke out** just after Christmas.*
• begin, spread, start
➤ **to break out of**
*The prisoner tried to **break out of** jail.*
• escape from, break loose from, abscond from
➤ **to break up**
*After the speeches, the crowd began to **break up**.*
• disperse, scatter, separate, split up, disintegrate

breakable ADJECTIVE
*Be careful! The parcel has **breakable** things in it.*
• fragile, delicate, brittle, frail
OPPOSITE unbreakable

breakdown NOUN
❶ *There has been a **breakdown** in the peace talks.*
• failure, collapse, fault
❷ *Can you give me a **breakdown** of the figures?*
• analysis

break-in NOUN
*There was a **break-in** at the local bank.*
• burglary, robbery, theft, raid

breakthrough NOUN
*Scientists have made a **breakthrough** in medicine.*
• advance, leap forward, discovery, development, revolution, progress
OPPOSITE setback

breath NOUN
*There wasn't a **breath** of wind in the air.*
• breeze, puff, waft, whiff, whisper, sigh

breathe VERB
To breathe in is to **inhale**.
To breathe out is to **exhale**.
To breathe heavily when you have been running is to **pant** or **puff**.
The formal word for breathing is **respiration**.

breathless ADJECTIVE
*Leo was **breathless** after the race.*
• out of breath, gasping, panting, puffing, tired out, wheezing

breed VERB
❶ *Salmon swim upstream to **breed** every year.*
• reproduce, have young, multiply, procreate, spawn
❷ *Bad hygiene **breeds** disease.*
• cause, produce, generate, encourage, promote, cultivate, induce

breed NOUN
*What **breed** of cat is that?*
• kind, sort, type, variety
The evidence of how a dog or cat has been bred is its **pedigree**.

a
b
c
d
e
f
g
h
i
j
k
l
m
n
o
p
q
r
s
t
u
v
w
x
y
z

A
B
C
D
E
F
G
H
I
J
K
L
M
N
O
P
Q
R
S
T
U
V
W
X
Y
Z

breezy *ADJECTIVE*
This morning the weather was bright and breezy.
• windy, blowy, blustery, gusty, fresh, draughty
see also **weather**

brew *VERB*
❶ *I'm just going to brew some tea.*
• make, prepare
When you brew beer it **ferments**.
❷ *It looks like a storm is brewing.*
• develop, form, loom, build up, gather, threaten

brew *NOUN*
The wizard stirred an evil-smelling brew.
• mixture, concoction

bridge *NOUN*
A bridge you can walk over is a footbridge.
A bridge to carry water is an **aqueduct**.
A long bridge carrying a road or railway is a **viaduct**.

brief *ADJECTIVE*
❶ *We paid a brief visit to our cousins on the way home.*
• short, quick, hasty, fleeting, temporary
❷ *Give me a brief account of what happened.*
• short, concise, abbreviated, condensed, compact, succinct
(OPPOSITES) long, lengthy

bright *ADJECTIVE*
❶ *We saw the bright lights of the town in the distance.*
• shining, brilliant, blazing, dazzling, glaring, gleaming
(OPPOSITES) dull, dim, weak
❷ *Bright colours will make the poster stand out.*
• strong, intense, vivid
Colours that shine in the dark are **luminous** colours.
(OPPOSITES) dull, faded, muted

❸ *Her teachers thought she was very bright.*
• clever, intelligent, gifted, sharp, quick-witted
(informal) brainy
A common simile is as **bright as a button**.
(OPPOSITES) stupid, dull-witted
❹ *Charlie gave me a bright smile.*
• cheerful, happy, lively, merry, jolly, radiant
(OPPOSITES) sad, gloomy
❺ *The day was cold, but bright.*
• sunny, fine, fair, clear, cloudless
(OPPOSITES) dull, cloudy, overcast

brighten *VERB*
It was a cloudy morning, but it brightened after lunch.
• become sunny, clear up, improve
➤ **to brighten up**
A new coat of paint will brighten up the room.
• cheer up, light up, enliven

brilliant *ADJECTIVE*
❶ *The fireworks gave off a brilliant light.*
• bright, blazing, dazzling, glaring, gleaming, glittering, glorious, shining, splendid, vivid
(OPPOSITES) dim, dull
❷ *Brunel was a brilliant engineer.*
• clever, exceptional, outstanding, gifted, talented
(OPPOSITES) incompetent, talentless
❸ *(informal) I saw a brilliant film last week.*
• excellent, marvellous, outstanding, wonderful, superb
(informal) fantastic, fabulous
see also **good**

brim *NOUN*
I filled my glass to the brim.
• top, rim, edge, brink, lip

bring *VERB* brings, bringing, brought
❶ *Can you bring the shopping in from the car?*
• carry, fetch, deliver, bear, transport
❷ *You can bring a friend to the party.*
• invite, conduct, escort, guide, lead

❸ *The war has* **brought** *great sorrow to our people.*
• cause, produce, lead to, result in, generate

➤ **to bring something about**
The new coach **brought about** *some changes.*
• cause, effect, create, introduce, be responsible for

➤ **to bring someone up**
In the story, Tarzan is **brought up** *by apes.*
• rear, raise, care for, foster, look after, nurture, educate, train

➤ **to bring something up**
I wish you hadn't **brought up** *the subject of money.*
• mention, talk about, raise, broach

brink NOUN
We stood on the **brink** *of a deep crater.*
• edge, lip, rim, verge, brim

brisk ADJECTIVE
❶ *Mrs Marawat went for a* **brisk** *walk every evening.*
• lively, fast-paced, energetic, invigorating, vigorous, refreshing, bracing
OPPOSITES slow, leisurely
❷ *The flower shop does a* **brisk** *trade around Easter.*
• busy, lively, bustling, hectic
OPPOSITES quiet, slack, slow

brittle ADJECTIVE
The bones of the skeleton were dry and **brittle**.
• breakable, fragile, delicate, frail
OPPOSITES soft, flexible

broad ADJECTIVE
❶ *The streets in the city were* **broad** *and straight.*
• wide, open, large, roomy, spacious, vast, extensive
OPPOSITE narrow
❷ *Just give me a* **broad** *outline of what happened.*
• general, rough, vague, loose, indefinite, imprecise
OPPOSITES specific, detailed

broaden VERB
I'm **broadening** *my interests by listening to jazz.*
• widen, extend, enlarge, expand, increase, develop, diversify

brochure NOUN
We got some holiday **brochures** *from the travel agent.*
• leaflet, pamphlet, booklet, catalogue

broke *past tense see* **break**

broken ADJECTIVE
❶ *Don't use that computer—it's* **broken**.
• faulty, defective, damaged, out of order
OPPOSITE working
❷ *After losing all his money, Forbes was a* **broken** *man.*
• crushed, defeated, beaten, spiritless

brood VERB
❶ *The hen was* **brooding** *her clutch of eggs.*
• hatch, incubate, sit on
❷ *He was still* **brooding** *over what I had said.*
• fret, mope, worry, dwell on

brought *past tense see* **bring**

brown ADJECTIVE, NOUN

WORD WEB

SOME SHADES OF BROWN:

• beige, bronze, buff, chestnut, chocolate, dun, fawn, khaki, russet, sepia, tan, tawny

browse VERB
❶ *I like* **browsing** *through toy catalogues.*
• flick through, leaf through, scan, skim
❷ *The cattle were* **browsing** *in the meadow.*
• graze, feed

a b c d e f g h i j k l m n o p q r s t u v w x y z

A
B
C
D
E
F
G
H
I
J
K
L
M
N
O
P
Q
R
S
T
U
V
W
X
Y
Z

bruise *VERB*
I fell and **bruised** my knee.
• mark, hurt, injure
for other types of injury see **injury**

brush *VERB*
❶ We spent ages **brushing** our three dogs.
• groom, comb, tidy
❷ A bird **brushed** against my cheek as it flew past.
• touch, contact, rub, scrape
➤ **to brush up**
I must **brush up** my Spanish before we go to Argentina.
• revise, improve, go over, refresh your memory of
(informal) swot up

brutal *ADJECTIVE*
The bandits launched a **brutal** attack.
• savage, vicious, cruel, barbaric, bloodthirsty, callous, ferocious, inhuman, merciless, pitiless, ruthless, sadistic
OPPOSITES gentle, humane

bubble *NOUN*
The bubbles in a fizzy drink are **effervescence**.
The bubbles made by soap or detergent are **lather** or **suds**.
Bubbles on top of a liquid are **foam** or **froth**.
The bubbles on top of beer are the **head**.

bubble *VERB*
A green liquid **bubbled** in the witch's cauldron.
• boil, seethe, gurgle, froth, foam

bubbly *ADJECTIVE*
❶ **Bubbly** drinks get up my nose.
• fizzy, sparkling, effervescent
❷ Sophie has a bright and **bubbly** personality.
• cheerful, lively, vivacious, spirited, animated

bucket *NOUN*
We took **buckets** and spades to the seaside.
• pail, can

buckle *NOUN*
The pirate wore a belt with a large silver **buckle**.
• clasp, fastener, fastening, clip, catch
buckle *VERB*
❶ Please **buckle** your seat belts.
• fasten, secure, clasp, clip, do up, hook up
❷ The bridge **buckled** when the giant stepped on to it.
• bend, warp, twist, crumple, cave in, collapse

bud *NOUN*
Buds are appearing on the apple trees.
• shoot, sprout

budge *VERB*
The window was stuck and wouldn't **budge**.
• give way, move, shift, stir

budget *VERB*
➤ **to budget for**
Have you **budgeted for** a holiday this year?
• allow for, plan for, provide for

bug *NOUN*
❶ Birds help to control **bugs** in the garden.
• insect, pest
❷ *(informal)* I can't get rid of this stomach **bug**.
• infection, virus, germ, disease, illness
❸ There are a few **bugs** in the computer program.
• fault, error, defect, flaw
(informal) gremlin
bug *VERB*
❶ The spy **bugged** their phone conversations.
• tap, listen in to, intercept
❷ *(informal)* I wish you'd stop **bugging** me with questions.
• bother, annoy, pester, trouble, harass

build *VERB* builds, building, built
We are going to **build** a shed in the garden.
• construct, erect, put together, put up, set up, assemble
➤ **to build up**
❶ I'm **building up** a collection of comic books.
• accumulate, assemble, collect, put together

❷ *We felt the tension **building up** in the crowd.*
• increase, intensify, rise, grow, mount up, escalate

build *NOUN*
*Charlotte had a strong **build**.*
• body, form, frame, figure, physique
see also **body**

building *NOUN*
*The new **building** will have seven storeys.*
• construction, structure, dwelling

WORD WEB

A person who designs buildings is an architect.

BUILDINGS WHERE PEOPLE LIVE:

• apartment, barracks, bungalow, castle, cottage, farmhouse, flat, fort, fortress, house, hut, mansion, palace, ranch, skyscraper, tenement, terrace, tower, villa
see also **house**

BUILDINGS WHERE PEOPLE WORK:

• factory, garage, lighthouse, mill, office, shop, store, warehouse

BUILDINGS WHERE PEOPLE WORSHIP:

• abbey, cathedral, chapel, church, monastery, mosque, pagoda, shrine, synagogue, temple
see also **church**

OTHER TYPES OF BUILDING:

• cabin, cafe, cinema, college, gallery, hotel, inn, library, museum, observatory, police station, post office, power station, prison, restaurant, school, shed, theatre

PARTS YOU MIGHT FIND INSIDE A BUILDING:

• balcony, basement, cellar, conservatory, corridor, courtyard, crypt, dungeon, foyer, gallery, lobby, porch, room, staircase, veranda
see also **room**

PARTS YOU MIGHT FIND OUTSIDE A BUILDING:

• arch, balustrade, bay window, bow window, buttress, chimney, colonnade, column, dome, dormer window, drainpipe, eaves, foundations, gable, gutter, masonry, parapet, pediment, pillar, pipes, quadrangle, roof, tower, turret, vault, wall, window, window sill
for parts of a castle see **castle**

WRITING TIPS

You can use these words to describe a building:
• airy, compact, cramped, crumbling, forbidding, grand, imposing, ramshackle, ruined, run-down, spacious, sprawling, squalid, stark, stately
They lived—Aunt Sponge, Aunt Spiker, and now James as well—in a queer ramshackle house on the top of a high hill in the south of England.—JAMES AND THE GIANT PEACH, Roald Dahl

bulge *NOUN*
*Asian elephants have two **bulges** on their foreheads.*
• bump, hump, lump, swelling, protuberance

bulge *VERB*
*Their eyes **bulged** with excitement.*
• stick out, swell, puff out, protrude

bulk *NOUN*
❶ *The sheer **bulk** of the iceberg was staggering.*
• size, dimensions, magnitude, mass, largeness, immensity
❷ *We spent the **bulk** of our holiday lazing on the beach.*
• most, most part, greater part, majority

bulky *ADJECTIVE*
*The parcel is too **bulky** to go through the letterbox.*
• big, large, hefty, substantial, sizeable, cumbersome, unwieldy
OPPOSITES small, compact

a
b
c
d
e
f
g
h
i
j
k
l
m
n
o
p
q
r
s
t
u
v
w
x
y
z

A
B
C
D
E
F
G
H
I
J
K
L
M
N
O
P
Q
R
S
T
U
V
W
X
Y
Z

bully *VERB*
Some of the children were afraid of being bullied.
• persecute, torment, intimidate, terrorize, push around

bump *VERB*
❶ *The baby bumped his head on the table.*
• hit, strike, knock, bang
❷ *My bicycle bumped up and down over the cobbles.*
• bounce, shake, jerk, jolt
➤ **to bump into**
❶ *The taxi bumped into the car in front of it.*
• collide with, bang into, run into, crash into
❷ *I bumped into one of my friends in the bookshop.*
• meet, come across, run into

bump *NOUN*
❶ *We felt a bump as the plane landed.*
• thud, thump, bang, blow, knock
❷ *How did you get that bump on your head?*
• lump, swelling, bulge

bumpy *ADJECTIVE*
❶ *The car jolted up and down on the bumpy road.*
• rough, uneven, irregular, lumpy
OPPOSITES smooth, even
❷ *We had a bumpy ride in a jeep over muddy tracks.*
• bouncy, jerky, jolting, lurching, choppy

bunch *NOUN*
❶ *The jailer jangled a bunch of keys.*
• bundle, cluster, collection, set
❷ *The child picked a bunch of flowers.*
• bouquet, posy, spray
❸ *(informal) They're a friendly bunch of people.*
• group, set, circle, band, gang, crowd

bundle *NOUN*
I found a bundle of old newspapers.
• bunch, batch, pile, stack, collection, pack, bale

bundle *VERB*
❶ *We bundled up the papers that were on the desk.*
• pack, tie, fasten, bind
❷ *The police bundled them into the back of their car.*
• move hurriedly, push, jostle

burden *NOUN*
❶ *Each mule was carrying a heavy burden.*
• load, weight, cargo
❷ *The captain has the burden of organizing the players.*
• responsibility, obligation, duty, pressure, stress, trouble, worry

burden *VERB*
I won't burden you with my own problems.
• bother, worry, trouble, distress, encumber, lumber
(informal) saddle

burglar *NOUN*
The burglars must have got in through the window.
• robber, thief, intruder

burglary *NOUN*
see **stealing**

burn *VERB* burns, burning, burnt or burned
❶ *We could see the campfire burning in the distance.*
• be alight, be on fire, blaze, flame, flare, flicker
To burn without flames is to **glow** or **smoulder**.
❷ *The captain ordered them to burn the enemy ship.*
• set fire to, incinerate, reduce to ashes
To start something burning is to **ignite**, **kindle** or **light** it.
To burn something slightly is to **char**, **scorch** or **singe** it.
To hurt someone with boiling liquid or steam is to **scald** them.
To burn a dead body is to **cremate** it.
To burn a mark on an animal is to **brand** it.

burrow *NOUN*
*The field was full of rabbit **burrows**.*
• hole, tunnel
A piece of ground with many burrows is
a **warren**.
A fox's burrow is called an **earth**.
A badger's burrow is called an **earth** or **sett**.
for other animal homes see **animal**

burrow *VERB*
*Rabbits have been **burrowing** under the fence.*
• tunnel, dig, excavate, mine

burst *VERB*
*The balloon **burst** when my brother sat on it.*
• puncture, rupture, break, give way,
split, tear

bury *VERB*
❶ *The document was **buried** under a pile of
old letters.*
• cover, conceal, hide, secrete
❷ *My great-grandparents are **buried** in that
graveyard.*
• inter, entomb

bush *NOUN*
*Birds often build their nests in **bushes**.*
• shrub

bushy *ADJECTIVE*
*The troll had **bushy** green eyebrows.*
• hairy, thick, dense, shaggy, bristly

business *NOUN*
❶ *My uncle runs a catering **business**.*
• company, firm, organization
❷ *The new bookshop does a lot of
business.*
• trade, trading, buying and selling,
commerce
❸ *What sort of **business** do you want to
go into?*
• work, job, career, employment, industry,
occupation, profession, trade
❹ *She left early to attend to some urgent
business.*
• matter, issue, affair, problem, point,
concern, question

bustle *VERB*
*We **bustled** about putting up decorations.*
• rush, dash, hurry, scurry, scuttle, fuss

busy *ADJECTIVE*
❶ *Dad is **busy** making my birthday cake
just now.*
• occupied, engaged, employed, working,
slaving away
(informal) hard at it, up to your eyes,
beavering away
A common simile is **as busy as a bee**.
OPPOSITE idle
❷ *Christmas is a very **busy** time for shops.*
• active, hectic, frantic, lively
OPPOSITES quiet, restful
❸ *Is the town always this **busy** on
Saturdays?*
• crowded, bustling, hectic, lively,
teeming
OPPOSITES quiet, peaceful

butt *VERB*
*The Minotaur **butted** Theseus against
the wall.*
• hit, bump, knock, push, ram, shove
➤ **to butt in**
*Please don't **butt in** when I'm talking.*
• interrupt, cut in

buy *VERB* buys, buying, bought
*I'm saving up to **buy** a skateboard.*
• get, pay for, purchase, acquire
OPPOSITE sell

buzz *NOUN, VERB*
for various sounds see **sound**

a
b
c
d
e
f
g
h
i
j
k
l
m
n
o
p
q
r
s
t
u
v
w
x
y
z

Cc

cabin NOUN
❶ *The outlaws hid in a cabin in the woods.*
• hut, shack, shed, lodge, chalet, shelter
❷ *The crew assembled in the captain's cabin.*
• berth, quarters, compartment

cable NOUN
❶ *The tent was held down with strong cables.*
• rope, cord, line, chain
❷ *Don't trip over the computer cable.*
• flex, lead, wire, cord

cafe NOUN
We had lunch in a cafe overlooking the river.
• cafeteria, coffee shop, tea room, snack bar, buffet, canteen, bistro, brasserie
for other places to eat see **restaurant**

cage NOUN
A large cage or enclosure for birds is an **aviary**.
A cage or enclosure for poultry is a **coop**.
A cage or enclosure for animals is a **pen**.
A cage or box for a pet rabbit is a **hutch**.

cake NOUN
Do you prefer carrot cake or chocolate cake?
• sponge, flan
A small individual cake is a **cupcake** or **fairy cake**.
*for puddings and other sweet foods
see* **food**

calamity NOUN
The fire in the warehouse was a calamity.
• disaster, catastrophe, tragedy, misfortune, mishap, blow

calculate VERB
I calculated that it would take an hour to walk home.
• work out, compute, figure out, reckon, add up, count, total
To calculate something roughly is to **estimate**.

call NOUN
❶ *We heard a call for help from inside the cave.*
• cry, exclamation, scream, shout, yell
❷ *Grandad made an unexpected call.*
• visit, stop, stay
❸ *There's not much call for suncream in winter.*
• demand, need

call VERB
❶ *'Stop that racket!' called the janitor.*
• cry out, exclaim, shout, yell
for other ways to say something see **say**
❷ *It was too late at night to call my friends.*
• phone, ring, telephone
❸ *The head teacher called me to his office.*
• summon, invite, send for, order
❹ *The doctor called to see if I was feeling better.*
• visit, pay a visit, drop in, drop by
❺ *They called the baby Marika.*
• name, baptize, christen, dub
❻ *What is your new book going to be called?*
• name, title, entitle
➤ **to call something off**
It was so rainy that we called off the barbecue.
• cancel, abandon, postpone
➤ **to call someone names**
It's not funny to call people names.
• insult, be rude to, make fun of, mock

calm ADJECTIVE
❶ *The weather was too calm to fly our kites.*
• still, quiet, peaceful, tranquil, serene, windless
OPPOSITE stormy, windy
❷ *The sea was calm, and we had a pleasant voyage.*
• smooth, still, flat, motionless, tranquil
OPPOSITE rough, choppy
❸ *I tried to stay calm before my judo exam.*
• cool, level-headed, patient, relaxed, sedate, unemotional, unexcitable, untroubled
OPPOSITE anxious, nervous

came *past tense see* **come**

camel *NOUN*
A camel with a single hump is a **dromedary**.
A camel with two humps is a **Bactrian**.

camp *NOUN*
From the hill we saw a camp in the field below us.
• campsite, camping ground, base
A military camp is an **encampment**.

campaign *NOUN*
❶ *Will you join our campaign to save the whale?*
• movement, crusade, drive, fight, effort, struggle
❷ *The army launched a campaign to recapture the city.*
• operation, offensive, action, war

cancel *VERB*
We had to cancel the race because of the weather.
• abandon, call off, scrap, drop, axe
(informal) scrub, ditch
To cancel something after it has already begun is to **abort** it.
To cancel something, but rearrange it for later, is to **postpone** it or **put it off**.
To cancel items on a list is to **cross out**, **delete** or **erase** them.

candidate *NOUN*
A candidate for a job is an **applicant**.
A candidate in an examination is an **entrant**.
A person competing with others in a contest is a **competitor**, **contender** or **contestant**.

canopy *NOUN*
We sheltered from the rain under a canopy.
• awning, cover, shade

cap *NOUN*
❶ *The tennis players wore caps because it was sunny.*
for various kinds of hat see **hat**
❷ *Who left the cap off the toothpaste?*
• cover, lid, top

cap *VERB*
Mount Everest is always capped with snow.
• cover, top, crown

capable *ADJECTIVE*
She is a capable chef.
• competent, able, accomplished, proficient, skilful, skilled, gifted, talented
OPPOSITE incompetent
➤ **to be capable of**
Do you think the professor is capable of murder?
• be able to do, be equal to, be up to
OPPOSITE be incapable of

capacity *NOUN*
❶ *Alice has a great capacity for making friends.*
• ability, power, potential, capability, competence, talent
(informal) knack
❷ *What is the capacity of this glass?*
• size, volume, space, extent, room
❸ *She spoke in her capacity as team leader.*
• position, function, role, office

cape *NOUN*
❶ *We could see the island from the cape.*
• headland, promontory, point, head
❷ *The lady wore a cape of black velvet.*
• cloak, shawl, wrap, robe
(old use) mantle

capital *NOUN*
❶ *New Delhi is the capital of India.*
• capital city, centre of government
❷ *We have enough capital to start a new business.*
• funds, money, finance, cash, assets, savings, means, resources
➤ **capital letter**
Start a new sentence with a capital letter.
• block capital, block letter

capsize *VERB*
The canoe capsized when it hit a rock.
• overturn, tip over, turn over, keel over
(informal) turn turtle

a b c d e f g h i j k l m n o p q r s t u v w x y z

A
B
C
D
E
F
G
H
I
J
K
L
M
N
O
P
Q
R
S
T
U
V
W
X
Y
Z

capsule NOUN

❶ *This capsule contains poison.*
• pill, tablet, lozenge
❷ *The space capsule is designed to orbit Mars.*
• module, craft, pod
for other words to do with space travel see **space**

captain NOUN

The captain brought his ship safely into harbour.
• commander, commanding officer, master, skipper

captive NOUN

The captives were thrown into the dungeon.
• prisoner, convict
A person who is held captive until demand is met is a **hostage**.

captive ADJECTIVE

The pirates held the crew captive for ten days.
• imprisoned, captured, arrested, detained, jailed
OPPOSITES free, released

captivity NOUN

The hostages have been released from captivity.
• imprisonment, confinement, detention, incarceration
OPPOSITE freedom

capture VERB

❶ *The bank robbers were captured by police this morning.*
• catch, arrest, apprehend, seize, take prisoner *(informal)* nab, nick
❷ *The castle has never been captured by enemy forces.*
• occupy, seize, take, take over, win

car NOUN

Our car is getting repaired in the garage.
• motor car, motor, vehicle
(North American) automobile

WORD WEB

An informal name for an old, noisy car is a **banger**.

SOME TYPES OF CAR:

• convertible, coupé, electric car, estate, four-wheel drive, hatchback, *(trademark)* Jeep, *(trademark)* Land Rover, limousine or *(informal)* limo, *(trademark)* Mini, patrol car or police car, people carrier, racing car, saloon, sports car, station wagon, SUV
Very early cars are **veteran** or **vintage** cars.

THE MAIN PARTS OF A CAR ARE:

• body, bonnet, boot, bumper, chassis, doors, engine, exhaust pipe, fuel tank, gearbox, headlamps, lights, mirrors, roof, tyres, undercarriage, wheels, windscreen, wings

THE MAIN CONTROLS IN A CAR ARE:

• accelerator, brake, choke, clutch, gear lever, handbrake, ignition key, indicators, speedometer, steering wheel, windscreen wipers
Now Commander Pott really trod hard down on the accelerator and the speedometer climbed up and hung around a hundred miles an hour.—CHITTY CHITTY BANG BANG, Ian Fleming
for other vehicles see **vehicle**

carcass NOUN

The lions fed on the carcass of the antelope.
• body, corpse, cadaver, remains

card NOUN

WORD WEB
CARDS TO SEND ON SPECIAL OCCASIONS:

❶ *Did you send her a birthday card?*
• birthday card, Christmas card, Diwali card, Easter card, get well card, greetings card, Hanukkah card, invitation, notelet, picture postcard, sympathy card, thank-you card, Valentine

SOME CARD GAMES:

❷ *The magician shuffled the pack of cards.*
• beggar-my-neighbour, blackjack, bridge, canasta, cribbage, happy families, old maid, patience, poker, pontoon, rummy, snap, solitaire, whist
A complete set of playing cards is a **pack**.
All the cards with the same sign on them are a **suit**.
The suits in a pack of cards are **clubs, diamonds, hearts** and **spades**.
Names for special cards are **king, queen, jack** or **knave, ace** and **joker**.
The king, queen and jack are called **court cards**.

care *NOUN*
❶ *Granny's face was full of care.*
• worry, anxiety, trouble, concern, burden, responsibility, sorrow, stress
❷ *I took great care with my handwriting.*
• attention, concentration, thoroughness, thought, meticulousness
OPPOSITE carelessness
❸ *Jake left his pet hamster in my care.*
• charge, keeping, protection, safe keeping, supervision
➤ **to take care**
Please take care crossing the road.
• be careful, be on your guard, look out, watch out
➤ **to take care of someone** or **something**
My grandparents take care of me after school.
• care for, look after, mind, watch over, attend to, tend

care *VERB*
Do you care which team wins the World Cup?
• mind, bother, worry, be interested, be troubled, be bothered, be worried
➤ **to care for someone** or **something**
❶ *The veterinary hospital cares for sick animals.*
• take care of, look after, attend to, tend, nurse
❷ *I don't really care for broccoli.*
• like, be fond of, be keen on, love

career *NOUN*
Ida had a successful career as a racing driver.
• job, occupation, profession, trade, business, employment, calling
for various careers see **job**

careful *ADJECTIVE*
❶ *You must be more careful with your spelling.*
• accurate, conscientious, thorough, thoughtful, meticulous, painstaking, precise
OPPOSITES careless, inaccurate
❷ *We kept a careful watch on the bonfire.*
• attentive, cautious, watchful, alert, wary, vigilant
OPPOSITES careless, inattentive
➤ **to be careful**
Please be careful with those scissors.
• take care, be on your guard, look out, watch out

careless *ADJECTIVE*
❶ *This is a very careless piece of work.*
• messy, untidy, thoughtless, inaccurate, slapdash, shoddy, scrappy, sloppy, slovenly
OPPOSITES careful, accurate
❷ *I was careless and cut my finger.*
• inattentive, thoughtless, absent-minded, heedless, irresponsible, negligent, reckless
OPPOSITES careful, attentive

caress *NOUN*
The mother bear gave each cub a caress.
• hug, kiss, embrace, pat, stroke, touch
caress *VERB*
The father gently caressed his child's hair.
• stroke, touch, smooth

cargo *NOUN*
Some planes carry cargo instead of passengers.
• goods, freight, merchandise

carnival *NOUN*
The whole village comes out for the annual carnival.
• fair, festival, fête, gala, parade, procession, show, celebration, pageant

a b c d e f g h i j k l m n o p q r s t u v w x y z

A
B
C
D
E
F
G
H
I
J
K
L
M
N
O
P
Q
R
S
T
U
V
W
X
Y
Z

carriage *NOUN*
for types of vehicle see **vehicle**

carry *VERB*
❶ *I helped Dad to carry the shopping to the car.*
• take, transfer, lift, fetch, bring, lug
❷ *Aircraft carry passengers and goods.*
• transport, convey
❸ *The rear axle carries the greatest weight.*
• bear, support, hold up
➤ **to carry on**
We carried on in spite of the rain.
• continue, go on, persevere, persist, keep on, remain, stay, survive
➤ **to carry something out**
The soldiers carried out the captain's orders.
• perform, do, execute, accomplish, achieve, complete, finish

cart *NOUN*
for types of vehicle see **vehicle**

carton *NOUN*
I put a carton of juice in my lunchbox.
• box, pack, package, packet

carve *VERB*
❶ *The statue was carved out of stone.*
• sculpt, chisel, hew
❷ *Mum carved the chicken for Sunday dinner.*
• cut, slice

case *NOUN*
❶ *I loaded my case into the boot of the car.*
• suitcase, trunk, bag
A number of suitcases that you take on a trip is your **baggage** or **luggage**.
❷ *What's in those cases in the attic?*
• box, chest, crate, carton, casket
❸ *This has been a clear case of mistaken identity.*
• instance, occurrence, example, illustration
❹ *It was one of Sherlock Holmes's most famous cases.*
• inquiry, investigation

❺ *They presented a good case against fox hunting.*
• argument, line of reasoning

cash *NOUN*
How much cash do you have?
• money, change, loose change, ready money, coins, notes, currency

cast *VERB* casts, casting, cast
❶ *The child cast a penny into the wishing-well.*
• throw, toss, drop, fling, lob, sling
❷ *The statue was cast in bronze.*
• form, mould, shape

castle *NOUN*

WORD WEB

CASTLES AND OTHER FORTIFIED BUILDINGS:

• château, citadel, fort, fortress, motte and bailey, palace, stronghold, tower

PARTS OF A CASTLE:

• bailey, barbican, battlement, buttress, courtyard, donjon, drawbridge, dungeon, gate, gateway, keep, magazine, moat, motte, parapet, portcullis, postern, rampart, tower, turret, wall, watchtower
Tiuri stood in the rain, looking at the river and the castle. An open drawbridge led to the gate, which was positioned between two large towers.—THE LETTER FOR THE KING, Tonke Dragt

casual *ADJECTIVE*
❶ *It was just a casual remark, so don't take it too seriously.*
• accidental, chance, unexpected, unintentional, unplanned
OPPOSITE deliberate
❷ *The restaurant had a casual atmosphere.*
• easy-going, informal, relaxed
OPPOSITE formal
❸ *The teacher complained about our casual attitude.*
• apathetic, careless, slack, unenthusiastic
OPPOSITE enthusiastic

casualty *NOUN*
Police are reporting heavy casualties from the fire.
• death, fatality, injury, loss, victim

cat *NOUN*

WORD WEB

A male cat is a **tom**.
A young cat is a **kitten**.
A cat with streaks in its fur is a **tabby**.
An informal word for a cat is **puss** or **pussy cat**.
A word meaning 'to do with cats' is **feline**.
I have a Gumbie Cat in mind, her name is Jennyanydots; Her coat is of the tabby kind, with tiger stripes and leopard spots.—OLD POSSUM'S BOOK OF PRACTICAL CATS, T. S. Eliot

SOME BREEDS OF CAT:

• Abyssinian, Burmese, chinchilla, Manx, Persian, Siamese

SOUNDS MADE BY CATS:

• mew, miaow, purr

SOME WILD ANIMALS OF THE CAT FAMILY:

• bobcat, cheetah, jaguar, leopard, lion, lynx, ocelot, puma, tiger, wild cat
see also **animal**

catastrophe *NOUN*
The drought is a catastrophe for the farmers.
• disaster, calamity, misfortune, mishap, tragedy

catch *VERB* catches, catching, caught
❶ *My friends yelled at me to catch the ball.*
• clutch, grab, grasp, grip, hang on to, hold, seize, snatch, take
❷ *One of the anglers caught a fish.*
• hook, net, trap
❸ *The police hoped to catch the thief red-handed.*
• arrest, capture, corner
(informal) nab
❹ *I hope you don't catch my cold.*
• become infected by, contract, get
(informal) go down with

❺ *You must hurry if you want to catch the bus.*
• be in time for, get on
➤ **to catch on**
Their latest record didn't catch on.
• become popular, do well, succeed
(informal) make it
➤ **to catch up with someone**
If we run we'll catch up with them.
• gain on, overtake

catch *NOUN*
❶ *The angler got a large catch of salmon.*
• haul
❷ *The car is so cheap that there must be a catch.*
• problem, obstacle, snag, difficulty, disadvantage, drawback, trap, trick
❸ *All the windows are fitted with safety catches.*
• fastening, latch, lock, bolt, hook

catching *ADJECTIVE*
Chickenpox is catching.
• contagious, infectious

category *NOUN*
I won first prize in the under-10s category.
• group, section, class, division, set

cater *VERB*
➤ **to cater for**
The hotel can cater for a hundred guests.
• cook for, provide food for, serve, supply

cattle *PLURAL NOUN*
Male cattle are **bulls**, **steers** or **oxen**.
Female cattle are **cows**.
Young male cattle are **calves** or **bullocks**.
Young female cattle are **calves** or **heifers**.
A word meaning 'to do with cattle' is **bovine**.
Farm animals in general are **livestock**.

caught *past tense see* **catch**

cause *NOUN*
❶ *What was the cause of the trouble?*
• origin, source, start
You can also talk about the **reasons** for the trouble.
❷ *You've got no cause to complain.*
• grounds, basis, motive, reason

a
b
c
d
e
f
g
h
i
j
k
l
m
n
o
p
q
r
s
t
u
v
w
x
y
z

❸ *The sponsored walk is for a good cause.*
• purpose, object

cause *VERB*
A single spark from the fire could cause an explosion.
• bring about, create, generate, lead to, give rise to, result in, provoke, arouse

caution *NOUN*
❶ *We decided to proceed with caution.*
• care, attention, watchfulness, wariness, vigilance
❷ *The traffic warden let him off with a caution.*
• warning, reprimand, telling-off
(informal) ticking-off

cautious *ADJECTIVE*
My grandad is a cautious driver.
• careful, attentive, watchful, wary, vigilant, hesitant
OPPOSITE reckless

cave *NOUN*
The cave walls were covered with prehistoric paintings.
• cavern, pothole, underground chamber

WORD WEB

A man-made cave with decorative walls is a **grotto**.

THINGS YOU MIGHT SEE IN A CAVE:

• cave painting, stalactite, stalagmite
The entrance to a cave is the **mouth**.
The top of a cave is the **roof** and the bottom is the **floor**.
Prehistoric people who lived in caves were **cavemen** and **cavewomen**, or **troglodytes**.
Someone who enjoys exploring caves is a **potholer** or a **spelunker**.

cave *VERB*
➤ **to cave in**
The miners had a lucky escape when the roof caved in.
• collapse, fall in

cavity *NOUN*
The map was lodged in a secret cavity in the wall.
• hole, hollow, space, chamber

cease *VERB*
The fighting ceased at midnight.
• come to an end, end, finish, stop, halt
OPPOSITE begin

ceaseless *ADJECTIVE*
The ceaseless noise of traffic kept me awake all night.
• constant, continual, continuous, never-ending, non-stop, incessant, interminable, endless, everlasting, permanent, perpetual, unending, persistent, relentless
OPPOSITE brief

celebrate *VERB*
❶ *Let's celebrate!*
• enjoy yourself, have a good time, be happy, rejoice
❷ *What shall we do to celebrate Granny's birthday?*
• commemorate, observe, keep

celebrated *ADJECTIVE*
Beatrix Potter is a celebrated author of children's books.
• famous, well-known, respected, renowned, eminent, distinguished, notable, outstanding, popular, prominent
OPPOSITE unknown

celebration *NOUN*
We had a big celebration for my cousin's wedding.
• festivity, party, feast, festival, banquet, jamboree

celebrity *NOUN*
The awards were handed out by a TV celebrity.
• famous person, personality, public figure, VIP, star, idol

cellar NOUN
We keep our bikes and sports gear in the cellar.
• basement, vault
see also **basement**

cemetery NOUN
A famous author is buried in the local cemetery.
• graveyard, burial ground, churchyard
A place where dead people are cremated is a **crematorium**.

central ADJECTIVE
❶ *We are now in the central part of the building.*
• middle, core, inner, interior
OPPOSITE outer
❷ *Who are the central characters in the story?*
• chief, crucial, essential, fundamental, important, main, major, principal, vital
OPPOSITE unimportant

centre NOUN
The library is in the centre of the town.
The burial chamber is in the centre of the pyramid.
• middle, heart, core, inside, interior
The centre of a planet or a piece of fruit is the **core**.
The centre of an atom or living cell is the **nucleus**.
The centre of a wheel is the **hub**.
The point at the centre of a see-saw is the **pivot**.
The edible part in the centre of a nut is the **kernel**.
OPPOSITES edge, outside, surface

ceremony NOUN
❶ *We watched the ceremony of the opening of parliament.*
• rite, ritual, formalities
A ceremony where someone is given a prize is a **presentation**.
A ceremony where someone is given a special honour is an **investiture**.
A ceremony to celebrate something new is an **inauguration** or **opening**.

A ceremony where someone becomes a member of a society is an **initiation**.
A ceremony to make a church or other building sacred is a **dedication**.
A ceremony to remember a dead person or a past event is a **commemoration**.
A ceremony held in a church is a **service**.
for ceremonies which can be held in a church see **church**
❷ *They had a quiet wedding without a lot of ceremony.*
• formality, pomp, pageantry, spectacle

certain ADJECTIVE
❶ *My dad was certain he would win the cookery competition.*
• confident, convinced, positive, sure, determined
OPPOSITE uncertain
❷ *We have certain proof that the painting is a forgery.*
• definite, clear, convincing, absolute, unquestionable, reliable, trustworthy, undeniable, infallible, genuine, valid
OPPOSITE unreliable
❸ *The damaged plane faced certain disaster.*
• inevitable, unavoidable
OPPOSITE possible
❹ *Her new book is certain to be a bestseller.*
• bound, sure
➤ **for certain**
I'll give you the money tomorrow for certain.
• certainly, definitely, for sure, without doubt, sure
➤ **to make certain**
Please make certain that you switch off the lights.
• make sure, ensure

certainly ADVERB
Baby dragons are certainly not timid.
• definitely, undoubtedly, unquestionably, assuredly, without a doubt

certificate NOUN
At the end of the course, you will receive a certificate.
• diploma, document, licence

chain NOUN
❶ *The anchor was attached to a chain.*
One ring in a chain is a **link**.
A chain used to link railway wagons together is a **coupling**.
❷ *The police formed a chain to keep the crowd back.*
• line, row, cordon
❸ *Holmes described the chain of events that led to the murder.*
• series, sequence, succession, string

chair NOUN
for furniture to sit on see **seat**

challenge VERB
I challenged Jo not to eat sweets for a week.
• dare, defy

champion NOUN
❶ *She is the current world champion at ice-skating.*
• title-holder, prizewinner, victor, winner, conqueror
❷ *Martin Luther King was a champion of civil rights.*
• supporter, advocate, defender, upholder, patron, backer

championship NOUN
Fifteen schools took part in the karate championship.
• competition, contest, tournament

chance NOUN
❶ *They say there's a chance of rain later.*
• possibility, likelihood, probability, prospect, danger, risk
❷ *I haven't had a chance to reply yet.*
• opportunity, time, occasion
❸ *The director took a chance in hiring an unknown actor.*
• gamble, risk
➤ **by chance**
I found the house quite by chance.
• by accident, accidentally, by coincidence
An unfortunate chance is **bad luck** or a **misfortune**.
A fortunate chance is **good luck** or a **fluke**.

change VERB
❶ *They've changed the programme for the concert.*
• alter, modify, rearrange, reorganize, adjust, adapt, vary
❷ *The town has changed a lot since Victorian times.*
• alter, become different, develop, grow, move on
❸ *Can I change these jeans for a bigger size, please?*
• exchange, replace, switch, substitute (informal) swap
➤ **to change into**
Tadpoles change into frogs.
• become, turn into, metamorphose into
change NOUN
There has been a slight change of plan.
• alteration, modification, variation, difference, break
A change to something worse is a **deterioration**.
A change to something better is an **improvement** or a **reform**.
A very big change is a **revolution**, **transformation** or U-turn.
A change in which one person or thing is replaced by another is a **substitution**.
A complete change made by some living things is a **metamorphosis**.

changeable ADJECTIVE
The weather has been changeable today.
• variable, unsettled, unpredictable, unreliable, inconsistent, erratic, unstable
If your loyalty is changeable you are **fickle**.
OPPOSITE steady

channel NOUN
❶ *The rainwater runs along this channel.*
• ditch, duct, gully, gutter, furrow, trough
❷ *How many TV channels do you get?*
• station

chaos NOUN
After the earthquake, the city was in chaos.
• confusion, disorder, mayhem, uproar, tumult, pandemonium, anarchy, bedlam, muddle, shambles
OPPOSITE order

A B C D E F G H I J K L M N O P Q R S T U V W X Y Z

chaotic ADJECTIVE
Alice finds that life in Wonderland is chaotic.
• confused, disorderly, disorganized, muddled, topsy-turvy, untidy, unruly, riotous
OPPOSITES orderly, organized

chapter NOUN
I read a chapter of my book last night.
• part, section, division
One section of a play is an **act** or **scene**.
One part of a serial is an **episode** or **instalment**.

character NOUN
❶ *Her character is quite different from her sister's.*
• personality, temperament, nature, disposition, make-up, manner
❷ *Our neighbour is a well-known character in our street.*
• figure, personality, individual, person
❸ *Who is your favourite character in 'Harry Potter'?*
• part, role
for ways to describe the characters in a story see **writing**

characteristic NOUN
The Martians had some odd physical characteristics.
• feature, peculiarity, attribute, trait, distinguishing feature

characteristic ADJECTIVE
Windmills are a characteristic feature of this area.
• typical, distinctive, recognizable, particular, special, unique, singular

charge NOUN
❶ *The admission charge is five euros.*
• price, rate
The charge made for a ride on public transport is the **fare**.
The charge made to post a letter or parcel is the **postage**.
A charge made to join a club is a **fee** or **subscription**.
A charge made for certain things by the government is a **duty** or a **tax**.
A charge made to use a private road, bridge or tunnel is a **toll**.
❷ *The robbers face several criminal charges.*
• accusation, allegation
❸ *Many soldiers were killed in the charge.*
• assault, attack, onslaught, raid
❹ *My best friend left her hamster in my charge.*
• care, keeping, protection, custody, trust
➤ **to be in charge of something**
An experienced sailor was in charge of the crew.
• manage, lead, command, direct, supervise, run

charge VERB
❶ *The library charges ten pence for a photocopy.*
• ask for, make you pay
❷ *A woman has been charged with attempted robbery.*
• accuse (of)
❸ *The cavalry charged the enemy line.*
• attack, assault, storm, rush

charm NOUN
❶ *In the painting, the girl's face is full of youthful charm.*
• attractiveness, appeal, charisma
❷ *The sorcerer recited a magic charm.*
• spell, incantation
for other words to do with magic see **magic**
❸ *The boy carried a crystal as a lucky charm.*
• talisman, mascot, amulet, trinket

charm VERB
Winnie the Pooh has charmed readers all over the world.
• bewitch, captivate, delight, enchant, entrance, fascinate, please

charming ADJECTIVE
We drove through some charming scenery.
• delightful, attractive, pleasant, pleasing, likeable, appealing

a b c d e f g h i j k l m n o p q r s t u v w x y z

chart *NOUN*
❶ *The explorer stopped to consult his chart.*
• map
❷ *This chart shows the average monthly rainfall.*
• diagram, graph, table

charter *VERB*
We chartered a minibus for our trip.
• hire, lease, rent

chase *VERB*
The wolves chased a deer through the forest.
• pursue, run after, follow, track, trail, hunt

chasm *NOUN*
From the bridge, we looked down at a deep chasm.
• hole, ravine, crevasse, canyon, gorge, abyss, gulf, fissure, pit, rift

chat or **chatter** *VERB*
see **talk**

chatty *ADJECTIVE*
Frank is usually shy, but today he's quite chatty.
• talkative, communicative
OPPOSITE silent

cheap *ADJECTIVE*
❶ *We got a cheap flight to Helsinki.*
• inexpensive, affordable, bargain, cut-price, discount, reasonable
❷ *These tyres are made from cheap rubber.*
• inferior, shoddy, second-rate, worthless, trashy
(informal) tacky, tatty
OPPOSITES superior, good-quality

cheat *VERB*
❶ *She was cheated into buying a fake diamond ring.*
• deceive, trick, swindle, double-cross, hoax, fool
(informal) con, diddle, fleece, rip-off
❷ *Anyone who cheats in the quiz will be disqualified.*
• copy, crib

cheat *NOUN*
Don't trust him—he's a cheat.
• cheater, deceiver, swindler, fraud, impostor, hoaxer, charlatan

check *VERB*
❶ *Have you checked your work carefully?*
• examine, inspect, look over, scrutinize
❷ *The heavy snow checked their progress towards the Pole.*
• hamper, hinder, block, obstruct, delay, hold back, slow, slow down, halt, stop
check *NOUN*
I need to run some checks on your computer.
• test, examination, inspection, check-up

cheeky *ADJECTIVE*
Don't be so cheeky!
• disrespectful, facetious, flippant, impertinent, impolite, impudent, insolent, insulting, irreverent, mocking, rude, saucy, shameless
OPPOSITE respectful

cheer *VERB*
❶ *We cheered when our team scored a goal.*
• clap, applaud, shout, yell
OPPOSITE jeer
❷ *The good news cheered us.*
• comfort, console, gladden, delight, please, encourage, uplift
OPPOSITE sadden
➤ **to cheer up**
The weather had cheered up by the afternoon.
• become more cheerful, brighten

cheerful *ADJECTIVE*
The sun was shining, and we set out in a cheerful mood.
• happy, good-humoured, light-hearted, merry, jolly, joyful, joyous, glad, pleased, optimistic, lively, elated, animated, bright, buoyant, jovial, gleeful, chirpy
OPPOSITE sad

cheese NOUN

WORD WEB

SOME TYPES OF CHEESE:

• blue cheese, Brie, cottage cheese, cream cheese, Cheddar, crowdie, mozzarella, parmesan, ricotta, Stilton
for other kinds of food see **food**

chemist NOUN

• pharmacist
(historical) apothecary, alchemist
A chemist's shop is a **dispensary** or **pharmacy**.

chess NOUN

WORD WEB

THE PIECES USED IN PLAYING CHESS ARE:

• bishop, castle or rook, king, knight, pawn, queen

SOME TERMS USED IN PLAYING CHESS:

• castle, check, checkmate, mate, move, stalemate, take
for other board games see **game**

chest NOUN

I found some old books in a chest in the attic.
• box, crate, case, trunk

chew VERB

Are you still chewing that toffee?
• eat, gnaw, munch
for other ways to eat see **eat**

chicken NOUN

A female chicken is a **hen**.
A male chicken is a **rooster**.
A young chicken is a **chick**.
A group of chickens is a **brood**.
A farm which keeps chickens is a **poultry farm**.

chief NOUN

The pirates chose Redbeard as their chief.
• leader, ruler, head, commander, captain, chieftain, master, governor, president, principal
(informal) boss

chief ADJECTIVE

❶ *The chief ingredients in a trifle are jelly, custard and cream.*
• main, central, key, principal, crucial, basic, essential, important, vital, major, primary, foremost, fundamental, indispensable, necessary, significant, predominant, prominent
OPPOSITES unimportant, minor, trivial
❷ *Albert was Queen Victoria's chief advisor.*
• head, senior

chiefly ADVERB

Kangaroos are found chiefly in Australia.
• mainly, mostly, predominantly, primarily, principally, especially

child NOUN

❶ *The book festival is aimed especially at children.*
• boy or girl, infant, juvenile, youngster, youth, lad or lass
(informal) kid, tot, nipper
❷ *How many children do you have?*
• son or daughter, descendant, offspring
A child who expects to inherit a title or fortune from parents is an **heir** or **heiress**.
A child whose parents are dead is an **orphan**.
A child looked after by a guardian is a **ward**.
see also **baby**

childhood NOUN

Neil spent much of his childhood by the sea.
• infancy, youth, boyhood or girlhood
The time when someone is a baby is their **babyhood**.
The time when someone is a teenager is their **adolescence** or **teens**.
OPPOSITE adulthood

a
b
c
d
e
f
g
h
i
j
k
l
m
n
o
p
q
r
s
t
u
v
w
x
y
z

childish *ADJECTIVE*
It's *childish* to make rude noises.
• babyish, immature, juvenile, infantile
OPPOSITE mature

chill *VERB*
Chill the pudding before serving it.
• freeze, cool, make cold, refrigerate
OPPOSITE warm

chilly *ADJECTIVE*
❶ It's a *chilly* evening, so wrap up well.
• cold, cool, frosty, icy, crisp, fresh, raw, wintry
(informal) nippy
OPPOSITE warm
❷ The librarian gave me a very *chilly* look.
• unfriendly, hostile, unwelcoming,
unsympathetic
OPPOSITE friendly

chime *VERB*
The church clock *chimed* at midnight.
• ring, sound, strike, peal, toll
for sounds made by a bell see **bell**

chimney *NOUN*
A chimney on a ship or steam engine is a
funnel.
A pipe to take away smoke and fumes is a **flue**.

chip *NOUN*
❶ There were *chips* of broken glass on the
pavement.
• bit, piece, fragment, scrap, sliver, splinter,
flake, shaving
❷ This mug's got a *chip* in it.
• crack, nick, notch, flaw

chip *VERB*
I *chipped* a cup while I was washing up.
• crack, nick, notch, damage

choice *NOUN*
❶ My bike had a flat tyre, so I had no *choice*
but to walk.
• alternative, option
❷ He wouldn't be my *choice* as team captain.
• preference, selection, pick, vote

❸ The greengrocer has a good *choice* of
vegetables.
• range, selection, assortment, array, mixture,
variety, diversity

choke *VERB*
❶ This tie is so tight it's *choking* me.
• strangle, suffocate, stifle, throttle
❷ Thick fumes made the firefighters
choke.
• cough, gasp

choose *VERB* chooses, choosing, chose,
chosen
❶ We had a show of hands to *choose*
a winner.
• select, appoint, elect, vote for
❷ I *chose* the biggest pizza on the menu.
• decide on, select, pick out, opt for,
plump for, settle on, single out
❸ Lola *chose* to stay at home.
• decide, make a decision, determine, prefer,
resolve

chop *VERB*
❶ *Chop* the celery into large chunks.
• cut, split
❷ They *chopped* down the undergrowth to
make a path.
• hack, slash
To chop down a tree is to **fell** it.
To chop a branch off a tree is to **lop** it.
To chop off an arm or leg is to **amputate** it.
To chop food into small pieces is to **dice** or
mince it.

chorus *NOUN*
❶ I'm singing in the *chorus* in the school
musical.
• choir
❷ I forgot the words to the song, so I just
sang the *chorus*.
• refrain

chubby *ADJECTIVE*
The baby chicks are fluffy and *chubby*.
• plump, tubby, podgy, dumpy

chunk NOUN
I bit a chunk out of my apple.
• piece, portion, lump, block, hunk, slab, wedge

church NOUN

WORD WEB

PLACES WHERE CHRISTIANS WORSHIP:

• abbey, cathedral, chapel, meeting house, parish church
for places where people of other religions worship see **building**

PARTS OF A CHURCH:

• aisle, belfry, chancel, cloister, crypt, nave, spire, steeple, transept, vestry

THINGS YOU MIGHT SEE IN A CHURCH:

• altar, crucifix, font, lectern, pews, pulpit

SERVICES WHICH MAY BE HELD IN A CHURCH:

• baptism or christening, communion, confirmation, funeral, mass, wedding

circle NOUN
❶ *We arranged the chairs in a circle.*
• ring, round, hoop, loop, band
A flat solid circle is a **disc**.
A three-dimensional round shape is a **sphere**.
An egg shape is an **oval** or **ellipse**.
for other shapes see **shape**
The distance round a circle is the **circumference**.
The distance across a circle is the **diameter**.
The distance from the centre to the circumference is the **radius**.
A circular movement is a **revolution** or **rotation**.
A circular trip round the world is a **circumnavigation**.
A circular trip round a planet is an **orbit**.
❷ *She has a wide circle of friends.*
• group, set, crowd

circle VERB
The vultures circled overhead.
• turn, go round, revolve, rotate, wheel

circular ADJECTIVE
The flying saucer was circular in shape.
• round, ring-shaped, disc-shaped

circulate VERB
❶ *Blood circulates in the body.*
• go round, move round
❷ *I asked friends to circulate our newsletter.*
• distribute, send round, issue

circumference NOUN
There is a fence around the circumference of the field.
• perimeter, border, boundary, edge, fringe

circumstances PLURAL NOUN
She described the circumstances which led to the accident.
• situation, conditions, background, causes, context, details, facts, particulars

citizen NOUN
The citizens of New York are proud of their city.
• resident, inhabitant

city NOUN
The main city of a country or region is the **metropolis**.
An area of houses outside the central part of a city is the **suburbs**.
A word meaning 'to do with a town or city' is **urban**.
A word meaning 'to do with a city and its suburbs' is **metropolitan**.
see also **town**

civilization NOUN
We are studying the civilization of ancient Egypt.
• culture, society, achievements, attainments

civilized ADJECTIVE
Trolls seldom behave in a civilized manner.
• polite, well-behaved, well-mannered, orderly, cultured, sophisticated, refined
OPPOSITE uncivilized

a b c d e f g h i j k l m n o p q r s t u v w x y z

claim *VERB*
❶ *You can claim your prize for the raffle here.*
• ask for, request, collect, demand, insist on
❷ *The professor claims to be an expert on dinosaurs.*
• declare, assert, allege, maintain, argue, insist

clamber *VERB*
We clambered over the rocks towards the sea.
• climb, scramble, crawl, move awkwardly

clap *VERB*
❶ *The audience clapped loudly at the end of the concert.*
• applaud, cheer
❷ *Suddenly, a hand clapped me on the shoulder.*
• slap, hit, pat, smack

clash *NOUN*
❶ *The clash of cymbals made me jump.*
• crash, bang, ringing
❷ *There was a clash between the president and her opponent during the debate.*
• argument, confrontation, conflict, fight, scuffle
(informal) scrap

clash *VERB*
❶ *The cymbals clashed.*
• crash, resound
❷ *Two good films clash on TV tonight.*
• coincide, happen at the same time
❸ *Demonstrators clashed with the police.*
• argue, fight, get into conflict, squabble

clasp *VERB*
❶ *My little brother clasped my hand.*
• grasp, grip, hold, squeeze, cling to
❷ *She clasped him in her arms.*
• embrace, hug

clasp *NOUN*
The cloak was held in place by a gold clasp.
• fastener, fastening, brooch, clip, pin, buckle, hook

class *NOUN*
❶ *There are 26 children in our class.*
• form, set, stream
The other pupils in your class are your classmates.
❷ *There are many different classes of plants.*
• category, group, classification, division, set, sort, type, kind, species
❸ *The ancient Romans divided people into social classes.*
• level, rank, status

classic *ADJECTIVE*
That was a classic tennis final this year.
• excellent, first-class, first-rate, top-notch, exceptional, fine, great, admirable, masterly, model, perfect
OPPOSITE ordinary
WHICH WORD? Note that classic is not the same as classical, which means either 'to do with the ancient Greeks and Romans' or 'to do with serious music written in the past'.

claw *VERB*
We could hear the monster clawing at the door.
• scratch, scrape, tear, savage

clean *ADJECTIVE*
❶ *Can you bring me a clean cup, please?*
• spotless, washed, scrubbed, swept, tidy, immaculate, hygienic, sanitary
An informal word meaning 'very clean' is squeaky-clean.
A common simile is as clean as a whistle.
OPPOSITE dirty
❷ *I began my diary on a clean piece of paper.*
• blank, unused, unmarked, empty, bare, fresh, new
OPPOSITE used
❸ *This plaster will keep the wound clean.*
• sterile, sterilized, uninfected
❹ *You can get clean water from this tap.*
• pure, clear, fresh, unpolluted, uncontaminated
❺ *The referee said she wanted a clean fight.*
• fair, honest, honourable, sporting, sportsmanlike
OPPOSITE dishonourable

clean VERB

❶ *We cleaned the house from top to bottom. I tried to clean the mud off my boots.*
• wash, wipe, mop, scour, scrub, polish, dust, sweep, vacuum, rinse, wring out, hose down, sponge, shampoo, swill
To clean clothes is to **launder** them.
OPPOSITE dirty, mess up

❷ *The nurse cleaned the wound with an antiseptic wipe.*
• cleanse, bathe, disinfect, sanitize, sterilize
OPPOSITES infect, contaminate

clear ADJECTIVE

❶ *We saw fish swimming in the clear pool.*
• clean, pure, colourless, transparent
A common simile is **as clear as crystal**.
OPPOSITE opaque

❷ *It was a beautiful clear day.*
• bright, sunny, cloudless, unclouded
A clear night is a **moonlit** or **starlit** night.
OPPOSITES cloudy, overcast

❸ *The instructions on the map were quite clear.*
• plain, understandable, intelligible, lucid, unambiguous
OPPOSITES ambiguous, confusing

❹ *The actor spoke his words with a clear voice.*
• distinct, audible
A common simile is **as clear as a bell**.
OPPOSITE muffled

❺ *The signature on this letter is not clear.*
• legible, recognizable, visible
OPPOSITE illegible

❻ *My camera takes nice clear pictures.*
• sharp, well defined, focused
OPPOSITE unfocused

❼ *Are you sure that your conscience is clear?*
• innocent, untroubled, blameless
OPPOSITE guilty

❽ *There's a clear difference between a male blackbird and a female.*
• obvious, definite, noticeable, conspicuous, perceptible, pronounced
OPPOSITE imperceptible

❾ *They made sure the road was clear for the ambulance.*
• open, empty, free, passable, uncrowded, unobstructed
OPPOSITE congested

clear VERB

❶ *I cleared the weeds from the flower bed.*
• get rid of, remove, eliminate, strip

❷ *The plumber cleared the blocked drain.*
• unblock, unclog, clean out, open up
To clear a channel is to **dredge** it.

❸ *I cleared the misty windows.*
• clean, wipe, polish

❹ *If the fire alarm goes, clear the building.*
• empty, evacuate

❺ *The fog cleared slowly.*
• disappear, vanish, disperse, evaporate, melt away

❻ *The forecast said that the weather will clear.*
• become clear, brighten, brighten up

❼ *He was cleared of all the charges against him.*
• acquit, free, release

❽ *The runners cleared the first hurdle.*
• go over, get over, jump over, pass over, vault

➤ **to clear up**
Please *clear up* this mess before you go.
• clean up, tidy up, put right, put straight

clench VERB

❶ *The warrior clenched her teeth and gripped her sword.*
• close tightly, squeeze together, grit

❷ *She clenched the coin tightly in her hand.*
• clasp, hold, grasp, grip

clever ADJECTIVE

❶ *Dr Hafiz is very clever and can read hieroglyphics.*
• intelligent, bright, gifted, able, knowledgeable
(informal) brainy, smart
OPPOSITE unintelligent
An informal name for a clever person is a **brainbox**.
An uncomplimentary synonym is **clever clogs** or **smarty pants**.

❷ *The elves were very clever with their fingers.*
• accomplished, capable, gifted, skilful, talented
If you are clever at a lot of things you are **versatile**.
OPPOSITE unskilful

a
b
c
d
e
f
g
h
i
j
k
l
m
n
o
p
q
r
s
t
u
v
w
x
y
z

A
B
C OPPOSITE stupid
D
E
F
G
H
I
J
K
L
M
N
O
P
Q
R
S
T
U
V
W
X
Y
Z

❸ *They are clever enough to get away with it.*
• quick, sharp, shrewd, smart
Uncomplimentary synonyms are artful, crafty, cunning, wily.
OPPOSITE stupid

client NOUN
The shop has a growing number of overseas clients.
• customer, user, buyer, consumer

cliff NOUN
The car rolled over the edge of a cliff.
• crag, precipice, rock face

climate NOUN
see **weather**

climax NOUN
The climax of the film is a stunning car chase.
• high point, highlight, peak
OPPOSITE anticlimax

climb VERB
❶ *It took us several hours to climb the mountain.*
• ascend, clamber up, go up, scale
❷ *The plane climbed into the clouds.*
• lift off, soar, take off
❸ *The road climbs steeply up to the castle.*
• rise, slope
➤ **to climb down**
❶ *It's harder to climb down the rock than to get up it.*
• descend, get down from
❷ *We all told him he was wrong, so he had to climb down.*
• admit defeat, give in, surrender

climb NOUN
It's a steep climb up to the castle.
• ascent, hill, gradient, rise, slope, incline

cling VERB clings, clinging, clung
➤ **to cling to someone** or **something**
❶ *The baby koala clung to its mother.*
• clasp, grasp, clutch, embrace, hug
❷ *Ivy clings to the wall.*
• adhere to, fasten on to, stick to

clip VERB
❶ *The sheets of paper were clipped together.*
• pin, staple
❷ *Dad clipped the hedges in the back garden.*
• cut, trim
To cut unwanted parts off a tree or bush is to **prune** it.

cloak NOUN
The girl wrapped her cloak tightly around herself.
• cape, coat, wrap
(old use) mantle

clock NOUN
for instruments used to measure time see **time**

clog VERB
The dead leaves are clogging the drain.
• block, choke, congest, obstruct, bung up, jam, stop up

close ADJECTIVE (say klohss)
❶ *Our house is close to the shops.*
• near, nearby, not far
To be actually by the side of something is to be **adjacent**.
OPPOSITES far, distant
❷ *Anisha and I are close friends.*
• intimate, dear, devoted, fond, affectionate
❸ *The police made a close examination of the stolen car.*
• careful, detailed, painstaking, minute, thorough
OPPOSITE casual
❹ *It was an exciting race because it was so close.*
• equal, even, level, well-matched
❺ *Open the window—it's very close in here.*
• humid, muggy, stuffy, clammy, airless, stifling, suffocating
OPPOSITE airy

close VERB (say klohz)
❶ *Don't forget to close the lid.*
• shut, fasten, seal, secure
❷ *The road has been closed to traffic for the parade.*
• barricade, block, obstruct, stop up

❸ *The band **closed** the concert with my favourite song.*
• finish, end, complete, conclude, stop, terminate
(informal) wind up

clot VERB
*If you cut yourself, the blood will **clot** and form a scab.*
• thicken, solidify

cloth NOUN
*The curtains were made of striped cotton **cloth**.*
• fabric, material
A word for cloth in general is **textiles**.
for types of cloth see **fabric**

clothe VERB
➤ to be clothed in
*The bridesmaids were **clothed in** white.*
• be dressed in, be wearing

clothes PLURAL NOUN
*What **clothes** are you taking on holiday?*
• clothing, garments, outfits, dress, attire, garb, finery
(informal) gear, togs, get-up
A set of clothes to wear is a **costume, outfit** or **suit**.
An official set of clothes worn for school or work is a **uniform**.

WORD WEB

SOME ITEMS OF CLOTHING:

• blouse, boubou, caftan, camisole, dashiki, dress, dungarees, frock, gown, hanbok, hijab, jeans, jersey, jumper, kaftan, kilt, kimono, leggings, miniskirt, pinafore, polo shirt, pullover, robe, sari, sarong, shirt, shorts, skirt, smock, suit, sweater, sweatshirt, trousers, trunks, T-shirt, tunic, waistcoat

OUTER CLOTHES:

• anorak, apron, blazer, cagoule, cape, cardigan, cloak, coat, dressing gown, duffel coat, fleece, gilet, hoody, greatcoat, jacket, mackintosh, oilskins, overalls, overcoat, parka, poncho, raincoat, shawl, shrug, stole, tracksuit

UNDERWEAR:

• boxer shorts, bra, briefs, crop top, drawers, knickers, pants, petticoat, slip, socks, stockings, tights, underpants, vest

CLOTHES FOR SLEEPING IN:

• nightdress or *(informal)* nightie, nightshirt, onesie, pyjamas or *(informal)* PJs

CLOTHES WORN IN THE PAST:

• corset, doublet, frock coat, gauntlet, ruff, toga

ACCESSORIES WORN WITH CLOTHES:

• belt, braces, cravat, earmuffs, gloves, sash, scarf, shawl, tie
see also **hat, shoe**

PARTS OF A GARMENT:

• bodice, button, buttonhole, collar, cuff, hem, lapel, pocket, seam, sleeve, waistband, zip

THINGS USED TO DECORATE CLOTHES:

• beads, frills, fringes, lace, ruffles, sequins, tassels

WRITING TIPS

You can use these words to describe **clothes**:
• baggy, casual, chic, dowdy, drab, fashionable, fine, flashy, flattering, frilly, frumpy, glamorous, ill-fitting, loose, luxurious, old-fashioned, ornate, ragged, roomy, shabby, skimpy, smart, sporty, stylish, tattered or in tatters, threadbare, tight-fitting, trendy, worn
The stranger was wearing an extremely shabby set of wizard's robes which had been darned in several places.—HARRY POTTER AND THE PRISONER OF AZKABAN, J. K. Rowling

a b c d e f g h i j k l m n o p q r s t u v w x y z

cloud NOUN
A *cloud* of steam billowed from the kettle.
• billow, puff, haze, mist

cloudy ADJECTIVE
❶ The day was cold and *cloudy*.
• dull, overcast, grey, dark, dismal, gloomy, sunless
OPPOSITE cloudless
see also **weather**
❷ We couldn't see any fish in the *cloudy* water.
• muddy, murky, hazy, milky
OPPOSITES clear, transparent

club NOUN
❶ The warrior brandished a wooden *club*.
• stick, baton, truncheon
❷ Would you like to join our book *club*?
• group, society, association, organization, circle, union

club VERB
The giant *clubbed* Jack on the head.
• hit, strike, thump, whack, batter
(informal) bash
for other ways of hitting see **hit**

clue NOUN
❶ I don't know the answer. Can you give me a *clue*?
• hint, suggestion, indication, pointer, tip, idea
❷ 'This footprint is an important *clue*,' said the detective.
• piece of evidence, lead
see also **detective**

clump NOUN
The owl flew into a *clump* of trees on the hill.
• group, thicket, cluster, collection
A clump of grass or hair is a **tuft**.

clumsy ADJECTIVE
The *clumsy* gnome was always breaking things.
• careless, awkward, ungainly, inept

An informal name for a clumsy person is butterfingers.
OPPOSITE graceful

cluster NOUN
A *cluster* of people waited outside the cinema.
• crowd, bunch, collection, assembly, gathering, knot
see also **group**

clutch VERB
The mountaineer *clutched* his rope.
• catch, clasp, cling to, grab, grasp, grip, hang on to, hold on to, seize, snatch

clutches PLURAL NOUN
The evil wizard had us in his *clutches*.
• grasp, power, control

clutter NOUN
We'll have to clear up all this *clutter*.
• mess, muddle, junk, litter, rubbish, odds and ends

coach NOUN
❶ We went to Cardiff by *coach*.
• bus
for other vehicles see **vehicle**
❷ Their football team has a new *coach*.
• trainer, instructor

coach VERB
He was *coached* by a former champion.
• train, teach, instruct

coarse ADJECTIVE
❶ The blanket was made of *coarse* woollen material.
• rough, harsh, scratchy, bristly, hairy
OPPOSITE soft
❷ We were shocked by their *coarse* table manners.
• rude, offensive, impolite, improper, indecent, crude, vulgar
OPPOSITES polite, refined

coast *NOUN*
After the disaster, oil was washed up along the coast.
• coastline, shore
see also **seashore**

coast *VERB*
I coasted down the hill on my bike.
• cruise, freewheel, glide

coat *NOUN*
❶ *The detective was wearing a thick winter coat.*
for coats and other garments see **clothes**
❷ *The fox had a reddish-brown coat.*
• hide, pelt, skin, fur, hair
A sheep's coat is a **fleece**.
❸ *The front door needs a coat of paint.*
• layer, coating, covering
(informal) lick

coat *VERB*
We ate marshmallows coated with chocolate.
• cover, spread, smear, glaze

coax *VERB*
Sam coaxed the hamster back into its cage.
• persuade, tempt, entice

code *NOUN*
❶ *There is a strict code of conduct for using the pool.*
• rules, regulations, laws
❷ *The message was written in a secret code.*
To put a message in code is to **encode** or **encrypt** it.
To understand a message in code is to **decode**, **decipher** or *(informal)* **crack** it.
A person who studies how to make and decipher codes is a **cryptographer**.

coil *NOUN*
The snake twisted itself into a coil.
• spiral, twist, curl, twirl, screw, corkscrew, whirl, whorl, roll, scroll
A coil of wool or thread is a **skein**.

coil *VERB*
The snake coiled itself round a branch.
• curl, loop, roll, spiral, turn, twist, twirl, wind, writhe

coin *NOUN*
Do you have a 50 pence coin?
• piece, bit

WORD WEB

SOME TYPES OF COIN USED IN THE PAST:

• daric, denarius, doubloon, ducat, farthing, florin, guinea, shilling, sovereign
A person who studies or collects coins is a **numismatist**.

---

coin *VERB*
We coined a new name for our group.
• invent, make up, think up, create, devise, produce

coincide *VERB*
My birthday coincides with the school holidays.
• clash, fall together, happen together

coincidence *NOUN*
➤ **by coincidence**
We met in town by coincidence.
• by accident, by chance, accidentally, unintentionally, by a fluke

cold *ADJECTIVE*
❶ *Wrap up warm in this cold weather.*
• freezing, chilly, frosty, icy, raw, arctic, bitter, cool, crisp, snowy, wintry
(informal) perishing
A common simile is **as cold as ice**.
OPPOSITES hot, warm
❷ *I tried to shelter from the cold wind.*
• biting, bitter, keen, penetrating, piercing
❸ *I was cold in spite of my woolly hat.*
• freezing, frozen, chilly, chilled, shivering, shivery
Hypothermia is a condition where someone is so cold that they become ill.
OPPOSITES hot, warm
❹ *The cyclops gave us a cold stare from his one eye.*
• unfriendly, unkind, unfeeling, distant, cool, heartless, indifferent, reserved, stony, uncaring, unemotional, unsympathetic
OPPOSITES warm, friendly

a
b
c
d
e
f
g
h
i
j
k
l
m
n
o
p
q
r
s
t
u
v
w
x
y
z

collaborate VERB
Several zoos collaborated on the rhino project.
• cooperate, work together

collapse VERB
❶ *Many buildings collapsed in the earthquake.*
• fall down, fall in, cave in, give way, crumble, crumple, buckle, disintegrate, tumble down
❷ *Some of the runners collapsed in the heat.*
• faint, pass out, fall over, keel over

colleague NOUN
The police officer discussed the plan with her colleagues.
• associate, partner, teammate, co-worker, workmate

collect VERB
❶ *Squirrels collect nuts for the winter.*
• gather, accumulate, hoard, heap, pile up, store up, stockpile, amass
❷ *A crowd collected to watch the fire.*
• assemble, gather, come together, converge
OPPOSITE scatter, disperse
❸ *We collected a large sum for charity.*
• raise, take in
❹ *She collected the car from the garage.*
• fetch, get, obtain, bring
OPPOSITE drop off, hand in

collection NOUN
Would you like to see my fossil collection?
• assortment, set, accumulation, array, hoard, pile
A collection of books is a **library**.
A collection of poems or short stories is an **anthology**.

collective noun NOUN
for collective nouns see **group**

college NOUN
for places where people study
see **education**

collide VERB
➤ **to collide with**
The runaway trolley collided with a wall.
• bump into, crash into, run into, smash into, hit, strike

collision NOUN
The collision dented the front wheel of my bike.
• bump, crash, smash, knock, accident
A collision involving a lot of vehicles is a **pile-up**.

colloquial ADJECTIVE
The book is written in a colloquial style.
• everyday, informal, conversational, slangy
OPPOSITE formal

colossal ADJECTIVE
A colossal statue towered above us.
• huge, enormous, gigantic, immense, massive, giant, mammoth, monumental, towering, vast
OPPOSITE small, tiny

colour NOUN
What do you call that colour?
• hue, shade, tint, tone, tinge

WORD WEB

NAMES OF VARIOUS COLOURS:

• black, blue, brown, cream, gold, golden, green, grey, lavender, orange, pink, purple, red, silver, turquoise, violet, white, yellow
The colours red, yellow and blue are known as **primary colours**.
for shades of colours see **black, blue, brown, green, red, white, yellow**

colour VERB
I coloured the icing deep pink.
• paint, dye, tint

colourful ADJECTIVE
❶ *The rose garden is colourful in the summer.*
• multicoloured, showy, vibrant, bright, brilliant, gaudy
OPPOSITE colourless
❷ *The book gives a colourful account of life on an island.*
• exciting, interesting, lively, vivid, striking, rich, picturesque
OPPOSITE dull

colourless ADJECTIVE
❶ *The flask contained a colourless liquid.*
• uncoloured, clear, transparent, neutral, pale
Something which has lost its colour is **bleached** or **faded**.
❷ *All the characters in the book are colourless.*
• dull, boring, uninteresting, unexciting, drab, dreary, lacklustre
OPPOSITES colourful, interesting

column NOUN
❶ *The roof of the temple was supported by stone columns.*
• pillar, post, support, shaft

❷ *A column of soldiers wound its way across the desert.*
• line, file, procession, row, string
❸ *I sometimes read the sports column in the newspaper.*
• article, piece, report, feature

comb VERB
❶ *I combed my hair and put it in a ponytail.*
• arrange, groom, tidy, untangle
❷ *The police combed the house in search of clues.*
• search thoroughly, hunt through, scour, ransack, rummage through

combat NOUN
Two hundred warriors were killed in combat.
• battle, war, warfare, fighting
see also **fight**

combat VERB
There's a new campaign to combat crime in the city.
• fight, oppose, resist, stand up to, tackle, battle against, grapple with

combine VERB
❶ *We combined our pocket money to buy a kite.*
• put together, add together, join, merge, unite, amalgamate
OPPOSITE divide
❷ *Combine the mixture with water to make a paste.*
• mix, stir together, blend, mingle, bind
OPPOSITE separate

come VERB comes, coming, came, come
❶ *We expect our guests to come in the afternoon.*
• arrive, appear, visit
OPPOSITE go
❷ *When you hear a cuckoo, you know that summer is coming.*
• advance, draw near
➤ **to come about**
Can you tell me how the accident came about?
• happen, occur, take place, result

75

A
B
C
D
E
F
G
H
I
J
K
L
M
N
O
P
Q
R
S
T
U
V
W
X
Y
Z

➤ **to come across**
I came across an old friend of mine.
• find, discover, chance upon, meet, bump into

➤ **to come round** or **to come to**
How long did it take me to come round after the operation?
• become conscious, revive, wake up

➤ **to come to**
❶ *Tell me when you come to the last chapter.*
• reach, get to, arrive at
❷ *What did the repair bill come to?*
• add up to, amount to, total

comfort NOUN
❶ *My teddy bear was a comfort to me when I was ill.*
• reassurance, consolation, encouragement, support, relief
❷ *If I had a million pounds, I could live in comfort.*
• ease, luxury, contentment, well-being, prosperity, affluence

comfort VERB
The coach tried to comfort the team after they lost.
• cheer up, console, reassure, encourage, hearten, sympathize with, soothe

comfortable ADJECTIVE
❶ *The bed was so comfortable I fell fast asleep.*
• cosy, snug, relaxing, easy, soft, warm, roomy, padded, plush
(informal) comfy
OPPOSITE uncomfortable
❷ *We'll need comfortable clothes for travelling.*
• casual, informal, loose-fitting
❸ *Our cat leads a comfortable life.*
• contented, happy, pleasant, agreeable, well-off, prosperous, luxurious, affluent

comic or **comical** ADJECTIVE
We laughed at his comic remarks.
• amusing, humorous, funny, hilarious, witty, diverting
(informal) hysterical
To be comical in a cheeky way is to be facetious.

To be comical in a silly way is to be absurd, farcical, ludicrous or ridiculous.
To be comical in a hurtful way is to be sarcastic.

command NOUN
❶ *The general gave the command to attack.*
• order, instruction, commandment, edict
❷ *Captain Nemo has command of the whole crew.*
• charge, control, authority (over), power (over), management, supervision
❸ *My sister has a good command of Spanish.*
• knowledge, mastery, grasp, understanding, ability (in), skill (in)

command VERB
❶ *The officer commanded his troops to fire.*
• order, instruct, direct, tell, bid
❷ *The captain commands the ship.*
• control, direct, be in charge of, govern, head, lead, manage, administer, supervise

commander NOUN
The commander decided to abandon the expedition.
• leader, chief, head, officer-in-charge

commence VERB
The flag is a signal for the race to commence.
• begin, start, embark (on)

commend VERB
The head commended us on our work.
• congratulate, compliment, praise, applaud
OPPOSITE criticize

comment NOUN
He made some nasty comments about his boss.
• remark, statement, observation, opinion, mention, reference
A hostile comment is a criticism.

commit VERB
The thieves were planning to commit another robbery.
• carry out, do, perform, execute

commitment NOUN
❶ *Our team certainly has the commitment to win.*
• determination, dedication, enthusiasm, keenness, passion, resolution
❷ *I've made a commitment to join the choir.*
• promise, pledge, vow, undertaking, guarantee

committee NOUN
The tennis club is run by a committee of volunteers.
• board, panel, council, body, cabinet

common ADJECTIVE
❶ *Colds are a common complaint in winter.*
• commonplace, everyday, frequent, normal, ordinary, familiar, well-known, widespread
OPPOSITE rare
❷ *'Good morning' is a common way to greet people.*
• typical, usual, regular, routine, standard, customary, conventional, habitual, traditional
OPPOSITE uncommon
❸ *My friends and I have a common interest in music.*
• shared, mutual, joint

commonplace ADJECTIVE
Computers are now commonplace in schools.
• common, everyday, frequent, usual, normal, ordinary, routine, familiar

commotion NOUN
A group of protesters were causing a commotion outside.
• disturbance, row, fuss, trouble, disorder, unrest, agitation, turmoil, uproar, racket, rumpus, upheaval, riot, fracas, furore, hullabaloo, brouhaha, pandemonium, bedlam

communal ADJECTIVE
The swimming pool has communal showers.
• shared, public, common
OPPOSITE private

communicate VERB
❶ *Steve communicated his boredom with a yawn.*
• express, make known, indicate, convey, disclose, announce, pass on, proclaim, publish, report
❷ *Nowadays, we communicate by email.*
• contact each other, correspond, be in touch

communication NOUN
❶ *Dolphins use sound for communication.*
• communicating, contact, understanding each other
❷ *I've received an urgent communication.*
• message, dispatch, letter, statement, announcement

WORD WEB

SOME FORMS OF SPOKEN COMMUNICATION:
• chat, conversation, dialogue, gossip, lecture, message, phone call, rumour, speech, talk, voicemail

SOME FORMS OF WRITTEN COMMUNICATION:
• blog, correspondence, email, greetings card, letter, memo or memorandum, note, notice, postcard, text, tweet

OTHER FORMS OF COMMUNICATION:
• body language, Braille, hand gesture, the Internet, Morse code, podcast, radio, semaphore, sign language or signing, social media, telepathy, television, vlog, website

community NOUN
The children grew up in a farming community.
• area, district, neighbourhood, locality

compact ADJECTIVE
This camera is light and compact.
• small, portable, petite
OPPOSITE large

companion *NOUN*
Zak's pony was his favourite *companion*.
• friend, partner, comrade
(informal) mate, buddy, pal, chum

company *NOUN*
❶ My cousin works for a computer *company*.
• business, firm, corporation, organization, establishment
❷ Shrek shunned the *company* of other ogres.
• fellowship, companionship, friendship, society

compare *VERB*
Can you *compare* these sets of figures?
• contrast, juxtapose, relate, set side by side
➤ **to compare with**
This copy can't *compare with* the original painting.
• compete with, rival, emulate, equal, match

comparison *NOUN*
❶ I put the two dresses side by side for *comparison*.
• comparing, contrast, juxtaposition
❷ There's no *comparison* between their team and ours.
• similarity, resemblance, likeness, match

compartment *NOUN*
The sewing box has *compartments* for needles and pins.
• section, division, area, space

compatible *ADJECTIVE*
The couple were never really *compatible*.
• well-suited, well-matched
OPPOSITE incompatible

compel *VERB*
You can't *compel* me to come with you.
• force, make

compete *VERB*
Five schools will be *competing* in the hockey tournament.
• participate, perform, take part, enter
➤ **to compete against**
We are *competing against* a strong team this week.
• oppose, play against, contend with

competent *ADJECTIVE*
You have to be a *competent* swimmer to join the club.
• able, capable, skilful, skilled, accomplished, proficient, experienced, expert, qualified, trained
OPPOSITE incompetent

competition *NOUN*

WORD WEB

SOME KINDS OF COMPETITION:

• championship, contest, game, knockout competition, match, quiz, race, rally, series, tournament, trial
see also **sport**

competitor *NOUN*
The *competitors* lined up for the start of the race.
• contestant, contender, challenger, participant, opponent, rival
People who take an exam are **candidates** or **entrants**.

complain *VERB*
The guests did nothing but *complain*.
• moan, protest, grumble, grouse, gripe, whinge, make a fuss
➤ **to complain about**
I wrote a letter *complaining about* the noise.
• protest about, object to, criticize, find fault with
OPPOSITE praise

complaint *NOUN*
❶ They received hundreds of *complaints* about the film.
• criticism, objection, protest, moan, grumble

❷ *You have a nasty stomach complaint.*
• disease, illness, ailment, sickness, infection

complement *VERB*
That shade of green complements your eyes.
• accompany, go with

complete *ADJECTIVE*
❶ *Your training as a doctor is not yet complete.*
• completed, ended, finished, accomplished, concluded
OPPOSITE unfinished
❷ *Have you got a complete set of cards?*
• whole, entire, full, intact
OPPOSITE incomplete
❸ *My birthday party was a complete disaster.*
• total, utter, sheer, absolute, thorough, downright, perfect, pure

complete *VERB*
We have completed all the tasks on the sheet.
• finish, end, conclude, carry out, perform

complex *ADJECTIVE*
Defusing a bomb is a complex task.
• complicated, difficult, elaborate, detailed, intricate, involved
(informal) fiddly
OPPOSITE simple

complexion *NOUN*
The elf had a greenish tinge to his complexion.
• skin, colour, colouring
for ways to describe complexion see **face**

complicated *ADJECTIVE*
The plot of the film is very complicated.
• complex, intricate, involved, difficult, elaborate, convoluted
OPPOSITES simple, straightforward

complimentary *ADJECTIVE*
❶ *My teacher made complimentary remarks on my playing.*
• appreciative, approving, admiring, positive, favourable, flattering
OPPOSITES critical, insulting, negative
❷ *We were given complimentary tickets for the game.*
• free, gratis

compliments *PLURAL NOUN*
It was nice to get compliments about my cooking.
• praise, appreciation, approval, congratulations, tribute
Compliments which you don't deserve are flattery.
OPPOSITE insults

component *NOUN*
The factory makes components for cars.
• part, bit, piece, element, spare part

compose *VERB*
Beethoven composed nine symphonies.
• create, devise, produce, make up, think up, write
➤ **to be composed of**
This quilt is composed of pieces of patchwork.
• be made of, consist of, comprise

composition *NOUN*
Is the song your own composition?
• piece, work, creation
(formal) opus
for types of musical composition see **music**

comprehend *VERB*
The crowd couldn't comprehend what was happening.
• understand, realize, appreciate, figure out, grasp, perceive, follow

a
b
c
d
e
f
g
h
i
j
k
l
m
n
o
p
q
r
s
t
u
v
w
x
y
z

A
B
C
D
E
F
G
H
I
J
K
L
M
N
O
P
Q
R
S
T
U
V
W
X
Y
Z

comprehensive *ADJECTIVE*
She gave us a comprehensive account of her travels.
• complete, full, thorough, detailed, extensive, inclusive, exhaustive, wide-ranging, encyclopedic
OPPOSITE selective

compress *VERB*
I tried to compress all my clothes into one bag.
• press, squeeze, cram, crush, jam, squash, stuff, flatten

comprise *VERB*
The team comprised athletes from several countries.
• be composed of, consist of, include, contain

compulsive *ADJECTIVE*
❶ *Suddenly, I felt a compulsive urge to laugh.*
• compelling, overwhelming, overpowering, irresistible, uncontrollable
❷ *We knew they were compulsive liars.*
• habitual, obsessive, incurable

compulsory *ADJECTIVE*
The wearing of seat belts is compulsory.
• required, obligatory, necessary
OPPOSITE optional

computer *NOUN*

WORD WEB

SOME KINDS OF COMPUTER:

• desktop, laptop, notebook, PC, server, tablet

SOME PARTS OF A COMPUTER SYSTEM:

• DVD drive, flash drive, games console, hard disk, keyboard, keypad, memory stick, microchip, microprocessor, monitor, motherboard, mouse, processor, screen, touchpad, touchscreen, USB port, webcam

OTHER TERMS USED IN COMPUTING:

• AI, app, attachment, back-up, broadband, browser, byte, CGI, cloud, cursor, data, database, directory, download, digital, email, file, folder, games console, gaming, gigabyte, hardware, hotspot, internet, megabyte, memory, menu, MP3, network, offline, online, printout, program, RAM, screenshot, software, spam, streaming, upload, virus, VR, web, window, wifi, wireless, word processor

concave *ADJECTIVE*
see **curved**
OPPOSITE convex

conceal *VERB*
❶ *The dog tried to conceal its bone.*
• hide, cover up, bury
❷ *We tried to conceal our hiding place.*
• disguise, mask, screen, camouflage, make invisible
❸ *Don't conceal the truth.*
• keep quiet about, keep secret, hush up, suppress

conceited *ADJECTIVE*
He was so conceited when he won first prize!
• boastful, arrogant, proud, vain, self-satisfied
(informal) big-headed, cocky
OPPOSITE modest

conceive *VERB*
❶ *Who conceived this silly plan?*
• think up, devise, invent, make up, originate, plan, produce, work out
(informal) dream up
❷ *I could not conceive how the plan would work.*
• imagine, see, envisage

concentrate *VERB*
❶ *I had to concentrate to hear what she was saying.*
• be attentive, think hard, focus

❷ *The crowds concentrated in the middle of town.*
• collect, gather, converge

concept *NOUN*
I find the concept of time travel fascinating.
• idea, thought, notion

concern *VERB*
❶ *This conversation doesn't concern you.*
• affect, involve, be important to, matter to, be relevant to, relate to
❷ *It concerns me that we are destroying the rainforests.*
• bother, distress, trouble, upset, worry

concern *NOUN*
❶ *My private life is no concern of theirs.*
• affair, business
❷ *Global warming is a great concern to us all.*
• worry, anxiety, fear
❸ *She's the head of a business concern.*
• company, firm, enterprise, establishment

concerned *ADJECTIVE*
❶ *After waiting an hour, Julia began to feel concerned.*
• worried, bothered, troubled, anxious, upset, distressed
❷ *We're writing a letter to all those concerned.*
• involved, connected, related, affected

concerning *PREPOSITION*
The head spoke to me concerning my future.
• about, regarding, relating to, with reference to, relevant to

concert *NOUN*
The jazz band is giving a concert tonight.
• recital, performance, show

concise *ADJECTIVE*
He gave the police a concise account of what happened.
• brief, short, condensed, succinct
A concise account of something is a precis or summary.
OPPOSITE long

conclude *VERB*
❶ *We concluded the Christmas concert with carols.*
• end, finish, complete, round off, wind up
❷ *The concert concluded with some carols.*
• close, terminate, culminate
❸ *They concluded that she was guilty.*
• decide, deduce, infer, suppose, assume, gather

conclusion *NOUN*
❶ *The conclusion of the film was a bit puzzling.*
• close, end, finale, finish, completion, culmination
❷ *'What is your conclusion, Inspector?'*
• decision, judgement, opinion, verdict, deduction

concrete *ADJECTIVE*
The police are looking for concrete evidence.
• real, actual, definite, firm, solid, substantial, physical, factual, objective
OPPOSITE abstract

condemn *VERB*
❶ *The manager condemned the behaviour of the players.*
• criticize, disapprove of, denounce, deplore, reproach
OPPOSITE praise
❷ *The judge condemned the men to death.*
• sentence
OPPOSITE acquit

condense *VERB*
❶ *I condensed my poem so that it fitted on one page.*
• reduce, shorten, compress, summarize
OPPOSITE expand
❷ *Steam condenses on a cold window.*
• become liquid, form condensation
OPPOSITE evaporate

a
b
c
d
e
f
g
h
i
j
k
l
m
n
o
p
q
r
s
t
u
v
w
x
y
z

condition NOUN
❶ *Is your bike in good condition?*
• state, order, repair
❷ *A dog needs exercise to stay in good condition.*
• fitness, health, shape
❸ *It's a condition of membership that you pay a subscription.*
• requirement, obligation, term
➤ **on condition that**
You can come on condition that you pay your own fare.
• provided, providing that, only if

conduct VERB
❶ *A guide conducted us round the museum.*
• guide, lead, take, accompany, escort
❷ *We asked the eldest girl to conduct our meeting.*
• lead, manage, control, run, administer, supervise, preside over, organize, handle
➤ **to conduct yourself**
The grown-ups did not conduct themselves well.
• behave, act, carry on

conduct NOUN
Our teacher congratulated us on our good conduct.
• behaviour, manners, attitude

confer VERB
❶ *They conferred the freedom of the city on the victorious team.*
• give (to), grant (to), present (to), award (to)
❷ *The president conferred with her advisors before making a decision.*
• consult, have a discussion, talk things over, converse

conference NOUN
All the witches were invited to a grand conference.
• meeting, consultation, discussion

confess VERB
The goblin confessed that she had stolen the gold.
• admit, own up to, acknowledge, reveal

confidence NOUN
❶ *We can face the future with confidence.*
• hope, optimism, faith
OPPOSITE doubt
❷ *I wish I had her confidence.*
• self-confidence, assurance, boldness, conviction

confident ADJECTIVE
❶ *I am confident that we will win.*
• certain, sure, positive, optimistic
OPPOSITE doubtful
❷ *She is a confident sort of person.*
• self-confident, assertive, bold, fearless, unafraid

confidential ADJECTIVE
The details of the plan are confidential.
• secret, private
OPPOSITE public

confine VERB
❶ *They confined their discussion to the weather.*
• limit, restrict
❷ *Our farm animals are not confined indoors.*
• enclose, surround, fence in, shut in, coop up, hem in

confirm VERB
❶ *The strange events confirmed his belief in ghosts.*
• prove, justify, support, back up, reinforce
OPPOSITE disprove
❷ *I phoned to confirm my appointment at the dentist.*
• verify, make official
OPPOSITE cancel

confiscate VERB
The janitor confiscated our ball.
• take away, take possession of, seize

conflict NOUN
There's a lot of conflict in their family.
• disagreement, quarrelling, fighting, hostility, friction, antagonism, opposition, strife, unrest

conflict VERB
➤ **to conflict with**
Her account of what happened conflicts with mine.
• disagree with, differ from, contradict, contrast with, clash with

conflicting ADJECTIVE
My brother and I have conflicting tastes in music.
• different, contrasting, contradictory, opposite, incompatible

conform VERB
➤ **to conform to** or **with**
The club expels anyone who doesn't conform with the rules.
• follow, keep to, obey, abide by, agree with, fit in with, submit to
OPPOSITE disobey

confront VERB
I decided to confront her and demand an apology.
• challenge, stand up to, face up to

confuse VERB
❶ *I was confused by the directions on the map.*
• puzzle, bewilder, mystify, baffle, perplex
❷ *You must be confusing me with someone else.*
• mix up, muddle

confusion NOUN
❶ *There was great confusion when the lights went out.*
• chaos, commotion, fuss, uproar, turmoil, pandemonium, bedlam, hullabaloo
❷ *There was a look of confusion on her face.*
• bewilderment, puzzlement, perplexity

congratulate VERB
We congratulated the winners.
• praise, applaud, compliment
OPPOSITE criticize

congregate VERB
The party guests congregated in the hall.
• gather, assemble, collect, come together
OPPOSITE disperse

connect VERB
❶ *What's the best way to connect these wires?*
• join, attach, fasten, link, couple, fix together, tie together
OPPOSITE separate
❷ *The fingerprints connected them with the crime.*
• make a connection between, associate, relate

connection NOUN
There is a close connection between our two families.
• association, relationship, link

conquer VERB
❶ *Extra troops were sent to conquer the enemy forces.*
• beat, defeat, overcome, vanquish, get the better of, overwhelm, crush, rout, thrash
❷ *Gaul was conquered by Julius Caesar.*
• seize, capture, take, win, occupy, possess
❸ *Several climbers have conquered Mount Everest.*
• climb, reach the top of

conqueror NOUN
Cheering crowds greeted the conquerors.
• victor, winner

conquest NOUN
The book gave an account of the Norman conquest.
• invasion, occupation, capture, possession

a
b
c
d
e
f
g
h
i
j
k
l
m
n
o
p
q
r
s
t
u
v
w
x
y
z

conscientious ADJECTIVE
Elves are very conscientious workers.
• hard-working, careful, dependable, reliable, responsible, dutiful, meticulous, painstaking, thorough
OPPOSITE careless

conscious ADJECTIVE
❶ *The patient was conscious throughout the operation.*
• awake, alert, aware
OPPOSITE unconscious
❷ *She made a conscious effort to improve her work.*
• deliberate, intentional, planned
OPPOSITE accidental

consent VERB
➤ **to consent to**
The head has consented to our request.
• agree to, grant, approve of, authorize
OPPOSITE refuse

consequence NOUN
❶ *He drank the potion without thinking of the consequences.*
• effect, result, outcome, upshot, sequel
❷ *The loss of a few pence is of no consequence.*
• importance, significance

conservation NOUN
Our group supports the conservation of wildlife.
• preservation, protection, maintenance, upkeep
OPPOSITE destruction

conservative ADJECTIVE
❶ *My parents have a very conservative taste in clothes.*
• old-fashioned, conventional, unadventurous, traditional
OPPOSITES progressive, up-to-date
❷ *At a conservative estimate, the work will take six months.*
• cautious, moderate, reasonable
OPPOSITE extreme

conserve VERB
The explorers had to conserve their water supply.
• save, preserve, be sparing with, use wisely, look after, protect
OPPOSITE waste

consider VERB
❶ *The detective considered the problem carefully.*
• think about, examine, contemplate, ponder on, reflect on, study, weigh up, meditate about
❷ *I consider this to be my best work.*
• believe, judge, reckon

considerable ADJECTIVE
1000 dollars is a considerable sum of money.
• big, large, significant, substantial, sizeable
OPPOSITES negligible, insignificant

considerate ADJECTIVE
It was considerate of you to lend me your umbrella.
• kind, kind-hearted, helpful, obliging, sympathetic, thoughtful, unselfish, caring, charitable, neighbourly
OPPOSITE selfish

consist VERB
➤ **to consist of**
❶ *The planet consists largely of craters.*
• be made of, be composed of, comprise, contain, include, incorporate
❷ *His job consists mostly of answering the phone.*
• involve

consistency NOUN
The mixture had the consistency of porridge.
• texture, thickness, density

consistent ADJECTIVE
❶ *These plants need to be kept at a consistent temperature.*
• steady, constant, regular, stable, unchanging
❷ *Fortunately, our goalkeeper is a consistent player.*
• predictable, dependable, reliable
OPPOSITE inconsistent

console *VERB*
He did his best to **console** me when my dog died.
• comfort, soothe, sympathize with, support

conspicuous *ADJECTIVE*
❶ The clock tower is a **conspicuous** landmark.
• prominent, notable, obvious, eye-catching, unmistakable, visible
❷ I had made some **conspicuous** mistakes.
• clear, noticeable, obvious, evident, glaring
OPPOSITE inconspicuous

constant *ADJECTIVE*
❶ There is a **constant** noise of traffic on the motorway.
• continual, continuous, never-ending, non-stop, ceaseless, incessant, interminable, endless, everlasting, permanent, perpetual, unending, persistent, relentless
OPPOSITE changeable
❷ My cat has been my **constant** friend for many years.
• faithful, loyal, dependable, reliable, firm, true, trustworthy, devoted
OPPOSITE unreliable

constitute *VERB*
In rugby, fifteen players **constitute** a team.
• make up, compose, comprise, form

construct *VERB*
We **constructed** a tree house in the back garden.
• build, erect, assemble, make, put together, put up, set up
OPPOSITE demolish

construction *NOUN*
❶ The **construction** of the tree house took all afternoon.
• building, erecting, erection, assembly, setting-up
❷ The hut was a flimsy **construction**.
• building, structure

consult *VERB*
❶ You should **consult** the dentist about your sore tooth.
• ask, get advice from, speak to
❷ If you don't know how to spell a word, **consult** your dictionary.
• refer to

consume *VERB*
❶ The birds **consumed** all the bread in ten minutes!
• eat, devour, gobble up, guzzle
❷ The truck **consumed** a great deal of fuel.
• use up
❸ The building was **consumed** by fire.
• destroy

contact *VERB*
I'll **contact** you when I have some news.
• call, call on, get in touch with, speak to, communicate with, notify, talk to, correspond with, phone, ring, write to

contagious *ADJECTIVE*
Mumps is a very **contagious** disease.
• catching, infectious

contain *VERB*
❶ This box **contains** various odds and ends.
• hold
❷ A dictionary **contains** words and definitions.
• include, incorporate, comprise, consist of

container *NOUN*
Put the leftover sauce in a **container**.
• vessel, receptacle, holder, box, case, canister, carton, pot, tub, tin

contaminate *VERB*
The river had been **contaminated** with chemicals.
• pollute, poison, infect
OPPOSITE purify

a
b
c
d
e
f
g
h
i
j
k
l
m
n
o
p
q
r
s
t
u
v
w
x
y
z

A
B
C
D
E
F
G
H
I
J
K
L
M
N
O
P
Q
R
S
T
U
V
W
X
Y
Z

contemplate *VERB*

❶ *Luca sat contemplating the clouds in the sky.*
• look at, view, observe, survey, watch, stare at, gaze at
❷ *The robbers contemplated what to do next.*
• think about, consider, ponder, study, reflect on, weigh up, meditate about

contemporary *ADJECTIVE*

Do you like contemporary music?
• current, fashionable, modern, up-to-date, the latest
(informal) trendy
OPPOSITE old-fashioned, out-of-date

contempt *NOUN*

The warrior stared at her enemy with a look of contempt.
• hatred, scorn, loathing, disgust, dislike, distaste
OPPOSITE admiration

contend *VERB*

I contend that I was right.
• declare, claim, argue, assert, maintain
➤ **to contend with**
❶ *The team had to contend with strong opposition.*
• compete with, fight against, oppose, grapple with, struggle against, strive against
❷ *We had to contend with bad weather and midges!*
• cope with, deal with, face, put up with

content *ADJECTIVE*

Fergus was perfectly content to sit reading a book.
• happy, contented, satisfied, pleased, willing
OPPOSITE unwilling

contented *ADJECTIVE*

After her meal, the cat looked very contented.
• happy, pleased, content, satisfied, fulfilled, serene, peaceful, relaxed, comfortable, tranquil, untroubled
OPPOSITE discontented

contents *PLURAL NOUN*

We all tried to guess the contents of the mystery parcel.
• elements, ingredients, parts

contest *NOUN*

The tennis final was an exciting contest.
• competition, challenge, fight, bout, encounter, struggle, game, match, tournament

contest *VERB*

Several players contested the referee's decision.
• challenge, disagree with, question, oppose, argue against, quarrel with

contestant *NOUN*

There are twenty contestants in the spelling competition.
• competitor, participant, player, contender

continual *ADJECTIVE*

I get sick of their continual arguing.
• constant, persistent, perpetual, repeated, frequent, recurrent, eternal, unending
see also continuous
OPPOSITE occasional

continue *VERB*

❶ *We continued our search until it got dark.*
• keep up, prolong, sustain, persevere with, pursue
(informal) stick at
❷ *This rain can't continue for long.*
• carry on, last, persist, endure, keep on, go on, linger
❸ *We'll continue our meeting after lunch.*
• resume, proceed with, pick up

continuous *ADJECTIVE*

We had continuous rain all through our holiday.
• never-ending, non-stop, ceaseless, everlasting, incessant, unbroken, unceasing, uninterrupted
An illness which continues for a long time is a chronic illness.
see also continual
OPPOSITE intermittent

contract *NOUN*

*The star has signed a **contract** for a new film.*
• agreement, deal, undertaking
A contract between two countries is an
alliance or **treaty**.
A contract to end a dispute about money is a
settlement.

contract *VERB*

❶ *Metal **contracts** when it gets colder.*
• reduce, lessen, shrink, tighten
OPPOSITE expand
❷ *The crew **contracted** a mysterious illness.*
• catch, develop, get

contradict *VERB*

*I didn't dare to **contradict** the referee.*
• challenge, disagree with,
speak against

contraption *NOUN*

*The inventor's house was full of weird
contraptions.*
• machine, device, gadget, invention,
apparatus, contrivance, mechanism
(informal) gizmo

contrary *ADJECTIVE*

*They had always been sulky, **contrary**
children.*
• awkward, difficult, stubborn, disobedient,
obstinate, uncooperative, unhelpful, wilful,
perverse
OPPOSITE cooperative
➤ **contrary to**
*Contrary to popular belief, snakes are
not slimy.*
• differing from, against, opposing,
in the face of, unlike

contrast *VERB*

❶ *We were asked to **contrast** two of our
favourite poems.*
• compare, juxtapose, distinguish
between
❷ *Her handwriting **contrasts** with mine.*
• differ (from), clash

contrast *NOUN*

*There is a sharp **contrast** between the two
paintings.*
• difference, distinction, opposition
OPPOSITE similarity

contribute *VERB*

*Will you **contribute** something to our charity
collection?*
• donate, give, provide
(informal) chip in
➤ **to contribute to**
*The sunny weather **contributed to** our
enjoyment.*
• add to, help, aid, encourage, enhance

contrive *VERB*

*They **contrived** a way to escape from the
dungeon.*
• think up, plan, make up, create,
invent

control *NOUN*

*The captain had complete **control** over the
crew.*
• authority, power, command, government,
management, direction, leadership,
guidance

control *VERB*

❶*The government **controls** the country's
affairs.*
• be in control of, be in charge of, manage,
run, command, direct, lead, guide, govern,
administer, regulate, rule, superintend,
supervise
❷ *Can't you **control** that dog?*
• manage, handle, restrain
❸ *They built a dam to **control** the floods.*
• check, curb, hold back, contain

controversial *ADJECTIVE*

*The decision to award a penalty was
controversial.*
• debatable, questionable, arguable

a
b
c
d
e
f
g
h
i
j
k
l
m
n
o
p
q
r
s
t
u
v
w
x
y
z

A
B
C
D
E
F
G
H
I
J
K
L
M
N
O
P
Q
R
S
T
U
V
W
X
Y
Z

controversy NOUN
There is much **controversy** about the election results.
• disagreement, debate, argument, dispute, quarrelling

convenient ADJECTIVE
❶ Is there a **convenient** place to put my umbrella?
• suitable, appropriate, available, nearby, accessible
OPPOSITE inconvenient
❷ Mum has a **convenient** tool for opening jars.
• handy, helpful, useful, labour-saving, neat

conventional ADJECTIVE
The **conventional** way to greet someone is to shake hands.
• customary, traditional, usual, accepted, common, normal, ordinary, everyday, routine, standard, regular, habitual, orthodox
OPPOSITE unconventional

converge VERB
The two rivers **converge** at this point.
• come together, join, meet, merge, combine, coincide
OPPOSITE divide

conversation NOUN
An informal conversation is a **chat** or **gossip**.
A more formal conversation is a **discussion**.
A very formal conversation is a **conference**.
Conversation in a play or novel is **dialogue**.

converse VERB
The travellers **conversed** happily for several minutes.
• chat, talk, have a conversation, engage in conversation
see also **talk**

convert VERB
❶ We have **converted** our attic into a games room.
• change, adapt, alter, transform
❷ I never used to like football, but my cousin **converted** me.
• change someone's mind, persuade, convince, win over

convex ADJECTIVE
see **curved**
OPPOSITE concave

convey VERB
❶ The breakdown truck **conveyed** our car to a garage.
• bring, carry, deliver, take, move, bear, transfer, transport
To convey something by sea is to **ferry** or **ship** it.
❷ What does his message **convey** to you?
• communicate, tell, reveal, indicate, signify, mean

convict NOUN
Four **convicts** have escaped from the prison.
• prisoner, criminal
convict VERB
The thieves were **convicted** and sent to prison.
• condemn, declare guilty, sentence
OPPOSITE acquit

convince VERB
The prisoner **convinced** them that he was innocent.
• persuade, assure, satisfy, make believe, win round

convincing ADJECTIVE
I tried to think of a **convincing** excuse.
• persuasive, believable, credible, plausible

cook VERB

WORD WEB

To cook food for guests or customers is to **cater** for them.
Cooking as a business is **catering**.
The art or skill of cooking is **cookery**.

SOME WAYS TO COOK FOOD:

• bake, barbecue, boil, braise, broil, casserole, curry, deep-fry, fry, grill, poach, roast, sauté, simmer, steam, stew, stir-fry, toast

OTHER WAYS TO PREPARE FOOD:

• baste, blend, chop, dice, grate, grind, infuse, knead, liquidize, marinade, mince, mix, peel, purée, sieve, sift, stir, whisk

SOME ITEMS THAT ARE USED FOR COOKING:

• baking tin or tray, barbecue, blender, bowl, carving knife, casserole, cauldron, chopping board, colander, cooker, dish, food processor, frying pan, grill, ladle, liquidizer, microwave, mincer, oven, pan, pot, rolling pin, saucepan, skewer, spatula, spit, strainer, toaster, whisk, wok, wooden spoon
see also **crockery, cutlery, kitchen**

cook NOUN

The chief cook in a restaurant or hotel is the **chef**.
A person who cooks food as a business is a **caterer**.

cool ADJECTIVE

❶ *The weather is cool for the time of year.*
• chilly, coldish
OPPOSITES hot, warm
❷ *Would you like a cool glass of lemonade?*
• chilled, iced, refreshing
OPPOSITE hot
❸ *Clifford remained cool when everyone else panicked.*
• calm, level-headed, relaxed, unexcitable, unflustered
(informal) laid-back
A common simile is **as cool as a cucumber**.
OPPOSITE frantic

❹ *(informal) Those roller skates are really cool!*
• chic, fashionable, smart
(informal) trendy

cooperate VERB

➤ **to cooperate with**
The scouts cooperated with each other to build a fire.
• work with, work together with, collaborate with, aid, assist, support

cope VERB

Shall I help you, or can you cope on your own?
• manage, carry on, get by, make do, survive
➤ **to cope with**
I can't cope with all this homework!
• deal with, handle, manage, get through

copy NOUN

That isn't the original painting—it's a copy.
• replica, reproduction, duplicate, imitation, likeness
A copy made to deceive someone is a **fake** or a **forgery**.
A living organism which is identical to another is a **clone**.

copy VERB

❶ *I copied the poem into my planner.*
• duplicate, reproduce, write out
To copy something in order to deceive is to **fake** or **forge** it.
❷ *My parrot can copy my voice.*
• imitate, impersonate, mimic

cord NOUN

The pilot pulled the cord to open her parachute.
• string, rope, tape, strap, line, cable, flex

core NOUN

It is very hot at the earth's core.
• centre, middle, inside, heart, nucleus

a
b
c
d
e
f
g
h
i
j
k
l
m
n
o
p
q
r
s
t
u
v
w
x
y
z

A
B
C
D
E
F
G
H
I
J
K
L
M
N
O
P
Q
R
S
T
U
V
W
X
Y
Z

corn *NOUN*
*The farmer was growing corn
in the field.*
• grain, cereal, wheat

corner *NOUN*
❶ *I'll meet you at the corner of the road.*
• turn, turning, junction, crossroads,
intersection
The place where two lines meet is an **angle**.
❷ *I sat in a quiet corner and read
her letter.*
• alcove, recess, nook

correct *ADJECTIVE*
❶ *Your answers are all correct.*
• right, accurate, exact, faultless
❷ *I hope he has given us correct
information.*
• true, genuine, authentic, precise, reliable,
factual
❸ *What is the correct way to address this
letter?*
• proper, acceptable, regular, appropriate,
suitable
OPPOSITE wrong

correct *VERB*
❶ *I have to correct my spelling mistakes.*
• alter, put right, rectify, improve
❷ *Miss Nicol spent the day correcting exam
papers.*
• mark

correspond *VERB*
➤ **to correspond with**
❶ *Her version of the story doesn't correspond
with mine.*
• agree with, match, be similar to,
be consistent with, tally with
❷ *Carol corresponds with a friend
in Paris.*
• write to, communicate with,
send letters to

corrode *VERB*
This acid will corrode metal.
• eat away, erode, rot, rust

corrupt *ADJECTIVE*
*Corrupt officials had accepted millions of
pounds in bribes.*
• dishonest, criminal, untrustworthy
(informal) bent, crooked
OPPOSITE honest

cost *VERB* costs, costing, cost
How much do these shoes cost?
• be worth, go for, sell for

cost *NOUN*
The bill shows the total cost.
• price, charge, amount, payment, fee, figure,
expense, expenditure, tariff
The cost of travelling on public transport is the
fare.

costly *ADJECTIVE*
*It would be too costly to repair
the car.*
• dear, expensive
OPPOSITE cheap

costume *NOUN*
*The Irish dancers were wearing national
costumes.*
• outfit, dress, clothing, suit, attire, garment,
garb
(informal) **get-up**
A costume you dress up in for a party
is **fancy dress**.
A set of clothes worn by soldiers or members
of an organization is a **uniform**.
see also **clothes**

cosy *ADJECTIVE*
*It's good to feel cosy in bed when it's cold
outside.*
• comfortable, snug, soft, warm, secure
OPPOSITE uncomfortable

couch *NOUN*
*My brother sat on the couch watching TV all
weekend.*
• settee, sofa
for other types of seat see **seat**

counsel *VERB*
His advisors counselled him
to surrender.
• advise, guide, direct, encourage,
recommend, urge

count *VERB*
❶ *I'm counting the days until my birthday.*
• add up, calculate, compute, estimate,
reckon, figure out, work out, total
❷ *It's playing well that counts, not*
winning.
• be important, be significant, matter
➤ **to count on**
You can count on me to support you.
• depend on, rely on, trust, bank on

countless *ADJECTIVE*
I've seen that film countless times.
• a great many, numerous, innumerable,
myriad, untold
OPPOSITE finite

country *NOUN*
❶ *England and Wales are separate countries.*
• nation, state, land, territory
A country ruled by a king or queen is a
kingdom, **monarchy** or **realm**.
A country governed by leaders elected by the
people is a **democracy**.
A democratic country with a president is a
republic.
❷ *We went for a picnic in the country.*
• countryside, landscape, outdoors
OPPOSITES town, city
A word meaning 'to do with the country' is
rural and its opposite is **urban**.

coupon *NOUN*
You can exchange these coupons for a free mug.
• token, voucher, ticket

courage *NOUN*
The rescue dogs showed great courage.
• bravery, boldness, daring, fearlessness,
nerve, pluck, valour, heroism, grit
(informal) guts
OPPOSITE cowardice

courageous *ADJECTIVE*
The warriors were always courageous in battle.
• brave, bold, daring, fearless, heroic, intrepid,
plucky, gallant, valiant
OPPOSITE cowardly

course *NOUN*
❶ *The hot-air balloon was drifting off its*
course.
• direction, path, route, way, progress, passage
❷ *The war changed the course of history.*
• development, progression, sequence,
succession
➤ **of course**
Of course you can come to my party.
• naturally, certainly, definitely, undoubtedly

courteous *ADJECTIVE*
I received a courteous reply to my letter.
• polite, respectful, well-mannered, civil,
considerate, friendly, helpful
OPPOSITE rude

cover *VERB*
❶ *A coat of paint will cover the graffiti.*
• conceal, disguise, hide, obscure, mask,
blot out
❷ *She covered her face with her hands.*
• shield, screen, protect, shade, veil
❸ *The hikers are hoping to cover twenty-five*
miles a day.
• progress, travel
❹ *An encyclopedia covers many subjects.*
• deal with, include, contain, incorporate
❺ *Will £50 cover your expenses?*
• be enough for, pay for
cover *NOUN*
❶ *The cover of the book was torn.*
• wrapper
A cover for a letter is an **envelope**.
A cover for a book is a **jacket**.
A cover to keep papers in is a **file** or **folder**.
❷ *On the bare hillside, there was no cover*
from the storm.
• shelter, protection, defence, shield, refuge,
sanctuary

A
B
C
D
E
F
G
H
I
J
K
L
M
N
O
P
Q
R
S
T
U
V
W
X
Y
Z

covering NOUN
There was a light **covering** of snow on the hills.
• coating, coat, layer, blanket, carpet, film, sheet, skin, veil

cowardly ADJECTIVE
It was **cowardly** to run away.
• timid, faint-hearted, spineless, gutless
(informal) yellow, chicken
OPPOSITE brave

cower VERB
A frightened creature was **cowering** in the corner.
• cringe, shrink, crouch, flinch, quail

crack NOUN
❶ There's a **crack** in this cup.
• break, chip, fracture, flaw, chink, split
❷ The outlaw hid in a **crack** between two rocks.
• gap, opening, crevice, rift, cranny
❸ The detective heard the **crack** of a pistol shot.
• bang, fire, explosion, snap, pop
❹ She gave the robber a **crack** on the head.
• blow, bang, knock, smack, whack
❺ I had a **crack** at writing a poem.
• try, attempt, shot, go

crack VERB
A brick fell down and **cracked** the pavement.
• break, fracture, chip, split, shatter, splinter

craft NOUN
❶ I'd like to learn the **craft** of weaving.
• art, skill, technique, expertise, handicraft
for names of arts and crafts see **art**
❷ All sorts of **craft** were in the harbour.
• boats, ships, vessels
for types of boat or ship see **boat**

crafty ADJECTIVE
The evil sorceress had a **crafty** plan.
• cunning, clever, shrewd, scheming, sneaky, sly, tricky, wily, artful

cram VERB
❶ We can't **cram** any more people in—the car is full.
• pack, squeeze, crush, force, jam, compress
❷ My sister is **cramming** for her maths exam.
• revise, study
(informal) swot

cramped ADJECTIVE
The seating on the train was a bit **cramped**.
• confined, narrow, restricted, tight, uncomfortable, crowded
(informal) poky
OPPOSITE roomy

crash NOUN
❶ I heard a loud **crash** from the kitchen.
• bang, smash
for other kinds of sound see **sound**
❷ We saw a nasty **crash** on the motorway.
• accident, collision, smash, bump
A crash involving a lot of vehicles is a **pile-up**.
A train crash may involve a **derailment**.

crash VERB
The car **crashed** into a lamp post.
• bump, smash, collide, knock

crate NOUN
We packed our belongings into **crates**.
• box, case, chest, packing case

crater NOUN
The surface of the moon is full of **craters**.
• pit, hole, hollow, cavity, chasm, opening, abyss

crawl VERB
I saw a caterpillar **crawling** along a leaf.
• creep, edge, inch, slither, clamber

craze NOUN
This game is the latest **craze** in the playground.
• fad, trend, vogue, fashion, enthusiasm, obsession, passion

crazy *ADJECTIVE*
❶ *The dog went* **crazy** *when it was stung by a wasp.*
• mad, insane, frenzied, hysterical, frantic, berserk, delirious, wild
(informal) loopy, nuts
❷ *It was a* **crazy** *idea to try to build a space rocket!*
• absurd, ridiculous, ludicrous, daft, idiotic, senseless, silly, stupid, foolhardy, preposterous
(informal) bonkers, barmy, wacky
OPPOSITE sensible

creamy *ADJECTIVE*
That ice cream is really **creamy***!*
• rich, smooth, thick, velvety

crease *NOUN*
Can you iron the **creases** *out of this shirt?*
• wrinkle, crinkle, pucker, fold, furrow, groove, line
A crease made deliberately in a skirt or other garment is a **pleat**.
crease *VERB*
Pack the clothes carefully, so you don't **crease** *them.*
• wrinkle, crinkle, crumple, crush, pucker

create *VERB*
❶ *The cats were* **creating** *a racket outside.*
• make, cause, produce
❷ *We have* **created** *a website for our chess club.*
• set up, start up, bring about, bring into existence, originate
You **write** a poem or story.
You **compose** music.
You **draw** or **paint** a picture.
You **carve** a statue.
You **invent** or **think up** a new idea.
You **design** a new product.
You **devise** a plan.
You **found** a new club or organization.
You **manufacture** goods.
You **generate** electricity.
You **build** or **construct** a model or a building.
OPPOSITE destroy

creation *NOUN*
❶ *The TV programme is about the* **creation** *of life on earth.*
• beginning, origin, birth, generation, initiation
❷ *They raised money for the* **creation** *of a sports centre.*
• building, construction, establishing, foundation
❸ *This pizza recipe is my own* **creation***.*
• concept, invention

creative *ADJECTIVE*
My aunt is a very **creative** *person.*
• artistic, imaginative, inventive, original, inspired
OPPOSITE unimaginative

creator *NOUN*
Walt Disney was the **creator** *of Mickey Mouse.*
• inventor, maker, originator, producer, deviser
The creator of a design is an **architect** or **designer**.
The creator of goods for sale is a **manufacturer**.

creature *NOUN*
A wild-looking **creature** *emerged from the swamp.*
• animal, beast, being
see also **animal**
for creatures found in myths and legends see **myth**

credible *ADJECTIVE*
The detective did not find the woman's story **credible***.*
• believable, convincing, persuasive, trustworthy, likely, possible, reasonable
OPPOSITE incredible

credit *NOUN*
The author is finally getting the **credit** *she deserves.*
• recognition, honour, praise, distinction, fame, glory, reputation
OPPOSITE dishonour

a
b
c
d
e
f
g
h
i
j
k
l
m
n
o
p
q
r
s
t
u
v
w
x
y
z

A
B
C
D
E
F
G
H
I
J
K
L
M
N
O
P
Q
R
S
T
U
V
W
X
Y
Z

credit *VERB*
It's hard to credit that they are brother and sister.
• believe, accept, have faith in, trust
OPPOSITE doubt

creed *NOUN*
Pupils of all races and creeds attend the school.
• religion, doctrine, faith, set of beliefs

creep *VERB* creeps, creeping, crept
❶ *I watched the lizard creep back into its hiding place.*
• crawl, edge, inch, slither, wriggle
❷ *I crept out of bed without waking the others.*
• move quietly, sneak, tiptoe, slip, slink, steal

creepy *ADJECTIVE*
There were creepy noises coming from the cellar.
• scary, frightening, eerie, ghostly, weird, sinister, uncanny, unearthly
(informal) spooky
see also **ghost**

crest *NOUN*
❶ *The bird had a large red crest on its head.*
• comb, plume, tuft
❷ *There was a wonderful view from the crest of the hill.*
• top, peak, summit, crown, head, brow

crevice *NOUN*
Moss was growing in the crevices in the rock.
• crack, cranny, gap, opening, rift, split
A deep crack in a glacier is a crevasse.

crew *NOUN*
for words for groups of people see **group**

cricket *NOUN*

WORD WEB

PEOPLE WHO PLAY CRICKET:

• batter, bowler, cricketer, fielder or fieldsman, wicketkeeper
The official who makes sure players keep to the rules is the **umpire**.

SOME OTHER TERMS USED IN CRICKET:

• boundary, crease, innings, maiden over, over, pitch, run, stump, wicket

crime *NOUN*
Robbing a bank is a serious crime.
• offence, lawbreaking, wrongdoing

criminal *NOUN*
Those responsible are known as criminals.
• lawbreaker, offender, wrongdoer
(informal) crook
A person who has been convicted of a crime is a **convict**.

WORD WEB

SOME TYPES OF CRIMINAL:

• assassin, bandit, blackmailer, brigand, burglar, cat burglar, con man, gangster, hacker, highwayman, hijacker, kidnapper, mugger, murderer, outlaw, pickpocket, pirate, poacher, robber, shoplifter, smuggler, terrorist, thief, thug, vandal

criminal *ADJECTIVE*
The gang were involved in many criminal schemes.
• illegal, unlawful, corrupt, dishonest, wrong
(informal) bent, crooked
OPPOSITE honest

cringe *VERB*
I cringed with embarrassment when my name was called.
• shrink, flinch, wince, cower

cripple *VERB*
❶ *The fall may have crippled the horse.*
• maim, lame
❷ *The country was nearly crippled by the war.*
• ruin, destroy, crush, wreck, damage, weaken

crisis *NOUN*
The election result caused a crisis in the country.
• emergency, problem, difficulty, predicament

crisp *ADJECTIVE*
❶ *Fry the tofu until it's crisp.*
• crispy, crunchy, brittle
OPPOSITES soft, soggy, limp
❷ *It was a crisp winter morning.*
• cold, fresh, frosty

critical *ADJECTIVE*
❶ *Some people made critical comments about my hairstyle.*
• negative, disapproving, derogatory, uncomplimentary, unfavourable
OPPOSITE complimentary
❷ *This match is critical for our team's chances of success.*
• crucial, important, vital, serious, decisive
OPPOSITE unimportant

criticize *VERB*
She criticized us for being so careless.
• blame, condemn, disapprove of, find fault with, reprimand, reproach, scold, berate
OPPOSITE praise

criticism *NOUN*
I think his criticism of my singing was unfair.
• attack, disapproval, reprimand, reproach

crockery *NOUN*
Please put the crockery away.
• china, dishes, plates

WORD WEB

SOME ITEMS OF CROCKERY:

• bowl, butter dish, cup, dinner plate, gravy boat, milk jug, mug, plate, saucer, side plate, sugar bowl, teacup, teapot, tureen

crooked *ADJECTIVE*
❶ *The wizard bent his wand into a crooked shape.*
• bent, twisted, warped, gnarled
OPPOSITE straight
❷ *(informal) The crooked salesman was selling fake diamonds.*
• criminal, dishonest, corrupt
(informal) bent
OPPOSITE honest

crop *NOUN*
We had a good crop of apples this year.
• harvest, yield, produce

crop *VERB*
Miss Marshall was cropping her garden hedge.
• cut, trim, clip, snip, shear
➤ **to crop up**
Several problems have cropped up.
• arise, appear, occur, emerge, come up, turn up

cross *VERB*
❶ *There is a bus stop where the two roads cross.*
• criss-cross, intersect
❷ *You can cross the river at the footbridge.*
• go across, pass over, traverse, ford, span

cross *ADJECTIVE*
They will be cross if we're late.
• angry, annoyed, upset, vexed, bad-tempered, ill-tempered, irritable, grumpy, testy, irate
see also **angry**
OPPOSITE pleased

a
b
c
d
e
f
g
h
i
j
k
l
m
n
o
p
q
r
s
t
u
v
w
x
y
z

A
B
C
D
E
F
G
H
I
J
K
L
M
N
O
P
Q
R
S
T
U
V
W
X
Y
Z

crouch *VERB*
*The outlaws **crouched** silently in the bushes.*
• squat, kneel, stoop, bend, duck, bob down, hunch, huddle

crowd *NOUN*
❶ *A **crowd** of people waited outside the theatre.*
• gathering, group, assembly, bunch, cluster, throng, mob, multitude, crush, horde, swarm
❷ *There was a huge **crowd** for the tennis final.*
• audience, spectators, gate, attendance

crowd *VERB*
❶ *People **crowded** on the pavement to watch the parade.*
• gather, collect, assemble, congregate, mass, flock, muster
❷ *Hundreds of people **crowded** into the hall.*
• push, pile, squeeze, pack, cram, crush, jam, bundle, herd

crowded *ADJECTIVE*
*The shops are always **crowded** at Christmas time.*
• full, packed, teeming, swarming, overflowing, jammed, congested
OPPOSITE empty

crown *NOUN*
*The royal **crown** was made of solid gold.*
• coronet, diadem, tiara

crown *VERB*
*Mary was **crowned** Queen of Scots when she was a baby.*
• enthrone, anoint
*A ceremony at which a king or queen is crowned is a **coronation**.*

crucial *ADJECTIVE*
*We are at a **crucial** point in our chess game.*
• important, critical, decisive, vital, serious, momentous
OPPOSITE unimportant

crude *ADJECTIVE*
❶ *The refinery processes **crude** oil.*
• raw, natural, unprocessed, unrefined
OPPOSITE refined
❷ *We made a **crude** shelter out of twigs.*
• rough, clumsy, makeshift, primitive
OPPOSITE skilful
❸ *The teacher told them to stop using **crude** language.*
• rude, coarse, dirty, foul, impolite, indecent, vulgar
OPPOSITE polite

cruel *ADJECTIVE*
*I think hunting is a **cruel** way to kill animals.*
• brutal, savage, vicious, fierce, barbaric, bloodthirsty, barbarous, heartless, ruthless, merciless, inhuman, sadistic, uncivilized, beastly
OPPOSITES kind, humane, gentle

crumb *NOUN*
*We put out some **crumbs** of bread for the birds.*
• bit, fragment, scrap, morsel
see also **bit**

crumble *VERB*
❶ *The walls of the castle were beginning to **crumble**.*
• disintegrate, break up, collapse, fall apart, decay, decompose
❷ *The farmer **crumbled** some bread into his soup.*
• crush, grind, pound, pulverize

crumpled *ADJECTIVE*
*Your shirt is **crumpled**.*
• creased, wrinkled, crinkled, crushed

crunch *VERB*
❶ *The dog was **crunching** on a bone.*
• chew, munch, chomp, grind
see also **eat**
❷ *I heard heavy footsteps **crunching** up the path.*
• crush, grind, pound, smash

crush VERB

❶ *He crushed his anorak into his school bag.*
• squash, squeeze, mangle, pound, press, bruise, crunch, scrunch
To crush something into a soft mess is to **mash** or **pulp** it.
To crush something into a powder is to **grind** or **pulverize** it.
To crush something out of shape is to **crumple** or **smash** it.
❷ *Our soldiers crushed the attacking army.*
• defeat, conquer, vanquish, overcome, overwhelm, quash, trounce, rout

crush NOUN

There was a crush of people at the front gates.
• crowd, press, mob, throng, jam, congestion

cry VERB

❶ *Someone was crying for help from the burning house.*
• call, shout, yell, exclaim, roar, bawl, bellow, scream, screech, shriek
❷ *The baby started to cry when she dropped her toy.*
• sob, weep, bawl, blubber, wail, shed tears, snivel
When someone starts to cry, their eyes **well up** with tears.

cry NOUN

The wounded man let out a cry of pain.
• call, shout, yell, roar, howl, exclamation, bellow, scream, screech, shriek, yelp

cuddle VERB

My baby brother cuddles a teddy bear in bed.
• hug, hold closely, clasp, embrace, caress, nestle against, snuggle against

cue NOUN

When I nod, that is your cue to speak.
• sign, signal, reminder

culprit NOUN

Police are searching for the culprits.
• criminal, offender, wrongdoer

cultivate VERB

❶ *Farmers have cultivated this land for centuries.*
• farm, work, till, plough, grow crops on
❷ *We want to cultivate good relations with our neighbours.*
• develop, encourage, promote, try to achieve, further, improve

cunning ADJECTIVE

The pirates had a cunning plan to seize the ship.
• clever, crafty, devious, wily, ingenious, shrewd, artful, scheming, sly, tricky

cup NOUN

A tall cup with straight sides is a **mug**.
A tall cup without a handle is a **beaker** or **tumbler**.
A decorative drinking cup is a **goblet**.
for other containers for drinks see **drink**

cupboard NOUN

There are some spare pillows in the cupboard.
• cabinet, dresser, sideboard
A cupboard for food is a **larder**.
for other items of furniture see **furniture**

curb VERB

You must try to curb your anger.
• control, restrain, suppress, check, hold back, limit, moderate, repress, restrict
OPPOSITE encourage

cure VERB

❶ *These pills will cure your headache.*
• ease, heal, help, improve, make better, relieve
OPPOSITE aggravate
❷ *No-one can cure the problem with my computer.*
• correct, mend, sort, repair, fix, put an end to, put right

cure NOUN

I wish they could find a cure for colds.
• remedy, treatment, antidote, medicine, therapy

a
b
c
d
e
f
g
h
i
j
k
l
m
n
o
p
q
r
s
t
u
v
w
x
y
z

curiosity NOUN
Babies are full of curiosity about the world.
• inquisitiveness, interest
Uncomplimentary words are nosiness, prying and snooping.

curious ADJECTIVE
❶ *We were all very curious about the secret chamber.*
• inquisitive, inquiring, interested, intrigued, agog
An uncomplimentary word is nosy.
OPPOSITE uninterested, indifferent
❷ *What is that curious smell?*
• odd, strange, peculiar, abnormal, queer, unusual, extraordinary, funny, mysterious, puzzling, weird

curl VERB
❶ *The snake curled itself around a branch.*
• wind, twist, loop, coil, wrap, curve, turn, twine
❷ *Steam curled upwards from the cauldron.*
• coil, spiral, twirl, swirl, furl, snake, writhe, ripple

curl NOUN
The girl's hair was a mass of golden curls.
• wave, ringlet, coil, loop, twist, roll, scroll, spiral

curly ADJECTIVE
My new doll has curly hair.
• curled, curling, wavy, frizzy, crinkly, ringletted
OPPOSITE straight

current NOUN
The wooden raft drifted along with the current.
• flow, tide, stream
A current of air is a draught.

current ADJECTIVE
❶ *The shop sells all the current teenage fashions.*
• modern, contemporary, present-day, up to date, topical, prevailing, prevalent
OPPOSITES past, old-fashioned

❷ *Have you got a current passport?*
• valid, usable, up to date
OPPOSITE out of date
❸ *Who is the current prime minister?*
• present, existing
OPPOSITES past, former

curse NOUN
❶ *Long ago, a wizard put a curse on the family.*
• jinx, hex
❷ *When the gardener hit his finger, he let out a curse.*
• swear word, oath

curve NOUN
Try to draw a straight line without any curves.
• bend, curl, loop, turn, twist, arch, arc, bow, bulge, wave
A curve in the shape of a new moon is a crescent.
A curve on a road surface is a camber.

curve VERB
The road ahead curves round to the right.
• bend, wind, turn, twist, curl, loop, swerve, veer, snake, meander

curved ADJECTIVE
The wall was painted with a series of curved lines.
• curving, curvy, curled, looped, coiled, rounded, bulging, bent, arched, bowed, twisted, crooked, spiral, winding, meandering, serpentine, snaking, undulating
A surface which is curved like the inside of a circle is concave.
A surface which is curved like the outside of a circle is convex.

cushion VERB
If you fall off the swing, the mat will cushion your fall.
• soften, reduce the effect of, absorb, muffle

custom NOUN

❶ *It's our custom to give presents at Christmas.*
• tradition, practice, habit, convention, fashion, routine, way
❷ *The shop is having a sale to attract more custom.*
• customers, buyers, trade, business

customary ADJECTIVE

It is customary to leave the waiter a tip.
• traditional, conventional, usual, normal, common, typical, expected, habitual, routine, regular, everyday, ordinary, prevailing, prevalent
OPPOSITE unusual

customer NOUN

There was a queue of customers at the checkout.
• buyer, shopper, client

cut VERB cuts, cutting, cut

❶ *The woodcutter cut the tree trunk to make logs.*
• chop, slit, split, chip, notch, axe, hack, hew, cleave
To cut off a limb is to **amputate** or **sever** it.
To cut down a tree is to **fell** it.
To cut branches off a tree is to **lop** them.
To cut twigs off a growing plant is to **prune** it.
To cut something up to examine it is to **dissect** it.
To cut stone to make a statue is to **carve** it.
To cut an inscription in stone is to **engrave** it.
❷ *The cook cut the apples into small pieces.*
• chop, slice, dice, grate, mince, shred
❸ *I'm going to get my hair cut in the holidays.*
• trim, clip, crop, snip, shave
To cut wool off a sheep is to **shear** it.

To cut grass is to **mow** it.
To cut corn is to **harvest** or **reap** it.
❹ *Josh cut his foot on a sharp stone.*
• gash, slash, nick, stab, pierce, wound
❺ *This letter is too long—I'll need to cut it.*
• shorten, condense, edit
❻ *The shop has cut its prices by 10%.*
• lower, reduce, decrease
If you cut something by half, you **halve** it.

cut NOUN

❶ *I got a nasty cut when I was slicing bread.*
• gash, wound, injury, nick, slash, scratch, slit, snip
❷ *There has been a cut in the price of petrol.*
• fall, reduction, decrease

cutlery NOUN

WORD WEB

SOME ITEMS OF CUTLERY:

• bread knife, butter knife, carving knife, cheese knife, chopsticks, dessert spoon, fish knife, fork, knife, ladle, spoon, steak knife, tablespoon, teaspoon

cutting ADJECTIVE

He made a cutting remark about my speech.
• sharp, hurtful, biting, stinging, vicious

cycle NOUN

see **bicycle**

a
b
c
d
e
f
g
h
i
j
k
l
m
n
o
p
q
r
s
t
u
v
w
x
y
z

Dd

A
B
C
D
E
F
G
H
I
J
K
L
M
N
O
P
Q
R
S
T
U
V
W
X
Y
Z

daily *ADJECTIVE*
*Walking to school is part of my **daily** exercise routine.*
• everyday, regular
OPPOSITES infrequent, irregular

dainty *ADJECTIVE*
*The doll's hair was tied with a **dainty** little ribbon.*
• delicate, neat, charming, fine, exquisite, bijou *(informal)* cute, dinky
OPPOSITE clumsy

dam *NOUN*
*Some beavers have built a **dam** in this river.*
• barrier, barrage, embankment, dyke, weir
dam *VERB*
*The river was **dammed** to make a reservoir.*
• block, check, hold back

damage *VERB*
*Many books were **damaged** in the fire.*
• harm, spoil, mar, break, impair, weaken, disfigure, deface, mutilate, scar
To damage something beyond repair is to destroy, ruin or wreck it.
To damage something deliberately is to sabotage or vandalize it.

damp *ADJECTIVE*
❶ *Don't wear those clothes if they are **damp**.*
• moist, soggy, clammy, dank
❷ *I don't like this **damp** weather.*
• drizzly, foggy, misty, rainy, wet
Weather which is both damp and warm is humid or muggy weather.
OPPOSITE dry

dampen *VERB*
❶ *Dampen the cloth with a little water.*
• moisten, wet
❷ *Nothing could **dampen** her enthusiasm.*
• make less, decrease, reduce

dance *NOUN*

WORD WEB

SOME KINDS OF DANCE OR DANCING:

• ballet, ballroom dancing, barn dance, belly-dancing, bolero, breakdancing, cancan, disco, flamenco, folk dance, Highland dancing, hornpipe, jazz dance, jig, jive dancing, limbo dancing, line-dancing, mazurka, morris dance, quadrille, reel, rumba, samba, Scottish country dancing, square dance, step dancing, street dance, tap-dancing, tarantella
A person who writes the steps for a dance is a choreographer.

SOME BALLROOM DANCES:

• foxtrot, minuet, polka, quickstep, tango, waltz

GATHERINGS WHERE PEOPLE DANCE:

• ball, ceilidh, disco

dance *VERB*
*I could have **danced** for joy.*
• caper, cavort, frisk, frolic, gambol, hop about, jig about, jump about, leap, prance, skip, whirl

danger *NOUN*
❶ *Who knows what **dangers** lie ahead?*
• peril, jeopardy, trouble, crisis, hazard, menace, pitfall, threat, trap
OPPOSITE safety
❷ *The forecast says there's a **danger** of frost.*
• chance, possibility, risk

dangerous *ADJECTIVE*
❶ *We were in a **dangerous** situation.*
• hazardous, perilous, risky, precarious, treacherous, unsafe, alarming, menacing *(informal)* hairy
❷ *The police arrested him for **dangerous** driving.*
• careless, reckless

❸ *A dangerous criminal had escaped from prison.*
• violent, desperate, ruthless, treacherous
❹ *It's wicked to empty dangerous chemicals into the river.*
• harmful, poisonous, deadly, toxic
OPPOSITES harmless, safe

dangle VERB
There was a bunch of keys dangling from the chain.
• hang, swing, sway, droop, wave about, flap, trail

dare VERB
❶ *I wouldn't dare to make a parachute jump.*
• have the courage, take the risk
❷ *They dared me to climb the tree.*
• challenge, defy

daring ADJECTIVE
It was a very daring plan.
• bold, brave, adventurous, courageous, fearless, intrepid, plucky, valiant
A daring person is a daredevil.
OPPOSITE timid

dark ADJECTIVE
❶ *It was a very dark night.*
• black, dim, murky, shadowy, gloomy, dingy
OPPOSITE bright
❷ *She wore a dark green coat.*
OPPOSITES pale, light

darken VERB
The sky darkened.
• become overcast, blacken, cloud over
OPPOSITE brighten

dash NOUN
❶ *When the storm broke, we made a dash for shelter.*
• run, rush, race, sprint
❷ *I like just a dash of milk in my tea.*
• drop, small amount, splash, spot

dash VERB
❶ *We dashed home because it was raining.*
• hurry, run, rush, race, hasten, sprint, speed, tear, zoom
❷ *She dashed her cup against the wall.*
• throw, hurl, knock, smash

data NOUN
I entered all the data into the computer.
• information, details, facts
Data can be in the form of figures, numbers or statistics.

date NOUN
I have a date with some friends this evening.
• meeting, appointment, engagement

dawn NOUN
❶ *I was woken at dawn by the birds singing outside.*
• daybreak, sunrise, first light
OPPOSITES dusk, sunset
❷ *It was the dawn of the modern age.*
• beginning, start, birth, origin

day NOUN
❶ *Badgers sleep during the day.*
• daytime
OPPOSITE night
❷ *Things were different in my grandfather's day.*
• age, time, era, epoch, period

WORD WEB

VARIOUS TIMES OF THE DAY:

• dawn or daybreak or sunrise, morning, noon or midday, afternoon, evening, nightfall or sunset, dusk or twilight, night, midnight

dazed ADJECTIVE
He had a dazed expression on his face.
• confused, bewildered, muddled, perplexed

A
B
C
D
E
F
G
H
I
J
K
L
M
N
O
P
Q
R
S
T
U
V
W
X
Y
Z

dazzle *VERB*
❶ *My eyes were dazzled by the bright lights.*
• daze, blind
❷ *The acrobats dazzled the audience with their skill.*
• amaze, astonish, impress, fascinate, awe

dead *ADJECTIVE*
❶ *A dead fish floated near the river's edge.*
• deceased, lifeless
Instead of 'the king who has just died', you can say 'the late king'.
A dead body is a **carcass** or **corpse**.
A common simile is **as dead as a doornail**.
OPPOSITE alive
❷ *Latin is a dead language.*
• extinct, obsolete
OPPOSITE living
❸ *This battery is dead.*
• flat, not working, worn out
❹ *The town centre is dead at this time of night.*
• dull, boring, uninteresting, slow
OPPOSITE lively

deaden *VERB*
❶ *The dentist gave me an injection to deaden the pain.*
• anaesthetize, lessen, reduce, suppress
OPPOSITE increase
❷ *Double glazing deadens the noise of the traffic.*
• dampen, muffle, quieten
OPPOSITE amplify

deadly *ADJECTIVE*
The witch gave her a deadly dose of poison.
• lethal, fatal, harmful, dangerous, destructive
OPPOSITE harmless

deafening *ADJECTIVE*
We complained about the deafening noise.
• loud, blaring, booming, thunderous, penetrating

deal *VERB* deals, dealing, dealt
❶ *Who is going to deal the cards?*
• give out, distribute, share out

❷ *My aunt used to deal in second-hand cars.*
• do business, trade
➤ **to deal with something**
❶ *I can deal with this problem.*
• cope with, sort out, attend to, see to, handle, manage, control, grapple with, look after, solve
❷ *The book deals with the history of Rome.*
• be concerned with, cover, explain about
deal *NOUN*
She made a deal with the garage for her new car.
• arrangement, agreement, contract, bargain
➤ **a good deal** or **a great deal**
We went to a great deal of trouble to do things properly.
• a lot, a large amount

dear *ADJECTIVE*
❶ *She is a very dear friend.*
• close, loved, valued, beloved
OPPOSITE distant
❷ *I didn't buy the watch because it was too dear.*
• expensive, costly
(informal) pricey
OPPOSITE cheap

death *NOUN*
❶ *The Vikings mourned the death of their chief.*
• dying, end, passing
❷ *The accident resulted in several deaths.*
• fatality

debate *NOUN*
We had a debate about animal rights.
• discussion, argument, dispute
Something which people argue about a lot is a **controversy**.
debate *VERB*
❶ *We debated whether it is right to kill animals for food.*
• discuss, argue
❷ *I debated what to do next.*
• consider, ponder, deliberate, weigh up, reflect on

debris NOUN
Debris from the crashed aircraft was scattered over a large area.
• remains, wreckage, fragments, pieces

decay VERB
Dead leaves fall to the ground and decay.
• decompose, rot, disintegrate, break down

deceit NOUN
I saw through their deceit.
• deception, trickery, dishonesty, fraud, duplicity, double-dealing, pretence, bluff, cheating, deceitfulness, lying
OPPOSITE honesty

deceitful ADJECTIVE
Don't trust her—she's a deceitful person.
• dishonest, underhand, insincere, duplicitous, false, cheating, hypocritical, lying, treacherous, two-faced, sneaky
OPPOSITE honest

deceive VERB
The spy had been deceiving them for years.
• fool, trick, delude, dupe, hoodwink, cheat, double-cross, mislead, swindle, take in *(informal)* con, diddle

decent ADJECTIVE
❶ *I did the decent thing and owned up.*
• honest, honourable
❷ *My friend's jokes were not decent.*
• polite, proper, respectable, acceptable, appropriate, suitable, fitting
OPPOSITE indecent
❸ *I haven't had a decent meal for ages!*
• satisfactory, agreeable, good, nice
OPPOSITE bad

deception NOUN
see **deceit**

deceptive ADJECTIVE
Appearances can be deceptive.
• misleading, unreliable, false

decide VERB
❶ *We decided to finish our work instead of going out to play.*
• choose, make a decision, make up your mind, opt, elect, resolve
❷ *The referee decided that the player was offside.*
• conclude, judge, rule
❸ *The last lap decided the result of the race.*
• determine, settle

decision NOUN
❶ *Can you tell me what your decision is?*
• choice, preference
❷ *The judge announced his decision.*
• conclusion, judgement, verdict, findings

decisive ADJECTIVE
❶ *A decisive piece of evidence proved that he was innocent.*
• crucial, convincing, definite
❷ *A referee needs to be decisive.*
• firm, forceful, strong-minded, resolute, quick-thinking
OPPOSITE hesitant

declare VERB
He declared that he was innocent.
• announce, state, assert, make known, pronounce, proclaim, swear

decline VERB
❶ *Our enthusiasm declined as the day went on.*
• become less, decrease, diminish, lessen, weaken, dwindle, flag, wane, tail off
OPPOSITE increase
❷ *Why did you decline my invitation to lunch?*
• refuse, reject, turn down
OPPOSITE accept

decode VERB
see **code**

decorate VERB
❶ *We decorated the Christmas tree with tinsel.*
• adorn, beautify, prettify, deck, festoon
To decorate a dish of food is to **garnish** it.

a b c d e f g h i j k l m n o p q r s t u v w x y z

To decorate clothes with lace or ribbon is to **trim** them.

❷ *I am going to decorate my bedroom next weekend.*
• paint, paper, wallpaper
(informal) do up, make over

❸ *The firefighters were decorated for their bravery.*
• award or give a medal to, honour, reward

decorative ADJECTIVE
The book had a decorative design on the cover.
• ornamental, elaborate, fancy, attractive, beautiful, colourful, pretty
OPPOSITE plain

decrease VERB
❶ *We decreased speed.*
• reduce, cut, lower, slacken
❷ *Our enthusiasm decreased as the day went on.*
• become less, decline, diminish, lessen, weaken, dwindle, flag, wane, tail off, shrink, subside
OPPOSITE increase

decrease NOUN
There has been a decrease in the number of sparrows this year.
• decline, drop, fall, cut, reduction
OPPOSITE increase

decree VERB
The king decreed that the day would be a holiday.
• order, command, declare, pronounce, proclaim

dedicate VERB
He dedicates himself entirely to his art.
• commit, devote

dedicated ADJECTIVE
A group of dedicated fans waited at the stage door.
• committed, devoted, keen, enthusiastic, faithful, zealous

deduce VERB
The detective deduced that the footprints were fresh.
• conclude, work out, infer, reason, gather

deduct VERB
Tax is deducted from your salary.
• subtract, take away, knock off
OPPOSITE add

deed NOUN
They thanked the rescue team for their heroic deed.
• act, action, feat, exploit, effort, achievement

deep ADJECTIVE
❶ *The pond is quite deep in the middle.*
OPPOSITE shallow
❷ *The letter expressed his deep regret.*
• intense, earnest, genuine, sincere
OPPOSITE insincere
❸ *Veronica fell into a deep sleep.*
• heavy, sound
OPPOSITE light
❹ *The actor spoke in a deep and sombre voice.*
• low, bass
OPPOSITE high

deer NOUN
A male deer is a **buck, hart, roebuck** or **stag**.
A female deer is a **doe** or **hind**.
A young deer is a **fawn**.
Deer's flesh used as food is **venison**.

defeat VERB
The Greeks attacked and defeated the Trojans.
• beat, conquer, vanquish, triumph over, win a victory over, overcome, overpower, crush, rout, trounce
To defeat someone in chess is to **checkmate** them.
To be defeated is to **lose**.

defeat NOUN
The team suffered a humiliating defeat.
• failure, humiliation, rout, trouncing
OPPOSITE victory

A B C D E F G H I J K L M N O P Q R S T U V W X Y Z

defect *NOUN*
*Cars are tested for **defects** before they leave the factory.*
• fault, flaw, imperfection, shortcoming, failure, weakness
A defect in a computer program is a bug.

defence *NOUN*
❶ *What was the accused woman's **defence**?*
• justification, excuse, explanation, argument, case
❷ *The castle was built as a **defence** against enemy attack.*
• protection, guard, safeguard, fortification, barricade, shield

defend *VERB*
❶ *They tried to **defend** themselves against the enemy.*
• protect, guard, keep safe
OPPOSITE attack
❷ *He gave a speech **defending** his actions.*
• justify, support, stand up for, make a case for
OPPOSITE accuse

defer *VERB*
*They **deferred** their departure until the weekend.*
• delay, put off, postpone

defiant *ADJECTIVE*
*The prisoner cursed with a **defiant** look in his eye.*
• rebellious, insolent, aggressive, challenging, disobedient, obstinate, quarrelsome, uncooperative, stubborn, mutinous
OPPOSITES submissive, compliant

deficient *ADJECTIVE*
*Their diet is **deficient** in vitamins.*
• lacking, wanting, short of, inadequate, insufficient, unsatisfactory
OPPOSITE adequate

define *VERB*
*A dictionary **defines** lots of words.*
• explain, give the meaning of, interpret, clarify

definite *ADJECTIVE*
❶ *Is it **definite** that we're going to move?*
• certain, sure, fixed, settled, decided
❷ *The doctor saw **definite** signs of improvement.*
• clear, distinct, noticeable, obvious, marked, positive, pronounced, unmistakable
OPPOSITE indefinite

definitely *ADVERB*
*I'll **definitely** phone you tomorrow.*
• certainly, for certain, positively, surely, unquestionably, without doubt, without fail
OPPOSITE perhaps

deflect *VERB*
*The goalkeeper was able to **deflect** the shot.*
• divert, turn aside, intercept, avert, fend off, ward off

deft *ADJECTIVE*
*She applied the paint with a **deft** flick of her brush.*
• skilful, agile, nimble, quick, clever, expert, proficient, adept
(informal) nifty
OPPOSITE clumsy

defy *VERB*
❶ *The rebel army decided to **defy** the king.*
• disobey, refuse to obey, resist, stand up to, confront
OPPOSITE obey
❷ *I **defy** you to come up with a better idea.*
• challenge, dare
❸ *The jammed door **defied** our efforts to open it.*
• resist, withstand, defeat, frustrate, beat

degrading *ADJECTIVE*
*Losing by ten goals to nil was a **degrading** experience.*
• shameful, humiliating, embarrassing, undignified

degree *NOUN*
*The young gymnast showed a high **degree** of skill.*
• standard, level, grade, measure, extent

a
b
c
d
e
f
g
h
i
j
k
l
m
n
o
p
q
r
s
t
u
v
w
x
y
z

A
B
C
D
E
F
G
H
I
J
K
L
M
N
O
P
Q
R
S
T
U
V
W
X
Y
Z

dejected ADJECTIVE
I felt *dejected* when I failed the test.
• depressed, disheartened, downhearted, unhappy, sad, low, gloomy, glum, melancholy, miserable, downcast, despondent, woeful, wretched, forlorn
(informal) fed up, down
OPPOSITES happy, cheerful

delay VERB
❶ Don't let me *delay* you.
• detain, hold up, keep waiting, make late, hinder, slow down
❷ The race was *delayed* because of bad weather.
• postpone, put off, defer
❸ You'll miss the bus if you *delay*.
• hesitate, linger, pause, wait, dawdle, loiter
(informal) hang about or around, drag your feet

delay NOUN
There has been a *delay* with the building work.
• hold-up, wait, pause

delete VERB
I *deleted* your email by mistake.
• remove, erase, cancel, cross out

deliberate ADJECTIVE
❶ That remark was a *deliberate* insult.
• intentional, planned, calculated, conscious, premeditated
OPPOSITES accidental, unintentional
❷ She walked with *deliberate* steps across the room.
• careful, steady, cautious, slow, unhurried
OPPOSITES hasty, careless

deliberately ADVERB
Did you say that *deliberately* to hurt my feelings?
• on purpose, intentionally
OPPOSITES accidentally, unintentionally

delicate ADJECTIVE
❶ The blouse has *delicate* embroidery on the cuffs.
• dainty, exquisite, intricate, neat
❷ Take care not to damage the *delicate* material.
• fragile, fine, flimsy, thin
❸ *Delicate* plants should be protected from frost.
• sensitive, tender
OPPOSITES tough, hardy, resilient
❹ The child was born with a *delicate* constitution.
• frail, weak, feeble, sickly, unhealthy
OPPOSITE strong
❺ The pianist's fingers had a *delicate* touch.
• gentle, light, soft
❻ He discussed the matter in a *delicate* way.
• tactful, sensitive, considerate, diplomatic, careful, discreet
OPPOSITE insensitive
❼ Can you help me with a *delicate* problem?
• awkward, embarrassing

delicious ADJECTIVE
The food at the banquet was *delicious*.
• tasty, appetizing, mouthwatering, delectable
(informal) yummy, scrumptious, moreish
for other ways to describe food see **food**
OPPOSITES horrible, disgusting

delight NOUN
Imagine my *delight* when I saw my friend again!
• happiness, joy, pleasure, enjoyment, bliss, ecstasy

delight VERB
The puppet show *delighted* the crowd.
• please, charm, entertain, amuse, divert, enchant, entrance, fascinate, thrill
OPPOSITE dismay

delighted ADJECTIVE
The *delighted* crowd cheered the winners.
• pleased, happy, joyful, thrilled, ecstatic, elated, exultant

delightful ADJECTIVE
The poem she wrote was **delightful**.
• lovely, pleasant, pleasing, beautiful, attractive, charming

deliver VERB
❶ Does anyone **deliver** mail to the island?
• convey, bring, hand over, distribute, present, supply, take round
❷ The head **delivered** a lecture on good behaviour.
• give, make, read out

delude VERB
He **deluded** us into thinking he was very rich.
• deceive, fool, trick, mislead, hoax, bluff (informal) con

delusion NOUN
Your belief that you are a great writer is a **delusion**!
• fantasy, dream, self-deception

demand VERB
❶ I **demanded** a refund for my train fare.
• insist on, claim, call for, require, want
❷ 'What do you want?' **demanded** a voice inside.
• ask, enquire, inquire

demand NOUN
❶ The king agreed to the **demands** of his people.
• request, claim, requirement
❷ There is not much **demand** for ice lollies in winter.
• need, call

demanding ADJECTIVE
❶ Toddlers can be very **demanding**.
• difficult, trying, tiresome, insistent
❷ The expedition leader had a very **demanding** job.
• difficult, challenging, exhausting, hard, tough, testing, taxing, onerous
OPPOSITE easy

demolish VERB
They **demolished** a building to make way for the road.
• destroy, flatten, knock down, level, pull down, tear down, bulldoze
OPPOSITES build, construct

demonstrate VERB
❶ The teacher **demonstrated** how warm air rises.
• show, exhibit, illustrate
❷ Animal rights campaigners were **demonstrating** in the street.
• protest, march, parade

demonstration NOUN
❶ I watched a **demonstration** of the new computer game.
• show, display, presentation
❷ Everyone joined the **demonstration** against world poverty.
• protest, rally, march, parade (informal) demo

demote VERB
The team may be **demoted** to a lower division.
• put down, relegate
OPPOSITE promote

den NOUN
We built a **den** in the garden.
• hideout, shelter, hiding place, secret place
The den of a wild animal is its lair.

denote VERB
What does this symbol **denote**?
• mean, indicate, signify, stand for, be a sign of, express

dense ADJECTIVE
❶ The accident happened in **dense** fog.
• thick, heavy
❷ A **dense** crowd waited in the square.
• compact, packed, solid
❸ I'm being rather **dense** today!
• stupid, slow

a b c d e f g h i j k l m n o p q r s t u v w x y z

A B C D E F G H I J K L M N O P Q R S T U V W X Y Z

dent *NOUN*
There was a large dent in the car door.
• indentation, depression, hollow, dip, dimple

dent *VERB*
A football hit the car door and dented it.
• make a dent in, knock in, push in

dentist *NOUN*
A dentist who specializes in straightening teeth is an **orthodontist**.
for other words to do with your teeth see **tooth**

deny *VERB*
❶ *The minister denied sharing the story with journalists.*
• reject, dispute, disagree with, contradict, dismiss, oppose
OPPOSITES admit, accept
❷ *Their parents don't deny them anything.*
• refuse, deprive of, withhold
OPPOSITE give

depart *VERB*
❶ *What time is the train due to depart?*
• leave, set off, get going, set out, start, begin a journey
OPPOSITES arrive, get in
❷ *It looks as if the robbers departed in a hurry.*
• leave, exit, go away, retreat, withdraw, make off
(informal) clear off, scram, scarper
OPPOSITE arrive

department *NOUN*
Mrs Ozcan works in the sales department.
• section, branch, division, office

depend *VERB*
➤ **to depend on someone**
I depend on you to help me.
• rely on, count on, bank on, trust
➤ **to depend on something**
My success will depend on good luck.
• be decided by, rest on, hinge on

dependable *ADJECTIVE*
Are these friends of yours dependable?
• reliable, trustworthy, loyal, faithful, trusty, honest, sound, steady
OPPOSITE unreliable

dependent *ADJECTIVE*
➤ **dependent on**
Everything is dependent on the weather.
• determined by, subject to, controlled by, reliant on

depict *VERB*
❶ *She depicted the landscape in watercolours.*
• draw, paint, sketch
❷ *The film depicts the horror of war.*
• show, represent, portray, describe, illustrate, outline

deplorable *ADJECTIVE*
Their rudeness was deplorable.
• disgraceful, shameful, scandalous, shocking, unforgivable, lamentable, reprehensible, inexcusable
OPPOSITE praiseworthy

deplore *VERB*
We all deplore cruelty to animals.
• condemn, disapprove of, hate

deport *VERB*
They were deported from Australia.
• exile, banish, expel, send abroad

deposit *NOUN*
❶ *Dad paid the deposit on a new car.*
• down-payment, first instalment, initial payment
❷ *There was a deposit of mud at the bottom of the river.*
• layer, sediment

depress *VERB*
The miserable weather was depressing us.
• sadden, discourage, dishearten, dispirit
OPPOSITE cheer

depressed ADJECTIVE
After his friends left, he began to feel depressed.
• disheartened, dejected, discouraged, downcast, downhearted, unhappy, sad, low, gloomy, glum, melancholy, miserable, despondent, desolate, in despair
(informal) down
OPPOSITE cheerful

depressing ADJECTIVE
It was a depressing situation to be in.
• discouraging, dispiriting, disheartening, gloomy, sad, dismal, dreary, sombre, bleak
OPPOSITE cheerful

depression NOUN
❶ *She sank into a state of depression.*
• despair, dejection, sadness, gloom, unhappiness, hopelessness, low spirits, melancholy, misery, desolation, pessimism, glumness
OPPOSITE cheerfulness
❷ *Most businesses do badly during a depression.*
• recession, slump
OPPOSITE boom
❸ *The rain had collected in several depressions in the ground.*
• hollow, indentation, dent, dip, hole, pit, rut
OPPOSITE bump

deprived ADJECTIVE
The charity tries to help deprived families.
• poor, needy, underprivileged
OPPOSITES wealthy, privileged

deputy NOUN
The sheriff appointed a new deputy.
• second-in-command, assistant, stand-in, substitute
WHICH WORD? Note that words beginning vice- usually mean 'the deputy for a particular person', for example the vice-captain or the vice-president.

derelict ADJECTIVE
They plan to pull down those derelict buildings.
• dilapidated, crumbling, decrepit, neglected, deserted, abandoned, ruined

deride VERB
The book was derided when it first came out.
• ridicule, mock, laugh at, dismiss
(informal) pooh-pooh
OPPOSITE praise

derive VERB
❶ *Bill derives a lot of pleasure from his garden.*
• get, obtain, receive, gain
❷ *She derived many of her ideas from books.*
• borrow, draw, pick up, take
(informal) lift

descend VERB
❶ *After admiring the view, we began to descend the mountain.*
• climb down, come down, go down, move down
To descend through the air is to **drop** or **fall**.
To descend through water is to **sink**.
❷ *The road descends gradually into the valley.*
• drop, fall, slope, dip, incline
OPPOSITE ascend
➤ **to be descended from someone**
She's descended from an Italian family.
• come from, originate from

descendant NOUN
A person's descendants are their **heirs** or **successors**.
OPPOSITE ancestor

descent NOUN
The path makes a steep descent into the valley.
• drop, fall, dip, incline
OPPOSITE ascent

describe VERB
❶ *An eyewitness described how the accident happened.*
• report, tell about, depict, explain, outline
❷ *Friends described him as a quiet, shy man.*
• portray, characterize, represent, present

a b c d e f g h i j k l m n o p q r s t u v w x y z

A
B
C
D
E
F
G
H
I
J
K
L
M
N
O
P
Q
R
S
T
U
V
W
X
Y
Z

description *NOUN*
❶ *I wrote a description of our day at the seaside.*
• report, account, story
❷ *Write a description of your favourite character in the play.*
• portrait, representation, sketch

descriptive *ADJECTIVE*
The author writes in a very descriptive style.
• expressive, colourful, detailed, graphic, vivid

desert *NOUN*

WORD WEB

THINGS YOU MIGHT SEE OR EXPERIENCE IN A DESERT:

• mirage, oasis, sand dune, sandstorm, whirlwind

SOME ANIMALS WHICH LIVE IN DESERTS:

• armadillo, camel, chameleon, coyote, desert rat, gerbil, lizard, locust, meerkat, rattlesnake, roadrunner, scorpion, tarantula, vulture

SOME PLANTS WHICH ARE FOUND IN DESERTS:

• cactus, date palm, grasses, prickly pear, sagebrush, tumbleweed
A group of people travelling together across a desert is a **caravan**.
People who live in the desert are often **nomads**.
for desert islands see **island**

desert *VERB*
He deserted his friends when they needed him most.
• abandon, leave, forsake, betray
(informal) walk out on
To desert someone in a place they can't get away from is to **maroon** or **strand** them.

deserted *ADJECTIVE*
By midnight, the streets of the town were deserted.
• empty, unoccupied, uninhabited, vacant
OPPOSITE crowded

deserve *VERB*
You deserve a break after all your hard work.
• be worthy of, be entitled to, have earned, merit, warrant

design *NOUN*
❶ *This is the winning design for the new art gallery.*
• plan, drawing, outline, blueprint, sketch
A first example of something, used as a model for making others, is a **prototype**.
❷ *Do you like the design of this wallpaper?*
• style, pattern, arrangement, composition
for types of art and design see **art**
design *VERB*
They design all their own clothes.
• create, develop, invent, devise, conceive, think up

desirable *ADJECTIVE*
❶ *The house has many desirable features.*
• appealing, attractive, interesting, tempting
OPPOSITE worthless
❷ *It is desirable to phone before you arrive.*
• advisable, sensible, prudent, wise
OPPOSITE unwise

desire *VERB*
The magic mirror will show you what you most desire.
• wish for, long for, want, crave, fancy, hanker after, yearn for, pine for, set your heart on, have a yen for
desire *NOUN*
My greatest desire is to swim with dolphins.
• wish, want, longing, ambition, craving, fancy, hankering, urge, yearning
A desire for food is **appetite** or **hunger**.
A desire for drink is **thirst**.
Excessive desire for money or other things is **greed**.

desolate ADJECTIVE
❶ *Mai felt desolate when her goldfish died.*
• depressed, dejected, miserable, sad, melancholy, hopeless, wretched, forlorn
OPPOSITE cheerful
❷ *No-one wants to live in that desolate place.*
• bleak, depressing, dreary, gloomy, dismal, cheerless, inhospitable, deserted, uninhabited, abandoned, godforsaken
OPPOSITE pleasant

despair NOUN
The lost children were overcome by despair.
• depression, desperation, gloom, hopelessness, misery, anguish, dejection, melancholy, pessimism, wretchedness
OPPOSITE hope

despatch NOUN, VERB
see **dispatch**

desperate ADJECTIVE
❶ *The shipwrecked crew were in a desperate situation.*
• difficult, critical, grave, serious, severe, drastic, dire, urgent, extreme
❷ *The hills were home to a band of desperate outlaws.*
• dangerous, violent, reckless

despicable ADJECTIVE
The pirates were known for despicable acts of cruelty.
• disgraceful, hateful, shameful, contemptible, loathsome, vile

despise VERB
I despise people who cheat at cards.
• hate, loathe, feel contempt for, deride, have a low opinion of, look down on, scorn, sneer at
OPPOSITE admire

despite PREPOSITION
We went for a walk despite the rain.
• in spite of, regardless of, notwithstanding
OPPOSITE because of

dessert NOUN
For dessert, there's apple pie and ice cream.
• pudding, sweet
(informal) afters

destination NOUN
The train arrived at its destination five minutes early.
• terminus, stop

destined ADJECTIVE
❶ *It was destined that he would become a famous musician.*
• fated, doomed, intended, meant, certain, inevitable, unavoidable, inescapable
❷ *This parcel is destined for Japan.*
• bound, directed, intended, headed

destiny NOUN
Was it destiny that brought us together?
• fate, fortune

destroy VERB
❶ *An avalanche destroyed the village.*
• demolish, devastate, crush, flatten, knock down, level, pull down, shatter, smash, sweep away
❷ *They tried to destroy the good work we had done.*
• ruin, wreck, sabotage, undo

destruction NOUN
❶ *The hurricane caused destruction all along the coast.*
• devastation, damage, demolition, ruin, wrecking
OPPOSITE creation
❷ *Global warming may cause the destruction of many animal species.*
• elimination, annihilation, obliteration, extermination, extinction
OPPOSITE conservation

destructive ADJECTIVE
Tornadoes have a great destructive power.
• damaging, devastating, catastrophic, disastrous, harmful, injurious, ruinous, violent

a b c d e f g h i j k l m n o p q r s t u v w x y z

A B C **D** E F G H I J K L M N O P Q R S T U V W X Y Z

detach VERB

*The camera lens can be **detached** for cleaning.*
• remove, separate, disconnect, take off, release, undo, unfasten, part
To detach a caravan from a vehicle is to **unhitch** it.
To detach railway wagons from a locomotive is to **uncouple** them.
To detach something by cutting it off is to **sever** it.
OPPOSITE attach

detail NOUN

*Her account of what happened was accurate in every **detail**.*
• fact, feature, particular, aspect, item, point, respect

detailed ADJECTIVE

*This book gives a **detailed** description of Victorian London.*
• precise, exact, specific, full, thorough, elaborate, comprehensive, exhaustive
OPPOSITES rough, vague

detain VERB

❶ *The police **detained** the suspect.*
• hold, arrest, capture, imprison, restrain
OPPOSITE release
❷ *I'll try not to **detain** you for long.*
• delay, hold up, hinder, keep waiting

detect VERB

*I could **detect** the smell of burning in the air.*
• identify, recognize, spot, find, discover, reveal, diagnose, track down

detective NOUN

Detective Dewar solved the case of the stolen tiara.
• investigator, sleuth
(informal) private eye

WORD WEB

THINGS A DETECTIVE MIGHT LOOK FOR:

• bloodstains, clues, evidence, eyewitness, fingerprints, footprints, murder weapon, proof, tracks, criminal, crook, culprit, felon, suspect, mastermind

THINGS DETECTIVES MIGHT NEED:

• bag, binoculars, disguises, gloves, magnifying glass, notebook, torch

THINGS A DETECTIVE MIGHT DO:

• analyse, comb (an area), deduce, deduct, detect, dig up, ferret out, follow a hunch, follow a lead or a tip-off, interrogate or question (a witness), investigate, pursue, shadow, solve (a case), stake out (a hiding place), tail or track down (a suspect)
An informal name for a story in which a detective solves a crime is a **whodunnit**.

deter VERB

*How can we **deter** birds from eating the pears?*
• discourage, put off, dissuade, prevent, stop
OPPOSITE encourage

deteriorate VERB

❶ *The president's health had begun to **deteriorate**.*
• worsen, decline, degenerate, get worse, go downhill
❷ *The walls will **deteriorate** if we don't maintain them.*
• decay, disintegrate, crumble
OPPOSITE improve

determination NOUN

*Marathon runners show great **determination**.*
• resolve, commitment, willpower, courage, dedication, drive, grit, perseverance, persistence, spirit
(informal) guts

determine VERB

*Our task was to **determine** the depth of the loch.*
• calculate, compute, figure out, work out, reckon, decide

determined *ADJECTIVE*
❶ *Boudicca must have been a determined woman.*
• resolute, decisive, firm, strong-minded, assertive, persistent, tough
OPPOSITE weak-minded
❷ *I'm determined to finish the race.*
• committed, resolved

detest *VERB*
I detest the smell of boiled cabbage.
• dislike, hate, loathe
Informal expressions are **can't bear** and **can't stand**.
OPPOSITE love

detour *NOUN*
I wasted time by taking a detour.
• diversion, indirect route, roundabout route

detrimental *ADJECTIVE*
Too much water can be detrimental to plants.
• damaging, harmful, destructive, adverse
OPPOSITE beneficial

devastate *VERB*
The earthquake devastated the island.
• destroy, wreck, ruin, demolish, flatten, level

devastating *ADJECTIVE*
The siege had a devastating effect on the town.
• overwhelming, stunning, shocking, shattering

develop *VERB*
❶ *The zoo is developing its education programme.*
• expand, extend, enlarge, build up, diversify
❷ *Her piano playing has developed this year.*
• improve, progress, evolve, advance, get better
❸ *The plants will develop quickly in the spring.*
• grow, flourish
❹ *How did he develop that posh accent?*
• get, acquire, pick up, cultivate

development *NOUN*
❶ *Were there any developments while I was away?*
• event, happening, incident, occurrence, change
❷ *We are pleased with the development of our website.*
• growth, expansion, improvement, progress, spread

deviate *VERB*
We were forced to deviate from our original plan.
• depart, diverge, differ, stray

device *NOUN*
The TV comes with a remote control device.
• tool, implement, instrument, appliance, apparatus, gadget, contraption
(informal) gizmo

devious *ADJECTIVE*
❶ *The mad professor had a devious plan to take over the world.*
• cunning, deceitful, dishonest, furtive, scheming, sly, sneaky, treacherous, wily
❷ *Because of the roadworks, we took a devious route home.*
• indirect, roundabout, winding, meandering
OPPOSITE direct

devise *VERB*
We need to devise a strategy for Saturday's game.
• conceive, form, invent, contrive, formulate, come up with, make up, plan, prepare, map out, think out, think up

devote *VERB*
My brother devotes all his free time to football.
• set aside, dedicate, assign, commit

devoted *ADJECTIVE*
She's a devoted supporter of our team.
• loyal, faithful, dedicated, enthusiastic, committed
OPPOSITE apathetic

a
b
c
d
e
f
g
h
i
j
k
l
m
n
o
p
q
r
s
t
u
v
w
x
y
z

A B C D E F G H I J K L M N O P Q R S T U V W X Y Z

devotion NOUN
Penguins show great devotion to their offspring.
• attachment, fondness, loyalty, dedication, commitment

devour VERB
He devoured a whole plateful of sandwiches.
• eat, consume, guzzle, gobble up, gulp down, swallow
(informal) scoff, wolf down
see also **eat**

diagram NOUN
We drew a diagram of the life cycle of a frog.
• chart, plan, sketch, outline

dial VERB
I dialled the number for a taxi.
• phone, call, ring, telephone

dialogue NOUN
The play consists of a series of dialogues.
• conversation, talk, discussion, exchange, debate, chat

diary NOUN
I wrote all about my birthday party in my diary.
• journal, daily record
A diary describing a voyage or mission is a **log** *or* **logbook.**
A diary in which you insert pictures and souvenirs is a **scrapbook.**
A diary published on a website is a **blog.**

dictate VERB
➤ **to dictate to someone**
You've got no right to dictate to me!
• order about, give orders to, command, bully
(informal) boss about, push around, lord it over

die VERB
❶ *My sister's hamster died last week.*
• expire, pass away, perish
(informal) snuff it, kick the bucket, croak
To die of hunger is to **starve.**
❷ *The flowers will die if they don't have water.*
• wither, wilt, droop, fade

➤ **to die down**
The flames will die down eventually.
• become less, decline, decrease, subside, weaken, dwindle, fizzle out, wane
➤ **to die out**
When did the dinosaurs die out?
• become extinct, cease to exist, come to an end, disappear, vanish

diet NOUN
Koalas live on a diet of eucalyptus leaves.
• food, nourishment, nutrition
In order to be healthy, you need to have a **balanced** *diet.*
A **vegetarian** *diet excludes meat.*
A **vegan** *diet excludes all animal products.*
see also **food**
➤ **a healthy diet**
We try to be healthy by including plenty of fruit and vegetables in our healthy diet.
• balanced, nutritious

differ VERB
The two men differed in their beliefs.
• disagree, conflict, argue, clash, contradict each other, oppose each other, quarrel
OPPOSITE agree
➤ **to differ from**
My style of painting differs from hers.
• be different from, contrast with

difference NOUN
❶ *Can you see any difference between these two colours?*
• contrast, distinction
OPPOSITE similarity
❷ *This money will make a difference to their lives.*
• change, alteration, modification, variation

different ADJECTIVE
❶ *We have different views about global warming.*
• differing, contradictory, opposite, clashing, conflicting
❷ *It's important that the teams wear different colours.*
• contrasting, dissimilar, distinguishable

❸ *The packet contains sweets of **different** flavours.*
• various, assorted, mixed, several, diverse, numerous, miscellaneous
❹ *Let's go somewhere **different** on holiday this year.*
• new, original, fresh
❺ *Everyone's handwriting is **different**.*
• distinct, distinctive, individual, special, unique
OPPOSITES identical, similar

difficult *ADJECTIVE*
❶ *This crossword is really **difficult**.*
*We were faced with a **difficult** problem.*
• hard, complicated, complex, involved, intricate, baffling, perplexing, puzzling
(informal) tricky, thorny, knotty
OPPOSITE simple
❷ *It is a **difficult** climb to the top of the hill.*
• challenging, arduous, demanding, taxing, exhausting, formidable, gruelling, laborious, strenuous, tough
OPPOSITE easy
❸ *Mum says I was a **difficult** child when I was little.*
• troublesome, awkward, trying, tiresome, annoying, disruptive, obstinate, stubborn, uncooperative, unhelpful
OPPOSITE cooperative

difficulty *NOUN*
❶ *The explorers were used to facing **difficulty**.*
• trouble, adversity, challenges, hardship
❷ *There are some **difficulties** with your application.*
• problem, complication, hitch, obstacle, snag

dig *VERB* digs, digging, dug
❶ *We spent the afternoon **digging** the garden.*
• cultivate, fork over, turn over
❷ *Rabbits **dig** holes in the ground.*
• burrow, excavate, tunnel, gouge out, hollow out, scoop out
❸ *Did you **dig** me in the back?*
• poke, prod, jab

dignified *ADJECTIVE*
*He was a very **dignified** man.*
• refined, stately, distinguished, noble, sedate, solemn, proper, grave, grand, august
OPPOSITE undignified

dignity *NOUN*
❶ *Their laughter spoilt the **dignity** of the occasion.*
• formality, seriousness, solemnity
❷ *She handled the problem with **dignity**.*
• calmness, poise, self-control

dilute *VERB*
*You need to **dilute** orange squash with water.*
• thin, water down, weaken
OPPOSITE concentrate

dim *ADJECTIVE*
❶ *I could see the **dim** outline of a figure in the mist.*
• indistinct, faint, blurred, fuzzy, hazy, shadowy, vague
OPPOSITE clear
❷ *The light in the cave was rather **dim**.*
• dark, dull, dingy, murky, gloomy
OPPOSITE bright

dimensions *PLURAL NOUN*
*We measured the **dimensions** of the room.*
• measurements, size, extent, capacity
for words used in measuring see **measurement**

diminish *VERB*
❶ *Don't **diminish** his confidence by making fun of him.*
• lessen, reduce, make smaller, minimize
❷ *Our water supply was **diminishing** rapidly.*
• become less, decrease, decline, subside, dwindle, wane
OPPOSITE increase

din *NOUN*
*I can't hear you because of that awful **din**!*
• noise, racket, row, clatter, hullabaloo, cacophony

a b c d e f g h i j k l m n o p q r s t u v w x y z

A
B
C
D
E
F
G
H
I
J
K
L
M
N
O
P
Q
R
S
T
U
V
W
X
Y
Z

dine *VERB*
*We will be **dining** at eight o'clock.*
• eat, have dinner, sup

dingy *ADJECTIVE*
*How can we brighten up this **dingy** room?*
• dull, drab, dreary, dowdy, colourless, dismal, gloomy, murky
OPPOSITE bright

dinosaur *NOUN*

WORD WEB

SOME TYPES OF DINOSAUR:

• apatosaurus, archaeopteryx, brachiosaurus, diplodocus, gallimimus, ichthyosaur, iguanodon, megalosaurus, pterodactyl, stegosaur, triceratops, T-rex or tyrannosaurus rex, velociraptor
*I could see at my very feet the glade of the iguanodons, and farther off was a round opening in the trees which marked the swamp of the pterodactyls.—*THE LOST WORLD, Arthur Conan Doyle

BODY PARTS WHICH A DINOSAUR MAY HAVE:

• dorsal plates, bony frill, fleshy fin, horn, wings, crest
A person who studies dinosaurs and other fossils is a **palaeontologist**.
for other prehistoric animals see **prehistoric**

dip *VERB*
❶ *I **dipped** my hand in the water.*
• immerse, lower, plunge, submerge, dunk
❷ *The road **dips** down into the valley.*
• descend, go down, slope down
dip *NOUN*
❶ *There was a **dip** in the road ahead.*
• hollow, hole, depression, slope
❷ *It was so hot we decided to have a **dip** in the sea.*
• swim, bathe

dire *ADJECTIVE*
❶ *The survivors were in a **dire** situation.*
• dreadful, terrible, awful, appalling, severe, grave, drastic, extreme
❷ *After weeks of drought, the garden is in **dire** need of rain.*
• urgent, desperate, pressing, sore

direct *ADJECTIVE*
❶ *It would be quicker to take the **direct** route.*
• straight, shortest
OPPOSITE indirect
❷ *Please give me a **direct** answer.*
• straightforward, frank, honest, sincere, blunt, plain, outspoken, candid, unambiguous
OPPOSITE evasive
direct *VERB*
❶ *Can you **direct** me to the station?*
• guide, point, show the way, give directions to
❷ *A new manager has been appointed to **direct** the company.*
• manage, run, be in charge of, control, administer, superintend, supervise, take charge of
To direct an orchestra is to **conduct** it.
❸ *The teacher **directed** the students to begin.*
• instruct, command, order, tell

direction *NOUN*
*Which **direction** did they go in?*
• way, route, course, path
➤ **directions**
*I read the **directions** for building the model.*
• instructions, guidance, guidelines, plans

director *NOUN*
*Who is the **director** of the company?*
• manager, head, chief, leader, president
(informal) boss

dirt *NOUN*
❶ *The floor was covered in **dirt**.*
• filth, grime, mess, muck, mud, dust
❷ *Chickens scratched about in the **dirt**.*
• earth, soil, clay, loam, mud

dirty *ADJECTIVE*

❶ *Those **dirty** clothes need to be washed.*
• unclean, filthy, grimy, grubby, soiled, stained, messy, mucky, muddy, sooty, foul *(informal)* grotty
OPPOSITE clean
❷ *We refused to drink the **dirty** water.*
• impure, polluted, murky, cloudy
OPPOSITE pure
❸ *The other team used **dirty** tactics.*
• unfair, dishonest, illegal, mean, unsporting
OPPOSITE honest
❹ *The comedian used a lot of **dirty** words.*
• rude, offensive, coarse, crude, improper, indecent
OPPOSITE decent

disability *NOUN*

*The Paralympics are open to athletes with **disabilities**.*
• incapacity, infirmity

disabled *ADJECTIVE*

*He has been **disabled** since the accident.*
• incapacitated
OPPOSITE able-bodied
An animal which is injured and cannot walk is **lame**.
A person who cannot move part of their body is **paralysed**.

disadvantage *NOUN*

*A big **disadvantage** was not having enough volunteers.*
• drawback, handicap, hindrance, inconvenience, downside, snag

disagree *VERB*

*My sister and I often **disagree** about music.*
• argue, differ, clash, quarrel, squabble, bicker, fall out
OPPOSITE agree
➤ **to disagree with**
❶ *He **disagrees with** everything I say.*
• argue with, contradict, oppose, object to
❷ *Broccoli **disagrees with** me.*
• have a bad effect on, upset

disagreeable *ADJECTIVE*

*There's no need to be so **disagreeable**.*
• unpleasant, horrible, nasty, offensive, horrid, revolting
OPPOSITE pleasant

disagreement *NOUN*

*We had a **disagreement** over who should pay for the meal.*
• argument, dispute, difference of opinion, quarrel, row, clash, squabble, conflict
OPPOSITE agreement

disappear *VERB*

❶ *The markings will **disappear** as the chicks grow older.*
• become invisible, vanish, fade, clear, disperse, dissolve
❷ *The thief **disappeared** around the corner.*
• run away, escape, flee, go away, withdraw
OPPOSITE appear

disappoint *VERB*

*She didn't want to **disappoint** her fans by cancelling the show.*
• let down, fail, dissatisfy, displease, upset
OPPOSITES please, satisfy

disappointed *ADJECTIVE*

*I'm **disappointed** that you can't come to my party.*
• saddened, unhappy, upset, let down, unsatisfied, displeased
OPPOSITES pleased, satisfied

disapprove *VERB*

➤ **to disapprove of**
*My aunt **disapproves of** watching television.*
• object to, take exception to, dislike, deplore, condemn, criticize, denounce, frown on *(informal)* take a dim view of
OPPOSITE approve of

a b c d e f g h i j k l m n o p q r s t u v w x y z

A
B
C
D
E
F
G
H
I
J
K
L
M
N
O
P
Q
R
S
T
U
V
W
X
Y
Z

disaster *NOUN*
There was a near disaster when the engine caught fire.
• catastrophe, calamity, tragedy

WORD WEB

SOME TYPES OF NATURAL DISASTER:

• avalanche, earthquake, epidemic, famine, fire, flood, hurricane, landslide, plague, tidal wave, tornado, tsunami, volcanic eruption

disastrous *ADJECTIVE*
The disastrous fire cost millions of pounds.
• catastrophic, devastating, calamitous, destructive, dire, dreadful, terrible, ruinous

disc *NOUN*
The full moon appears as a disc in the sky.
see **circle**

discard *VERB*
I discarded some of my old toys.
• get rid of, throw away, throw out, reject, cast off, dispose of, dump, scrap

discharge *VERB*
❶ *The accused was found not guilty and discharged.*
• free, release, clear, acquit, let off, allow to leave, liberate
❷ *The chimney discharged thick smoke.*
• expel, emit, give out, pour out, eject, belch, produce

disciple *NOUN*
The religious leader had many disciples.
• follower, supporter, admirer, devotee
In Christianity, the disciples of Jesus are called the **apostles**.

discipline *NOUN*
Discipline is important in the army.
• order, control

disclose *VERB*
The witness disclosed the truth.
• reveal, tell, make known, confess, make public
OPPOSITE conceal

discomfort *NOUN*
He still experiences a lot of discomfort from his injury.
• pain, soreness, distress, unease

disconnect *VERB*
We need to disconnect the cooker before we can move it.
• detach, cut off, unplug, unhook

discontented *ADJECTIVE*
She felt very discontented with her job.
• dissatisfied, miserable, unhappy, upset
(informal) fed up
OPPOSITES happy, satisfied

discontinue *VERB*
That style of shoe has been discontinued.
• stop, end, terminate
OPPOSITES introduce, establish

discount *NOUN*
I got a discount on the full price.
• deduction, reduction, cut, concession, allowance

discourage *VERB*
❶ *Don't let her criticism discourage you.*
• demoralize, depress
(informal) put you off
❷ *The burglar alarm will discourage thieves.*
• deter, dissuade, prevent, restrain, stop, hinder
OPPOSITE encourage

discover *VERB*
I discovered some old toys in the attic.
• find, come across, spot, stumble across, uncover
To discover something that has been buried is to **unearth** it.
To discover something that has been under water is to **dredge it up.**
To discover something you have been pursuing is to **track it down.**
OPPOSITE hide

discovery *NOUN*
Scientists have made an exciting new discovery.
• find, breakthrough

discreet ADJECTIVE
I asked a few discreet questions about her illness.
• tactful, sensitive, delicate, careful, cautious, diplomatic, wary
OPPOSITE tactless

discriminate VERB
It's sometimes hard to discriminate between poisonous mushrooms and edible ones.
• distinguish, tell the difference
➤ **to discriminate against**
It's wrong to discriminate against people because of their age.
• be biased against, be intolerant of, be prejudiced against

discrimination NOUN
❶ *The school has a policy against racial discrimination.*
• prejudice, bias, intolerance, unfairness
Discrimination against people because of their sex is **sexism**.
Discrimination against people because of their race is **racism**.
❷ *They show discrimination in their choice of music.*
• good taste, good judgement

discuss VERB
I discussed the idea with my parents.
• talk about, confer about, debate

discussion NOUN
We had a lively discussion about pocket money.
• conversation, argument, exchange of views
A formal discussion is a **conference** or **debate**.

disease NOUN
He was suffering from a serious disease.
• illness, ailment, sickness, complaint, affliction
(informal) bug
see also **illness**

diseased ADJECTIVE
Gardeners throw away diseased plants.
• unhealthy, sickly, infected
OPPOSITE healthy

disembark VERB
The passengers disembarked from the ferry.
• go ashore
OPPOSITE embark

disgrace NOUN
❶ *He never got over the disgrace of being caught cheating.*
• humiliation, shame, embarrassment, dishonour
❷ *The way she treats them is a disgrace!*
• outrage, scandal

disgraceful ADJECTIVE
We were shocked by her disgraceful behaviour.
• shameful, shocking, appalling, outrageous, scandalous
OPPOSITE honourable

disguise VERB
I tried to disguise my feelings.
• conceal, hide, cover up, camouflage, mask
➤ **to disguise yourself as**
The spy disguised herself as a hotel porter.
• dress up as, pretend to be

disguise NOUN
I didn't recognize him in that disguise.
• costume, camouflage, make-up, mask

disgust NOUN
The sight of the carcass filled me with disgust.
• repulsion, repugnance, distaste, dislike, horror, loathing, detestation
OPPOSITE liking

disgust VERB
The smell of rotten eggs disgusts me.
• repel, revolt, sicken, appal, offend, distress, shock, horrify
(informal) put you off, turn your stomach
OPPOSITE please

disgusting ADJECTIVE
The brew in the cauldron looked disgusting.
• repulsive, revolting, horrible, nasty, loathsome, repellent, repugnant, offensive, appalling, sickening, nauseating
(informal) gross
OPPOSITES delightful, pleasing

a
b
c
d
e
f
g
h
i
j
k
l
m
n
o
p
q
r
s
t
u
v
w
x
y
z

A B C **D** E F G H I J K L M N O P Q R S T U V W X Y Z

dish *NOUN*
❶ *Dad served the trifle in a large glass dish.*
• bowl, basin, plate, platter
A dish to serve soup from is a **tureen**.
see also **crockery**
❷ *What's your favourite dish?*
• food, recipe, meal

dishevelled *ADJECTIVE*
His clothes were a mess and his hair was dishevelled.
• messy, untidy, scruffy, unkempt, bedraggled, slovenly
OPPOSITES neat, tidy

dishonest *ADJECTIVE*
❶ *They were taken in by a dishonest salesman.*
• deceitful, cheating, corrupt, disreputable, untrustworthy, immoral, lying, swindling, thieving
(informal) bent, crooked, dodgy, shady
❷ *The author makes some dishonest claims.*
• false, misleading, untruthful, fraudulent, devious
OPPOSITE honest

dishonesty *NOUN*
The MP was accused of dishonesty.
• deceit, cheating, corruption, insincerity, lying, deviousness
(informal) crookedness
OPPOSITE honesty

disinfect *VERB*
The nurse disinfected my wound.
• cleanse, sterilize
OPPOSITE infect
To disinfect an infected place is to **decontaminate** it.
To disinfect a room using fumes is to **fumigate** it.

disintegrate *VERB*
The cloth is so old that it's starting to disintegrate.
• break up, fall apart, break into pieces, crumble, decay, decompose

disinterested *ADJECTIVE*
A referee must be disinterested.
• impartial, neutral, unbiased, unprejudiced, detached, fair
OPPOSITE biased

disk *NOUN*
see **disc**

dislike *NOUN*
His colleagues regarded him with intense dislike.
• hatred, loathing, detestation, disapproval, disgust, revulsion
OPPOSITE liking

dislike *VERB*
I dislike people who hunt wild animals.
• hate, loathe, detest, disapprove of
OPPOSITE like

dislodge *VERB*
The wind dislodged some tiles on the roof.
• displace, move, shift, disturb

disloyal *ADJECTIVE*
The rebels were accused of being disloyal to the government.
• unfaithful, treacherous, faithless, false, unreliable, untrustworthy
OPPOSITE loyal

dismal *ADJECTIVE*
❶ *How can we brighten up this dismal room?*
• dull, drab, dreary, dingy, colourless, cheerless, gloomy, murky
OPPOSITES bright, cheerful
❷ *(informal) It was a dismal performance by the home team.*
• dreadful, awful, terrible, feeble, useless, hopeless
(informal) pathetic
OPPOSITES brilliant, splendid

dismantle *VERB*
After the school fair, we had to dismantle all the stalls.
• take apart, take down
To dismantle your group's tents is to **strike camp**.
OPPOSITE assemble

dismay *NOUN*
We listened with **dismay** to the bad news.
• distress, alarm, shock, concern, anxiety, gloom

dismayed *ADJECTIVE*
I was **dismayed** by the failure of our plan.
• distressed, discouraged, depressed, devastated, shocked, appalled
OPPOSITE encouraged

dismiss *VERB*
❶ The teacher **dismissed** the class.
• send away, discharge, free, let go, release
❷ The firm **dismissed** ten workers.
• sack, give the sack, give notice to, make redundant
(informal) fire
❸ The weather was so bad that we **dismissed** the idea of having a picnic.
• discard, drop, reject

dismount *VERB*
The knight **dismounted** from her horse.
• descend, get off

disobedient *ADJECTIVE*
The teacher said he had never known such a **disobedient** child.
• naughty, badly behaved, undisciplined, uncontrollable, unmanageable, unruly, ungovernable, troublesome, defiant, disruptive, mutinous, rebellious, contrary
OPPOSITE obedient

disobey *VERB*
❶ You will be penalized if you **disobey** the rules.
• break, ignore, disregard, defy, violate
❷ Soldiers are trained never to **disobey**.
• be disobedient, rebel, revolt, mutiny
OPPOSITE obey

disorder *NOUN*
❶ The public meeting broke up in **disorder**.
• disturbance, uproar, commotion, quarrelling, rioting, brawling, fighting, lawlessness, anarchy

❷ It's time I tidied up the **disorder** in my room.
• mess, muddle, untidiness, chaos, confusion, clutter, jumble
OPPOSITE order

disorderly *ADJECTIVE*
The class were behaving in a **disorderly** manner.
• badly behaved, disobedient, unruly, uncontrollable, undisciplined, ungovernable, unmanageable
OPPOSITE orderly

dispatch *NOUN*
The messenger brought a **dispatch** from headquarters.
• message, communication, report, letter, bulletin

dispatch *VERB*
The parcel has already been **dispatched**.
• post, send, transmit

dispense *VERB*
➤ to dispense with
Now that I have new trainers, I can **dispense** with the old ones.
• get rid of, dispose of, do without, remove

disperse *VERB*
❶ The police **dispersed** the crowd.
• break up, send away, drive away, separate, send in different directions
❷ The crowd **dispersed** quickly after the match.
• scatter, spread out, disappear, dissolve, melt away, vanish
OPPOSITE gather

displace *VERB*
❶ The gales have **displaced** some of the roof tiles.
• dislodge, put out of place, shift, disturb
❷ A brilliant new player **displaced** me in the team.
• replace, take the place of, succeed

a
b
c
d
e
f
g
h
i
j
k
l
m
n
o
p
q
r
s
t
u
v
w
x
y
z

display VERB
We planned the best way to display our work.
• demonstrate, exhibit, present, put on show, set out, show, show off
To display something boastfully is to flaunt it.

display NOUN
We set out a display of our art work.
• exhibition, show, presentation, demonstration

displease VERB
I must have done something to displease her.
• annoy, irritate, upset, anger, exasperate, vex

dispose VERB
➤ **to dispose of something**
Let's dispose of this old carpet.
• get rid of, discard, throw away, give away, scrap
(*informal*) dump
➤ **to be disposed to do something**
He didn't seem disposed to help us.
• be willing to, be inclined to, be ready to, be likely to

disposition NOUN
Our kitten has a very friendly disposition.
• character, nature, personality

dispute NOUN
We settled the dispute about who should wash the dishes.
• argument, disagreement, quarrel, debate, controversy, difference of opinion

disqualify VERB
Two athletes have been disqualified from the competition.
• bar, prohibit

disregard VERB
I disregarded the doctor's advice.
• ignore, pay no attention to, take no notice of, reject
OPPOSITE heed

disrespectful ADJECTIVE
She was very disrespectful towards her parents.
• rude, bad-mannered, insulting, impolite, insolent, cheeky
OPPOSITE respectful

disrupt VERB
Bad weather has disrupted the hockey tournament.
• interrupt, upset, interfere with, throw into confusion or disorder

dissatisfied ADJECTIVE
I was dissatisfied with my violin playing.
• displeased, disappointed, discontented, frustrated, annoyed
OPPOSITE satisfied

dissolve VERB
Stir your tea until the sugar dissolves.
• disperse, disintegrate, melt

dissuade VERB
➤ **to dissuade someone from doing something**
We tried to dissuade him from going out in the storm.
• discourage someone from, persuade someone not to, deter someone from, warn someone against
OPPOSITE persuade

distance NOUN
What is the distance from Earth to the Sun?
• measurement, space, extent, reach, mileage
The distance across something is the breadth or width.
The distance along something is the length.
The distance between two points is a gap or interval.
for units for measuring distance
see **measurement**

distant ADJECTIVE
❶ *I'd love to travel to distant countries.*
• faraway, remote, out of the way, inaccessible, exotic
OPPOSITE close

❷ *His **distant** manner puts me off.*
• unfriendly, unapproachable, formal, reserved, withdrawn, cool, haughty, aloof
OPPOSITE friendly

distinct ADJECTIVE
❶ *There is a **distinct** improvement in your handwriting.*
• definite, evident, noticeable, obvious, perceptible
OPPOSITE imperceptible
❷ *It was a small photo, but the details were quite **distinct**.*
• clear, distinguishable, plain, recognizable, sharp, unmistakable, visible, well defined
OPPOSITE indistinct
❸ *Organize your essay into **distinct** sections.*
• individual, separate

distinction NOUN
❶ *There's a clear **distinction** between the real diamond and the fake.*
• difference, contrast, distinctiveness
❷ *He had the **distinction** of being the team captain.*
• honour, glory, merit, credit, prestige

distinctive ADJECTIVE
*We spotted the **distinctive** footprints of a yeti in the snow.*
• characteristic, recognizable, unmistakable, special, unique

distinguish VERB
❶ *It was impossible to **distinguish** one twin from the other.*
• tell apart, pick out, discriminate, differentiate, make a distinction, decide
❷ *In the dark we couldn't **distinguish** who was walking past.*
• identify, tell, make out, determine, perceive, recognize, single out

distinguished ADJECTIVE
❶ *The school has a **distinguished** academic record.*
• excellent, first-rate, outstanding, exceptional
OPPOSITE ordinary

❷ *She is a very **distinguished** actor.*
• famous, celebrated, well-known, eminent, notable, prominent, renowned
OPPOSITES unknown, obscure

distort VERB
❶ *When my bike hit the kerb, it **distorted** the wheel.*
• bend, buckle, twist, warp, contort
❷ *The newspaper **distorted** the facts of the story.*
• twist, slant, misrepresent

distract VERB
*Don't **distract** the bus driver.*
• divert the attention of, disturb, put off

distress NOUN
*The trapped animal was clearly in **distress**.*
• suffering, torment, anguish, dismay, anxiety, grief, misery, pain, sadness, sorrow, worry, wretchedness

distress VERB
*We could see that the bad news **distressed** him.*
• upset, disturb, trouble, worry, alarm, dismay, torment
OPPOSITE comfort

distribute VERB
❶ *The coach **distributed** water to the players at half-time.*
• give out, hand round, circulate, dispense, issue, share out, take round
(informal) dish out, dole out
❷ *Distribute the seeds evenly.*
• scatter, spread, disperse

district NOUN
*Granny lives in a quiet **district**.*
• area, neighbourhood, locality, region, vicinity

distrust VERB
*I **distrusted** the professor from the moment I met him.*
• doubt, mistrust, question, suspect, be suspicious or wary of, be sceptical about, feel uncertain or uneasy or unsure about
OPPOSITE trust

a
b
c
d
e
f
g
h
i
j
k
l
m
n
o
p
q
r
s
t
u
v
w
x
y
z

disturb VERB
❶ Don't **disturb** the baby when she's asleep.
• bother, interrupt, annoy, pester
❷ They were **disturbed** by the bad news.
• distress, trouble, upset, worry, alarm, frighten
❸ Please don't **disturb** the papers on my desk.
• muddle, mix up, move around,
mess about with

disused ADJECTIVE
They made the **disused** railway line into a
cycle track.
• abandoned, unused, closed down

ditch NOUN
We dug a **ditch** to drain away the water.
• trench, channel, drain, gully

dither VERB
Stop **dithering** and make up your mind!
• hesitate, waver, be in two minds
(informal) shilly-shally

dive VERB
❶ The mermaid **dived** into the water.
• plunge, jump, leap
A dive in which you land flat on your front
is a **bellyflop**.
❷ The eagle **dived** towards its prey.
• pounce, swoop

diver NOUN
A diver who wears a rubber suit and flippers
and breathes air from a portable tank is a
scuba diver or **frogman**.

diverse ADJECTIVE
People from many **diverse** cultures live in
the area.
• different, differing, varied, various,
contrasting

diversion NOUN
❶ The police had set up a traffic **diversion**.
• detour, indirect route, roundabout route
❷ There were lots of **diversions** at the
holiday camp.
• entertainment, amusement, recreation

divert VERB
❶ They **diverted** the plane to another airport.
• redirect, switch
❷ She **diverted** herself by practising
handstands.
• entertain, amuse, occupy, interest,
keep happy

divide VERB
❶ We **divided** the class into two groups.
• separate, split, break up, move apart, part
OPPOSITE combine
❷ I **divided** the cake between my friends.
• distribute, share out, give out, allot,
deal out, dispense
❸ Which way do we go? The path **divides** here.
• branch, fork
OPPOSITE converge

divine ADJECTIVE
❶ The temple is used for **divine** worship.
• holy, religious, sacred, spiritual
❷ The Greeks believed **divine** beings lived on
Mount Olympus.
• godlike, immortal, heavenly
❸ (informal) These fairy cakes taste **divine**!
• excellent, wonderful, superb

division NOUN
❶ The map shows the **division** of Europe after
the war.
• dividing, splitting, separation, partition
❷ There was a **division** in the government.
• disagreement, split, feud
❸ There is a movable **division** between the two
classrooms.
• partition, divider, dividing wall, screen
❹ They work in different **divisions** of the
same company.
• branch, department, section, unit

dizzy ADJECTIVE
Going on a roundabout makes me feel **dizzy**.
• dazed, giddy, faint, reeling, unsteady

do VERB does, doing, did, done
❶ My friend always knows what to **do** in a crisis.
• act, behave, conduct yourself

❷ *The vet has a lot of work to do this morning.*
• attend to, cope with, deal with, handle, look after, perform, undertake
❸ *It took me half an hour to do the washing-up.*
• accomplish, achieve, carry out, complete, execute, finish
❹ *I need to do all of these sums.*
• answer, puzzle out, solve, work out
❺ *Staring at the sun can do damage to your eyes.*
• bring about, cause, produce, result in
❻ *If you don't have lemonade, water will do.*
• be acceptable, be enough, be satisfactory, be sufficient, serve

➤ **to do away with**
I wish our school would do away with homework.
• get rid of, abolish, eliminate, end, put an end to

➤ **to do up**
These jeans are too tight to do up.
• button up, fasten

docile *ADJECTIVE*
Don't be afraid of the dog—he's quite docile.
• tame, gentle, meek, obedient, manageable, safe, submissive
OPPOSITE fierce

dock *NOUN*
A boat was waiting for us at the end of the dock.
• harbour, quay, jetty, wharf, landing stage, dockyard, pier, port, marina

dock *VERB*
We can't disembark until the ship docks.
• moor, tie up

doctor *NOUN*
for people who practise medicine see **medicine**

document *NOUN*
The library contains many old documents.
• paper, record, file, certificate, deed

dodge *VERB*
I just managed to dodge the snowball.
• avoid, evade, side-step

dog *NOUN*

WORD WEB

A female dog is a **bitch**.
A young dog is a **pup, puppy** or **whelp**.
Informal words for a dog are **mutt** and **pooch**.
An uncomplimentary word for a dog is **cur**.
A dog of pure breed with known ancestors has a **pedigree**.
A dog of mixed breeds is a **mongrel**.
A dog used for hunting is a **hound**.
A word meaning 'to do with dogs' is **canine**.

SOME BREEDS OF DOG:

• Afghan hound, basset hound, beagle, bloodhound, boxer, bulldog, bull terrier, cairn terrier, chihuahua, cocker spaniel, collie, corgi, dachshund, Dalmatian, Dobermann, fox terrier, German shepherd, Great Dane, greyhound, husky, Irish setter, Labrador, mastiff, Pekinese or Pekingese, Pomeranian, poodle, pug, golden retriever, Rottweiler, St Bernard, schnauzer, setter, sheepdog, spaniel, terrier, West Highland terrier, whippet, wolfhound, Yorkshire terrier

SOUNDS MADE BY DOGS:

• bark, growl, snap, snarl, woof, yap, yelp
The Sheepdog barked a low, cautious bark. He was answered by a high, shrill bark. Then he heard a yelp, as if some dog had been cuffed.—THE HUNDRED AND ONE DALMATIANS, Dodie Smith
see also **animal**

domestic *ADJECTIVE*
❶ *At weekends I do various domestic chores.*
• household, family
❷ *Cats and dogs are popular domestic animals.*
• domesticated, tame

a b c d e f g h i j k l m n o p q r s t u v w x y z

A B C D E F G H I J K L M N O P Q R S T U V W X Y Z

dominant *ADJECTIVE*
❶ *The captain plays a **dominant** role in the team.*
• leading, main, chief, major, powerful, principal, important, influential
OPPOSITE minor
❷ *The castle is a **dominant** feature in the landscape.*
• conspicuous, prominent, obvious, large, imposing, eye-catching
OPPOSITE insignificant

dominate *VERB*
*The visiting team **dominated** the game.*
• control, direct, monopolize, govern, take control of, take over

donate *VERB*
*Will you **donate** something to our collection?*
• give, contribute

donation *NOUN*
*The museum relies on **donations** from the public.*
• contribution, gift, offering

done *ADJECTIVE*
❶ *All my thank-you letters are **done** now.*
• finished, complete, over
❷ *The cake will be brown on top when it's **done**.*
• cooked, ready

donor *NOUN*
*A generous **donor** gave us money for new sports equipment.*
• benefactor, contributor, sponsor

doomed *ADJECTIVE*
*The expedition was **doomed** from the start.*
• ill-fated, condemned, fated, cursed, jinxed, damned

door *NOUN*
A door in a floor or ceiling is a **hatch** or **trapdoor**.
The plank or stone underneath a door is the **threshold**.
The beam or stone above a door is the **lintel**.
The opening into which a door fits is the **doorway**.
The device on which a door turns when it opens is the **hinge**.
To leave a door slightly open is to leave it **ajar**.

dose *NOUN*
*The nurse gave me a **dose** of the medicine.*
• measure, correct amount, dosage, portion

dot *NOUN*
*He was furious when he saw **dots** of paint on the carpet.*
• spot, speck, fleck, point, mark
The dot you always put at the end of a sentence is a **full stop**.
➤ **on the dot** *(informal)*
We left the house at nine o'clock on the dot.
• exactly, precisely

double *ADJECTIVE*
*You enter the room through a **double** set of doors.*
• dual, twofold, paired, twin, matching, duplicate

double *NOUN*
*She's so like you—she's almost your **double**.*
• twin
(informal) lookalike, spitting image, dead ringer
A living organism created as an exact copy of another living organism is a **clone**.

doubt *NOUN*
❶ *Have you any **doubt** about his honesty?*
• distrust, suspicion, mistrust, hesitation, reservation, scepticism
OPPOSITE confidence
❷ *There is no **doubt** that you will pass your exam.*
• question, uncertainty, ambiguity, confusion
OPPOSITE certainty

doubt *VERB*
*There is no reason to **doubt** her story.*

• distrust, feel uncertain or uneasy or unsure about, question, mistrust, suspect, be sceptical about, be suspicious or wary of

OPPOSITE trust

doubtful ADJECTIVE

❶ He looked doubtful, but agreed to let us go.
• unsure, uncertain, unconvinced, hesitant, distrustful, sceptical, suspicious

OPPOSITE certain

❷ The referee made a doubtful decision there.
• questionable, debatable, arguable

downfall NOUN

After the government's downfall, there was a general election.
• collapse, fall, ruin

downward ADJECTIVE

We took the downward path into the valley.
• downhill, descending

OPPOSITE upward

doze VERB

The cat often dozes in the evening.
• rest, sleep, nod off
(informal) drop off

drab ADJECTIVE

The curtains were faded and drab.
• dull, dingy, dreary, cheerless, colourless, dismal, gloomy, grey

OPPOSITES bright, cheerful

draft NOUN

I jotted down a draft of my story.
• outline, plan, sketch, rough version

draft VERB

I began to draft my story.
• outline, plan, prepare, sketch, work out

drag VERB

The tractor dragged the car out of the ditch.
• pull, tow, tug, draw, haul, lug

OPPOSITE push

dragon NOUN

A fearsome dragon once lived in these hills.

WORD WEB

SOME WAYS TO DESCRIBE A DRAGON:

• ancient, fearsome, fiery, fire-breathing, legendary, mighty, monstrous, scaly, winged
 And there was the Horntail … crouched low over her clutch of eggs, her wings half furled, her evil, yellow eyes upon him, a monstrous, scaly black lizard, thrashing her spiked tail.
—HARRY POTTER AND THE GOBLET OF FIRE, J. K. Rowling

BODY PARTS A DRAGON MIGHT HAVE:

• barbed tail, bat-like wings, claws, crest, forked tail or tongue, pointed teeth, scales, spikes or spines, talons

A DRAGON'S SCALES MIGHT BE:

• dazzling, iridescent, patterned, shimmering

A DRAGON'S BREATH MIGHT BE:

• fiery, flaming, scorching, searing

THINGS A DRAGON MIGHT DO:

• breathe fire, change shape, curl its body, furl or unfurl its wings, puff smoke, roar, snort, soar, swoop, thrash its tail

PLACES WHERE A DRAGON MIGHT LIVE:

• cave, den, lair
for other creatures found in myths and legends see myth

drain NOUN

Surplus water runs away along a drain.
• ditch, channel, drainpipe, gutter, pipe, sewer

drain VERB

❶ If they drain the marsh, lots of waterbirds will die.
• dry out, remove water from
❷ She drained the oil from the engine.
• draw off, empty

a b c d e f g h i j k l m n o p q r s t u v w x y z

A
B
C
D
E
F
G
H
I
J
K
L
M
N
O
P
Q
R
S
T
U
V
W
X
Y
Z

❸ *The water slowly drained away.*
• trickle, ooze, seep
❹ *The tough climb drained my energy.*
• use up, consume, exhaust

drama *NOUN*
❶ *Drama is one of my favourite subjects.*
• acting
see also **theatre**
❷ *I witnessed the drama of a real robbery.*
• action, excitement, suspense, spectacle

dramatic *ADJECTIVE*
We watched the dramatic rescue on TV.
• exciting, eventful, thrilling, sensational, spectacular, gripping

drank *past tense see* **drink**

drastic *ADJECTIVE*
After being without food for three days, the explorers needed to take drastic action.
• desperate, extreme, radical, harsh, severe
OPPOSITE moderate

draught *NOUN*
I felt a draught of air from the open window.
• breeze, current, movement, puff

draw *VERB* **draws, drawing, drew, drawn**
❶ *I drew some pictures of the flowers in our garden.*
• sketch, trace, doodle
❷ *I'm not very good at drawing faces.*
• depict, portray, represent
❸ *The horse was drawing a cart.*
• pull, tow, drag, haul, tug, lug
❹ *We expect tomorrow's match to draw a big crowd.*
• attract, bring in, pull in
❺ *The two teams drew 1-1.*
• finish equal, tie
➤ **to draw near**
As the spaceship drew near, I began to get nervous.
• approach, advance, come near

draw *NOUN*
Kinds of prize draw are a **lottery** and a **raffle**.

drawback *NOUN*
One drawback of electric cars is the price.
• disadvantage, difficulty, handicap, obstacle, inconvenience, hindrance, downside, snag

drawing *NOUN*

WORD WEB

SOME TYPES OF DRAWING:

• caricature, cartoon, design, doodle, illustration, outline, sketch

TOOLS USED FOR DRAWING:

• chalk, charcoal, crayon, ink, pastel, pen, pencil

dread *NOUN*
Our teacher has a dread of spiders.
• fear, horror, terror, phobia (about), anxiety (about)

dreadful *ADJECTIVE*
❶ *There has been a dreadful accident at sea.*
• horrible, terrible, appalling, horrendous, distressing, shocking, upsetting, tragic, grim
❷ *The weather at the weekend was dreadful.*
• bad, awful, terrible, abysmal, abominable, dire, foul, nasty
OPPOSITES good, pleasant

dream *NOUN*
A bad dream is a **nightmare**.
A dreamlike experience you have while awake is a **daydream**, **fantasy** or **reverie**.
Something you see in a dream or daydream is a **vision**.
The dreamlike state when you are hypnotized is a **trance**.
Something you think you see that is not real is a **hallucination** or **illusion**.

dream *VERB* **dreams, dreaming, dreamt or dreamed**
I dreamed that I was a mermaid.
• daydream, imagine, fancy, fantasize

dreary *ADJECTIVE*
❶ *The newsreader had a very dreary voice.*
• dull, boring, flat, tedious, unexciting, uninteresting
OPPOSITE lively
❷ *When will this dreary weather end?*
• depressing, dismal, dull, gloomy, cheerless, murky, overcast
OPPOSITES bright, sunny

drench *VERB*
The rain drenched me to the skin.
• soak, wet thoroughly

dress *NOUN*
❶ *What kind of dress are you wearing to the party?*
• frock, gown
❷ *The invitation said to wear casual dress.*
• clothes, clothing, outfit, costume, garments
see also **clothes**

dress *VERB*
❶ *I helped to dress my little brother.*
• clothe, put clothes on
OPPOSITE undress
❷ *A nurse dressed my wound.*
• bandage, put a dressing on, bind up

dressing *NOUN*
The nurse put a dressing on the wound.
• bandage, plaster

drew *past tense see* **draw**

dribble *VERB*
❶ *Careful, the baby's dribbling on your jumper.*
• drool
❷ *Water dribbled out of the hole in the tank.*
• drip, trickle, leak, ooze, seep

drift *VERB*
❶ *The boat drifted downstream.*
• float, be carried, move slowly

❷ *The crowd lost interest and drifted away.*
• stray, wander, meander, ramble, walk aimlessly
❸ *The snow will drift in this wind.*
• pile up, accumulate, make drifts

drift *NOUN*
❶ *The car was stuck in a snow drift.*
• bank, heap, mound, pile, ridge
❷ *Did you understand the drift of the speech?*
• gist, main idea, point

drill *NOUN*
❶ *There will be a fire drill at school next week.*
• practice, training
❷ *Do you all know the drill for erecting a tent?*
• procedure, routine, system

drill *VERB*
It took a long time to drill through the wall.
• bore, penetrate, pierce

drink *NOUN*

WORD WEB

SOME HOT DRINKS:

• chocolate, cocoa, coffee, tea

SOME NON-ALCOHOLIC COLD DRINKS:

• barley water, cola, cordial, fruit juice, ginger beer, iced tea, lemonade, milk, milkshake, mineral water, smoothie, soda water, squash, water

SOME ALCOHOLIC DRINKS:

• beer, brandy, champagne, cider, gin, port, punch, rum, sherry, vodka, whisky, wine
Very strong alcoholic drinks are **spirits**.

CONTAINERS FOR DRINKS:

• beaker, bottle, can, cup, glass, goblet, mug, tankard, tumbler, wine glass
bottle, cup

a b c d e f g h i j k l m n o p q r s t u v w x y z

drink *VERB* **drinks, drinking, drank, drunk**
To drink greedily is to **gulp**, **guzzle** or **swig**.
To drink noisily is to **slurp**.
To drink a small amount at a time is to **sip**.
To drink with the tongue as a cat does is to **lap**.

drip *NOUN*
The mechanic was worried by the **drips** of oil underneath the car.
• spot, dribble, splash, trickle
drip *VERB*
The oil **dripped** on to the garage floor.
• drop, leak, dribble, splash, trickle

drive *VERB* **drives, driving, drove, driven**
❶ The dog **drove** the sheep through the gate.
• direct, guide, herd
❷ I couldn't **drive** the spade into the hard ground.
• push, thrust, hammer, plunge, ram
❸ When can I learn to **drive** a car?
• control, handle, manage
❹ Lack of money **drove** him to steal.
• force, compel, oblige
➤ **to drive someone out**
The invading soldiers **drove** the people **out**.
• eject, expel, throw out
To drive people out of their homes is to **evict** them.
To drive people out of their country is to **banish** or **exile** them.
drive *NOUN*
❶ We went for a **drive** in the country.
• ride, trip, journey, outing, excursion, jaunt
❷ Have you got the **drive** to succeed?
• ambition, determination, keenness, motivation, energy, zeal

driver *NOUN*
Many **drivers** go too fast.
• motorist
A person who drives someone's car as a job is a **chauffeur**.

droop *VERB*
Plants tend to **droop** in dry weather.
• sag, wilt, bend, flop, be limp

drop *NOUN*
❶ Large **drops** of rain began to fall.
• drip, droplet, spot, bead, blob
❷ Could I have another **drop** of milk in my tea?
• dash, small quantity
❸ We expect a **drop** in the price of fruit in the summer.
• decrease, reduction, cut
❹ There's a **drop** of two metres on the other side of the wall.
• fall, descent, plunge
drop *VERB*
❶ The hawk **dropped** on to its prey.
• descend, dive, plunge, swoop
❷ I **dropped** to the ground exhausted.
• collapse, fall, sink, subside, slump, tumble
❸ Why did you **drop** me from the team?
• omit, eliminate, exclude, leave out
❹ They **dropped** the plan for a new bypass.
• abandon, discard, reject, give up, scrap
➤ **to drop in**
Drop in on your way home.
• visit, call, pay a call
➤ **to drop out**
Why did you **drop out** of the race at the last minute?
• withdraw, back out, pull out
(informal) quit

drove *past tense see* **drive**

drown *VERB*
The music from upstairs **drowned** our conversation.
• overwhelm, overpower, drown out

drowsy *ADJECTIVE*
If you feel **drowsy**, why not go to bed?
• sleepy, tired, weary

drug *NOUN*
A new **drug** has been discovered for back pain.
• medicine, remedy, treatment
A drug which relieves pain is an **analgesic** or **painkiller**.
A drug which calms you down is a **sedative** or **tranquillizer**.
Drugs which make you more active are **stimulants**.

drum NOUN

WORD WEB

SOME TYPES OF DRUM:

• bass drum, bhodrán, bongo drum, djembe, kettledrum or timpani, snare drum, tabor, tambour, timpani, tom-tom
for other musical instruments see **music**

dry ADJECTIVE
❶ *Nothing will grow in this dry soil.*
• arid, parched, moistureless, waterless, dehydrated, desiccated, barren
OPPOSITE wet
A common simile is **as dry as a bone.**
When your throat feels very dry, you are **parched.**
❷ *He gave rather a dry speech.*
• dull, boring, dreary, tedious, uninteresting
OPPOSITE interesting
❸ *I can't understand his dry sense of humour.*
• ironic, wry, witty, subtle

dry VERB
❶ *If it's sunny, I'll hang the clothes out to dry.*
• get dry, dry out
❷ *Will you please dry the dishes?*
• wipe dry
When you dry food to preserve it, you **dehydrate** it.

dual ADJECTIVE
The building has a dual purpose: it can be either a cinema or a theatre.
• double, twofold, twin, combined

dubious ADJECTIVE
I'm a bit dubious about getting a snake for a pet.
• doubtful, uncertain, unsure, hesitant
OPPOSITES certain, sure

duck NOUN
A male duck is a **drake.**
A young duck is a **duckling.**

duck VERB
❶ *Oliver ducked to avoid the snowball.*
• bend down, bob down, crouch, stoop

❷ *My friends threatened to duck me in the pool.*
• dip, immerse, plunge, submerge

due ADJECTIVE
❶ *The train is due in five minutes.*
• expected, anticipated
❷ *Subscriptions are now due.*
• owed, owing, payable
❸ *I give her due credit for what she did.*
• fitting, proper, appropriate, suitable, deserved, well-earned

dug past tense see dig

dull ADJECTIVE
❶ *I don't like the dull colours in this room.*
• dim, dingy, drab, dreary, dismal, faded, gloomy, sombre, subdued
OPPOSITES bright, colourful
❷ *The sky was dull that day.*
• cloudy, overcast, grey, sunless, murky
OPPOSITE clear
❸ *I heard a dull thud from upstairs.*
• indistinct, muffled, muted
OPPOSITE distinct
❹ *He's rather a dull student.*
• stupid, slow, unintelligent, dim, unimaginative, dense, obtuse *(informal)* thick
OPPOSITE clever
❺ *The play was so dull that I fell asleep.*
• boring, dry, monotonous, tedious, uninteresting, unexciting, lacklustre
OPPOSITE interesting
A common simile is **as dull as ditchwater.**

dumb ADJECTIVE
❶ *The spectators were struck dumb with amazement.*
If you do not speak, you are **mute** or **silent.**
If you cannot speak because you are surprised, confused or embarrassed, you are **speechless** or **tongue-tied.**
If you find it hard to express yourself, you are **inarticulate.**

a b c d e f g h i j k l m n o p q r s t u v w x y z

❷ *(informal) That was a dumb question!*
• stupid, unintelligent, dim, slow, dense, obtuse
(informal) daft

dummy ADJECTIVE
There was a dummy door at the side of the stage.
• imitation, fake, copy, toy

dump VERB
❶ *I decided to dump some of my old toys.*
• get rid of, throw away, throw out, discard, dispose of, scrap
❷ *Just dump your things in the bedroom.*
• put down, set down, deposit, place, drop, throw down, tip

duplicate NOUN
We made a duplicate of the original document.
• copy, photocopy, reproduction, replica
An exact copy of a historic document or manuscript is a **facsimile**.
A person who looks like you is your **double** or **twin**.
A living organism which is a duplicate of another living organism is a **clone**.

duration NOUN
We slept in a tent for the duration of the holiday.
• length, period, extent

dusk NOUN
Bats begin to emerge at dusk.
• twilight, nightfall, sunset, sundown
OPPOSITE dawn

dust NOUN
There was a lot of dust on the furniture.
• dirt, grime, particles, powder, grit

dust VERB
❶ *I dusted the bookshelves.*
• wipe over, clean, polish

❷ *The baker dusted the top of the cake with icing sugar.*
• powder, sprinkle

dusty ADJECTIVE
The books we found in the attic were very dusty.
• dirty, grimy
OPPOSITE clean

duty NOUN
❶ *I have a duty to help my parents.*
• responsibility, obligation
❷ *I carried out my duties conscientiously.*
• job, task, assignment, chore
❸ *The government has increased the duty on petrol.*
• charge, tax

dwell VERB dwells, dwelling, dwelt
➤ to dwell in
It is said that bandits dwell in these caves.
• live in, inhabit, occupy, reside in
➤ to dwell on
Try not to dwell on things that happened in the past.
• keep thinking about, worry about, brood over

dwelling NOUN
see **house**

dwindle VERB
Our enthusiasm dwindled as the day went on.
• become less, diminish, decline, decrease, lessen, subside, wane, weaken
OPPOSITE increase

dynamic ADJECTIVE
The team has a new, dynamic captain.
• energetic, lively, enthusiastic, vigorous, active, forceful, powerful
OPPOSITE apathetic

Ee

eager ADJECTIVE
He is always eager to help.
• keen, enthusiastic, desperate, anxious
OPPOSITE unenthusiastic

early ADJECTIVE
❶ *The bus was early today.*
• ahead of time, ahead of schedule
OPPOSITE late
❷ *The early computers were huge machines.*
• first, old, primitive, ancient
OPPOSITES recent, new

earn VERB
❶ *Bob earns extra pocket money washing cars.*
• work for, receive, get, make, obtain, bring in
❷ *She trained hard and earned her success.*
• deserve, merit

earnest ADJECTIVE
He's a terribly earnest young man.
• serious, sincere, solemn, thoughtful, grave
OPPOSITES casual, flippant

earth NOUN
The earth was so dry that many plants died.
• ground, land, soil
Rich, fertile earth is **loam.**
The top layer of fertile earth is **topsoil.**
Rich earth consisting of decayed plants is **humus.**
A heavy, sticky kind of earth is **clay.**

earthquake NOUN
When there is an earthquake, you feel a **shock** or **tremor.**
An instrument which detects and measures earthquakes is a **seismograph.**

ease NOUN
❶ *She swam ten lengths of the pool with ease.*
• facility, skill, speed
OPPOSITE difficulty
❷ *Lady Deadwood leads a life of ease.*
• comfort, contentment, leisure, peace, quiet, relaxation, rest, tranquillity
OPPOSITE stress

ease VERB
❶ *The doctor gave her some pills to ease her pain.*
• relieve, lessen, soothe, moderate
OPPOSITE aggravate
❷ *After taking the pills, the pain began to ease.*
• decrease, reduce, slacken
OPPOSITE increase
❸ *We eased the piano into position.*
• edge, guide, manoeuvre, inch, slide, slip

east NOUN, ADJECTIVE, ADVERB
The parts of a country or continent in the east are the **eastern** parts.
In the past, the countries of east Asia, east of the Mediterranean, were called **orient**al countries.
To travel towards the east is to travel **eastward** or **eastwards** or **in an easterly direction.**
A wind from the east is an **easterly** wind.

easy ADJECTIVE
❶ *Tonight's homework is really easy.*
• undemanding, effortless, light
An informal word for an easy task is a **doddle.**
❷ *The instructions were easy to understand.*
• simple, straightforward, clear, plain, elementary
A common simile is **as easy as ABC.**
❸ *Our cat has an easy life.*
• carefree, comfortable, peaceful, relaxed, leisurely, restful, tranquil, untroubled
OPPOSITE difficult

a
b
c
d
e
f
g
h
i
j
k
l
m
n
o
p
q
r
s
t
u
v
w
x
y
z

A B C D E F G H I J K L M N O P Q R S T U V W X Y Z

eat *VERB* eats, eating, ate, eaten
Hannah was eating a cheese sandwich.
• consume, devour
(informal) scoff
When cattle eat grass they are **grazing**.
A person who eats a large amount is said
to **eat like a horse**.
for various things to eat see **food**

OVERUSED WORD

Try to vary the words you use for **eat**.
Here are some other words you could use.

TO EAT GREEDILY OR QUICKLY:

• guzzle, gobble, gulp, gorge, bolt down,
polish off, wolf down
*Because I is refusing to gobble up human
beans like the other giants, I must spend
my life guzzling up icky-poo snozzcumbers
instead.*—THE BFG, Roald Dahl

TO EAT NOISILY:

• munch, chomp, crunch, gnash, gnaw,
slurp
Rabbits like to chomp raw carrots.

TO EAT IN SMALL AMOUNTS:

• nibble, peck, pick at or pick away at,
taste
Do you have any biscuits we could nibble?

TO EAT WITH ENJOYMENT:

• relish, savour, tuck into
He was savouring a sausage roll.

TO EAT A FORMAL MEAL:

• dine, feast, banquet
The guests will be dining in the great hall.

ebb *VERB*
❶ *The fishermen waited for the tide to ebb.*
• recede, retreat, flow back, fall, go down
❷ *She fell ill and her strength began to ebb.*
• decline, weaken, lessen, fade, wane

eccentric *ADJECTIVE*
Uncle Otto had always been a little eccentric.
• odd, peculiar, strange, weird, abnormal,
unusual, curious, unconventional, unorthodox,
quirky
(informal) way-out, dotty, crackpot
OPPOSITES conventional, orthodox

echo *VERB*
❶ *The sound echoed across the valley.*
• resound, reverberate
❷ *'He's gone home.' 'Gone home?' she echoed.*
• repeat, imitate, mimic

edge *NOUN*
The edge of a cliff or other steep place is
the **brink**.
The edge of a cup or other container is the
brim or **rim**.
The line round the edge of a circle is the
circumference.
The line round the edge of any other·shape is
its **outline**.
The distance round the edge of an area is the
perimeter.
The stones along the edge of a road are
the **kerb**.
Grass along the edge of a road is the **verge**.
The space down the edge of a page is the
margin.
The space round the edge of a picture is a
border.
Something that fits round the edge of a picture
is a **frame**.
The edge of a garment is the **hem**.
An edge with threads or hair hanging loosely
down is a **fringe**.
The edge of a crowd is the **fringe** of the crowd.
The area round the edge of a city is the
outskirts or **suburbs**.
The edge of a cricket field is the **boundary**.
The edge of a football pitch is the **touchline**.

edge *VERB*
❶ *We edged away from the lion's den.*
• creep, inch, move stealthily, steal, slink
❷ *The shirt was edged with black lace.*
• trim, hem

edgy *ADJECTIVE*
Horses become edgy during thunderstorms.
• nervous, restless, anxious, agitated, excitable, tense, jumpy, fidgety
(informal) uptight, jittery
OPPOSITE calm

edible *ADJECTIVE*
Are these toadstools edible?
• eatable, fit to eat, good to eat, safe to eat
OPPOSITES poisonous, uneatable

edit *VERB*
The letters were edited before they were published.
• revise, correct, adapt, rework, rewrite, rephrase, proofread

edition *NOUN*
We're preparing a Christmas edition of our magazine.
• copy, issue, number, version

educate *VERB*
The job of a school is to educate young people.
• teach, train, inform, instruct, tutor

educated *ADJECTIVE*
She is an educated woman.
• knowledgeable, learned, literate, well read, well-informed, cultivated, cultured

education *NOUN*
This school is for the education of young witches and wizards.
• schooling, teaching, training, instruction, tuition, tutoring, coaching
A programme of education is the **curriculum** or **syllabus**.

WORD WEB

PEOPLE WHO PROVIDE EDUCATION:

• coach, counsellor, governess, head teacher, instructor, lecturer, professor, teacher, teaching assistant, trainer, tutor

PLACES TO RECEIVE EDUCATION:

• academy, college, kindergarten, nursery, playgroup, primary school, secondary school, sixth-form college, university

eerie *ADJECTIVE*
I heard some eerie sounds in the night.
• strange, weird, uncanny, mysterious, frightening, creepy, ghostly, sinister, unearthly, unnatural
(informal) scary, spooky

effect *NOUN*
❶ *One effect of global warming is that the ice caps are melting.*
• result, consequence, outcome, sequel, upshot
❷ *The magic potion was beginning to have an effect.*
• impact, influence
❸ *The lighting gives an effect of warmth.*
• feeling, impression, sense, illusion

effective *ADJECTIVE*
❶ *I wish they could find an effective cure for colds.*
• successful
❷ *Our team needs an effective goalkeeper.*
• competent, able, capable, proficient, skilled
❸ *He presented an effective argument against hunting.*
• convincing, persuasive, compelling, impressive, telling
OPPOSITE useless

efficient *ADJECTIVE*
❶ *An efficient worker can do the job in an hour.*
• effective, competent, able, capable, proficient
❷ *We tried to work out an efficient way of heating our house.*
• economic, productive
OPPOSITE inefficient

a b c d e f g h i j k l m n o p q r s t u v w x y z

135

A
B
C
D
E
F
G
H
I
J
K
L
M
N
O
P
Q
R
S
T
U
V
W
X
Y
Z

effort *NOUN*
❶ *A lot of effort went into making the film.*
• work, trouble, exertion, industry, labour, toil
❷ *She congratulated us on a good effort.*
• attempt, try, endeavour, go, shot

eject *VERB*
❶ *Lava was ejected from the volcano when it erupted.*
• discharge, emit
❷ *The caretaker ejected an intruder from the building.*
• remove, expel, evict, banish, kick out, throw out, turn out

elaborate *ADJECTIVE*
The plot of the book is so elaborate that I got lost halfway through.
• complicated, complex, detailed, intricate, involved, convoluted
OPPOSITE simple

elated *ADJECTIVE*
We were elated when we won the match.
• delighted, pleased, thrilled, joyful, ecstatic, gleeful, exultant, delirious
(informal) over the moon

elbow *VERB*
We elbowed our way to the front of the long queue.
• push, shove, nudge, jostle

elder *ADJECTIVE*
My elder sister is in the football team.
• older

elderly *ADJECTIVE*
I helped the elderly couple to get on the bus.
• aged, aging, old, senior
OPPOSITE young

eldest *ADJECTIVE*
Jane is my eldest sister.
• oldest

elect *VERB*
We elected a new captain.
• vote for, appoint

election *NOUN*
We had an election to choose a new captain.
• vote, ballot, poll

elegant *ADJECTIVE*
The director always wears elegant clothes.
• graceful, stylish, fashionable, chic, smart, tasteful, sophisticated
OPPOSITE inelegant

element *NOUN*
They discussed various elements of the book.
• part, component, feature, constituent
➤ **to be in your element**
Doug was in his element at a computer.
• be at home, be comfortable, be happy, enjoy yourself

eligible *ADJECTIVE*
Children over twelve are not eligible to enter this race.
• qualified, allowed, authorized, suitable
OPPOSITE ineligible

eliminate *VERB*
The government wants to eliminate crime.
• get rid of, put an end to
To be eliminated from a competition is to be **knocked out**.

elude *VERB*
The police chased her, but she managed to elude them.
• avoid, evade, escape from, get away from

embark *VERB*
The passengers embarked in time for the ship to sail at high tide.
• board, go aboard
OPPOSITE disembark
➤ **to embark on something**
Today we embarked on a big project.
• begin, start, commence, undertake

embarrass *VERB*
*Will it embarrass you if I tell people
our secret?*
• humiliate, distress, mortify,
make you blush

embarrassed *ADJECTIVE*
*Don't feel embarrassed—it happens to
everyone!*
• humiliated, ashamed, awkward,
uncomfortable, bashful, distressed, flustered,
mortified, self-conscious

emblem *NOUN*
The dove is an emblem of peace.
• sign, symbol, motif

embrace *VERB*
❶ *The mother gorilla embraced her baby.*
• hug, clasp, cuddle, hold
❷ *She's always ready to embrace new ideas.*
• welcome, accept, adopt, take on
❸ *The syllabus embraces all aspects of the
subject.*
• include, incorporate, take in

emerge *VERB*
*He didn't emerge from his bedroom until
ten o'clock.*
• appear, come out

emergency *NOUN*
Try to keep calm in an emergency.
• crisis, serious situation, danger, difficulty

emigrant *NOUN*
*Millions of emigrants crossed the Atlantic for
a new life.*
Someone who has had to leave their country
because of war or disaster is a **refugee**.
OPPOSITE immigrant

emigrate *VERB*
*During the famine, many Irish people were
forced to emigrate to America.*
• leave the country, move abroad
OPPOSITE immigrate

emit *VERB*
❶ *The exhaust pipe emitted clouds of smoke.*
• discharge, expel, belch, blow out, give off
❷ *The satellite was emitting radio signals.*
• transmit, give out, send out

emotion *NOUN*
His voice was full of emotion.
• feeling, passion, sentiment, fervour

emotional *ADJECTIVE*
❶ *She made an emotional farewell speech.*
• moving, touching
❷ *The music for the love scenes was very
emotional.*
• romantic, sentimental
❸ *He's a very emotional person.*
• passionate, intense
OPPOSITES unemotional, cold

emphasis *NOUN*
*In the word 'aardvark' the emphasis is on the
first syllable.*
• stress, accent, weight

emphasize *VERB*
She emphasized the important points.
• highlight, stress, focus on, dwell on, underline

employ *VERB*
❶ *The new factory plans to employ
100 workers.*
• hire, engage, give work to, take on
❷ *The factory will employ the latest methods.*
• use, utilize

employee *NOUN*
100 employees will work at the new factory.
• worker
A word for all the employees of an
organization is **staff** or **workforce**.

employment *NOUN*
He's still looking for suitable employment.
• work, a job, an occupation, a profession,
a trade
for various kinds of employment see **job**

a
b
c
d
e
f
g
h
i
j
k
l
m
n
o
p
q
r
s
t
u
v
w
x
y
z

A
B
C
D
E
F
G
H
I
J
K
L
M
N
O
P
Q
R
S
T
U
V
W
X
Y
Z

empty *ADJECTIVE*
❶ *Please put the empty bottles in the recycling.*
`OPPOSITE` full
❷ *The house next to ours has been empty for weeks.*
• unoccupied, uninhabited, vacant, deserted
`OPPOSITE` occupied
❸ *There is still some empty space on the wall.*
• blank, bare, clear, unused

empty *VERB*
❶ *Empty the dirty water into the sink.*
• drain, pour out
`OPPOSITE` fill
❷ *Did you empty all the shopping from the trolley?*
• remove, unload
❸ *The room slowly began to empty.*
• clear, be vacated

enable *VERB*
❶ *The fine weather enabled us to do the job quickly.*
• allow, make it possible for, help, aid, assist
❷ *A passport enables you to travel abroad.*
• allow, entitle, permit, authorize
`OPPOSITE` prevent

enchanting *ADJECTIVE*
The ballet dancers were enchanting.
• delightful, charming, appealing, attractive, bewitching, spellbinding

enchantment *NOUN*
❶ *The forest had an air of enchantment.*
• magic, wonder, delight, pleasure
❷ *The witch recited an enchantment.*
• spell, incantation
see also **magic**

enclose *VERB*
❶ *The documents were enclosed in a brown paper envelope.*
• contain, insert, wrap, bind, sheathe
❷ *The animals were enclosed within a wire fence.*
• confine, restrict, fence in, shut in, imprison

enclosure *NOUN*
An animal's enclosure with bars is a **cage**.
An enclosure for chickens is a **coop** or **run**.
An enclosure for cattle and other animals is a **pen** or **corral**.
An enclosure for horses is a **paddock**.
An enclosure for sheep is a **fold**.

encounter *VERB*
❶ *He encountered her outside the station.*
• meet, come across, run into, bump into, come face to face with
❷ *We encountered some problems.*
• experience, come upon, confront, be faced with

encourage *VERB*
❶ *We went to the match to encourage our team.*
• inspire, support, motivate, cheer, spur on, egg on, empower
❷ *The poster encourages people to eat healthily.*
• persuade, urge
❸ *Is advertising likely to encourage sales?*
• increase, boost, stimulate, further, promote, help, aid
`OPPOSITE` discourage

encouragement *NOUN*
Our team needs some encouragement.
• reassurance, inspiration, incitement, stimulation, urging, incentive, stimulus, support

encouraging *ADJECTIVE*
The results of the tests were encouraging.
• hopeful, positive, promising, reassuring, optimistic, cheering, favourable

end *NOUN*
❶ *The fence marks the end of the garden.*
• boundary, limit
❷ *The end of the film was the most exciting part.*
• ending, finish, close, conclusion, culmination

The last part of a show or piece of music is the **finale**.
A section added at the end of a letter is a **postscript**.
A section added at the end of a story is an **epilogue**.
❸ *I was tired by the time we got to the **end** of the journey.*
• termination, destination
❹ *We arrived late and found ourselves at the **end** of the queue.*
• back, rear, tail
❺ *What **end** did you have in view when you started?*
• aim, purpose, intention, objective, plan, outcome, result

end *VERB*
❶ *The meeting should **end** in time for lunch.*
• finish, complete, conclude, break off, halt *(informal)* round off
❷ *When did they **end** public executions?*
• abolish, do away with, get rid of, put an end to, discontinue, eliminate
❸ *The festival **ended** with a show of fireworks.*
• close, come to an end, stop, cease, terminate, culminate, wind up

endanger *VERB*
*Bad driving **endangers** other people.*
• put at risk, threaten
OPPOSITE protect

endeavour *VERB*
*Please **endeavour** to behave well.*
• try, attempt, aim, strive, make an effort

ending *NOUN*
*The **ending** of the film was the most exciting part.*
• end, finish, close, conclusion, culmination, last part
The ending of a show or piece of music is the **finale**.

endless *ADJECTIVE*
❶ *Teachers need **endless** patience.*
• unending, limitless, infinite, inexhaustible, unlimited

❷ *There's an **endless** procession of cars along the main road.*
• continual, continuous, constant, incessant, interminable, perpetual, unbroken, uninterrupted, everlasting, ceaseless

endurance *NOUN*
The climb was a test of their endurance.
• perseverance, persistence, determination, resolution, stamina

endure *VERB*
❶ *She had to **endure** a lot of pain.*
• bear, stand, suffer, cope with, experience, go through, put up with, tolerate, undergo
❷ *These traditions have **endured** for centuries.*
• survive, continue, last, persist, carry on, keep going

enemy *NOUN*
They used to be friends but now they are bitter enemies.
• opponent, adversary, foe, rival
OPPOSITES friend, ally

energetic *ADJECTIVE*
❶ *She's a very **energetic** person.*
• dynamic, spirited, enthusiastic, animated, active, zestful
OPPOSITES inactive, lethargic
❷ *It was a very **energetic** exercise routine.*
• lively, vigorous, brisk, fast, quick moving, strenuous
OPPOSITES slow-paced, sluggish

energy *NOUN*
❶ *The dancers had tremendous **energy**.*
• liveliness, spirit, vitality, vigour, life, drive, zest, verve, enthusiasm, dynamism *(informal)* get-up-and-go, zip
OPPOSITE lethargy
❷ *Wind power is a renewable source of energy.*
• power, fuel

a
b
c
d
e
f
g
h
i
j
k
l
m
n
o
p
q
r
s
t
u
v
w
x
y
z

A B C D E F G H I J K L M N O P Q R S T U V W X Y Z

enforce VERB
The umpire's job is to enforce the rules.
• carry out, administer, apply, implement, put into effect, impose, insist on

engage VERB
❶ *The builder engaged extra workers in order to complete the job on time.*
• employ, hire, take on
❷ *The general decided to engage the enemy at dawn.*
• attack, start fighting

engaged ADJECTIVE
❶ *The painter was engaged in his work.*
• busy, occupied, employed, tied up, immersed, absorbed, engrossed
❷ *I tried to phone but the line was engaged.*
• busy, being used, unavailable
OPPOSITES free, available

engagement NOUN
She has a business engagement this afternoon.
• meeting, appointment, commitment, date

engine NOUN
The lawnmower needs a new engine.
• motor, mechanism, turbine
A railway engine is a **locomotive**.

engrossed ADJECTIVE
Rajiv was engrossed in his book.
• absorbed, busy, occupied, preoccupied, engaged, immersed

engulf VERB
The floods engulfed several villages.
• flood, drown, immerse, inundate, overwhelm, submerge, swallow up, swamp

enhance VERB
The team's victory enhanced their reputation.
• improve, strengthen

enjoy VERB
I really enjoyed the film.
• like, love, get pleasure from, be pleased by, admire, appreciate

enjoyable ADJECTIVE
It was an enjoyable party.
• pleasant, agreeable, delightful, entertaining, amusing
OPPOSITE unpleasant

enlarge VERB
The zoo is going to enlarge the lion enclosure.
• expand, extend, develop, make bigger
To make something wider is to **broaden** or **widen** it.
To make something longer is to **extend**, **lengthen** or **stretch** it.
To make something seem larger is to **magnify** it or **zoom in**.
OPPOSITE reduce

enormous ADJECTIVE
Enormous waves battered the ship.
• huge, gigantic, immense, colossal, massive, monstrous, monumental, mountainous, towering, tremendous, vast
(informal) whopping
OPPOSITE small

enough DETERMINER
Is there enough food for ten people?
• sufficient, adequate, ample

enquire VERB
➤ to enquire about
I enquired about train times to Bristol.
• ask for, get information about, request, investigate

enquiry NOUN
The librarian helped me with my enquiry.
• question, query, request, investigation, research

enrage VERB
I was enraged by their stupidity.
• anger, infuriate, madden, incense, exasperate, provoke
OPPOSITE pacify

enrol VERB
*I **enrolled** as a member of the drama club.*
• join, sign up, put your name down, volunteer

ensure VERB
*Please **ensure** that you lock the door.*
• make certain, make sure, confirm, see

enter VERB
❶ *Silence fell as I **entered** the room.*
• come in, walk in
OPPOSITE leave
To enter a place without permission is to invade it.
❷ *The arrow **entered** his shoulder.*
• go into, penetrate, pierce
❸ *Can I **enter** my name on the list?*
• insert, record, register, put down, set down, sign, write, inscribe
OPPOSITE cancel
❹ *Our class decided to **enter** the competition.*
• take part in, enrol in, sign up for, go in for, join in, participate in, volunteer for
OPPOSITE withdraw from

enterprise NOUN
❶ *She showed **enterprise** in starting her own business.*
• drive, initiative
❷ *The expedition was a very rash **enterprise**.*
• adventure, operation, project, undertaking, venture, effort, mission

entertain VERB
❶ *The storyteller **entertained** us with scary ghost stories.*
• amuse, divert, keep amused, make you laugh, please, cheer up
OPPOSITE bore
❷ *You can **entertain** friends in the private dining room.*
• receive, welcome, cater for, give hospitality to

entertainer NOUN

> **WORD WEB**
>
> **SOME KINDS OF ENTERTAINER:**
>
> • acrobat, actor, actress, ballet dancer, busker, clown, comedian or comic, conjuror, dancer, escape artist or escapologist, juggler, magician, mime artist, musician, singer, street entertainer, stuntman or stuntwoman, trapeze artist, TV presenter, ventriloquist, vlogger
> A famous entertainer is a **star** or **superstar**.
> *for types of musician see* **music**
>
> **ENTERTAINERS IN THE PAST:**
>
> • fool or jester, gladiator, minstrel

entertainment NOUN
*Our hosts had arranged some **entertainment** for us.*
• amusements, recreation, diversions, enjoyment, fun, pastimes

enthusiasm NOUN
❶ *The young athletes showed plenty of **enthusiasm**.*
• keenness, commitment, ambition, drive, zeal, zest
OPPOSITE apathy
❷ *Collecting fossils is one of my **enthusiasms**.*
• interest, passion, pastime, hobby, craze, diversion, fad

enthusiast NOUN
*My family are football **enthusiasts**.*
• fan, fanatic, devotee, lover, supporter, addict
(informal) freak, nut

enthusiastic ADJECTIVE
❶ *He's an **enthusiastic** supporter of our local team.*
• keen, passionate, avid, devoted, energetic, fervent, zealous

a b c d e f g h i j k l m n o p q r s t u v w x y z

A
B
C
D
E
F
G
H
I
J
K
L
M
N
O
P
Q
R
S
T
U
V
W
X
Y
Z

❷ *The audience burst into* **enthusiastic** *applause.*
• eager, excited, lively, vigorous, exuberant, hearty
OPPOSITES unenthusiastic, apathetic

entire *ADJECTIVE*
My friends spent the **entire** *evening watching television.*
• complete, whole, total, full

entirely *ADVERB*
I'm not **entirely** *sure that I agree with you.*
• completely, absolutely, wholly, totally, utterly, fully, perfectly, quite

entitle *VERB*
The voucher **entitles** *you to claim a discount.*
• permit, allow, enable, authorize

entrance *NOUN (say* en-transs*)*
❶ *Please pay at the* **entrance**.
• entry, way in, access, door, gate
When you go through the entrance to a building, you cross the **threshold**.
❷ *I'll meet you in the* **entrance**.
• entrance hall, foyer, lobby, porch
❸ *Her sudden* **entrance** *took everyone by surprise.*
• entry, arrival, appearance
OPPOSITE exit

entrance *VERB (say* en-transs*)*
The crowd were **entranced** *by the fireworks display.*
• charm, delight, please, enchant

entrant *NOUN*
A prize will be awarded to the winning **entrant**.
• contestant, competitor, contender, candidate, participant

entry *NOUN*
❶ *A van was blocking the* **entry** *to the school.*
• way in, entrance, access, door, gate
❷ *Every evening I write an* **entry** *in my diary.*
• item, note

envelop *VERB*
Mist **enveloped** *the top of the mountain.*
• cover, hide, mask, conceal

envious *ADJECTIVE*
He was **envious** *of his brother's success.*
• jealous, resentful

environment *NOUN*
Animals should live in their natural **environment**, *not in cages.*
• habitat, surroundings, setting, conditions, situation
➤ **the environment**
We must do all we can to protect the **environment**.
• the natural world, nature, the earth, the world

envy *NOUN*
I didn't feel any **envy**, *even when I saw how rich she was.*
• jealousy, resentment, bitterness
envy *VERB*
We **envied** *their expensive holiday.*
• be jealous of, begrudge, grudge, resent

episode *NOUN*
❶ *I paid for the broken window, and I want to forget the whole* **episode**.
• event, incident, experience
❷ *I missed last night's* **episode** *of 'Dr Who'.*
• instalment, part

equal *ADJECTIVE*
❶ *Give everyone an* **equal** *amount.*
• equivalent, identical, matching, similar, corresponding, fair
❷ *The scores were* **equal** *at half-time.*
• even, level, the same, square
To make the scores equal is to **equalize**.

equip *VERB*
All the bedrooms are **equipped** *with a colour television.*
• provide, supply
To equip soldiers with weapons is to **arm** them.
To equip a room with furniture is to **furnish** it.

equipment NOUN
The shed is full of gardening **equipment**.
• apparatus, gear, kit, tackle, tools, implements, instruments, materials, machinery, paraphernalia, things
Computing equipment is **hardware**.

equivalent ADJECTIVE
A metre is **equivalent** to a hundred centimetres.
• matching, similar, corresponding, identical, the same as

era NOUN
Shakespeare lived in the Elizabethan **era**.
• age, period, time, epoch

erase VERB
I **erased** the writing on the blackboard.
• delete, remove, rub out, wipe out, get rid of

erect ADJECTIVE
The dog stood with its ears **erect**.
• upright, vertical, perpendicular
erect VERB
The town hall was **erected** in 1890.
• build, construct, raise, put up, set up
To erect a tent is to **pitch** it.

erode VERB
The flood water **eroded** the river bank.
• wear away, eat away, destroy

errand NOUN
I went on an **errand** to the corner shop.
• job, task, assignment, trip, journey

erratic ADJECTIVE
The team's performance has been **erratic** this season.
• inconsistent, irregular, uneven, variable, changeable, fluctuating, unpredictable
OPPOSITE consistent

error NOUN
❶ The accident was the result of an **error** by the driver.
• mistake, fault, lapse, blunder

❷ I think there is an **error** in your argument.
• flaw, inaccuracy, misunderstanding, inconsistency
The error of leaving something out is an **omission** or **oversight**.

erupt VERB
Smoke began to **erupt** from the volcano.
• be discharged, be emitted, pour out, issue, spout, gush, spurt, belch

escape VERB
❶ Why did you let him **escape**?
• get away, get out, run away, break free, break out
(informal) give you the slip
A performer who escapes from chains, etc. is an **escape artist** or **escapologist**.
❷ She always **escapes** the nasty jobs.
• avoid, get out of, evade, dodge, shirk
escape NOUN
❶ The prisoner's **escape** was filmed by security cameras.
• getaway, breakout, flight
❷ The explosion was caused by an **escape** of gas.
• leak, leakage, seepage

escort NOUN
❶ The president always has an **escort** to protect him.
• bodyguard, guard
❷ The actor appeared with their **escort**.
• companion, partner
escort VERB
The queen was **escorted** by a number of attendants.
• accompany, guard, protect, look after

especially ADVERB
I like apple pie, **especially** with ice cream.
• above all, chiefly, most of all

espionage NOUN
see **spy**

a
b
c
d
e
f
g
h
i
j
k
l
m
n
o
p
q
r
s
t
u
v
w
x
y
z

A
B
C
D
E
F
G
H
I
J
K
L
M
N
O
P
Q
R
S
T
U
V
W
X
Y
Z

essential *ADJECTIVE*
Fruit and vegetables are an **essential** *part of our diet.*
• important, necessary, basic, vital, principal, fundamental, chief, crucial, indispensable

establish *VERB*
❶ *He plans to* **establish** *a new business.*
• set up, start, begin, create, found, initiate, institute, introduce, launch, originate
❷ *The police have not managed to* **establish** *their guilt.*
• prove, show to be true, confirm, verify

estate *NOUN*
❶ *There's a new housing* **estate** *near our school.*
• area, development, scheme
❷ *The castle is sited on a large* **estate**.
• land, grounds
❸ *The millionaire left her* **estate** *to charity.*
• property, fortune, wealth, possessions

estimate *NOUN*
What is your **estimate** *of how much it will cost?*
• assessment, calculation, evaluation, guess, judgement, opinion
An official estimate of the value of something is a **valuation**.
An official estimate of what a job is going to cost is a **quotation** or tender.

estimate *VERB*
The builders **estimate** *that the work will take four months.*
• calculate, assess, work out, compute, count up, evaluate, judge, reckon, think out

eternal *ADJECTIVE*
❶ *The magic fountain was said to give* **eternal** *youth.*
• everlasting, infinite, lasting, unending, timeless
Beings with eternal life are said to be **immortal**.
❷ *I'm sick of your* **eternal** *quarrelling!*
• constant, continual, never-ending, non-stop, persistent, perpetual, endless, ceaseless, incessant, unceasing

evacuate *VERB*
❶ *The firefighters* **evacuated** *everyone from the building.*
• remove, clear, send away, move out
❷ *We were told to* **evacuate** *the building.*
• leave, quit, abandon, withdraw from, empty, vacate

evade *VERB*
Don't try to **evade** *your responsibilities.*
• avoid, dodge, shirk, escape from, steer clear of, fend off
OPPOSITE confront

even *ADJECTIVE*
❶ *You need an* **even** *surface for ice skating.*
• level, flat, smooth, straight
OPPOSITE uneven
❷ *The runners kept up an* **even** *pace.*
• regular, steady, unvarying, rhythmical, monotonous
OPPOSITE irregular
❸ *Mrs Torres has an* **even** *temper.*
• calm, cool, placid, unexcitable
OPPOSITE excitable
❹ *The scores were* **even** *at half time.*
• equal, level, matching, identical, the same, square
OPPOSITE different
❺ *The numbers 2, 4 and 6 are* **even** *numbers.*
OPPOSITE odd

even *VERB*
➤ **to even something up**
If you join their team, that will **even up** *the numbers.*
• equalize, level, balance, match, square

evening *NOUN*
Towards **evening** *it clouded over and began to rain.*
• dusk, nightfall, sundown, sunset, twilight

event *NOUN*
❶ *Her autobiography describes the main* **events** *of her life.*
• happening, incident, occurrence

❷ *There was an **event** to mark the launch of the new film.*
• function, occasion, ceremony, entertainment, party, reception
❸ *The Paralympics is an important sporting event.*
• competition, contest, fixture, engagement, meeting, game, match, tournament

eventful *ADJECTIVE*
*We had an **eventful** journey.*
• interesting, exciting, busy, lively, active
OPPOSITES uneventful, dull

eventual *ADJECTIVE*
*We were happy with our **eventual** score.*
• final, ultimate, resulting, overall, ensuing

eventually *ADVERB*
*The journey took ages, but **eventually** we arrived safely.*
• finally, at last, in the end, ultimately

evergreen *ADJECTIVE*
*Most pine trees are **evergreen**.*
OPPOSITE deciduous

everyday *ADJECTIVE*
*Don't dress up—just wear your **everyday** clothes.*
• normal, ordinary, usual, regular, customary

evidence *NOUN*
*This piece of paper is **evidence** that he is lying.*
• proof, confirmation
Evidence that someone accused of a crime was not there when the crime was committed is an **alibi**.
Evidence given in a law court is a **testimony**.
To give evidence in court is to **testify**.

evident *ADJECTIVE*
*It was **evident** that someone had been in the room.*
• clear, obvious, apparent, plain, certain, unmistakable, undeniable, noticeable, perceptible, visible

evidently *ADVERB*
*The woman was **evidently** upset.*
• clearly, obviously, apparently, plainly, undoubtedly

evil *ADJECTIVE*
❶ *The charm was used to keep away **evil** spirits.*
• malevolent, fiendish, diabolical
❷ *Who would do such an **evil** deed?*
• wicked, immoral, cruel, sinful, villainous, malicious, foul, hateful, vile
OPPOSITE good

evil *NOUN*
❶ *Heroes fight against **evil**.*
• wickedness, badness, wrongdoing, sin, immorality, villainy, malevolence, malice
❷ *The people had to endure the **evils** of famine and drought.*
• disaster, misfortune, suffering, pain, affliction, curse

evolve *VERB*
*Life **evolved** on Earth over millions of years.*
• develop, grow, progress, emerge, mature

exact *ADJECTIVE*
❶ *I gave the police an **exact** account of what happened.*
• accurate, precise, correct, true, faithful, detailed, meticulous, strict
❷ *Is this an **exact** copy of the original document?*
• identical, perfect, indistinguishable
OPPOSITE inaccurate

exactly *ADVERB*
*At what time **exactly** did you leave the house?*
• precisely, specifically, accurately, correctly, strictly
OPPOSITES roughly, inaccurately
A phrase meaning 'exactly on time' is to be **on the dot**.

exaggerate *VERB*
*He tends to **exaggerate** his problems.*
• magnify, inflate, overdo, make too much of
OPPOSITE minimize

a b c d e f g h i j k l m n o p q r s t u v w x y z

A
B
C
D
E
F
G
H
I
J
K
L
M
N
O
P
Q
R
S
T
U
V
W
X
Y
Z

examination NOUN
❶ *The results of the examinations will be announced next month.*
• test, assessment
(informal) exam
❷ *The judge made a thorough examination of the facts.*
• investigation, inspection, study, analysis, survey, review, appraisal
❸ *He was sent to hospital for an examination.*
• check-up
A medical examination of a dead person is a **post-mortem**.

examine VERB
❶ *The judge examined the evidence.*
• inspect, study, investigate, analyse, look closely at, pore over, scrutinize, probe, survey, review, weigh up, sift
❷ *They were examined on their knowledge of history.*
• question, interrogate, quiz
To examine someone rigorously is to **grill** them.

example NOUN
❶ *Give me an example of what you mean.*
• instance, illustration, sample, specimen, case
❷ *She's an example to us all.*
• model, ideal

exasperate VERB
Her constant questions began to exasperate me.
• annoy, irritate, upset, frustrate, anger, madden, vex

exceed VERB
He exceeded the previous race record by two seconds.
• beat, better, outdo, pass, surpass, go over

excel VERB
She's a good all-round athlete, but she excels at sprinting.
• do best, stand out, shine

excellent ADJECTIVE
That's an excellent idea!
• first-class, first-rate, outstanding, exceptional, remarkable, tremendous, wonderful, superb, great, fine, marvellous, superior, superlative, top-notch
(informal) brilliant, fantastic, terrific, fabulous, sensational, super
for other ways to describe something good
see **good**
(OPPOSITES) bad, awful, second-rate

except PREPOSITION
Everyone got a prize except me.
• apart from, but, with the exception of, excluding

exception NOUN
➤ **to take exception to something**
They took exception to the way they were treated by the authorities.
• dislike, object to, complain about, disapprove of, be upset by

exceptional ADJECTIVE
It is exceptional to have such cold weather in June.
• unusual, extraordinary, uncommon, unexpected, amazing, rare, odd, peculiar, strange, surprising, special, abnormal, phenomenal, unheard-of, bizarre
(OPPOSITES) normal, usual

excerpt NOUN
We recited an excerpt from the poem.
• extract, passage, part, section
A short excerpt is a **quotation**.
The most interesting excerpts from something are the **highlights**.
Excerpts from a film are **clips**.

excess NOUN
If there is an excess of something, so that it is hard to sell it, there is a **glut**.
When a business has an excess of income over its expenses, it has a **profit** or a **surplus**.

excessive ADJECTIVE
❶ *I think their enthusiasm for football is excessive.*
• extreme, exaggerated, fanatical
❷ *We prepared excessive amounts of food for the party.*
• unnecessary, needless, superfluous, extravagant, wasteful, unreasonable

exchange VERB
The shop will exchange faulty goods.
• change, replace
To exchange goods for other goods without using money is to **barter.**
To exchange an old thing for part of the cost of a new one is to **trade** it **in.**
To exchange things with your friends is to **swap** them.
To exchange players for other players in a football match, etc., is to **substitute** them.

excite VERB
The prospect of going to Italy excited Miss MacKillop.
• thrill, enthuse, stimulate, electrify, rouse, stir up
OPPOSITE calm

excited ADJECTIVE
On Christmas Eve, my little brother was too excited to sleep.
• agitated, lively, enthusiastic, exuberant, thrilled, elated, eager, animated
OPPOSITE calm

excitement NOUN
I could hardly bear the excitement!
• suspense, tension, drama, thrill

exciting ADJECTIVE
The last minutes of the match were the most exciting of all!
• dramatic, eventful, thrilling, gripping, sensational, stirring, rousing, stimulating, electrifying
OPPOSITES dull, boring

exclaim VERB
'Get out of my house!' she exclaimed.
• call, shout, cry out, yell
for other ways to say something see **say**

exclamation NOUN
Holmes gave an exclamation of surprise.
• cry, shout, yell
An impolite exclamation is an **oath** or **swear** word.

WRITING TIPS

SOMEONE WHO IS ANGRY OR ANNOYED MIGHT SAY:

• blast, bother, drat, fiddlesticks
'Fiddlesticks!' said Merlin. 'I've forgotten the spell!'

SOMEONE WHO IS SURPRISED OR ALARMED MIGHT SAY:

• blimey, crikey, crumbs, golly, goodness me, good gracious, good heavens, gosh, my goodness, my word, yikes
My goodness!' said Commander Pott anxiously. 'Now we've had it!'–CHITTY CHITTY BANG BANG, Ian Fleming

exclude VERB
❶ *Adults are excluded from joining our club.*
• ban, bar, prohibit, keep out, banish, reject
❷ *He had to exclude dairy products from his diet.*
• leave out, omit
OPPOSITE include

excluding PREPOSITION
The gardens are open every day excluding Christmas.
• except, except for, with the exception of, apart from, bar

exclusive ADJECTIVE
They stayed at a very exclusive hotel.
• select, private, snobbish, upmarket
(informal) posh, fancy

a b c d e f g h i j k l m n o p q r s t u v w x y z

A
B
C
D
E
F
G
H
I
J
K
L
M
N
O
P
Q
R
S
T
U
V
W
X
Y
Z

excursion NOUN
We went on an *excursion* to the seaside.
• trip, journey, outing, expedition, jaunt

excuse NOUN
What is your *excuse* for being so late?
• reason, explanation, defence, justification

excuse VERB
I can't *excuse* this bad behaviour.
• forgive, overlook, pardon
OPPOSITE punish

➤ **to be excused something**
May I *be excused* swimming?
• be exempt from, be let off, be released from

execute VERB
❶ In some countries, criminals may still be *executed*.
• put to death
Someone who executes people is an executioner.
To execute someone unofficially without a proper trial is to **lynch** them.
❷ She *executed* a perfect somersault.
• perform, carry out, produce, complete, accomplish

exercise NOUN
❶ *Exercise* helps to keep you fit.
• physical activity, working out, keep-fit, training
❷ Doing *exercises* will improve your guitar playing.
• practice, training, drill

exercise VERB
❶ If you *exercise* regularly, you will keep fit.
• keep fit, train, exert yourself
❷ I sometimes *exercise* our neighbour's dog.
• take for a walk, take out, walk
❸ We must *exercise* patience.
• show, use, apply, display, employ

exert VERB
He *exerted* all his strength to lift the box.
• use, apply, employ

exertion NOUN
The *exertion* of climbing the stairs made him sweat.
• effort, hard work, labour, toil

exhale VERB
The doctor asked me to *exhale* slowly.
• breathe out
OPPOSITE inhale

exhaust NOUN
The *exhaust* from cars damages the environment.
• fumes, smoke, emissions, gases

exhaust VERB
❶ The steep climb up the hill *exhausted* me.
• tire, wear out
❷ We had *exhausted* our food supply by midday.
• finish, go through, use up, consume
(informal) polish off

exhausted ADJECTIVE
After a hard race, we lay *exhausted* on the grass.
• tired, weary, worn out, fatigued, breathless, gasping, panting
(informal) all in, done in, bushed, zonked

exhausting ADJECTIVE
Digging the garden is *exhausting* work.
• tiring, demanding, hard, laborious, strenuous, difficult, gruelling, wearisome
OPPOSITE easy

exhaustion NOUN
We were overcome by sheer *exhaustion*.
• tiredness, fatigue, weariness, weakness

exhibit *VERB*
❶ *Her paintings were exhibited in galleries all over South America.*
• display, show, present, put up, set up, arrange
❷ *He was exhibiting signs of anxiety.*
• show, demonstrate, reveal
OPPOSITE hide

exhibition *NOUN*
We went to see an exhibition of paintings by Picasso.
• display, show

exile *VERB*
As a result of the war, many people were exiled from their own country.
• banish, expel, drive out, deport, eject, send away

exile *NOUN*
He returned to his country after 24 years of exile.
• banishment, expulsion, deportation
A person who has been exiled is an **exile** or a **refugee**.

exist *VERB*
❶ *Some people claim that ghosts actually exist.*
• be real, occur
❷ *We can't exist without food.*
• live, remain alive, survive, keep going, last, continue, endure

existence *NOUN*
❶ *Do you believe in the existence of ghosts?*
• reality
❷ *Most plants depend on sunlight for their existence.*
• life, survival

existing *ADJECTIVE*
❶ *There are only two existing species of elephants.*
• surviving, living, remaining
❷ *Next year, the existing rules will be replaced by new ones.*
• present, current

exit *NOUN*
❶ *I'll wait for you by the exit.*
• door, way out, doorway, gate, barrier
OPPOSITE entrance
❷ *The robbers made a hurried exit.*
• departure
OPPOSITE entrance

exit *VERB*
The actors exited from the left of the stage.
• go out, leave, depart, withdraw
OPPOSITE enter

exotic *ADJECTIVE*
I have travelled to many exotic places.
• remote, foreign, alien, different, exciting, romantic, strange, unfamiliar, wonderful
OPPOSITE familiar

expand *VERB*
Their computer business is expanding rapidly.
• increase, enlarge, extend, build up, develop, make bigger
To become larger is to **grow** or **swell**.
To become wider is to **broaden**, **thicken** or **widen**.
To become longer is to **extend**, **lengthen** or **stretch**.
OPPOSITES contract, reduce

expanse *NOUN*
The explorers crossed a large expanse of desert.
• area, stretch, tract
An expanse of water or ice is a **sheet**.

expect *VERB*
❶ *I expect that it will rain today.*
• anticipate, imagine, forecast, predict, foresee, prophesy
❷ *She expects me to do everything for her!*
• require, want, count on, insist on, demand
❸ *I expect they missed the bus.*
• believe, imagine, guess, suppose, presume, assume, think

a
b
c
d
e
f
g
h
i
j
k
l
m
n
o
p
q
r
s
t
u
v
w
x
y
z

A
B
C
D
E
F
G
H
I
J
K
L
M
N
O
P
Q
R
S
T
U
V
W
X
Y
Z

expedition *NOUN*
An expedition into unknown territory is an exploration.
An expedition to carry out a special task is a mission.
An expedition to find something is a **quest**.
An expedition to worship at a holy place is a pilgrimage.
An expedition to see or hunt wild animals is a safari.
see also **explorer**

expel *VERB*
❶ *A fan expels the stale air and fumes.*
• send out, force out
❷ *They were expelled from school.*
• dismiss, ban, remove, throw out, send away
To expel someone from their home is to **eject** or **evict** them.
To expel someone from their country is to **banish** or **exile** them.
To expel evil spirits is to **exorcise** them.

expense *NOUN*
She was worried about the expense of the holiday.
• cost, charges, expenditure

expensive *ADJECTIVE*
Houses are very expensive in this area.
• dear, costly
OPPOSITE cheap

experience *NOUN*
❶ *Have you had any experience of singing in a choir?*
• practice, involvement, participation
❷ *I had an unusual experience today.*
• happening, event, occurrence, incident
An exciting experience is an **adventure**.
An unpleasant experience is an **ordeal**.

experienced *ADJECTIVE*
He's an experienced actor who has been in many films.
• skilled, qualified, expert, knowledgeable, trained, professional
OPPOSITE inexperienced

experiment *NOUN*
We carried out a scientific experiment.
• test, trial
A series of experiments is **research** or an investigation.

experiment *VERB*
They experimented to see if their robot would work.
• do tests
To experiment on or with something is to **test** it or **try it out.**

expert *NOUN*
She's an expert at chess.
• specialist, authority, genius, wizard
(informal) dab hand, geek, whizz

expert *ADJECTIVE*
Only an expert sailor could cross the ocean.
• brilliant, capable, clever, competent, experienced, knowledgeable, professional, proficient, qualified, skilful, skilled, specialized, trained
OPPOSITES amateur, unskilful

expertise *NOUN*
Do you have the expertise to restore the painting?
• skill, ability, competence, knowledge, know-how, training

expire *VERB*
❶ *The television licence expires next month.*
• finish, run out, come to an end, become invalid
❷ *The animal expired before the vet arrived.*
• die, pass away

explain *VERB*
❶ *The doctor explained the procedure carefully.*
• make clear, give an explanation of, clarify, describe
❷ *Can you explain your strange behaviour?*
• give reasons for, account for, excuse, make excuses for, justify

explanation *NOUN*
❶ *They could find no* **explanation** *for the accident.*
• reason, excuse, justification
❷ *She gave a brief* **explanation** *of how her invention worked.*
• account, description, demonstration

explode *VERB*
❶ *The firework* **exploded** *with a bang.*
• blow up, make an explosion, go off, burst, shatter
❷ *The slightest movement might* **explode** *the bomb.*
• detonate, set off

exploit *NOUN*
The book describes her **exploits** *as a secret agent.*
• adventure, deed, feat, venture, escapade

exploit *VERB*
The council plans to **exploit** *the area as a tourist attraction.*
• make use of, take advantage of, use, develop, profit from
(informal) cash in on

explore *VERB*
❶ *The spacecraft will* **explore** *the solar system.*
• search, survey, travel through, probe
❷ *We must* **explore** *all the possibilities.*
• examine, inspect, investigate, look into, research, analyse, scrutinize

explorer *NOUN*
The **explorers** *were looking for the legendary Lost City.*
• traveller, voyager, discoverer, wanderer

WORD WEB

THINGS AN EXPLORER MIGHT FIND:

• catacombs, cave, cavern, chest, hieroglyphics, inscription, labyrinth, maze, mummy, parchment, pyramid, riddle, sarcophagus, seal, secret passage, skeleton, stone tablet, temple, tomb, treasure, tunnel, underground chamber

THINGS AN EXPLORER MIGHT USE OR CARRY:

• binoculars, chart, compass, machete, map, penknife, rope, rucksack, telescope, tent, torch, water bottle
Stella checked and re-checked her pockets and her explorer's bag ... to make sure she had her telescope, compass, magnifying glass, pocket map, emergency mint cake, matches and ball of string.—THE POLAR BEAR EXPLORERS' CLUB, Alex Bell
for explorers in polar regions see **polar**
for explorers in space see **astronaut**

explosion *NOUN*
The **explosion** *rattled the windows.*
• blast, bang
An explosion from a volcano is an **eruption**.
An explosion of laughter is an **outburst**.
The sound of a gun going off is a **report**.

export *VERB*
The factory **exports** *most of the cars it makes.*
• sell abroad, send abroad, ship overseas
 OPPOSITE import

expose *VERB*
❶ *He yawned,* **exposing** *a set of white teeth.*
• uncover
❷ *The truth about his past was* **exposed** *in the newspaper.*
• make known, publish, reveal, disclose

express *VERB*
He's always quick to **express** *his opinions.*
• voice, communicate, convey, put into words, phrase
To express yourself by word of mouth is to **speak**.
To express yourself on paper is to **write**.
To express your feelings forcefully is to **give vent** to them.

A B C D E F G H I J K L M N O P Q R S T U V W X Y Z

expression *NOUN*
❶ *'Tickled pink' is a colloquial expression.*
• phrase, saying, term, wording
An expression that people use too much is a cliché.
❷ *Did you see her expression when I told her the news?*
• look, appearance, countenance, face
❸ *Rhona plays the piano with great expression.*
• feeling, emotion, sympathy, understanding

WORD WEB

EXPRESSIONS YOU MIGHT SEE ON A FACE:

• beam, frown, glare, glower, grimace, grin, leer, long face, pout, scowl, smile, smirk, sneer, wide-eyed look, wince, yawn
see also **face**
Mr Coombes was looking grim. His hammy pink face had taken on that dangerous scowl which only appeared when he was extremely cross and somebody was for the high-jump.
—BOY, Roald Dahl

---

expressive *ADJECTIVE*
❶ *The old wizard gave me an expressive look.*
• meaningful, significant, revealing, telling
❷ *An actor needs to have an expressive voice.*
• lively, varied, eloquent
OPPOSITES expressionless, flat

exquisite *ADJECTIVE*
There was some exquisite lace on the collar.
• beautiful, fine, delicate, intricate, dainty

extend *VERB*
❶ *Stopping for lunch will extend our journey by an hour.*
• lengthen, make longer, prolong, delay, draw out
OPPOSITE shorten
❷ *They have recently extended their website.*
• enlarge, expand, increase, build up, develop, add to, widen the scope of
OPPOSITE reduce

❸ *He sat back and extended his legs.*
• stretch out, hold out, put out, reach out, stick out
❹ *We extended a warm welcome to the visitors.*
• give, offer

extension *NOUN*
They are building an extension to the runway.
• continuation, addition

extensive *ADJECTIVE*
The palace gardens cover an extensive area.
• big, large, broad, wide, spread out
OPPOSITE small

extent *NOUN*
❶ *The map shows the extent of the island.*
• area, dimensions, expanse, spread, breadth, length, limits, measurement
❷ *After the storm we went out to see the extent of the damage.*
• amount, degree, level, size, scope, magnitude, range

exterior *NOUN*
She painted the exterior of her house.
• outside
OPPOSITE interior

exterminate *VERB*
They used poison to exterminate the rats.
• destroy, kill, get rid of, annihilate, wipe out

external *ADJECTIVE*
In external appearance, the house was rather gloomy.
• exterior, outside, outer
OPPOSITE internal

extinct *ADJECTIVE*
An extinct species is one that has **died out** or **vanished**.
An extinct volcano is an **inactive** volcano.

extinguish *VERB*
We extinguished the campfire before we went to bed.
• put out, quench, smother
OPPOSITE ignite

extra *ADJECTIVE*
❶ *There is an extra charge for taking your bike on the train.*
• additional, further, added, supplementary, excess
❷ *There is extra food in the kitchen if you need it.*
• more, spare, surplus, reserve

extract *NOUN*
There's an extract from the new Jacqueline Wilson book in the magazine.
• excerpt, passage, part, section
A short extract is a **quotation.**
Especially interesting extracts from something are the **highlights.**
An extract from a newspaper is a **cutting.**
An extract from a film is a **clip.**

extract *VERB*
❶ *The dentist decided to extract my tooth.*
• pull out, remove, take out, draw out, withdraw
(informal) whip out
❷ *The following passages are extracted from the book.*
• derive, get, gather, obtain, quote, select

extraordinary *ADJECTIVE*
The astronauts saw many extraordinary sights.
• amazing, astonishing, remarkable, outstanding, exceptional, incredible, fantastic, marvellous, miraculous, phenomenal, rare, special, strange, surprising, unheard of, unusual, weird, wonderful, abnormal, curious
OPPOSITE ordinary

extravagant *ADJECTIVE*
He held a large, extravagant party for all his friends.
• expensive, lavish, wasteful
Someone who spends money in an extravagant way is a **spendthrift.**
OPPOSITE modest

extreme *ADJECTIVE*
❶ *Polar bears can withstand extreme cold.*
• great, intense, severe, acute, excessive
❷ *She lives on the extreme edge of the town.*
• farthest, furthest

eye *NOUN*

WORD WEB

PARTS OF YOUR EYE:

• cornea, eyeball, eyebrow, eyelash, eyelid, iris, lens, pupil, retina
A person who tests your eyesight is an **optician.**
A word meaning 'to do with eyes' is **optical.**
A person with good eyesight is said to have **eyes like a hawk** or to be **eagle-eyed.**

WRITING TIPS

You can use these words to describe **eyes:**

• beady, bulbous, bulging, deep-set, glassy, heavy-lidded, hooded, protuberant, saucer-like, sunken; cloudy, misty, moist, piercing, steely, tearful, watery
Bod did not look up. If he had, he would have seen a pair of watery blue eyes watching him intently from a bedroom window.
—THE GRAVEYARD BOOK, Neil Gaiman

eye *VERB*
The dog eyed the sausages hungrily.
• look at, regard, stare at, watch, gaze at, contemplate

a
b
c
d
e
f
g
h
i
j
k
l
m
n
o
p
q
r
s
t
u
v
w
x
y
z

Ff

A B C D E F G H I J K L M N O P Q R S T U V W X Y Z

fabric *NOUN*
This fabric will make a lovely dress for my doll.
• cloth, material, stuff
A plural word for different kinds of fabric is textiles.

WORD WEB

SOME TYPES OF FABRIC:

• canvas, chiffon, corduroy, cotton, damask, denim, felt, flannel, gingham, jersey, linen, *(trademark)* Lycra, muslin, nylon, polyester, rayon, satin, silk, taffeta, tweed, velvet, wool

fabulous *ADJECTIVE*
❶ *(informal) We had a fabulous time at the party.*
• excellent, first-class, marvellous, outstanding, superb, tremendous, wonderful *(informal)* brilliant, fantastic, smashing
❷ *Dragons are fabulous creatures.*
• fictitious, imaginary, legendary, mythical

face *NOUN*
❶ *We saw the anger in the warrior's face.*
• expression, features, look, countenance
❷ *The face of the clock had been smashed.*
• front
❸ *A cube has six faces.*
• side, surface

WRITING TIPS

You can use these words to describe a **face**:

TO DESCRIBE ITS SHAPE:

• flat, long, oval, round, rounded; lantern-jawed, square-jawed

TO DESCRIBE ITS FEATURES:

• chiselled, chubby, craggy, delicate, fine, gaunt, haggard, hollow, pinched, prominent, puffy, skeletal, sunken, thin
*Their faces were **gaunt** and **pinched** from hunger.*

TO DESCRIBE ITS SKIN OR COLOUR:

• clear, dark, fair, flushed, freckled, fresh, glowing, healthy, rosy, ruddy, tanned; ashen, grey, leaden, pale, pallid, pasty, sallow, sickly, unhealthy, wan; flabby, saggy, shrivelled, weather-beaten, wizened, wrinkled, wrinkly; disfigured, pimply, pock-marked, scarred, spotty, unshaven
Doc Spencer ... was a tiny man with tiny hands and feet and a tiny round face. The face was as brown and wrinkled as a shrivelled apple.–
DANNY THE CHAMPION OF THE WORLD, Roald Dahl

TO DESCRIBE THE LOOK ON A FACE:

• cheeky, cheerful, radiant, sunny; grave, grim, serious; sulky, sullen, surly; blank, deadpan, faceless, impassive, unmoving, vacant
*The guard stared ahead, his face **unmoving**.*
see also **expression**
for parts of a face see **eye** and **nose**

face *VERB*
❶ *Stand and face your partner.*
• be opposite to, look towards
❷ *The astronauts had to face many dangers.*
• cope with, deal with, face up to, stand up to, tackle, meet, encounter, confront
OPPOSITE avoid

fact *NOUN*
It is a fact that dodos are now extinct.
• reality, truth, certainty
OPPOSITE fiction
➤ **the facts**
*The detective considered **the facts** in the case.*
• details, particulars, information, data
Facts which are useful in trying to prove something are **evidence**.
Facts expressed as numbers are **statistics**.

factual ADJECTIVE
*Anne Frank wrote a **factual** account of her life during the war*
• real, true, truthful, accurate, authentic, faithful, genuine, objective, reliable
A film or story based on a person's life is **biographical**.
A film or story based on history is **historical**.
A film telling you about real events is a **documentary**.
OPPOSITES made-up, fictional

fade VERB
❶ *Sunlight has **faded** the curtains.*
• make paler, bleach, blanch, whiten, dim
OPPOSITE brighten
❷ *Those flowers will **fade** in a few days.*
• wither, wilt, droop, flag, shrivel
OPPOSITE flourish
❸ *Gradually, the light began to **fade**.*
• weaken, decline, diminish, dwindle, fail, wane, disappear, melt away, vanish
OPPOSITE increase

fail VERB
❶ *Their plan to steal the crown jewels **failed** miserably.*
• be unsuccessful, go wrong, fall through, founder, come to grief, miscarry
(informal) flop, bomb
OPPOSITE succeed
❷ *The rocket engine **failed** before take-off.*
• break down, cut out, give up, stop working
❸ *By late afternoon, the light had begun to **fail**.*
• weaken, decline, diminish, dwindle, fade, get worse, deteriorate
OPPOSITE improve
❹ *The professor **failed** to warn us of the danger.*
• neglect, forget, omit
OPPOSITE remember
❺ *I hope I don't **fail** my violin exam.*
(informal) flunk
OPPOSITE pass

failure NOUN
❶ *The storm caused a power **failure**.*
• breakdown, fault, malfunction, crash, loss, collapse, stoppage
❷ *Their attempt to reach the North Pole was a **failure**.*
• defeat, disappointment, disaster, fiasco
(informal) flop, washout
OPPOSITE success

faint ADJECTIVE
❶ *The details in the photograph are very **faint**.*
• faded, dim, unclear, indistinct, vague, blurred, hazy, pale, shadowy, misty
OPPOSITES clear, distinct
❷ *There was a **faint** smell of burning in the air.*
• delicate, slight
OPPOSITE strong
❸ *We heard a **faint** cry for help.*
• weak, low, muffled, distant, hushed, muted, soft, thin
OPPOSITE loud
❹ *Gordon was so hungry that he felt **faint**.*
• dizzy, giddy, light-headed, unsteady, weak, exhausted, feeble
(informal) woozy

faint VERB
*The explorers nearly **fainted** from exhaustion.*
• become unconscious, collapse, pass out, black out
(old use) swoon

fair ADJECTIVE
❶ *I think the referee made a **fair** decision.*
• just, proper, right, fair-minded, honest, honourable, impartial, unbiased, unprejudiced, disinterested
OPPOSITE unfair
❷ *The twins both have **fair** hair.*
• blond or blonde, light, golden, yellow
OPPOSITE dark
❸ *Our team has a **fair** chance of winning the cup.*
• reasonable, moderate, average, acceptable, adequate, satisfactory, passable, respectable, tolerable
❹ *The weather should be **fair** today.*
• dry, fine, sunny, bright, clear, cloudless, pleasant, favourable

a b c d e g h i j k l m n o p q r s t u v w x y z

A B C D E F G H I J K L M N O P Q R S T U V W X Y Z

fair NOUN
❶ *My sister won a teddy bear at the fair.*
• fairground, funfair, carnival, fete, gala
❷ *Our school is holding a book fair next week.*
• show, exhibition, display, market, bazaar

fairly ADVERB
❶ *The competition will be judged fairly.*
• honestly, properly, justly, impartially
❷ *The ground is still fairly wet.*
 I'm fairly certain that we are heading north.
• quite, rather, somewhat, slightly, moderately, up to a point, reasonably, tolerably
(informal) pretty

fairy NOUN

WORD WEB

THINGS A FAIRY MIGHT HAVE OR USE:

• fairy dust, lantern, wand, wings

A FAIRY'S WINGS OR CLOTHES MIGHT BE:

• diaphanous, feathery, glittering, glowing, gossamer, lustrous, sheer, sparkling, translucent, transparent

PLACES WHERE A FAIRY MIGHT LIVE:

• dell, glen, magic forest, magic tree, glade, mound, toadstool
Fairies, as envisaged by the Muggle, inhabit tiny dwellings fashioned out of flower petals, hollowed-out toadstools and similar.
—FANTASTIC BEASTS AND WHERE TO FIND THEM, J. K. Rowling

SOME CREATURES SIMILAR TO FAIRIES:

• brownie, elf, imp, leprechaun, nymph, pixie, sprite
for other creatures found in myths and legends see **myth**

faith NOUN
❶ *The acrobat had complete faith in his assistant.*
• belief, trust, confidence
OPPOSITE doubt

❷ *In our school, we have pupils of many different faiths.*
• religion, creed, doctrine, belief

faithful ADJECTIVE
❶ *My dog, Scruffy, is my faithful friend.*
• loyal, devoted, reliable, trustworthy, dependable, firm, constant, close
OPPOSITE unfaithful
❷ *Is this a faithful copy of the map?*
• accurate, exact, precise, true

fake NOUN
That's not a real Roman coin—it's a fake.
• copy, imitation, reproduction, replica, forgery
(informal) phoney
An event that is a fake is a **hoax**, **sham** or **simulation**.
A person who pretends to be another person is an **impostor**.

fake VERB
The spy tried to fake a foreign accent.
• imitate, copy, pretend, put on, reproduce, simulate
To fake someone's signature is to **forge** it.

fall VERB falls, falling, fell, fallen
❶ *The acrobat fell off a ladder and broke his leg.*
• tumble, topple, crash down, pitch, plunge
❷ *Snow was beginning to fall quite thickly.*
• drop, come down, descend, rain down, plummet
❸ *The level of the river had fallen since March.*
• go down, subside, recede, sink, ebb
❹ *The temperature in the cave fell to below freezing.*
• go down, become lower, decrease, decline, lessen, diminish, dwindle
❺ *After a long siege, the town fell to the enemy.*
• give in, surrender
❻ *Millions of soldiers fell in the war.*
• die, be killed, perish
(old use) be slain
❼ *We arrived at the camp as night was falling.*
• happen, occur, come, take place

➤ to fall in
The roof of the cabin fell in during the storm.
• cave in, collapse, give way

➤ to fall out
The twins are always falling out with each other.
• argue, disagree, quarrel, squabble, bicker

➤ to fall through
Our holiday plans have fallen through again.
• come to nothing, fail, collapse, founder

fall NOUN
❶ *Rukhia had a fall and cut her knee.*
• tumble
❷ *We noticed a sharp fall in the temperature.*
• drop, lowering
OPPOSITE rise
❸ *There has been a fall in the price of coffee.*
• decrease, reduction, decline
OPPOSITE increase
❹ *This is a story about the fall of Troy.*
• defeat, surrender

false ADJECTIVE
❶ *The smugglers gave us false information about the treasure.*
• wrong, incorrect, untrue, inaccurate, mistaken, erroneous, faulty, invalid, misleading, deceptive
OPPOSITE correct
❷ *The spy was travelling with a false passport.*
• fake, bogus, sham, counterfeit, forged
OPPOSITES genuine, authentic
❸ *Mrs Gummidge put in her false teeth.*
• artificial, imitation
OPPOSITES real, natural
❹ *The Green Knight turned out to be a false ally.*
• unfaithful, disloyal, unreliable, untrustworthy, deceitful, dishonest, treacherous
OPPOSITES faithful, loyal

falter VERB
❶ *The horse faltered as it approached the jump.*
• hesitate, flinch, hold back, pause, stumble, waver, get cold feet
To falter in your speech is to **stammer** or **stutter**.
❷ *The knight's courage began to falter.*
• weaken, diminish, flag, wane

fame NOUN
Her Olympic medal brought her international fame.
• celebrity, stardom, renown, glory, reputation, name, standing, stature, prominence
Fame that you get for doing something bad is **notoriety**.

familiar ADJECTIVE
❶ *Seagulls are a familiar sight on the beach.*
• common, everyday, normal, ordinary, usual, regular, customary, frequent, mundane, routine
OPPOSITE rare
❷ *It seems a bit familiar to call her by her first name.*
• informal, friendly, intimate, relaxed, close
OPPOSITES formal, unfriendly

➤ to be familiar with something
Are you familiar with the rules of chess?
• be acquainted with, be aware of, know

family NOUN
Some members of my family live in Hong Kong.
• relations, relatives

WORD WEB

An old-fashioned term for your family is your **kin**.
The official term for your closest relative is **next of kin**.
A group of related Scottish families is a **clan**.
A succession of people from the same powerful family is a **dynasty**.
In certain societies, a group of families living together is a **tribe**.
A single stage in a family is a **generation**.
The line of ancestors from which a family is descended is its **ancestry**.
A diagram showing how people in your family are related is a **family tree**.
The study of family history is **genealogy**.
A family of young birds is a **brood**.
A family of kittens or puppies is a **litter**.

a b c d e f g h i j k l m n o p q r s t u v w x y z

A B C D E **F** G H I J K L M N O P Q R S T U V W X Y Z

MEMBERS OF A FAMILY MAY INCLUDE:

• adopted child, aunt, brother, child, cousin, daughter, father, foster child, foster parent, grandchild, grandparent, guardian, husband, mother, nephew, niece, parent, partner, sister, son, spouse, stepbrother, stepchild, stepfather, stepmother, stepsister, uncle, ward, wife

famished ADJECTIVE
What's for dinner? I'm famished!
• hungry, ravenous, starving
If you are slightly hungry, you are peckish.

famous ADJECTIVE
Venus Williams is a very famous tennis player.
• well-known, celebrated, renowned, acclaimed, notable, prominent, distinguished, eminent
To be famous for doing something bad is to be **notorious**.
OPPOSITES unknown, obscure

fan NOUN
❶ *Can you switch on the fan, please?*
• ventilator, blower, extractor, air-conditioner
❷ *I'm a big fan of science fiction.*
• enthusiast, admirer, devotee, follower, supporter

fanatic NOUN
My sister is a rugby fanatic.
• enthusiast, addict, devotee
(informal) freak, nut

fanatical ADJECTIVE
We are fanatical about football.
• enthusiastic, extreme, fervent, over-enthusiastic, passionate, rabid, zealous
OPPOSITE moderate

fanciful ADJECTIVE
I like reading fanciful stories about dragons.
• fantastic, unrealistic, whimsical, imaginary, fictitious, made-up
OPPOSITE realistic

fancy ADJECTIVE
I used fancy writing for the cover.
• elaborate, decorative, ornamental, ornate
OPPOSITE plain

fancy VERB
❶ *What do you fancy to eat?*
• feel like, want, wish for, desire, prefer
❷ *I fancied I heard a noise downstairs.*
• imagine, think, believe, suppose

fantastic ADJECTIVE
❶ *The story is full of fantastic creatures.*
• fanciful, extraordinary, strange, odd, weird, outlandish, far-fetched, incredible, imaginative
OPPOSITE realistic
❷ *(informal) We had a fantastic time at camp.*
• excellent, first-class, outstanding, superb, wonderful, tremendous, marvellous
(informal) brilliant, fabulous, smashing

fantasy NOUN
Rosie had a fantasy about being a mermaid.
• dream, daydream, delusion, fancy

far ADJECTIVE
❶ *The castle stood in the far north of the country.*
• distant, faraway, remote
OPPOSITE nearby
❷ *The ferry took us to the far side of the river.*
• opposite, other
OPPOSITE near

fare NOUN
Do you have enough money for the bus fare?
• price, charge, cost, payment, fee

farm NOUN

WORD WEB

The formal word for farming is **agriculture**.
A farm which uses no artificial fertilizers or chemicals is an **organic farm**.
A very small farm is a **smallholding**.

A small farm growing fruit and vegetables is a **market garden**.
A small farm in Scotland is a **croft**.
A large cattle farm in America is a **ranch**.

FARM BUILDINGS:

• barn, byre or cowshed, dairy, farmhouse, granary, outhouse, pigsty, stable

OTHER PARTS OF A FARM:

• barnyard or farmyard, cattle pen, fields, haystack, meadow, paddock, pasture, sheep fold, silo

ITEMS OF FARM EQUIPMENT:

• baler, combine harvester, cultivator, drill, harrow, harvester, mower, planter, plough, tractor, trailer

PEOPLE WHO WORK ON A FARM:

• agricultural worker, *(old use)* dairymaid, farmer, farm labourer, shepherd, stockbreeder, tractor driver

SOME FARM ANIMALS:

• bull, bullock, chicken or hen, cow, duck, goat, goose, horse, pig, sheep, turkey
Birds kept on a farm are **poultry**.
Cows kept for milk or beef are **cattle**.
Farm animals in general are **livestock**.

farm *VERB*
The MacDonalds had **farmed** the land for centuries.
• cultivate, work, till, plough

fascinate *VERB*
We were **fascinated** by the inventor's workshop.
• interest, engross, captivate, enthral, absorb, beguile, entrance, attract, charm, enchant, delight
OPPOSITE bore

fashion *NOUN*
❶ The Martians behaved in a peculiar **fashion**.
• way, manner

❷ I dress according to the latest **fashion**.
• trend, vogue, craze, fad, style, look

fashionable *ADJECTIVE*
Zayn has a **fashionable** new hairstyle.
• stylish, chic, up-to-date, popular, elegant, smart
(informal) trendy, hip, in
OPPOSITE unfashionable, out-of-date

fast *ADJECTIVE*
The robbers made a **fast** exit when they heard us coming.
• quick, rapid, speedy, swift, brisk, hurried, hasty, high-speed, headlong, breakneck
(informal) nippy
OPPOSITE slow, unhurried
Something which goes faster than sound is **supersonic**.
A common simile is as fast as lightning.

fast *ADVERB*
❶ Mr Toad was driving too **fast** in his motor car.
• quickly, speedily, swiftly, rapidly, briskly
❷ The boat was stuck **fast** on the rocks.
• firmly, securely, tightly
❸ Be quiet! The baby is **fast** asleep.
• deeply, sound, soundly, completely

fasten *VERB*
❶ They **fastened** their ropes to the rock face.
• tie, fix, attach, connect, join, link, bind, hitch, clamp, pin, clip, tack, stick
To fasten a boat is to **anchor** or **moor** it.
To fasten an animal is to **tether** it.
❷ They **fastened** the gate with a heavy chain.
• secure, seal, lock, bolt, make fast

fat *ADJECTIVE*
❶ Your cat will get **fat** if you overfeed it.
• overweight, obese, chubby, plump, podgy, dumpy, flabby, portly, stout, round, rotund
❷ The witch opened a big, **fat** book of spells.
• thick, bulky, chunky, weighty, substantial
OPPOSITE thin

a b c d e f g h i j k l m n o p q r s t u v w x y z

A
B
C
D
E
F
G
H
I
J
K
L
M
N
O
P
Q
R
S
T
U
V
W
X
Y
Z

fatal *ADJECTIVE*
❶ *The knight delivered a fatal wound to her enemy.*
• deadly, lethal, mortal
A fatal illness is an **incurable** or **terminal** illness.
❷ *Leaving the door unlocked was a fatal mistake.*
• disastrous, catastrophic, dreadful, calamitous

fate *NOUN*
❶ *The shipwrecked crew were in the hands of fate.*
• fortune, destiny, providence, chance, luck
❷ *The prisoner met with a terrible fate.*
• death, end

fatigue *NOUN*
Some of the runners were overcome with fatigue.
• exhaustion, tiredness, weariness, weakness

fatigued *ADJECTIVE*
We were all fatigued by the time we got home.
• exhausted, tired, worn out, weary
(informal) all in

fault *NOUN*
❶ *This software has a fault in it.*
• defect, flaw, malfunction, snag, problem, weakness
❷ *It was my fault that we missed our bus.*
• responsibility, liability

faultless *ADJECTIVE*
The dancer's movements were faultless.
• perfect, flawless, ideal, impeccable
OPPOSITE imperfect

faulty *ADJECTIVE*
The TV was faulty, so we took it back to the shop.
• broken, not working, defective, out of order, unusable, damaged
OPPOSITE perfect

favour *NOUN*
❶ *I asked my friend to do me a favour.*
• good deed, good turn, kindness, service, courtesy
❷ *The captain's plan found favour with most of the crew.*
• approval, support, liking, goodwill
➤ **to be in favour of something**
We're all in favour of longer holidays.
• agree to, approve of, support, like the idea of

favour *VERB*
Do you favour the idea of free school meals?
• approve of, support, back, advocate, choose, like, opt for, prefer
(informal) fancy, go for
OPPOSITE oppose

favourable *ADJECTIVE*
❶ *The weather conditions are favourable for sailing.*
• advantageous, helpful, beneficial
OPPOSITE unfavourable
❷ *The film has received favourable reviews.*
• good, positive, complimentary, encouraging, enthusiastic, sympathetic, approving, agreeable
OPPOSITE critical, hostile, negative

favourite *ADJECTIVE*
What is your favourite book?
• best-loved, preferred, treasured, dearest, special, top

fear *NOUN*
When Garth heard the monster, he trembled with fear.
• fright, terror, horror, alarm, panic, dread, anxiety, apprehension, trepidation
OPPOSITE courage
A formal word for a special type of fear is **phobia**.
A fear of open spaces is **agoraphobia**.
A fear of spiders is **arachnophobia**.
A fear of enclosed spaces is **claustrophobia**.
A fear or dislike of foreigners is **xenophobia**.

fear *VERB*
❶ *My sister **fears** snakes and spiders.*
• be frightened of, be afraid of, be scared of, dread
❷ *I **fear** we may be too late.*
• suspect, expect, anticipate

fearful *ADJECTIVE*
❶ *The young warrior had a **fearful** look in his eyes.*
• frightened, scared, terrified, afraid, panicky, nervous, anxious, timid
OPPOSITE brave
❷ *The erupting volcano was a **fearful** sight.*
• frightening, terrifying, shocking, fearsome, ghastly, dreadful, appalling, terrible

fearless *ADJECTIVE*
*The **fearless** explorers entered the dark cave.*
• brave, courageous, daring, heroic, valiant, intrepid, plucky
OPPOSITE cowardly

fearsome *ADJECTIVE*
*The dragon yawned, revealing a **fearsome** set of teeth.*
• frightening, fearful, horrifying, terrifying, dreadful, awesome
(informal) scary

feasible *ADJECTIVE*
*Is it **feasible** to fly to Paris and back in a day?*
• possible, practicable, practical, achievable, realistic, workable
OPPOSITES impractical, impossible

feast *NOUN*
*The king held a great **feast** to celebrate his birthday.*
• banquet, dinner
(informal) spread

feat *NOUN*
*The trapeze artists performed many daring **feats**.*
• act, action, deed, exploit, achievement, performance

feather *NOUN*
A large feather is a **plume**.
All the feathers on a bird are its **plumage**.
Soft, fluffy feathers are **down**.
A feather used as a pen is a **quill**.
for ways to describe a bird's feathers see **bird**

feature *NOUN*
❶ *The room has several unusual **features**.*
• characteristic, detail, point, aspect, quality, peculiarity, trait, facet
A person's features are their **face**.
for ways to describe facial features see **face**
❷ *There was a **feature** about our school in the newspaper.*
• article, report, story, item, piece

feature *VERB*
❶ *The film **features** some thrilling car chases.*
• give prominence to, highlight, spotlight, show off
❷ *A new cartoon character **features** in this film.*
• appear, take part, figure, star

fee *NOUN*
*The club charges an annual membership **fee**.*
• charge, cost, payment, price
A fee to use a private road or bridge is a **toll**.

feeble *ADJECTIVE*
❶ *The elderly horse looked tired and **feeble**.*
• weak, frail, infirm, delicate, poorly, sickly, puny, weary, weedy
OPPOSITES strong, powerful
❷ *I made a **feeble** attempt to stop the ball.*
*Do you expect me to believe that **feeble** excuse?*
• weak, poor, ineffective, inadequate, unconvincing, tame, flimsy, lame

feed *VERB* feeds, feeding, fed
*We have enough sandwiches to **feed** six people.*
• provide for, cater for, give food to, nourish
➤ **to feed on**
*The leopard was **feeding on** its prey.*
• eat, consume, devour

a b c d e f g h i j k l m n o p q r s t u v w x y z

feel VERB feels, feeling, felt
❶ *I felt the llama's soft, woolly fur.*
• touch, caress, stroke, fondle
❷ *When the candle went out, we had to feel our way out of the cave.*
• grope, fumble
❸ *It feels colder today.*
• appear, seem, strike you as
❹ *I tend to feel the cold.*
• notice, be aware of, be conscious of, experience, suffer from
❺ *I feel that it's time we made a start.*
• think, believe, consider
➤ **to feel like**
Do you feel like going for a walk?
• want, wish for, desire
(informal) fancy

WRITING TIPS

You can use these words to describe how something feels:
• bristly, coarse, creamy, crinkly, crunchy, dry, feathery, fibrous, fine, fluffy, grainy, hairy, knobbly, lumpy, moist, mushy, papery, rough, rubbery, runny, silky, smooth, soft, spongy, springy, squashy, sticky, stiff, stringy, velvety, watery, woolly
(informal) gooey, squishy
The ground felt spongy under their feet, sucking at them gently at every step that seemed taken only just in time to keep from sinking.—THE EAGLE OF THE NINTH, Rosemary Sutcliff

feel NOUN
I love the feel of warm sand between my toes.
• feeling, sensation, touch

feeling NOUN
❶ *The cat had lost all feeling in its paw.*
• sense of touch, sensation, sensitivity
❷ *I didn't mean to hurt your feelings.*
• emotion, passion, sentiment

❸ *I have a feeling that something is wrong.*
• suspicion, notion, inkling, hunch, idea, impression, fancy, intuition
❹ *There was a good feeling at the party.*
• atmosphere, mood, air, aura

fell *past tense see* **fall**

female ADJECTIVE
for female human beings see **woman**
for female animals see **animal**
OPPOSITE male

feminine ADJECTIVE
I like to dress in a feminine style.
• womanly, ladylike, girlish
(informal) girly
OPPOSITE masculine

fence NOUN
The mansion was surrounded by a tall fence.
• railing, barrier, wall, paling, stockade, hedge
fence VERB
The field was fenced with a thorn hedge.
• enclose, surround, bound, encircle

fend VERB
➤ **to fend for yourself**
The lion cubs will soon have to fend for themselves.
• look after, take care of, care for
➤ **to fend someone** or **something off**
Cara raised her shield to fend off the blow.
• repel, resist, ward off, fight off, hold off, thwart

ferocious ADJECTIVE
The mansion was guarded by a ferocious dog.
• fierce, fearsome, savage, wild, vicious, violent, bloodthirsty, brutal
OPPOSITE tame

fertile ADJECTIVE
The surrounding countryside was green and fertile.
• fruitful, productive, rich, fecund
OPPOSITES barren, sterile

fertilize VERB
If you want good crops, you must **fertilize** the soil.
• enrich, feed, manure

fervent ADJECTIVE
My gran is a **fervent** supporter of the local team.
• eager, keen, avid, ardent, committed, enthusiastic, fanatical, passionate, zealous
OPPOSITES apathetic, lukewarm

festival NOUN
The town holds a **festival** every summer.
• carnival, fiesta, fête, gala, fair, celebration, jamboree
A celebration of a special anniversary is a jubilee.
for religious festivals see **religion**

festive ADJECTIVE
Chinese New Year is a **festive** occasion.
• cheerful, happy, merry, jolly, cheery, joyful, joyous, jovial, light-hearted, celebratory
OPPOSITES gloomy, sombre

fetch VERB
❶ I **fetched** the shopping from the car.
• get, bring, carry, collect, transfer, transport, convey, pick up, retrieve, obtain
❷ If we sell our car, how much will it **fetch**?
• make, raise, sell for, go for, bring in, earn

feud NOUN
There has been a **feud** between our families for years.
• quarrel, dispute, conflict, hostility, enmity, rivalry, strife, antagonism
A feud that lasts a long time is a **vendetta**.

feverish ADJECTIVE
❶ I felt **feverish** with the cold.
When you are feverish you are **hot** and **shivery**.
With a bad fever you may become **delirious**.
❷ There was **feverish** activity in the kitchen.
• frenzied, frantic, frenetic, excited, agitated, hectic, busy, hurried, impatient, restless

few DETERMINER
I've only been abroad a **few** times.
Few astronauts have walked on the moon.
• not many, hardly any, a small number of, a handful of
OPPOSITE many

fibre NOUN
Rope is made by twisting **fibres** together.
• thread, strand, hair, filament

fickle ADJECTIVE
Some **fickle** supporters deserted the team when they lost.
• changeable, disloyal, unfaithful, unreliable, erratic, inconsistent, unpredictable, inconstant
OPPOSITE loyal

fiction NOUN
❶ Roald Dahl wrote **fiction** for both children and adults.
for various kinds of literature see **writing**
❷ Their account of what happened was pure **fiction**.
• fantasy, invention, fabrication, lies
OPPOSITE fact

fictional ADJECTIVE
Harry Potter is a **fictional** character.
• imaginary, made-up, invented, fanciful
OPPOSITES factual, real

fictitious ADJECTIVE
The spy was using a **fictitious** name.
• false, fake, fabricated, fraudulent, bogus, assumed, spurious, unreal
OPPOSITES genuine, real

fiddle VERB
❶ Who's been **fiddling** with the controls?
• tinker, meddle, tamper, play about, mess about, twiddle
❷ (informal) They had been **fiddling** the bank account for years.
• falsify, alter, rig
(informal) cook the books

a b c d e f g h i j k l m n o p q r s t u v w x y z

A
B
C
D
E
F
G
H
I
J
K
L
M
N
O
P
Q
R
S
T
U
V
W
X
Y
Z

fiddly *ADJECTIVE*
*Icing a cake can be a **fiddly** job.*
• intricate, complicated, awkward, involved
OPPOSITE simple

fidget *VERB*
*I begin to **fidget** when I'm bored.*
• be restless, fiddle about, play about,
mess about

fidgety *ADJECTIVE*
*After waiting an hour, we began to get
fidgety.*
• restless, unsettled, impatient, agitated,
jumpy, nervy
OPPOSITE calm

field *NOUN*
❶ *Cattle were grazing in the **field**.*
• meadow, pasture
A small field for horses is a **paddock**.
An area of grass in a village is a **green**.
❷ *The **field** is too wet to play football.*
• ground, pitch, playing field
❸ *Electronics is not my **field**.*
• special interest, speciality, area of study

fierce *ADJECTIVE*
❶ *The travellers were killed in a **fierce** attack
by armed bandits.*
• vicious, ferocious, savage, brutal, violent,
wild, cruel, merciless, ruthless, pitiless
❷ *Our team will face **fierce** opposition in the
final.*
• strong, keen, eager, aggressive, competitive,
passionate, relentless
❸ *The explorers braved the **fierce** heat of the
desert sun.*
• blazing, intense, raging

fiery *ADJECTIVE*
❶ *It's best to avoid the **fiery** heat of the
midday sun.*
• blazing, burning, hot, intense, fierce, raging,
flaming, red-hot, glowing
❷ *My cousin has always had a **fiery** temper.*
• violent, passionate, excitable, angry, furious

fight *NOUN*
❶ *The warriors faced each other for a **fight** to
the death.*
Fighting is **combat** or **hostilities**.
A fight between armies is a **battle**.
A minor unplanned battle is a **skirmish**.
A series of battles is a **campaign** or **war**.
A minor fight is a **brawl**, **scrap**, **scuffle**
or **tussle**.
A fight arranged between two people is
a **duel**.
❷ *We support the **fight** to save the rainforest.*
• campaign, crusade, struggle

fight *VERB* fights, fighting, fought
❶ *Two seagulls were **fighting** over a scrap of
bread.*
• have a fight, scrap, scuffle, exchange blows,
come to blows
❷ *The two countries **fought** each other in
the war.*
• do battle with, wage war with, attack
Fighting with swords is **fencing**.
Fighting with fists is **boxing**.
Fighting in which you try to throw your
opponent to the ground is **wrestling**.
Fighting sports such as karate and judo are
martial arts.
❸ *We will **fight** the decision to close our
local library.*
• protest against, oppose, resist,
make a stand, take a stand against,
campaign against

fighter *NOUN*

WORD WEB

PEOPLE WHO FIGHT IN A WAR OR CONFLICT:

• guerrilla, soldier, warrior
see also **soldier**

PEOPLE WHO FOUGHT IN PAST TIMES:

• archer, gladiator, knight, ninja, samurai

PEOPLE WHO FIGHT AS A SPORT:

• boxer, fencer, kick-boxer, wrestler

figure NOUN
❶ *Please write the figure '8' on the board.*
• number, numeral, digit, integer
❷ *What figure would you put on your old bike?*
• price, value, amount, sum, cost
❸ *We saw a tall figure approaching through the rain.*
• body, build, form, shape
❹ *Inside the temple were several clay figures.*
• statue, carving, sculpture
❺ *The figure on page 22 shows the annual rainfall for Wales.*
• diagram, graph, illustration, drawing

figure VERB
Donald Duck figures in many cartoons.
• appear, feature, take part
➤ **to figure out**
We couldn't figure out what the riddle meant.
• work out, make out, understand, see

figure of speech NOUN

WORD WEB
SOME COMMON FIGURES OF SPEECH:
• alliteration, metaphor, onomatopoeia, personification, simile

file NOUN
❶ *I keep all my award certificates in a file.*
• folder, binder, cover
A file containing information, especially secret information, is a **dossier**.
❷ *Please walk in a single file.*
• line, row, column, rank, queue, procession

file VERB
❶ *I file all my letters in a pink folder.*
• organize, put away, store
❷ *We filed into the hall for assembly.*
• walk in a line, march, troop, parade

fill VERB
❶ *Dad filled the trolley with shopping.*
• load, pack, stuff, cram, top up
To fill a tyre with air is to **inflate** it.
OPPOSITE empty
❷ *What can I use to fill this hole?*
• close up, plug, seal, block up, stop up
❸ *Sightseers filled the streets.*
• crowd, jam, block, obstruct
(informal) bung up

filling NOUN
The filling started to ooze out of my sandwich.
• stuffing, insides, innards, padding

film NOUN
❶ *There is a good film on TV tonight.*
• picture, video, DVD
(North American) movie
A long film is a **feature film**.
A short excerpt from a film is a **clip**.
A script for a film is a **screenplay** and a writer of screenplays is a **screenwriter**.
A well-known film actor is a **film star**.
A theatre where films are shown is a **cinema**, **picture house** or *(North American)* **movie theatre**.
❷ *There was a film of oil on the water.*
• coat, coating, layer, covering, sheet, skin
A large patch of oil floating on water is a **slick**.

filth NOUN
The walls of the dungeon were covered with filth.
• dirt, grime, muck, mess, mud, sludge, scum, slime

filthy ADJECTIVE
❶ *Those trainers are filthy!*
• dirty, mucky, messy, grimy, grubby, muddy, soiled, stained
OPPOSITE clean
❷ *Don't drink the filthy water from the well.*
• cloudy, contaminated, foul, impure, polluted, slimy, smelly, stinking
OPPOSITE pure

a b c d e **f** g h i j k l m n o p q r s t u v w x y z

165

A

B

C

D

E

F

G

H

I

J

K

L

M

N

O

P

Q

R

S

T

U

V

W

X

Y

Z

final *ADJECTIVE*
❶ *The final moments of the match were very tense.*
• last, closing, concluding
OPPOSITE opening
❷ *What was the final result?*
• eventual, ultimate

finally *ADVERB*
I've finally managed to finish my book.
• eventually, at last, in the end

finances *PLURAL NOUN*
Are your finances doing well?
• money, bank account, funds, resources, assets, wealth

find *VERB* finds, finding, found
❶ *Did you find any fossils on the beach?*
• come across, discover, see, spot, locate, encounter, stumble across, unearth
❷ *The children never found the secret door again.*
• trace, track down, recover, retrieve
OPPOSITE lose
❸ *Did the doctor find what was wrong?*
• find out, detect, identify, diagnose, ascertain
❹ *You will find that building a tree house is hard work.*
• find out, become aware, realize, learn, recognize, notice, observe

findings *PLURAL NOUN*
The detective told us of his findings.
• judgement, conclusion, verdict, decision

fine *ADJECTIVE*
❶ *The young musicians gave a fine performance.*
• excellent, first-class, superb, splendid, admirable, commendable, good
OPPOSITE bad
❷ *As the weather was fine, we took a picnic.*
• sunny, fair, bright, clear, cloudless, pleasant
OPPOSITE dull

❸ *Spiders spin very fine thread for their webs.*
• delicate, fragile, thin, flimsy, slender, slim
OPPOSITE thick
❹ *The desert dunes were made of fine sand.*
• dusty, powdery
OPPOSITE coarse

fine *NOUN*
They had to pay a fine for dropping litter.
• penalty, charge, damages

finger *NOUN*
Your short fat finger is your **thumb**.
The finger next to your thumb is your **index finger**, because it is the finger you point with or indicate things with.
The next finger is your **middle finger**.
The next finger is your **ring finger**, because you can wear a wedding or engagement ring on that finger of your left hand.
Your small thin finger is your **little finger** or *(Scottish & North American)* **pinkie**.
The joints in your fingers are your **knuckles**.

finger *VERB*
Please don't finger the food on the table.
• touch, feel, poke, fondle

finish *VERB*
❶ *When are you likely to finish your homework?*
• complete, reach the end of, cease, round off
❷ *The film should finish around nine o'clock.*
• end, stop, conclude, terminate
(informal) wind up
❸ *I've already finished my bag of crisps.*
• consume, use up, get through, exhaust
(informal) polish off
OPPOSITE start

finish *NOUN*
We stayed to watch the parade until the finish.
• end, close, conclusion, completion, result, termination
OPPOSITE start

fire *NOUN*
The campers toasted marshmallows in the fire.
• blaze, flames, burning, combustion
A very big hot fire is an **inferno**.

An open fire out of doors is a **bonfire**.
An enclosed fire which produces great heat is a **furnace**.
An enclosed fire for cooking food is an **oven**.
An enclosed fire for making pottery is a **kiln**.
A team of people whose job is to put out fires is a **fire brigade**.
A member of a fire brigade is a **firefighter**.

fire VERB
❶ *The clay will harden if you fire it in a kiln.*
• bake, harden, heat
❷ *The soldier aimed his rifle and fired two shots.*
• shoot, discharge, let off, set off
To fire a missile is to **launch** it.
❸ *(informal) Miss Stark fired her assistant for being late for work.*
• dismiss, sack

firm NOUN
Mrs Sakho owns a firm that makes biscuits.
• company, business, organization, enterprise

firm ADJECTIVE
❶ *The surface of the planet was dry and firm.*
• hard, solid, dense, compact, rigid, set
OPPOSITE soft
❷ *Make sure the knots in the rope are firm.*
• secure, tight, strong, stable, fixed, sturdy, steady
❸ *Zelda had a firm belief in the power of magic.*
• definite, certain, sure, decided, determined, resolute, unshakeable, unwavering
OPPOSITE unsure
❹ *The two girls have become firm friends.*
• close, devoted, faithful, loyal, constant, dependable, reliable

first ADJECTIVE
❶ *The first inhabitants of the area were Picts.*
• earliest, original
❷ *The first thing to do in an emergency is to keep calm.*
• principal, key, main, fundamental, basic, chief
➤ **at first**
At first, we thought the dog was asleep.
• at the beginning, to start with, initially, originally

first-class or **first-rate** ADJECTIVE
That was a first-class game of chess.
• excellent, first rate, outstanding, superb, exceptional, superior, superlative, top-notch
OPPOSITES second-rate, mediocre

fish NOUN

WORD WEB

SOME TYPES OF FISH:

• brill, carp, catfish, chub, cod, conger eel, dace, eel, flounder, goldfish, grayling, gudgeon, haddock, hake, halibut, herring, lamprey, ling, mackerel, minnow, mullet, perch, pike, pilchard, piranha, plaice, roach, salmon, sardine, sawfish, shark, skate, sole, sprat, squid, stickleback, sturgeon, swordfish, trout, tuna, turbot, whitebait, whiting
for types of shellfish see **shellfish**
Young fish are **fry**.
An informal word for a very small fish is a **tiddler**.
A large number of fish swimming together is a **shoal**.
A person who sells fish is a **fishmonger**.
The sport or job of catching fish is **fishing**.
Fishing with a rod and a line is **angling** and a person who does this is an **angler**.
Fishing with nets from a boat is **trawling**.
Fishing equipment is **tackle**.

fit ADJECTIVE
❶ *Our menu was fit for royalty.*
• suitable, appropriate, fitting, right, good enough, worthy
OPPOSITE unsuitable
❷ *I walk to school every day to keep fit.*
• healthy, well, strong, robust
(old use) hale and hearty
OPPOSITE unhealthy
A common simile is **as fit as a fiddle**.
❸ *After a long ride, the horses were fit to collapse.*
• ready, liable, likely, about

Alphabet tab column: a b c d e **f** g h i j k l m n o p q r s t u v w x y z

fit VERB

❶ *We need to fit a new lock on the door.*
• install, put in place, position
❷ *This key doesn't fit the lock.*
He fits the description of the missing man.
• match, correspond to, go together with, tally with
❸ *Her speech perfectly fitted the occasion.*
• be suitable for, be appropriate to, suit

fit NOUN

My friend and I had a fit of the giggles.
• attack, bout, outburst, spell

fitting ADJECTIVE

Scoring the winning goal was a fitting end to his career.
• suitable, appropriate, apt, proper
OPPOSITE inappropriate

fix VERB

❶ *The soldier fixed a bayonet to the end of her rifle.*
• fasten, attach, connect, join, link
❷ *We fixed the tent poles in the ground.*
• set, secure, make firm, stabilize
❸ *Let's fix a time for the party.*
• decide on, agree on, set, arrange, settle, determine, specify, finalize
❹ *(informal) Dad says he can fix my bike.*
• repair, mend
(informal) sort, put right

fix NOUN

(informal) Can you help me? I'm in a fix.
• difficulty, mess, predicament, plight
(informal) jam, hole

fizz VERB

The lemonade fizzed when I opened the bottle.
• hiss, bubble, foam, froth

fizzy ADJECTIVE

Could I have a bottle of fizzy water, please?
• sparkling, bubbly, effervescent, gassy, foaming
OPPOSITE still

flabby ADJECTIVE

This exercise is good for flabby thighs.
• fat, fleshy, sagging, slack, loose, floppy, limp
OPPOSITE firm

flag NOUN

The street was decorated with flags for the carnival.
• banner, pennant, streamer
The flag of a regiment is its **colours** or **standard.**
A flag flown on a ship is an **ensign.**
Decorative strips of small flags are **bunting.**

flag VERB

By evening, our energy was starting to flag.
• diminish, lessen, decrease, decline, weaken, slump, fade, dwindle, wane

flap VERB

The sail flapped in the wind.
• flutter, sway, swing, wave about, thrash about

flare VERB

➤ to flare up
❶ *The fire flared up when we blew on it.*
• blaze, burn brightly, flame
❷ *They flare up at the slightest thing.*
• become angry, lose your temper

flash VERB

We saw a light flash from an upstairs window.
• shine, beam, blaze, flare, glare, gleam, glint, flicker, glimmer, sparkle

flash NOUN

There were flashes of lightning in the sky.
• blaze, flare, beam, ray, shaft, burst, gleam, glint, flicker, glimmer, sparkle
for other ways to describe light see **light**

flat ADJECTIVE

❶ *You need a flat surface to write on.*
• even, level, smooth, plane
A common simile is **as flat as a pancake.**
OPPOSITE uneven
❷ *I lay flat on the ground.*
• horizontal, outstretched, spread out

A B C D E F G H I J K L M N O P Q R S T U V W X Y Z

To be lying face downwards is to be **prone**.
To be lying face upwards is to be **supine**.
OPPOSITE upright
❸ *The robot spoke in a **flat**, electronic voice.*
• dull, boring, lifeless, uninteresting,
monotonous, tedious
OPPOSITE lively
❹ *The front tyre of my bike was **flat**.*
• deflated, punctured
OPPOSITE inflated
❺ *Our request met with a **flat** refusal.*
• outright, straight, positive, absolute, total,
utter, point-blank

flat *NOUN*
for places where people live see **building**

flatten *VERB*
❶ *We **flattened** the crumpled map on the desk.*
• smooth, press, roll out, iron out
❷ *The earthquake **flattened** several buildings.*
• demolish, destroy, knock down, pull down,
level
❸ *The young plants were **flattened** by the rain.*
• squash, crush, trample,
(informal) squish

flaunt *VERB*
*They are always **flaunting** their wealth.*
• show off, display, parade, exhibit

flavour *NOUN*
❶ *I don't like the **flavour** of raw onions.*
• taste, tang
for ways to describe flavour see **food**
❷ *Which **flavour** of ice cream do you like best?*
• kind, sort, variety

flavour *VERB*
*The sauce was **flavoured** with garlic and herbs.*
• season, spice

flaw *NOUN*
❶ *Pride was the only **flaw** in his character.*
• weakness, fault, shortcoming, failing, lapse
❷ *I can see a **flaw** in your argument.*
• error, inaccuracy, mistake, slip
❸ *There is a tiny **flaw** in this glass.*
• imperfection, defect, blemish, break,
chip, crack

fleck *NOUN*
*There were a few **flecks** of paint on the carpet.*
• spot, speck, flake, dot, dab
see also **bit**

flee *VERB* flees, fleeing, fled
*When they heard the alarm, the robbers **fled**.*
• run away, bolt, fly, escape, get away,
take off, hurry off
(informal) clear off, make off, scarper

fleet *NOUN*
A fleet of boats or small ships is a **flotilla**.
A fleet of warships is an **armada**.
A military fleet belonging to a country is
its **navy**.

fleeting *ADJECTIVE*
*I only caught a **fleeting** glimpse of the badger.*
• brief, momentary, quick, short, passing
OPPOSITES lengthy, lasting

flesh *NOUN*
• tissue, muscle, fat
An animal's flesh used for food is **meat**.
The decaying flesh of a dead animal is **carrion**.

flew *past tense see* **fly**

flex *NOUN*
*Don't trip over the **flex** of the iron!*
• cable, lead, wire

flexible *ADJECTIVE*
❶ *I need a pair of trainers with **flexible** soles.*
• bendable, supple, pliable, bendy, elastic,
springy
OPPOSITES rigid, inflexible
❷ *My working hours are very **flexible**.*
• adjustable, adaptable, variable, open
OPPOSITE fixed

flicker *VERB*
*The candlelight **flickered** in the draught.*
• twinkle, glimmer, waver, flutter, blink,
shimmer

a
b
c
d
e
f
g
h
i
j
k
l
m
n
o
p
q
r
s
t
u
v
w
x
y
z

A B C D E F G H I J K L M N O P Q R S T U V W X Y Z

flight NOUN
❶ *He is an expert on the history of flight.*
• flying, aviation, aeronautics
for other words to do with flying see **aircraft**
❷ *No-one saw the king's flight from the battlefield.*
• escape, getaway, retreat

flimsy ADJECTIVE
❶ *The kite was so flimsy that it broke apart.*
• fragile, delicate, frail, brittle, weak, wobbly, shaky, rickety,
OPPOSITE sturdy, robust
❷ *The fairy wore a dress of the flimsiest silk.*
• thin, fine, light, lightweight, floaty

flinch VERB
She flinched as an arrow flew past her head.
• back off, draw back, falter, recoil, shrink back, start, wince

fling VERB flings, flinging, flung
I flung a stone into the pond.
• throw, cast, sling, toss, hurl, pitch
(informal) chuck, bung

flip VERB
We flipped a coin to decide who should go first.
• toss, flick, spin

float VERB
We watched the twigs float gently down the river.
• sail, drift, glide, slip, slide, waft

flock NOUN
for groups of animals see **group**

flock VERB
People flocked round to see what was happening.
• crowd, gather, collect, herd, jostle

flood NOUN
❶ *The flood of water swept away the bridge.*
• deluge, inundation, rush, torrent, spate
❷ *The restaurant has received a flood of complaints.*
• succession, barrage, storm, volley

flood VERB
❶ *The river burst its banks and flooded the valley.*
• drown, swamp, inundate, submerge, immerse, engulf
❷ *We have been flooded with entries for our competition.*
• overwhelm, swamp, besiege

floor NOUN
❶ *The children in the audience sat on the floor.*
• ground, flooring, base
A floor on a ship is a **deck.**
❷ *Doreen's flat is on the top floor.*
• storey, level, tier, stage

flop VERB
❶ *I was so tired that I just flopped on to my bed.*
• collapse, drop, fall, slump
❷ *The plants will flop if you don't water them.*
• dangle, droop, hang down, sag, wilt
❸ *(informal) The first film flopped, but the sequel was a big hit.*
• be unsuccessful, fail, founder, fall flat

floppy ADJECTIVE
The rabbit had long, floppy ears.
• droopy, limp, saggy, soft
OPPOSITES stiff, rigid

flounder VERB
The soldiers floundered through the mud.
• struggle, stumble, stagger, fumble, wallow, blunder, falter

flourish VERB
❶ *My tomato plants are flourishing this year.*
• grow well, thrive, bloom, blossom, flower
OPPOSITE die
❷ *Sales on our website have continued to flourish.*
• be successful, do well, prosper, thrive, boom, succeed, progress, develop, increase
OPPOSITE fail
❸ *Ted flourished a newspaper to attract my attention.*
• wave, brandish, wield, shake

flow *VERB*
The rainwater flowed along the gutter.
• run, stream, pour, glide
To flow slowly is to **dribble, drip, ooze, seep** or **trickle.**
To flow fast is to **cascade, gush** or **sweep.**
To flow with sudden force is to **spurt** or **squirt.**
To flow over the edge of something is to **overflow** or **spill.**
When blood flows from someone, they **bleed.**
When the tide flows out, it **ebbs.**

flow *NOUN*
❶ *It's hard work rowing against the flow.*
• current, tide, drift
❷ *There was a steady flow of water into the pond.*
• stream, flood, cascade, gush, rush, spate

flower *NOUN*

WORD WEB

A single flower is a **bloom.**
A mass of small flowers growing together on a tree is **blossom.**
Flowers in a vase are an **arrangement.**
A bunch of flowers arranged for a special occasion is a **bouquet, posy** or **spray.**
Flowers arranged in a circle are a **garland** or **wreath.**
A person who sells and arranges flowers is a **florist.**

SOME BRITISH WILD FLOWERS:

• bluebell, buttercup, catkin, clover, cornflower, cowslip, daisy, dandelion, foxglove, harebell, heather, orchid, poppy, primrose

SOME POPULAR CULTIVATED FLOWERS:

• azalea, begonia, carnation, chrysanthemum, crocus, cyclamen, daffodil, dahlia, forget-me-not, freesia, fuchsia, geranium, gladiolus, hollyhock, hyacinth, iris, lilac, lily, lupin, marigold, nasturtium, pansy, peony, petunia, phlox, rose, snowdrop, sunflower, tulip, violet, water lily

THE MAIN PARTS OF A FLOWER ARE:

• anther, filament, ovary, petal, pistil, pollen, sepal, stamen, stigma, style
The sweet liquid collected by bees from flowers is **nectar.**

flower *VERB*
Most plants flower in the summer.
• bloom, blossom, bud

fluffy *ADJECTIVE*
Four fluffy ducklings were swimming in the pond.
• feathery, downy, furry, fuzzy, hairy, woolly, shaggy, soft

fluid *NOUN*
An oily fluid oozed from the pipe.
• liquid, solution, juice
OPPOSITE solid

fluke *NOUN*
It was a fluke that the ball went into the net.
• chance, accident, stroke of good luck

flush *VERB*
Rory flushed with embarrassment.
• blush, go red, colour, redden, burn

flustered *ADJECTIVE*
I get flustered when I have to read in assembly.
• confused, upset, bothered, agitated, unsettled, ruffled
(informal) rattled
OPPOSITE calm

flutter *VERB*
A moth fluttered about the light bulb.
• flap, beat, flicker, quiver, tremble, vibrate

fly *NOUN*
for various insects see **insect**

a
b
c
d
e
f
g
h
i
j
k
l
m
n
o
p
q
r
s
t
u
v
w
x
y
z

A
B
C
D
E
F
G
H
I
J
K
L
M
N
O
P
Q
R
S
T
U
V
W
X
Y
Z

fly *VERB* **flies, flying, flew, flown**
❶ *Two swallows were **flying** high in the sky.*
• glide, swoop, flit, hover, float
for ways to describe how birds move see **bird**
❷ *Suddenly the eagle **flew** into the air.*
• rise, soar, mount, take off
❸ *The ship was **flying** the British flag.*
• display, show, hoist, raise
❹ *Doesn't time **fly**!*
• go quickly, pass quickly, rush by

foam *NOUN*
The bath water was covered with pinkish foam.
• bubbles, froth, suds, lather
Foam made by seawater is **surf** or **spume**.

foam *VERB*
*The mixture in the cauldron **foamed** and gurgled.*
• froth, bubble, fizz, boil, seethe, lather

focus *NOUN*
❶ *Can you adjust the **focus** on your camera?*
• clarity, sharpness
❷ *The new lion cubs were the **focus** of everyone's attention.*
• centre, focal point, target, core, pivot
focus *VERB*
➤ **to focus on**
*Our teacher wants us to **focus on** our spelling.*
• concentrate on, think about, examine, look at

fog *NOUN*
*The top of the mountain was covered with **fog**.*
Thin fog is **haze** or **mist**.
A thick mixture of fog and smoke is **smog**.

foggy *ADJECTIVE*
❶ *It was too **foggy** to see through the windows.*
• misty, hazy, murky, cloudy, smoggy
❷ *My photo of the horses came out **foggy**.*
• blurred, fuzzy, indistinct, out of focus
OPPOSITES clear, in focus

foil *VERB*
*The guard-dog **foiled** their plan to break into the house.*
• frustrate, thwart, block, prevent, obstruct, stop, check, halt

fold *VERB*
Fold the paper along the dotted line.
• bend, double over, crease, pleat
fold *NOUN*
❶ *She smoothed the soft **folds** of her dress.*
• crease, furrow, layer
A fold which is pressed into a garment is a **pleat**.
❷ *The dog drove the sheep into the **fold**.*
• enclosure, pen

folder *NOUN*
*I keep all my art work in a **folder**.*
• file, binder, wallet, portfolio

follow *VERB*
❶ *Why does thunder always **follow** lightning?*
• come after, succeed, replace
OPPOSITE precede
❷ *I think that car is **following** us!*
• go after, chase, pursue, track, trail, tail, stalk, hunt, shadow
❸ *Follow this path until you reach the river.*
• go along, keep to
❹ *I **followed** the instructions on the packet.*
• carry out, comply with, heed, obey, observe
❺ *Which football team do you **follow**?*
• be a fan of, support
❻ *We found it hard to **follow** what the creature was saying.*
• understand, comprehend, grasp, take in, catch
❼ *Although we are the same age, it doesn't **follow** that we are friends.*
• mean, happen, result, ensue, arise, come about

follower *NOUN*
Someone who follows you in a job is your **successor**.
Someone who follows a person or animal to try to catch them is a **hunter** or **pursuer**.

Someone who continually follows a person about is a **stalker**.

Someone who follows a person's teaching is a **disciple**.

Someone who follows a football team, etc. is a **fan** or **supporter**.

fond ADJECTIVE

❶ *Mrs Walker gave her pet poodle a fond kiss.*

• loving, tender, affectionate

❷ *Anna had a fond hope that she would become a film star.*

• foolish, silly, unrealistic, fanciful

➤ **to be fond of**

I'm very fond of chocolate cake.

• be keen on, be partial to, like, love

food NOUN

The banquet table was laid out with all kinds of food.

• foodstuffs, rations, provisions, refreshments, eatables, nourishment, nutrition

(informal) grub, nosh

for meat and foods made from meat see **meat**

The food that you normally eat or choose to eat is your **diet**.

A diet which includes no meat is a **vegetarian** diet.

A diet which includes no animal products is a **vegan** diet.

Food which includes fish or shellfish is **seafood**.

Foods made from milk, butter or cheese are **dairy foods**.

Food for farm animals is **fodder**.

WORD WEB

SOME TYPES OF SEAFOOD:

• bloater, bream, caviar, cod, crab, eel, haddock, halibut, herring, kipper, lobster, mackerel, monkfish, mussels, oysters, pilchard, plaice, prawn, salmon, sardine, scampi, sea bass, shrimp, sole, sprat, trout, tuna, whelks, whitebait, whiting

SOME DAIRY FOODS:

• butter, cheese, cream, curds, ice cream, kefir, milk, yoghurt

for types of cheese see **cheese**

FOODS MADE FROM FLOUR OR CEREALS:

• bagel, batter, biscuits or *(North American)* cookies, bread, bun, chapatti, cornflakes, cracker, crispbread, dumpling, flatbread, muesli, nan, oatcake, pancake, pastry, pitta bread, poppadom, popcorn, porridge, rice cake, roll, scone, toast, tortilla, waffle

SOME PREPARED DISHES OF FOOD:

• balti, barbecue, broth, burger, casserole, chilli, chips or *(North American)* French fries, couscous, crisps, curry, dhal, falafel, fritter, goulash, hummus, jollof, kebab, lasagne, meatball, nachos, noodles, omelette, pakora, panini, pasta, pie, pizza, quiche, risotto, samosa, sandwich, shawarma, soup, stew, stir-fry, sushi, teriyaki

for types of pasta see **pasta**

SOME PUDDINGS AND OTHER SWEET FOODS:

• barfi, brownie, cake, chocolate, crumble, cupcake, custard, gateau, honey, jalebi, jam, jelly, marmalade, marzipan, meringue, mousse, muffin, sponge, steamed pudding, sugar, tart, treacle, trifle

For fruits and vegetables see **fruit, vegetable**

SOME FLAVOURINGS AND SAUCES FOR FOOD:

• chilli, chutney, French dressing, garlic, gravy, herbs, ketchup, mayonnaise, mustard, pepper, peri-peri, pesto, pickle, salsa, salt, soy sauce, spices, sriracha, vinegar

Things like salt and pepper which you add to food are **condiments** or **seasoning**.

a b c d e f g h i j k l m n o p q r s t u v w x y z

A
B
C
D
E
F
G
H
I
J
K
L
M
N
O
P
Q
R
S
T
U
V
W
X
Y
Z

WRITING TIPS

You can use these words to describe **food:**

TO DESCRIBE HOW IT LOOKS OR FEELS:

• chewy, creamy, crispy, crumbly, crunchy, doughy, dry, flaky, greasy, juicy, leathery, lumpy, milky, mushy, rubbery, runny, slimy, sloppy, smooth, soggy, soupy, spongy, sticky, stodgy, stringy, syrupy, velvety, watery
(informal) gooey
Stella was delighted to see that they were having ice cream, complete with sprinkles, fudge sticks and gooey chocolate toffee sauce.—THE POLAR BEAR EXPLORERS' CLUB, Alex Bell

TO DESCRIBE HOW IT TASTES:

• bitter, bland, fiery, flavoursome, fresh, fruity, hot, mellow, mild, peppery, piquant, pungent, refreshing, salty, savoury, sharp, sour, spicy, strong, sugary, sweet, syrupy, tangy, tart, vinegary
*The sauce was **hot**, but not too **spicy**.*
for ways to describe how food smells see **smell**

TO DESCRIBE FOOD YOU LIKE:

• appetizing, delicious, luscious, mouthwatering, tasty, tempting, well-cooked
(informal) scrumptious, yummy
Something especially tasty to eat is a **delicacy** or **titbit**.
'I've eaten many strange and scrumptious dishes in my time, Like jellied gnats and dandyprats and earwigs cooked in slime...'
—JAMES AND THE GIANT PEACH, Roald Dahl

TO DESCRIBE FOOD YOU DON'T LIKE:

• disgusting, flavourless, indigestible, inedible, nauseating, stomach-turning, tasteless, unappetizing, uneatable; charred, mouldy, overcooked, stale, undercooked
(informal) gross
Measle didn't think the food was very good. The stew was watery and tasteless and the vegetables were soggy and overcooked.
—MEASLE AND THE DOOMPIT, Ian Ogilvy

fool NOUN
❶ *Only a **fool** would believe that ridiculous story.*
• idiot, buffoon, clown, halfwit, dimwit, dunce, simpleton, blockhead, clot, dunderhead, imbecile, moron, ass
(informal) twit, chump, nitwit, nincompoop
❷ *(historical) The king's **fool** entertained the court.*
• jester, clown

fool VERB
*The spy **fooled** everyone with her disguises.*
• deceive, trick, mislead, hoax, dupe, hoodwink
(informal) con, kid, have you on, take you in, pull the wool over your eyes
➤ **to fool about** or **around**
*We were told not to **fool about** in the swimming pool.*
• play about, mess about, misbehave

foolish ADJECTIVE
*It would be **foolish** to stand too close to the lions.*
• stupid, silly, idiotic, senseless, ridiculous, nonsensical, unwise, ill-advised, half-witted, unintelligent, absurd, crazy, mad, hare-brained
(informal) daft
OPPOSITE sensible

foot NOUN
❶ *Rhona walked on the sand in her bare **feet**.*
The foot of an animal that has claws is a **paw**.
The foot of a cow, deer or horse is a **hoof**.
A pig's foot is a **trotter**.
A bird's feet are its **claws**.
The feet of a bird of prey are its **talons**.
❷ *We set up camp at the **foot** of the mountain.*
• base, bottom

football NOUN

WORD WEB

Football is also known as **soccer**.
Someone who plays football is a **footballer**.
Football is played on a **field** or **pitch** in a **ground**, **park** or **stadium**.

MEMBERS OF A FOOTBALL TEAM:

• captain, defender, full back, forward, goalkeeper or *(informal)* goalie, midfielder, striker, substitute, sweeper, winger

OTHER PEOPLE INVOLVED IN FOOTBALL:

• ballboy or ballgirl, coach, manager, referee, referee's assistants

SOME MOVES A FOOTBALLER MIGHT MAKE:

• chip, dribble, dummy, header, kick, mazy run, miss, pass, score, shot, tackle, volley
for ways to hit or kick a ball see **ball**

SOME OTHER TERMS USED IN FOOTBALL:

• corner, crossbar, deflection, dugout, equalizer, extra time, final whistle, foul, free kick, goal, goalposts, half-time, kick-off, net, offside, penalty, penalty shoot-out, red or yellow card, sending off, throw-in

footprint *NOUN*
We followed the **footprints** in the snow.
• footmark, track, print
The tracks left by an animal are also called a spoor.

footstep *NOUN*
I heard **footsteps** crunching up the garden path.
• step, footfall, tread

forbidden *ADJECTIVE*
Skateboarding is **forbidden** in the playground.
• banned, barred, prohibited, disallowed, outlawed
OPPOSITE allowed

forbidding *ADJECTIVE*
The haunted tower had a dark, **forbidding** look.
• gloomy, grim, menacing, ominous, stern, threatening, unfriendly, unwelcoming
OPPOSITE friendly

force *NOUN*
❶ The firefighters had to use **force** to open the door.
• strength, power, might, muscle, vigour, effort, energy
❷ The **force** of the explosion broke all the windows.
• impact, effect, shock, intensity
❸ The soldiers are part of a peace-keeping **force**.
• group, unit, team, corps, army, troops
force *VERB*
❶ The prisoners were **forced** to work in the mines.
• compel, make, order, require, oblige, pressurize, coerce
❷ The king **forced** a new law upon the country.
• impose, inflict
❸ The firefighters had to **force** the door.
• break open, burst open, prise open, smash, wrench
(informal) yank

forceful *ADJECTIVE*
The director has a very **forceful** personality.
• strong, powerful, dynamic, commanding, assertive, overbearing
OPPOSITE weak

forecast *NOUN*
The weather **forecast** is for snow tomorrow.
• outlook, prediction
forecast *VERB* forecasts, forecasting, forecast or forecasted
Snow has been **forecast** for Tuesday.
• foresee, foretell, predict

foreground *NOUN*
I took a photo of our house with my mum in the **foreground**.
• front
OPPOSITE background

foreign *ADJECTIVE*
❶ Lots of **foreign** tourists visit Edinburgh in the summer.
• overseas, international
OPPOSITES native, domestic

❷ *I like travelling to **foreign** countries.*
• overseas, distant, faraway, exotic, remote, far-flung
❸ *The idea of work was completely **foreign** to the princess.*
• unnatural, unfamiliar, strange, alien

foreigner *NOUN*
*Many **foreigners** have come to live in the city.*
• overseas visitor, stranger, outsider, newcomer
A formal word is **alien**.
A word describing people who come from abroad to live in a country is **immigrant**.

foremost *ADJECTIVE*
*Hans Christian Andersen was one of the **foremost** writers of fairy tales.*
• best known, leading, most important, greatest, principal, chief, major

foresee *VERB* foresees, foreseeing, foresaw, foreseen
*Do you **foresee** any problems with our plan?*
• anticipate, expect, predict, forecast, prophesy, foretell

forest *NOUN*
*for places where trees grow see **tree***

foretell *VERB* foretells, foretelling, foretold
❶ *The fortune-teller **foretold** that I would go on a voyage.*
• predict, prophesy, forecast, foresee
❷ *The cold wind **foretold** a change in the weather.*
• herald, signify

forever *ADVERB*
*Timmy is **forever** complaining about something.*
• constantly, continually, always, perpetually

forge *VERB*
❶ *The blacksmith **forged** a new horseshoe.*
• cast, hammer out, beat into shape
❷ *That signature has been **forged**.*
• fake, copy, counterfeit

➤ **to forge ahead**
*After a slow start, the rowing team was **forging ahead**.*
• advance, make progress, make headway

forgery *NOUN*
*One of these paintings is a **forgery**.*
• fake, copy, imitation, reproduction, replica *(informal)* phoney

forget *VERB* forgets, forgetting, forgot, forgotten
❶ *I **forgot** my toothbrush when I packed my suitcase.*
• leave out, leave behind, overlook
❷ *I **forgot** to switch off the computer.*
• omit, neglect, fail
OPPOSITE remember

forgetful *ADJECTIVE*
*As the professor grew older, he became more **forgetful**.*
• absent-minded, careless, inattentive, oblivious, vague, dreamy, lax

forgive *VERB* forgives, forgiving, forgave, forgiven
*Please **forgive** me for being so rude.*
• excuse, pardon, let off, overlook, spare

fork *VERB*
*The path ahead widened and then **forked** into two.*
• split, branch, divide

forlorn *ADJECTIVE*
*Aisha felt **forlorn** after her friends had left.*
• sad, unhappy, lonely, dejected, miserable, sorrowful
OPPOSITE cheerful

form *NOUN*
❶ *I made out the **form** of a man through the mist.*
• shape, figure, outline, silhouette
❷ *Ice is a **form** of water.*
• kind, sort, type, variety

❸ *My brother moves up into a higher form next term.*
• class, year, grade, set
❹ *If you want to join the club, sign this form.*
• document, paper, sheet, questionnaire

form *VERB*
❶ *The sculptor formed the clay into the shape of a bird.*
• shape, mould, model, fashion, work, cast
❷ *My friends and I have formed a chess club.*
• set up, establish, found, create, start
❸ *Icicles had formed on the roof of the cave.*
• appear, develop, grow, emerge, take shape

formal *ADJECTIVE*
❶ *I was invited to the formal opening of the museum.*
• official, ceremonial
❷ *The letter was written in a very formal style.*
• correct, proper, conventional, dignified, solemn
OPPOSITES informal, casual

former *ADJECTIVE*
In former times, the castle was surrounded by a moat.
• earlier, previous, past, bygone

formula *NOUN*
The inventor was working on a new formula for toothpaste.
• recipe, prescription

forsake *VERB* forsakes, forsaking, forsook, forsaken
Ben knew that his old sheepdog would never forsake him.
• abandon, desert, leave

fort *NOUN*
A few soldiers were left to defend the fort.
• fortress, fortification, stronghold, castle, citadel, tower
see also **castle**

fortify *VERB*
❶ *The townspeople built fences to fortify the town.*
• defend, protect, secure, reinforce
❷ *A good breakfast will fortify you for the morning.*
• strengthen, support, sustain, bolster, boost, invigorate
OPPOSITE weaken

fortunate *ADJECTIVE*
We were fortunate to have good weather.
• lucky, in luck
OPPOSITES unfortunate, unlucky

fortune *NOUN*
❶ *By good fortune, I stumbled across a secret doorway.*
• chance, luck, accident, fate
❷ *The millionaire left her fortune to charity.*
• wealth, riches, possessions, property, assets, estate
(informal) millions

fortune-teller *NOUN*
The fortune-teller gazed into her crystal ball.
• clairvoyant, soothsayer, seer

forward *ADJECTIVE*
❶ *We need to do some forward planning for the camping trip.*
• advance, early, future
❷ *Would it be too forward to send him an email?*
• bold, cheeky, brash, familiar, impudent, presumptuous

forwards *ADVERB*
❶ *The queue moved forwards very slowly.*
• on, onwards, along
❷ *All the seats face forwards.*
• to or toward the front, ahead
OPPOSITE backwards

a b c d e f g h i j k l m n o p q r s t u v w x y z

A B C D E F G H I J K L M N O P Q R S T U V W X Y Z

fossil *NOUN*
Isla found a fossil on the beach.

WORD WEB

SOME TYPES OF FOSSIL:

• ammonite, dinosaur bone, petrified wood, trilobite
A person who looks for fossils is a **fossil hunter**.
A person who studies fossils is a **palaeontologist**.

foster *VERB*
My aunt has decided to foster a child.
• bring up, rear, raise, care for, look after, take care of
To **adopt** a child is to make the child legally a full member of your family.

fought *past tense see* **fight**

foul *ADJECTIVE*
❶ *The knight fainted at the foul smell of the dragon's breath.*
• disgusting, revolting, repulsive, rotten, stinking, offensive, unpleasant, loathsome, nasty, horrible, vile
OPPOSITE pleasant
❷ *The walls and floor of the dungeon were foul.*
• dirty, unclean, filthy, mucky, messy
OPPOSITE clean, pure
❸ *The player was sent off for using foul language.*
• rude, offensive, insulting, abusive, improper, indecent
❹ *The referee blew her whistle for a foul tackle.*
• illegal, prohibited, unfair
OPPOSITE fair

found *past tense see* **find**

found *VERB*
The school was founded a hundred years ago.
• establish, set up, start, begin, create, originate, initiate, institute

foundation *NOUN*
❶ *There's no foundation for the rumour they are spreading.*
• basis, grounds
❷ *It's a hundred years since the foundation of the museum.*
• founding, beginning, establishment, setting up

founder *VERB*
❶ *The ship struck a rock and foundered.*
• go under, sink, submerge
❷ *The project foundered because of lack of money.*
• fail, fall through, collapse, come to nothing
(informal) fold, flop, bomb

fountain *NOUN*
A fountain of water shot into the air.
• jet, spout, spray, spring

fox *NOUN*
A male fox is a **dog**.
A female fox is a **vixen**.
A young fox is a **cub**.
A fox lives in an **earth**.
A word meaning 'to do with foxes' is **vulpine**.

fox *VERB*
The last clue in the crossword foxed me completely.
• puzzle, baffle, bewilder, mystify, perplex
(informal) flummox, floor

fraction *NOUN*
Only a fraction of an iceberg shows above the water.
• bit, part, portion

fracture *VERB*
Steve fell off his bike and fractured his wrist.
• break, crack, split, splinter

fracture *NOUN*
The X-ray showed a fracture in the bone.
• break, breakage, crack, split, fissure

fragile ADJECTIVE
Fossil dinosaur bones are very fragile.
• breakable, delicate, frail, brittle, easily damaged, weak
OPPOSITE strong

fragment NOUN
❶ *I dug up a fragment of broken pottery.*
• bit, piece, chip, sliver, shard
❷ *She overheard fragments of their conversation.*
• part, portion, scrap, snippet

fragrant ADJECTIVE
The room was fragrant with the smell of roses.
• sweet-smelling, perfumed, scented, aromatic

frail ADJECTIVE
❶ *My grandad felt frail after his illness.*
• weak, infirm, feeble
❷ *That step-ladder looks a bit frail.*
• flimsy, fragile, delicate, rickety, unsound
OPPOSITES strong, robust

frame NOUN
❶ *The frame of the house is made of timber.*
• framework, structure, shell, skeleton
❷ *I put the photo of my friend in a frame.*
• mount, mounting, surround, border, setting, edging

frank ADJECTIVE
We had a very frank discussion about money.
• honest, direct, sincere, genuine, candid, outspoken, plain, blunt, straightforward, truthful
OPPOSITE insincere

frantic ADJECTIVE
❶ *I was frantic with worry when our kitten got lost.*
• beside yourself, fraught, desperate, distraught, hysterical, worked up, berserk
❷ *There was frantic activity on the day of the wedding.*
• excited, hectic, frenzied, feverish, wild, mad
OPPOSITE calm

fraud NOUN
❶ *The bank manager was found guilty of fraud.*
• deceit, deception, dishonesty, swindling, cheating
❷ *The prize draw was just a fraud—nobody won anything.*
• swindle, trick, hoax, pretence, sham
(informal) con, scam
❸ *The salesman turned out to be a fraud.*
• cheat, swindler, trickster, hoaxer
(informal) con artist, phoney

fraudulent ADJECTIVE
Beware of fraudulent email messages.
• dishonest, illegal, criminal, corrupt, swindling, bogus, sham
(informal) crooked, phoney
OPPOSITE honest

frayed ADJECTIVE
The old woman wore a cloak of frayed tartan cloth.
• tattered, ragged, worn, threadbare

free ADJECTIVE
❶ *You are free to wander anywhere in the building.*
• able, allowed, permitted, at liberty
OPPOSITE restricted
❷ *After ten years in jail, the prisoners were free at last.*
• freed, liberated, released, emancipated, at large, on the loose
A common simile is as free as a bird.
OPPOSITES imprisoned, enslaved
❸ *I got a free drink with my sandwich.*
• complimentary, free of charge, gratis, on the house
❹ *Are you free this weekend?*
• available, unoccupied
OPPOSITE busy, occupied
❺ *The bathroom is free now.*
• available, unoccupied, vacant, empty
OPPOSITE engaged
❻ *Jack is very free with his money.*
• generous, lavish, liberal
OPPOSITE mean

a
b
c
d
e
f
g
h
i
j
k
l
m
n
o
p
q
r
s
t
u
v
w
x
y
z

A
B
C
D
E
F
G
H
I
J
K
L
M
N
O
P
Q
R
S
T
U
V
W
X
Y
Z

free VERB

❶ *The soldiers freed the prisoners of war.*
• release, liberate, set free, deliver
To free slaves is to **emancipate** them.
To free prisoners by paying money to their
captors is to **ransom** them.
OPPOSITE imprison
❷ *We freed the dogs and let them
run about.*
• loose, turn loose, let go, untie, unchain
OPPOSITE confine
❸ *The escapologist tried to free his arms from
the chains.*
• undo, untangle, work loose

freedom NOUN

*The animals have a lot of freedom in the
safari park.*
• liberty, independence

freeze VERB freezes, freezing, froze,
frozen

❶ *Water begins to freeze at 0°C.*
• become ice, ice over, harden, solidify
❷ *If you freeze food, you can store it for a
long time.*
• deep-freeze, chill, refrigerate
❸ *Season-ticket prices have been frozen for
another year.*
• fix, hold, peg, keep as they are

freezing ADJECTIVE

It's freezing outside in winter.
• chilly, frosty, icy, wintry, raw, bitter

frequent ADJECTIVE

❶ *I send frequent email messages to my
friends.*
• numerous, constant, continual, recurring,
recurrent, repeated, countless
OPPOSITE infrequent
❷ *Badgers are frequent visitors to the garden.*
• regular, habitual, common, familiar,
persistent
OPPOSITE rare

frequent VERB

Office workers frequent the park at lunchtime.
• visit, attend, haunt

fresh ADJECTIVE

❶ *This pudding is made with fresh fruit.*
• natural, raw, unprocessed
❷ *The shop bakes fresh bread every day.*
• new
OPPOSITES old, stale
❸ *Sally went outside to get some fresh air.*
• clean, cool, crisp, refreshing
OPPOSITE stuffy
❹ *Have you put fresh sheets on the bed?*
• new, clean, laundered, washed
OPPOSITE dirty
❺ *Having a shower makes me feel nice and fresh.*
• refreshed, revived, restored, invigorated
❻ *We need some fresh ideas for our magazine.*
• new, original, different, novel, innovative
OPPOSITE old

fret VERB

My sister is fretting about her piano exam.
• worry, fuss, agonize, become stressed,
get worked up

friction NOUN

❶ *You can make fire from the friction of
rubbing sticks together.*
• rubbing, chafing, abrasion
❷ *There was some friction between the two
teams.*
• conflict, disagreement, hostility, rivalry,
antagonism, discord, quarrelling

friend NOUN

I am inviting four friends to my birthday party.
• companion, comrade
(informal) mate, pal, buddy, chum
A friend you play games with is a **playmate**.
A friend you write to but don't normally meet
is a **penfriend**.
A friend you know only slightly is an
acquaintance.
OPPOSITE enemy

friendly ADJECTIVE

❶ *Our neighbour's pet dog is very friendly.*
• affectionate, loving, good-natured, likeable,
amiable, approachable, kind-hearted,
kindly, amicable, genial, sociable, outgoing,
sympathetic

❷ *Those two are very **friendly** with each other.*
• close, familiar, intimate
(informal) pally, chummy
❸ *I like this cafe—it has a very **friendly** atmosphere.*
• warm, welcoming, hospitable, cordial, neighbourly
OPPOSITES unfriendly, hostile

friendship *NOUN*
*Their **friendship** has lasted for many years.*
• closeness, affection, fondness, familiarity, intimacy, attachment, comradeship, fellowship
OPPOSITE hostility
*A formal friendship between countries or parties is an **alliance**.*

fright *NOUN*
❶ *The children jumped up in **fright** and began to scream.*
• fear, terror, alarm, horror, panic, dread
❷ *The explosion gave us an awful **fright**!*
• scare, shock, surprise, start, turn, jolt

frighten *VERB*
*Sorry—I didn't mean to **frighten** you.*
• scare, terrify, startle, alarm, shock, panic, petrify

frightened *ADJECTIVE*
*Mia always felt **frightened** in the dark.*
• afraid, scared, terrified, alarmed, fearful, panicky, petrified
*see also **afraid***

frightening *ADJECTIVE*
*The ghost story she told was quite **frightening**.*
• terrifying, horrifying, alarming, nightmarish, chilling, spine-chilling, hair-raising, bloodcurdling, eerie, sinister, fearsome
(informal) scary, creepy, spooky

frill *NOUN*
❶ *The shirt has **frills** under the collar.*
• ruffle, ruff, flounce, fringe
❷ *Our hotel was basic with no **frills**.*
• extra, luxury

fringe *NOUN*
❶ *My scarf has a beaded **fringe** at each end.*
• border, edging, frill, trimming
❷ *We live on the **fringe** of the town.*
• edge, border, margin, outskirts

frisky *ADJECTIVE*
*The new lion cubs in the zoo are very **frisky**.*
• playful, lively, high-spirited, sprightly

fritter *VERB*
➤ to **fritter away**
*Luke **frittered away** his pocket money on sweets.*
• waste, squander, spend unwisely, use up

frivolous *ADJECTIVE*
❶ *We were in a **frivolous** mood before we went on holiday.*
• playful, lively, high-spirited, jaunty
OPPOSITES serious, sombre
❷ *Don't waste my time asking **frivolous** questions.*
• foolish, silly, ridiculous, shallow, superficial, pointless, unimportant, trivial, petty
OPPOSITES serious, important

frock *NOUN*
*for items of clothing see **clothes***

frog *NOUN*
*A young frog is a **tadpole**.*
*Frogs' eggs are **frogspawn**.*
*The sound a frog makes is a **croak** or ribbit.*

frolic *VERB*
*Lambs were **frolicking** in the field.*
• jump about, leap about, bound, caper, prance, gambol, romp, skip

front *NOUN*
❶ *We stood at the **front** of the queue.*
• head, start, beginning, lead, top
❷ *The **front** of the house was painted white.*
• face, facing, frontage, facade
OPPOSITE back, rear
*The front of a ship is the **bow** or prow.*
*The front of a picture is the **foreground**.*

A
B
C
D
E
F
G
H
I
J
K
L
M
N
O
P
Q
R
S
T
U
V
W
X
Y
Z

front ADJECTIVE

❶ *The front runners came into sight round the corner.*
• first, leading, most advanced
OPPOSITE back
❷ *The horse had injured one of its front legs.*
• fore
OPPOSITES back, rear, hind

frontier NOUN

We crossed the frontier between France and Belgium.
• border, boundary

frosty ADJECTIVE

❶ *It was a clear, frosty night.*
• cold, crisp, icy, freezing, wintry
❷ *The shopkeeper gave us a frosty stare.*
• unfriendly, unwelcoming, cold, cool, stony
OPPOSITES warm, friendly

froth NOUN

I like a lot of froth on my hot chocolate.
• foam, bubbles, head
The froth on top of soapy water is **lather** or **suds**.
Dirty froth is **scum**.

frown NOUN

On Christmas Eve, Scrooge had a frown on his face.
• scowl, glare, grimace, glower
for other facial expressions see **expression**

frown VERB

Zahara frowned when the program didn't work.
• scowl, glare, grimace, glower, knit your brow, look sullen

frugal ADJECTIVE

❶ *Mrs Koulibaly was always frugal with her money.*
• thrifty, sparing, economical, prudent
OPPOSITES wasteful, spendthrift
❷ *They ate a frugal meal of bread crusts.*
• meagre, paltry, plain, simple
OPPOSITE lavish

fruit NOUN

WORD WEB

SOME COMMON VARIETIES OF FRUIT:

• apple, apricot, avocado, banana, bilberry, blackberry, blackcurrant, blueberry, bramble, cherry, coconut, cranberry, damson, date, fig, gooseberry, grape, guava, kiwi fruit, loganberry, lychee, mango, melon, nectarine, pawpaw or papaya, peach, pear, pineapple, plum, pomegranate, quince, raspberry, redcurrant, rose hip, sloe, strawberry, tomato, watermelon

CITRUS FRUITS:

• clementine, grapefruit, kumquat, lemon, lime, mandarin, orange, satsuma, tangerine

DRIED FRUITS:

• currant, prune, raisin, sultana
Rhubarb is not a fruit, although it is cooked and eaten like one.
A person who sells fruit and vegetables is a **greengrocer**.

fruitful ADJECTIVE

Did you have a fruitful shopping trip?
• successful, productive, useful, worthwhile, profitable, rewarding
OPPOSITE fruitless

fruitless ADJECTIVE

The detectives spent a fruitless morning searching for clues.
• unsuccessful, unprofitable, unproductive, futile, pointless, useless, vain
OPPOSITE successful

frustrate VERB

❶ *It frustrated us to have to wait in the long queue.*
• exasperate, discourage, dispirit, irritate

❷ *Our plan for the day was frustrated by the weather.*
• block, foil, thwart, defeat, check, hinder, prevent

fry *VERB*
for ways to cook things see **cook**

fugitive *NOUN*
Police searched everywhere for the fugitives.
• runaway, escapee, outlaw, deserter
Someone who is a fugitive from war or persecution is a **refugee**.

fulfil *VERB*
❶ *She fulfilled her ambition to represent her country at the Olympics.*
• achieve, realize, accomplish, attain, carry out, complete, succeed in
❷ *To join the club, you must fulfil these conditions.*
• meet, satisfy, conform to

full *ADJECTIVE*
❶ *My suitcase is full to the brim.*
• filled, loaded, topped up
OPPOSITE empty
❷ *The shopping centre was full on Saturday.*
• busy, crowded, jammed, packed, crammed, congested
OPPOSITE empty
❸ *The detective gave a full account of his findings.*
• complete, detailed, comprehensive, thorough, exhaustive
OPPOSITE incomplete
❹ *The horses were galloping at full speed.*
• top, maximum, greatest, highest
OPPOSITE minimum
❺ *The wedding dress has a very full skirt.*
• wide, broad, voluminous
OPPOSITE tight

fun *NOUN*
We had great fun at the beach on our holiday.
• amusement, diversion, enjoyment, entertainment, games, jokes, laughter, merriment, play, pleasure, recreation, sport

➤ **to make fun of someone**
It was cruel to make fun of him when he fell over.
• jeer at, laugh at, mock, ridicule, taunt, tease

function *NOUN*
❶ *The function of a vet is to cure sick animals.*
• duty, role, task, job, responsibility, purpose
❷ *The hall is being used for an official function.*
• event, occasion, party, reception
function *VERB*
This camera doesn't function properly.
• work, go, operate, run, perform

fundamental *ADJECTIVE*
He taught me the fundamental rules of chess.
• basic, elementary, essential, important, main, necessary, principal

funds *PLURAL NOUN*
The school used some of its funds to buy a minibus.
• money, cash, savings, capital, reserves

funny *ADJECTIVE*
❶ *There are some very funny jokes in the film.*
• amusing, humorous, comic, comical, hilarious, witty, entertaining, diverting
(informal) hysterical, priceless
OPPOSITE serious
❷ *There's a funny smell in here.*
• strange, odd, peculiar, curious, puzzling, weird, queer, bizarre

fur *NOUN*
Arctic foxes have thick white fur in the winter.
• hair, coat, hide, pelt

furious *ADJECTIVE*
❶ *The manager was furious when his team lost.*
• angry, mad, enraged, infuriated, incensed, livid, fuming, raging, seething

a b c d e **f** g h i j k l m n o p q r s t u v w x y z

❷ *The elves worked at a **furious** rate to finish their work.*
• frantic, hectic, frenzied, extreme, intense
OPPOSITE calm

furniture NOUN

WORD WEB

SOME ITEMS OF FURNITURE:

• armchair, bed, bookcase, bureau, chair, chest of drawers, coffee table, couch, cupboard, desk, dresser, dressing table, filing cabinet, futon, settee, sideboard, sofa, sofa bed, stool, table, wardrobe
The soft covering on a chair or sofa is upholstery.
Old and valuable pieces of furniture are antiques.

furrow NOUN
*The tractor wheels had made deep **furrows** in the mud.*
• groove, rut, ditch, channel, trench

furry ADJECTIVE
*A small, **furry** creature was curled inside the box.*
• hairy, fleecy, woolly, fuzzy, downy, feathery

further ADJECTIVE
*Look on our website for **further** information.*
• more, extra, additional, supplementary

furtive ADJECTIVE
*The spy cast a **furtive** glance around the room.*
• secretive, stealthy, surreptitious, underhand, crafty, sneaky, sly

fury NOUN
❶ *The **fury** of the creature showed in its eyes.*
• anger, rage, wrath, indignation
❷ *There was no shelter from the **fury** of the storm.*
• ferocity, fierceness, intensity, severity, violence, turbulence, savagery

fuse VERB
*The metals had **fused** together into a solid mass.*
• blend, combine, merge, unite, join, melt
To fuse metals together when you are making or mending something is to **solder** or **weld** them.

fuss NOUN
*There was a lot of **fuss** when the queen arrived.*
• bother, commotion, excitement, trouble, hullabaloo

fuss VERB
*Please don't **fuss**!*
• worry, fret, bother, get worked up

fussy ADJECTIVE
❶ *Our cat is **fussy** about its food.*
• finicky, hard to please, particular *(informal)* choosy, picky
An informal name for a fussy person is a **fusspot**.
❷ *I don't like clothes with **fussy** designs.*
• fancy, elaborate, ornate, florid

futile ADJECTIVE
*The residents made a **futile** attempt to put out the fire.*
• fruitless, pointless, unsuccessful, useless, ineffectual, vain, wasted
OPPOSITE successful

future NOUN
*She has a bright **future** as an engineer.*
• outlook, prospects
OPPOSITE past

fuzzy ADJECTIVE
❶ *The TV picture has gone **fuzzy**.*
• blurred, bleary, unfocused, unclear, indistinct, hazy, cloudy
OPPOSITE clear
❷ *Mia was wearing a **fuzzy** cardigan.*
• fluffy, frizzy, furry, woolly, fleecy

Gg

gadget NOUN
My pocket torch is a handy little **gadget**.
• tool, instrument, implement, device, contraption
(informal) gizmo

gain VERB
❶ Martha **gained** a reputation as an excellent cook.
• get, acquire, obtain, earn, win
OPPOSITE lose
❷ We **gained** our target of raising £200.
• reach, get to, arrive at, achieve, attain

game NOUN
❶ My favourite **game** is hide-and-seek.
• amusement, pastime, sport, activity, recreation
❷ The big **game** is on this Saturday.
• match, contest, competition, tournament

WORD WEB

INDOOR GAMES:

• backgammon, bagatelle, battleships, billiards, bingo, board game, cards, chess, darts, dice, dominoes, draughts, go, hangman, ludo, mah-jong, pool, snakes and ladders, snooker, table tennis or (informal) ping-pong, tiddlywinks, video game
for names of card games see **card**

PARTY GAMES:

• charades, hide-and-seek, I-spy, musical chairs, pass the parcel

PLAYGROUND AND OTHER OUTDOOR GAMES:

• conkers, hopscotch, leapfrog, marbles, skipping, skittles, tag
for more indoor and outdoor games see **sport**

---

gang NOUN
❶ The sea was swarming with **gangs** of pirates.
• group, band, crowd, pack, set, mob
❷ A **gang** of workers dug a hole in the road.
• team, unit, crew, squad, party

gap NOUN
❶ The animals escaped through a **gap** in the fence.
• opening, space, hole, breach, break, crack, rift
❷ She returned to work after a **gap** of two years.
• break, interval, interruption, pause, lull

gaping ADJECTIVE
The meteor left a **gaping** hole in the ground.
• wide, broad, yawning, vast, cavernous

garden NOUN
A small area of garden is a **plot** or **patch**.
A rented garden for growing vegetables is an **allotment**.
A garden planted with trees is an **orchard**.
A formal word for gardening is **horticulture**.
A word meaning 'to do with gardens or gardening' is **horticultural**.
for tools used for gardening see **tool**

garment NOUN
see **clothes**

gas NOUN
The mixture gave off an evil-smelling **gas**.
• vapour, fumes

gash NOUN
The broken glass made a nasty **gash** in my foot.
• cut, slash, wound, slit

gasp VERB
At the end of the race we lay **gasping** for breath.
• gulp, pant

a b c d e f **g** h i j k l m n o p q r s t u v w x y z

gate *NOUN*
People waited at the **gate** to be let in.
• gateway, doorway, entrance, portal

gather *VERB*
❶ A crowd **gathered** to watch the performers.
• assemble, collect, come together, congregate
OPPOSITE disperse
❷ The captain **gathered** her team to give them a talk.
• bring together, round up, muster
❸ We **gathered** daisies to make into chains.
• pick, pluck, collect, harvest
❹ I **gather** that you've been on holiday.
• understand, hear, learn, believe

gathering *NOUN*
There was a family **gathering** for granny's birthday.
• assembly, meeting, crowd, party, get-together

gaudy *ADJECTIVE*
The newsreader wore a rather **gaudy** tie.
• flashy, showy, loud, glaring, garish, lurid

gauge *VERB*
They're trying to **gauge** the size of the volcano.
• measure, calculate, judge, assess, estimate, reckon

gaunt *ADJECTIVE*
The sorceress had a **gaunt** face and stringy hair.
• haggard, drawn, thin, skinny, scraggy, scrawny, wasted, skeletal

gave past tense see **give**

gaze *VERB*
The dog **gazed** hungrily at the food.
• stare, look, gape

gear *NOUN*
We put our fishing **gear** in the back of the car.
• equipment, stuff, things, paraphernalia, tackle

gem *NOUN*
The crown was made of solid gold, studded with **gems**.
• jewel, precious stone
for names of gem stones see **jewel**

general *ADJECTIVE*
❶ There was a **general** air of gloom about the abbey.
• widespread, extensive, broad, sweeping, overall, prevalent
❷ I've only got a **general** idea of where we are.
• rough, approximate, indefinite, vague, loose

generally *ADVERB*
I **generally** travel to school by bus.
• usually, normally, as a rule, chiefly, mostly, mainly, commonly, on the whole

generate *VERB*
Our website has **generated** a lot of interest.
• create, produce, bring about, give rise to

generous *ADJECTIVE*
❶ It was **generous** of you to give me your seat.
• unselfish, charitable, kind-hearted
OPPOSITE selfish
❷ We each got a **generous** helping of ice cream.
• ample, large, lavish, plentiful
OPPOSITE meagre

genial *ADJECTIVE*
The housekeeper greeted us with a **genial** smile.
• friendly, kind, warm, warm-hearted, kindly, good-natured, pleasant, agreeable, cordial
OPPOSITE unfriendly

genius *NOUN*
Nila is a **genius** at maths.
• expert, master, mastermind, wizard, ace

gentle *ADJECTIVE*
❶ The vet is very **gentle** with sick animals.
• kind, tender, good-tempered, humane
❷ Grasses swayed in the **gentle** breeze.
• light, slight, mild, soft, faint
OPPOSITE strong

❸ *There is a gentle slope to the top of the hill.*
• slight, gradual, easy
OPPOSITE steep

genuine ADJECTIVE
❶ *Is that a genuine diamond?*
• real, actual, true, authentic
OPPOSITE fake
❷ *Your friend seems like a very genuine person.*
• honest, sincere, frank, earnest
OPPOSITE false

gesture NOUN
She opened her arms in a gesture of welcome.
• sign, signal, motion, movement

get VERB gets, getting, got
❶ *We're getting a goldfish for our class.*
• acquire, obtain, buy, purchase
❷ *Can you get me another blanket, please?*
• bring, fetch, collect, pick up, retrieve
❸ *Cara got a medal for swimming.*
• receive, gain, earn, win, achieve
❹ *What time did you get home?*
• arrive at, reach, come to
OPPOSITE leave
❺ *It was starting to get dark outside.*
• become, grow, turn
❻ *I got a stomach bug on holiday last year.*
• catch, develop, pick up, come down with
❼ *You'll never get Oscar to eat celery.*
• persuade, urge, influence, coax
❽ *I don't get the point of that film.*
• understand, follow, comprehend, grasp

➤ **to get on** or **along**
How are you getting on with playing the guitar?
• manage, fare, cope, prosper, succeed

➤ **to get out of**
My brother got out of doing the washing up.
• avoid, evade, shirk

➤ **to get over**
He hasn't got over the accident yet.
• get better from, recover from, shake off, survive

ghastly ADJECTIVE
The boy's face turned a ghastly shade of green.
• appalling, awful, dreadful, frightful, grim, grisly, horrible, horrifying, shocking, monstrous, terrible

ghost NOUN
Meldrop House was haunted by several ghosts.
• spirit, spectre, phantom, ghoul, apparition, shade, wraith
(informal) spook
A ghost that makes a lot of noise is a poltergeist.

WORD WEB

A GHOST OR GHOSTLY EXPERIENCE MIGHT BE:

• bloodcurdling, chilling, grisly, gruesome, hair-raising, macabre, nightmarish, spine-chilling, spine-tingling

THINGS A GHOST MIGHT DO:

• flit, float, glide, glow, haunt a person or place, hover, lurk, materialize, pass through walls, rattle or drag chains, shimmer, vanish, waft, wander

NOISES A GHOST MIGHT MAKE:

• cackle, clang, clank, creak, groan, hoot, howl, moan, screech, sigh, sob, wail
The air was filled with phantoms, wandering hither and thither in restless haste, and moaning as they went. Every one of them wore chains like Marley's Ghost.–A CHRISTMAS CAROL, Charles Dickens

PLACES A GHOST MIGHT BE FOUND:

• catacombs, crypt, haunted house or mansion, graveyard, sepulchre, tomb, vault

OTHER THINGS THAT MIGHT BE IN A HAUNTED HOUSE:

• bats, candles, cellar, cobwebs, dungeon, gargoyle, mummy, owl, secret door or passage, skeleton, skull, trapdoor, turret

a
b
c
d
e
f
g
h
i
j
k
l
m
n
o
p
q
r
s
t
u
v
w
x
y
z

ghostly ADJECTIVE
*The candlelight cast **ghostly** shadows on the wall.*
• spectral, phantom, ghoulish, unearthly, eerie, sinister, uncanny
(informal) spooky, creepy

giant NOUN
*The castle belonged to a fearsome **giant**.*
for creatures found in myths and legends see myth

giant ADJECTIVE
*A **giant** tree towered above us.*
• gigantic, huge, enormous, massive, immense, mammoth, colossal, monstrous
see also big
OPPOSITE tiny

giddy ADJECTIVE
*I felt **giddy** when I stood at the edge of the cliff.*
• dizzy, faint, unsteady

gift NOUN
❶ *I received some nice **gifts** on my birthday.*
• present
❷ *Elsa has a **gift** for music.*
• talent, ability, flair, knack, genius

gifted ADJECTIVE
*There are some **gifted** players in the team.*
• talented, able, accomplished, capable, skilful, expert

gigantic ADJECTIVE
*The dragon reared its **gigantic** head.*
• huge, giant, enormous, massive, colossal, immense, mammoth, monstrous
(informal) whopping
OPPOSITE tiny

giggle VERB
*Ailsa and I couldn't stop **giggling**.*
• snigger, titter, chuckle, laugh

girl NOUN
A synonym used in some parts of Britain is lass.
Old-fashioned words are damsel, maid *and* maiden.

give VERB gives, giving, gave, given
❶ *Santa Claus **gave** each child a present.*
• deal out, distribute, issue, supply, offer, present, hand over, pass, award
❷ *Will you **give** something to our collection for charity?*
• contribute, donate
❸ *The giant **gave** a loud sneeze.*
• utter, emit, let out
❹ *We are **giving** a concert at the end of term.*
• present, put on, lay on, organize, arrange
❺ *Will this branch **give** if I sit on it?*
• collapse, give way, bend, break, buckle
➤ **to give in**
*The boxer **gave in** after a long fight.*
• surrender, yield, submit, quit
➤ **to give up**
*He **gave up** trying to start the car.*
• abandon, stop, cease, quit

glad ADJECTIVE
*I'm **glad** to hear that you're feeling better.*
• pleased, happy, delighted, thrilled
OPPOSITE sad

glamorous ADJECTIVE
*All the guests at the awards ceremony looked very **glamorous**.*
• beautiful, attractive, gorgeous, elegant, stylish, fashionable

glance VERB
*The bus driver **glanced** quickly at his watch.*
• look quickly, peek, peep, glimpse

glare VERB
*The troll **glared** at us from under his bushy eyebrows.*
• stare, frown, scowl, glower

glare NOUN
❶ *The **glare** of the lights dazzled me.*
• dazzle, blaze, brightness, brilliance
❷ *The teacher silenced the children with an angry **glare**.*
• stare, scowl, glower, frown, nasty look

glasses PLURAL NOUN
She put on her glasses to read the letter.
• spectacles
(informal) specs

WORD WEB

OTHER INSTRUMENTS WITH LENSES:

• binoculars, camera, magnifying glass, microscope, telescope
An old word for a telescope is a **spyglass**. A lens that you wear over one eye is a **monocle**.

gleam NOUN
I saw a gleam of moonlight between the clouds.
• glimmer, glint, flash, ray, shaft

gleam VERB
The lights gleamed on the water.
• glimmer, glint, glisten, shimmer, shine

glide VERB
The boat glided gently across the lake.
• move smoothly, slide, slip, drift, float, coast

glimmer VERB
The city lights glimmered in the distance.
• gleam, glint, glow, glisten, shimmer, flicker, blink

glimpse VERB
I glimpsed a deer running through the forest.
• catch sight of, spot, spy, sight

glimpse NOUN
We caught a glimpse of a dolphin's tail.
• peek, peep, glance, sighting, view

glint VERB
Sunlight glinted on the windows.
• flash, glitter, sparkle, twinkle

glisten VERB
The pavement glistened with frost.
• gleam, shine, glint, shimmer, glimmer

glitter VERB
The jewels glittered under the bright lights.
• sparkle, twinkle, shimmer, glimmer, glint, glisten, flash, shine

gloat VERB
He was gloating about winning the poetry prize.
• boast, brag, crow, show off

global ADJECTIVE
The Internet is a global network of computers.
• worldwide, international, universal

globe NOUN
❶ *I'd like to travel all round the globe.*
• world, planet, earth
❷ *The fortune teller used a crystal globe.*
• ball, sphere, orb

gloom NOUN
❶ *We could hardly see in the gloom of the cave.*
• darkness, dimness, shade, shadow, murk
The gloomy light late in the evening is **dusk** or **twilight**.
❷ *There was an air of gloom in the abandoned tower.*
• depression, sadness, unhappiness, melancholy, misery, despair

gloomy ADJECTIVE
❶ *It was cold and gloomy in the cellar.*
• dark, dingy, dim, dismal, dreary, sombre, cheerless, murky, shadowy
OPPOSITE bright
❷ *Eeyore was feeling gloomy again.*
• depressed, sad, unhappy, glum, miserable, melancholy, low, downcast, dejected
(informal) down in the dumps
OPPOSITE cheerful

glorious ADJECTIVE
Look at that glorious sunset!
• magnificent, splendid, stunning, spectacular, superb, magnificent, wonderful, marvellous

glossy ADJECTIVE
The bear had a thick, glossy coat of black fur.
• shiny, sleek, silky, shining, gleaming, lustrous
OPPOSITE dull

glove NOUN
for items of clothing see **clothes**

glow NOUN
The soft glow of burning candles lit the room.
• brightness, shine, gleam, radiance

glow VERB
The embers of the bonfire were still glowing.
• shine, gleam, burn
Something that glows in the dark is **luminous** or **phosphorescent**.

glower VERB
The jailer glowered at the prisoners.
• glare, scowl, frown, stare angrily

glue NOUN
Put a blob of glue on each corner of the paper.
• adhesive, paste, gum

glue VERB
Glue the edges of the box together.
• stick, paste, bond, seal

glum ADJECTIVE
Why are you looking so glum?
• depressed, sad, unhappy, gloomy, miserable, melancholy, low, downcast, dejected
OPPOSITE cheerful

gnarled ADJECTIVE
The branches of the tree were gnarled with age.
• bent, twisted, crooked, distorted, knobbly, knotty

gnaw VERB
The wolves gnawed at a pile of bones.
• chew, bite, nibble, munch

go VERB goes, going, went, gone
❶ *A carriage was going slowly along the road.*
• move, progress, proceed
see also **move**
❷ *My granny has always wanted to go to China.*
• travel, journey
❸ *Some of the guests had already gone.*
• leave, depart, get away, withdraw
❹ *By morning, the ice had all gone.*
• disappear, vanish
❺ *The canal goes all the way from Inverness to Fort William.*
• extend, lead, reach, stretch, run
❻ *The mountaineer's face went blue with cold.*
• become, turn, grow
❼ *Is that old grandfather clock still going?*
• function, operate, work, run
❽ *Cups and saucers go on the bottom shelf.*
• belong, be kept, be placed
❾ *Time goes slowly when you're stuck indoors.*
• pass, go by, elapse

➤ **to go back**
Sarah has gone back to the house.
• return, retreat, retrace your steps

➤ **to go in for**
I'm not going in for the race this year.
• enter, take part in, participate in

➤ **to go off**
❶ *A bomb went off nearby.*
• explode, blow up, detonate
❷ *The milk will go off if it's not in the fridge.*
• turn sour, go bad, rot

➤ **to go on**
❶ *What's going on over there?*
• happen, occur, take place
❷ *Please go on with your story.*
• carry on, continue, keep going, proceed

➤ **to go with**
Does this scarf go with my coat?
• match, suit, blend with

go NOUN
Would you like to have a go on my computer?
• try, turn, chance, opportunity
(informal) shot, bash, stab

goal NOUN

❶ *The goal of the society is to protect wildlife.*
• aim, ambition, intention, object, objective, purpose, target

❷ *We managed to get a goal just before half-time.*
Three goals scored by the same player is known as a **hat-trick**.

gobble VERB

Ladybirds love to gobble greenfly.
• guzzle, gulp, bolt, devour

god or goddess NOUN

Zeus was one of the gods of ancient Greece.
• deity
A word meaning 'to do with a god or goddess' is **divine**.

gold NOUN

Something that is made of gold is **golden** or **gilded**.
A thin covering of gold is **gilt**.

good ADJECTIVE

That is a really good idea!
• excellent, fine, lovely, nice, wonderful *(informal)* fantastic, great, super, cool, fantabulous, splendiferous
OPPOSITE bad

OVERUSED WORD

Try to vary the words you use for **good**. Here are some other words you could use.

FOR A GOOD PERSON OR GOOD CREATURE:

• honest, worthy, honourable, moral, decent, virtuous, noble, kind, kindly, humane, generous, charitable, merciful
There was once a kindly old wizard who used his magic generously and wisely for the benefit of his neighbours.—THE TALES OF BEEDLE THE BARD, J. K. Rowling
OPPOSITES evil, wicked
A good character in a story or film is a **hero** or **heroine** or *(informal)* **goody**.

FOR GOOD BEHAVIOUR:

• well-behaved, obedient, angelic, exemplary
The children are well-behaved.
A common simile is **as good as gold**.
OPPOSITES naughty, disobedient

FOR A GOOD FRIEND:

• true, loyal, loving, reliable, trusty, trustworthy
My dog, Rusty, is a loyal companion.

FOR A GOOD FEELING OR GOOD MOOD:

• happy, cheerful, light-hearted, positive, contented
Mr Fox was in a cheerful mood after his tea.

FOR A GOOD EXPERIENCE OR GOOD NEWS:

• pleasant, enjoyable, delightful, agreeable, pleasing
OPPOSITES unpleasant, disagreeable
The girls had an enjoyable time at the party.
The letter contained some pleasing news.

FOR A GOOD PERFORMER OR GOOD WORK:

• capable, skilful, clever, able, talented, competent, commendable, sound
My friend, Chris, is a talented dancer.
OPPOSITES poor, awful

FOR GOOD FOOD OR A GOOD MEAL:

• delicious, tasty, healthy, nourishing, nutritious, well-cooked, wholesome, substantial, hearty
The crew ate a hearty breakfast together.

FOR A GOOD EXCUSE OR GOOD REASON:

• acceptable, valid, proper, satisfactory, legitimate
I hope you have a valid excuse for being late.
OPPOSITES poor, unacceptable

FOR GOOD TIMING:

• convenient, suitable, fortunate, appropriate, opportune
Is this a convenient time for a chat?
OPPOSITES inconvenient, unsuitable

a
b
c
d
e
f
g
h
i
j
k
l
m
n
o
p
q
r
s
t
u
v
w
x
y
z

A
B
C
D
E
F
G
H
I
J
K
L
M
N
O
P
Q
R
S
T
U
V
W
X
Y
Z

FOR GOOD WEATHER:

• fine, favourable
*We are hoping for **fine** weather tomorrow.*
OPPOSITES harsh, adverse

goodbye *NOUN*
*The astronauts said **goodbye** to their families.*
• farewell
(informal) cheerio
A formal phrase meaning 'to say goodbye' is
to bid farewell.

good-looking *ADJECTIVE*
*I think your cousin is quite **good-looking**.*
• attractive, handsome, pretty
OPPOSITES ugly

goods *PLURAL NOUN*
*The smugglers hid the stolen **goods** in a cave.*
• property, merchandise, wares, cargo

gorgeous *ADJECTIVE*
*The gardens look **gorgeous** in the summer.*
• beautiful, glorious, dazzling, stunning,
splendid, superb, glamorous, handsome

gossip *VERB*
*Two neighbours were **gossiping** over the fence.*
• chatter, tell tales
(informal) natter
gossip *NOUN*
❶ *Don't believe all the **gossip** you hear.*
• chatter, rumour, hearsay, scandal
(informal) tittle-tattle
❷ *Our next-door neighbour is a dreadful **gossip**.*
• busybody, chatterbox, telltale,
scandalmonger

gouge *VERB*
*The builders **gouged** a hole in the wall.*
• dig, hollow out, scoop out, excavate

govern *VERB*
*The ancient Romans **governed** a vast empire.*
• rule, run, administer, direct, command,
manage, be in charge of

gown *NOUN*
*The mermaid wore a **gown** made of seaweed
and pearls.*
• dress, robe, frock

grab *VERB*
*The cowboy **grabbed** the reins of the runaway
horse.*
• seize, grasp, catch, clutch, grip, get hold of,
snatch

graceful *ADJECTIVE*
*The gymnast made a **graceful** landing.*
• elegant, beautiful, stylish, smooth, flowing,
agile, nimble
OPPOSITES clumsy, graceless

gracious *ADJECTIVE*
*The film star waved and gave a **gracious** smile.*
• polite, courteous, good-natured, pleasant,
agreeable, civil

grade *NOUN*
*My sister has reached the top **grade** in judo.*
• class, standard, level, stage, rank, degree
grade *VERB*
*Eggs are **graded** according to size.*
• group, sort, classify

gradual *ADJECTIVE*
*There's been a **gradual** change in the weather.*
• steady, slow, gentle, moderate, regular, even
OPPOSITE sudden

grain *NOUN*
❶ *Some **grains** of sand stuck to my toes.*
• bit, particle, speck, granule
❷ *The **grain** will be made into bread.*
• cereals, corn

grand *ADJECTIVE*
❶ *The wedding was a **grand** occasion.*
• magnificent, splendid, stately, impressive,
big, great, important, imposing
❷ *(informal) Keep going—you're doing a
grand job!*
• excellent, fine, good, first-class

grant *VERB*
The king granted the prisoners their freedom.
• give, allow, permit, award

grapple *VERB*
The guards grappled with the intruders, but they got away.
• struggle, wrestle, fight, tussle

grasp *VERB*
❶ *The climber grasped the end of the rope.*
• clutch, grab, grip, seize, catch, snatch, take hold of, hang on to
❷ *The ideas were quite difficult to grasp.*
• understand, comprehend, follow, take in
grasp *NOUN*
Rita has a good grasp of mathematics.
• understanding, comprehension, knowledge, mastery

grass *NOUN*
People were told not to walk on the grass.
• lawn, turf, green

grate *VERB*
❶ *I grated the cheese on to the pizza.*
• shred, grind
❷ *The chalk grated on the blackboard.*
• scrape, scratch
➤ **to grate on**
That man's voice grates on my nerves.
• annoy, irritate, jar on

grateful *ADJECTIVE*
I'm grateful for your help.
• thankful, appreciative, obliged, indebted
OPPOSITE ungrateful

gratitude *NOUN*
We sent some flowers to show our gratitude.
• thanks, appreciation

grave *NOUN*
see **tomb**

grave *ADJECTIVE*
❶ *They looked grave when they heard the news.*
• grim, sad, serious, thoughtful
OPPOSITE cheerful
❷ *She made a grave mistake.*
• crucial, important, serious, vital
OPPOSITE trivial

graveyard *NOUN*
He was buried in the local graveyard.
• burial ground, cemetery, churchyard

graze *VERB*
I grazed my knee when I fell off my bike.
• scrape, cut, scratch, scuff

greasy *ADJECTIVE*
I don't like greasy food.
• fatty, oily

great *ADJECTIVE*
❶ *The inventor had made a great discovery.*
• important, significant, major, leading, noteworthy
OPPOSITES insignificant, minor
❷ *Mozart was a great composer.*
• famous, notable, celebrated, eminent, distinguished, outstanding, brilliant
❸ *Their voices echoed round the great hall.*
• big, huge, large, enormous, vast, immense, gigantic, extensive, cavernous
OPPOSITE small
❹ *Orla took great care over the designs.*
• considerable, extreme, exact
OPPOSITE little
❺ *(informal) That is a great idea!*
• very good, excellent, marvellous, outstanding, superb, tremendous, wonderful *(informal)* brilliant, fantastic, super, smashing, terrific
OPPOSITES bad, awful

greed *NOUN*
The king wanted more gold to satisfy his greed.
• avarice, selfishness, hunger, craving, gluttony

a
b
c
d
e
f
g
h
i
j
k
l
m
n
o
p
q
r
s
t
u
v
w
x
y
z

greedy ADJECTIVE
❶ *The children were so greedy that they ate all the cakes.*
• gluttonous
(informal) piggish
A common simile is **as greedy as a pig.**
❷ *Scrooge is very greedy with his money.*
• selfish, miserly, tight-fisted, grasping

green ADJECTIVE, NOUN

WORD WEB

SOME SHADES OF GREEN:

• bottle-green, emerald, jade, khaki, lime, olive, pea-green

greens PLURAL NOUN
see **vegetable**

greet VERB
The driver greeted us with a friendly wave.
• welcome, hail, receive, salute

grew past tense see **grow**

grey ADJECTIVE
❶ *The old wizard had a bushy grey beard.*
• silver, silvery, grizzly, hoary, whitish
❷ *The mother's face was grey with worry.*
• ashen, pale, leaden, wan
❸ *The day began cold and grey.*
• dull, cloudy, overcast

grief NOUN
He couldn't hide his grief at his friend's death.
• sorrow, sadness, mourning, unhappiness, distress, anguish, heartache
OPPOSITE joy

grieve VERB
❶ *The family is still grieving over her death.*
• mourn, lament, weep
OPPOSITE rejoice
❷ *It grieves me to leave so soon.*
• sadden, upset, distress, hurt
OPPOSITE please

grim ADJECTIVE
❶ *The judge wore a grim expression on her face.*
• stern, severe, harsh, bad-tempered, sullen
OPPOSITE cheerful
❷ *The detective made the grim discovery of the body.*
• unpleasant, horrible, dreadful, terrible, hideous, shocking, gruesome, grisly
OPPOSITE pleasant

grime NOUN
There was a layer of grime on the floor.
• dirt, filth, muck, mire, mess

grimy ADJECTIVE
Don't wipe those grimy feet on the carpet!
• dirty, filthy, grubby, mucky, soiled
OPPOSITE clean

grin NOUN, VERB
Mark arrived with a silly grin on his face.
• smile, beam, smirk
A large grin is a **broad**, **wide** or **cheesy** grin.

grind VERB grinds, grinding, ground
❶ *Grind the spices into a fine powder.*
• crush, pound, powder, pulverize, mill
❷ *This tool is used for grinding knives.*
• sharpen, file, hone, whet

grip VERB
❶ *Grip the handle tightly.*
• grasp, seize, clutch, clasp, hold
❷ *The audience was gripped by the film.*
• fascinate, engross, absorb, enthral

grisly ADJECTIVE
We found the grisly remains of a dead sheep.
• gruesome, gory, ghastly, hideous, nasty, revolting, sickening

grit NOUN
❶ *I've got some grit in my shoe.*
• gravel, dust, sand
❷ *The marathon runners showed real grit.*
• bravery, courage, toughness, spirit, pluck
(informal) guts

groan *VERB*
The wounded soldier groaned with pain.
• cry out, moan, sigh, wail

groove *NOUN*
Thick grooves had been carved in the stone wall.
• channel, furrow, rut, cut, scratch, slot

grope *VERB*
I groped in the dark for the light switch.
• fumble, feel about, flounder

gross *ADJECTIVE*
❶ *That is a gross exaggeration!*
• extreme, glaring, obvious, sheer, blatant, outright
❷ *Most ogres have gross table manners.*
• offensive, rude, coarse, vulgar

ground *past tense see* **grind**

ground *NOUN*
❶ *I planted some seeds in the ground.*
• earth, soil, land
❷ *The ground was too wet to play on.*
• field, pitch, park, stadium, arena

group *NOUN*
❶ *Japan consists of a group of islands.*
• collection, set, batch, cluster, clump
❷ *A group of children was waiting at the bus stop.*
• crowd, bunch, gathering, band, body, gang
❸ *The book group meets once a month.*
• club, society, association, circle
❹ *We sorted the fossils into different groups.*
• category, class, type, kind, sort

WORD WEB

WORDS FOR GROUPS OF PEOPLE:

a **band** of musicians
a **class** of pupils
a **company** or **troupe** of actors
a **congregation** of worshippers in church
a **coven** of witches
a **crew** of sailors
a **gang** of workers
a **horde** of invaders
a **team** of players

WORDS FOR GROUPS OF ANIMALS:

an **army** or **colony** of ants
a **band** of gorillas
a **brood** of chicks
a **covey** of partridges
a **flock** of sheep or birds
a **gaggle** of geese
a **herd** of cattle or elephants
a **litter** of pigs or puppies
a **pack** of wolves
a **pride** of lions
a **school** or **pod** of dolphins or whales
a **shoal** of fish
a **swarm** of insects
a **troop** of monkeys

WORDS FOR GROUPS OF THINGS:

a **battery** of guns
a **bunch** of flowers
a **clump** of trees
a **clutch** of eggs in a nest
a **constellation** or **galaxy** of stars
a **convoy** or **fleet** of ships

grow *VERB* grows, growing, grew, grown
❶ *The puppies have grown since I last saw them.*
• get bigger, put on growth, spring up, sprout
❷ *The number of children in the school has grown.*
• increase, develop, enlarge, expand, build up
OPPOSITE decrease
❸ *Our neighbour grows orchids in her greenhouse.*
• cultivate, produce, raise, farm
❹ *It is growing dark outside.*
• become, get, turn

grown-up *ADJECTIVE*
The female cheetah has two grown-up cubs.
• adult, mature, fully grown
OPPOSITE young

grown-up *NOUN*
Don't tell the grown-ups.
• adult
OPPOSITES young person, child

a b c d e f g h i j k l m n o p q r s t u v w x y z

growth *NOUN*
❶ *There's been a **growth** of interest in golf for kids.*
• increase, rise, spread, expansion, development, enlargement
❷ *The doctor examined the **growth** on my foot.*
• lump, swelling, tumour

grub *NOUN*
*I found a **grub** on the cabbage leaf.*
• larva, maggot, caterpillar

grubby *ADJECTIVE*
*My hands were **grubby** from working in the garden.*
• dirty, filthy, grimy, messy, mucky, soiled
(OPPOSITE) clean

grudge *NOUN*
*Captain Hook bore a **grudge** against Peter Pan.*
• grievance, bitterness, resentment, hard feelings, ill will, spite

gruelling *ADJECTIVE*
*The marathon is a **gruelling** race.*
• hard, tough, demanding, exhausting, challenging, difficult, laborious, strenuous, backbreaking, punishing
(OPPOSITE) easy

gruesome *ADJECTIVE*
*The battlefield was a **gruesome** sight.*
• grisly, gory, ghastly, hideous, monstrous, revolting, sickening, appalling, dreadful, frightful, shocking, abominable

gruff *ADJECTIVE*
*The ogre spoke in a **gruff** voice.*
• harsh, rough, hoarse, husky, throaty

grumble *VERB*
*You're always **grumbling** about the weather!*
• complain, moan, groan, protest, whine, gripe

grumpy *ADJECTIVE*
*I was **grumpy** because I had a headache.*
• bad-tempered, cross, irritable, testy, tetchy, cantankerous
(informal) grouchy
(OPPOSITE) good-humoured

guarantee *VERB*
*I **guarantee** that you will enjoy the show.*
• promise, assure, pledge, vow

guard *VERB*
*The cave was **guarded** by a one-eyed giant.*
• protect, defend, stand guard over, patrol, safeguard, shield, watch over

guard *NOUN*
*A **guard** was on duty at the gate.*
• sentry, sentinel, warder, lookout, watchman

guardian *NOUN*
*The **guardian** of the treasure was a fierce dragon.*
• defender, protector, keeper, minder, custodian

guess *NOUN*
*My **guess** is that it will rain tomorrow.*
• estimate, prediction, feeling, hunch

guess *VERB*
❶ *There was a prize for **guessing** the weight of the cake.*
• estimate, judge, work out, gauge, predict, reckon
❷ *I **guess** you must be tired after your journey.*
• suppose, imagine, expect, assume, think

guest *NOUN*
*We are having **guests** for tea on Sunday.*
• visitor, caller, company

guide *NOUN*
❶ *Our **guide** showed us around the zoo.*
• courier, escort, leader, chaperone
❷ *We bought a useful **guide** to the city.*
• guidebook, handbook, manual

guide *VERB*
*The explorers used the stars to **guide** them at night.*
• direct, lead, steer, conduct, escort, show the way

guilt *NOUN*
❶ *The prisoner admitted his **guilt**.*
• responsibility, liability, blame, wrongdoing
(OPPOSITE) innocence

❷ *You could see the look of **guilt** on her face.*
• shame, remorse, regret, penitence, disgrace, dishonour

guilty *ADJECTIVE*
❶ *The prisoner was found **guilty** of the crime.*
• responsible, to blame, at fault, in the wrong, liable
OPPOSITE innocent
❷ *You have a **guilty** look on your face!*
• ashamed, guilt-ridden, remorseful, sorry, conscience-stricken, repentant, shamefaced, sheepish
OPPOSITE unrepentant

gulp *VERB*
*Peter **gulped** down the cake in one go.*
• swallow, bolt, gobble, guzzle, devour
for other ways to eat see **eat**
gulp *NOUN*
*Amanda took a long **gulp** of lemonade.*
• swallow, mouthful
(informal) swig

gun *NOUN*
for various weapons see **weapon**

gurgle *VERB*
*The mountain stream **gurgled** over the rocks.*
• burble, babble

gush *NOUN*
*There was a **gush** of water from the pipe.*
• rush, stream, torrent, cascade, flood, jet, spout, spurt
gush *VERB*
*Water **gushed** from the broken pipe.*
• rush, stream, flow, pour, flood, spout, spurt, squirt

gust *NOUN*
*A **gust** of wind carried the kite into the sky.*
• blast, rush, puff, squall, flurry

guzzle *VERB*
*The seagulls **guzzled** all the bread.*
• gobble, gulp, bolt, devour
for other ways to eat see **eat**

Hh

habit *NOUN*
❶ *It's her **habit** to go for a walk each morning.*
• custom, practice, routine, rule
❷ *My dog has a **habit** of scratching his ear.*
• mannerism, way, tendency, inclination, quirk

hack *VERB*
*We **hacked** our way through the thick undergrowth.*
• chop, cut, hew, slash, lop

had *past tense see* **have**

haggard *ADJECTIVE*
*The warriors looked **haggard** after the battle.*
• drawn, gaunt, thin, pinched, wasted, shrunken, wan
OPPOSITE healthy

haggle *VERB*
*The men **haggled** over the price of the gems.*
• bargain, negotiate, argue, wrangle

hair *NOUN*
*Rapunzel's **hair** reached down to the ground.*
• locks, tresses
(informal) mop
A single piece of hair is a **strand**.
A bunch of hair is a **hank**, **lock** or **tress**.
A mass of bushy hair is a **shock** of hair.
False hair is a **hairpiece**, **toupee** or **wig**.
An area without hair is a **bald patch**.
The way hair is cut is a **hairstyle** or *(informal)* **hairdo** or *(formal)* **coiffure**.
Hair is cut or styled by a **hairdresser** or **hairstylist**.
Men's hair is also cut by a **barber**.

a b c d e f **g** **h** i j k l m n o p q r s t u v w x y z

A B C D E F G **H** I J K L M N O P Q R S T U V W X Y Z

WORD WEB

SOME HAIRSTYLES:

• Afro, bob, braids, bun, bunches, chignon, cornrows, crew cut, curls, dreadlocks, fishtail, French braid or plait, fringe, Mohican, mullet, perm, pigtail, plaits, ponytail, quiff, ringlets, short back and sides, sideburns, skinhead, topknot

HAIR ON AN ANIMAL:

• bristles, coat, down, fleece, fur, mane, whiskers

WRITING TIPS

You can use these words to describe **hair**:

TO DESCRIBE ITS COLOUR:

• auburn, blond or blonde, brunette, *(informal)* carroty, dark, fair, flaxen, ginger, grey, grizzled, hoary, mousy, platinum blonde, raven, red, silver
He was a man of fifty, with a shock of grizzled hair, a broad but not unkindly face of regular features, bushy eyebrows, and the finest forehead that I ever saw.—MOONFLEET, J. Meade Faulkner

TO DESCRIBE HOW IT LOOKS OR FEELS:

• bristly, bushy, coarse, curly, dishevelled, fine, frizzy, glossy, greasy, lank, limp, matted, ringletted, shaggy, shiny, silky, spiky, straggly, straight, stringy, tangled, thick, tousled, tuggy, unkempt, wavy, windswept, wispy
The hair on Mr Twit's face didn't grow smooth and matted as it does on most hairy-faced men. It grew in spikes that stuck out straight like the bristles of a nailbrush.—THE TWITS, Roald Dahl
for ways to describe animal hair see **animal**

hairy ADJECTIVE
Mammoths were like elephants with thick hairy coats.
• shaggy, bushy, bristly, woolly, fleecy, furry, fuzzy, long-haired, hirsute

hall NOUN
❶ *The hall was full for the concert.*
• assembly hall, auditorium, concert hall, theatre
❷ *You can use the coat stand in the hall.*
• entrance hall, hallway, lobby, foyer

halt VERB
❶ *The car halted at the red light.*
• stop, come to a halt, draw up, pull up, wait
❷ *A traffic jam halted the traffic.*
• stop, check, obstruct
❸ *Work halted when the whistle went.*
• end, cease, terminate, break off
OPPOSITES start, go

halve VERB
❶ *Halve the tomatoes and scoop out the seeds.*
• cut in half, divide into halves, split in two
❷ *The workforce has been halved in the last five years.*
• cut by half, reduce by half

hammer VERB
I hammered on the door, but no one answered.
• strike, beat, knock, batter, pummel, pound

hamper VERB
Bad weather hampered the rescuers.
• hinder, hold up, obstruct, impede, restrict, handicap, frustrate
OPPOSITE help

hand NOUN
When you clench your hand you make a **fist**.
The flat part of the inside of your hand is the **palm.**
Work that you do with your hands is **manual** work.

hand VERB
The postman handed me several letters.
• give, pass, present, offer, deliver
➤ **to hand something down**
This brooch has been handed down from generation to generation.
• pass down, pass on, bequeath

handicap *NOUN*
Lack of experience can be a handicap in some jobs.
• disadvantage, drawback, hindrance, obstacle, problem, difficulty, limitation
OPPOSITE advantage

handicap *VERB*
The search was handicapped by bad weather.
• hamper, hinder, hold up, restrict, impede
OPPOSITE help

handle *NOUN*
The door handle is broken.
• grip, handgrip, knob, shaft
The handle of a sword is the hilt.

handle *VERB*
❶ *Please don't handle the exhibits.*
• touch, feel, hold, stroke, fondle, finger, grasp
❷ *The referee handled the game well.*
• manage, control, conduct, deal with, cope with, tackle

handsome *ADJECTIVE*
❶ *Prince Charming was very handsome.*
• attractive, good-looking, nice-looking, gorgeous
(informal) dishy
OPPOSITES ugly, unattractive
❷ *They sold their house for a handsome profit.*
• big, large, substantial, sizeable
OPPOSITE slight

handy *ADJECTIVE*
❶ *This handy gadget is for peeling potatoes.*
• useful, helpful, convenient, practical
OPPOSITE awkward
❷ *I always keep my umbrella handy.*
• accessible, available, close at hand, nearby, ready
OPPOSITE inaccessible

hang *VERB* hangs, hanging, hung
❶ *A monkey was hanging from the tree branch.*
• dangle, be suspended, swing, sway
❷ *The dog had hair hanging down over his eyes.*
• droop, drape, flop, trail, cascade

❸ *I hung the picture on the wall.*
• fix, attach, fasten, stick, peg
❹ *Smoke hung in the air.*
• float, hover, drift, linger, cling
➤ **to hang about** or **around**
Don't hang about; we'll miss the bus.
• delay, dawdle, linger, loiter
➤ **to hang on** *(informal)*
Try to hang on a bit longer.
• carry on, continue, stay, remain, persist, keep going, persevere
➤ **to hang on to something**
❶ *Hang on to the rope.*
• hold, grip, grasp
❷ *Hang on to your bus ticket.*
• keep, retain, save

happen *VERB*
Did anything interesting happen today?
• take place, occur, arise, come about, crop up, emerge, result

happening *NOUN*
There have been strange happenings here lately.
• event, occurrence, incident, phenomenon

happiness *NOUN*
The bride's face glowed with happiness.
• joy, joyfulness, delight, jubilation, pleasure, contentment, gladness, cheerfulness, merriment, ecstasy, bliss
OPPOSITE sorrow

happy *ADJECTIVE*

OVERUSED WORD

Try to vary the words you use for **happy**. Here are some other words you could use.

FOR A HAPPY MOOD OR HAPPY PERSON:

• cheerful, cheery, joyful, jolly, merry, delighted, light-hearted, contented, gleeful
Dr Mead ... was a tall, broad-shouldered man with kind grey eyes, and a cheerful smile. Pollyanna liked him at once, and told him so.
—POLLYANNA, Eleanor H. Porter
A common simile is as happy as a lark.
OPPOSITES unhappy, sad

A
B
C
D
E
F
G
H
I
J
K
L
M
N
O
P
Q
R
S
T
U
V
W
X
Y
Z

FOR A VERY HAPPY MOOD:

• thrilled, ecstatic, elated, overjoyed
(informal) over the moon, thrilled to bits,
tickled pink
*Megan was ecstatic when she won
first prize.*

FOR A HAPPY TIME OR HAPPY EXPERIENCE:

• enjoyable, joyous, glorious, blissful,
heavenly, idyllic
They spent a glorious summer on the island.

FOR A HAPPY COINCIDENCE:

• lucky, fortunate, favourable
*By a lucky coincidence, we took the same
train.*
OPPOSITE unfortunate

TO BE HAPPY TO DO SOMETHING:

• pleased, glad, willing, delighted
I would be glad to help organize the party.
OPPOSITE unwilling

harass *VERB*
I keep being harassed with junk email.
• pester, trouble, bother, annoy, disturb,
plague, torment, badger, hound, hassle

harbour *NOUN*
Several yachts were tied up in the harbour.
• port, dock, mooring, quay, pier, wharf

hard *ADJECTIVE*

OVERUSED WORD

Try to vary the words you use for **hard**.
Here are some other words you could use.

FOR HARD GROUND OR A HARD SURFACE:

• solid, firm, dense, compact, rigid, stiff
The ground was solid and covered with frost.
Common similes are **as hard as nails** and
as hard as a rock.
OPPOSITE soft

FOR A HARD PULL OR HARD PUSH:

• strong, forceful, heavy, powerful, violent
Try giving the door a heavy push.
OPPOSITE light

FOR HARD WORK:

• tough, gruelling, strenuous, tiring,
exhausting, laborious, back-breaking
Digging the tunnel was strenuous work.
OPPOSITE easy

FOR A HARD WORKER:

• energetic, keen, diligent
At first, the apprentice was very diligent.
OPPOSITE lazy

FOR A HARD PERSON OR HARD TREATMENT:

• strict, stern, harsh, severe, cruel,
hard-hearted, heartless, unfeeling, unkind
*'How dare you say I'm freckled and redheaded?
You are a rude, impolite, unfeeling woman!'*
—ANNE OF GREEN GABLES, L. M. Montgomery
OPPOSITE mild

FOR A HARD PROBLEM OR HARD QUESTION:

• difficult, complicated, complex,
intricate, perplexing, puzzling, baffling,
knotty, thorny
None of us could solve the complex riddle.
OPPOSITE simple

hard *ADVERB*
❶ *Ros is working hard at learning Mandarin.*
• strenuously, energetically, diligently, keenly,
intently
❷ *It has been raining hard all afternoon.*
• heavily, steadily
(informal) cats and dogs

harden *VERB*
We left the cement to harden.
• set, solidify, stiffen
If you harden clay in a kiln, you bake or fire it.
OPPOSITE soften

hardly *ADVERB*
I could hardly see in the fog.
• barely, scarcely, only just, with difficulty

hardship *NOUN*
They suffered years of hardship during the war.
• suffering, trouble, difficulty, distress, misery, misfortune, need, want

hardy *ADJECTIVE*
You must be hardy to go camping in winter.
• tough, strong, robust, sturdy, resilient, rugged
OPPOSITE tender

harm *VERB*
❶ *His captors didn't harm him.*
• hurt, injure, ill-treat, wound
❷ *Too much direct sunlight may harm this plant.*
• damage, spoil, ruin
harm *NOUN*
I didn't mean to cause him any harm.
• damage, hurt, injury, pain
OPPOSITE benefit

harmful *ADJECTIVE*
Junk food can be harmful to your health.
• damaging, dangerous, destructive, injurious, unhealthy
OPPOSITES harmless, beneficial

harmless *ADJECTIVE*
❶ *You can drink the potion—it is quite harmless.*
• safe, non-toxic, innocuous
OPPOSITES harmful, dangerous
❷ *It was just a bit of harmless fun.*
• innocent, inoffensive

harsh *ADJECTIVE*
❶ *The trumpet sounded loud and harsh.*
• rough, rasping, grating, jarring, shrill, raucous
OPPOSITES soft, gentle
❷ *We blinked in the harsh light.*
• bright, brilliant, dazzling, glaring
OPPOSITES soft, subdued
❸ *The rescue team braved the harsh weather.*
• severe, strict, cruel, hard, tough, bleak
OPPOSITE mild
❹ *The coach had some harsh words to say.*
• strong, sharp, unkind, unfriendly

harvest *NOUN*
There was a good harvest of apples this year.
• crop, yield, return
Things grown on a farm are **produce**.
A plentiful harvest is a **bumper harvest**.

haste *NOUN*
The elves worked with great haste.
• hurry, rush, speed, urgency

hasty *ADJECTIVE*
❶ *The robbers made a hasty exit.*
• fast, hurried, quick, sudden, swift, rapid, speedy
OPPOSITE slow
❷ *The king regretted his hasty decision.*
• rash, reckless, impatient, foolhardy, thoughtless
OPPOSITES careful, measured

hat *NOUN*

WORD WEB

SOME KINDS OF HAT:

• balaclava, baseball cap, beanie, bearskin, beret, bicycle helmet, bonnet, bowler hat, cap, deerstalker, hard hat, helmet, mitre, mortar board, panama hat, skullcap, sombrero, sou'wester, Stetson, sun hat, tam o' shanter, top hat, trilby, turban, woolly hat

hatch *VERB*
The gang hatched a plot to rob a bank.
• plan, develop, conceive, think up, devise
(informal) cook up, dream up

hate *VERB*
❶ *Eddie hates broccoli and peas.*
• dislike, detest, despise, loathe
❷ *I hate to bother you.*
• be sorry, be reluctant, regret
OPPOSITES like, love
hate *NOUN*
Washing dishes is one of my pet hates.
• dislike

a b c d e f g h i j k l m n o p q r s t u v w x y z

hatred NOUN
The evil wizard stared with hatred in his eyes.
• hate, loathing, dislike, hostility, enmity, contempt, detestation
OPPOSITE love

haughty ADJECTIVE
Celia sniffed and gave us a haughty look.
• proud, arrogant, conceited, lofty, superior, pompous, disdainful
(informal) stuck-up
OPPOSITE modest

haul VERB
Eric hauled his bike out of the shed.
• drag, pull, tow, draw

haunt VERB
for things a ghost might do see **ghost**

have VERB has, having, had
❶ *I have my own phone now.*
• own, possess
❷ *Our house has three bedrooms.*
• consist of, comprise, include, incorporate
❸ *We are having a barbecue at the weekend.*
• hold, organize, provide, host, throw
❹ *We had trouble finding a place to park.*
• experience, go through, meet with, run into, face, suffer
❺ *Did you have a good time at the party?*
• experience, enjoy
❻ *The BBC has had lots of emails.*
• receive, get, be given, be sent
❼ *Sharon had the last slice of cake.*
• take, consume, eat
❽ *One of the giraffes has had a baby.*
• give birth to, bear, produce
❾ *I have to be home by six o'clock.*
• must, need, ought, should

haven NOUN
The lake is a haven for wild birds.
• refuge, shelter, retreat, sanctuary

havoc NOUN
The pixies were causing havoc in the kitchen.
• chaos, mayhem, disorder, disruption

hazard NOUN
The road through the mountains is full of hazards.
• danger, risk, threat, trap, pitfall, snag

hazardous ADJECTIVE
The explorers made the hazardous journey to the South Pole.
• dangerous, risky, unsafe, perilous, precarious
OPPOSITE safe

haze NOUN
I could hardly see through the haze.
• fog, mist, cloud, steam, vapour

hazy ADJECTIVE
❶ *The face in the photograph was rather hazy.*
• blurred, misty, unclear, dim, faint
OPPOSITES clear, sharp
❷ *I have a hazy memory of that day.*
• uncertain, vague
OPPOSITE clear, strong

head NOUN
❶ *My dad hit his head on the attic ceiling.*
• skull, crown
(informal) nut
for other parts of your body see **body**
❷ *Can you add up these figures in your head?*
• brain, mind, intellect, intelligence
❸ *There is a new head of the music department.*
• chief, leader, manager, director, controller
(informal) boss
❹ *The girls waited at the head of the queue.*
• front, lead, top
OPPOSITES back, rear

head VERB
The professor was chosen to head the expedition.
• lead, be in charge of, direct, command, manage, oversee, supervise

➤ **to head for**
At the end of the day we headed for home.
• go towards, make for, aim for

heading NOUN
Each chapter had a different **heading**.
• title, caption, headline

headlong ADJECTIVE
We made a **headlong** dash to get under cover.
• quick, hurried, hasty, breakneck

headquarters PLURAL NOUN
The spy contacted **headquarters** for instructions.
• base, head office
(informal) HQ

head teacher NOUN
The **head teacher** runs the school.
• headmaster or headmistress, principal

heal VERB
❶ It took two months for my leg to **heal** properly.
• get better, mend, recover
❷ Part of a vet's job is to **heal** sick animals.
• cure, make better, treat, restore

health NOUN
The puppies are in excellent **health**.
• condition, fitness, shape, strength, vigour, well-being
for various medical treatments see **medicine**

healthy ADJECTIVE
❶ Neil has always been a **healthy** child.
• well, fit, strong, sturdy, vigorous, robust
(informal) in good shape
(OPPOSITES) ill, sickly
❷ Porridge makes a very **healthy** breakfast.
• health-giving, wholesome, invigorating
(OPPOSITE) unhealthy

heap NOUN
There was an untidy **heap** of clothes on the floor.
• mound, pile, stack, mountain, collection, mass

heap VERB
We **heaped** up all the rubbish in the corner.
• pile, stack, collect, bank, mass

hear VERB hears, hearing, heard
❶ Did you **hear** what she said?
• catch, listen to, make out, pick up, overhear, pay attention to
A sound that you can hear is **audible**.
A sound that you cannot hear is **inaudible**.
❷ Have you **heard** the news?
• be told, discover, find out, learn, gather

heart NOUN
❶ Have you no **heart**?
• compassion, feeling, sympathy, tenderness, affection, humanity, kindness, love
❷ The hotel is located right in the **heart** of the city.
• centre, middle, hub
❸ They tried to get to the **heart** of the problem.
• core, essence

heartless ADJECTIVE
How could she be so **heartless**?
• hard-hearted, callous, cruel, inhuman, unfeeling, unkind, pitiless, ruthless
(OPPOSITE) kind

hearty ADJECTIVE
❶ He gave me a **hearty** slap on the back.
• strong, forceful, vigorous
(OPPOSITE) feeble
❷ The girls had a **hearty** appetite after their walk.
• big, healthy
(OPPOSITE) poor
❸ Our friends gave us a **hearty** welcome.
• enthusiastic, sincere, warm
(OPPOSITE) unenthusiastic

heat NOUN
❶ The cat basked in the **heat** of the fire.
• warmth, glow
❷ Last summer, the **heat** made me feel ill.
• hot weather, high temperatures, closeness
A long period of hot weather is a **heatwave**.

heave VERB
The men **heaved** the sacks onto a lorry.
• haul, drag, pull, draw, tow, tug, hoist, lug, lift, raise, throw

a
b
c
d
e
f
g
h
i
j
k
l
m
n
o
p
q
r
s
t
u
v
w
x
y
z

A B C D E F G **H** I J K L M N O P Q R S T U V W X Y Z

heavy *ADJECTIVE*
❶ *The box was too **heavy** for me to lift.*
• weighty, massive, dense, bulky
❷ *Digging the garden is **heavy** work.*
• hard, tough, gruelling, back-breaking, strenuous
❸ *This book makes **heavy** reading.*
• serious, intense, demanding
❹ *The rain has caused **heavy** flooding.*
• severe, extreme, torrential
❺ *Both sides suffered **heavy** losses in the battle.*
• large, substantial, considerable
❻ *A **heavy** mist hung over the landscape.*
• dense, thick
OPPOSITE light
➤ **with a heavy heart**
*She said goodbye **with a heavy heart**.*
• unhappily, sadly, sorrowfully, gloomily, in low spirits

hectic *ADJECTIVE*
*The days before the wedding were **hectic**.*
• busy, frantic, feverish, frenzied, chaotic
(informal) manic
OPPOSITE quiet, leisurely

heed *VERB*
*The sailors didn't **heed** the captain's warning.*
• listen to, pay attention to, take notice of, attend to, regard, obey, follow, mark, mind, note
OPPOSITE ignore

hefty *ADJECTIVE*
❶ *Sasha was carrying a **hefty** parcel.*
• big, large, weighty, massive, bulky
❷ *The wrestler was a **hefty** man.*
• strong, sturdy, muscular, powerful, brawny, burly, hulking
(informal) beefy
OPPOSITE slight

height *NOUN*
❶ *The plane was flying at its normal **height**.*
• altitude, elevation
❷ *His **height** wasn't a problem.*
• tallness, size, stature

held *past tense see* **hold**

help *NOUN*
❶ *Thank you for your **help**.*
• aid, assistance, support, guidance, cooperation, advice
OPPOSITE hindrance
❷ *Would a torch be of any **help** to you?*
• use, benefit

help *VERB*
❶ *Could you please **help** me with my luggage?*
• aid, assist, cooperate with
(informal) give a hand to
❷ *The Red Cross is an organization that **helps** people in need.*
• be helpful to, support, serve, stand by
❸ *This medicine will **help** your cough.*
• make better, cure, ease, relieve, improve
OPPOSITES aggravate, worsen
❹ *I can't **help** coughing.*
• stop, avoid, prevent, refrain from

helpful *ADJECTIVE*
❶ *The staff were friendly and **helpful**.*
• obliging, cooperative, kind, considerate, thoughtful, sympathetic
OPPOSITE unhelpful
❷ *The shop assistant gave us some **helpful** advice.*
• useful, valuable, worthwhile, beneficial, profitable
OPPOSITE worthless

helping *NOUN*
*I got a huge **helping** of ice cream.*
• serving, portion, plateful, amount, share, ration

helpless *ADJECTIVE*
*Kittens are born blind and **helpless**.*
• powerless, weak, feeble, dependent, defenceless, vulnerable
OPPOSITE independent, strong

hem *VERB*
➤ **to hem someone in**
*The bus was **hemmed** in by some parked cars.*
• shut in, box in, encircle, enclose, surround

herb NOUN

WORD WEB

SOME COMMON HERBS:

• basil, chamomile, caraway, chervil, chicory, chive, coriander, cumin, dill, fennel, fenugreek, hyssop, lemon balm, liquorice, lovage, marjoram, mint, oregano, parsley, peppermint, rosemary, sage, tarragon, thyme

herd NOUN
for groups of animals see **group**

heroic ADJECTIVE
The firefighters made a heroic effort to put out the blaze.
• bold, brave, courageous, daring, fearless, noble, selfless, valiant
OPPOSITE cowardly
for words to describe superheroes see **superhero**

hesitant ADJECTIVE
The puppy was hesitant about going outside.
• uncertain, unsure, doubtful, cautious, tentative, timid, shy, wary
OPPOSITE confident

hesitate VERB
I hesitated for a moment before ringing the doorbell.
• pause, delay, wait, hold back, dither, falter, waver
(informal) think twice

hidden ADJECTIVE
❶ *The giant kept his gold hidden in a wooden chest.*
• concealed, out of sight, unseen, invisible, covered, disguised
OPPOSITE visible
❷ *There's a hidden message in the riddle.*
• secret, mysterious, obscure, coded, cryptic
OPPOSITE obvious

hide VERB hides, hiding, hid, hidden
❶ *Quick! Someone's coming—we'd better hide.*
• go into hiding, take cover, take refuge, keep out of sight, lie low, go to ground
❷ *They hid the jewels in a secret drawer.*
• conceal, secrete, bury
(informal) stash
OPPOSITE expose
❸ *The clouds hid the sun.*
• blot out, cover, screen, shroud, veil, mask
OPPOSITE uncover
❹ *I tried to hide my feelings.*
• disguise, keep secret, suppress, camouflage, cloak
OPPOSITE show

hideous ADJECTIVE
The troll had a hideous grin on his face.
• repulsive, revolting, ugly, grotesque, monstrous, ghastly, gruesome, horrible, appalling, dreadful, frightful
OPPOSITE beautiful

high ADJECTIVE
❶ *The castle was surrounded by a high wall.*
• tall, towering, elevated, lofty
OPPOSITE low
❷ *Sir Grinalot was a knight of high rank and status.*
• senior, top, leading, important, prominent, powerful
OPPOSITES low, junior
❸ *House prices are very high at the moment.*
• expensive, dear, costly, excessive
OPPOSITE low
❹ *A high wind was blowing.*
• strong, powerful, forceful, extreme
OPPOSITE gentle
❺ *The pixie spoke in a high squeaky voice.*
• high-pitched, sharp, shrill, piercing
OPPOSITE deep
A high singing voice is **soprano** or **treble**.

highlight NOUN
The highlight of the holiday was spotting a wild dolphin.
• high point, high spot, best moment, climax

A
B
C
D
E
F
G
H
I
J
K
L
M
N
O
P
Q
R
S
T
U
V
W
X
Y
Z

highly *ADVERB*
It is highly unusual to see badgers during the day.
• very, extremely, exceptionally, considerably, decidedly

hike *VERB, NOUN*
We often go hiking across the moors.
• trek, walk, ramble, tramp

hilarious *ADJECTIVE*
The boys thought the cartoon was hilarious.
• funny, amusing, comical
(informal) hysterical

hill *NOUN*
❶ *From the top of this hill you can see for miles.*
• mount, peak, ridge
A small hill is a **hillock** or **mound**.
The top of a hill is the **summit**.
❷ *Jenny pushed her bike up the steep hill.*
• slope, rise, incline, ascent, gradient

hinder *VERB*
The snowstorm hindered the rescue attempt.
• hamper, hold up, obstruct, impede, slow down, stand in the way of, restrict, handicap
OPPOSITE help

hindrance *NOUN*
The sharks were a hindrance to the divers.
• obstacle, obstruction, handicap, inconvenience, difficulty, disadvantage, drawback
OPPOSITE help

hint *NOUN*
❶ *I don't know the answer—can you give me a hint?*
• clue, indication, sign, suggestion, inkling
❷ *The magazine offers handy hints for decorating.*
• tip, pointer

hint *VERB*
Mum hinted that we might be getting a puppy.
• give a hint, suggest, imply, indicate

hire *VERB*
If you hire a bus or aircraft you **charter** it.
If you hire someone to do a job you **engage** or **employ** them.
If you hire a building for a time you **lease** or **rent** it.

historic *ADJECTIVE*
The first landing on the moon was a historic event.
• famous, notable, celebrated, important, renowned, momentous, significant, major
OPPOSITE unimportant
WHICH WORD? Note that **historic** is not the same as **historical**. A **historic** event is important in history, whereas a **historical** event simply happened in the past.

historical *ADJECTIVE*
Robin Hood may have been a historical character.
• real, real-life, true, actual, authentic
OPPOSITE fictitious
WHICH WORD? Note that **historical** is not the same as **historic**. A **historical** event simply happened in the past, whereas a **historic** event is important in history.

history *NOUN*
❶ *Dr Marashi is an expert on Persian history.*
• heritage, past, antiquity, past times, olden days
❷ *She wrote a history of the First World War.*
• account, chronicle, record
The history of a person's life is their **biography**.
The history of your own life is your **autobiography** or **memoirs**.

hit *NOUN*
❶ *Matt got a nasty hit on the head.*
• bump, blow, bang, knock, whack
A hit with your fist is a **punch**.
A hit with your open hand is a **slap** or **smack**.
A hit with a bat or club is a **drive**, **stroke** or **swipe**.
❷ *Their new release was an instant hit.*
• success, triumph
(informal) winner

hit VERB hits, hitting, hit
❶ *Auntie Flo hit the burglar on the head with her umbrella.*
• strike, knock, bang, bash, thump, bump, crack, rap, slam, swipe, slog, cuff
(informal) whack, wham, wallop, sock, clout, clobber, belt, biff
(old use) smite
To hit with your fist is to **punch**.
To hit with the palm of your hand is to **slap** or **smack**.
To punish someone by hitting them is to **beat** them.
To hit someone with a stick is to **club** them.
To hit your toe on something is to **stub** it.
To kill an insect by hitting it is to **swat** it.
To hit something repeatedly is to **batter, buffet** or **pound** it.
To hit something gently is to **tap** it.
for ways to hit a ball see **ball**
❷ *The drought has hit many farms in the area.*
• affect, damage, harm, hurt

hoard NOUN
Hamish keeps a hoard of sweets in his desk.
• cache, store, stock, supply, pile, stockpile
A hoard of treasure is a **treasure trove**.

hoard VERB
Squirrels hoard nuts for the winter.
• store, collect, gather, save, put by, pile up, stockpile
(informal) stash away

hoarse ADJECTIVE
My voice was hoarse from shouting.
• rough, harsh, husky, croaky, throaty, gruff, rasping, gravelly

hoax NOUN
The telephone call was a hoax.
• joke, practical joke, prank, trick, spoof
(informal) con, scam

hobby NOUN
My favourite hobby is snorkelling.
• pastime, pursuit, interest, activity, recreation

hoist VERB
The crane hoisted the crates on to a ship.
• lift, pull up, raise, heave, winch up

hold NOUN
The vet took a firm hold of the dog's collar.
• grip, grasp, clutch, clasp

hold VERB holds, holding, held
❶ *Please hold the dog's lead.*
• clasp, grasp, grip, cling to, hang on to, clutch, seize
❷ *Can I hold the baby?*
• embrace, hug, cradle
❸ *They held the suspect until the police arrived.*
• confine, detain, keep
❹ *Will the ladder hold my weight?*
• bear, support, carry, take
❺ *If our luck holds, we could reach the final.*
• continue, last, carry on, persist, stay
❻ *She holds strong opinions.*
• believe in, maintain, stick to
➤ **to hold out**
❶ *The robot held out one of his arms.*
• extend, reach out, stick out, stretch out
❷ *Our supplies won't hold out much longer.*
• keep going, last, carry on, continue, endure
➤ **to hold something up**
❶ *Please hold up your hand.*
• lift, put up, raise
❷ *The accident held up the traffic.*
• delay, hinder, slow down

hole NOUN
❶ *The meteor created a massive hole in the ground.*
• pit, hollow, crater, dent, depression, cavity, chasm, abyss
❷ *The rabbits escaped through a hole in the fence.*
• gap, opening, breach, break, cut, slit, gash, split, tear, vent

holiday NOUN
We spent our summer holiday in Ireland.
• vacation, break, leave, time off

hollow ADJECTIVE
Tennis balls are hollow.
• empty, unfilled
OPPOSITE solid

hollow NOUN
The ball rolled into a hollow in the ground.
• dip, dent, depression, hole, pit, crater
A hollow between two hills is a **valley**.

a
b
c
d
e
f
g
h
i
j
k
l
m
n
o
p
q
r
s
t
u
v
w
x
y
z

A
B
C
D
E
F
G
H
I
J
K
L
M
N
O
P
Q
R
S
T
U
V
W
X
Y
Z

hollow *VERB*
*We **hollowed** out a pumpkin to make a Halloween lantern.*
• dig, excavate, gouge, scoop

holy *ADJECTIVE*
❶ *The pilgrims knelt to pray in the **holy** shrine.*
• sacred, blessed, revered
❷ *The pilgrims were **holy** people.*
• religious, spiritual, devout, pious, godly, saintly

home *NOUN*
*The hurricane forced people to flee their **homes**.*
• house, residence, dwelling, abode, lodging
A home for the sick is a **convalescent home** or **nursing home**.
A place where a bird or animal lives is its **habitat**.
see also **house**
for homes of wild animals see **animal**

homely *ADJECTIVE*
*The hotel was small with a **homely** atmosphere.*
• friendly, informal, cosy, familiar, relaxed, easy-going, comfortable, simple

honest *ADJECTIVE*
❶ *He's an **honest** boy, so he gave the money back.*
• good, honourable, law-abiding, moral, trustworthy, upright, virtuous
OPPOSITE dishonest
❷ *Please give me your **honest** opinion.*
• sincere, genuine, truthful, direct, frank, candid, plain, straightforward, unbiased
OPPOSITE insincere

honour *NOUN*
❶ *Her success brought **honour** to the school.*
• credit, good reputation, good name, respect, praise, acclaim
❷ *It's an **honour** to meet you.*
• privilege, distinction
honour *VERB*
*The winners were **honoured** at a special ceremony.*
• praise, celebrate, salute, give credit to, pay tribute to, glorify

honourable *ADJECTIVE*
❶ *The knight was an **honourable** man.*
• good, honest, sincere, noble, principled, moral, righteous, trustworthy, upright, virtuous, worthy, decent, fair, trusty
❷ *It was an **honourable** thing to do.*
• noble, admirable, praiseworthy, decent
OPPOSITE unworthy

hook *VERB*
❶ *Mum **hooked** the trailer to the car.*
• attach, fasten, hitch, connect, couple
❷ *The angler **hooked** an enormous fish.*
• catch, land, take

hop *VERB*
*The goblins **hopped** about in excitement.*
• jump, leap, skip, spring, prance, caper, bound, dance

hope *VERB*
*I **hope** to see you again soon.*
• wish, trust, expect, look forward
hope *NOUN*
❶ *Her dearest **hope** was to see her family again.*
• ambition, dream, desire, wish
❷ *There's **hope** of better weather tomorrow.*
• prospect, expectation, likelihood

hopeful *ADJECTIVE*
❶ *I am feeling **hopeful** about tomorrow's match.*
• optimistic, confident, positive, expectant
OPPOSITE pessimistic
❷ *The future is beginning to look more **hopeful**.*
• promising, encouraging, favourable, reassuring
OPPOSITE discouraging

hopeless *ADJECTIVE*
❶ *The shipwrecked crew were in a **hopeless** situation.*
• desperate, wretched, beyond hope
OPPOSITE hopeful
❷ *I'm **hopeless** at ice-skating.*
• bad, poor, incompetent
(informal) useless, rubbish
OPPOSITES good, competent

horde NOUN
Hordes of people were queuing for tickets.
• crowd, throng, mob, swarm, gang, group

horizontal ADJECTIVE
Lay the pole on the ground in a horizontal position.
• flat, level
OPPOSITE vertical

horrible ADJECTIVE
What a horrible smell!
• awful, terrible, dreadful, appalling, unpleasant, disagreeable, offensive, objectionable, disgusting, repulsive, revolting, horrendous, horrid, nasty, hateful, odious, loathsome, beastly, ghastly
OPPOSITE pleasant

horrific ADJECTIVE
The film has some horrific scenes of battle.
• horrifying, terrifying, shocking, gruesome, dreadful, appalling, ghastly, hideous, atrocious, grisly, sickening

horrify VERB
We were horrified by the sight of the monster.
• appal, shock, terrify, frighten, alarm, scare, sicken, disgust

horror NOUN
❶ *The children screamed in horror when they saw the snake.*
• terror, fear, fright, alarm, dread
❷ *The film depicts the full horror of war.*
• awfulness, hideousness, gruesomeness, ghastliness, frightfulness

horse NOUN

WORD WEB

A male horse is a **stallion** and a female is a **mare**.
A young horse is a **foal**, **colt** (male) or **filly** (female).
An uncomplimentary word for a horse is **nag**.
A poetic word for a horse is **steed**.
A word meaning 'to do with horses' is **equine**.
A cross between a donkey and a horse is a **mule**.

SOME TYPES OF HORSE:
• bronco, carthorse, Clydesdale, mustang, piebald, pony, racehorse, Shetland pony, shire horse, war horse

SOUNDS MADE BY HORSES:
• neigh, nicker, snort, whinny
In the eerie silence of no man's land all that could be heard was the jingle of the harness and the snorting of the horses.—WAR HORSE, Michael Morpurgo

WAYS A HORSE CAN MOVE:
• canter, gallop, trot, walk

PARTS OF A HORSE'S HARNESS:
• bit, blinker, bridle, girth, noseband, pommel, rein, saddle, stirrups

SPORTS AND ACTIVITIES INVOLVING HORSES:
• gymkhana, horse racing, jousting, rodeo, polo, showjumping, steeplechase
To get on a horse before riding is to **mount** and to get off a horse is to **dismount**.
A person who rides a horse in a race is a **jockey**.
A word meaning 'to do with horse riding' is **equestrian**.
Soldiers who fight on horseback are **cavalry**.
An old word for a cavalry horse was a **charger**.

hospital NOUN

WORD WEB

PLACES WHERE PEOPLE GO FOR MEDICAL TREATMENT:
• clinic, convalescent home, hospice, infirmary, nursing home, sanatorium

PARTS OF A HOSPITAL:
• accident and emergency, dispensary, intensive care unit, operating theatre, outpatients, pharmacy, X-ray department, ward
see also **medicine**

a b c d e f g h i j k l m n o p q r s t u v w x y z

hostile ADJECTIVE

❶ *The warriors shook their weapons in a hostile manner.*
• aggressive, antagonistic, unfriendly, unwelcoming, warlike, malevolent
OPPOSITE friendly

❷ *The North Pole has a very hostile climate.*
• harsh, unfavourable, adverse, bad
OPPOSITE favourable

hostility NOUN

The hostility between the two players was obvious.
• dislike, enmity, hate, hatred, aggression, antagonism, bad feeling, detestation, ill will, unfriendliness, malice
OPPOSITE friendship

hot ADJECTIVE

❶ *The weather has been hot this summer.*
• warm, balmy, blazing, roasting, scorching, blistering, sweltering, stifling
OPPOSITES cold, cool

❷ *Careful—the soup's really hot.*
• burning, boiling, baking hot, piping hot, scalding, searing, sizzling, steaming
OPPOSITES cold, cool

❸ *I like curry, but only if it's not too hot.*
• spicy, peppery, fiery
OPPOSITE mild

❹ *The politician has a hot temper.*
• fierce, fiery, violent, passionate, raging, angry, intense
OPPOSITES calm, mild

house NOUN

WORD WEB

WORDS FOR THE PLACE YOU LIVE IN:

• abode, dwelling, home, lodging, quarters, residence

BUILDINGS WHERE PEOPLE LIVE:

• apartment, bungalow, chalet, cottage, council house, croft, detached house, farmhouse, flat, hovel, hut, igloo, lodge, manor, manse, mansion, rectory, semi-detached house, shack, shanty, tenement, terraced house, thatched house, vicarage, villa
for rooms in a house see **room**

house VERB

The farm animals are housed indoors during the winter.
• accommodate, lodge, shelter, take in, quarter, board

hover VERB

❶ *A flock of seagulls hovered overhead.*
• fly, flutter, float, hang, drift

❷ *He hovered outside the room, afraid to knock.*
• linger, pause, wait about, hesitate, dally, loiter, dither
(informal) hang about

however ADVERB

❶ *I couldn't lift the stone, however hard I tried.*
• no matter how

❷ *Spiders' silk is thin; however, it is also strong.*
• nevertheless, nonetheless, yet, still, even so

howl VERB

❶ *The injured boy howled in pain.*
• cry, yell, scream, yelp, shriek, wail

❷ *They heard wolves howling in the night.*
• bay, yowl

huddle VERB

The penguins huddled together to get warm.
• crowd, gather, flock, cluster, squeeze, pack, nestle, cuddle, snuggle
OPPOSITE scatter

hue NOUN

Elliot's face turned a greenish hue.
• colour, shade, tint, tone, tinge
for various colours see **colour**

hug VERB

Rohan was hugging his favourite teddy bear.
• cuddle, clasp, embrace, cling to, hold close, squeeze

huge *ADJECTIVE*
Elephants are huge animals.
• enormous, gigantic, massive, colossal, giant, immense, vast, mighty, mammoth, monumental, hulking, great, big, large
(informal) whopping, ginormous
OPPOSITES small, little, tiny

hum *VERB*
We heard insects humming in the air.
• buzz, drone, murmur, purr, whirr

humane *ADJECTIVE*
A humane society should treat animals well.
• kind, compassionate, sympathetic, civilized, benevolent, kind-hearted, charitable, loving, merciful
OPPOSITE cruel

humans *PLURAL NOUN*
Humans have smaller brains than whales.
• human beings, the human race, humanity, mankind, people

humble *ADJECTIVE*
❶ *The gentle giant was both humble and kind.*
• modest, meek, unassuming, polite, respectful, submissive
OPPOSITE proud
❷ *Hansel and Gretel lived in a humble cottage.*
• simple, modest, plain, ordinary, commonplace, lowly
OPPOSITE grand

humid *ADJECTIVE*
I don't like this humid weather.
• muggy, clammy, close, sticky, steamy, sweaty
OPPOSITE fresh

humiliate *VERB*
He was humiliated in front of his friends.
• embarrass, disgrace, shame, make ashamed, humble, crush, degrade
(informal) put you in your place, take you down a peg

humiliating *ADJECTIVE*
The team suffered a humiliating defeat.
• embarrassing, crushing, degrading, humbling, undignified
OPPOSITE glorious

humorous *ADJECTIVE*
My friend told me a humorous story.
• amusing, funny, comic, witty, entertaining
OPPOSITE serious

humour *NOUN*
❶ *I liked the humour in the film.*
• comedy, wit, amusement, jokes
❷ *The ogre was in a very bad humour.*
• mood, temper, disposition, frame of mind, spirits

hump *NOUN*
Camels have humps on their backs.
• bump, lump, bulge, swelling

hunch *NOUN*
The detective had a hunch about the murder case.
• feeling, intuition, inkling, guess, impression, suspicion, idea

hunch *VERB*
Will hunched his shoulders to keep out the cold.
• arch, bend, curve, hump, shrug, curl up

hung *past tense see* **hang**

hunger *NOUN*
After a week without food, the crew were faint with hunger.
• lack of food, starvation, famine
Bad health caused by not having enough food is **malnutrition**.

hungry *ADJECTIVE*
Our cat always seems to be hungry.
• starving, famished, ravenous
(informal) peckish

hunt *NOUN*
Police have begun the hunt for clues.
• search, quest, chase, pursuit

a b c d e f g h i j k l m n o p q r s t u v w x y z

A
B
C
D
E
F
G
H
I
J
K
L
M
N
O
P
Q
R
S
T
U
V
W
X
Y
Z

hunt *VERB*
❶ *Endangered animals are **hunted** illegally.*
• chase, pursue, track, trail, hound, stalk
An animal which hunts other animals for food
is a **predator**.
❷ *I **hunted** in the attic for our old photos.*
• search, seek, look, rummage, ferret,
root around

hurdle *NOUN*
❶ *The horse jumped over the **hurdle** easily.*
• fence, barrier, jump, barricade, obstacle
❷ *The biggest **hurdle** facing the team is lack
of experience.*
• difficulty, problem, handicap, hindrance,
snag, stumbling block

hurl *VERB*
*I **hurled** the ball as far as I could.*
• throw, fling, pitch, toss, cast, sling, launch
(informal) chuck

hurry *VERB*
❶ *If you want to catch the bus, you'd
better **hurry**.*
• be quick, hasten, make speed
(informal) get a move on step on it
`OPPOSITE` dawdle
❷ *Alice saw the White Rabbit **hurrying** past.*
• rush, dash, fly, speed, hurtle, scurry
`OPPOSITES` amble, stroll
❸ *It's no good trying to **hurry** a donkey.*
• quicken, speed up, urge on
`OPPOSITES` slow down

hurry *NOUN*
*In our **hurry**, we forgot the tickets.*
• rush, haste, speed, urgency

hurt *VERB*
❶ *Be careful not to **hurt** yourself with the
scissors.*
• harm, injure, damage, wound, maim
To hurt someone deliberately is to **torment** or
torture them.
❷ *My feet **hurt**.*
• be sore, be painful, ache, throb, sting, smart
❸ *Your letter **hurt** me deeply.*
• upset, distress, offend, grieve

hurtful *ADJECTIVE*
*That was a very **hurtful** remark.*
• upsetting, unkind, cruel, mean, painful,
spiteful, nasty

hurtle *VERB*
*The train **hurtled** along at top speed.*
• rush, speed, race, dash, fly, charge, tear,
shoot, zoom

husband *NOUN*
*Hugh is Mrs Hart's fourth **husband**.*
Another word for a person's husband or wife is
spouse.

hush *VERB*
*The speaker tried his best to **hush** the crowd.*
• silence, quieten, settle, still, calm
➤ **to hush something up**
*They tried to **hush** up the scandal.*
• cover up, hide, conceal, keep quiet,
keep secret, suppress

husky *ADJECTIVE*
*The wizard spoke in a **husky** voice.*
• hoarse, throaty, gruff, rasping, gravelly,
rough, croaky

hut *NOUN*
*The walkers came across a **hut** in the forest.*
• shed, shack, cabin, den, shelter, shanty,
hovel

hygienic *ADJECTIVE*
*Always use a **hygienic** surface for chopping
food.*
• sanitary, clean, disinfected, sterilized, sterile,
germ-free, healthy
`OPPOSITE` unhygienic

hysterical *ADJECTIVE*
❶ *The fans became **hysterical** when the band
appeared.*
• crazy, frenzied, mad, delirious, raving, wild,
uncontrollable
❷ *(informal) We laughed at the **hysterical**
jokes in the film.*
• hilarious, funny, amusing, comical

Ii

ice NOUN

WORD WEB

VARIOUS FORMS OF ICE:

• black ice, floe, frost, glacier, iceberg, ice sheet, icicle

WAYS TO DESCRIBE ICE:

• brittle, cracked, frozen solid, glacial, glassy, gleaming, glinting, hard, packed, slippery or *(informal)* slippy, smooth, treacherous

THINGS YOU MIGHT DO ON ICE:

• glide, skate, skid, slide, slip, slither

SPORTS THAT ARE PLAYED ON ICE:

• curling, figure skating, ice skating, ice hockey, speed skating
Ice sports are played on an **ice rink**.

icy ADJECTIVE
❶ *You need to dress warmly in icy weather.*
• cold, freezing, frosty, wintry, arctic, bitter, biting
❷ *Icy roads are dangerous.*
• frozen, slippery, glacial, glassy
(informal) slippy

idea NOUN
❶ *I've got a great idea!*
• plan, scheme, proposal, suggestion, inspiration
❷ *She has some funny ideas about life.*
• belief, notion, opinion, view, theory, concept, conception, hypothesis
❸ *What's the main idea of this poem?*
• point, meaning, intention, thought
❹ *Give me an idea of what you are planning.*
• clue, hint, inkling, impression

ideal ADJECTIVE
It's ideal weather for a picnic.
• perfect, excellent, the best, faultless, suitable

identical ADJECTIVE
The twins were wearing identical clothes.
• matching, similar, alike, indistinguishable
OPPOSITE different

identify VERB
❶ *The police asked if I could identify the thief.*
• recognize, name, distinguish, pick out, single out
❷ *The doctor couldn't identify what was wrong.*
• diagnose, discover, spot
(informal) put a name to
➤ **to identify with**
Can you identify with the hero of the story?
• sympathize with, feel for, understand
(informal) put yourself in the shoes of

idiotic ADJECTIVE
That was an idiotic thing to do.
• stupid, silly, foolish, unwise, senseless, ridiculous, half-witted, unintelligent, crazy, mad, hare-brained
(informal) daft
OPPOSITE sensible

idle ADJECTIVE
❶ *The ogre was an idle, foul-smelling creature.*
• lazy, indolent, slothful, work-shy
OPPOSITE hard-working
❷ *The computers lay idle all week.*
• inactive, unused, inoperative
OPPOSITE busy, active

idol NOUN
❶ *The floor of the temple was littered with broken idols.*
• god, deity, image, statue
❷ *He was a pop idol of the fifties.*
• star, celebrity, icon, pin-up, favourite

a b c d e f g h i j k l m n o p q r s t u v w x y z

idolize *VERB*
*Kirsty **idolizes** her big brother.*
• adore, love, worship, be devoted to, look up to

ignite *VERB*
*The matches were wet and would not **ignite**.*
• light, catch fire, burn, kindle, spark

ignorant *ADJECTIVE*
*Trolls are often described as **ignorant** creatures.*
• uneducated, simple, stupid
➤ **ignorant of**
*Detective Miles was **ignorant of** the facts in the case.*
• unaware of, unfamiliar with, unacquainted with, aware of

ignore *VERB*
Ignoring the weather, Lynn went for a walk.
• disregard, take no notice of, overlook, neglect, spurn, snub
(informal) turn a blind eye to

ill *ADJECTIVE*
❶ *I missed school for a week when I was **ill**.*
• sick, unwell, poorly, sickly, ailing, infirm, unfit, indisposed, diseased, infected, nauseous, queasy, off colour, peaky
(informal) under the weather
for common illnesses see **illness**
OPPOSITES healthy, well
❷ *Did the plants suffer **ill** effects in the frost?*
• bad, harmful, adverse, damaging
OPPOSITE good

illegal *ADJECTIVE*
*Stealing is **illegal**.*
• unlawful, against the law, banned, prohibited, criminal, forbidden, wrong
OPPOSITE legal

illegible *ADJECTIVE*
*The signature on the letter was **illegible**.*
• unreadable, indecipherable, unclear, indistinct
OPPOSITES legible, readable

illness *NOUN*
*What kind of **illness** is he suffering from?*
• affliction, ailment, attack, complaint, condition, disease, disorder, health problem, infection, infirmity, sickness, virus
(informal) bug, upset
A sudden illness is an **attack** or fit.
A period of illness is a **bout of illness**.
A general outbreak of illness in a particular area is an **epidemic**.
An outbreak of an illness in a whole country or the whole world is a **pandemic**.

WORD WEB

SOME COMMON ILLNESSES:

• allergy, appendicitis, asthma, bronchitis, chickenpox, chill, cold, cough, diarrhoea, eczema, fever, flu, glandular fever, hay fever, headache, indigestion, influenza, jaundice, laryngitis, measles, migraine, mumps, stomach-ache, tonsillitis, ulcer, whooping cough
for ways to treat illness see **medicine**

illustrate *VERB*
❶ *I used some photos to **illustrate** my story.*
• depict, picture, portray
❷ *The accident **illustrates** the importance of road safety.*
• show, demonstrate, make clear

illustration *NOUN*
❶ *I like books with lots of **illustrations**.*
• picture, photograph, drawing, sketch, diagram
❷ *I'll give you an **illustration** of what I mean.*
• example, instance, demonstration, specimen

image *NOUN*
❶ *The film contained frightening **images** of war.*
• picture, portrayal, depiction, representation
❷ *The temple contained **images** of the gods.*
• figure, idol, statue, carving
❸ *You can see your **image** in the mirror.*
• reflection, likeness
❹ *She is the **image** of her mother.*
• double, twin

imaginary *ADJECTIVE*
The story takes place in an imaginary universe.
• imagined, non-existent, unreal, made-up, invented, fanciful, fictitious, fictional
OPPOSITE real

imagination *NOUN*
Use your imagination to draw an alien spacecraft.
• creativity, inventiveness, ingenuity, inspiration, originality, vision, artistry, fancy

imaginative *ADJECTIVE*
Roald Dahl wrote highly imaginative stories.
• creative, inventive, inspired, original, artistic, fanciful, ingenious, clever
OPPOSITES unimaginative, dull

imagine *VERB*
❶ *Imagine what it would be like to visit Mars.*
• picture, visualize, pretend, think up, dream up, fancy, conjure up, envisage
❷ *I imagine you'd like something to eat.*
• suppose, assume, presume, believe, guess

imitate *VERB*
Parrots can imitate the human voice.
• copy, reproduce, mimic, mirror, echo, simulate, impersonate, follow, match
(informal) send up, take off

imitation *ADJECTIVE*
The coat was made from imitation leather.
• artificial, synthetic, fake, sham, mock
OPPOSITES real, genuine

imitation *NOUN*
This is an imitation of a Viking helmet.
• copy, replica, reproduction, duplicate
An imitation made to deceive someone is a fake or a forgery.

immature *ADJECTIVE*
Tess is quite immature for her age.
• childish, babyish, infantile, juvenile
OPPOSITE mature

immediate *ADJECTIVE*
❶ *Please can I have an immediate reply.*
• instant, instantaneous, prompt, speedy, swift, urgent, quick, direct
(informal) snappy
OPPOSITE slow
❷ *Are you friends with your immediate neighbours?*
• closest, nearest, adjacent, next
OPPOSITE distant

immediately *ADVERB*
You must call a doctor immediately!
• at once, now, straight away, right away, instantly, promptly, directly

immense *ADJECTIVE*
The giant wiggled one of his immense toes.
• huge, great, massive, enormous, colossal, vast, giant, gigantic, mighty, mammoth, monumental
(informal) whopping, ginormous
OPPOSITE tiny

immobile *ADJECTIVE*
The dog stood immobile at the vet's door.
• unmoving, motionless, stationary, still
OPPOSITE mobile

immoral *ADJECTIVE*
It would be immoral to steal the money.
• wrong, wicked, bad, sinful, dishonest, corrupt
OPPOSITES moral, right

immortal *ADJECTIVE*
The ancient Greeks believed their gods were immortal.
• undying, ageless, eternal, everlasting
OPPOSITE mortal

impact *NOUN*
❶ *The crater was caused by the impact of a meteor.*
• crash, collision, smash, blow, bump, bang, knock, jolt
❷ *Computers have a big impact on our lives.*
• effect, influence

a b c d e f g h i j k l m n o p q r s t u v w x y z

A
B

impair *VERB*
Very loud noise can impair your hearing.
• damage, harm, injure, weaken

C
D
E
F

impartial *ADJECTIVE*
Referees must be impartial.
• neutral, detached, objective, unbiased, unprejudiced, disinterested, independent, fair, fair-minded, just, even-handed, open-minded
OPPOSITE biased

G
H
I

impatient *ADJECTIVE*
❶ *As time went on, Henry grew more and more impatient.*
• restless, agitated, anxious, edgy, fidgety, irritable, snappy, testy, jumpy
OPPOSITE patient
❷ *The crowd were impatient for the show to begin.*
• anxious, eager, in a hurry, keen
(informal) itching

J
K
L

imperfect *ADJECTIVE*
The items on this shelf are imperfect.
• damaged, faulty, defective, flawed, broken, incomplete
OPPOSITE perfect

M
N
O

impertinent *ADJECTIVE*
The elf made some rather impertinent remarks.
• rude, cheeky, impolite, impudent, insolent, disrespectful
OPPOSITES respectful, polite

P
Q
R
S

implement *NOUN*
The shed is full of garden implements.
• tool, appliance, device, utensil, gadget, instrument
see also **tool**

T
U
V

implore *VERB*
Jack implored the giant not to eat him.
• beg, entreat, plead with

W
X
Y
Z

imply *VERB*
Are you implying that I am a liar?
• suggest, hint, indicate

WHICH WORD? Note there is a difference between **imply** and **infer**. To **infer** something is to deduce or work it out.

impolite *ADJECTIVE*
It would be impolite to refuse the invitation.
• rude, bad-mannered, discourteous, disrespectful, insulting
OPPOSITE polite

import *VERB*
The UK imports tea and coffee.
• bring in, ship in
OPPOSITE export

important *ADJECTIVE*
❶ *The World Cup is an important sporting event.*
• major, significant, big, central, momentous, outstanding, historic
❷ *I have some important business to attend to.*
• serious, urgent, pressing, weighty, vital, essential, crucial
❸ *The prime minister is an important person.*
• prominent, powerful, influential, notable, eminent, distinguished
OPPOSITES unimportant, minor

impose *VERB*
The government imposed a tax on fuel.
• introduce, enforce, fix, inflict, prescribe, set
➤ **to impose on**
I don't want to impose on you.
• inconvenience, intrude on, take advantage of

imposing *ADJECTIVE*
The castle is an imposing building.
• grand, great, impressive, stately, magnificent, splendid, majestic, dignified, striking
OPPOSITE insignificant

impossible *ADJECTIVE*
We used to think that space travel was impossible.
• impractical, unthinkable, unrealistic, unachievable, unworkable, out of the question
OPPOSITE possible

impress *VERB*
Aysha impressed the coach with her netball skills.
• make an impression on, influence, leave its mark on, stick in your mind

impression *NOUN*
❶ *I had the impression that something was wrong.*
• feeling, idea, sense, notion, suspicion, hunch
❷ *The film made a big impression on them.*
• effect, impact, influence, mark
❸ *My sister does a good impression of the head teacher.*
• imitation, impersonation, *(informal)* send-up

impressive *ADJECTIVE*
The film includes some impressive special effects.
• striking, effective, powerful, remarkable, spectacular, exciting, inspiring
OPPOSITES unimpressive, uninspiring

imprison *VERB*
The thief was imprisoned for two years.
• send to prison, jail, lock up, incarcerate, confine, detain
(informal) put away, send down, put under lock and key
OPPOSITE liberate

improve *VERB*
❶ *Her work improved during the term.*
• get better, advance, progress, develop, move on
OPPOSITE deteriorate
❷ *Has he improved since his illness?*
• get better, recover, recuperate, pick up, rally, revive
OPPOSITE get worse
❸ *How can I improve this story?*
• make better, enhance, refine, amend, revise, correct, upgrade

improvement *NOUN*
❶ *Your handwriting shows signs of improvement.*
• getting better, advance, progress, development, recovery, upturn
❷ *The author made some improvements to the book.*
• amendment, correction, revision, modification, enhancement

impudent *ADJECTIVE*
The pixie had an impudent grin on his face.
• cheeky, insolent, rude, impolite, impertinent, disrespectful
OPPOSITES respectful, polite

impulse *NOUN*
I had a sudden impulse to sing out loud.
• desire, instinct, urge

impulsive *ADJECTIVE*
He regretted his impulsive decision to dye his hair.
• hasty, rash, reckless, sudden, spontaneous, thoughtless, unthinking, impetuous
OPPOSITE deliberate

inaccessible *ADJECTIVE*
The caves were in an inaccessible part of the island.
• unreachable, isolated, remote, out of the way, hard to find
OPPOSITE accessible

inaccurate *ADJECTIVE*
That spelling of my surname is inaccurate.
• wrong, incorrect, mistaken, false, inexact, untrue
OPPOSITE accurate

inadequate *ADJECTIVE*
The campers had brought an inadequate supply of matches.
• insufficient, not enough, limited, scarce, scanty, meagre
OPPOSITE adequate

a
b
c
d
e
f
g
h
i
j
k
l
m
n
o
p
q
r
s
t
u
v
w
x
y
z

A
B
C
D
E
F
G
H
I
J
K
L
M
N
O
P
Q
R
S
T
U
V
W
X
Y
Z

inappropriate *ADJECTIVE*
It's inappropriate to call the teacher by their first name.
• unsuitable, improper, out of place, unfitting, unseemly
OPPOSITE appropriate

inaudible *ADJECTIVE*
see **hear**

incapable *ADJECTIVE*
➤ **incapable of**
He is incapable of making a decision.
• unable to, incompetent at, unfit to, unsuited to, ineffective at
OPPOSITE capable of

incident *NOUN*
There was an amusing incident at school this morning.
• event, happening, occurrence, episode, affair

incidental *ADJECTIVE*
Tell us the main story without the incidental details.
• unimportant, minor, inessential, secondary, subordinate
OPPOSITE essential

incline *NOUN*
The house was at the top of a steep incline.
• hill, slope, rise, gradient

inclined *ADJECTIVE*
➤ **to be inclined to**
Ogres are inclined to eat too much.
• be disposed to, have a habit of, be liable to, tend to

include *VERB*
Does the cost include postage and packing?
• contain, incorporate, comprise, involve, take in, allow for, take into account, cover
OPPOSITE exclude

income *NOUN*
What is your average monthly income?
• pay, salary, wages, earnings
OPPOSITE expenditure

incompetent *ADJECTIVE*
The actor was so incompetent that he forgot his lines.
• unskilful, inept, ineffective, unsatisfactory, useless, hopeless
OPPOSITE competent

incomplete *ADJECTIVE*
The new football stadium is still incomplete.
• unfinished, uncompleted, not ready
OPPOSITE complete

inconsiderate *ADJECTIVE*
It's inconsiderate to play the radio so loudly.
• selfish, unthinking, thoughtless, insensitive, rude, tactless, unkind, uncaring
OPPOSITE considerate

inconsistent *ADJECTIVE*
❶ *Her performance has been inconsistent this season.*
• changeable, unreliable, variable, unpredictable, erratic, fickle
❷ *The stories of the two witnesses are inconsistent.*
• contradictory, conflicting, different
OPPOSITE consistent

inconspicuous *ADJECTIVE*
The spy wore plain clothes to be inconspicuous.
• unnoticed, unobtrusive, camouflaged, out of sight
OPPOSITE conspicuous

inconvenient *ADJECTIVE*
The guests arrived at an inconvenient moment.
• awkward, difficult, unsuitable, unfortunate, untimely, inopportune
OPPOSITE convenient

incorporate *VERB*
The show incorporates some well-known tunes.
• include, contain, embrace, take in
OPPOSITE exclude

incorrect *ADJECTIVE*
Nine out of ten of her answers were incorrect.
• wrong, mistaken, inaccurate, false
OPPOSITE correct

increase VERB

❶ *They've increased the size of the tennis courts.*
• make bigger, enlarge, expand, develop, add to, widen, broaden
❷ *She increased the cooking time in the recipe.*
• extend, lengthen, prolong
❸ *The police increased their efforts to find the murderer.*
• intensify, step up
❹ *Will you be increasing the bus fares?*
• put up, raise
❺ *Can you increase the volume of the TV?*
• turn up, amplify, boost
❻ *The number of cars on the roads continues to increase.*
• grow, mount, go up, rise, soar, build up, escalate, multiply
for opposites see **decrease**

incredible ADJECTIVE

❶ *Do you expect us to believe that incredible story?*
• unbelievable, unlikely, improbable, far-fetched, absurd, implausible
OPPOSITE credible
❷ *The Forth Bridge is an incredible feat of engineering.*
• extraordinary, amazing, astounding, magnificent, marvellous, spectacular

independence NOUN

The islanders value their independence.
• freedom, liberty, autonomy
OPPOSITE dependence

independent ADJECTIVE

❶ *My granny is a very independent person.*
• free, liberated, self-sufficient, self-reliant
OPPOSITE dependent
❷ *Luxembourg is an independent country.*
• autonomous, self-governing
❸ *We need an independent opinion on the matter.*
• impartial, neutral, objective, unbiased
OPPOSITE biased

indicate VERB

❶ *The usher indicated where we should sit.*
• point to or out, specify, show, reveal, make known
❷ *A red light indicates danger.*
• mean, stand for, denote, express, signal, signify, communicate, convey

indication NOUN

He gave no indication that he felt ill.
• sign, signal, hint, clue, inkling, evidence, warning, symptom, token

indifferent ADJECTIVE

❶ *I felt indifferent as I watched the game.*
• uninterested, detached, uncaring, unenthusiastic, unmoved, uninvolved, unconcerned
OPPOSITE enthusiastic
❷ *The food in the restaurant was indifferent.*
• mediocre, ordinary, unexciting, average
OPPOSITE excellent

indignant ADJECTIVE

The player was indignant when she was sent off.
• annoyed, angry, cross, affronted, offended, outraged, piqued

indirect ADJECTIVE

The bus took an indirect route into town.
• roundabout, winding, meandering, rambling, zigzag
OPPOSITE direct

indistinct ADJECTIVE

❶ *The photo was rather indistinct.*
• unclear, blurred, blurry, fuzzy, hazy, vague, indefinite, obscure, shadowy
OPPOSITE clear
❷ *The audience heard indistinct sounds of people talking.*
• muffled, mumbled, muted, faint, weak, inaudible, unintelligible, incoherent
OPPOSITE distinct

a
b
c
d
e
f
g
h
i
j
k
l
m
n
o
p
q
r
s
t
u
v
w
x
y
z

individual *ADJECTIVE*
*Her singing has an **individual** style.*
• characteristic, distinct, distinctive, special, unique, personal, singular

individual *NOUN*
*Who was that odd **individual**?*
• person, character, man, woman

induce *VERB*
❶ *I couldn't **induce** her to come to the party.*
• persuade, convince, prevail on, coax, tempt
❷ *Some headaches are **induced** by stress.*
• cause, produce, provoke, bring on, lead to, give rise to

indulge *VERB*
*They **indulged** their children too much.*
• spoil, pamper, mollycoddle
➤ **to indulge in**
*I **indulged in** a nice hot bath.*
• enjoy, revel in, wallow in

indulgent *ADJECTIVE*
*They are very **indulgent** towards their grandchildren.*
• tolerant, patient, permissive, lenient, easy-going, generous, liberal
OPPOSITE strict

industry *NOUN*
❶ *Many people in the area work in the car industry.*
• business, trade, commerce, manufacturing, production
❷ *The elves' workshop was a hive of **industry**.*
• hard work, effort, energy, diligence, application, busyness
OPPOSITE laziness

ineffective *ADJECTIVE*
*He was an **ineffective** captain of the team.*
• incompetent, inadequate, unsuccessful, inept *(informal)* useless, hopeless
OPPOSITE effective

inefficient *ADJECTIVE*
❶ *Our old vacuum cleaner was very **inefficient**.*
• ineffective, unproductive, useless, slow, sloppy

❷ *The car is **inefficient** in its use of fuel.*
• wasteful, uneconomical, extravagant
OPPOSITE efficient

inevitable *ADJECTIVE*
*If it rains, it is **inevitable** that the pitch will get wet.*
• certain, sure, definite, unavoidable, inescapable

inexpensive *ADJECTIVE*
*We bought some **inexpensive** clothes in the market.*
• cheap, low-priced, low-cost, cut-price, affordable
OPPOSITE expensive

infamous *ADJECTIVE*
*Dick Turpin was an **infamous** highwayman.*
• notorious, villainous, wicked

infant *NOUN*
*He had blond, curly hair as an **infant**.*
• baby, small child, tot, toddler

infect *VERB*
*A virus may have **infected** the water supply.*
• contaminate, pollute, poison

infection *NOUN*
*The **infection** spread rapidly.*
• disease, virus, contagion, contamination

infectious *ADJECTIVE*
*Chickenpox is highly **infectious**.*
• contagious, catching

infer *VERB*
*What can you **infer** from the tone of her letter?*
• conclude, deduce, gather, assume, guess, work out
WHICH WORD? Note there is a difference between **infer** and **imply**. To **imply** something is to suggest or hint at it.

inferior *ADJECTIVE*
❶ *The clothes were of inferior quality.*
• poor, bad, second-rate, mediocre, cheap, shoddy
❷ *Officers can give orders to those of inferior rank.*
• lesser, lower, junior, subordinate

infested *ADJECTIVE*
The attic was infested with mice.
• swarming, teeming, crawling, overrun, plagued

infiltrate *VERB*
Spies infiltrated the enemy's camp.
• enter secretly, penetrate

infinite *ADJECTIVE*
You need infinite patience to train a puppy.
• endless, limitless, unlimited, boundless, never-ending, unending, inexhaustible
OPPOSITE finite

infirm *ADJECTIVE*
Most of the patients are elderly and infirm.
• frail, weak, feeble, poorly, ill, unwell
OPPOSITE healthy
People who have to stay in bed are **bedridden**.

inflammation *NOUN*
This ointment will soothe the inflammation.
• swelling, redness, soreness, infection

inflate *VERB*
The tyres need to be inflated.
• blow up, pump up
OPPOSITE deflate

inflict *VERB*
I hate seeing anyone inflict pain on an animal.
• administer, deal out, apply, impose

influence *NOUN*
Rock music had a big influence on her life.
• effect, impact, power, dominance, guidance, authority, control

influence *VERB*
The money he was offered influenced his decision.
• affect, have an effect on, direct, guide, control, motivate

influential *ADJECTIVE*
She knows some very influential people.
• important, leading, powerful, significant
OPPOSITE unimportant

inform *VERB*
Please inform us if you move house.
• tell, let know, notify, advise

informal *ADJECTIVE*
❶ *The party will be a very informal event.*
• casual, relaxed, easy-going, friendly, homely, natural
❷ *Emails are usually written in an informal style.*
• colloquial, familiar, chatty, personal
OPPOSITE formal

information *NOUN*
There is more information on our website.
• details, particulars, facts, data, advice, guidance, knowledge
(informal) info

informative *ADJECTIVE*
That book you lent me was very informative.
• helpful, useful, instructive, illuminating, revealing
OPPOSITE unhelpful

infuriate *VERB*
He was infuriated by the umpire's decision.
• anger, enrage, incense, madden, exasperate

ingenious *ADJECTIVE*
It seemed like an ingenious plan.
• clever, brilliant, inspired, inventive, imaginative, original, crafty, cunning, shrewd

inhabit *VERB*
People inhabited the caves thousands of years ago.
• live in, occupy, dwell in, reside in, populate, settle in

a b c d e f g h i j k l m n o p q r s t u v w x y z

A B C D E F G H I J K L M N O P Q R S T U V W X Y Z

inhabitant *NOUN*
The island has fewer than thirty inhabitants.
• resident, dweller, native, occupier, occupant
An inhabitant of a particular city or country is a **citizen**.
The inhabitants of a place are its **population**.

inhabited *ADJECTIVE*
Is the island inhabited?
• occupied, lived-in
OPPOSITE uninhabited

inherit *VERB*
She inherited the farm from her uncle.
• succeed to, be left, come into

inherited *ADJECTIVE*
Eye colour is an inherited characteristic.
• hereditary, passed down

inhuman *ADJECTIVE*
I think it's inhuman to hunt animals.
• barbaric, cruel, inhumane, merciless, heartless
OPPOSITE humane

initial *ADJECTIVE*
My initial reaction was to run away and hide.
• first, earliest, preliminary, opening, introductory
OPPOSITES final, eventual

initially *ADVERB*
Initially, I didn't like swimming.
• at first, in the beginning, to begin with, to start with, at the outset

initiative *NOUN*
You must use your initiative on the treasure hunt.
• resourcefulness, inventiveness, originality, enterprise

injection *NOUN*
The nurse gave me an injection.
• inoculation, vaccination
(informal) jab

injure *VERB*
Was anyone injured in the accident?
• hurt, harm, wound
To injure someone causing permanent damage is to **maim** them.

injury *NOUN*
She escaped without any serious injury.
• wound, harm, hurt

WORD WEB

SOME TYPES OF INJURY:

• bite, bruise, burn, cut, fracture, gash, graze, scald, scratch, sprain, sting, strain

inner *ADJECTIVE*
❶ *A passageway led to the inner chamber.*
• central, inside, interior, internal, middle
OPPOSITES outer, exterior
❷ *She tries to hide her inner feelings.*
• innermost, inward, personal, private, intimate, secret, hidden, concealed
OPPOSITES outward, external

innocent *ADJECTIVE*
❶ *The jury found the man innocent.*
• guiltless, blameless, free from blame
OPPOSITE guilty
❷ *Baby tigers look so innocent.*
• angelic, harmless, faultless, virtuous, pure, simple, inexperienced, naive
OPPOSITE wicked

innumerable *ADJECTIVE*
There are innumerable stars in the sky.
• countless, numberless, uncountable, untold

inquire *VERB*
➤ **to inquire into**
Detectives are inquiring into the robbery.
• look into, investigate, examine, explore

inquiry *NOUN*
There will be an official inquiry into the accident.
• investigation, inspection, examination

inquisitive ADJECTIVE
Chimpanzees are naturally inquisitive.
• curious, questioning, inquiring, probing
for uncomplimentary synonyms see **nosy**

insane ADJECTIVE
❶ *It was rumoured that the king had gone insane.*
• mentally ill, mad, crazy, deranged, demented, disturbed, unhinged
(informal) off your head, out of your mind
OPPOSITE sane
❷ *It would be insane to swim in the sea in January!*
• crazy, mad, daft, senseless, stupid, foolish, idiotic
OPPOSITES sensible, wise

inscription NOUN
The professor read the inscription on the tomb.
• engraving, carving, writing

insect NOUN

WORD WEB

SOME TYPES OF INSECT:
• ant, aphid, bee, beetle, bluebottle, bumblebee, butterfly, cicada, cockroach, crane fly or daddy-long-legs, cricket, dragonfly, earwig, firefly, flea, fly, glow-worm, gnat, grasshopper, greenfly, hornet, horsefly, ladybird, locust, louse, mantis, mayfly, midge, mosquito, moth, stick insect, termite, tsetse fly, wasp, weevil
see also **bee**
for groups of insects see **group**

LIFE STAGES OF SOME INSECTS:
• caterpillar, chrysalis, grub, larva, maggot, pupa

PARTS OF INSECTS' BODIES:
• abdomen, antennae, head, legs, thorax, wings

SOME CREATURES SIMILAR TO INSECTS:
• centipede, earthworm, millipede, slug, spider, woodlouse, worm

insecure ADJECTIVE
❶ *Be careful—that scaffolding is insecure.*
• unsafe, unsteady, unstable, loose, shaky, wobbly, dangerous, hazardous, precarious
❷ *Ollie felt insecure on his first day at school.*
• anxious, nervous, worried, apprehensive, uneasy, uncertain, unconfident
OPPOSITE secure

insensitive ADJECTIVE
I'm sorry if my comments were insensitive.
• thoughtless, tactless, unfeeling, uncaring, unsympathetic, callous
OPPOSITE sensitive

insert VERB
Please insert a coin in the slot.
• put in, place, push in, stick in, install, implant

inside ADJECTIVE
The inside doors are all painted green.
• indoor, inner, interior, internal
OPPOSITE outside

inside NOUN
The inside of the nest was lined with feathers.
• interior, inner surface, centre, core, heart, middle
OPPOSITE outside

insignificant ADJECTIVE
The author made a few insignificant changes.
• unimportant, minor, trivial, negligible, slight, meaningless
OPPOSITE significant

insincere ADJECTIVE
The butler welcomed us with an insincere smile.
• false, pretended, hypocritical, dishonest, deceitful, deceptive, lying
(informal) two-faced
OPPOSITE sincere

a
b
c
d
e
f
g
h
i
j
k
l
m
n
o
p
q
r
s
t
u
v
w
x
y
z

insist *VERB*
She insisted that she had already paid.
• declare, state, assert, maintain, stress, emphasize, swear, vow, claim
➤ **to insist on**
The magician insisted on silence before he began.
• demand, require

insolent *ADJECTIVE*
The child gave the teacher an insolent stare.
• rude, impudent, disrespectful, impolite, impertinent, arrogant, brazen
(informal) cheeky
OPPOSITES polite, respectful

inspect *VERB*
They inspected the damage done by the storm.
• check, examine, investigate, look over, study, survey, scrutinize

inspection *NOUN*
There will be a safety inspection this afternoon.
• check, check-up, examination, review, survey

inspiration *NOUN*
❶ *What was the inspiration behind your story?*
• impulse, motivation, stimulus
❷ *The scientist had a sudden inspiration.*
• idea, thought

inspire *VERB*
The crowd inspired the team to play well.
• motivate, prompt, stimulate, encourage, stir, arouse, spur on, empower

install *VERB*
We are getting a new bathroom installed.
• put in, set up, fix, place, position, establish
OPPOSITE remove

instalment *NOUN*
I missed the first instalment of 'Dr Who'.
• episode, part

instance *NOUN*
Give me an instance of what you mean.
• example, illustration, case, sample

instant *ADJECTIVE*
Gardeners don't expect instant results.
• immediate, quick, rapid, fast, prompt, snappy, speedy, swift, direct
instant *NOUN*
The shooting star was gone in an instant.
• moment, second, split second, flash
(informal) tick, jiffy

instinct *NOUN*
The detective always followed his own instincts.
• impulse, inclination, intuition, hunch, feeling, urge

instinctive *ADJECTIVE*
Most people have an instinctive fear of sharks.
• intuitive, natural, innate, inherent, automatic, involuntary, reflex, spontaneous, impulsive, unconscious, unthinking
OPPOSITES deliberate, conscious

instruct *VERB*
❶ *All the staff are instructed in first aid.*
• teach, train, coach, tutor
❷ *The police officer instructed the cars to wait.*
• tell, order, direct, command

instructions *PLURAL NOUN*
Please follow the instructions carefully.
• directions, guidelines, orders, commands

instructor *NOUN*
The swimming instructor also teaches life-saving.
• teacher, trainer, coach

instrument *NOUN*
Dentists use special instruments to check your teeth.
• tool, implement, utensil, appliance, device, gadget, contraption
for musical instruments see **music**

insufficient *ADJECTIVE*
The plants died because they had insufficient water.
• inadequate, deficient, not enough, too little, scant, scanty
OPPOSITES enough, excessive

insult VERB
He was insulted not to be invited to the wedding.
• offend, outrage, be rude to, hurt, injure, slight, snub

insult NOUN
It is considered an insult to refuse a gift.
• rudeness, offence, affront, slight, slur, snub

insulting ADJECTIVE
They made insulting comments about the food.
• offensive, rude, impolite, derogatory, scornful
OPPOSITE complimentary

intact ADJECTIVE
The vase has remained intact for centuries.
• unbroken, whole, undamaged, unharmed, complete, perfect
(informal) in one piece

integrate VERB
They decided to integrate the two orchestras.
• bring together, combine, join, merge, unite, unify, amalgamate
OPPOSITE separate

integrity NOUN
Do you have any reason to doubt his integrity?
• honesty, honour, loyalty, trustworthiness, reliability, goodness, sincerity, virtue, fidelity
OPPOSITE dishonesty

intelligence NOUN
❶ *The robot shows some signs of intelligence.*
• cleverness, understanding, comprehension, reason, sense, wisdom, brainpower, wits
(informal) brains
❷ *The spy was sent to gather secret intelligence.*
• information, knowledge, data, facts, reports

intelligent ADJECTIVE
The aliens from Planet Zog are highly intelligent.
• clever, bright, smart, quick, sharp, perceptive, shrewd, able, brilliant, rational, thinking
(informal) brainy
OPPOSITES unintelligent, stupid

intelligible ADJECTIVE
The language of the Martians was not intelligible.
• understandable, comprehensible, meaningful, straightforward, unambiguous, clear, legible, plain, lucid
OPPOSITE incomprehensible

intend VERB
❶ *What do you intend to do?*
• plan, aim, mean, have in mind, plot, propose
❷ *The class is intended for non-swimmers.*
• design, set up, aim (at)

intense ADJECTIVE
❶ *I felt a sudden, intense pain in my chest.*
• extreme, acute, severe, sharp, great, strong, violent
OPPOSITES slight, mild
❷ *The contest aroused intense feelings.*
• deep, passionate, powerful, strong, profound
OPPOSITE mild

intensive ADJECTIVE
Police carried out an intensive search of the area.
• detailed, thorough, concentrated
OPPOSITE superficial

intent ADJECTIVE
He read the letter with an intent look on his face.
• concentrating, absorbed, engrossed, preoccupied, interested
➤ **intent on**
The detective was intent on solving the mystery.
• determined to, resolved to, eager to, fixed on, bent on

intention NOUN
It's her intention to play cricket for Australia.
• aim, objective, target, goal, ambition, plan, intent

intentional ADJECTIVE
He was penalized for an intentional foul.
• deliberate, conscious, calculated, planned, intended, wilful
OPPOSITE accidental

a
b
c
d
e
f
g
h
i
j
k
l
m
n
o
p
q
r
s
t
u
v
w
x
y
z

intercept VERB
The defender managed to intercept the pass.
• check, stop, catch, cut off, head off, deflect

interest VERB
Politics doesn't interest me at all.
• appeal to, attract, capture your imagination, excite, fascinate, stimulate, absorb
OPPOSITE bore

interest NOUN
❶ *The dog showed no interest in the bone.*
• curiosity, attention, concern, involvement
❷ *The information was of no interest to anyone.*
• importance, significance, consequence, value
❸ *My interests include judo and playing the trombone.*
• hobby, pastime, pursuit, activity, diversion

interesting ADJECTIVE
Everyone wanted to hear about our interesting adventures.
• fascinating, absorbing, enthralling, intriguing, engrossing, stimulating, riveting, gripping, entertaining, diverting
OPPOSITES boring, dull

interfere VERB
➤ **to interfere in**
Don't interfere in other people's affairs.
• intervene in, intrude in, meddle in, pry into, encroach on, butt in on
➤ **to interfere with**
The bad weather interfered with our plans.
• hamper, hinder, get in the way of, obstruct

interior ADJECTIVE, NOUN
see **inside**

intermediate ADJECTIVE
Should I join the intermediate or the advanced class?
• middle, midway, halfway, transitional

internal ADJECTIVE
Scoop out the internal parts of the tomato.
• inner, inside, interior
OPPOSITE external

international ADJECTIVE
Interpol are international police.
• global, worldwide, intercontinental

internet NOUN
I booked tickets on the internet.
• the web, online

interpret VERB
Can you interpret this old writing?
• explain, make sense of, make clear, translate, clarify, decipher, decode

interrogate VERB
The police interrogated the suspect for several hours.
• question, interview, examine, cross-examine
(informal) quiz, grill

interrupt VERB
❶ *Please don't interrupt while I am speaking.*
• intervene, interject, break in, butt in, cut in
❷ *Heavy rain interrupted the tennis match.*
• stop, suspend, disrupt, break off, cut short

interruption NOUN
He wrote for an hour without any interruption.
• break, pause, stop, gap, halt, disruption

interval NOUN
❶ *There will be a short interval after the first act.*
• break, pause, wait, delay, lapse, lull
Another word for an interval in a play or film is **interlude** or **intermission**.
An interval in a meeting is a **recess**.
An interval when you take a rest is a **breather** or **breathing space**.
❷ *There were signs at regular intervals along the road.*
• space, gap, distance

intervene VERB
A man intervened to stop the fight.
• step in, interfere, interrupt, butt in

interview *VERB*
He interviewed the author about their new book.
• question, talk to, interrogate, examine

intimate *ADJECTIVE*
❶ *They have been intimate friends for years.*
• close, cherished, dear, friendly, informal
OPPOSITE distant
❷ *The newspaper printed intimate details about her life.*
• personal, private, confidential, secret

intimidate *VERB*
You can't intimidate me into telling a lie.
• bully, threaten, frighten, menace, scare, terrify, terrorize, persecute

intrepid *ADJECTIVE*
The intrepid explorers finally reached the North Pole.
• daring, bold, fearless, courageous, brave, valiant, heroic, plucky

intricate *ADJECTIVE*
The clock has an intricate mechanism.
• complex, complicated, elaborate, sophisticated, involved
OPPOSITE simple

intriguing *ADJECTIVE*
The results of the experiment are intriguing.
• interesting, attractive, fascinating, captivating, beguiling

introduce *VERB*
❶ *Let me introduce you to my friend.*
• present, make known
❷ *The director stood up to introduce the film.*
• give an introduction to, announce, lead into
❸ *The council are introducing a new bus service next year.*
• set up, start, begin, create, establish, initiate, bring in

introduction *NOUN*
Something which happens as an introduction to a bigger event is a **prelude**.
An introduction to a book is a **preface**.
An introduction to a play is a **prologue**.
A piece played as an introduction to a concert or opera is an **overture**.

intrude *VERB*
➤ **to intrude on**
I don't mean to intrude on your privacy.
• break in on, encroach on, interrupt, butt in on, interfere with, intervene in

intruder *NOUN*
Some intruders broke into the building last night.
• trespasser, prowler, burglar

invade *VERB*
The Vikings invaded many parts of Europe.
• attack, enter, occupy, overrun, march into, raid

invalid *ADJECTIVE*
❶ *The ticket is invalid because it is out of date.*
• unacceptable, unusable, worthless
❷ *That is an invalid argument.*
• false, unsound, unreasonable, illogical, irrational, unconvincing
OPPOSITE valid

invaluable *ADJECTIVE*
Steph is an invaluable member of the hockey team.
• indispensable, irreplaceable, crucial, essential, useful, valuable
OPPOSITE worthless
WHICH WORD? Note that **invaluable** and **valuable** mean the same thing. They are not opposites!

invasion *NOUN*
Fortunately, the Martian invasion never happened.
• attack, raid

invent *VERB*
James Dewar invented the Thermos flask.
• create, devise, think up, conceive, design, originate

a
b
c
d
e
f
g
h
i
j
k
l
m
n
o
p
q
r
s
t
u
v
w
x
y
z

A
B
C
D
E
F
G
H
I
J
K
L
M
N
O
P
Q
R
S
T
U
V
W
X
Y
Z

invention NOUN
❶ *This computer program is my own invention.*
• creation, design, discovery
(informal) brainchild
❷ *The witness's account of what happened was pure invention.*
• fantasy, fiction, lies, deceit

inventive ADJECTIVE
Roald Dahl's stories are full of inventive characters.
• creative, original, imaginative, ingenious, inspired

inventor NOUN
Josephine Cochrane was the inventor of the dishwasher.
• creator, designer, originator, discoverer

investigate VERB
Police are investigating the cause of the accident.
• examine, explore, inquire into, look into, study, consider, follow up, probe, research, scrutinize
(informal) go into

investigation NOUN
An investigation showed how the accident happened.
• examination, inquiry, inspection, study, review, survey

invigorating ADJECTIVE
We went for an invigorating walk before breakfast.
• refreshing, stimulating, reviving, bracing, healthy
OPPOSITE tiring

invisible ADJECTIVE
The wizard was invisible when he wore his magic cloak.
• out of sight, unseen, unnoticed, hidden, concealed, covered, obscured, camouflaged, disguised, undetectable, unnoticeable, inconspicuous
OPPOSITE visible

invite VERB
Our neighbours invited us round for tea.
• ask, request your company, welcome, summon

inviting ADJECTIVE
An inviting smell came from the kitchen.
• attractive, appealing, pleasant, welcoming, agreeable, appetizing, tempting
OPPOSITE repulsive

involve VERB
❶ *My job involves a lot of travel.*
• include, comprise, require, demand, necessitate, mean
❷ *Protecting the environment involves us all.*
• affect, concern, interest, touch

involved ADJECTIVE
❶ *The film has a long and involved plot.*
• complex, complicated, elaborate, intricate, confusing, difficult, convoluted
OPPOSITE simple
❷ *Are you involved in the theatre?*
• concerned, participating, engaged, caught up, mixed up

irrational ADJECTIVE
My aunt has an irrational fear of buttons.
• unreasonable, illogical, senseless, nonsensical, absurd, crazy
OPPOSITE rational

irregular ADJECTIVE
❶ *The bricks were arranged in an irregular pattern.*
• varying, erratic, haphazard, random, unpredictable, fitful
OPPOSITE regular
❷ *It is highly irregular to eat pizza with a spoon!*
• abnormal, unusual, exceptional, unconventional, improper
OPPOSITE normal

irrelevant ADJECTIVE
Some of the information in the book is irrelevant.
• inappropriate, unnecessary, inessential, pointless, unrelated, unconnected, beside the point
OPPOSITE relevant

irresistible *ADJECTIVE*
I had an irresistible urge to burst out laughing.
• overwhelming, overpowering, uncontrollable, unavoidable, powerful, compelling

irresponsible *ADJECTIVE*
It's irresponsible to drive too fast.
• reckless, rash, thoughtless, inconsiderate, uncaring, unthinking, negligent
OPPOSITE responsible

irritable *ADJECTIVE*
After a bad night, he woke in an irritable mood.
• bad-tempered, grumpy, short-tempered, cross, impatient, snappy, touchy, testy, prickly, peevish
(informal) stroppy, shirty
OPPOSITES good-humoured, cheerful

irritate *VERB*
The noise from next door began to irritate me.
• annoy, bother, exasperate, anger, provoke, madden, vex
(informal) get on your nerves, bug

island *NOUN*

WORD WEB

A small island is an **islet**.
A coral island is an **atoll**.
A group of islands is an **archipelago**.
An uninhabited island is a **desert island**.
An island which is not on a map is **uncharted**.
A person who is stranded on a desert island is a **castaway**.

ON A DESERT ISLAND YOU MIGHT BE:

• cast adrift, beached, marooned, shipwrecked, stranded, washed ashore

THINGS YOU MIGHT FIND OR USE ON A DESERT ISLAND:

• beach, cave, driftwood, flotsam, footprints, lagoon, message in a bottle, palm trees, raft, shelter, tree house

isolated *ADJECTIVE*
❶ *The hikers sheltered in an isolated cave in the mountains.*
• remote, out of the way, secluded, outlying, inaccessible, cut off, deserted
OPPOSITE accessible
❷ *There have been a few isolated cases of cheating.*
• single, uncommon, unusual, abnormal, exceptional, unique
OPPOSITE common

issue *VERB*
❶ *They issued blankets to the refugees.*
• give out, distribute, supply
❷ *They have issued a new set of stamps.*
• bring out, put out, produce, publish, release, circulate, print
❸ *Green smoke issued from the dragon's nostrils.*
• come out, emerge, appear, flow out, gush, erupt

issue *NOUN*
❶ *The new issue of the magazine comes out this week.*
• edition, number, instalment, copy
❷ *Journalists post stories about local issues on the website.*
• matter, subject, topic, affair, concern, question, problem

itch *NOUN*
❶ *I had an annoying itch on my foot.*
• tickle, tingling, prickle
❷ *Olga had a great itch to travel.*
• desire, longing, urge, wish, yearning, ache, impulse

item *NOUN*
❶ *I bought a few items in the jumble sale.*
• thing, object, article
❷ *There was an item about our school in the paper.*
• article, piece, report, feature

a b c d e f g h i j k l m n o p q r s t u v w x y z

Jj

jab *VERB*
A passer-by *jabbed* me in the ribs.
• poke, prod, elbow, nudge, stab, thrust

jagged *ADJECTIVE*
This dinosaur had *jagged* teeth.
• rough, uneven, ragged, spiky, toothed, serrated
OPPOSITE smooth

jail *NOUN*
see **prison**

jam *NOUN*
❶ We got stuck in a *jam* on the motorway.
• traffic jam, hold-up, tailback, blockage
❷ *(informal)* I'm in a bit of a *jam*.
• difficulty, mess, predicament, plight
(informal) fix, tight corner

jam *VERB*
❶ Someone had *jammed* the door open.
• prop, wedge, stick
❷ The roads are *jammed* at rush hour.
• block, clog, obstruct, congest
(informal) bung up
❸ I *jammed* my things into a backpack.
• cram, pack, stuff, squeeze, squash, crush, ram, crowd

jangle *VERB*
Silver bracelets *jangled* on her wrists.
• jingle, chink, clink, tinkle

jar *NOUN*
We collected some tadpoles in a glass *jar*.
• pot, jug, pitcher, vase

jar *VERB*
❶ He *jarred* his back badly when he fell.
• jolt, jerk, shake, shock

❷ Those paint colours *jar* with each other.
• clash, conflict, be at odds

jaunty *ADJECTIVE*
The seven dwarves whistled a *jaunty* tune.
• cheerful, lively, bright, jolly, perky, breezy, sprightly
OPPOSITE gloomy

jealous *ADJECTIVE*
They were *jealous* of her success.
• envious, resentful, grudging

jeer *VERB*
Some of the audience whistled and *jeered*.
• boo, hiss, sneer, taunt, mock, scoff, ridicule
OPPOSITE cheer

jerk *VERB*
The rider *jerked* on the horse's reins.
• pull, tug, yank, pluck, wrench, tweak

jerky *ADJECTIVE*
The tractor came to a *jerky* halt.
• jolting, jumpy, shaky, bouncy, bumpy, uneven
OPPOSITE steady

jester *NOUN*
The king's *jester* kept the court amused.
• fool, joker, clown

jet *NOUN*
A *jet* of water shot high in the air.
• spout, spurt, squirt, gush, stream, fountain

jewel and **jewellery** *NOUN*

WORD WEB

SOME ITEMS OF JEWELLERY:

• anklet, bangle, beads, body piercing, bracelet, brooch, chain, charm, choker, cufflinks, earring, engagement ring, locket, medallion, necklace, pendant, pin, ring, tiara, tiepin, wedding ring

STONES OR GEMS USED TO MAKE JEWELLERY:

• agate, amber, amethyst, aquamarine, coral, diamond, emerald, garnet, jade, jasper, jet, lapis lazuli, onyx, moonstone, opal, pearl, ruby, sapphire, topaz, turquoise

METALS USED TO MAKE JEWELLERY:

• gold, platinum, silver

jingle VERB
Some coins jingled in his back pocket.
• jangle, chink, clink, tinkle

job NOUN
❶ *My sister has a job as a TV reporter.*
• post, position, profession, occupation, employment, trade, work, career
The job you particularly want to do is your **mission** or **vocation**.
❷ *Whose job is it to do the washing-up?*
• duty, task, assignment, chore, errand

WORD WEB

SOME JOBS:

• actor, architect, artist, astronaut, author, banker, barber, blogger, bookseller, builder, bus driver, carer, chef, cleaner, coach, cook, curator, dancer, dentist, detective, doctor, editor, electrician, engineer, explorer, farmer, firefighter, fisherman, flight attendant, florist, footballer, gamer, gardener, hairdresser, imam, influencer, janitor, joiner, journalist, lawyer, lexicographer, librarian, mechanic, midwife, miner, minister, model, musician, nurse, office worker, optician, painter, paramedic, pharmacist, photographer, pilot, plumber, police officer, politician, postal delivery worker, priest, printer, professor, programmer, psychiatrist, rabbi, receptionist, reporter, sailor, scientist, secretary, shepherd, shopkeeper, singer, soldier, solicitor, surgeon, tailor, teacher, train driver, translator, TV presenter, undertaker, vet, vlogger, waiter or waitress, web designer, writer, zookeeper

jog VERB
❶ *We jog round the park every morning.*
• go jogging, run, trot
❷ *A boy sitting next to me jogged my elbow.*
• nudge, prod, jolt, knock, bump, jar, jostle
❸ *The photograph may jog her memory.*
• prompt, stir, arouse, set off, stimulate

join VERB
❶ *Our families joined together to buy the present.*
• combine, come together, merge, unite, amalgamate
OPPOSITE separate
❷ *Join one piece of rope to the other.*
• connect, fasten, attach, fix, link, put together, tack on
OPPOSITE detach
❸ *The two roads join here.*
• meet, merge, converge
OPPOSITE divide
❹ *I joined the crowd going into the cinema.*
• follow, go with, tag along with
OPPOSITE leave
❺ *We have joined a local sports club.*
• become a member of, enrol in, sign up for
To join the army is to **enlist**.
OPPOSITES leave, resign from

join NOUN
If you look hard, you can still see the join.
• joint, connection, link, mend, seam

joint ADJECTIVE
The preparation of the meal was a joint effort.
• combined, shared, common, communal, cooperative, united, collective, mutual
OPPOSITE individual

joke NOUN
Do you know any good jokes?
• jest, quip, crack, witticism, wisecrack *(informal)* gag

joke VERB
Those two are always laughing and joking.
• jest, clown, have a laugh, make jokes

a
b
c
d
e
f
g
h
i
j
k
l
m
n
o
p
q
r
s
t
u
v
w
x
y
z

jolly *ADJECTIVE*
We had a jolly time on holiday.
• cheerful, merry, happy, joyful, pleasant, enjoyable
OPPOSITE gloomy

jolt *VERB*
The car jolted over the bumps in the road.
• jerk, jog, bump, bounce, shake, shudder

jostle *VERB*
The film star was jostled by photographers.
• push, shove, hustle, press, crowd in on

jot *VERB*
➤ **to jot down**
I quickly jotted down some ideas.
• make a note of, write down, take down, note, scribble

journal *NOUN*
❶ *The newsagent sells a few journals.*
• magazine, newspaper, paper, periodical, publication
❷ *The captain kept a journal of the voyage.*
• diary, log, record, account, chronicle

journalist *NOUN*
She works as a journalist on the local paper.
• reporter, correspondent, columnist, writer

journey *NOUN*
On their journey, the astronauts will pass the Moon.
• voyage, trip, expedition, travels, tour, route

jovial *ADJECTIVE*
Our guests were in a jovial mood.
• cheerful, happy, jolly, good-humoured, merry, joyful
OPPOSITE sad

joy *NOUN*
I remember the sheer joy of scoring a goal!
• happiness, joyfulness, delight, cheerfulness, gladness, mirth, glee, jubilation, gaiety, rejoicing, bliss, ecstasy, elation
OPPOSITE sorrow

joyful *ADJECTIVE*
The wedding was a joyful occasion.
• happy, cheerful, merry, joyous, jolly, jovial, good-humoured
OPPOSITE sad

judge *NOUN*
A judge in a local court is a **magistrate**.
A judge in a competition is an **adjudicator**.
A judge in a sport is a **referee** or **umpire**.
judge *VERB*
❶ *The umpire judged that the ball was out.*
• rule, decide, decree, adjudicate
❷ *Who's judging the flower show this year?*
• decide on, assess, evaluate, appraise
❸ *He judged the coin to be about 1000 years old.*
• reckon, suppose, consider, gauge, guess, estimate

judgement *NOUN*
❶ *What is the judgement of the court?*
• decision, finding, ruling, verdict, decree
❷ *His comments show a lack of judgement.*
• wisdom, common sense, understanding, discrimination
❸ *In my judgement, you're making a big mistake.*
• opinion, view, belief, assessment, estimate

juice *NOUN*
Squeeze the juice from the lemons.
• liquid, fluid, sap

jumble *NOUN*
There was a jumble of clothes on the floor.
• mess, muddle, clutter, chaos, confusion, disorder

jumble *VERB*
Please don't jumble the pages.
• muddle, mix up, mess up, disorganise, shuffle
OPPOSITE arrange

jump *VERB*
❶ *Suddenly a rabbit jumped in front of us.*
• leap, spring, bound, bounce, hop
When a cat jumps it **pounces**.
❷ *All the horses jumped the first hurdle.*
• leap over, vault, clear
❸ *The loud bang made them all jump.*
• start, flinch, jolt

jump *NOUN*
❶ *With a jump, the grasshopper landed on the leaf.*
• leap, spring, bound, vault, hop
❷ *The horse easily cleared the last jump.*
• hurdle, fence, gate, barrier, obstacle

junction *NOUN*
There are traffic lights at the road junction.
• intersection, crossing, interchange

jungle *NOUN*
Jungles are home to over half of the world's plant and land animal species.
• rainforest, tropical forest

WORD WEB

THINGS YOU MIGHT SEE IN THE JUNGLE:

• canopy, ferns, foliage, forest floor, lagoons, mist, moss, rainfall, rivers, rocks, streams, swamp, tall trees, undergrowth, understory, vines, waterfalls

SOME ANIMALS WHICH LIVE IN THE JUNGLE:

• alligator, ant, anteater, armadillo, bird of paradise, butterfly, chameleon, crocodile, gorilla, hummingbird, jaguar, leopard, macaw, monkey, mosquito, parrot, piranha, porcupine, snake, tarantula, tiger, toucan, tree frog

SOME PLANTS WHICH ARE FOUND IN THE JUNGLE:

• banana tree, cacao, creeper or liana, mangrove, orchid, palm tree, rubber tree
see also **explorer**

junior *ADJECTIVE*
❶ *I'm a member of the junior hockey team.*
• younger
❷ *He's only a junior employee in the firm.*
• low-ranking, minor, lesser, subordinate
OPPOSITE senior

junk *NOUN*
The garage is full of old junk.
• rubbish, clutter, garbage, jumble, trash, waste, scrap, odds and ends

just *ADJECTIVE*
It was a just punishment, considering the crime.
• fair, fitting, appropriate, deserved, proper, reasonable, justified
OPPOSITES unjust, unfair

justice *NOUN*
❶ *The prisoners demanded to be treated with justice.*
• fairness, justness, fair play, right, honesty, impartiality
OPPOSITE injustice
❷ *They were tried in a court of justice.*
• law

justify *VERB*
How can you justify spending so much money?
• defend, excuse, account for, explain

jut *VERB*
➤ **to jut out**
A large nail jutted out from the wall.
• stick out, project, protrude, extend, overhang

juvenile ADJECTIVE
❶ *This part of the library is for juvenile fiction.*
• children's, young people's
OPPOSITE adult
❷ *His jokes are really juvenile.*
• childish, babyish, immature
OPPOSITE mature

Kk

keen ADJECTIVE
❶ *Rhona is a keen hockey player.*
• enthusiastic, eager, fervent, avid, devoted, committed, motivated
A common simile is as keen as mustard.
OPPOSITE unenthusiastic
❷ *A carving knife should have a keen edge.*
• sharp, razor-sharp, cutting
OPPOSITE blunt
❸ *Owls have keen eyesight.*
• sharp, acute, piercing
OPPOSITE poor
❹ *A keen wind was blowing from the east.*
• bitter, cold, icy, penetrating
OPPOSITE mild

keep VERB keeps, keeping, kept
❶ *Let's keep the rest of the cake for later.*
• save, conserve, preserve, retain, hang on to, hold on to, guard, store
❷ *Please keep still.*
• stay, remain
❸ *A man in the audience kept coughing.*
• persist in, go on, carry on, continue
❹ *You're late. What kept you?*
• delay, detain, hold up, keep waiting
❺ *Where do you keep the knives and forks?*
• store, house, put, stow
❻ *Will the milk keep until tomorrow?*
• last, be usable, stay good
❼ *It costs money to keep a pet.*
• support, maintain, provide for, pay for
➤ **to keep something up**
Keep up the good work!
• carry on, continue, maintain

key NOUN
Have you found the key to the riddle?
• answer, solution, explanation, clue

keyboard NOUN
for keyboard instruments see **music**

kick NOUN
Ben closed the gate with a kick.
• strike, boot, hit, blow
kick VERB
The goalkeeper kicked the ball into the air.
• strike, boot, hit, drive, send
for other ways to strike a ball see **ball**

kidnap VERB
In the story, a boy is kidnapped by bandits.
• abduct, capture, seize, carry off, snatch

kill VERB
Several people were killed in the explosion.
(informal) bump off, do away with
(old use) slay
To kill someone deliberately is to **murder** them.
To kill someone brutally is to **butcher** them.
To kill large numbers of people is to **massacre** or **slaughter** them.
To kill someone as a punishment is to **execute** them or **put them to death**.
To kill someone for political reasons is to **assassinate** them.

kind *NOUN*
What kind of music do you like to play?
• sort, type, variety, style, category, class, set

kind *ADJECTIVE*
It was very kind of you to help me.
• kind-hearted, caring, good-natured, kindly, affectionate, warm, genial, loving, sweet, gentle, lenient, amiable, friendly, generous, sympathetic, thoughtful, obliging, considerate, understanding, compassionate, unselfish, giving, gracious, merciful, benevolent, charitable, humane, neighbourly
OPPOSITE unkind

king *NOUN*
Neptune is the mythological King of the Sea.
• monarch, sovereign

kingdom *NOUN*
King Brian the Bald ruled over a vast kingdom.
• realm, monarchy

kiss *NOUN*
She gave him a kiss on the cheek.
(informal) peck

kit *NOUN*
I've forgotten my games kit.
• gear, outfit, equipment, paraphernalia, tools, tackle

kitchen *NOUN*

WORD WEB

EQUIPMENT YOU MIGHT FIND IN A KITCHEN:

• apron, blender, bread bin, cooker, crockery, cutlery, dishwasher, draining board, food processor, freezer, fridge, grill, kettle, liquidizer, microwave, mixer, oven, oven gloves, refrigerator, scales, sink, toaster
for other things used for cooking see **cook, cutlery**

kitten *NOUN*
see **cat**

knack *NOUN*
George has a knack for taking photographs.
• skill, talent, gift, flair

knead *VERB*
Knead the dough until it is smooth.
• work, press, squeeze, pummel

knew *past tense see* **know**

knife *NOUN*

WORD WEB

SOME KINDS OF KNIFE:

• cleaver, dagger, dirk, machete, penknife, scalpel
for kitchen knives see **cutlery**

knight *NOUN*

WORD WEB

THINGS A MEDIEVAL KNIGHT MIGHT WEAR OR CARRY:

• armour, baldric (leather belt), chain mail, coat of arms, falcon or hawk, helmet, lance, mace (metal club), pennant, shield, surcoat, sword, tabard, tunic
for parts of a suit of armour see **armour**
He was equipped for battle, with helmet and chain mail, lance and sword. His tabard, shield, and the feathers on his helmet were as red as blood.—THE LETTER FOR THE KING, Tonke Dragt
A fight between knights on horseback was a **joust**.
A series of sporting contests between knights was a **tournament**.
A boy training to be a knight was first a **page** and then a **squire**.
An expedition made by a knight was a **quest**.

a b c d e f g h i j **k** l m n o p q r s t u v w x y z

A
B
C
D
E
F
G
H
I
J
K
L
M
N
O
P
Q
R
S
T
U
V
W
X
Y
Z

knob *NOUN*
❶ *The knob had fallen off the door.*
• handle
❷ *Melt a knob of butter in a pan.*
• lump, piece, bit

knobbly *ADJECTIVE*
Crocodiles have thick and knobbly skin.
• lumpy, bumpy, gnarled

knock *VERB*
*I knocked my head as I came out of
the car.*
• bump, bang, hit, strike, thump
(informal) bash

knot *VERB*
The sailors knotted the two ropes together.
• tie, bind, fasten, join, entwine, lash
OPPOSITE untie

know *VERB* knows, knowing, knew,
known
❶ *Do you know how to mend a puncture?*
• understand, have knowledge of,
comprehend
❷ *As soon as she saw the unicorn, she knew
what it was.*
• recognize, realize, appreciate, be aware of
❸ *Do you know Oliver well?*
• be acquainted with, be familiar with,
be a friend of

knowledge *NOUN*
❶ *She has a good knowledge of Italian.*
• understanding, grasp, command,
familiarity (with)
❷ *An encyclopedia contains a lot of
knowledge.*
• information, data, facts, learning,
know-how, wisdom, scholarship

knowledgeable *ADJECTIVE*
*My sister is very knowledgeable about
guitars.*
• familiar (with), well-informed, educated,
learned
OPPOSITE ignorant

Ll

label *NOUN*
The washing instructions are on the label.
• tag, ticket, sticker
label *VERB*
*I've labelled all the boxes, so we'll know what's
in them.*
• put a label on, tag, mark, name, identify

laborious *ADJECTIVE*
*It was a laborious climb to the top of
the hill.*
• hard, tough, strenuous, difficult, stiff, tiring,
exhausting, gruelling
OPPOSITE easy

labour *NOUN*
❶ *The workers were paid for their labour.*
• work, effort, industry, exertion, toil
❷ *The factory took on extra labour.*
• workers, employees
labour *VERB*
*They laboured to get the job finished
on time.*
• work hard, exert yourself, toil
(informal) slave away, slog

lack *NOUN*
*The judge dismissed the case because of a
lack of evidence.*
• absence, shortage, scarcity, want
A general lack of food is a **famine.**
A general lack of water is a **drought.**
OPPOSITE abundance
lack *VERB*
The game lacked excitement.
• be short of, be without, want, need,
require, miss

lady *NOUN*
see **woman**

236

lag *VERB*
*One runner was **lagging** behind the others.*
• straggle, trail, fall behind, drop behind, dawdle, linger, loiter

laid *past tense see* **lay**

lair *NOUN*
*The hunters tracked the animal back to its **lair**.*
• den, refuge, shelter, hideout, hiding place

lake *NOUN*
*We rowed across the **lake**.*
• pond, pool, *(Scottish)* loch
A saltwater lake is a **lagoon**.
A lake used to supply water is a **reservoir**.

lame *ADJECTIVE*
❶ *The **lame** horse had to be withdrawn from the race.*
• crippled, limping
❷ *I didn't believe their **lame** excuses.*
• feeble, flimsy, poor, unconvincing, inadequate, weak, tame

lamp *NOUN*
see **light**

land *NOUN*
❶ *The castle is surrounded by several acres of **land**.*
• grounds, estate, property
❷ *The **land** here is good for growing strawberries.*
• ground, soil, earth
❸ *China is a **land** with an ancient history.*
• country, nation, state, region, territory

land *VERB*
❶ *The plane **landed** exactly on time.*
• touch down, arrive
 OPPOSITE take off
❷ *The ship will **land** at Dover.*
• dock, berth, come ashore
❸ *How did these papers **land** on my desk?*
• arrive, turn up, end up, wind up, settle

landscape *NOUN*
*We sat on the hill and admired the **landscape**.*
• countryside, scenery, view, scene, outlook, prospect

lane *NOUN*
see **road**

language *NOUN*
❶ *The scroll was written in an ancient **language**.*
• tongue, speech, dialect
❷ *The author uses very poetic **language**.*
• wording, phrasing, vocabulary, expression, style
The words of a language are its **vocabulary**.
see also **writing**

lap *NOUN*
❶ *My cat, Snowy, likes to sit on my **lap**.*
• knee, knees, thighs
❷ *The cars were on the last **lap** of the race.*
• circuit, round, loop

lapse *NOUN*
❶ *The official made a mistake because of a **lapse** in concentration.*
• failure, error, fault, slip, flaw, weakness, shortcoming
❷ *I've started swimming again after a **lapse** of a year.*
• break, gap, interval, interruption, lull, pause

large *ADJECTIVE*
❶ *Elephants are **large** animals.*
• big, huge, enormous, colossal, giant, gigantic, immense, great, massive, bulky, heavy, hefty, weighty, mighty, towering *(informal)* whopping, ginormous
❷ *The cook gave me a **large** helping of pudding.*
• ample, generous, plentiful, abundant, lavish
❸ *Is this room **large** enough for dancing in?*
• spacious, roomy, sizeable
❹ *The gales caused damage over a **large** area.*
• wide, broad, extensive, widespread, vast
❺ *The meeting was attended by a **large** number of people.*
• considerable, substantial
 OPPOSITE small

a
b
c
d
e
f
g
h
i
j
k
l
m
n
o
p
q
r
s
t
u
v
w
x
y
z

A **B** **C** **D** **E** **F** **G** **H** **I** **J** **K** **L** **M** **N** **O** **P** **Q** **R** **S** **T** **U** **V** **W** **X** **Y** **Z**

largely *ADVERB*
The driver was largely to blame for the accident.
• mainly, chiefly, mostly, principally, to a large extent

last *ADJECTIVE*
❶ *Z is the last letter of the alphabet.*
• final, closing, concluding, terminating, ultimate
(OPPOSITE) first
❷ *Did you see his last film?*
• latest, most recent
(OPPOSITE) next

last *NOUN*
➤ **at last**
The holidays are here at last!
• finally, eventually, in the end

last *VERB*
❶ *Let's hope the fine weather lasts.*
• carry on, continue, keep on, stay, remain, persist, endure, hold
❷ *The plants won't last long without water.*
• hold out, keep going, live, survive

late *ADJECTIVE*
❶ *The bus is late.*
• delayed, overdue
(OPPOSITE) early, punctual, on time
❷ *Mr Pettigrew showed us a portrait of his late wife.*
• dead, deceased, departed

lately *ADVERB*
There has been a lot of snow lately.
• recently, latterly, of late

later *ADJECTIVE*
We'll study that poem in a later class.
• future, following, subsequent

later *ADVERB*
I'm busy now, but I'll phone you later.
• afterwards, in a while, subsequently, next

laugh *VERB*
❶ *The children laughed when the clown fell over.*
• chuckle, giggle, titter, burst out laughing, roar or scream with laughter, roll or fall about laughing, guffaw
(informal) have hysterics, be in stitches
❷ *It's rude to laugh at his way of singing.*
• make fun of, mock, ridicule, scoff at, tease, deride

laughter *NOUN*
We heard bursts of laughter coming from the kitchen.
• laughing, amusement, hilarity, mirth, merriment

launch *VERB*
❶ *The space shuttle will be launched tomorrow.*
• send off, set off, blast off, fire
❷ *The new website was launched in the summer.*
• begin, start, set up, open, establish, found, initiate

lavatory *NOUN*
The girls' lavatories are at the end of the corridor.
• toilet, bathroom, WC, cloakroom, washroom
(informal) loo

lavish *ADJECTIVE*
The king put on a lavish feast for his birthday.
• generous, extravagant, sumptuous, luxurious, opulent, grand, abundant, copious, plentiful, bountiful
(OPPOSITES) meagre, paltry

law *NOUN*
A law passed by parliament is an **act**.
A proposed law to be discussed by parliament is a **bill**.
The laws of a game are **regulations** or **rules**.
A regulation which must be obeyed is a **commandment**, **decree**, **edict** or **order**.

lay *past tense see* **lie**

lay *VERB* lays, laying, laid
❶ *He laid the parchment carefully on his desk.*
• put down, set down, place, position, spread, deposit, leave
❷ *Please lay the table for dinner.*
• set out, arrange

layer *NOUN*
❶ *The walls needed two layers of paint.*
• coat, coating, covering, thickness, film, sheet, skin
❷ *You can see various layers of rock in the cliff.*
• seam, stratum

laze *VERB*
We spent the day lazing in the garden.
• be lazy, idle, loaf, lounge, lie about, relax, loll

lazy *ADJECTIVE*
My lazy little cousin stayed in bed all day!
• idle, inactive, lethargic, slack, slothful, indolent
An informal name for a lazy person is lazybones.

lead *VERB* leads, leading, led
❶ *The rescuers led the climbers to safety.*
• guide, conduct, escort, usher, steer, pilot, shepherd
OPPOSITE follow
❷ *Dr Martez will lead the expedition to Peru.*
• be in charge of, direct, command, head, manage, supervise
❸ *The Slovenian cyclist led from the start of the race.*
• be in front, be in the lead, head the field
❹ *The animals in the zoo lead a peaceful life.*
• have, pass, spend, experience

lead *NOUN*
❶ *The team followed the captain's lead.*
• example, guidance, leadership, direction
❷ *The Hungarian swimmer is in the lead.*
• first place, front position
❸ *Ria was given the lead in the play.*
• main part, starring role, title role

❹ *Keep the dog on a lead.*
• leash, strap, chain, tether, rein
❺ *Don't trip over the electrical lead.*
• cable, flex, wire

leader *NOUN*
The leader of the pirates was Captain Cutlass.
• head, chief, commander, captain, director, principal, ruler
(informal) boss
The leader of a group of wrongdoers is the ringleader.

leaf *NOUN*
❶ *Deciduous trees lose their leaves in autumn.*
A mass of leaves is foliage or greenery.
❷ *A single leaf had been torn out of the book.*
• page, sheet

leak *NOUN*
The plumber mended a leak in the water tank.
• crack, hole, opening, drip
A leak in a tyre is a puncture.

leak *VERB*
❶ *The juice had leaked all over my school bag.*
• escape, drip, seep, ooze, trickle
❷ *Details of a secret plan were leaked to the newspaper.*
• reveal, disclose, make known, pass on, give away, let out

lean *VERB* leans, leaning, leaned or leant
❶ *I leaned against the wall.*
• recline, rest, prop yourself, support yourself
❷ *The yacht leaned to one side in the wind.*
• slope, tilt, tip, incline, slant, list, bank

lean *ADJECTIVE*
The athlete has a strong, lean figure.
• slim, slender, thin, wiry
OPPOSITE fat

leap *VERB* leaps, leaping, leapt or leaped
The dog leaped in the air to catch the ball.
• jump, spring, bound, vault

a b c d e f g h i j k l m n o p q r s t u v w x y z

A
B
C
D
E
F
G
H
I
J
K
L
M
N
O
P
Q
R
S
T
U
V
W
X
Y
Z

learn VERB learns, learning, learnt or learned
❶ We are *learning* about the Vikings this term.
• discover, find out, gather, grasp, pick up
❷ I've got to *learn* the words of this song.
• learn by heart, memorize, master

learner NOUN
This swimming class is for *learners* only.
• beginner, starter, novice
Someone learning things at school or college is a **pupil** or **student**.
Someone learning a trade is an **apprentice** or **trainee**.

least ADJECTIVE, DETERMINER
❶ Who got the *least* number of points?
• fewest, lowest
❷ The *least* amount of this poison is deadly.
• slightest, smallest, tiniest

leave VERB leaves, leaving, left
❶ Do you have to *leave* now?
• go, go away, depart, withdraw, take your leave, go out, set off, say goodbye
(informal) take off, disappear
OPPOSITE arrive
❷ The doctor *left* the room in a hurry.
• exit, go out of, depart from, quit, vacate
OPPOSITE enter
❸ Don't *leave* me here on my own!
• abandon, desert, forsake
❹ The crew *left* the sinking ship.
• evacuate, get out of
❺ My sister has *left* her job at the bank.
• give up, quit, resign from
(informal) walk out of
❻ *Leave* the milk bottles by the front door.
• place, position, put down, set down, deposit
❼ I'll just *leave* all the arrangements to you.
• pass on, hand over, refer, entrust
❽ Lady Bigwig *left* all her money to charity.
• bequeath, hand down, will, endow
➤ **to leave someone** or **something out**
Eric was *left out* of the basketball team.
• miss out, omit, exclude, reject

leave NOUN
❶ The prime minister is away on *leave*.
• holiday, vacation, time off

❷ Will you give me *leave* to speak?
• permission, freedom, liberty

lecture NOUN
❶ There is a *lecture* about dinosaurs at the museum today.
• talk, lesson, speech, address
❷ The teacher gave us a *lecture* on how to behave.
• reprimand, warning
(informal) telling-off

led past tense see **lead**

ledge NOUN
The climbers rested on a *ledge* of rock.
• shelf, projection
A ledge under a window is a **windowsill**.

left past tense see **leave**

left ADJECTIVE
The left side of a ship when you face forwards is the **port** side.
see also **right**

leg NOUN
❶ Boris fell and bruised his *leg*.
for parts of your body see **body**
❷ The rowers completed the first *leg* of the race.
• part, stage, section, phase, stretch

legal ADJECTIVE
Is it *legal* to park here on Sundays?
• lawful, legitimate, permissible, permitted, allowed
OPPOSITE illegal

legend NOUN
I like reading *legends* about ancient heroes.
• myth, story, folk tale, fairy tale, fable, tradition, saga
for creatures found in myths and legends see **myth**

legendary ADJECTIVE
Unicorns are *legendary* beasts.
• mythical, fabulous, fabled, fictional, fictitious, invented, made-up
OPPOSITE real

legible *ADJECTIVE*
Although the letter is old, the handwriting is legible.
• readable, clear, distinct, neat
OPPOSITE illegible

legitimate *ADJECTIVE*
Are you the legitimate owner of this car?
• legal, proper, rightful, authorized, licensed, permitted

leisure *NOUN*
Grandad has plenty of leisure since he retired.
• free time, spare time, relaxation, recreation, rest

leisurely *ADJECTIVE*
We went for a leisurely stroll in the park.
• gentle, relaxed, relaxing, unhurried, restful, slow
OPPOSITE fast

lend *VERB*
Can you lend me some money until the weekend?
• loan, advance, let you have
OPPOSITE borrow

length *NOUN*
❶ *My heart sank when I saw the length of the queue.*
• extent, size
❷ *We only had to wait a short length of time.*
• space, period, stretch

lengthen *VERB*
❶ *Is it possible to lengthen these curtains?*
• extend, make longer, increase, stretch
❷ *The days lengthen in spring.*
• draw out, get longer, stretch out
OPPOSITE shorten

lengthy *ADJECTIVE*
There was a lengthy argument over who was to blame.
• long, drawn-out, extended, prolonged, time-consuming
OPPOSITE short

lenient *ADJECTIVE*
The teacher was lenient and let us off.
• easy-going, soft-hearted, tolerant, forgiving, indulgent, kind, merciful
OPPOSITE strict

lessen *VERB*
❶ *This medicine will lessen the pain.*
• minimize, reduce, relieve
❷ *The storm lessened during the night.*
• diminish, decrease, dwindle, subside, weaken, ease off, tail off, die away or down
OPPOSITE increase

lesson *NOUN*
My piano lesson is on Friday afternoon.
• class, period, tutorial, instruction

let *VERB* lets, letting, let
❶ *Abby's parents let her go to the party.*
• allow, give permission to, permit, consent to, agree to
OPPOSITE forbid
❷ *Our friends are letting their house for the summer.*
• lease, rent out, hire out

lethal *ADJECTIVE*
This bottle contains a lethal potion.
• deadly, fatal, mortal, poisonous

letter *NOUN*
❶ *There are twenty-six letters in the alphabet.*
• character, symbol, sign, figure
The letters a, e, i, o, u, and sometimes y, are **vowels**.
The other letters are **consonants**.
❷ *Did you remember to sign your letter?*
• note, message, communication
Letters that people send each other are **correspondence**.

level *ADJECTIVE*
❶ *You need a level field for playing rounders.*
• even, flat, horizontal, smooth
OPPOSITE uneven
❷ *At half-time the scores were level.*
• equal, even, the same, matching
(informal) neck-and-neck

a
b
c
d
e
f
g
h
i
j
k
l
m
n
o
p
q
r
s
t
u
v
w
x
y
z

level *VERB*
❶ *Dad levelled the garden to make a lawn.*
• even out, flatten, smooth
❷ *A serious earthquake levelled the town.*
• knock down, demolish, destroy, devastate

level *NOUN*
❶ *The water had reached a high level.*
• height
❷ *The lift takes you up to the sixth level.*
• floor, storey, tier
❸ *What level have you reached in judo?*
• grade, standard, stage, rank, degree

lever *VERB*
Slowly, I levered open the lid of the chest.
• prise, wrench, force

liable *ADJECTIVE*
❶ *You're liable to make mistakes when you're tired.*
• likely, inclined, disposed, prone, ready
OPPOSITE unlikely
❷ *If you break anything, you'll be liable for the cost.*
• responsible, answerable, accountable

liberal *ADJECTIVE*
❶ *We each got a liberal helping of ice cream.*
• generous, ample, plentiful, lavish, abundant, copious, bountiful
OPPOSITES meagre, miserly
❷ *She has a liberal attitude towards most things.*
• broad-minded, easy-going, lenient, tolerant, permissive
OPPOSITE strict

liberate *VERB*
The prisoners were liberated at the end of the war.
• free, release, set free, emancipate, discharge, let go, set loose
OPPOSITE imprison

liberty *NOUN*
❶ *The animals have liberty to wander around the park.*
• freedom, independence
❷ *The king granted the prisoners their liberty.*
• liberation, release, emancipation

licence *NOUN*
He has a licence to practise as a doctor.
• permit, certificate, authorization, warrant

license *VERB*
Are you licensed to drive this vehicle?
• permit, allow, authorize, entitle

lid *NOUN*
Can you help me get the lid off this jar?
• cap, cover, covering, top

lie *VERB* lies, lying, lay, lain
❶ *Jamal was lying on his bed, reading.*
• recline, stretch out, lounge, sprawl, rest
To lie face down is to be **prone**.
To lie face upwards is to be **supine**.
❷ *The castle lies in a valley.*
• be sited, be situated, be located, be found

lie *VERB* lies, lying, lied
I don't trust them—I think they're lying.
• deceive someone, bluff
(informal) fib

lie *NOUN*
He accused the newspaper of printing lies.
• deceit, falsehood, dishonesty
(informal) fib
OPPOSITE truth

life *NOUN*
❶ *My hamster, Fluffy, leads a very easy life.*
• existence, being, way of life
❷ *Our lives depended on finding water.*
• survival
❸ *You seem to be full of life today!*
• energy, liveliness, vigour, vitality, spirit, sprightliness, animation
❹ *I'm reading a life of Elvis Presley.*
• life story, autobiography, biography

lift *VERB*
❶ *The removal team lifted the piano carefully.*
• pick up, raise, elevate, pull up, hoist
❷ *The plane lifted off the ground.*
• rise, ascend, soar

lift *NOUN*
Take the lift to the top floor.
A North American word is **elevator**.

light NOUN

WORD WEB

SOME KINDS OF NATURAL LIGHT:

• daylight, moonlight, starlight, sunlight, twilight

SOURCES OF ARTIFICIAL LIGHT:

• bulb, candle, chandelier, floodlight, fluorescent lamp, headlamp or headlight, lamp, lantern, laser, neon light, searchlight, spotlight, street light, torch

VARIOUS FORMS OF LIGHT:

• beam, flash, flicker, glow, halo, lustre, radiance, ray, reflection, shaft

WRITING TIPS

You can use these words to describe **light**.

TO DESCRIBE HOW LIGHT APPEARS:

• bright, brilliant, harsh, luminous, lustrous, strong, diffused, dim, muted, soft, warm

LIGHT MAY:

• beam, blaze, dazzle, flash, flicker, glare, gleam, glimmer, glint, glisten, glitter, glow, shimmer, shine, sparkle, twinkle
In the still woods, the only movements were bars of sunlight glinting like green glass through the leafy canopy.—PAX, Sara Pennypacker

light ADJECTIVE

❶ *The artist worked in a **light** and airy studio.*
• bright, well-lit, illuminated
OPPOSITES dim, gloomy
❷ *She was wearing **light** blue jeans.*
• pale
OPPOSITE dark
❸ *The parcel looks big, but it is quite **light**.*
• lightweight, portable, weightless, slight
A common simile is as **light** as a feather.
OPPOSITE heavy

❹ *A **light** wind rippled the surface of the water.*
• gentle, faint, slight
OPPOSITE strong
❺ *We had a **light** meal before we went out.*
• small, modest, simple, insubstantial
OPPOSITES heavy, substantial
❻ *I brought a book for some **light** reading.*
• undemanding, entertaining, lightweight
OPPOSITE serious

light VERB lights, lighting, lit or lighted
❶ *We **lit** the candles on my birthday cake.*
• ignite, kindle, set alight, set fire to, switch on
OPPOSITE extinguish
❷ *The fireworks **lit** the sky.*
• light up, brighten, illuminate, shed light on, shine on
OPPOSITE darken

like VERB

OVERUSED WORD

Try to vary the words you use for **like**. Here are some other words you could use.

TO LIKE A PERSON OR ANIMAL:

• be fond of, be attached to, care for, love, adore, cherish, esteem, admire, hold dear *(informal)* have a soft spot for
*Lauren is very **attached** to her new puppy.*

TO LIKE SOMETHING OR LIKE DOING SOMETHING:

• be keen on, be partial to, be interested in, delight in, enjoy, appreciate, prefer, relish
*I'm not very **keen** on broccoli.*
*What sort of films do you **enjoy**?*
OPPOSITE dislike

like PREPOSITION
*The witch's hand looked **like** a knobbly tree.*
• similar to, the same as, resembling, identical to
OPPOSITE unlike

a
b
c
d
e
f
g
h
i
j
k
l
m
n
o
p
q
r
s
t
u
v
w
x
y
z

likely ADJECTIVE
It's likely that the shop will be closed tomorrow.
• probable, expected, anticipated, predictable, foreseeable
OPPOSITE unlikely

likeness NOUN
❶ *There's a strong likeness between the two sisters.*
• resemblance, similarity, correspondence
OPPOSITE difference
❷ *This photo is a good likeness of my grandfather.*
• image, representation, picture, portrait, copy

liking NOUN
Ray has a liking for classical music.
• fondness, taste, love, affection, preference
OPPOSITE dislike

limb NOUN
Your limbs are your arms and legs.
Birds have **wings**.
Seals, whales and dolphins have **flippers**.
An octopus has **tentacles**.
The limbs of a tree are its **boughs or branches**.

limit NOUN
❶ *There is a limit of twenty pupils for this class.*
• maximum, restriction, threshold, ceiling, cut-off point
A limit on time is a **deadline** or **time limit**.
❷ *The fence marks the limit of the school grounds.*
• border, boundary, edge, perimeter, frontier
limit VERB
I had to limit the invitations to my party.
• put a limit on, restrict, control, ration

limited ADJECTIVE
❶ *The crew had a limited supply of water.*
• restricted, short, inadequate, insufficient, rationed, finite, fixed
❷ *It was hard to move about in the limited space.*
• small, cramped, narrow, confined
OPPOSITE limitless

limp VERB
She limped off the pitch with an injured ankle.
• hobble, hop, falter, stumble

limp ADJECTIVE
The leaves on the plant are looking limp.
• drooping, floppy, sagging, wilting, soft, flabby, slack
OPPOSITE rigid

line NOUN
❶ *I drew a pencil line across the page.*
• stroke, rule, underline, stripe, streak, band, bar, dash
A line that is cut into a surface is a **groove**, **score** or **scratch**.
A line on a person's skin is a **wrinkle**.
A deep groove or wrinkle is a **furrow**.
A line on fabric is a **crease**.
❷ *There was a long line of people waiting at the bus stop.*
• queue, row, file, column, rank, procession, chain
A line of police officers forming a barrier is a **cordon**.
A line of schoolchildren walking in pairs is a **crocodile**.
❸ *The clothes were drying on the washing line.*
• cord, rope, string, thread, wire, cable, flex, lead

linger VERB
❶ *The smell of burning wood lingered in the air.*
• continue, remain, stay, last, persist
OPPOSITE disappear
❷ *Don't linger outside in this cold weather.*
• hang about, wait about, loiter, dawdle, dally, delay
OPPOSITE hurry

link NOUN
The two schools have close links with each other.
• relationship, association, connection, bond, tie
link VERB
The farmer linked the trailer to the tractor.
• attach, connect, fasten, join, couple
OPPOSITE separate

A B C D E F G H I J K L M N O P Q R S T U V W X Y Z

lion NOUN

A female lion is a **lioness**.
A young lion is a **cub**.
A group of lions is a **pride**.
The fur collar on a male lion is its **mane**.

liquid ADJECTIVE

Pour the liquid jelly into a mould.
• runny, watery, wet, fluid, flowing, running, sloppy
To make something liquid by heating it is to **melt** it.
Liquid metal or rock is **molten**.
OPPOSITE solid

liquid NOUN

The flask contained a frothy green liquid.
• fluid, solution, juice
The liquid inside a plant is **sap**.

list NOUN

A list of people's names is a **roll** or **register**.
A list of people who have tasks to do is a **rota**.
A list of books in the library or of goods for sale is a **catalogue**.
A list of topics mentioned in a book is an **index**.
A list of things to choose from is a **menu**.
A list of things to do or remember is a **checklist**.

list VERB

❶ *I helped to list the books in the library.*
• record, write down, catalogue, index, register
❷ *The damaged ship listed to one side.*
• lean, tilt, tip, slope, incline

listen VERB

➤ **to listen to something**
The spy listened carefully to the instructions.
• pay attention to, take notice of, attend to, heed
To listen secretly to a private conversation is to eavesdrop.

literature NOUN

❶ *The bookshop specializes in children's literature.*
• books, writing
for various kinds of literature see **writing**

❷ *The travel agent gave us some literature to read.*
• brochures, leaflets, pamphlets, handouts

litter NOUN

The street was covered with litter.
• rubbish, waste, refuse, garbage, junk, clutter, mess, odds and ends

litter VERB

The desk was littered with scrunched-up paper.
• scatter, strew

little ADJECTIVE, DETERMINER

OVERUSED WORD

Try to vary the words you use for **little**.
Here are some other words you could use.

FOR SOMETHING LITTLE IN SIZE:

• mini, miniature, minute, petite, small, tiny, compact
(informal) teeny, titchy
(Scottish) wee
As stoves went it was a very small one, with a barred grate and a miniature oven of the kind which are built into caravans.–THE BORROWERS AFIELD, Mary Norton
OPPOSITES big, large
see also **small**

FOR SOMEONE LITTLE IN AGE:

• small, young, *(Scottish)* wee
My granny lived in India when she was young.
OPPOSITES big, old

FOR A LITTLE TIME OR A LITTLE WHILE:

• brief, short, fleeting, passing
It was a short while before our friends arrived.
OPPOSITES lengthy, long

FOR LITTLE FOOD OR LITTLE MONEY:

• hardly any, scarcely any, insufficient, meagre, paltry
There was scarcely any food left in the house.
OPPOSITES ample, plenty

a b c d e f g h i j k l m n o p q r s t u v w x y z

➤ a little
*Would you like **a little** milk in your tea?*
• some, a bit of, a spot of, a touch of
*I'm feeling **a little** tired now.*
• a bit, slightly, rather, somewhat

live VERB *(rhymes with give)*
*Will these plants **live** through the winter?*
• stay alive, survive, exist, flourish, last, continue, remain
OPPOSITE die
➤ to live in a place
*They **live** in a basement flat.*
• inhabit, occupy, dwell in, reside in
➤ to live on
*Koalas **live on** eucalyptus leaves.*
• eat, feed on

live ADJECTIVE *(rhymes with hive)*
*The fishermen caught a **live** octopus in their nets.*
• alive, living, breathing
OPPOSITE dead

lively ADJECTIVE
❶ *The toddlers were in a **lively** mood.*
• active, energetic, animated, spirited, boisterous, excited, vivacious, sprightly, frisky, chirpy, perky
OPPOSITE inactive
❷ *The city centre is always **lively** at night.*
• busy, bustling, crowded, exciting, buzzing
OPPOSITES quiet, dead

livid ADJECTIVE
*Antonio was **livid** when he saw the damage to his bike.*
• angry, furious, fuming, incensed, enraged, seething, raging

living ADJECTIVE
❶ *Leilani had no **living** relatives.*
• alive
OPPOSITE dead
❷ *There are no dinosaurs still **living**.*
• existing, surviving
OPPOSITE extinct

living NOUN
❶ *He makes a **living** from painting.*
• income, livelihood
❷ *What does she do for a **living**?*
• job, occupation, profession, trade, career

load NOUN
❶ *Camels can carry heavy **loads**.*
• burden, weight
❷ *The lorry delivered its **load** to the supermarket.*
• cargo, consignment, goods, freight
load VERB
❶ *We **loaded** the suitcases into the car.*
• pack, pile, heap, stow
❷ *He was **loaded** with shopping bags.*
• weigh down, burden, saddle

loan NOUN
*She needs a **loan** to pay for her holiday.*
• advance
A system which allows you to pay for something later is **credit**.
A loan to buy a house is a **mortgage**.

loathe VERB
*My friend **loathes** parties.*
• hate, detest, dislike, despise
OPPOSITES love, adore

local ADJECTIVE
*Our **local** shop delivers newspapers.*
• neighbourhood, nearby, neighbouring

locate VERB
❶ *I can't **locate** the book you asked for.*
• find, discover, track down, detect, unearth, lay your hands on
OPPOSITE lose
❷ *The art gallery is **located** in the city centre.*
• place, position, put, situate, set up, build, establish, station

location NOUN
*The pilot made a note of her **location**.*
• position, situation, whereabouts, place, spot

lock *NOUN*
❶ *There was a heavy lock on the lid of the chest.*
• fastening, clasp, padlock, bolt, latch
❷ *The sorceress cut a lock from her hair.*
• tress, curl, tuft

lock *VERB*
Make sure you lock the door when you go out.
• fasten, secure, bolt, close, shut, seal

lodge *VERB*
❶ *Where are you lodging at present?*
• live, stay, reside, dwell
❷ *The animals are lodged indoors in the winter.*
• house, accommodate, board, put up
❸ *The ball was lodged in a tree.*
• get caught, get stuck, jam, wedge, fix, embed

log *NOUN*
❶ *They collected logs to burn on the fire.*
for various types of wood see **wood**
❷ *The astronauts kept a log of their voyage.*
• diary, journal, record, account

logical *ADJECTIVE*
The robot always gave a logical answer.
• rational, reasonable, sensible, sound, valid, intelligent, clear, lucid, methodical, systematic
OPPOSITE illogical

lone *ADJECTIVE*
A lone rider galloped past.
• single, solitary, unaccompanied, isolated

lonely *ADJECTIVE*
❶ *Cara felt lonely while her friends were away.*
• alone, friendless, lonesome, solitary, abandoned, neglected, forlorn, forsaken
❷ *The climbers sheltered in a lonely hut.*
• deserted, isolated, remote, secluded, out of the way

long *ADJECTIVE*
It seemed a long time before the bus came.
• lengthy, prolonged, extended, extensive, long-lasting
OPPOSITE short

long *VERB*
➤ **to long for something**
I'm longing for a drink.
• yearn for, crave, want, wish for, desire, fancy, hunger for, pine for, hanker after, itch for
(informal) be dying for

look *VERB*
❶ *If you look carefully, you'll see an owl in the tree.*
• watch, observe, view, regard, keep your eyes open
❷ *My pet snake looks a bit hungry.*
• appear, seem
➤ **to look after someone** or **something**
We looked after their house when they went on holiday.
• care for, keep an eye on, mind, tend, watch, watch over, guard, protect
To look after sick people is to **nurse** them.
➤ **to look for something**
He spent ages looking for his keys.
• hunt for, search for, seek
➤ **to look out**
If you don't look out, you'll get wet.
• beware, pay attention, take care, watch out, keep an eye open

OVERUSED WORD

Try to vary the words you use for **look**. Here are some other words you could use.

TO LOOK QUICKLY:
• glance, glimpse, peek, peep
The secret agent glanced at her watch.

TO LOOK CAREFULLY OR INTENTLY:
• stare, peer, study, scrutinize, examine, inspect, take a good look at
Daniel peered out of the window, which was tinted sepia so that the outside world looked like an old photograph.—THE NOWHERE EMPORIUM, Ross MacKenzie

TO LOOK ANGRILY:
• glare, glower, frown, scowl, grimace
The two men glowered at each other with menace.

a b c d e f g h i j k **l** m n o p q r s t u v w x y z

To look steadily is to **gaze**.
To look in amazement is to **gape**.
To look over a wide area is to **scan**
or **survey** it.

look NOUN
❶ *Did you have a look at what they were wearing?*
• glance, glimpse, peep, sight, view
❷ *The guard had an unfriendly look.*
• appearance, bearing, manner, air, expression, face

lookout NOUN
Lookouts were posted along the wall.
• sentry, guard, sentinel, watchman

loom VERB
❶ *A figure loomed out of the mist.*
• appear, emerge, arise, take shape
❷ *The haunted mansion loomed above us.*
• rise, tower, stand out, hang over

loop NOUN
Make a loop in the string and then tie a knot.
• coil, hoop, circle, ring, noose, bend, curl, kink, twist
loop VERB
The cowboy looped the reins round a fence post.
• coil, wind, curl, bend, turn, twist

loose ADJECTIVE
❶ *Some of the cobbles on the road are loose.*
• insecure, unfixed, movable, unsteady, shaky, wobbly
OPPOSITES firm, secure
❷ *The fire was started by a loose wire.*
• disconnected, unattached, detached
❸ *These jeans are loose around the waist.*
• slack, baggy, roomy, loose-fitting
OPPOSITE tight
❹ *The chickens wander loose about the farm.*
• free, at large, at liberty, on the loose, unconfined, unrestricted
OPPOSITE confined

loosen VERB
Can you loosen these knots?
• undo, unfasten, untie, free, loose, slacken, release, ease
OPPOSITE tighten

loot NOUN
The thieves buried their loot in a safe place.
• haul, plunder, takings
loot VERB
Rioters looted the shops.
• raid, ransack, rob, steal from, pillage, plunder

lorry NOUN
for types of vehicle see **vehicle**

lose VERB loses, losing, lost
❶ *Valentina has lost one of her gloves.*
• be unable to find, mislay, misplace
OPPOSITE find
❷ *Unfortunately, we lost the game on Saturday.*
• be defeated, get beaten, suffer a defeat
OPPOSITE win

loss NOUN
❶ *She is experiencing loss of memory.*
• failure, disappearance, deprivation
❷ *The farmer was upset by the loss of his sheepdog.*
• death, decease, passing

lot NOUN
We are having another lot of visitors this weekend.
• group, batch, set, crowd, collection
➤ **a lot of**
I needed a lot of help with my spelling.
• a large amount of, a good or great deal of, plenty of
➤ **lots of**
There are lots of toys to choose from in the shop.
• a great number of, many, numerous, plenty of *(informal)* loads of, tons of, masses of, oodles of, hundreds of

loud ADJECTIVE

❶ *The whole house was kept awake by the loud music.*
• noisy, blaring, booming, deafening, rowdy, resounding, thunderous, penetrating, piercing
A noise which is loud enough to hear is **audible**.
OPPOSITES quiet, soft
❷ *The tourists wore rather loud shirts.*
• bright, gaudy, garish, showy, flashy
OPPOSITES muted, subdued

lounge VERB

The guests lounged in the garden all day.
• relax, be lazy, idle, laze, sprawl, lie around, loll, take it easy, waste time

lovable ADJECTIVE

Our friends have a lovable new kitten.
• adorable, dear, sweet, charming, likeable, lovely, appealing, attractive, cuddly, enchanting, endearing
OPPOSITE hateful

love NOUN

She often mentions her love of the outdoors.
• liking, passion, fondness, affection, devotion, admiration, adoration
(informal) soft spot for

love VERB

❶ *They love each other and want to get married.*
• be in love with, care for, adore, cherish, hold dear, treasure, worship, idolize
A relationship between two people who love each other is a **romance**.
❷ *My friend, Dot, loves knitting.*
• like, have a passion for, be fond of, be partial to, enjoy
OPPOSITE hate

lovely ADJECTIVE

OVERUSED WORD

Try to vary the words you use for **lovely**. Here are some other words you could use.

FOR A LOVELY PERSON:

• charming, delightful, lovable, likeable, dear, sweet, enchanting, endearing

'I told you they loved singing!' cried Mr Wonka. 'Aren't they delightful? Aren't they charming? But you mustn't believe a word they said. It's all nonsense, every bit of it!'—CHARLIE AND THE CHOCOLATE FACTORY, Roald Dahl

FOR A LOVELY DAY OR LOVELY VIEW:

• fine, glorious
It's a glorious day for a bicycle trip.

FOR A LOVELY EXPERIENCE:

• pleasant, pleasing, enjoyable
The girls had an enjoyable time camping.
OPPOSITE nasty

FOR SOMETHING THAT LOOKS LOVELY:

• appealing, attractive, beautiful, pretty
The roses look attractive in that vase.

loving ADJECTIVE

Rohan gave his teddy bear a loving hug.
• affectionate, kind, friendly, warm, tender, fond, devoted, passionate
OPPOSITE unfriendly

low ADJECTIVE

❶ *The garden is surrounded by a low wall.*
• short, shallow, sunken
❷ *They were soldiers of low rank in the army.*
• junior, inferior, lowly, modest, humble
❸ *We spoke in low whispers.*
• quiet, soft, muted, subdued, muffled
❹ *The tuba plays low notes.*
• bass, deep
OPPOSITE high

lower VERB

❶ *The supermarket lowered its prices.*
• reduce, cut, bring down, decrease, lessen
(informal) slash
❷ *Please lower the volume of your radio.*
• quieten, turn down
❸ *At the end of the Olympic Games, they lower the flag.*
• take down, let down, dip
OPPOSITE raise

a
b
c
d
e
f
g
h
i
j
k
l
m
n
o
p
q
r
s
t
u
v
w
x
y
z

loyal ADJECTIVE
Lin had always been a loyal friend.
• true, trusty, faithful, steadfast, reliable, dependable, devoted, constant, sincere
OPPOSITE disloyal

luck NOUN
❶ *He found the secret entrance by luck.*
• accident, chance, coincidence, fluke, fate, destiny
❷ *She had a bit of luck today.*
• good fortune, success

lucky ADJECTIVE
❶ *I got the right answer by a lucky guess.*
• accidental, chance, unintentional, unplanned
❷ *Some lucky person won a million pounds.*
• fortunate, favoured, successful
OPPOSITE unlucky

ludicrous ADJECTIVE
They laughed at such a ludicrous idea.
• ridiculous, absurd, laughable, idiotic, foolish, crazy, daft, senseless

luggage NOUN
The luggage can go in the boot of the car.
• baggage, cases, suitcases, bags

lull VERB
She lulled the baby by rocking it gently.
• calm, soothe, hush, quieten, pacify, subdue
lull NOUN
There was a brief lull in the conversation.
• pause, break, gap, interval, calm
(informal) let-up

lumber VERB
❶ *A rhinoceros lumbered towards them.*
• move clumsily, trundle, trudge, tramp, blunder, shamble
❷ *(informal) Why am I lumbered with the washing up?*
• burden
(informal) saddle

lump NOUN
❶ *Lumps of sticky clay stuck to his boots.*
• chunk, piece, cluster, clump, wad, mass, hunk, wedge, block
A round lump of something is a **ball**.
A lump of gold is a **nugget**.
A lump of earth is a **clod**.
A lump of blood is a **clot**.
❷ *I could feel a lump where I'd bumped my head.*
• bump, swelling, bulge, protrusion
lump VERB
➤ **to lump things together**
The books and toys are all lumped together.
• put together, combine, merge, bunch up

lunge VERB
Robin lunged at the sheriff with his sword.
• thrust, charge, rush, dive, pounce, throw yourself

lurch VERB
❶ *The bus passengers lurched from side to side.*
• reel, sway, rock, stagger, stumble, totter
❷ *The ship lurched as the waves pounded it.*
• pitch, roll, heave, lean, list

lure VERB
Spiders lure insects into their webs.
• attract, entice, tempt, coax, draw, invite, persuade
Something used to lure an animal into a trap is **bait**.

lurk VERB
The jaguar lurked in wait for its prey.
• skulk, loiter, prowl, crouch, hide, lie in wait, lie low

lush ADJECTIVE
Rainforests have lush vegetation.
• rich, dense, thick, rampant, abundant

luxurious ADJECTIVE
The dress was trimmed with luxurious lace.
• grand, lavish, lush, rich, expensive, costly, de luxe, plush, magnificent, splendid, sumptuous
OPPOSITES simple, austere

luxury NOUN
The millionaire lived a life of luxury.
• affluence, wealth, richness, splendour, comfort, ease
OPPOSITE poverty

Mm

machine NOUN
Do you know how this machine works?
• apparatus, appliance, device, engine, contraption

mad ADJECTIVE
❶ *You must be mad to go out on a day like this.*
• crazy, daft, insane, senseless, stupid, foolish, idiotic
(informal) out of your mind, potty, nuts
OPPOSITE sensible, wise
❷ *The emperor was mad with rage.*
• angry, furious, beside yourself, frenzied, hysterical
❸ *(informal) Sandra is mad about horses.*
• enthusiastic, fanatical, passionate

made *past tense see* **make**

magazine NOUN
I bought a magazine to read on the train.
• journal, periodical, paper, comic

magic ADJECTIVE
❶ *My grandpa taught me some magic tricks.*
• conjuring
❷ *The castle was surrounded by a magic spell.*
• magical, supernatural

magic NOUN
Do you believe in magic?
• sorcery, witchcraft, wizardry, spells, charms, enchantments

WORD WEB

PEOPLE WHO USE MAGIC:

• enchanter or enchantress, magician, sorcerer or sorceress, sorcerer's apprentice, warlock, witch, wizard
see also **fairy**

THINGS WHICH A WITCH OR WIZARD MIGHT DO:

• bewitch, enchant, cast or undo a spell, become invisible or vanish, brew a potion, put a curse on you, brandish or flick their wand

THINGS WHICH A WITCH OR WIZARD MIGHT USE:

• amulet, broomstick, cauldron, charm, curse or hex, elixir, magic potion, magic spell or incantation, spellbook, talisman, wand
Neville had somehow managed to melt Seamus's cauldron into a twisted blob and their potion was seeping across the stone floor, burning holes in people's shoes.—HARRY POTTER AND THE PHILOSOPHER'S STONE, J. K. Rowling

for magical creatures see **myth**

magical ADJECTIVE
see **magic**

magician NOUN
❶ *The magician pulled a scarf out of her hat.*
• conjuror
❷ *King Arthur was helped by the magician, Merlin.*
• sorcerer, witch, wizard

magnificent ADJECTIVE
❶ *The mountain scenery was magnificent.*
• beautiful, glorious, splendid, spectacular, impressive, majestic
❷ *The film star lived in a magnificent house.*
• grand, imposing, stately
(informal) posh
❸ *That was a magnificent meal!*
• excellent, first-class, marvellous, superb
(informal) fabulous, fantastic
OPPOSITE ordinary

magnify VERB
Objects are magnified through binoculars.
• enlarge, make larger
(informal) blow up
OPPOSITES reduce, minimize

mail *NOUN*
The mail arrived early this morning.
• post, delivery, letters and parcels

mail *VERB*
Can you mail this letter for me?
• post, send, dispatch

maim *VERB*
see **injure**

main *ADJECTIVE*
❶ *What was the main point of the story?*
• central, chief, most important, basic, essential, fundamental, primary, predominant
❷ *This is the main shopping area in the town.*
• major, principal, biggest, foremost, largest, leading, prime
OPPOSITES minor, unimportant

mainly *ADVERB*
Chimpanzees eat mainly fruit and vegetables.
• largely, mostly, chiefly, principally, predominantly, primarily

maintain *VERB*
❶ *The referee tried to maintain order.*
• keep, preserve
❷ *A team of gardeners maintain the grounds.*
• look after, take care of, keep in order
❸ *How much does it cost to maintain a family?*
• support, keep, provide for
❹ *She still maintains that she's innocent.*
• claim, declare, assert, insist, state, contend

majestic *ADJECTIVE*
The town was dominated by the majestic castle.
• grand, magnificent, splendid, impressive, stately, imposing, noble

major *ADJECTIVE*
❶ *There are delays on all the major roads into the city.*
• chief, principal, primary, leading
❷ *Writing her first novel was a major achievement.*
• big, great, considerable, significant, important
OPPOSITE minor

majority *NOUN*
➤ **the majority of**
The majority of children walk to school.
• the greater number of, the bulk of, most
OPPOSITE minority

make *VERB* **makes, making, made**
❶ *We made a shelter out of leaves and branches.*
• build, construct, assemble, put together, produce, manufacture
❷ *Those two are always making trouble.*
• cause, bring about, give rise to, provoke
❸ *They made me captain.*
• appoint, elect, nominate
❹ *They've made the attic into a games room.*
• change, turn, convert, modify, transform, alter
❺ *She'll make a good actress when she's older.*
• become, grow into, turn into, change into
❻ *The regulations were made to protect children.*
• establish, fix, decide on, agree
❼ *You made me jump!*
• cause you to
❽ *We can't make her go if she doesn't want to.*
• force, compel, order
❾ *He made a lot of money last year.*
• gain, get, obtain, acquire, receive, earn, win
❿ *The ship finally made land.*
• reach, arrive at, get to, get as far as
⓫ *What time do you make it?*
• calculate, estimate, reckon
⓬ *2 and 2 make 4.*
• add up to, come to, total
⓭ *I'll make you an offer for your old bike.*
• propose, suggest
⓮ *Have you made your bed this morning?*
• arrange, tidy
➤ **to make off**
The thieves made off in a stolen car.
• leave, escape, get away, run away, disappear *(informal)* clear off
➤ **to make someone** or **something out**
I can't make out why everything went wrong.
• understand, work out, comprehend, fathom, make sense of
➤ **to make up**
I made up a new flavour of ice cream.
• create, invent, think up, concoct

make NOUN
What make of computer do you have?
• brand, model, label

male ADJECTIVE
for male human beings see **man**
for male animals see **animal**
OPPOSITE female

malicious ADJECTIVE
Someone had spread a malicious rumour.
• malevolent, hostile, malign, spiteful, vindictive, vicious, hurtful

mammal NOUN
for various kinds of animal see **animal**

man NOUN
A polite word for a man is **gentleman**.
Informal words are **bloke, chap, fellow** and **guy**.
A married man is a **husband**.
A man who has children is a **father**.
An unmarried man is a **bachelor**.
A man whose wife has died is a **widower**.
A man on his wedding day is a **groom**.
A man who is engaged to be married is a **fiancé**.
Words for a young man are **boy, lad** and **youth**.

manage VERB
❶ *His daughter manages the business now.*
• be in charge of, run, direct, lead, control, govern, rule, supervise, oversee, preside over
❷ *I can't manage any more work this week.*
• cope with, deal with, take on, carry out
❸ *We'll have to manage without the car.*
• cope, make do, get along, get by

manager NOUN
If you have a problem, talk to the manager.
• chief, director, proprietor
(informal) boss

mania NOUN
A mania for the pop group swept the country.
• craze, hysteria, obsession, passion, fixation, fad

manipulate VERB
❶ *She manipulated the dials on the robot.*
• operate, work, handle, control
(informal) twiddle
❷ *He uses his charm to manipulate people.*
• take advantage of, use, exploit, impose on

manner NOUN
❶ *They did the work in an efficient manner.*
• way, style, fashion, method
❷ *I was put off by her frosty manner.*
• behaviour, conduct, attitude, disposition, air, look, bearing
➤ **manners**
Trolls have no manners at all!
• politeness, courtesy, graces

manoeuvre NOUN
❶ *Parking a bus is a difficult manoeuvre.*
• move, operation
❷ *The opposing team used a clever manoeuvre.*
• strategy, tactic, trick, dodge, plan, plot, scheme

manoeuvre VERB
How do you manoeuvre a hot-air balloon?
• guide, move, pilot, steer, navigate

manufacture VERB
The factory manufactures pine furniture.
• make, build, assemble, fabricate

many DETERMINER
I've been on an aeroplane many times.
• a lot of, plenty of, numerous, frequent, countless, innumerable, myriad, untold
(informal) umpteen, lots of
OPPOSITE few

map NOUN
The travel agent gave us a free map of Dakar.
• chart, diagram, plan
A book of maps is an **atlas**.
A person who draws maps is a **cartographer**.

mar VERB
The film was marred by a terrible soundtrack.
• spoil, ruin, harm, impair, tarnish

a
b
c
d
e
f
g
h
i
j
k
l
m
n
o
p
q
r
s
t
u
v
w
x
y
z

march *VERB*
The brass band marched down the High Street.
• parade, file, troop, stride, pace

margin *NOUN*
Don't write in the margin of the paper.
• border, edge

marginal *ADJECTIVE*
There is a marginal difference between the two signatures.
• slight, small, minimal, minor, unimportant, negligible, borderline
OPPOSITE great

mark *NOUN*
❶ *There were muddy paw marks all over the kitchen floor.*
• spot, stain, blemish, blotch, blot, smear, smudge, streak
A mark left by a pen or pencil is a **scribble**.
A mark left by fingers is a **fingermark**.
A mark on your skin that you are born with is a **birthmark**.
❷ *They stood in silence as a mark of respect.*
• sign, token, indication, symbol, emblem
❸ *What mark did you get in the spelling test?*
• score, grade
mark *VERB*
❶ *Please be careful not to mark the photographs.*
• stain, smudge, dirty, blot
❷ *The teacher had a pile of essays to mark.*
• correct, grade, assess
❸ *There will be trouble, you mark my words!*
• mind, heed, attend to, listen to, note, take note of

marked *ADJECTIVE*
There's a marked difference in style between the paintings.
• noticeable, considerable, pronounced, clear, obvious, distinct, decided
OPPOSITES slight, minor

market *NOUN*
see **shop**

marriage *NOUN*
❶ *My grandparents celebrated 40 years of marriage.*
• matrimony, wedlock
❷ *Today is the anniversary of their marriage.*
• wedding
see also **wedding**

marry *VERB*
In what year did your grandparents marry?
• get married, wed
(informal) tie the knot, get hitched
A couple who have promised to marry are **engaged** to each other.
A man who is engaged to be married is a **fiancé** and a woman who is engaged to be married is a **fiancée**.

marsh *NOUN*
Wading birds are found in coastal marshes.
• swamp, bog, wetland, marshland, fen

marvel *NOUN*
It is one of the marvels of modern science.
• wonder, miracle
marvel *VERB*
➤ **to marvel at**
The crowd marvelled at the juggler's skill.
• admire, wonder at, be amazed by, be astonished by

marvellous *ADJECTIVE*
❶ *The professor showed us his marvellous inventions.*
• amazing, remarkable, extraordinary, incredible, miraculous, astonishing, phenomenal
OPPOSITE ordinary
❷ *We had a marvellous day at the zoo.*
• excellent, superb, tremendous, wonderful, splendid
(informal) brilliant, fantastic, terrific, super, smashing
OPPOSITES bad, awful

masculine *ADJECTIVE*
The singer had a deep, masculine voice.
• male, manly, macho
OPPOSITE feminine

A B C D E F G H I J K L M N O P Q R S T U V W X Y Z

mash VERB
Mash the potatoes until they're smooth.
• crush, pound, pulp, smash, squash
To make something into powder is to **grind** or **pulverize** it.

mask VERB
The entrance was masked by an overhanging tree.
• conceal, hide, cover, obscure, screen, veil, shroud, camouflage

mass NOUN
She sifted through the mass of papers on her desk.
• heap, pile, mound, stack, collection, quantity, accumulation
(informal) load

massacre VERB
see **kill**

massive ADJECTIVE
see **huge**

master NOUN
❶ *We played a game in which I was master of the castle.*
• lord, ruler, governor, chief
❷ *Sherlock Holmes was a master of disguises.*
• expert (at), genius, ace, wizard

master VERB
❶ *Have you mastered chess yet?*
• grasp, learn, understand
(informal) get the hang of, get to grips with
❷ *I've managed to master my fear of heights.*
• overcome, conquer, defeat, triumph over, get the better of, control, curb, subdue, tame

match NOUN
❶ *The semi-final was a really exciting match.*
• game, contest, competition, fixture, tournament, tie
❷ *The hat and gloves are a good match.*
• combination, pair

match VERB
Does this tie match my shirt?
• go with, suit, fit with, blend with, tone in with
OPPOSITE contrast with

matching ADJECTIVE
The bed cover comes with a matching pillowcase.
• coordinating, corresponding, complementary, twin
OPPOSITE contrasting

mate NOUN (informal)
❶ *Gary is one of my best mates.*
• friend
(informal) pal, chum, buddy
❷ *She's got a job as a plumber's mate.*
• assistant, helper, apprentice

material NOUN
❶ *I'm collecting material for the school magazine.*
• information, facts, data, ideas, notes
❷ *The cleaning materials are in the cupboard.*
• stuff, substances, things
❸ *The kite is made of lightweight material.*
• cloth, fabric
for kinds of cloth see **fabric**

mathematics NOUN
This computer game makes mathematics fun!
• sums
(informal) maths

WORD WEB
BRANCHES OF MATHS:
• algebra, arithmetic, geometry, statistics

THINGS YOU MIGHT DO IN MATHS:
• adding, calculating, counting, dividing, measuring, multiplying, subtracting

SOME INSTRUMENTS USED FOR MATHS:
• calculator, compasses, computer, dividers, ruler, set square
for other words used in maths see **measurement, shape**

255

A
B
C
D
E
F
G
H
I
J
K
L
M
N
O
P
Q
R
S
T
U
V
W
X
Y
Z

matted *ADJECTIVE*
The dog's coat was dirty and matted.
• knotted, tangled, uncombed

matter *NOUN*
❶ *The manager will deal with this matter.*
• affair, concern, issue, business, situation, incident, subject, topic, thing
❷ *Peat consists mainly of plant matter.*
• material, stuff, substance
❸ *What's the matter with the car?*
• problem, difficulty, trouble, worry

matter *VERB*
Will it matter if I'm late?
• be important, count, make a difference

mature *ADJECTIVE*
❶ *The zoo has two mature gorillas.*
• adult, fully grown, well-developed
OPPOSITE young
❷ *He is very mature for his age.*
• grown-up, responsible, sensible
OPPOSITES immature, childish

maximum *ADJECTIVE*
What is the maximum speed of the rocket?
• greatest, top, highest, fullest, biggest, largest
OPPOSITE minimum

maximum *NOUN*
The heat is at its maximum at midday.
• highest point, peak, top, upper limit, ceiling

maybe *ADVERB*
Maybe you'll be picked for the football team.
• perhaps, possibly
OPPOSITE definitely

maze *NOUN*
We were lost in a maze of underground tunnels.
• labyrinth, network, web, tangle

meadow *NOUN*
Cows were grazing in the meadow.
• field, pasture

meagre *ADJECTIVE*
The prisoners were given meagre rations of food.
• scant, sparse, poor, scanty, inadequate, insufficient, skimpy, paltry
(informal) measly, stingy
OPPOSITES generous, ample

meal *NOUN*

WORD WEB

MEALS YOU HAVE AT VARIOUS TIMES OF DAY:

• afternoon tea, breakfast, brunch, dinner, lunch, supper, tea
A big formal meal is a **banquet** or **feast**.
A quick informal meal is a **snack**.
A meal you eat out of doors is a **barbecue** or **picnic**.
A meal where you help yourself to food is a **buffet**.
A meal you buy ready cooked is a **takeaway**.

VARIOUS COURSES OF A MEAL:

• starter, main course; dessert, pudding, sweet
(informal) afters
see also **food**

mean *VERB* means, meaning, meant
❶ *A red traffic light means that cars have to stop.*
• indicate, signify, denote, express, imply, convey, communicate, stand for, symbolize
❷ *I mean to get better at swimming this year.*
• intend, plan, aim, propose, want

mean *ADJECTIVE*
❶ *Scrooge was too mean to buy any presents.*
• selfish, miserly, uncharitable
(informal) stingy, tight-fisted, penny-pinching
OPPOSITE generous
❷ *That was a mean trick to play.*
• unkind, unpleasant, nasty, spiteful, vicious, cruel, malicious
OPPOSITE kind

meaning *NOUN*
What is the meaning of this riddle?
• sense, significance, explanation, interpretation, definition

meaningful *ADJECTIVE*
The two friends exchanged a meaningful look.
• pointed, suggestive, significant, expressive
OPPOSITE meaningless

means *NOUN*
Text is a popular means of communication.
• method, mode, medium, channel, course, way

means *PLURAL NOUN*
They don't have the means to buy a house.
• money, resources, funds, finance, income, wherewithal

measure *VERB*
Measure the height of the wall.
• calculate, gauge, assess, survey
To measure the weight of something is to weigh it.

measure *NOUN*
❶ *At least we now know the measure of the problem.*
• size, extent, magnitude
❷ *They are taking measures to improve the park.*
• step, action, course, procedure, means

measurement *NOUN*
What are the measurements of this room?
• dimensions, size, extent, proportions

WORD WEB

UNITS FOR MEASURING DISTANCE:

• millimetre, centimetre, metre, kilometre; inch, foot, yard, mile
The distance of an object in space is measured in **light years**.
The depth of the sea is measured in **fathoms**.

UNITS FOR MEASURING AREA:

• square centimetre or square metre, hectare; square inch or square foot, acre

UNITS FOR MEASURING VOLUME:

• millilitre, litre, kilolitre; pint, quart, gallon

UNITS FOR MEASURING WEIGHT:

• milligram, gram, kilo or kilogram, tonne, ounce, pound, stone, ton

UNITS FOR MEASURING TIME:

• second, minute, hour, day, week, month, year, decade, century

UNITS FOR MEASURING SPEED:

• kilometres per hour, miles per hour
The speed of a boat or ship is measured in knots.

UNITS FOR MEASURING TEMPERATURE:

• degrees Celsius, degrees centigrade, degrees Fahrenheit

OTHER MEASUREMENTS USED IN COOKING:

• cup or cupful, dessertspoon, pinch, spoonful, teaspoon, tablespoon

meat *NOUN*

WORD WEB

SOME KINDS OF MEAT:

• bacon, beef, chicken, duck, game, gammon, goat, goose, ham, lamb, mutton, pork, turkey, veal, venison

CUTS OR JOINTS OF MEAT:

• breast, brisket, chop, cutlet, fillet, leg, loin, rib, rump, sirloin, steak

FOODS MADE FROM MEAT:

• burger, chop, corned beef, cutlet, haggis, hamburger, kebab, meatball, mince, pasty, paté, pie, sausage, sausage roll

medal *NOUN*
Our team won a bronze medal in the relay race.
• award, prize, trophy
A person who wins a medal is a medallist.

A
B
C
D
E
F
G
H
I
J
K
L
M
N
O
P
Q
R
S
T
U
V
W
X
Y
Z

meddle VERB
❶ *He is always meddling in other people's affairs.*
• interfere, intrude, intervene, pry
(informal) poke your nose in
❷ *Don't meddle with my things.*
• fiddle about, tinker

medicine NOUN
❶ *Did you take your cough medicine?*
• drug, medication, treatment, remedy
An amount of medicine taken at one time is a dose.
Medicine which a doctor gives you is a prescription.
❷ *My cousin is studying herbal medicine.*
• therapy, treatment, healing

WORD WEB

SOME TYPES OF MEDICINE:

• anaesthetic, antibiotic, antidote, antiseptic, gargle, herbs, painkiller, sedative, tincture, tonic, tranquillizer

FORMS IN WHICH YOU TAKE MEDICINE:

• capsule, inhaler, injection, lotion, lozenge, ointment, pill, tablet

INSTRUMENTS AND OTHER THINGS USED IN MEDICINE:

• bandage, dressing, forceps, gauze, lint, plaster, poultice, scalpel, sling, splint, stethoscope, syringe, thermometer, tweezers

PLACES WHERE YOU CAN GET MEDICAL TREATMENT:

• clinic, doctor's surgery, health centre, hospital, infirmary, nursing home, sickbay

SOME FORMS OF ALTERNATIVE MEDICINE:

• acupuncture, aromatherapy, herbal medicine, homeopathy, reflexology

PEOPLE WHO PRACTISE MEDICINE:

A person trained to heal sick people is a doctor or physician.

A person trained to look after sick people is a nurse.
Someone who performs medical operations is a surgeon.
A person who puts you to sleep during operations is an anaesthetist.
A person who takes X-rays is a radiographer.
A person who tests your eyes is an optician.
A person who tests your hearing is an audiologist.
People who look after your teeth are dentists and hygienists.
A person who practises herbal medicine is a herbalist.
A specialist in children's health is a paediatrician.
A specialist in mental illnesses is a psychiatrist.
A person who treats you using massage and exercise is a physiotherapist.

mediocre ADJECTIVE
I thought the film was rather mediocre.
• ordinary, average, commonplace, indifferent, second-rate, run-of-the-mill, undistinguished, uninspiring
OPPOSITE outstanding

medium ADJECTIVE
The man was of medium height.
• average, middle, middling, standard, moderate, normal

medium NOUN
The Internet is a great medium of communication.
• means, mode, method, way, channel

meek ADJECTIVE
Koalas look meek, but they have fierce claws.
• gentle, mild, tame, submissive, modest, docile, quiet, humble
OPPOSITE aggressive

meet VERB meets, meeting, met
❶ *I met an old friend at the party.*
• come across, encounter, run into, see
(informal) bump into

❷ *My parents met me at the station.*
• greet, pick up, welcome
❸ *We're meeting outside the cinema at eight.*
• gather, assemble, collect, muster, rally
❹ *The two roads meet here.*
• come together, merge, connect, join, cross, intersect
❺ *She meets all the requirements for the job.*
• fulfil, satisfy, match, answer, comply with

meeting *NOUN*
The bandits held a meeting to discuss their plan.
• gathering, assembly, council, forum, congress, conference
A large outdoor public meeting is a **rally**.
A formal meeting with a king or queen is an **audience**.

melancholy *ADJECTIVE*
The princess sat alone with a melancholy look on her face.
• sad, unhappy, miserable, gloomy, mournful, sorrowful, sombre, cheerless, woeful, dejected, depressed
OPPOSITE cheerful

melody *NOUN*
The pianist played my favourite melody.
• tune, air, theme

melt *VERB*
The ice began to melt in the sun.
• thaw, soften, unfreeze
To melt frozen food is to **defrost** it.
To melt ore to get metal from it is to **smelt** it.
Rock or metal that has melted because of great heat is **molten**.
OPPOSITE freeze

member *NOUN*
➤ **to be a member of something**
Are you a member of the book club?
• belong to, subscribe to

memorable *ADJECTIVE*
The concert should be a memorable event.
• unforgettable, notable, noteworthy, impressive, remarkable, outstanding
OPPOSITE ordinary

memorize *VERB*
I have to memorize my words for the play.
• learn, learn by heart, remember
OPPOSITE forget

memory *NOUN*
She has happy memories of her childhood in Wales.
• recollection, remembrance, reminiscence, reminder, impression

menace *NOUN*
❶ *Sharks can be a menace to divers.*
• danger, threat
❷ *That cat is an absolute menace!*
• nuisance, annoyance, irritation, inconvenience

mend *VERB*
Workers were mending the pavement.
• fix, repair, put right, restore, renovate, patch

mention *VERB*
❶ *Please don't mention the idea to anyone.*
• refer to, speak about, touch on, hint at
❷ *You mentioned that you spoke Japanese.*
• say, remark, reveal, disclose
(informal) let out
❸ *The director mentioned all the cast.*
• name, acknowledge, list

mercy *NOUN*
The evil queen showed no mercy.
• compassion, humanity, sympathy, pity, leniency, kindness, charity
OPPOSITE cruelty

merge *VERB*
❶ *The academy plans to merge the two schools.*
• join together, combine, integrate, put together, unite, amalgamate
❷ *Two streams merge here to form a river.*
• come together, converge, join, meet
OPPOSITE separate

merit *NOUN*
She's a scientist of great merit.
• excellence, quality, distinction, worth, talent, virtue, value

a
b
c
d
e
f
g
h
i
j
k
l
m
n
o
p
q
r
s
t
u
v
w
x
y
z

A B C D E F G H I J K L **M** N O P Q R S T U V W X Y Z

merit *VERB*
*The project **merits** our full attention.*
• deserve, justify, be entitled to, earn, rate, warrant

merry *ADJECTIVE*
*The postman was whistling a **merry** tune.*
• cheerful, happy, jolly, bright, joyful, light-hearted, lively, spirited
OPPOSITE gloomy

mess *NOUN*
❶ *Please clear up this **mess**.*
• muddle, untidiness, chaos, disorder, confusion, clutter, jumble, litter, dirt
(informal) shambles
❷ *Zainab made a **mess** of her audition.*
• disaster, botch
(informal) hash
❸ *They got into a **mess** over money.*
• difficulty, problem, dilemma, plight
(informal) fix, jam

mess *VERB*
➤ **to mess about**
*We spent the day **messing about** on the beach.*
• play about, fool around, lounge about
(informal) muck about
➤ **to mess things up**
*I hope you haven't **messed up** my felt tips.*
• confuse, mix up, muddle, jumble, make a mess of, tangle
➤ **to mess something up**
*I think I **messed up** my interview.*
• bungle, botch
(informal) make a hash of

message *NOUN*
*Did you get my **message**?*
• note, letter, communication
for types of message see **communication**
for secret messages see **code**

messy *ADJECTIVE*
*My bedroom is really **messy**!*
• muddled, untidy, disorderly, chaotic, dirty, filthy, grubby, mucky
(informal) higgledy-piggledy
OPPOSITE neat

met *past tense see* **meet**

metal *NOUN*

WORD WEB

SOME COMMON METALS:

• aluminium, brass, bronze, copper, gold, iron, lead, magnesium, mercury, nickel, pewter, platinum, silver, steel, tin, zinc
A bar of metal is an **ingot**.
A lump of metal is a **nugget**.
Something that looks or sounds like metal is **metallic**.

method *NOUN*
*My granny has a secret **method** for making jam.*
• technique, way, procedure, process
An especially skilful method for doing something is a **knack**.

methodical *ADJECTIVE*
*Inspector Wadia is always very **methodical**.*
• organized, orderly, systematic, meticulous, careful, deliberate, efficient, businesslike, painstaking
OPPOSITE careless

middle *ADJECTIVE*
*The **middle** lane is reserved for buses.*
• central, inner, inside, midway
middle *NOUN*
*A scarecrow stood in the **middle** of the field.*
• centre, core, heart, midpoint
The middle of a wheel is the **hub**.
The middle part of an atom or cell is the **nucleus**.

might *NOUN*
*I banged at the door with all my **might**.*
• strength, power, energy, force, vigour

mighty *ADJECTIVE*
*The dragon let out a **mighty** roar.*
• powerful, forceful, vigorous, ferocious, violent, great, enormous, hefty
OPPOSITE weak

mild *ADJECTIVE*
❶ *He's a mild person who never complains.*
• amiable, docile, easy-going, gentle, good-tempered, harmless, kind, lenient, merciful, placid, soft-hearted
❷ *The weather has been mild for this time of year.*
• pleasant, warm, temperate
OPPOSITE severe

milk *NOUN*
Foods made from milk are **dairy products**.
see also **food**

milky *ADJECTIVE*
The flask contained a milky liquid.
• whitish, cloudy, misty, chalky, opaque
OPPOSITE clear

mimic *VERB*
My dad is good at mimicking famous people.
• do impressions of, imitate, impersonate, pretend to be
(informal) take off
If you mimic people especially to make fun of them, you **caricature** or **parody** them.

mind *NOUN*
❶ *Her mind was as sharp as ever.*
• brain, intelligence, intellect, head, sense, understanding, wits, judgement, mental powers, reasoning
❷ *Are you sure you won't change your mind?*
• wishes, intention, fancy, inclination, opinion, outlook, point of view
mind *VERB*
❶ *Will you mind my bag for a minute?*
• guard, look after, watch, care for
(informal) keep an eye on
❷ *Mind the step.*
• look out for, watch out for, beware of, pay attention to, heed, note
❸ *They won't mind if I'm late.*
• bother, care, worry, be upset, take offence, object, disapprove

mine *NOUN*
A coal mine is a **colliery** or **pit**.
A place where coal is removed from the surface of the ground is an **opencast mine**.
A place where stone or slate is removed is a **quarry**.

mingle *VERB*
The secret agent mingled with the crowd.
• mix in, circulate, blend, combine, merge, fuse

miniature *ADJECTIVE*
A piccolo looks like a miniature flute.
• tiny, minute, diminutive, small-scale, baby, mini
see also **small**

minimum *ADJECTIVE*
Set the oven to the minimum temperature.
• least, smallest, littlest, lowest
OPPOSITE maximum

minor *ADJECTIVE*
I only had a minor part in the play.
• small, unimportant, insignificant, inferior, subordinate, trivial, petty
OPPOSITE major

minute *ADJECTIVE*
You can hardly see the minute crack.
• tiny, minuscule, microscopic, negligible
OPPOSITE large

miraculous *ADJECTIVE*
The patient made a miraculous recovery.
• amazing, astonishing, astounding, extraordinary, incredible, marvellous, unbelievable, wonderful, mysterious, inexplicable

misbehave *VERB*
My puppy has been misbehaving again!
• behave badly, be naughty, be disobedient, get up to mischief
OPPOSITE behave

miscellaneous *ADJECTIVE*
The bag contained miscellaneous balls of wool.
• assorted, various, different, mixed

mischief *NOUN*
The friends are always getting up to mischief.
• naughtiness, bad behaviour, disobedience, playfulness, roguishness

a
b
c
d
e
f
g
h
i
j
k
l
m
n
o
p
q
r
s
t
u
v
w
x
y
z

A
B
C
D
E
F
G
H
I
J
K
L
M
N
O
P
Q
R
S
T
U
V
W
X
Y
Z

miserable *ADJECTIVE*
❶ *You look miserable—what's the matter?*
• sad, unhappy, sorrowful, gloomy, glum, downhearted, despondent, dejected, depressed, melancholy, mournful, tearful
OPPOSITES cheerful, happy
❷ *The poor animals lived in miserable conditions.*
• distressing, uncomfortable, wretched, pitiful, pathetic, squalid
OPPOSITE comfortable
❸ *The weather was cold and miserable.*
• dismal, dreary, depressing, unpleasant
OPPOSITE pleasant

miserly *ADJECTIVE*
He was too miserly to donate any money.
• mean, selfish
(informal) grasping, stingy, tight-fisted, penny-pinching
OPPOSITE generous

misery *NOUN*
The slaves must have led a life of misery.
• sadness, sorrow, unhappiness, grief, distress, despair, anguish, wretchedness, suffering, torment, heartache, depression
OPPOSITE happiness

misfortune *NOUN*
I heard about her family's misfortune.
• bad luck, trouble, hardship, adversity, affliction, setback, mishap
OPPOSITE good luck

mishap *NOUN*
We had a slight mishap with the car.
• accident, problem, difficulty, setback

mislay *VERB* mislays, mislaying, mislaid
I seem to have mislaid my purse.
• lose
OPPOSITE find

misleading *ADJECTIVE*
The directions he gave were quite misleading.
• confusing, unreliable, deceptive, ambiguous, unclear

miss *VERB*
❶ *I missed the bus.*
• be too late for
❷ *The arrow missed the target.*
• fall short of, go wide of
❸ *If we leave now, we should miss the traffic.*
• avoid
❹ *I missed Dad when he was in hospital.*
• long for, yearn for, pine for
➤ **to miss something out**
I missed out the boring bits of the story.
• leave out, omit, ignore, overlook, skip

missile *NOUN*
see **weapon**

missing *ADJECTIVE*
She found the missing keys in a drawer.
• lost, mislaid, misplaced, absent, straying

mission *NOUN*
❶ *Our mission in life is to help those in need.*
• aim, purpose, objective, task, job, campaign
❷ *The astronauts are on a mission to Mars.*
• expedition, journey, voyage, exploration

mist *NOUN*
❶ *We drove slowly through the mist.*
• fog, haze, cloud, drizzle
❷ *I can't see because of the mist on my glasses.*
• condensation, steam

mistake *NOUN*
This piece of writing is full of mistakes.
• error, inaccuracy, blunder, slip, slip-up, lapse
A spelling mistake is a **misspelling**.
A mistake where something is left out is an **omission**.
A mistake in a printed book is a **misprint**.
mistake *VERB* mistakes, mistaking, mistook, mistaken
She mistook my meaning entirely.
• misunderstand, get wrong, mix up

mistrust *VERB*
Do you have any reason to mistrust him?
• distrust, have doubts about, suspect
OPPOSITE trust

misty ADJECTIVE
❶ *If it's misty outside, take a torch.*
• foggy, hazy
❷ *I can't see through the misty window.*
• steamy, cloudy, smoky, opaque
❸ *We saw a misty shape approaching.*
• faint, fuzzy, blurred, dim, indistinct, shadowy, vague
OPPOSITE clear

misunderstand VERB misunderstands, misunderstanding, misunderstood
I think you misunderstood what I said.
• mistake, get wrong, miss the point of
OPPOSITE understand

mix VERB
Mix the ingredients in a bowl.
• combine, blend, mingle
➤ **to mix something up**
Please don't mix up my books.
• muddle, jumble, confuse
To mix up playing cards is to **shuffle** them.

mixed ADJECTIVE
Add a teaspoon of mixed herbs.
• assorted, various, different, miscellaneous
OPPOSITE separate

mixture NOUN
❶ *Put the cake mixture in a baking tin.*
• mix, blend, combination
A mixture of metals is an **alloy**.
A mixture of two different species of plant or animal is a **hybrid**.
❷ *There's an odd mixture of things in the drawer.*
• assortment, collection, variety, jumble, conglomeration
A confused mixture is a **mishmash**.

moan VERB
❶ *The wounded warrior moaned in pain.*
• cry, groan, sigh, wail, howl, whimper
❷ *Ned's always moaning about the food.*
• complain, grumble, grouse, whine
(informal) whinge

mob NOUN
An angry mob stormed the gates of the castle.
• crowd, horde, throng, mass, rabble, gang, pack, herd, bunch

mob VERB
Autograph hunters mobbed the pop star.
• crowd round, swarm round, surround, besiege, hem in, jostle

mobile ADJECTIVE
❶ *A mobile library visits once a fortnight.*
• movable, travelling
Something that you can carry about is portable.
OPPOSITE stationary
❷ *A week after the injury, she was mobile again.*
• moving about, active
(informal) up and about
OPPOSITE immobile

mock VERB
It was mean of them to mock his singing.
• jeer at, laugh at, make fun of, scoff at, sneer at, ridicule, scorn, deride
(informal) take the mickey out of

model ADJECTIVE
❶ *We went to an exhibition of model railways.*
• miniature, toy
❷ *He's a model pupil.*
• ideal, perfect

model NOUN
❶ *I'm building a model of a space rocket.*
• copy, replica, toy
❷ *This is the latest model of skateboard.*
• design, type, version
❸ *She's a model of good behaviour.*
• example, ideal

model VERB
The artist models figures in clay.
• make, mould, shape, construct, fashion

moderate ADJECTIVE
The first book was a moderate success.
• average, fair, modest, medium, reasonable, passable, tolerable
OPPOSITE exceptional

a b c d e f g h i j k l **m** n o p q r s t u v w x y z

A B C D E F G H I J K L M N O P Q R S T U V W X Y Z

moderately *ADVERB*
He answered the questions moderately well.
• fairly, reasonably, quite, rather, somewhat
(informal) pretty

modern *ADJECTIVE*
❶ *All the equipment in their kitchen was modern.*
• up to date, contemporary, advanced, the latest
OPPOSITE out of date
❷ *She always dresses in modern clothes.*
• fashionable, stylish, modish
(informal) trendy, hip
OPPOSITE old-fashioned

modest *ADJECTIVE*
❶ *He's very modest about his success.*
• humble, quiet, reserved, shy, bashful, coy
OPPOSITE conceited
❷ *There has been a modest increase in sales.*
• moderate, reasonable, average, medium

modify *VERB*
We've had to modify our travel plans.
• adapt, alter, change, adjust, refine, revise, vary

moist *ADJECTIVE*
❶ *The walls of the dungeon were moist.*
• damp, wet, watery, clammy, dank
❷ *Tropical plants grow well in a moist atmosphere.*
• humid, muggy, steamy, rainy
OPPOSITE dry

moisture *NOUN*
There is still a lot of moisture on the ground.
• wetness, dampness, damp, dew, condensation, humidity

moment *NOUN*
❶ *I'll be ready in a moment.*
• minute, second, instant, flash
(informal) jiffy, tick
❷ *It was a great moment in the history of space travel.*
• time, occasion, period

momentary *ADJECTIVE*
He felt a momentary stab of pain.
• brief, short, fleeting, temporary
OPPOSITE permanent

monarch *NOUN*
see **ruler**

money *NOUN*
How much money do you have with you?
• cash, currency, funds, finance
(informal) dough, dosh
A large amount of money is a **fortune**,
riches or wealth.

monster *NOUN*
A sea monster reared its head above the waves.
• beast, giant, ogre, brute

monstrous *ADJECTIVE*
❶ *The town was engulfed by a monstrous wave.*
• huge, gigantic, enormous, immense, massive, colossal, great, hulking, mighty, towering, vast
❷ *The nation was shocked by the monstrous crime.*
• horrifying, shocking, wicked, evil, hideous, horrible, terrible, atrocious, dreadful, gruesome, outrageous, scandalous

mood *NOUN*
What sort of mood is he in today?
• temper, humour, state of mind, disposition

moody *ADJECTIVE*
They've been moody and withdrawn for weeks.
• sulky, sullen, grumpy, bad-tempered, temperamental, touchy, miserable, gloomy, glum
OPPOSITE cheerful

moon *NOUN*

WORD WEB

FORMS IN WHICH WE SEE THE MOON:
• crescent moon, full moon, new moon; moonbeam, moonlight

THINGS YOU MIGHT FIND OR DO ON THE MOON:
• crater, moon dust, moon rock, moonscape, moonwalk
A word meaning 'to do with the moon' is **lunar**.

The time when the moon rises is **moonrise**.
The time when the moon sets is **moonset**.
see also **astronaut, space**

moor *NOUN*
The tower stood on a windswept moor.
• moorland, heath, fell

moor *VERB*
We moored the boat in the harbour.
• tie up, secure, fasten, anchor, berth, dock

moral *ADJECTIVE*
She tried her best to lead a moral life.
• good, honest, truthful, upright, decent, honourable, principled, ethical, virtuous, righteous
OPPOSITE immoral

moral *NOUN*
The moral of this story is that crime doesn't pay.
• lesson, message, meaning

morale *NOUN*
The new coach has improved the team's morale.
• confidence, spirit, state of mind, attitude, mood

more *DETERMINER*
The soup needs more pepper.
• extra, further, added, additional
OPPOSITE less

morning *NOUN*
The expedition set off in the early morning.
• daybreak, dawn, first light, sunrise
for other times of the day see **day**

morsel *NOUN*
They hadn't eaten a morsel of food all day.
• bite, crumb, mouthful, taste, nibble, piece, scrap, fragment

mortal *ADJECTIVE*
❶ *All human beings are mortal.*
OPPOSITE immortal
❷ *The knight had received a mortal wound.*
• deadly, fatal, lethal

mostly *ADVERB*
I spend my money mostly on books and games.
• mainly, largely, chiefly, primarily, generally, usually, normally, typically, principally, predominantly

motion *NOUN*
He summoned the waiter with a motion of his hand.
• gesture, movement

motivate *VERB*
What motivated you to write a book?
• prompt, drive, stimulate, urge, provoke, spur, influence, induce

motive *NOUN*
The police can find no motive for the crime.
• cause, motivation, reason, purpose, grounds

motor *NOUN*
The toy train had an electric motor.
• engine

motto *NOUN*
Her motto has always been, 'Keep smiling'.
• catchphrase, proverb, saying, slogan, golden rule

mould *VERB*
The sculptor moulded the figures from clay.
• shape, form, fashion, model, cast

mouldy *ADJECTIVE*
All I found in the fridge was some mouldy cheese.
• rotten, rotting, decaying, musty, damp

a b c d e f g h i j k l **m** n o p q r s t u v w x y z

A
B
C
D
E
F
G
H
I
J
K
L
M
N
O
P
Q
R
S
T
U
V
W
X
Y
Z

mound *NOUN*
❶ *Her desk was covered with* **mounds**
of paper.
• heap, pile, stack, mass
❷ *There used to be a castle on top of that*
mound.
• hill, hillock, rise, hump
An ancient mound of earth over a grave
is a **barrow**.

mount *VERB*
❶ *She* **mounted** *the pony and rode off.*
• get on, jump on to
❷ *The butler slowly* **mounted** *the*
stairs.
• go up, climb, ascend
❸ *The gallery is* **mounting** *a new*
exhibition.
• put up, set up, display
❹ *The tension began to* **mount**
in the crowd.
• grow, increase, rise, intensify

mountain *NOUN*

WORD WEB

The top of a mountain is the **peak**
or **summit**.
A line of mountains is a **range**.
A long, narrow mountain is a **ridge**.
A mountain with a hole at the top caused
by an eruption is a **volcano**.

**THINGS YOU MIGHT SEE ON OR NEAR A
MOUNTAIN:**

• avalanche, boulder, cave, cliff, crag,
crevice, glacier, gorge, ledge, mountain
pass, mountain stream, precipice, rocks,
slope, valley or *(Scottish)* glen

SOME WORDS TO DESCRIBE A MOUNTAIN:

• barren, craggy, forbidding, jagged, lofty,
massive, misty, rocky, rugged,
snow-capped, soaring, towering,
treacherous
An area of land with many mountains is
mountainous.

mourn *VERB*
He was still **mourning** *the loss*
of his friend.
• grieve for, lament for

mouth *NOUN*
❶ *The crocodile slept with its* **mouth** *wide open.*
• jaws
A dog's nose and mouth is its **muzzle**.
A word meaning 'to do with your mouth' is **oral**.
❷ *They lived in a village at the* **mouth** *of the*
river.
• outlet
A wide river mouth is an **estuary** or
(Scottish) **firth**.
❸ *The* **mouth** *of the cave was hidden*
by trees.
• entrance, opening

move *NOUN*
❶ *Don't make a* **move**!
• movement
❷ *The spy was watching their every*
move.
• action, step, deed, manoeuvre
❸ *Is it my* **move** *next?*
• turn, go, chance, opportunity
move *VERB*

OVERUSED WORD

Try to vary the words you use for
move. Here are some other words you
could use.

TO MOVE FROM ONE PLACE TO ANOTHER:

• carry, remove, transfer, transport, shift
They **shifted** *the piano into the front*
room.

TO MOVE FROM A POSITION:

• go, leave, depart, quit, budge
The camel stared and refused to **budge**.

TO MOVE RESTLESSLY:

• toss, turn, stir, twist, shake, fidget,
twitch, flap
Please stop **twitching** *in your seat.*

TO MOVE FROM SIDE TO SIDE:

• sway, swing, wave, wag, wiggle
*The knight **swung** a sword above his helmet.*

TO MOVE ALONG:

• travel, walk, proceed
*Few people **travel** on these roads after dark.*

TO MOVE QUICKLY:

• hurry, dash, dart, race, run, rush, hasten, hurtle, career, speed, sprint, streak, scurry, whizz, zoom
The next stone went whizzing through a big web, snapping its cords, and taking off the spider sitting in the middle of it, whack, dead.
—THE HOBBIT, J. R. R. Tolkien
see also **run**

TO MOVE SLOWLY:

• amble, stroll, saunter, dawdle, slouch, crawl, drift
*Yawning and grumbling, the Weasleys **slouched** outside with Harry behind them.*—HARRY POTTER AND THE CHAMBER OF SECRETS, J. K. Rowling

TO MOVE TOWARDS SOMETHING:

• advance, approach, come, proceed, progress
*The lookout saw a pirate ship **approaching**.*

TO MOVE BACK OR MOVE AWAY:

• back, retreat, reverse, withdraw
*The serpent **retreated**, hissing, into its lair.*

TO MOVE DOWNWARDS:

• drop, descend, dive, fall, sink, swoop
*A pair of vultures **swooped** down from the sky.*

TO MOVE UPWARDS:

• rise, ascend, climb, mount, soar, arise
*A hot-air balloon **mounted** into the air.*

TO MOVE GRACEFULLY:

• flow, glide, dance
*Some swans **glided** gently across the pond.*

TO MOVE CLUMSILY:

• stumble, stagger, flounder, lurch, lumber, shuffle, totter, trundle, trip
*The ogre **stumbled** up the narrow steps.*

TO MOVE STEALTHILY:

• creep, crawl, edge, inch, slink
*The secret agent **edged** carefully along the wall.*
for ways to describe how an animal or bird moves see **animal, bird**

movement NOUN
❶ *The robot made a sudden, jerky **movement**.*
• motion, move, action, gesture
❷ *Has there been any **movement** in their attitude?*
• progress, development, change, shift
❸ *She was involved in the peace **movement**.*
• organization, group, party, campaign

movie NOUN
see **film**

moving ADJECTIVE
*The story was so **moving** that I started to cry.*
• emotional, inspiring, stirring, touching
(informal) tear-jerking

muck NOUN
*They cleared the **muck** out of the stable.*
• dirt, filth, grime, mud, sludge, dung, manure

mucky ADJECTIVE
*My football boots are all **mucky**.*
• dirty, messy, muddy, grimy, grubby, filthy, foul, soiled, squalid
OPPOSITE clean

a b c d e f g h i j k l m n o p q r s t u v w x y z

A
B
C
D
E
F
G
H
I
J
K
L
M
N
O
P
Q
R
S
T
U
V
W
X
Y
Z

mud *NOUN*
*The tractor left a trail of **mud** on the road.*
• dirt, muck, mire, sludge, clay, soil

muddle *NOUN*
❶ *There was a **muddle** over the date of the party.*
• confusion, misunderstanding
(informal) mix-up
❷ *There was a **muddle** of clothes on the floor.*
• jumble, mess, tangle

muddle *VERB*
❶ *Who **muddled** the papers on my desk?*
• mix up, mess up, disorder, jumble up, shuffle, tangle
OPPOSITE tidy
❷ *They got **muddled** and took the wrong turning.*
• confuse, bewilder, puzzle, perplex

muddy *ADJECTIVE*
❶ *Take off your **muddy** shoes before you come in.*
• dirty, messy, mucky, filthy, caked, soiled
OPPOSITE clean
❷ *I got filthy walking across the **muddy** ground.*
• boggy, marshy, waterlogged, wet, sodden
OPPOSITE dry, firm

muffle *VERB*
❶ *We **muffled** ourselves up to play in the snow.*
• wrap, cover
❷ *She tried to **muffle** her sneeze.*
• stifle, smother, suppress, silence, deaden, dull

muffled *ADJECTIVE*
*They heard **muffled** voices from the next room.*
• faint, indistinct, unclear, muted, deadened
OPPOSITE clear

mug *NOUN*
see **cup**

muggy *ADJECTIVE*
*The weather is often **muggy** before a storm.*
• humid, close, clammy, sticky, moist, damp, oppressive
OPPOSITE fresh

multiply *VERB*
*Her problems seemed to be **multiplying**.*
• increase, grow, spread, mount up

mumble *VERB*
*We couldn't hear the actor as he was **mumbling**.*
• mutter, talk indistinctly

munch *VERB*
*Kim sat **munching** popcorn all through the film.*
• chew, crunch
for other ways to eat see **eat**

murder *VERB*
see **kill**

murky *ADJECTIVE*
*A creature loomed out of the **murky** waters of the loch.*
• dark, clouded, cloudy, dim, dull, dingy, gloomy, grey, foggy, misty
OPPOSITE clear

murmur *VERB*
*We heard voices **murmuring** in the room above.*
• mutter, mumble, whisper

muscular *ADJECTIVE*
*The wrestler had a **muscular** body.*
• brawny, beefy, athletic, sinewy, strapping, strong, well-built
OPPOSITES puny, weak

museum *NOUN*
*There's a new Viking exhibition at the **museum**.*
• academy, gallery
A person who works in a museum and looks after its collection is a **curator**.
A person who studies ancient civilizations by digging for the remains of buildings and artefacts is an **archaeologist**.

A person who studies the civilization of ancient Egypt is an **Egyptologist**.

WORD WEB

THINGS YOU MIGHT SEE IN A MUSEUM:

• artefact, collection, display case, exhibit

SOME MUSEUM ARTEFACTS:

• amphora, amulet, casket, figurine, frieze, mask, mosaic, papyrus, runes, seal, sceptre, statue, terracotta
see also **prehistoric, pyramid**

music NOUN

WORD WEB

VARIOUS KINDS OF MUSIC:

• bhangra, blues, calypso, classical music, country and western, dance music, disco music, folk music, gospel, hiphop, jazz, orchestral music, pop music, punk, ragtime, rap, reggae, rock, soul, swing

TERMS USED IN MUSIC:

• chord, counterpoint, discord, harmony, melody, note, octave, pitch, rhythm, scale, semitone, tempo, theme, tone, tune

NAMES OF NOTES AND SIGNS IN WRITTEN MUSIC:

• clef, crotchet, flat, key signature, minim, natural, quaver, semibreve, semiquaver, sharp, stave, time signature

TYPES OF MUSICAL COMPOSITION:

• anthem, ballad, carol, concerto, folk song, fugue, hymn, lullaby, march, melody, musical, opera, operetta, sonata, song, symphony, tune

FAMILIES OF MUSICAL INSTRUMENTS:

• brass, keyboard, percussion, strings, woodwind

STRINGED INSTRUMENTS THAT CAN BE PLAYED WITH A BOW:

• cello, double bass, viola, violin or fiddle

STRINGED INSTRUMENTS PLAYED BY PLUCKING OR STRUMMING:

• banjo, cittern, guitar, harp, lute, lyre, mandolin, sitar, ukulele, zither

BRASS INSTRUMENTS:

• bugle, cornet, euphonium, flugelhorn, French horn, trombone, trumpet, tuba

OTHER INSTRUMENTS PLAYED BY BLOWING:

• bagpipes, bassoon, clarinet, cor anglais, flute, harmonica or mouth organ, oboe, piccolo, recorder, saxophone

KEYBOARD INSTRUMENTS:

• accordion, harmonium, harpsichord, keyboard, organ, piano, synthesizer

PERCUSSION INSTRUMENTS:

• bass drum, bongo drum, castanets, cymbals, drum, glockenspiel, gong, kettledrum, maracas, marimba, rattle, snare drum, tabor, tambour, tambourine, timpani, tom-tom, triangle, tubular bells, vibraphone, xylophone

PEOPLE WHO PLAY VARIOUS INSTRUMENTS:

• bugler, cellist, clarinettist, drummer, fiddler, flautist, guitarist, harpist, lutenist, oboist, organist, percussionist, pianist, piper, timpanist, trombonist, trumpeter, violinist

SOME OTHER MUSICIANS:

• accompanist, composer, conductor, instrumentalist, singer, vocalist
for types of singing voice see **sing**

GROUPS OF MUSICIANS:

• band, choir or chorus, duet or duo, ensemble, group, orchestra, quartet, quintet, trio

a b c d e f g h i j k l **m** n o p q r s t u v w x y z

A
B
C
D
E
F
G
H
I
J
K
L
M
N
O
P
Q
R
S
T
U
V
W
X
Y
Z

musical *ADJECTIVE*
Helena has a very musical voice.
• tuneful, melodic, melodious, harmonious, sweet-sounding
for types of musical instrument see music

musty *ADJECTIVE*
There was a musty smell in the cellar.
• damp, dank, mouldy, stale, stuffy, airless
OPPOSITE fresh

mute *ADJECTIVE*
We stared in mute amazement at the volcano.
• silent, speechless, dumb, tongue-tied

mutilate *VERB*
His right hand was mutilated by a firework.
• maim, disfigure, injure, wound, mangle

mutiny *NOUN*
The crew were plotting a mutiny against the captain.
• rebellion, revolt, uprising

mutter *VERB*
The goblin sat muttering to himself in the corner.
• mumble, murmur, whisper

mutual *ADJECTIVE*
It is in our mutual interest to work together.
• joint, common, shared, reciprocal

mysterious *ADJECTIVE*
The investigators uncovered a mysterious sign on the wall.
• strange, puzzling, baffling, mystifying, perplexing, obscure, unexplained, incomprehensible, inexplicable, curious, weird

mystery *NOUN*
What really happened was a mystery.
• puzzle, riddle, secret

mystify *VERB*
We were mystified by the curious message.
• puzzle, baffle, bewilder, perplex

myth *NOUN*

WORD WEB

CREATURES FOUND IN MYTHS AND LEGENDS

• Abominable Snowman, Anansi, banshee, basilisk, brownie, bunyip, chimera, centaur, Cerberus, cyclops, dragon, elf, fairy, genie, giant, gnome, goblin, gremlin, gryphon, hippogriff, imp, kelpie, kraken, leprechaun, mermaid, merman, Minotaur, nymph, ogre, Pegasus, phoenix, pixie, rakshasa, selkie, serpent, shapeshifter, siren, sphinx, sprite, troll, unicorn, vampire, werewolf, yeti, yowie
A native of Tibet, the yeti is believed to be related to the troll, though no one has yet got close enough to conduct the necessary tests.
—FANTASTIC BEASTS AND WHERE TO FIND THEM, J. K. Rowling
see also **dragon, fairy**

mythical *ADJECTIVE*
The unicorn is a mythical beast.
• fabulous, fanciful, imaginary, invented, fictional, legendary, mythological, non-existent, unreal
OPPOSITE real

Nn

nag *VERB*
He was always **nagging** them to work harder.
• badger, pester, scold

naive *ADJECTIVE*
He's so **naive** that he believes their promises.
• innocent, inexperienced, unsophisticated, artless, gullible, simple

naked *ADJECTIVE*
He walked **naked** into the bathroom.
• bare, nude, unclothed, undressed
OPPOSITE clothed

name *NOUN*
The official names you have are your **first names** or **forenames**, and **surname**.
Names a Christian is given at baptism are **Christian names**.
A false name is an **alias**.
A name people use instead of your real name is a **nickname**.
A false name an author uses is a **pen name** or **pseudonym**.
The name of a book or film is its **title**.

name *VERB*
The zoo **named** the new lion cubs Kiara and Kovu.
• call
To name someone at the ceremony of baptism is to **baptize** or **christen** them.

nap *NOUN*
Granny always takes a **nap** on Sunday afternoons.
• rest, sleep, doze, lie-down, siesta (informal) snooze, forty winks

narrate *VERB*
The famous actor **narrated** the story of his life.
• tell, recount, relate

narrative *NOUN*
The sailor wrote an exciting **narrative** of her voyage.
• account, history, story, tale, chronicle (informal) yarn

narrow *ADJECTIVE*
The rabbit squeezed through a **narrow** opening in the fence.
• thin, slender, slim
OPPOSITE wide

nasty *ADJECTIVE*
❶ Ogres have a thoroughly **nasty** temper.
• unkind, unpleasant, unfriendly, disagreeable, objectionable, odious, mean, malicious, cruel, spiteful, vicious
❷ A **nasty** smell wafted from the laboratory.
• unpleasant, offensive, disgusting, repulsive, revolting, horrible, foul, rotten, sickening
OPPOSITE agreeable, pleasant
❸ The weather suddenly turned **nasty**.
• unpleasant, rough, stormy, squally
for other ways to describe something you don't like see **bad**

nation *NOUN*
People from many **nations** compete in the Olympic Games.
• country, state, land, race, population

national *ADJECTIVE*
The programme will be broadcast on **national** television.
• nationwide
OPPOSITE local

natural *ADJECTIVE*
❶ Karen has a **natural** gift for music.
• born, inborn, instinctive, intuitive, native
❷ It's only **natural** to be nervous before an exam.
• normal, common, understandable, reasonable, predictable
OPPOSITE unnatural

a
b
c
d
e
f
g
h
i
j
k
l
m
n
o
p
q
r
s
t
u
v
w
x
y
z

A
B
C
D
E
F
G
H
I
J
K
L
M
N
O
P
Q
R
S
T
U
V
W
X
Y
Z

nature *NOUN*
❶ *I like TV programmes about **nature**.*
• natural history, wildlife
❷ *The old sheepdog has a very kind **nature**.*
• character, disposition, personality, manner
❸ *I collect coins, medals and things of that nature.*
• kind, sort, type, description, variety

naughty *ADJECTIVE*
*The puppies were quite **naughty** when they were young.*
• bad, badly behaved, disobedient, mischievous, uncontrollable, unmanageable, troublesome, unruly
OPPOSITE well-behaved
➤ **to be naughty**
• misbehave, behave badly, disobey

navigate *VERB*
*The captain **navigated** her ship between the dangerous rocks.*
• steer, direct, guide, manoeuvre, pilot

navy *NOUN*
see **armed forces**

near *ADJECTIVE*
❶ *We get on well with our **near** neighbours.*
• next-door, nearby, close, adjacent, surrounding
❷ *My birthday is **near**.*
• approaching, coming
(informal) round the corner
❸ *We sent cards to all our **near** relatives.*
• close, dear, familiar, intimate
OPPOSITE distant

nearly *ADVERB*
*Thank goodness, it's **nearly** dinner time!*
• almost, practically, virtually, just about, approaching

neat *ADJECTIVE*
❶ *Please leave the room as **neat** as possible.*
• clean, orderly, tidy, uncluttered, immaculate
(informal) spick and span

❷ *Gethin always looks **neat** in his school uniform.*
• smart, elegant, spruce, trim
❸ *His handwriting is very **neat**.*
• precise, skilful, well-formed
OPPOSITE untidy

necessary *ADJECTIVE*
*The recipe lists all the **necessary** ingredients.*
• essential, required, needed, needful, compulsory, obligatory, unavoidable
OPPOSITE unnecessary

need *NOUN*
*There's a **need** for more shops in our area.*
• call, demand, requirement

need *VERB*
❶ *I **need** a pound coin for the locker.*
• require, want, be short of, lack
❷ *The charity **needs** our support.*
• depend on, rely on

needless *ADJECTIVE*
*They went to a lot of **needless** expense.*
• unnecessary, unwanted, uncalled for, excessive, superfluous

needlework *NOUN*
*You need good eyesight for **needlework**.*
• sewing

WORD WEB

SOME TYPES OF NEEDLEWORK:

• appliqué, beadwork, cross-stitch, embroidery, patchwork, quilting, tapestry
for other arts and crafts see **art**

---

needy *ADJECTIVE*
*They set up a fund to help **needy** children.*
• poor, deprived, badly off, hard up
OPPOSITE rich

negative *ADJECTIVE*
*He has a very **negative** attitude to his job.*
• pessimistic, uncooperative, unenthusiastic, grudging, unhelpful, unwilling
OPPOSITE positive

neglect *VERB*
She's been neglecting her work.
• forget, ignore, overlook, abandon, disregard, pay no attention to, shirk

negligible *ADJECTIVE*
There is a negligible difference in price.
• tiny, slight, insignificant, unimportant, trivial
OPPOSITE considerable

negotiate *VERB*
❶ *She negotiated with the car salesman.*
• bargain, haggle, deal, confer
❷ *The skier negotiated the course with ease.*
• get past, get round, manoeuvre round

neighbourhood *NOUN*
They live in a very nice neighbourhood.
• area, district, community, locality, vicinity

neighbouring *ADJECTIVE*
The journey will take them to Mexico and neighbouring countries.
• nearby, bordering, adjacent, adjoining, surrounding, nearest, next-door

neighbourly *ADJECTIVE*
It was very neighbourly of her to offer to feed the cat.
• friendly, helpful, kind, obliging, sociable
OPPOSITE unfriendly

nerve *NOUN*
❶ *Acrobats need to have a lot of nerve.*
• bravery, courage, daring, pluck
(informal) bottle
❷ *He had the nerve to ask for more money!*
• cheek, impudence, rudeness, impertinence

nervous *ADJECTIVE*
Students often feel nervous before an exam.
• anxious, worried, apprehensive, concerned, uneasy, fearful, edgy, fraught, tense, troubled
(informal) uptight, jittery
OPPOSITE calm

nestle *VERB*
The cubs nestled against their mother.
• cuddle, curl up, snuggle

neutral *ADJECTIVE*
❶ *A referee has to be neutral.*
• impartial, unbiased, unprejudiced, even-handed
OPPOSITES biased, prejudiced
❷ *The room was decorated in neutral colours.*
• dull, drab, indefinite, colourless
OPPOSITES vibrant, distinctive

new *ADJECTIVE*
❶ *Start on a new sheet of paper.*
• clean, fresh, unused, brand-new
Something new and unused is in mint condition.
❷ *They went to the motor show to see the new models.*
• latest, current, modern, recent, up to date
❸ *They've found a new bug in the computer program.*
• additional, extra, unexpected, unfamiliar
❹ *Haven't you got any new ideas?*
• fresh, original, novel, innovative, creative, different
OPPOSITE old

news *NOUN*
What's the latest news?
• information, word, report, bulletin
(old use) tidings

next *ADJECTIVE*
❶ *He lives in the house next to the chip shop.*
• adjacent, closest, nearest
OPPOSITE distant
❷ *If you miss this bus, you can catch the next one.*
• following, subsequent
OPPOSITE previous

nice *ADJECTIVE*
❶ *That's not a very nice thing to say!*
• pleasant, agreeable
OPPOSITE nasty
❷ *There is a nice distinction between borrowing and stealing.*
• delicate, fine, precise, subtle

a
b
c
d
e
f
g
h
i
j
k
l
m
n
o
p
q
r
s
t
u
v
w
x
y
z

A
B
C
D
E
F
G
H
I
J
K
L
M
N
O
P
Q
R
S
T
U
V
W
X
Y
Z

OVERUSED WORD

Try to vary the words you use for **nice**. Here are some other words you could use.

FOR A NICE PERSON:

• good, kind, friendly, helpful, generous, likeable, amiable, charming, polite, genial
'Come with me, dear Ratty, and your amiable friend also, if he will be so very good, just as far as the stable-yard, and you shall see what you shall see!'–THE WIND IN THE WILLOWS, Kenneth Grahame

FOR A NICE EXPERIENCE:

• delightful, enjoyable, wonderful, marvellous, splendid
*Did you have an **enjoyable** time in Cuba?*

FOR SOMETHING THAT LOOKS NICE:

• beautiful, attractive, pleasing, lovely
*There is an **attractive** view from the upstairs window.*

FOR A NICE SMELL:

• fragrant, sweet-smelling
*The **fragrant** scent of lavender filled the garden.*

FOR NICE FOOD:

• delicious, tasty, appetizing, satisfying
*They serve **tasty** sandwiches in the cafe.*

FOR NICE WEATHER:

• fine, sunny, warm
*The weather has been **fine** all week.*

for other ways to describe something you like see **good**

---

night *NOUN*
*Badgers usually come out at **night**.*
• night-time, dark
Animals which are active at night are **nocturnal** animals.

nimble *ADJECTIVE*
*The elves sewed the shoes with their **nimble** fingers.*
• agile, skilful, quick, deft
OPPOSITE clumsy

nip *VERB*
❶ *She **nipped** her finger in the door.*
• pinch, squeeze, clip, catch
❷ *The dog **nipped** my leg.*
• bite, peck, snip
❸ *(informal) I'll just **nip** along to the post office.*
• dash, run, rush
(informal) pop

noble *ADJECTIVE*
❶ *Lady Sarah belonged to an ancient **noble** family.*
• aristocratic, high-born, upper-class
❷ *The rescuers were congratulated for their **noble** efforts.*
• brave, heroic, courageous, honourable, worthy, virtuous, gallant
OPPOSITES cowardly, unworthy

nod *VERB*
*Simon **nodded** his head in agreement.*
• bob, bow, dip, lower
➤ **to nod off**
*He sometimes **nods off** in front of the television.*
• fall asleep, doze off, drop off, have a nap

noise *NOUN*
*Where is that dreadful **noise** coming from?*
• din, racket, row, uproar, commotion, tumult, cacophony, hullabaloo, pandemonium

noisy *ADJECTIVE*
❶ *The people next door were playing **noisy** music.*
• loud, blaring, booming, deafening, ear-splitting, thunderous
❷ *The children are very **noisy** this morning.*
• rowdy, raucous, chattering, talkative
OPPOSITE quiet

nominate *VERB*
They nominated her as captain.
• appoint, elect, choose, select, name

nonsense *NOUN*
Stop talking nonsense!
• rubbish, drivel, balderdash, piffle, gibberish, claptrap, gobbledegook
(informal) rot, tripe, twaddle

non-stop *ADJECTIVE*
❶ *Their non-stop chattering annoyed her.*
• constant, continual, continuous, endless, ceaseless, incessant, never-ending
❷ *They took a non-stop train from Glasgow to Edinburgh.*
• direct, express, fast

normal *ADJECTIVE*
❶ *He had a normal kind of day at work.*
• average, common, customary, familiar, habitual, ordinary, predictable, regular, routine, standard, typical, unsurprising, usual
❷ *No normal person would sleep on a bed of nails.*
• healthy, rational, reasonable, sane
OPPOSITE abnormal

north *NOUN, ADJECTIVE, ADVERB*
The parts of a continent or country in the north are the **northern** parts.
To travel towards the north is to travel **northward** or **northwards** or **in a northerly direction.**
A wind from the north is a **northerly** wind.
A person who lives in the north of a country is a **northerner**.

nose *NOUN*
❶ *Someone punched Roger on the nose.*
(informal) hooter
The openings in your nose are your **nostrils**.
A word meaning 'to do with your nose' is **nasal**.
Words for an animal's nose are **muzzle** and **snout**.

❷ *I sat in the nose of the boat hoping to spot a dolphin.*
• front, bow, prow

WRITING TIPS
YOU CAN USE THESE WORDS TO DESCRIBE A NOSE:

• beak-like, bulbous, button, classical or Roman, crooked, pointed, snub, upturned
The troll had bushy eyebrows and a red, bulbous nose.

nosy *ADJECTIVE (informal)*
Stop being so nosy and asking all these questions!
• inquisitive, curious, prying, snooping, intrusive
An informal name for a nosy person is a nosy parker.

notable *ADJECTIVE*
❶ *Many notable artists lived and worked in Paris.*
• famous, celebrated, renowned, noted, distinguished, eminent, prominent
❷ *The fireworks concert this year was a notable event.*
• memorable, noteworthy, significant, major, important, remarkable
OPPOSITES insignificant, minor

notch *NOUN*
The forester cut a notch in the tree trunk.
• cut, nick, groove, score, incision

note *NOUN*
❶ *I sent a note thanking him for the present.*
• message, letter, communication
❷ *There was a note of anger in her voice.*
• sound, tone, feeling, quality
note *VERB*
❶ *The detective noted the address on a scrap of paper.*
• jot down, make a note of, write down, record, scribble
❷ *Did you note what they were wearing?*
• notice, see, take note of, pay attention to, heed, mark, observe

a
b
c
d
e
f
g
h
i
j
k
l
m
n
o
p
q
r
s
t
u
v
w
x
y
z

A
B
C
D
E
F
G
H
I
J
K
L
M
N
O
P
Q
R
S
T
U
V
W
X
Y
Z

nothing NOUN
Four minus four equals nothing.
• nought, zero
In cricket a score of nothing is a **duck**, in tennis it is **love**, and in football it is **nil**.

notice NOUN
Someone put up a notice about the meeting.
• sign, advertisement, placard, poster, warning
➤ **to take notice of something**
They took no notice of the warning.
• heed, pay attention to

notice VERB
❶ *Did you notice what he was wearing?*
• note, see, take note of, pay attention to, heed, mark, observe
❷ *I noticed a funny smell in the room.*
• become aware of, detect

noticeable ADJECTIVE
❶ *There has been a noticeable improvement in the weather.*
• definite, distinct, notable, measurable, perceptible, significant
❷ *The tower is noticeable for miles around.*
• visible, conspicuous
❸ *He spoke with a noticeable foreign accent.*
• obvious, pronounced, unmistakable, audible
OPPOSITE imperceptible

notion NOUN
Aunt Zia has some strange notions about life.
• belief, idea, view, thought, opinion, theory, concept

notorious ADJECTIVE
They are notorious liars.
• infamous, well-known, disgraceful, scandalous

nought NOUN
see **nothing**

nourish VERB
Plants are nourished by water drawn up through their roots.
• feed, sustain, support

nourishing ADJECTIVE
The penguins live on a nourishing diet of fish and squid.
• nutritious, wholesome, healthy, health-giving

novel ADJECTIVE
The inventor had a novel idea for building a robot.
• original, new, innovative, fresh, different, imaginative, creative, unusual, unconventional
OPPOSITE familiar

novel NOUN
for various forms of writing see **writing**

now ADVERB
❶ *My cousins are now living in Melbourne.*
• at present, at the moment, currently, nowadays
❷ *I'll give them a ring now.*
• immediately, at once, straight away, without delay, instantly

nude ADJECTIVE
The artist painted from a nude model.
• naked, bare, undressed, unclothed
OPPOSITE clothed

nudge VERB
She nudged me with her elbow.
• poke, prod, shove, bump, jog, jolt

nuisance NOUN
The traffic noise is a real nuisance.
• annoyance, irritation, inconvenience, bother, menace, pest, drawback

numb ADJECTIVE
My toes are numb with cold.
• unfeeling, deadened, frozen, insensitive, paralysed
OPPOSITE sensitive

number NOUN
❶ *Add the **numbers** together to get the answer.*
• figure, numeral
Any of the numbers from 0 to 9 is a **digit**.
A negative or positive whole number is an **integer**.
An amount used in measuring or counting is a **unit**.
❷ *A large **number** of people applied for the job.*
• amount, quantity, collection, crowd
❸ *I've ordered the latest **number** of the magazine.*
• edition, issue
❹ *The band played some well-known **numbers**.*
• song, piece, tune

numerous ADJECTIVE
*There are **numerous** spelling mistakes on this page.*
• many, plenty of, abundant, countless, innumerable, myriad, untold
OPPOSITE few

nurse NOUN
for people who practise medicine see **medicine**

nurse VERB
*The aid workers **nursed** the sick children.*
• look after, care for, tend, treat

nut NOUN

WORD WEB

SOME KINDS OF NUT:

• almond, Brazil nut, cashew, chestnut, coconut, hazelnut, macadamia, peanut, pecan, pine nut, pistachio, walnut

Oo

oath NOUN
❶ *The knights swore an **oath** of honour.*
• pledge, promise, vow
❷ *He let out an **oath** when he banged his head.*
• swear word, curse, blasphemy

obedient ADJECTIVE
*The dog seems very **obedient**.*
• well-behaved, disciplined, manageable, dutiful, docile
OPPOSITE disobedient

obey VERB
❶ *The dog **obeyed** its owner's commands.*
• follow, carry out, execute, implement, observe, adhere to, heed
❷ *The soldiers **obeyed** without question.*
• do what you are told, take orders, be obedient, conform
OPPOSITE disobey

object NOUN
❶ *We saw some strange **objects** in the museum.*
• article, item, thing
❷ *What is the **object** of this exercise?*
• point, purpose, aim, goal, intention, objective

object VERB
➤ **to object to something**
*Several residents have **objected to** the plan.*
• complain about, be opposed to, disapprove of, take exception to, protest against
OPPOSITES accept, agree to

objection NOUN
*Do you have any **objection** to my sitting here?*
• protest, complaint, disapproval, opposition

objectionable ADJECTIVE
*The drains were giving off an **objectionable** smell.*
• unpleasant, disagreeable, disgusting, foul, offensive, repellent, revolting, obnoxious, nasty
OPPOSITE acceptable

a
b
c
d
e
f
g
h
i
j
k
l
m
n
o
p
q
r
s
t
u
v
w
x
y
z

objective *ADJECTIVE*
He gave an objective account of what happened.
• disinterested, factual, impartial, rational, unbiased, unemotional, unprejudiced
OPPOSITE subjective

objective *NOUN*
Their objective was to reach the top of the hill.
• aim, goal, intention, target, ambition, object, purpose

obligatory *ADJECTIVE*
The wearing of seat belts is obligatory.
• compulsory, necessary, required
OPPOSITE optional

oblige *VERB*
Would you oblige me by watering the plants?
• help, assist, do you a favour

obliged *ADJECTIVE*
❶ *He felt obliged to help them.*
• bound, compelled, expected, required
❷ *I'm much obliged to you for your kindness.*
• thankful, grateful, indebted

oblong *NOUN*
• rectangle
for other shapes see **shape**

obscure *ADJECTIVE*
❶ *An obscure figure emerged from the mist.*
• dim, murky, shadowy, misty, blurred, unclear, vague, indistinct
OPPOSITE clear
❷ *His joke seemed rather obscure.*
• confusing, puzzling, incomprehensible
OPPOSITE obvious
❸ *Henry Kirke White is an obscure poet.*
• unknown, unheard of, unimportant, forgotten, minor
OPPOSITE famous

obscure *VERB*
A tall hedge obscured the view.
• block out, cover, hide, mask, screen, shroud
OPPOSITE reveal

observant *ADJECTIVE*
If you're observant, you might see a badger.
• alert, attentive, sharp-eyed, vigilant, watchful
OPPOSITE inattentive

observation *NOUN*
❶ *They took him to hospital for observation.*
• study, watching, scrutiny
❷ *The detective made an observation.*
• comment, remark, statement

observe *VERB*
❶ *Astronomers observed the eclipse last night.*
• watch, look at, view, study
❷ *I have observed a change in his behaviour.*
• notice, note, see, detect, spot, discern, perceive, witness
❸ *It's important to observe the rules.*
• follow, abide by, adhere to, heed, keep to, obey
❹ *My friend observed that I had grown taller.*
• mention, say, comment, remark, declare

obsessed *ADJECTIVE*
I am obsessed with cars.
• infatuated, fixated, preoccupied, engrossed

obsession *NOUN*
She has an obsession with birds.
• passion, fixation, addiction, mania

obsolete *ADJECTIVE*
That computer software is now obsolete.
• out of date, outdated, antiquated, dated
OPPOSITE current

obstacle *NOUN*
❶ *They drove around the obstacles in the road.*
• obstruction, barrier, barricade
❷ *Their age proved to be an obstacle.*
• problem, difficulty, hindrance, hurdle, snag, catch

obstinate *ADJECTIVE*
The obstinate camel refused to budge.
• stubborn, uncooperative, wilful, headstrong
OPPOSITE cooperative

A
B
C
D
E
F
G
H
I
J
K
L
M
N
O
P
Q
R
S
T
U
V
W
X
Y
Z

obstruct *VERB*
The path was obstructed by a fallen tree.
• block, jam, make impassable

obstruction *NOUN*
The fallen tree was causing an obstruction.
• blockage, barrier, barricade

obtain *VERB*
You must obtain a permit before you can park here.
• get, get hold of, acquire
(informal) pick up

obvious *ADJECTIVE*
❶ *It was silly to make so many obvious mistakes.*
• glaring, noticeable, pronounced
❷ *The castle is an obvious landmark.*
• conspicuous, notable, prominent, visible
OPPOSITE inconspicuous
❸ *It was obvious that the woman was a spy.*
• clear, evident, apparent, plain, undeniable, unmistakable
OPPOSITE hidden

occasion *NOUN*
❶ *I've been to Italy on several occasions.*
• time, moment, instance, opportunity, chance
❷ *The wedding was a happy occasion.*
• affair, event, happening, incident, occurrence

occasional *ADJECTIVE*
The weather forecast said there would be occasional showers.
• intermittent, odd, scattered, irregular, infrequent
OPPOSITES frequent, regular

occasionally *ADVERB*
The dragon occasionally lifted its head and roared.
• sometimes, now and again, once in a while, every so often
OPPOSITES frequently, often

occupant *NOUN*
The only occupants of the castle were a family of bats.
• inhabitant, occupier, resident, tenant

occupation *NOUN*
❶ *He's not happy with his present occupation.*
• job, post, employment, profession, trade, work
for various occupations see **job**
❷ *Vita's favourite occupation is reading.*
• activity, hobby, pastime, pursuit

occupied *ADJECTIVE*
She's very occupied in her work just now.
• absorbed, involved, engrossed, busy, engaged
OPPOSITE idle

occupy *VERB*
❶ *They occupy the house next door.*
• live in, reside in, dwell in, inhabit
❷ *We sold the piano because it occupied too much space.*
• fill, take up, use up
❸ *The rebel army occupied the town.*
• capture, seize, take over, conquer, invade

occur *VERB*
❶ *She told us what had occurred.*
• happen, take place, come about, arise
❷ *The disease only occurs in certain plants.*
• develop, crop up, turn up

occurrence *NOUN*
An eclipse of the sun is an unusual occurrence.
• event, happening, incident, phenomenon

ocean *NOUN*

WORD WEB

THE OCEANS OF THE WORLD ARE:

• Antarctic, Arctic, Atlantic, Indian, Pacific
for creatures that live in the ocean see **sea**

a b c d e f g h i j k l m n o p q r s t u v w x y z

A
B
C
D
E
F
G
H
I
J
K
L
M
N
O
P
Q
R
S
T
U
V
W
X
Y
Z

odd ADJECTIVE
❶ Her behaviour seemed very **odd**.
• strange, unusual, abnormal, peculiar, curious, puzzling, queer, unconventional, eccentric, funny, weird
OPPOSITE normal
❷ He could only find a couple of **odd** socks.
• left over, single, spare
❸ He does **odd** jobs to earn money.
• occasional, casual, irregular, various

odour NOUN
There's a nasty **odour** coming from the fridge.
• smell, scent
A pleasant odour is a **fragrance** or **perfume**.
An unpleasant odour is a **reek**, **stench** or **stink**.
see also **smell**

offence NOUN
❶ The thief was punished for her **offence**.
• crime, wrongdoing, misdeed, fault, sin
In games, an offence is a **foul** or an **infringement**.
❷ I didn't mean to cause any **offence**.
• hurt, anger, annoyance, displeasure, hard feelings, disgust

offend VERB
❶ I hope my letter didn't **offend** you.
• give or cause offence to, insult, upset, hurt your feelings, anger, displease, annoy, affront, disgust, vex
❷ You'll be punished if you **offend** again.
• break the law, do wrong

offensive ADJECTIVE
❶ The gas produces an **offensive** smell.
• unpleasant, repellent, disgusting, revolting, nasty
OPPOSITE pleasant
❷ He apologized for his **offensive** remarks.
• insulting, impolite, rude, abusive

offer VERB
❶ A reward was **offered** for the capture of the outlaws.
• propose, put forward, suggest, make available

❷ He **offered** to help with the washing-up.
• volunteer

offer NOUN
Their **offer** of help was gratefully received.
• proposal, suggestion

office NOUN
❶ The boss won't be in the **office** today.
• workplace, bureau, department
❷ Penny will take up the **office** of treasurer.
• post, position, appointment, role, function

officer NOUN
for officers in the police force see **police officer**

official ADJECTIVE
The **official** opening of the museum is next month.
• formal, authentic, authorized, legitimate, proper, genuine, approved
OPPOSITE unofficial

official NOUN
We spoke to an **official** of the organization.
• officer, office-holder, representative, executive

often ADVERB
It **often** rains in April.
• frequently, regularly, repeatedly, time after time, many times, again and again, constantly

oil VERB
She **oiled** the hinge to stop it squeaking.
• grease, lubricate

oily ADJECTIVE
Fried food is too **oily** for me.
• fatty, greasy

ointment NOUN
The chemist gave her some **ointment** for the rash.
• cream, lotion

old ADJECTIVE

OVERUSED WORD

Try to vary the words you use for **old**.
Here are some other words you could use.

FOR AN OLD PERSON:

• elderly, aged, senior
Bus tickets are free for elderly people.
OPPOSITE young

FOR AN OLD BUILDING OR OLD DOCUMENT:

• ancient, early, historical, original
The ancient Norman church is to be restored.
Something that you respect because it is
old is **venerable**.
OPPOSITE new

FOR AN OLD STYLE OR OLD TECHNOLOGY:

• old-fashioned, out of date, antiquated,
obsolete
*His clothes were curiously old-fashioned,
mostly brown and black, the sort of thing
people wore two or three hundred years ago.*
—BILLY AND THE MINPINS, Roald Dahl
Things which are valuable because they are
old are **antique** or **vintage**.
OPPOSITES up to date, current

FOR SOMETHING OLD AND WORN-OUT:

• worn, scruffy, shabby, threadbare
I put on scruffy jeans to do some gardening.

FOR THE OLD DAYS OR OLD TIMES:

• past, former, earlier, previous, bygone,
olden
*We did a project on how children lived
in former times.*
Times before written records were kept
were **prehistoric** times.
OPPOSITE modern

old-fashioned ADJECTIVE

That hairstyle is quite old-fashioned now.
• out of date, outdated, outmoded, antiquated
OPPOSITES modern, up to date

omit VERB

❶ *His article was omitted from the magazine.*
• exclude, leave out, miss out, cut, eliminate,
overlook, skip
❷ *Don't omit to turn off the lights.*
• forget, fail, neglect

one-sided ADJECTIVE

*The driver gave a one-sided account of the
accident.*
• biased, prejudiced, unbalanced, unfair

ooze VERB

The filling started to ooze from my wrap.
• leak, seep, escape, dribble, drip

opaque ADJECTIVE

The dirt had turned the window opaque.
• cloudy, obscure, unclear, dull, hazy, muddy,
murky
OPPOSITE transparent

open ADJECTIVE

❶ *The puppy escaped through the open door.*
• unlocked, unfastened, ajar, gaping
OPPOSITE closed
❷ *The jam jar had been left open.*
• uncovered, unsealed
❸ *There is a view of open country from the
back window.*
• clear, unrestricted, unenclosed, extensive
OPPOSITE enclosed
❹ *We were open about what we had done wrong.*
• frank, honest, sincere, straightforward,
candid
OPPOSITE deceitful
❺ *The captain faced open rebellion from
the crew.*
• unconcealed, undisguised, obvious, plain
OPPOSITE concealed

open VERB

❶ *Please open the door.*
• unfasten, unlock, unbolt
❷ *I can't wait to open my birthday presents!*
• undo, unwrap, untie, unseal
To open an umbrella is to **unfurl** it.
To open a wine bottle is to **uncork** it.
To open a map is to **unfold** or **unroll** it.
To open a computer program is to **launch** it.

a b c d e f g h i j k l m n o p q r s t u v w x y z

A ❸ *The jumble sale opens at 10 a.m.*
• begin, start, commence
B *(informal)* get going
OPPOSITE close

opening *NOUN*
❶ *The sheep got out through an opening in the fence.*
• gap, hole, breach, break, split
❷ *The film has a very dramatic opening.*
• beginning, start, commencement
❸ *We are invited to the opening of the new sports centre.*
• launch, initiation
❹ *The job offers a good opening for a keen young person.*
• chance, opportunity

operate *VERB*
❶ *This watch operates even under water.*
• work, function, go, perform
❷ *Do you know how to operate this machine?*
• use, work, drive, handle, manage, deal with
❸ *The surgeon operated to remove her appendix.*
• carry out an operation, perform surgery

operation *NOUN*
❶ *Astronauts control the operation of the spacecraft.*
• performance, working, functioning
❷ *He had an operation to remove his appendix.*
• surgery
❸ *Trying to defuse a bomb is a dangerous operation.*
• task, activity, action, exercise, manoeuvre, process, procedure

opinion *NOUN*
What was your honest opinion of the film?
• view, judgement, impression, belief, attitude, point of view, thought, conclusion, assessment, notion, feeling, idea

opponent *NOUN*
The knight fought bravely against his opponent.
• enemy, foe, rival, adversary, challenger
Your opponents in a game are the **opposition**.
OPPOSITE ally

opportunity *NOUN*
❶ *There were few opportunities to relax.*
• chance, occasion, moment, time
❷ *The job offers a good opportunity for a keen young person.*
• opening
(informal) break

oppose *VERB*
Many people opposed the building of the new road.
• object to, disapprove of, be against, be hostile towards, argue against, fight against, attack, resist
OPPOSITES support, defend

opposite *ADJECTIVE*
❶ *Our families have opposite views about politics.*
• contrasting, conflicting, contradictory, opposed, opposing, different, contrary
OPPOSITE similar
❷ *My friend lives on the opposite side of the road.*
• facing

opposite *NOUN*
She says one thing and does the opposite.
• contrary, reverse, converse

opposition *NOUN*
❶ *There was fierce opposition to the new road.*
• hostility, resistance, disapproval, unfriendliness, scepticism
OPPOSITE support
❷ *The opposition were stronger than our team expected.*
• opponents, rivals

optical *ADJECTIVE*
for optical instruments see **glasses**

optimistic *ADJECTIVE*
She's optimistic about her chances of success.
• hopeful, positive, confident, expectant, cheerful, buoyant
OPPOSITE pessimistic

A B C D E F G H I J K L M N O P Q R S T U V W X Y Z

option NOUN
He had the option of staying or leaving.
• choice, alternative, possibility

optional ADJECTIVE
The holiday includes an optional tour of the city.
• voluntary, possible
OPPOSITE compulsory

oral ADJECTIVE
She had to take an oral exam in French.
• spoken, verbal
OPPOSITE written

orbit VERB
The earth orbits the sun in about 365 days.
• circle, travel round

ordeal NOUN
The shipwrecked sailor told us about his ordeal.
• suffering, troubles, trial, anguish, torture, nightmare

order NOUN
❶ *The captain gave the order to abandon ship.*
• command, instruction, direction
❷ *I've put in an order for the new book.*
• request, demand, reservation, booking
❸ *The police restored order after the riot.*
• peace, calm, control, quiet, harmony, law and order
❹ *My books are arranged in alphabetical order.*
• arrangement, sequence, series, succession
❺ *She keeps her bike in good order.*
• condition, state

order VERB
❶ *She ordered them to be quiet.*
• command, instruct, require, tell
❷ *He ordered the new magazine.*
• request, reserve, apply for, book

orderly ADJECTIVE
❶ *The library has an orderly system for sorting books.*
• organized, ordered, tidy, neat, systematic, methodical
OPPOSITE untidy

❷ *Please form an orderly queue.*
• well-behaved, controlled, disciplined
OPPOSITE disorderly

ordinary ADJECTIVE
❶ *It was just an ordinary sort of day.*
• normal, typical, usual, customary, habitual, everyday
❷ *This is more than just an ordinary robot.*
• standard, average, common, conventional, regular
❸ *It was a very ordinary game.*
• mediocre, unexceptional, run-of-the-mill, routine
OPPOSITES special, unusual

organization NOUN
❶ *She works for a charitable organization.*
• institution, operation, enterprise, company
(informal) outfit, set-up
❷ *Who was responsible for the organization of the conference?*
• coordination, planning, arrangement, running

organize VERB
❶ *It took her ages to organize the party.*
• coordinate, plan, make arrangements for, see to, set up, run
❷ *The librarian has to organize the books in the library.*
• arrange, put in order, classify, sort out, tidy up

origin NOUN
❶ *We know very little about the origin of life on earth.*
• beginning, creation, start, birth, source, cause
OPPOSITE end
❷ *He became very rich, despite his humble origins.*
• background, ancestry, descent, family, parentage, pedigree, stock

a b c d e f g h i j k l m n o p q r s t u v w x y z

A B C D E F G H I J K L M N O P Q R S T U V W X Y Z

original *ADJECTIVE*
❶ *The settlers drove out the original inhabitants.*
• earliest, first, initial, native, aboriginal
❷ *The story was very original.*
• inventive, new, novel, creative, fresh, imaginative, unusual, unconventional
❸ *Is that an original work of art or a copy?*
• genuine, real, authentic, unique

originate *VERB*
❶ *Where did the idea originate?*
• begin, start, commence, emerge, crop up
❷ *They originated a new style of dancing.*
• invent, create, design, conceive, introduce, launch

ornament *NOUN*
A few ornaments will make the room more attractive.
• decoration, adornment, trinket, bauble

ornamental *ADJECTIVE*
There were a few ornamental statues in the garden.
• decorative, fancy, pretty, ornate

ornate *ADJECTIVE*
The furniture in the palace was very ornate.
• elaborate, fancy, showy, ornamental, decorative

orthodox *ADJECTIVE*
She wasn't taught to play the piano in the orthodox way.
• conventional, accepted, customary, usual, standard, traditional, regular, established, approved, recognized, official
OPPOSITE unorthodox, unconventional

outbreak *NOUN*
❶ *The townspeople feared an outbreak of violence.*
• outburst, upsurge (in), flare-up, spate
An outbreak of disease that spreads quickly is an epidemic.
❷ *The armies prepared for the outbreak of war.*
• beginning, start, onset

outburst *NOUN*
There was an outburst of laughter from the next room.
• explosion, eruption, outbreak, storm

outcome *NOUN*
What was the outcome of the meeting?
• result, consequence, effect, upshot

outcry *NOUN*
There was an outcry over the closure of the hospital.
• protest, complaint, uproar, fuss, furore

outdoor *ADJECTIVE*
The hotel had an outdoor swimming pool.
• open-air, out of doors, outside

outer *ADJECTIVE*
The fishermen wore waterproof outer garments.
• external, exterior, outside
OPPOSITE inner

outfit *NOUN*
❶ *Katie bought a new outfit for the wedding.*
• clothes, costume, suit, ensemble *(informal)* get-up
❷ *The puncture repair outfit is in the boot.*
• equipment, kit, gear

outing *NOUN*
They've gone on their annual outing to London.
• trip, excursion, expedition, jaunt

outlaw *NOUN*
A band of outlaws held up the train.
• bandit, brigand, robber, highwayman, criminal, fugitive

outlet *NOUN*
❶ *The basin has an outlet for excess water.*
• opening, vent, channel, way out, exit, mouth
OPPOSITE inlet
❷ *The company has outlets throughout the UK.*
• shop, store, market

outline NOUN
❶ We could see the **outline** of some trees in the distance.
• profile, shape, silhouette, form, shadow
❷ He gave us a brief **outline** of his plan.
• summary, sketch, framework, precis, rough idea

outline VERB
The detective **outlined** her plan.
• summarize, sketch out

outlook NOUN
❶ The cottage has a beautiful **outlook** over the loch.
• view, prospect, sight, vista
❷ He has a rather gloomy **outlook** on life.
• point of view, view, attitude, frame of mind
❸ The **outlook** for the weekend is bright and sunny.
• forecast, prediction, prospect

outrage NOUN
❶ There was public **outrage** at the government's decision.
• anger, fury, disgust, indignation, horror
❷ He said it was an **outrage** that so much money has been wasted.
• disgrace, scandal, crime, atrocity

outrageous ADJECTIVE
❶ The behaviour of the trolls was **outrageous**.
• disgraceful, scandalous, shocking, atrocious, appalling, monstrous, shameful
❷ They charge **outrageous** prices at that shop.
• excessive, unreasonable
OPPOSITE acceptable, reasonable

outside ADJECTIVE
Lookouts were stationed on the **outside** wall of the castle.
• exterior, external, outer

outside NOUN
Insects have their skeletons on the **outside** of their bodies.
• exterior, shell, surface
OPPOSITE inside

outsider NOUN
She's lived in the village for years, but still feels like an **outsider**.
• newcomer, stranger, alien, foreigner, immigrant, incomer

outskirts PLURAL NOUN
We live on the **outskirts** of town.
• edge, fringe, outer areas
The outskirts of a big town are the **suburbs**.
OPPOSITE centre

outspoken ADJECTIVE
She's always been **outspoken** in her views.
• frank, honest, plain, blunt, straightforward

outstanding ADJECTIVE
❶ He will be an **outstanding** tennis player in a few years.
• excellent, exceptional, superb, extraordinary, superlative, brilliant, great, fine, distinguished, celebrated, remarkable, superior, striking, notable
OPPOSITE ordinary
❷ There are still some **outstanding** bills to pay.
• overdue, unpaid, owing

outward ADJECTIVE
In **outward** appearance, the castle was dark and dingy.
• outer, outside, external, exterior, visible

outwit VERB
Anya managed to **outwit** her dad at chess.
• outsmart, get the better of, beat, defeat

oval ADJECTIVE
The sandwiches were arranged on an **oval** platter.
• egg-shaped, elliptical

oven NOUN
The meat was roasting in the **oven**.
• cooker, stove
A special oven for firing pottery is a **kiln**.

overcast ADJECTIVE
The sky has been **overcast** all day.
• cloudy, dull, grey, sunless, dark, leaden
see also **weather**

a
b
c
d
e
f
g
h
i
j
k
l
m
n
o
p
q
r
s
t
u
v
w
x
y
z

A
B
C
D
E
F
G
H
I
J
K
L
M
N
O
P
Q
R
S
T
U
V
W
X
Y
Z

overcome VERB overcomes, overcoming, overcame, overcome
❶ He managed to **overcome** his fear of flying.
• conquer, defeat, master, get the better of
❷ Some people in the building were **overcome** by fumes.
• overpower, overwhelm

overflow VERB
Someone left the tap on and the bath overflowed.
• spill over, run over, pour over, flood

overgrown ADJECTIVE
The back garden was completely **overgrown**.
• unkempt, untidy, tangled, weedy, wild

overhaul VERB
The boiler was recently **overhauled**.
• service, check over, inspect, repair, restore, refurbish

overhead ADVERB
A flock of geese flew **overhead**.
• above, high up, in the sky

overlook VERB
❶ He seems to have **overlooked** one important fact.
• miss, fail to see
❷ I am willing to **overlook** the error.
• excuse, forget about, ignore, disregard, pardon, pay no attention to
(informal) turn a blind eye to
❸ The front room of the house **overlooks** the garden.
• have a view of, look on to, face

overpowering ADJECTIVE
I felt an **overpowering** urge to giggle.
• overwhelming, powerful, strong, compelling, irresistible, uncontrollable

overrun VERB overruns, overrunning, overran, overrun
The barn was **overrun** with rats and mice.
• invade, take over, spread over, swarm over

overtake VERB overtakes, overtaking, overtook, overtaken
We **overtook** the car in front.
• pass, leave behind, pull ahead of, outstrip

overthrow VERB overthrows, overthrowing, overthrew, overthrown
The rebels **overthrew** the President.
• bring down, topple, oust, defeat, drive out, depose

overturn VERB
❶ The boat **overturned**.
• capsize, tip over, turn over, turn turtle
❷ She leapt to her feet, **overturning** her chair.
• knock over, tip over, topple, upset, spill

overwhelm VERB
❶ The troops were **overwhelmed** by the enemy forces.
• defeat, overcome, overpower, crush
❷ A tidal wave **overwhelmed** the village.
• engulf, flood, inundate, submerge, swallow up, bury

overwhelming ADJECTIVE
She was elected by an **overwhelming** majority.
• decisive, devastating, crushing, huge, massive, great
An overwhelming victory at an election is a landslide.

owe VERB
If you owe money to someone, you are in debt.

owing ADJECTIVE
➤ owing to
Owing to the rain, the match is cancelled.
• because of, on account of, as a result of, thanks to

own VERB
It was the first bike he had **owned**.
• be the owner of, have, possess
➤ to own up to
No one **owned up to** breaking the window.
• confess to, admit to, tell the truth about
(informal) come clean about

Pp

pace *NOUN*
❶ *Move forward two paces.*
• step, stride
❷ *The front runner set a fast pace.*
• rate, speed
A formal word is **velocity**.

pacify *VERB*
*The zookeeper managed to pacify
the polar bear.*
• calm, quieten, soothe, humour, appease
OPPOSITE anger, annoy

pack *NOUN*
❶ *There were four candles in each pack.*
• package, packet, bundle, bale
❷ *The hikers picked up their packs and
trudged off.*
• rucksack, backpack, knapsack
pack *VERB*
❶ *She packed her suitcase and called a taxi.*
• fill, load up
❷ *I forgot to pack my hairdryer.*
• stow away, wrap up
❸ *They tried to pack too many passengers on
to the train.*
• cram, crowd, squeeze, stuff, jam, wedge

package *NOUN*
*The postman delivered a big
package.*
• parcel, packet, bundle

pad *NOUN*
❶ *He put a pad of cotton wool over
the wound.*
• wad
A pad to make a chair or bed comfortable
is a **cushion** or **pillow**.
❷ *There's a pad for messages next
to the phone.*
• jotter, notebook, writing pad

pad *VERB*
The seats are padded with foam rubber.
• stuff, fill, pack
To put covers and padding on furniture is to
upholster it.

padding *NOUN*
The padding is coming out of this cushion.
• stuffing, filling
The covers and padding on furniture are
upholstery.

paddle *VERB*
❶ *The children paddled at the water's edge.*
• dabble, splash about
To walk through deep water is to **wade**.
❷ *She paddled her canoe along the canal.*
To move a boat along with two oars is to **row** it.

page *NOUN*
❶ *Several pages have been torn out of
this book.*
• sheet, leaf
❷ *He wrote two pages of notes.*
• side

paid *past tense see* **pay**

pain *NOUN*
Dana felt a sudden jabbing pain in her foot.
• anguish, suffering
A dull pain is an **ache** or **soreness**.
Severe pain is **agony**, **torment** or **torture**.
A slight pain is **discomfort**.
A slight pain which doesn't last long is a **twinge**.
A sudden pain is a **pang** or **stab**.
Pain in your head is a **headache**.
Pain in your teeth is **toothache**.

painful *ADJECTIVE*
❶ *My shoulder is still really painful.*
• sore, aching, tender, hurting, smarting,
stinging, throbbing
OPPOSITE painless
❷ *The conversation brought back many
painful memories.*
• unpleasant, upsetting, distressing,
disagreeable, traumatic

a b c d e f g h i j k l m n o **p** q r s t u v w x y z

287

A
B
C
D
E
F
G
H
I
J
K
L
M
N
O
P
Q
R
S
T
U
V
W
X
Y
Z

painless *ADJECTIVE*
❶ *The treatment is quite painless.*
• comfortable, pain-free
OPPOSITE painful
❷ *This is a quick and painless way to make a cake.*
• easy, simple, effortless, undemanding

paint *NOUN*

WORD WEB

KINDS OF PAINT FOR DECORATING:

• emulsion, undercoat, whitewash
A layer of paint is a **coat** of paint.
Paint which stays shiny when it dries is **gloss** paint.
Paint which goes dull when it dries is **matt** paint.

KINDS OF PAINT FOR ARTWORK:

• acrylic, finger paint, oil paint, poster paint, watercolour

paint *VERB*
❶ *The bedroom walls were painted green.*
• colour, decorate
❷ *Samantha painted the flowers in bright colours.*
• depict, portray, represent

painter *NOUN*
A person who paints houses is a **decorator**.
A person who paints pictures is an **artist**.

painting *NOUN*
A picture painted on a wall is a **fresco** or a **mural**.
A picture painted by a famous artist of the past is an **old master**.
see also **picture**

pair *NOUN*
A pair of people who go out together are a **couple**.
Two people who sing or play music together are a **duet** or a **duo**.

Two people who work together are **partners** or a **partnership**.
Two babies born together are **twins**.

palace *NOUN*
for types of building see **building**

pale *ADJECTIVE*
❶ *Are you all right? You're looking a little pale.*
• white, pallid, pasty, wan, ashen, sallow, anaemic
OPPOSITE ruddy, flushed
To go pale with fear is to **blanch**.
❷ *That shade of pink is too pale.*
• light, pastel, faded, faint, dim, bleached, colourless
OPPOSITE bright

pamper *VERB*
The twins' grandparents liked to pamper them.
• spoil, indulge, cosset, mollycoddle, humour

pamphlet *NOUN*
We were given a pamphlet about road safety.
• leaflet, booklet, brochure

pan *NOUN*
for things used for cooking see **cook**

panel *NOUN*
A panel of experts judged the contest.
• group, team, board, committee

panic *NOUN*
People fled the streets in panic.
• alarm, fright, terror, frenzy, hysteria
panic *VERB*
If a fire starts, don't panic!
• be alarmed, take fright, become hysterical
(informal) lose your head, get in a flap
To panic is also to be **panic-stricken**.

pant *VERB*
Some of the runners were panting by the last lap.
• breathe quickly, gasp, wheeze, puff

pants *PLURAL NOUN*
for underwear see **clothes**

paper *NOUN*
❶ *She started her diary on a fresh sheet of paper.*
A piece of paper is a **leaf** or a **sheet**.
❷ *The doctor had some important papers to sign.*
• document, deed, certificate
❸ *The story made the front page of the local paper.*
• newspaper, journal
(informal) rag

paper *NOUN*

WORD WEB

MATERIALS FOR WRITING OR DRAWING ON:

• card, cardboard, cartridge paper, notepaper, postcard, stationery, tracing paper, writing paper

EARLY MATERIALS FOR WRITING ON:

• papyrus, parchment, vellum

OTHER KINDS OF PAPER:

• greaseproof paper, tissue paper, toilet paper, wallpaper, wrapping paper

parade *NOUN*
A circus parade passed along the street.
• procession, march, spectacle, show, display
A parade of vehicles or of people on horseback is a **cavalcade**.
A parade of people in costume is a **pageant**.

parade *VERB*
The brass band paraded through the town.
• march, troop, file past

paralyse *VERB*
His right arm was paralysed in the accident.
• disable, immobilize, cripple, deaden, numb

parcel *NOUN*
The postman delivered a bulky parcel.
• package, packet

parched *ADJECTIVE*
❶ *Nothing was growing in the parched earth.*
• dry, arid, baked, scorched, barren, sterile, waterless
❷ *I need a drink of water—I'm parched!*
• thirsty

pardon *VERB*
The king decided to pardon the prisoners.
• release, free, set free, let off, spare, excuse, forgive
To pardon someone who is condemned to death is to **reprieve** them.

parent *NOUN*
for family relationships see **family**

park *NOUN*
At lunchtime, we went for a walk in the park.
• public gardens, recreation ground
A park with fields and trees around a big house is an **estate** or **parkland**.

WORD WEB

SOME KINDS OF PARK:

• adventure park, amusement park, botanical gardens, nature reserve, play park or playground, safari park, skate park, theme park

EQUIPMENT YOU MIGHT FIND IN A PLAY PARK:

• chute or slide, climbing frame, flying fox, monkey bars, rope ladder, roundabout, sandpit, see-saw, swings, trampoline

park *VERB*
The plumber parked her van around the corner.
• leave, position, station

a
b
c
d
e
f
g
h
i
j
k
l
m
n
o
p
q
r
s
t
u
v
w
x
y
z

part NOUN
❶ *All the parts of the engine are now working properly.*
• bit, component, constituent
❷ *I only saw the first part of the programme.*
• section, piece, portion, element
❸ *Which part of the business do they own?*
• branch, department, division
❹ *Granny lives in another part of the town.*
• area, district, region, neighbourhood, sector
❺ *He's just right to act the part of Peter Pan.*
• character, role

part VERB
❶ *It was the first time she'd been parted from her parents.*
• separate, divide, remove
OPPOSITE join
❷ *They exchanged a final kiss before parting.*
• go away, leave, depart, say goodbye
OPPOSITE meet

partial ADJECTIVE
The play was only a partial success.
• limited, imperfect, incomplete
OPPOSITE complete
➤ **to be partial to**
Becky is very partial to chocolate cake.
• be fond of, be keen on, enjoy, like

participate VERB
Our school is participating in the mini-marathon.
• take part, join in, be involved, cooperate, help, share

particle NOUN
The camera lens was covered with particles of dust.
• speck, grain, fragment, bit, piece, scrap, shred, sliver
see also bit

particular ADJECTIVE
❶ *The tickets must be used on a particular day.*
• specific, certain, distinct, definite, exact

❷ *She took particular care not to damage the parcel.*
• special, exceptional, unusual, extreme, marked, notable
❸ *The cat's very particular about his food.*
• fussy, finicky, hard to please
(informal) choosy, picky

particulars PLURAL NOUN
The police officer took down all the particulars.
• details, facts, information, circumstances

partition NOUN
A partition separates the two classrooms.
• room divider, screen

partly ADVERB
It was partly my fault that we were late.
• in part, to some extent, up to a point
OPPOSITE entirely

partner NOUN
The two women have been business partners for years.
• colleague, associate, ally
In marriage, your partner is your **spouse**, or your **husband** or **wife**.
An animal's partner is its **mate**.

party NOUN
❶ *We had a class party at the end of term.*
• celebration, festivity, function, gathering, reception
(informal) get-together, do
❷ *A party of tourists was going round the museum.*
• group, band, crowd, gang
❸ *They have formed a new political party.*
• alliance, association, faction, league
party NOUN

WORD WEB

SOME KINDS OF PARTY:

• ball, banquet, barbecue, bar mitzvah, birthday party, ceilidh, Christmas party, cocktail party, dance, dinner party, disco, Diwali party, Eid party, fancy dress party, garden party, Halloween party, house-warming, picnic, sleepover, tea party, wedding

THINGS YOU MIGHT SEE AT A PARTY:

• balloons, birthday cake, birthday candles, bunting, party bags, poppers, sparklers, streamers
for party games see **game**

pass *VERB*
❶ *We watched the parade as it passed.*
• go by, move past
❷ *She tried to pass the car in front.*
• overtake, go ahead of
❸ *We passed over the bridge.*
• go, advance, proceed, progress
❹ *Could you pass me the sugar, please?*
• hand, give, deliver, offer, present
❺ *Do you think you will pass your music exam?*
• be successful in, get through, succeed in
❻ *How did you pass the time on holiday?*
• spend, use, occupy, fill, while away
❼ *Three years passed before we met again.*
• go by, elapse
❽ *The pain will soon pass.*
• go away, come to an end, disappear, fade
➤ **to pass out**
One of the runners passed out in the heat.
• faint, lose consciousness, black out

pass *NOUN*
❶ *We had a pass to get into the concert for free.*
• permit, licence, ticket
❷ *The horses filed through a pass between the hills.*
• gap, gorge, ravine, canyon, valley

passage *NOUN*
❶ *A secret passage led from the chamber to the outside.*
• passageway, corridor, tunnel
❷ *The guards forced a passage through the crowd.*
• path, route, way
❸ *A sea passage takes longer than going by air.*
• journey, voyage, crossing

❹ *Our homework is to choose a favourite passage from a book.*
• episode, excerpt, extract, piece, quotation, section
❺ *He hadn't changed, despite the passage of time.*
• passing, progress, advance

passenger *NOUN*
The bus has seats for 55 passengers.
• traveller
Passengers who travel regularly to work are commuters.

passion *NOUN*
❶ *'Romeo and Juliet' is a story of youthful passion.*
• love, emotion
❷ *She has a passion for sports.*
• enthusiasm, eagerness, appetite, desire, craving, urge, zest, thirst, mania

passionate *ADJECTIVE*
❶ *The captain gave a passionate speech before the battle.*
• emotional, intense, moving, heartfelt
OPPOSITE unemotional
❷ *They are passionate followers of football.*
• eager, keen, avid, enthusiastic, fanatical, fervent
OPPOSITE apathetic

passive *ADJECTIVE*
Owls are normally passive during the daytime.
• inactive, docile
OPPOSITE active

past *NOUN*
In the past, things were different.
• past times, old days, olden days, days gone by
The study of what happened in the past is history.
The things and ideas that have come down to us from the past are our heritage or traditions.
OPPOSITE future

past *ADJECTIVE*
Things were very different in past centuries.
• earlier, former, previous, old
OPPOSITE future

a
b
c
d
e
f
g
h
i
j
k
l
m
n
o
p
q
r
s
t
u
v
w
x
y
z

A
B
C
D
E
F
G
H
I
J
K
L
M
N
O
P
Q
R
S
T
U
V
W
X
Y
Z

pasta NOUN

WORD WEB

SOME TYPES OF PASTA:

• cannelloni, lasagne, linguine, macaroni, noodles, penne, ravioli, spaghetti, tagliatelle, tortellini
for other kinds of food see **food**

paste NOUN
I used some **paste** to stick things into my scrapbook.
• glue, gum, adhesive

pastime NOUN
Shona's favourite **pastime** is swimming.
• activity, hobby, recreation, amusement, diversion, entertainment, relaxation, game, sport
see also **game, sport**

pasture NOUN
Cattle were grazing on the **pasture**.
• field, meadow, grassland

pat VERB
Andy **patted** the Shetland pony on the head.
• tap, touch, stroke, pet
To touch something quickly and lightly is to **dab** it.
To stroke someone with an open hand is to **caress** them.

patch VERB
I need some material to **patch** my jeans.
• mend, repair
Another way to mend holes in clothes is to **darn** them or **stitch** them up.

patchy ADJECTIVE
There will be **patchy** outbreaks of rain overnight.
• irregular, inconsistent, uneven, varying, unpredictable

path NOUN
Please keep to the **path** as you walk through the gardens.
• pathway, track, trail, footpath, walk, walkway, lane
A path for horse-riding is a **bridleway**.
A path by the side of a road is a **pavement**.
A path above a beach is an **esplanade** or **promenade**.
A path along a canal is a **towpath**.
A path between buildings is an **alley**.
see also **road**

pathetic ADJECTIVE
❶ The abandoned kittens were a **pathetic** sight.
• moving, touching, pitiful, distressing, heartbreaking, sad, sorry
❷ The goalie made a **pathetic** attempt to stop the ball.
• hopeless, useless, weak, feeble, inadequate, incompetent

patience NOUN
She waited with great **patience** for an hour.
• calmness, tolerance, self-control, endurance, restraint, perseverance, persistence, resignation
OPPOSITE impatience

patient ADJECTIVE
❶ The nurse was very **patient** with the children.
• calm, composed, even-tempered, easy-going, tolerant, lenient, mild, quiet, uncomplaining, resigned, long-suffering
❷ It took hours of **patient** work to restore the painting.
• persevering, persistent, unhurried, untiring, steady, determined
OPPOSITE impatient

patrol VERB
Police **patrolled** the area all night.
• guard, keep watch over, inspect, tour

patter NOUN, VERB
for various sounds see **sound**

pattern *NOUN*
Do you like the pattern on this wallpaper?
• design, decoration

WORD WEB

SOME KINDS OF PATTERN:

• batik, checked, criss-cross, dotted or dotty, floral or flowery, geometric, gingham, paisley, polka dot, spotted or spotty, striped or stripey, tartan, wavy, zigzag

pause *NOUN*
There was a pause while the singers got their breath back.
• break, gap, halt, rest, lull, stop, wait, interruption, stoppage
A pause in the middle of a performance is an **interlude** or **interval**.
A pause in the middle of a cinema film is an **intermission**.

pause *VERB*
❶ *The stranger paused at the door before knocking.*
• hesitate, wait, delay, hang back
❷ *The cyclists paused to let the others catch up.*
• halt, stop, rest, take a break, break off

paw *NOUN*
The cat had a mouse under its paw.
• foot
A horse's foot is a **hoof**.
A pig's feet are its **trotters**.
A bird's feet are its **claws**.

pay *VERB* pays, paying, paid
❶ *How much did you pay for your new bike?*
• spend, give out, hand over
(informal) fork out
❷ *Who's going to pay the bill?*
• pay off, repay, settle, clear, refund
❸ *They had to pay for all the damage they caused.*
• compensate, pay back

❹ *Do you think the new business is likely to pay?*
• be profitable
❺ *I'll make you pay for this!*
• suffer

pay *NOUN*
We should get an increase in pay next year.
• wages, salary, income, earnings
A payment someone gets for doing a single job is a **fee**.

payment *NOUN*
A voluntary payment to a charity is a **contribution** or **donation**.
The payment you make to travel on public transport is the **fare**.
A payment you have to make as a punishment is a **fine**.
A payment made to free a hostage or prisoner is a **ransom**.
A payment you get as a prize is a **reward**.
A payment to join a club is a **subscription**.
A voluntary payment to a waiter or waitress is a **tip**.
Payment that you receive regularly from your parents is **pocket money**.
A payment you get if you paid too much for something is a **refund**.

peace *NOUN*
❶ *After the war there was a period of peace.*
• agreement, harmony, friendliness
❷ *He enjoys the peace of the countryside.*
• calmness, peacefulness, quiet, tranquillity, calm, stillness, serenity, silence

peaceful *ADJECTIVE*
We enjoyed a peaceful day fishing.
• calm, quiet, relaxing, tranquil, restful, serene, undisturbed, untroubled, gentle, placid, soothing, still
OPPOSITE noisy, troubled

peak *NOUN*
❶ *The peak of the mountain was covered in snow.*
• summit, cap, crest, crown, pinnacle, top, tip, point
❷ *She is at the peak of her career as an athlete.*
• top, height, highest point, climax

a b c d e f g h i j k l m n o p q r s t u v w x y z

peal *VERB*
for sounds made by a bell see **bell**

peculiar *ADJECTIVE*
❶ What's that **peculiar** smell?
• strange, unusual, odd, curious,
extraordinary, abnormal, funny, weird, bizarre
OPPOSITE ordinary
❷ He recognized her **peculiar** way of writing.
• characteristic, distinctive, individual,
particular, personal, special, unique,
identifiable

pedigree *NOUN*
They have a complete record of the dog's
pedigree.
• ancestry, descent, family history

peel *NOUN*
Orange **peel** is used in marmalade.
• rind, skin

peep and **peer** *VERB*
see **look**

peg *NOUN*
Leave your coat and scarf on the **peg**.
• hook, knob

pelt *VERB*
❶ The boys **pelted** each other with snowballs.
• attack, bombard, shower
see also **throw**
❷ The rain was **pelting** down outside.
• pour, teem

pen *NOUN*
❶ My **pen** has run out of ink.
• ballpoint, felt-tip pen, fountain pen, gel pen
❷ The dog drove the sheep into the **pen**.
• enclosure, fold

penalize *VERB*
In football, you are **penalized** if you handle
the ball.
• punish

penalty *NOUN*
The **penalty** for this crime is ten years in
prison.
• punishment
OPPOSITE reward

penetrate *VERB*
❶ The bullet had **penetrated** the man's chest.
• make a hole in, pierce, bore through
When something penetrates a tyre, it
punctures it.
❷ The soldiers **penetrated** the enemy's
defences.
• get past, get through, infiltrate

penniless *ADJECTIVE*
The family was left **penniless** and without a
home.
• poor, impoverished, poverty-stricken
OPPOSITE rich

people *PLURAL NOUN*
❶ How many **people** are you inviting?
• persons, individuals
People as opposed to animals are **humans**,
human beings or **mankind**.
❷ The government is elected by the **people** of
the country.
• population, citizens, the public, society,
nation, race

perceive *VERB*
❶ We **perceived** a figure moving along the
horizon.
• make out, notice, become aware of,
catch sight of, recognize
❷ I began to **perceive** what she meant.
• realize, understand, comprehend, grasp

perceptive *ADJECTIVE*
It was very **perceptive** of you to spot my
mistake.
• observant, clever, sharp, shrewd, quick, alert
OPPOSITE unobservant

perch *VERB*
A robin was **perching** on top of the postbox.
• sit, settle, rest, balance

percussion NOUN
for percussion instruments see **music**

perfect ADJECTIVE
❶ *Each petal on the flower was perfect.*
• faultless, flawless, ideal, intact, undamaged, complete, whole
❷ *The coat is a perfect fit.*
• exact, faithful, precise, accurate, correct
OPPOSITE imperfect
❸ *I received a letter from a perfect stranger.*
• complete, total, absolute, utter

perfect VERB
Gymnasts spend years perfecting their technique.
• make perfect, improve, refine, polish

perform VERB
❶ *Is this your first time performing on stage?*
• act, appear, play, dance, sing
❷ *The class performed a play about pirates.*
• present, stage, produce, put on
❸ *Soldiers are expected to perform their duty.*
• do, carry out, execute, fulfil
To perform a crime is to **commit** a crime.

performance NOUN
❶ *Tonight's performance is already sold out.*
• show, production, presentation
❷ *He congratulated the players on their outstanding performance.*
• effort, work, endeavour, exertion, behaviour, conduct

performer NOUN
see **entertainer**

perfume NOUN
The perfume of roses filled the room.
• smell, scent, fragrance

perhaps ADVERB
Perhaps the weather will improve soon.
• maybe, possibly
OPPOSITE definitely

peril NOUN
The crew faced many perils on their voyage.
• danger, hazard, risk, menace, threat
OPPOSITE safety

perimeter NOUN
There is a fence round the perimeter of the field.
• edge, border, boundary
The distance round the edge of something is the **circumference**.

period NOUN
❶ *After a long period of hard work they had a rest.*
• time, span, spell, stretch
❷ *The book is about the Victorian period.*
• age, era, epoch

perish VERB
❶ *Many birds perish in cold weather.*
• die, be killed, pass away
❷ *The old tyres have started to perish with age.*
• disintegrate, crumble away, rot, decay, decompose

permanent ADJECTIVE
❶ *Sugar can do permanent damage to your teeth.*
• lasting, long-lasting, long-term, everlasting, enduring
❷ *Traffic noise is a permanent problem in the city centre.*
• never-ending, perpetual, persistent, chronic, perennial
❸ *She has been offered a permanent job in the firm.*
• stable, steady, fixed, lifelong
OPPOSITE temporary

permission NOUN
They had the teacher's permission to leave.
• consent, agreement, approval
(informal) go-ahead

a b c d e f g h i j k l m n o p q r s t u v w x y z

A
B
C
D
E
F
G
H
I
J
K
L
M
N
O
P
Q
R
S
T
U
V
W
X
Y
Z

permit *VERB*
The council doesn't permit fishing in the lake.
• allow, consent to, give permission for, authorize, license, grant, tolerate, admit

permit *NOUN*
You need a permit to fish in the river.
• licence, pass, ticket

perpetual *ADJECTIVE*
The machine produces a perpetual hum.
• constant, continual, continuous, never-ending, non-stop, endless, ceaseless, incessant, persistent, unceasing, unending
OPPOSITE temporary

perplexing *ADJECTIVE*
'This is the most perplexing case I've seen,' said the detective.
• puzzling, confusing, bewildering, baffling, mystifying

persecute *VERB*
People were persecuted for their religious beliefs.
• oppress, discriminate against, harass, intimidate, bully, terrorize, torment

persevere *VERB*
The rescuers persevered despite the bad weather.
• continue, carry on, keep going, persist *(informal)* keep at it, stick at it
OPPOSITE give up

persist *VERB*
If your headache persists, you should see a doctor.
• continue, carry on, last, linger, remain, endure
OPPOSITE stop
➤ **to persist in**
He persists in wearing that awful tie!
• keep on, insist on

persistent *ADJECTIVE*
❶ *There was a persistent drip from the tap in the kitchen.*
• constant, continual, incessant, never-ending, steady, non-stop
❷ *That dog is very persistent—it won't go away.*
• determined, persevering, tireless, resolute, steadfast, stubborn, obstinate

person *NOUN*
Not a single person has replied to my email.
• individual, human being, character, soul

personal *ADJECTIVE*
❶ *The book is based on the writer's personal experience.*
• own, individual, particular
❷ *The contents of the letter are personal.*
• confidential, private, secret, intimate

personality *NOUN*
❶ *Like all ogres, she has an ugly personality.*
• character, nature, disposition, temperament, make-up
❷ *The show was introduced by a TV personality.*
• celebrity, star, VIP

perspire *VERB*
He perspires a lot in hot weather.
• sweat

persuade *VERB*
I persuaded my friend to join the choir.
• convince, coax, induce
To persuade someone to do something is also to **talk them into** doing it.
OPPOSITE dissuade

persuasive *ADJECTIVE*
She used some very persuasive arguments.
• convincing, effective, sound, strong, forceful, compelling, valid
OPPOSITE unconvincing

pessimistic *ADJECTIVE*
The players are **pessimistic** about their
chances of winning.
• negative, unhopeful, gloomy, despairing,
resigned, cynical
OPPOSITE optimistic

pest *NOUN*
❶ I'm trying an organic method to get rid of
garden **pests**.
Pests in general are **vermin**.
An informal word for insect pests is **bugs**.
A pest which lives on or in another creature is
a **parasite**.
❷ Don't be a **pest**!
• nuisance, bother, annoyance
(informal) pain

pester *VERB*
Please don't **pester** me while I'm busy!
• annoy, bother, trouble, harass, badger,
hound, nag
(informal) bug

pet *NOUN*

WORD WEB

SOME ANIMALS COMMONLY KEPT AS PETS:

• budgerigar, canary, cat, dog, ferret,
fish, gerbil, goldfish, guinea pig, hamster,
mouse, parrot, pigeon, rabbit, rat, tortoise

petrified *ADJECTIVE*
Jack stood **petrified** as the monster lumbered
towards him.
• terrified, horrified, terror-struck, paralysed,
frozen
see also **afraid**

petty *ADJECTIVE*
There were a lot of annoying **petty** rules.
• minor, trivial, unimportant, insignificant
OPPOSITE important

phase *NOUN*
Going to school is the start of a new **phase** in
your life.
• period, time, stage, step

phenomenal *ADJECTIVE*
The winner of the quiz had a **phenomenal**
memory.
• amazing, incredible, outstanding,
remarkable, exceptional, extraordinary
(informal) fantastic
OPPOSITE ordinary

phenomenon *NOUN*
❶ Snow is a common **phenomenon** in winter.
• happening, occurrence, event, fact
❷ The six-year-old pianist was quite a
phenomenon.
• wonder, curiosity, marvel

phobia *NOUN*
see **fear**

phone *NOUN*
Is there a **phone** in the building?
• telephone
A portable phone is a **mobile phone** or **mobile**.
A phone that you use to access the Internet is
a **smartphone**.
A message left on a phone is **voicemail**.

phone *VERB*
He **phoned** to say that he'd be late.
• call, ring, telephone, dial

photograph *NOUN*
We're having our class **photograph** taken
today.
• photo, snap or snapshot, shot, picture
A photograph that you take of yourself on a
phone camera is a **selfie**.
A photograph that is printed on paper is a
print.
The art of taking photographs is **photography**.

photograph *VERB*
Dad **photographed** some birds in the
garden.
• take a picture of, shoot, snap

A
B
C
D
E
F
G
H
I
J
K
L
M
N
O
P
Q
R
S
T
U
V
W
X
Y
Z

WORD WEB

SOME OTHER TERMS USED IN PHOTOGRAPHY:

• aperture, digital camera, film, flash, focus, pinhole camera, pixel, shutter, viewfinder, wide-angle lens, zoom lens

phrase *NOUN*
'Bon voyage' is a French phrase meaning 'have a good journey'.
• expression, saying

phrase *VERB*
I tried to phrase my letter carefully.
• express, put into words

physical *ADJECTIVE*
❶ *There's a lot of physical contact in rugby.*
• bodily
Physical punishment is **corporal** punishment.
❷ *Ghosts have no physical presence.*
• earthly, material, solid, substantial

pick *VERB*
❶ *They've picked the players for the hockey team.*
• choose, select, decide on, settle on, opt for, single out
❷ *Irene picked some flowers from the garden.*
• gather, collect, cut
❸ *I picked an apple off the tree.*
• pluck, pull off, take
➤ **to pick up**
❶ *He was too weak to pick up the box.*
• lift, raise, hoist
❷ *I'll pick up some milk on the way home.*
• get, collect, fetch

picture *NOUN*
❶ *There's a picture of a pyramid in this book.*
• illustration, image, print
A picture which represents a particular person is a **portrait**.
A picture which represents the artist himself or herself is a **self-portrait**.
A picture which represents a group of objects is a **still life**.

A picture which represents a country scene is a **landscape**.
Pictures on a computer are **graphics**.
see also **painting, portrait**
❷ *Mum took some pictures of us building a sandcastle.*
• photo, photograph, snapshot, snap

picture *VERB*
❶ *The girl is pictured against a background of flowers.*
• depict, illustrate, represent, show, portray
❷ *Can you picture what the world will be like in 100 years?*
• imagine, visualize

picturesque *ADJECTIVE*
❶ *They stayed in a picturesque thatched cottage.*
• attractive, pretty, charming, quaint
OPPOSITE ugly
❷ *He wrote a picturesque account of his trip to Morocco.*
• colourful, descriptive, imaginative, expressive, lively, poetic, vivid

piece *NOUN*
❶ *They collected pieces of wood to build a raft.*
• bar, block, length, stick, chunk, lump, hunk, bit, chip, fragment, particle, scrap, shred
❷ *I've only got two pieces of chocolate left.*
• bit, portion, part, section, segment, share, slice
❸ *I always have a piece of fruit in my snack box.*
• item
A piece of clothing is an **article** of clothing.
❹ *I've lost one of the pieces of the jigsaw.*
• part, element, unit, component, constituent
❺ *There's a piece about our school in the local paper.*
• article, item, report, feature

pier *NOUN*
The passengers waited at the pier to board the ship.
• quay, wharf, jetty, landing stage

pierce *VERB*
The arrow had pierced the knight's armour.
• enter, go through, make a hole in, penetrate, bore through
To pierce a hole through paper is to **punch** a hole in it or **perforate** it.
To pierce a hole in a tyre is to **puncture** it.
To pierce someone with a spike is to **impale** or **spear** them.

piercing *ADJECTIVE*
I heard a piercing scream from inside the house.
• high-pitched, shrill, penetrating, loud, shattering, deafening, ear-splitting

pig *NOUN*
An old word for pigs is **swine**.
A wild pig is a **wild boar**.
A male pig is a **boar** or **hog**.
A female pig is a **sow**.
A young pig is a **piglet**.
A family of piglets is a **litter**.
The smallest piglet in a litter is the **runt**.

pile *NOUN*
❶ *Where did this pile of rubbish come from?*
• heap, mound, mountain, stack, hoard, mass, quantity, collection, assortment
❷ *(informal) I've still got piles of homework to do.*
• plenty, a lot, a great deal
(informal) lots, masses

pile *VERB*
Pile everything in the corner and we'll sort it out later.
• heap, stack, collect, gather, assemble, hoard
➤ **to pile up**
The bills are beginning to pile up.
• build up, mount up, accumulate

pill *NOUN*
Take one pill every four hours.
• tablet, capsule, pellet

pillar *NOUN*
The roof was supported by tall pillars.
• column, pier, post, prop, support

pillow *NOUN*
A long kind of pillow is a **bolster**.
A kind of pillow for a chair or sofa is a **cushion**.

pilot *VERB*
He piloted the hot-air balloon back to safety.
• fly, steer, guide, lead, navigate

pimple *NOUN*
The troll had a pimple on the end of his nose.
• spot, boil, swelling

pin *NOUN*
A decorative pin to wear is a **brooch**.
A pin to fix something on a noticeboard is a **drawing pin**.
A pin to fix clothing in place is a **safety pin**.

pinch *VERB*
❶ *The baby pinched my arm and wouldn't let go.*
• nip, squeeze, press, tweak, grip
❷ *(informal) Who's pinched my calculator?*
• steal, take, snatch, pilfer
(informal) nick, swipe, make off with

pine *VERB*
The dog pined when its owner died.
• mope, languish, sicken, waste away
➤ **to pine for**
She was pining for her old house by the sea.
• long for, yearn for, miss, crave, hanker after

pip *NOUN*
Make sure there are no pips in the lemon juice.
• seed

pipe *NOUN*
The water flows away along this pipe.
• tube
A pipe used for watering the garden is a **hose**.
A pipe in the street which supplies water for fighting fires is a **hydrant**.
A pipe which carries oil, etc., over long distances is a **pipeline**.
The system of water pipes in a house is the **plumbing**.

a b c d e f g h i j k l m n o **p** q r s t u v w x y z

A B C D E F G H I J K L M N O P Q R S T U V W X Y Z

pipe VERB
❶ *Water is piped from the reservoir to the town.*
• carry, convey, channel, funnel
❷ *She began to pipe a tune on her recorder.*
• play, blow, sound, whistle

pirate NOUN
The ship was overrun by bloodthirsty pirates.
• buccaneer, marauder

WORD WEB

THINGS YOU MIGHT FIND ON A PIRATE SHIP:

• barrels, cabin, crow's nest, deck,
hammock, lantern, mast, plank, pirate
flag, rigging, sail, treasure chest, wheel
A pirate flag is a **Jolly Roger** or
skull-and-crossbones.
A pirate ship might sail on the **high seas** or
the **Spanish Main**.
see also **boat**

PEOPLE YOU MIGHT FIND ON A PIRATE SHIP:

• cabin boy or girl, captain, captives, cook,
crew, first mate, lookout, stowaway

PIRATE TREASURE MIGHT CONTAIN:

• **doubloons** or **ducats, gold bullion, pieces
of eight**
Goods or treasure seized by pirates is **booty**.
see also **treasure**

WEAPONS A PIRATE MIGHT USE:

• **cannon, cutlass, dagger, gunpowder,
musket, pistol**
*Silver had two guns slung about him—one
before and one behind—besides the great
cutlass at his waist, and a pistol in each
pocket of his square-tailed coat.*—TREASURE
ISLAND, Robert Louis Stevenson

**OTHER THINGS A PIRATE MIGHT WEAR
OR CARRY:**

• **bandanna** or **kerchief, bottle of rum,
breeches, cocked hat, earrings, eye patch,
hook, parrot** or **cockatoo, pigtail,
sea chart, spyglass** or **telescope,
treasure map, wooden leg** or **peg leg**

SOME WORDS TO DESCRIBE A PIRATE:

• barbaric, bloodthirsty, cut-throat,
daring, dastardly, fearless, heartless,
lawless, merciless, murderous, pitiless,
ruthless, savage, swashbuckling, vengeful,
vicious, villainous

pit NOUN
❶ *They dug a deep pit to bury the treasure.*
• hole, crater, cavity, hollow, depression,
pothole, chasm, abyss
❷ *Coal used to be mined from the pits
in this area.*
• mine, coal mine, colliery, quarry

pitch NOUN
❶ *The pitch was waterlogged, so the match
was called off.*
• ground, field, playing field
❷ *She can sing at a very high pitch.*
• tone, frequency

pitch VERB
❶ *Hinna pitched the ball back over
the fence.*
• throw, toss, fling, hurl, sling, cast, lob
(informal) chuck
❷ *It was hard trying to pitch the tent
in the rain!*
• erect, put up, set up
❸ *He lost his balance and pitched headlong
into the water.*
• plunge, dive, drop, topple, plummet
❹ *The rowing boat pitched about in the
storm.*
• lurch, rock, roll, toss

pitfall NOUN
*The author described some of the pitfalls of
being famous.*
• difficulty, problem, hazard, danger, snag,
catch, trap

pitiful ADJECTIVE
❶ *We could hear pitiful cries for help.*
• sad, sorrowful, mournful, pathetic, plaintive,
heart-rending, moving, touching

② *The goalie made a pitiful attempt to stop the ball.*
• hopeless, useless, feeble, inadequate, incompetent, pathetic

pity NOUN
The pirates showed no pity towards the captives.
• mercy, compassion, sympathy, humanity, kindness, concern, feeling
OPPOSITE cruelty

➤ **a pity**
It's a pity that you have to leave so early.
• a shame, unfortunate, bad luck

pity VERB
We pitied anyone who was caught up in the storm.
• feel sorry for, feel for, sympathize with, take pity on

pivot NOUN
The point on which a lever turns is the **fulcrum.**
The point on which a spinning object turns is its **axis.**
The point on which a wheel turns is the axle or **hub.**

place NOUN
❶ *This is a good place to park.*
• site, venue, spot, location, position, situation
❷ *They are looking for a quiet place to live.*
• area, district, locality, neighbourhood, region, vicinity
❸ *Save me a place on the bus.*
• seat, space

place VERB
❶ *The hotel is placed next to the beach.*
• locate, situate, position, station
❷ *You can place your coats on the bed.*
• put down, set down, leave, deposit, lay
(informal) dump

placid ADJECTIVE
❶ *The dog has a placid nature and would make an ideal pet.*
• calm, composed, unexcitable, even-tempered
OPPOSITE excitable

② *The sea was placid at that time of the day.*
• calm, quiet, tranquil, peaceful, undisturbed, unruffled
OPPOSITE stormy

plague NOUN
❶ *Doctors worked hard to prevent the plague from spreading.*
• pestilence, epidemic, contagion, outbreak
❷ *There was a plague of wasps this summer.*
• invasion, infestation, swarm

plague VERB
❶ *Stop plaguing me with questions!*
• bother, pester, trouble, annoy, badger, harass
(informal) nag, bug
❷ *Celia has been plagued by bad luck recently.*
• afflict, beset, torment, hound

plain ADJECTIVE
❶ *The furniture in the room was very plain.*
• simple, modest, basic
OPPOSITE elaborate
❷ *Some people say he looks plain compared with his brother.*
• unattractive, ordinary
OPPOSITE attractive
❸ *It is plain to me that you are not interested.*
• clear, evident, obvious, apparent, unmistakable
OPPOSITE unclear
❹ *She told us what she thought in very plain terms.*
• direct, frank, blunt, outspoken, honest, sincere, straightforward
❺ *We need to wear a plain T-shirt for sports.*
• self-coloured

plain NOUN
A grassy plain in a hot country is called **savannah.**
The large plains of North America are the **prairies.**
The large plains of Russia are the **steppes.**

a b c d e f g h i j k l m n o p q r s t u v w x y z

A
B
C
D
E
F
G
H
I
J
K
L
M
N
O
P
Q
R
S
T
U
V
W
X
Y
Z

plan *NOUN*
❶ *The captain explained her plan to the rest of the team.*
• idea, proposal, scheme, strategy, project, suggestion, proposition
A plan to do something bad is a **plot**.
❷ *The committee looked at the plans for the new sports centre.*
• design, diagram, chart, map, drawing, blueprint

plan *VERB*
❶ *The outlaws planned an attack upon the sheriff.*
• scheme, design, devise, work out, formulate, prepare, organize
To plan to do something bad is to **plot**.
❷ *What do you plan to do next?*
• aim, intend, propose, mean

plane *NOUN*
see **aircraft**

planet *NOUN*
The new space probe will travel to distant planets.
• world

WORD WEB

THE PLANETS OF THE SOLAR SYSTEM (IN ORDER FROM THE SUN) ARE:

• Mercury, Venus, Earth, Mars, Jupiter, Saturn, Uranus, Neptune
The path followed by a planet is its **orbit**.
Minor planets orbiting the sun are **asteroids**.
Pluto is classified as a **dwarf planet**.
A planet, such as Jupiter or Saturn, that is made up of gases is a **gas giant**.
Something which orbits a planet is a **satellite**.
The earth's large satellite is the **Moon**.
see also **space**

WRITING TIPS

You can use these words to describe an alien planet:
• Earth-like, gaseous, inhospitable, uninhabitable, uninhabited

TO DESCRIBE ITS SURFACE:

• barren, desolate, dusty, frozen, icy, molten, rocky, volcanic

TO DESCRIBE ITS ATMOSPHERE OR AIR:

• airless, noxious, poisonous, thin, toxic, unbreathable

TO DESCRIBE ITS LIFE:

• beings, extraterrestrials, inhabitants, life forms
see also **alien**
On Uriel there had been the magnificent creatures. On Camazotz the inhabitants had at least resembled people. But what were these three strange things approaching?—A WRINKLE IN TIME, Madeleine L'Engle

plant *NOUN*

WORD WEB

SOME TYPES OF PLANT:

• algae, bush, cactus, cereal, evergreen, fern, flower, fungus, grass, herb, house plant, ivy, lichen, moss, pot plant, shrub, tree, vegetable, vine, weed, wildflower
see also **flower, fruit, herb, tree, vegetable**

PARTS OF VARIOUS PLANTS:

• bloom, blossom, branch, bud, flower, fruit, leaf, petal, pod, root, shoot, stalk, stem, trunk, twig
A young plant is a **seedling**.
A piece cut off a plant to form a new plant is a **cutting**.
A word for plants in general is **vegetation**.
A person who studies plants is a **botanist**.
A word meaning 'to do with plants' is **botanical**.

plant *VERB*
These seeds should be planted in the spring.
• sow, put in the ground
To move a plant from where it was growing and plant it somewhere else is to **transplant** it.

plaster *NOUN*
The nurse put a plaster on the cut.
• dressing, sticking plaster, bandage

plate *NOUN*
❶ *They piled our plates with food.*
for items of crockery see **crockery**
❷ *The robot's body was formed of metal plates.*
• panel, sheet
❸ *The book includes colour plates of various flowers.*
• illustration, photo, picture

platform *NOUN*
The conductor stood on a platform to address the audience.
• dais, podium, stage, stand

play *NOUN*
❶ *The school play this year is 'Peter Pan'.*
• drama, performance, production
❷ *It is important to balance work and play.*
• playing, recreation, amusement, fun, games, sport
for various games and sports see **game, sport**

play *VERB*
❶ *We went out to play after lunch.*
• amuse yourself, have fun, romp about
❷ *My sister loves playing basketball.*
• take part in, participate in, compete in
❸ *We're playing the home team next week.*
• compete against, oppose, challenge, take on
❹ *I'm learning to play the guitar.*
• perform on
❺ *Who will be playing Peter Pan?*
• act, take the part of, portray, represent

player *NOUN*
❶ *You need four players for this game.*
• contestant, participant, competitor
❷ *How many players are in the orchestra?*
• performer, instrumentalist, musician
Someone who plays music on their own is a **soloist**.
for various performers see **entertainer, music**

playful *ADJECTIVE*
The kittens were in a playful mood.
• lively, spirited, frisky, mischievous, roguish, impish, joking, teasing
OPPOSITE serious

playground *NOUN*
for playground games see **game**

playing field *NOUN*
There is a training session on the playing field tomorrow.
• ground, pitch, sports ground

play park *NOUN*
see **park**

plea *NOUN*
The king ignored the captives' plea for mercy.
• appeal, request, entreaty, petition

plead *VERB*
➤ **to plead with**
The children pleaded with the witch to let them go.
• beg, entreat, implore, appeal to, ask, request, petition

pleasant *ADJECTIVE*
❶ *The owner of the shop is always pleasant to us.*
• kind, friendly, likeable, charming, amiable, amicable, cheerful, genial, good-natured, good-humoured, approachable, hospitable, welcoming
❷ *We spent a very pleasant evening playing cards.*
• pleasing, enjoyable, agreeable, delightful, lovely, entertaining
❸ *The weather is quite pleasant today.*
• fine, mild, sunny, warm
OPPOSITE unpleasant

please *VERB*
❶ *I hope my present will please you.*
• give pleasure to, make happy, satisfy, delight, amuse, entertain
❷ *Do as you please.*
• want, wish

a
b
c
d
e
f
g
h
i
j
k
l
m
n
o
p
q
r
s
t
u
v
w
x
y
z

pleased *ADJECTIVE*
Why do you look so pleased today?
• contented, delighted, elated, glad, grateful, happy, satisfied, thankful, thrilled
OPPOSITE annoyed

pleasure *NOUN*
❶ *Mr Unnikrishnan gets a lot of pleasure from his garden.*
• delight, enjoyment, happiness, joy, satisfaction, comfort, contentment, gladness
Very great pleasure is **bliss** or **ecstasy**.
❷ *He talked about the pleasures of living in the country.*
• joy, comfort, delight

pleat *NOUN*
It takes ages to iron the pleats in the skirt.
• crease, fold, tuck

pledge *NOUN*
The knights swore a pledge of loyalty to the king.
• oath, vow, promise, word

plentiful *ADJECTIVE*
There is a plentiful supply of berries in the forest.
• abundant, ample, generous, inexhaustible, lavish, liberal, profuse
OPPOSITE scarce

plenty *NOUN*
Don't buy any milk—there's plenty in the fridge.
• a lot, a large amount, an abundance, a profusion
A lot more than you need is a **glut** or **surplus**.
OPPOSITE scarcity
➤ **plenty of**
We've still got plenty of time.
• a lot of, lots of, ample, abundant
(informal) loads of, masses of, tons of

plight *NOUN*
He was concerned about the plight of the homeless.
• predicament, trouble, difficulty, problem, dilemma

plod *VERB*
❶ *The hikers plodded on through the mud.*
• tramp, trudge, lumber
❷ *She's still plodding away at her violin lessons.*
• slog, labour, persevere

plot *NOUN*
❶ *Guy Fawkes was part of a plot against the government.*
• conspiracy, scheme, secret plan
❷ *It was hard to follow the plot of the film.*
• story, storyline, narrative, thread
for ways to describe a plot or storyline
see **writing**
❸ *They bought a plot of ground to build a new house.*
• area, piece, lot, patch
A plot of ground for growing flowers or vegetables is an **allotment**.
A large plot of land is a **tract** of land.

plot *VERB*
❶ *The gang were plotting a daring bank raid.*
• plan, devise, concoct, hatch
(informal) cook up
❷ *They were accused of plotting against the queen.*
• conspire, intrigue, scheme
❸ *The captain plotted the course of the ship.*
• chart, map, mark

plough *VERB*
❶ *Tractors are used to plough the fields.*
• cultivate, till, turn over
❷ *Are you still ploughing through that book?*
• wade, labour, toil

pluck *VERB*
❶ *They plucked the apples off the tree.*
• pick, pull off, gather, collect, harvest
❷ *A seagull plucked the sandwich out of her hand.*
• grab, seize, snatch, jerk, pull, tug, yank
❸ *The guitarist plucked the strings very gently.*
To run your finger or plectrum across the strings of a guitar is to **strum**.
To pluck the strings of a violin or cello is to play **pizzicato**.

plug *NOUN*
They removed the **plug** in the side of the barrel.
• stopper, cork, bung

plug *VERB*
❶ The plumber managed to **plug** the leak in the pipe.
• stop up, block, close, fill, seal, bung up
❷ (informal) We asked the local radio station to **plug** our concert.
• advertise, publicize, promote, push

plump *ADJECTIVE*
The goblin was short and **plump**, with pointy ears.
• chubby, dumpy, fat, tubby, podgy, round, stout, portly
OPPOSITE skinny

plunder *VERB*
Viking raiders **plundered** the village.
• loot, pillage, raid, ransack, rob, steal from

plunge *VERB*
❶ One by one, the girls **plunged** into the pool.
• dive, jump, leap, throw yourself
❷ As the wind died down, the kite **plunged** to the ground.
• drop, fall, pitch, tumble, plummet, swoop
❸ I **plunged** my hand in the cold water.
• dip, lower, sink, immerse, submerge
❹ Finn **plunged** his spear into the dragon's throat.
• thrust, stab, push, stick, shove, force

plural *ADJECTIVE*
OPPOSITE singular

poem *NOUN*
We each wrote a **poem** about the seaside.
• rhyme
Poems are **poetry** or **verse**.
A group of lines forming a section of a poem is a **stanza**.
A pair of rhyming lines within a poem is a **couplet**.
The rhythm of a poem is its **metre**.

WORD WEB

SOME KINDS OF POEM:

• ballad, concrete poem, elegy, epic, free verse, haiku, limerick, lyric, narrative poem, nonsense verse, nursery rhyme, ode, sonnet

poetic *ADJECTIVE*
The opening chapter is written in a **poetic** style.
• expressive, imaginative, lyrical, poetical
An uncomplimentary synonym is **flowery**.

point *NOUN*
❶ Be careful—that knife has a very sharp **point**.
• tip, end, spike, prong
❷ The stars looked like **points** of light in the sky.
• dot, spot, speck, fleck
❸ He marked on the map the exact **point** where the treasure lay.
• location, place, position, site
❹ At that **point** the rain started to come down.
• moment, instant, time
❺ I agree with your last **point**.
• idea, argument, thought
❻ Her sense of humour is one of her good **points**.
• characteristic, feature, attribute
❼ There is no **point** in phoning at this hour.
• purpose, reason, aim, object, use, usefulness
❽ I think I missed the **point** of that film.
• meaning, essence, core, gist

point *VERB*
❶ She **pointed** the way.
• draw attention to, indicate, point out, show, signal
❷ Can you **point** me in the right direction for the station?
• aim, direct, guide, lead, steer

a b c d e f g h i j k l m n o p q r s t u v w x y z

A
B
C
D
E
F
G
H
I
J
K
L
M
N
O
P
Q
R
S
T
U
V
W
X
Y
Z

pointless *ADJECTIVE*
It's pointless to argue with him—he's so stubborn.
• useless, futile, vain
OPPOSITE worthwhile

poise *NOUN*
The young actor showed great poise for her age.
• calmness, composure, assurance, self-confidence

poised *ADJECTIVE*
The jaguar was poised to pounce on its prey.
• ready, waiting, prepared, set

poison *NOUN*
A poison to kill plants is herbicide or weedkiller.
A poison to kill insects is insecticide or pesticide.
The poison in a snake bite is venom.
A substance which can save you from the effects of a poison is an antidote.

poisonous *ADJECTIVE*
Some of those mushrooms may be poisonous.
• toxic, venomous, deadly, lethal

poke *VERB*
Someone poked me in the back with an umbrella.
• prod, dig, jab, stab, thrust
➤ **to poke out**
The kitten's head was poking out of the basket.
• stick out, project, protrude

polar *ADJECTIVE*
The polar expedition will study birds and sea life.
• Antarctic or Arctic

WORD WEB

THINGS YOU MIGHT SEE IN POLAR REGIONS:

• glacier, iceberg, ice field or ice cap, moss, permafrost, pack ice, sheet ice, tundra
see also **ice**

SOME ANIMALS WHICH LIVE IN POLAR REGIONS:

• albatross, arctic fox, arctic tern, narwhal, penguin, polar bear, reindeer, seal, walrus, whale, wolf

THINGS A POLAR EXPLORER MIGHT USE:

• goggles, huskies, ice pick, kayak, mittens, parka, skis, ski pole, sledge, snowmobile, snowshoes

pole *NOUN*
Four poles marked the corners of the field.
• post, bar, rod, stick, shaft
A pole that you use when walking or as a weapon is a **staff.**
A pole for a flag to fly from is a **flagpole.**
A pole to support sails on a boat or ship is a **mast** or **spar.**
A pole with a pointed end to stick in the ground is a **stake.**
Poles which a circus entertainer walks on are **stilts.**

police officer *NOUN*
Several police officers were patrolling the football ground.
• policeman or policewoman, officer, constable
(informal) cop, copper
Police officers of higher rank are **sergeant, inspector** and **superintendent.**
The head of a police force is the **chief constable.**
Someone training for the police force is a **cadet.**
Someone who investigates crimes is a **detective.**
see also **detective**

policy *NOUN*
The leaflet explains the school's policy on bullying.
• approach, strategy, stance, plan of action

polish *VERB*
Beeswax is used to polish furniture.
• rub down, shine, buff, burnish, wax

> **to polish something off**
*The children **polished off** a whole plate
of sandwiches.*
• finish, get through, eat up

polish *NOUN*
*The silverware had been cleaned to give
it a good **polish**.*
• shine, sheen, gloss, lustre, sparkle,
brightness, glaze, finish

polished *ADJECTIVE*
❶ *She could see her face in the **polished**
surface.*
• shining, shiny, bright, glassy, gleaming,
glossy, lustrous
OPPOSITE dull, tarnished
❷ *The orchestra gave a **polished** performance.*
• accomplished, skilful, faultless, perfect,
well-prepared

polite *ADJECTIVE*
*The children are **polite** to visitors.*
• courteous, well-mannered, respectful, civil,
well-behaved, gracious, gentlemanly or
ladylike, chivalrous, gallant
OPPOSITE rude, impolite

politics *NOUN*

WORD WEB

SOME WORDS USED IN POLITICS:

• alliance, assembly, ballot, by-election,
cabinet, campaign, council, election,
first minister, government, left-wing,
lobby, majority, manifesto, minister, MP,
MSP, parliament, party, poll, president,
prime minister, referendum, right-wing,
senator, vote

poll *NOUN*
*The result of the **poll** has been declared.*
• election, vote, ballot
A vote on a particular question by all the
people in a country is a **referendum**.
An official survey to find out about the
population is a **census**.

pollute *VERB*
*The river has been **polluted** by chemicals.*
• contaminate, infect, poison

pompous *ADJECTIVE*
*The giant spoke in a rather **pompous** manner.*
• arrogant, self-important, haughty,
snobbish
(informal) stuck-up
OPPOSITE modest

pond *NOUN*
see **pool**

pool *NOUN*
❶ *The surface of the **pool** was covered with
frogspawn.*
• pond
A larger area of water is a **lake** or (in Scotland)
a **loch**.
A small shallow area of water is a **puddle**.
A pool of water in the desert is an **oasis**.
A pool among rocks on a seashore is a **rock pool**.
❷ *The sports centre has an indoor and an
outdoor **pool**.*
• swimming pool, swimming baths
A public open-air swimming pool is a **lido**.

poor *ADJECTIVE*
❶ *You can't afford luxuries if you're **poor**.*
• impoverished, poverty-stricken, penniless,
needy, badly off, hard up
OPPOSITE rich
❷ *His handwriting is very **poor**.*
• bad, inferior, inadequate, incompetent,
unsatisfactory, shoddy, weak, worthless
OPPOSITE good, superior
❸ *They pitied the **poor** animals standing in
the rain.*
• unlucky, unfortunate, pitiful,
wretched
OPPOSITE lucky

poorly *ADJECTIVE*
*He stayed at home because he felt **poorly**.*
• ill, sick, unwell, unfit
OPPOSITE well

a
b
c
d
e
f
g
h
i
j
k
l
m
n
o
p
q
r
s
t
u
v
w
x
y
z

A
B
C
D
E
F
G
H
I
J
K
L
M
N
O
P
Q
R
S
T
U
V
W
X
Y
Z

pop *NOUN, VERB*
for various sounds see **sound**

popular *ADJECTIVE*
❶ *Disney has made a lot of popular children's films.*
• well-liked, well-loved, celebrated, favourite
OPPOSITE unpopular
❷ *Rollerblades are very popular just now.*
• fashionable, widespread, current, in demand
(informal) trendy
OPPOSITE unpopular

population *NOUN*
About ten per cent of the world's population is left-handed.
• inhabitants, residents, occupants, citizens, people, community

pore *VERB*
➤ **to pore over**
The detective pored over the evidence on his desk.
• examine, study, inspect, look closely at, scrutinize

port *NOUN*
A large cruise ship sailed into the port.
• harbour, dock, anchorage
A harbour for yachts and pleasure boats is a **marina**.

portable *ADJECTIVE*
We bought a portable picnic table.
• transportable, mobile, compact, lightweight
A portable phone is a **mobile phone** or **mobile**.
A portable computer is a **laptop** or **notebook**.

portion *NOUN*
Violet asked for a large portion of trifle.
• helping, serving, ration, share, quantity, piece, part, bit, slice

portrait *NOUN*
There's a portrait of the Queen on every stamp.
• picture, image, likeness, representation
A portrait which shows a side view of someone is a **profile**.
A portrait which shows just the outline of someone is a **silhouette**.
A portrait which exaggerates some aspect of a person is a **caricature**.

portray *VERB*
The film portrays life in Victorian England.
• depict, represent, show, describe, illustrate

pose *VERB*
The film star posed in front of the camera.
• model, sit
➤ **to pose as someone**
The spy posed as a newspaper reporter.
• impersonate, pretend to be, pass yourself off as

posh *ADJECTIVE*
We went to a posh restaurant for a treat.
• smart, stylish, high-class, elegant, fashionable, up-market, luxurious, luxury, de luxe, plush
(informal) classy, swanky, swish, snazzy

position *NOUN*
❶ *Mark the position on the map.*
• location, place, point, spot, site, whereabouts
❷ *He shifted his position to avoid getting cramp.*
• pose, posture, stance
❸ *Losing all her money put her in a difficult position.*
• situation, state, condition, circumstances
❹ *A referee should adopt a neutral position.*
• opinion, attitude, outlook, view
❺ *Being a head teacher is an important position.*
• job, post, appointment, function

positive ADJECTIVE
❶ *The detective was positive that the cook was lying.*
• certain, sure, convinced, assured, confident
OPPOSITE uncertain
❷ *Miss Andrews made some positive comments on my singing.*
• helpful, useful, worthwhile, beneficial, constructive
OPPOSITE negative

possess VERB
❶ *They don't possess a computer.*
• have, own
❷ *What possessed you to take up diving?*
• make you think of, come over you

possessions PLURAL NOUN
They lost all of their possessions in the flood.
• belongings, goods, property

possibility NOUN
There's a possibility that it may rain later.
• chance, likelihood, danger, risk

possible ADJECTIVE
❶ *Is it possible that life exists on other planets?*
• likely, probable, conceivable, credible
❷ *It wasn't possible to shift the piano.*
• feasible, practicable, practical
OPPOSITE impossible

possibly ADVERB
'Will you finish your homework today?' 'Possibly.'
• maybe, perhaps

post NOUN
❶ *The farmer put up some posts for a new fence.*
• pole, pillar, shaft, stake, support, prop
❷ *The post was delivered late.*
• mail, letters, delivery
❸ *Are you thinking of applying for the post?*
• job, position, situation, appointment, vacancy

post VERB
❶ *Did you post those letters?*
• mail, send, dispatch
❷ *The names of the winners will be posted on the noticeboard.*
• display, put up, announce, advertise

poster NOUN
We saw a poster about a missing cat.
• advertisement, announcement, bill, notice, sign, placard

postpone VERB
The match was postponed because of bad weather.
• put off, defer, delay
To stop a meeting or game that you intend to start again later is to **adjourn** or **suspend** it.

pot NOUN
On the table were little pots of jam and honey.
• jar, dish, bowl, pan

potent ADJECTIVE
❶ *The magic potion is very potent, so you only need a single drop.*
• strong, powerful, intoxicating, pungent, heady
❷ *She persuaded us with her potent arguments.*
• effective, forceful, strong, compelling
OPPOSITE weak

potential ADJECTIVE
❶ *He's a potential champion.*
• budding, future, likely, possible, probable, promising
❷ *These floods are a potential disaster for the farmers.*
• looming, threatening

potion NOUN
A magic potion was brewing in the wizard's cauldron.
• drug, medicine, mixture

a b c d e f g h i j k l m n o **p** q r s t u v w x y z

A B C D E F G H I J K L M N O P Q R S T U V W X Y Z

pottery *NOUN*

WORD WEB

Someone who creates pottery is a **potter**.
A formal word for pottery is **ceramics**.

TYPES OF POTTERY:

• bone china, china, earthenware, porcelain, stoneware, terracotta
The kind of pottery we eat and drink from is **crockery**.

pouch *NOUN*
The pirate kept his gunpowder in a leather pouch.
• bag, purse, sack

poultry *NOUN*

WORD WEB

KINDS OF POULTRY:

• bantam, chicken, duck, fowl, goose, guinea fowl, hen, pullet, turkey
A male chicken specially fattened for eating is a **capon**.

pounce *VERB*
➤ **to pounce on**
The cat pounced on the mouse.
• jump on, leap on, spring on, swoop down on, lunge at, ambush, attack

pound *VERB*
Huge waves pounded the stranded ship.
• beat, hit, batter, smash
To pound something hard until it is powder is to **crush**, **grind** or **pulverize** it.
To pound something soft is to **knead**, **mash** or **pulp** it.

pour *VERB*
❶ *Water poured through the hole.*
• flow, run, gush, stream, spill, spout
❷ *I poured some milk into my cup.*
• tip, serve

poverty *NOUN*
Many of the townspeople were living in poverty.
• pennilessness, hardship, need, want
Extreme poverty is **abject poverty**.
OPPOSITE wealth

powder *NOUN*
The fairy sprinkled some magic powder in the air.
• dust, particles

powdery *ADJECTIVE*
The wind blew the powdery soil away.
• dusty, fine, loose, grainy, sandy

power *NOUN*
❶ *The crowds were amazed by the power of the robot.*
• strength, force, might, energy
❷ *The storyteller has the power to enthral an audience.*
• skill, talent, ability, competence
❸ *A policeman has the power to arrest someone.*
• authority, right
❹ *The empress had power over all the people.*
• authority, command, control, dominance, domination

powerful *ADJECTIVE*
❶ *Sir Joustalot was the most powerful knight in the kingdom.*
• influential, leading, commanding, dominant, high-powered
❷ *The wrestler had a powerful punch.*
• strong, forceful, hard, mighty, vigorous, formidable, potent
❸ *He used some powerful arguments.*
• strong, convincing, effective, persuasive, impressive
OPPOSITE weak

powerless *ADJECTIVE*
The good witch was powerless to undo the spell. .
• helpless, ineffective, weak, feeble, defenceless

practical ADJECTIVE
❶ *I'll ask Katie what to do—she is always very practical.*
• down-to-earth, matter-of-fact, sensible, level-headed
OPPOSITE impractical
❷ *The robbers' plan was not very practical.*
• workable, realistic, sensible, feasible, viable, achievable
OPPOSITE impractical
❸ *Do you have any practical experience of child-minding?*
• real, actual, hands-on
OPPOSITE theoretical

practically ADVERB
Keep going—we're practically there!
• almost, just about, nearly, virtually

practice NOUN
❶ *We have extra hockey practice this week.*
• training, exercises, preparation, rehearsal, drill
❷ *Is it the practice amongst ogres to eat grubs for breakfast?*
• custom, habit, convention, routine
➤ **in practice**
What will the plan involve in practice?
• in effect, in reality, actually, really

practise VERB
❶ *My piano teacher asked me to practise for longer.*
• do exercises, rehearse, train, drill
To practise just before the start of a performance is to **warm up**.
❷ *My sister wants to practise veterinary medicine.*
• do, perform, carry out, put into practice, follow, pursue, work in

praise VERB
The critics praised the actress for her outstanding performance.
• commend, applaud, admire, compliment, congratulate, pay tribute to
(informal) rave about
OPPOSITE criticize

praise NOUN
He received a lot of praise for his painting.
• approval, admiration, compliments, congratulations, applause

prance VERB
Milly started prancing about in a silly way.
• dance, skip, hop, leap, romp, cavort, caper, frolic, gambol

precarious ADJECTIVE
❶ *The diver was in a precarious situation, surrounded by sharks.*
• dangerous, perilous, risky
OPPOSITE safe
❷ *Take care—that ladder looks precarious!*
• unsafe, unstable, unsteady, insecure, shaky, wobbly, rickety
OPPOSITE secure

precede VERB
A fireworks display preceded the concert.
• come before, go before, lead
OPPOSITE follow, succeed

precious ADJECTIVE
❶ *Her most precious possession was an old photograph.*
• treasured, cherished, valued, prized, dearest, beloved
❷ *The throne glittered with precious gems and gold.*
• valuable, costly, expensive, priceless
for precious stones see **jewel**
OPPOSITE worthless

precise ADJECTIVE
❶ *Can you tell me the precise time, please?*
• exact, accurate, correct, true, right
OPPOSITE rough
❷ *The map gave precise directions for finding the treasure.*
• careful, detailed, specific, particular, definite
OPPOSITE vague

a b c d e f g h i j k l m n o p q r s t u v w x y z

A
B
C
D
E
F
G
H
I
J
K
L
M
N
O
P
Q
R
S
T
U
V
W
X
Y
Z

predict *VERB*
*You can't **predict** what may happen in the future.*
• forecast, foresee, foretell, prophesy

predictable *ADJECTIVE*
*It was **predictable** that it would rain.*
• expected, foreseeable, likely, probable
[OPPOSITE] unpredictable

preface *NOUN*
*The story behind the book is explained in the **preface**.*
• introduction, prologue

prefer *VERB*
*Would you **prefer** juice or lemonade?*
• rather have, go for, opt for, plump for, choose, fancy

preferable *ADJECTIVE*
➤ **preferable to**
*She finds country life **preferable to** living in the city.*
• better than, superior to, more attractive than, more suitable than

preference *NOUN*
❶ *Sandy has a **preference** for sweet things.*
• liking, fancy, inclination
❷ *My **preference** is to walk rather than take the bus.*
• choice, option, selection, pick, wish

prefix *NOUN*
[OPPOSITE] suffix

pregnant *ADJECTIVE*
*One of the giraffes in the zoo is **pregnant**.*
• expecting a baby, carrying a baby
(informal) expecting
A pregnant woman is an expectant mother.

prehistoric *ADJECTIVE*

WORD WEB

PREHISTORIC REMAINS YOU MIGHT VISIT:

• barrow or tumulus, cromlech or stone circle, dolmen, hill fort, menhir or standing stone
A person who studies prehistory by excavating and analysing remains is an archaeologist.

NAMES OF PREHISTORIC PERIODS:

The best tools and weapons were made of stone in the **Stone Age**, of bronze in the **Bronze Age**, and of iron in the **Iron Age**. Formal names for the Old, Middle and New Stone Ages are **Palaeolithic**, **Mesolithic** and **Neolithic** periods.
Prehistoric people who lived during the Stone Age were **Neanderthals**.
Most of the earth's surface was covered with ice in the **Ice Age**.
see also **cave**

SOME PREHISTORIC ANIMALS:

• cave bear, dinosaur, glyptodont, ground sloth, sabre-toothed cat or smilodon, sabre-toothed squirrel, woolly mammoth, woolly rhinoceros
A person who studies fossils of prehistoric life is a **palaeontologist**.
see also **dinosaur**

prejudice *NOUN*
*The school does not tolerate any form of **prejudice**.*
• bias, discrimination, intolerance, narrow-mindedness, bigotry
Prejudice against other races is **racism**.
Prejudice against other nations is **xenophobia**.
Prejudice against people because of their sex is **sexism**.
[OPPOSITE] fairness, tolerance

preliminary *ADJECTIVE*
*They were knocked out in the **preliminary** round of the competition.*
• first, initial, introductory, early, opening, preparatory

prelude *NOUN*
see **introduction**

premises *PLURAL NOUN*
*Keep out—these are private **premises**.*
• buildings, property, grounds

preoccupied *ADJECTIVE*
➤ **preoccupied with something**
*She was so **preoccupied** with her work that she forgot the time.*
• absorbed in, engrossed in, wrapped up in, intent on, obsessed with

prepare *VERB*
*The museum staff are **preparing** for the new exhibition.*
• get ready, make arrangements for, organize, plan, set up
To prepare for a play is to **rehearse**.
To prepare to take part in a sport is to **train**.

prepared *ADJECTIVE*
*The knights were **prepared** to fight for the Queen.*
• be able, be ready, be willing

presence *NOUN*
*Your **presence** is required upstairs.*
• attendance

present *ADJECTIVE (say* prez-ent*)*
❶ *Is everyone **present**?*
• here, in attendance, at hand
❷ *Who is the **present** world chess champion?*
• current, existing

present *NOUN (say* prez-ent*)*
*What would you like for your birthday **present**?*
• gift
(informal) prezzie

present *VERB (say* pri-zent*)*
❶ *The head **presents** the prizes on sports day.*
• award, hand over
❷ *Our class is **presenting** a play about the Vikings.*
• put on, perform, stage, mount
❸ *Dr Smart **presented** her amazing invention to the world.*
• put forward, show, display, exhibit, make known

preserve *VERB*
❶ *It's more difficult to **preserve** food in hot weather.*
• keep, save, store
❷ *It's important to **preserve** wildlife.*
• look after, protect, conserve, defend, safeguard, maintain

press *VERB*
❶ ***Press** the fruit through a sieve to get rid of the seeds.*
• push, force, squeeze, squash, crush, shove, cram, compress
❷ *He **pressed** his shirt for the party.*
• iron, flatten, smooth
❸ *Our friends **pressed** us to stay a bit longer.*
• beg, urge, entreat, implore

press *NOUN*
❶ *We read about the competition in the **press**.*
• newspapers, magazines
❷ *The **press** came to the opening of the new arts centre.*
• journalists, reporters, the media

pressure *NOUN*
❶ *The nurse applied **pressure** to the wound.*
• force, compression, squeezing, weight, load
❷ *In the final, the home team were under a lot of **pressure**.*
• stress, strain, tension

prestige *NOUN*
*There's a lot of **prestige** in winning an Olympic medal.*
• credit, glory, fame, honour, renown, distinction, status, kudos

a
b
c
d
e
f
g
h
i
j
k
l
m
n
o
p
q
r
s
t
u
v
w
x
y
z

A
B
C
D
E
F
G
H
I
J
K
L
M
N
O
P
Q
R
S
T
U
V
W
X
Y
Z

presume *VERB*
❶ *I presume you'd like something to eat.*
• assume, take it, imagine, suppose, think, believe, guess
❷ *He wouldn't presume to tell her what to do!*
• be bold enough, dare, venture

pretend *VERB*
She's not really crying—she's only pretending.
• put on an act, bluff, fake, sham, pose
(informal) kid, put it on

pretend *ADJECTIVE*
That's not a real spider—it's just a pretend one!
• fake, false, artificial, made-up
OPPOSITE real

pretty *ADJECTIVE*
The doll was dressed in a pretty blue outfit.
• attractive, beautiful, lovely, nice, pleasing, charming, dainty, picturesque, quaint
(informal) cute
A common simile is **as pretty as a picture.**
OPPOSITE ugly

prevent *VERB*
❶ *The driver could do nothing to prevent the accident.*
• stop, avert, avoid, head off
❷ *The police prevented an attempted bank raid.*
• block, foil, frustrate, thwart
❸ *There's not much you can do to prevent colds.*
• stave off, ward off

previous *ADJECTIVE*
❶ *The couple had met on a previous occasion.*
• earlier, former, preceding, prior
❷ *The previous owners of the house have gone abroad.*
• former
OPPOSITE subsequent

prey *NOUN*
The lion killed its prey.
• quarry, victim

prey *VERB*
➤ **to prey on**
Owls prey on small animals.
• hunt, kill, feed on

price *NOUN*
What is the price of a return ticket to Sydney?
• cost, amount, figure, expense, payment, sum, charge, rate
The price you pay for a journey on public transport is the **fare.**
The price you pay to send a letter is the **postage.**
The price you pay to use a private road, bridge or tunnel is a **toll.**

priceless *ADJECTIVE*
❶ *The museum contained many priceless antiques.*
• precious, rare, valuable, costly, expensive, dear
❷ *(informal) The joke she told was priceless.*
• funny, amusing, comic, hilarious, witty

prick *VERB*
Jamie burst the balloon by pricking it with a pin.
• pierce, puncture, stab, jab, perforate

prickle *NOUN*
A hedgehog uses its prickles for defence.
• spike, spine, needle, barb, thorn
The prickles on a hedgehog or porcupine are also called **quills.**

prickly *ADJECTIVE*
Holly leaves are very prickly.
• spiky, spiny, thorny, bristly, sharp, scratchy

pride *NOUN*
❶ *Mrs Reyes takes great pride in her garden.*
• satisfaction, pleasure, delight
❷ *The medal winner was a source of great pride to his family.*
• self-esteem, self-respect, dignity, honour
❸ *Pride comes before a fall.*
• arrogance, conceit, big-headedness, vanity, snobbery
OPPOSITE humility

priest NOUN

*The **priest** conducted the wedding ceremony.*
• minister, vicar, pastor, padre
A Buddhist religious leader is a **lama**.
A Hindu or Sikh religious leader is a **guru**.
A Jewish religious leader is a **rabbi**.
A Muslim religious leader is an **imam**.
An ancient Celtic priest was a **Druid**.

prim ADJECTIVE

*Aunt Jemima is always very **prim** and proper.*
• prudish, strait-laced, formal, demure

primarily ADVERB

*The website is aimed **primarily** at teenagers.*
• chiefly, especially, mainly, mostly, predominantly, principally, above all

primary ADJECTIVE

*Their **primary** aim was to win the match.*
• main, chief, principal, foremost, major, most important, top, prime
for primary colours see **colour**

prime ADJECTIVE

❶ *The penguins' **prime** concern is to protect their chicks.*
see also **primary**
❷ *The dish is made with **prime** cuts of meat.*
• best, superior, first-class, choice, select, top

primitive ADJECTIVE

❶ *__Primitive__ humans were hunters rather than farmers.*
• ancient, early, prehistoric, primeval
OPPOSITE civilized
❷ *These days steam engines seem very primitive.*
• crude, basic, simple, rudimentary, undeveloped
OPPOSITE advanced

prince and princess NOUN

see **royalty**

principal ADJECTIVE

*The **principal** aim of the race is to raise money for charity.*
• main, chief, primary, foremost, most important, leading, major, dominant, fundamental, supreme, top

principle NOUN

*Both teams agreed to follow the **principles** of fair play.*
• rule, standard, code, ethic

print NOUN

❶ *He found the tiny **print** difficult to read.*
• lettering, letters, printing, type, characters
❷ *The detective searched the building for prints.*
• mark, impression, footprint, fingerprint
❸ *Is that a **print** or an original painting?*
• copy, reproduction, duplicate

priority NOUN

*Traffic on the main road has **priority**.*
• precedence, right of way

prise VERB

*She tried to **prise** the lid off the treasure chest.*
• lever, force, wrench

prison NOUN

*She was sentenced to six months in **prison**.*
• jail, imprisonment, confinement

prisoner NOUN

*The **prisoner** tried to escape from jail.*
• convict, captive, inmate
A person who is held prisoner until a demand is met is a **hostage**.

private ADJECTIVE

❶ *Everything I write in my diary is **private**.*
• secret, confidential, personal, intimate
Secret official documents are **classified** documents.
❷ *Can we go somewhere a little more private?*
• quiet, secluded, hidden, concealed
OPPOSITE public

privilege *NOUN*
Club members enjoy special privileges.
• advantage, benefit, concession, right

privileged *ADJECTIVE*
She comes from a privileged family background.
• advantaged, wealthy, fortunate, affluent, prosperous

prize *NOUN*
Our team won first prize in the relay race.
• award, reward, trophy
Money that you win as a prize is your **winnings**.
Prize money that keeps increasing until someone wins it is a **jackpot**.

prize *VERB*
Chrissie prized her grandmother's ring above all else.
• treasure, value, cherish, hold dear, esteem, revere
OPPOSITE dislike

probable *ADJECTIVE*
A burst pipe was the most probable cause of the flood.
• likely, feasible, possible, predictable, expected
OPPOSITE improbable

probe *VERB*
❶ *The submarine can probe the depths of the ocean.*
• explore, penetrate, see into, plumb
❷ *Detectives probed the circumstances surrounding the crime.*
• investigate, inquire into, look into, examine, study

problem *NOUN*
❶ *Our maths teacher set us a difficult problem.*
• puzzle, question
(informal) brain-teaser, poser
❷ *I'm having a problem with my computer.*
• difficulty, trouble, snag, worry
(informal) headache

procedure *NOUN*
The recipe explains the procedure for making bread.
• method, process, system, technique, way
A procedure which you follow regularly is a **routine**.

proceed *VERB*
❶ *The sheep proceeded slowly along the path.*
• go on, advance, move forward, progress
❷ *We advised them not to proceed with their plan.*
• go ahead, carry on

proceedings *PLURAL NOUN*
A thunderstorm interrupted the day's proceedings.
• events, happenings, activities, affairs
(informal) goings-on

proceeds *PLURAL NOUN*
The committee added up the proceeds from the jumble sale.
• income, takings, money, earnings, profit

process *NOUN*
The inventor showed us a new process for creating electricity.
• method, procedure, operation, system, technique

process *VERB*
The dairy processes milk to make butter and cheese.
• deal with, prepare, treat, refine, transform

procession *NOUN*
The procession made its way slowly down the hill.
• parade, march, column, line

proclaim *VERB*
The judges proclaimed that the winner was disqualified.
• declare, announce, pronounce

prod *VERB*
Someone prodded me in the back with an umbrella.
• poke, dig, jab, nudge, push

produce VERB
❶ *Some lorries **produce** a lot of fumes.*
• create, generate, cause, give rise to
❷ *The tree **produced** a good crop of apples this year.*
• yield, grow
❸ *The factory **produces** cars and vans.*
• make, manufacture, construct
❹ *The referee's decision **produced** cheers from the crowd.*
• provoke, result in, arouse, stimulate
❺ *The writers have **produced** an award-winning comedy.*
• compose, invent, think up
❻ *The magician **produced** a rabbit from his hat.*
• bring out, present, reveal

produce NOUN
*The shop sells organic **produce**.*
• food, crops, fruit and vegetables

product NOUN
❶ *The company launched a new range of beauty **products**.*
• item, article, substance
❷ *The famine is the **product** of years of drought.*
• result, consequence, outcome, upshot

production NOUN
❶ ***Production** at the factory has increased this year.*
• output
❷ *We went to see a **production** of 'The Sound of Music'.*
• performance, show

productive ADJECTIVE
❶ *The soil here is rich and **productive**.*
• fertile, fruitful
❷ *It wasn't a very **productive** meeting.*
• useful, valuable, worthwhile, constructive, profitable, fruitful
OPPOSITE unproductive

profession NOUN
*Nursing is a worthwhile **profession**.*
• career, job, occupation, work, employment, business

professional ADJECTIVE
❶ *The plans were drawn by a **professional** architect.*
• qualified, skilled, trained, experienced
❷ *This is a very **professional** piece of work.*
• skilled, expert, proficient, competent, efficient
OPPOSITE incompetent
❸ *His ambition is to be a **professional** footballer.*
• paid, full-time
OPPOSITE amateur

proficient ADJECTIVE
*Olga is a **proficient** tap dancer.*
• skilful, skilled, accomplished, capable, expert, able
OPPOSITE incompetent

profile NOUN
see portrait

profit NOUN
*They sold the business and bought a yacht with the **profit**.*
• gain, surplus, excess
The extra money you get on your savings is interest.
OPPOSITE loss

programme NOUN
❶ *We worked out a **programme** for sports day.*
• plan, schedule, timetable
A list of things to be done at a meeting is an agenda.
❷ *There was a really good **programme** on TV last night.*
• broadcast, show, production, transmission

progress NOUN
❶ *I traced their **progress** on the map.*
• journey, route, movement, travels
❷ *I'm not making much **progress** learning Dutch.*
• advance, development, growth, improvement, headway
An important piece of progress is a breakthrough.

a b c d e f g h i j k l m n o **p** q r s t u v w x y z

progress *VERB*
Work on the new building is progressing well.
• proceed, advance, move forward, make progress, make headway, continue, develop, improve
(informal) come along

prohibit *VERB*
Skateboarding is prohibited in the school grounds.
• ban, forbid, outlaw, rule out, veto
OPPOSITE permit, allow

project *NOUN*
❶ *We did a history project on the Victorians.*
• activity, task, assignment, piece of research
❷ *There is a project to create a bird sanctuary in the area.*
• plan, proposal, scheme

project *VERB*
❶ *A narrow ledge projects from the cliff.*
• extend, protrude, stick out, jut out, overhang
❷ *The lighthouse projects a beam of light.*
• cast, shine, throw out

prolong *VERB*
Our guests prolonged their visit by a few days.
• extend, lengthen, make longer, stretch out, draw out
OPPOSITE shorten

prominent *ADJECTIVE*
❶ *The clown had a very prominent nose.*
• noticeable, conspicuous, obvious, striking, eye-catching
OPPOSITE inconspicuous
❷ *He is a prominent Hollywood actor.*
• well-known, famous, celebrated, major, leading, notable, distinguished, eminent
OPPOSITE unknown

promise *NOUN*
❶ *We had promises of help from many people.*
• assurance, pledge, guarantee, commitment, vow, oath, word of honour
❷ *That young pianist shows promise.*
• potential, talent

promise *VERB*
Mum and Dad promised that we'd go camping this summer.
• assure someone, give your word, guarantee, swear, take an oath, vow

promising *ADJECTIVE*
❶ *The weather looks promising for tomorrow.*
• encouraging, hopeful
❷ *Sheena is a promising young singer.*
• bright, talented, gifted, budding
(informal) up-and-coming

promote *VERB*
❶ *Gareth has been promoted to captain.*
• move up, advance, upgrade, elevate
❷ *The singer is here to promote her new album.*
• advertise, publicize, market, push, sell
(informal) plug
❸ *The school is trying to promote healthy eating.*
• encourage, foster, advocate, back, support

prompt *ADJECTIVE*
I received a prompt reply to my email.
• punctual, quick, rapid, swift, immediate, instant
OPPOSITE delayed

prompt *VERB*
Having a dog prompted her to take more exercise.
• cause, lead, induce, motivate, stimulate, encourage, provoke

prone *ADJECTIVE*
❶ *The victim was lying prone on the floor.*
• face down, on the front
To lie face upwards is to be **supine**.
❷ *He is prone to exaggerate his health problems.*
• inclined, apt, liable, likely

pronounce *VERB*
❶ *Try to pronounce the words clearly.*
• say, speak, utter, articulate, sound
❷ *The doctor pronounced her fully recovered.*
• declare, announce, proclaim, judge

pronounced *ADJECTIVE*
*She spoke with a **pronounced** Australian accent.*
• clear, marked, distinct, definite, noticeable, obvious, striking, unmistakable, prominent
OPPOSITE imperceptible

proof *NOUN*
*There is no **proof** that he is a secret agent.*
• evidence, confirmation

prop *NOUN*
*The bridge is supported by steel **props**.*
• support, strut
A stick to prop yourself on when you hurt a leg is a **crutch**.
Part of a building which props up a wall is a **buttress**.

prop *VERB*
*Kenny **propped** his bike against the kerb.*
• lean, rest, stand

➤ **to prop something up**
*The shelf was **propped up** with sticks of wood.*
• support, hold up, reinforce

propel *VERB*
*The steamboat was **propelled** by a huge paddle wheel.*
• drive forward, push forward, power, impel

proper *ADJECTIVE*
❶ *The nurse showed them the **proper** way to tie a bandage.*
• correct, right, accurate, precise, true, genuine
OPPOSITE wrong, incorrect
❷ *It's only **proper** that he should pay for the broken window.*
• fair, just, fitting, appropriate, deserved, suitable
OPPOSITE inappropriate
❸ *It's not **proper** to speak with your mouth full.*
• decent, respectable, tasteful
OPPOSITE rude
❹ *(informal) I looked a **proper** idiot wearing two different socks!*
• complete, total, utter, absolute, thorough

property *NOUN*
❶ *This office deals with lost **property**.*
• belongings, possessions, goods
❷ *The website lists **property** that is for sale in the city.*
• buildings, houses, land, premises
❸ *Many herbs have healing **properties**.*
• quality, characteristic, feature, attribute, trait

prophecy *NOUN*
*The witch's **prophecy** came true.*
• prediction, forecast

prophesy *VERB*
*The witch **prophesied** that there would be a great battle.*
• predict, forecast, foresee, foretell

proportion *NOUN*
❶ *A large **proportion** of wild elephants live on nature reserves.*
• part, section, share, fraction
❷ *What is the **proportion** of girls to boys in your class?*
• balance, ratio

➤ **proportions**
*The dining hall was a room of large **proportions**.*
• measurements, size, dimensions

proposal *NOUN*
*What do you think of the **proposal** to build a skate park?*
• plan, project, scheme, suggestion, recommendation

propose *VERB*
❶ *He **proposed** a change in the rules.*
• suggest, ask for, recommend
❷ *How do you **propose** to pay for the holiday?*
• intend, mean, plan, aim
❸ *The class **proposed** two pupils to represent them on the school council.*
• nominate, put forward

a b c d e f g h i j k l m n o p q r s t u v w x y z

proprietor *NOUN*
*Who is the **proprietor** of the
bicycle shop?*
• manager, owner
(informal) boss

prosecute *VERB*
*Anyone caught shoplifting will be **prosecuted**.*
• bring to trial, charge, take to court
To take someone to court to try to get money
from them is to **sue** them.

prospect *NOUN*
❶ *What are their **prospects** of winning
the tournament?*
• chance, hope, expectation, likelihood,
possibility, probability
❷ *The hotel has a lovely **prospect** across
the valley.*
• outlook, view, vista

prosper *VERB*
*We expect our business to **prosper**
this year.*
• do well, be successful, flourish, succeed,
thrive, grow, boom
OPPOSITE fail

prosperity *NOUN*
*Tourism has brought **prosperity** to the region.*
• wealth, affluence, growth, success
(informal) boom

prosperous *ADJECTIVE*
*She is a very **prosperous** architect.*
• wealthy, rich, well-off, well-to-do, affluent,
successful, thriving
OPPOSITE poor

protect *VERB*
❶ *A sentry was posted outside to **protect**
the palace.*
• defend, guard, safeguard, keep safe,
secure
❷ *I wore a hat to **protect** myself from the sun.*
• shield, shade, screen, insulate

protection *NOUN*
*The waterproof hood gives **protection** from
the rain.*
• shelter, cover, defence, insulation

protest *NOUN*
❶ *There were **protests** at the plan to close
the cinema.*
• complaint, objection
A general protest is an **outcry**.
❷ *Some streets will be closed for a **protest**
in the city centre.*
• demonstration, march, rally
(informal) demo

protest *VERB*
*We wrote a letter **protesting** about the
closure of the cinema.*
• complain, make a protest, object (to),
take exception (to), express disapproval (of)

protrude *VERB*
*His stomach **protrudes** above his
waistband.*
• stick out, poke out, bulge, swell, project,
stand out, jut out

proud *ADJECTIVE*
❶ *Comfort's father was very **proud** when she
passed her music exam.*
• delighted (with), pleased (with)
A common simile is **as proud as
a peacock**.
❷ *He's too **proud** to mix with the likes
of us!*
• conceited, big-headed, arrogant, vain,
haughty, self-important, snobbish,
superior
(informal) stuck-up
OPPOSITE humble

prove *VERB*
*The evidence will **prove** that he is
innocent.*
• confirm, demonstrate, establish,
verify
OPPOSITE disprove

A B C D E F G H I J K L M N O P Q R S T U V W X Y Z

proverb NOUN
see **saying**

provide VERB
❶ *We'll provide the juice if you bring the sandwiches.*
• bring, contribute, arrange for, lay on
To provide food and drink for people is to **cater** for them.
❷ *The ski centre can provide you with boots and skis.*
• supply, equip, furnish

provisions PLURAL NOUN
We had enough provisions for two weeks.
• food, rations, stores, supplies

provoke VERB
❶ *Don't do anything to provoke the lions!*
• annoy, irritate, anger, incense, infuriate, exasperate, tease, taunt, goad
(informal) wind up
OPPOSITE pacify
❷ *The referee's decision provoked anger from the crowd.*
• arouse, produce, prompt, cause, generate, induce, stimulate, spark off, stir up, whip up

prowl VERB
Guard dogs prowled about the grounds of the palace.
• roam, slink, sneak, creep, steal

prudent ADJECTIVE
It would be prudent to start saving some money.
• wise, sensible, shrewd, thoughtful, careful, cautious
OPPOSITE reckless, unwise

prune VERB
Mum prunes her roses every spring.
• cut back, trim

pry VERB
I didn't mean to pry, but I overheard your conversation.
• be curious, be inquisitive, interfere
(informal) be nosy, nose about or around, snoop
➤ **to pry into something**
They are always prying into other people's business.
• interfere in, meddle in, spy on
(informal) poke your nose into

psychological ADJECTIVE
The doctor thinks the illness is psychological.
• mental, emotional
OPPOSITE physical

public ADJECTIVE
❶ *The public entrance is at the front of the gallery.*
• common, communal, general, open, shared
OPPOSITE private
❷ *The name of the author is now public knowledge.*
• well-known, acknowledged, published, open, general, universal
OPPOSITE secret

public NOUN
➤ **the public**
This part of the castle is not open to the public.
• people in general, everyone, the community, society, the nation

publication NOUN
She's celebrating the publication of her first novel.
• issuing, printing, production
Various publications are **books** and **magazines**.

publicity NOUN
❶ *Did you see the publicity for the book fair?*
• advertising, advertisements, promotion
❷ *Famous people don't always enjoy publicity.*
• fame, exposure, limelight

a
b
c
d
e
f
g
h
i
j
k
l
m
n
o
p
q
r
s
t
u
v
w
x
y
z

A
B
C
D
E
F
G
H
I
J
K
L
M
N
O
P
Q
R
S
T
U
V
W
X
Y
Z

publish VERB
❶ *The magazine is published every week.*
• issue, print, produce, bring out, release, circulate
❷ *When will they publish the results?*
• announce, declare, disclose, make known, make public, report, reveal
To publish information on radio or TV is to **broadcast** it.

pudding NOUN
Do you want any pudding?
• dessert, sweet
(informal) afters
for types of pudding see **food**

puff NOUN
❶ *A puff of wind caught his hat.*
• gust, breath, flurry
❷ *A puff of smoke rose from the chimney.*
• cloud, whiff

puff VERB
❶ *The dragon puffed green smoke from its nostrils.*
• blow out, send out, emit, belch
❷ *By the end of the race I was puffing.*
• breathe heavily, pant, gasp, wheeze
❸ *The sails puffed out as the wind rose.*
• become inflated, billow, swell

pull VERB
❶ *She pulled her chair nearer to the desk.*
• drag, draw, haul, lug, trail, tow
OPPOSITE push
❷ *Be careful—you nearly pulled my arm off!*
• tug, rip, wrench, jerk, pluck

➤ **to pull out**
❶ *The dentist pulled out one of my teeth.*
• extract, take out, remove
❷ *He had to pull out of the race.*
• back out, withdraw, retire

➤ **to pull someone's leg**
I hope you aren't pulling my leg!
• make fun of, play a trick, tease

➤ **to pull through**
It was a bad accident, but the doctors expect him to pull through.
• get better, recover, revive, survive

➤ **to pull up**
The bus pulled up at the traffic lights.
• draw up, stop, halt

pulse NOUN
You can feel the pulse of blood in your veins.
• beat, throb, drumming

pump VERB
The fire brigade pumped water out of the cellar.
• drain, draw off, empty
To move liquid from a higher container to a lower one through a tube is to **siphon** it.

punch VERB
❶ *I got punched in the eye by accident.*
• jab, poke, prod, thump
for other ways of hitting see **hit**
❷ *I need to punch a hole through the card.*
• bore, pierce

punctual ADJECTIVE
The bus was punctual today.
• in good time, on time, prompt
OPPOSITE late

punctuation NOUN

WORD WEB

PUNCTUATION MARKS:

• apostrophe, brackets, colon, comma, dash, exclamation mark, full stop, hyphen, question mark, quotation marks or speech marks, semicolon, square brackets

OTHER SYMBOLS USED IN WRITING:

• accent, asterisk, bullet point, emoji, hashtag, slash

puncture NOUN
❶ *I had a puncture on the way home.*
• burst tyre, flat tyre
❷ *I found the puncture in my tyre.*
• hole, leak

puncture *VERB*
A nail punctured my tyre.
• perforate, pierce, deflate, let down

punish *VERB*
Those responsible for the crime will be punished.
• penalize, discipline, chastise

punishment *NOUN*
The punishment for dropping litter is a hefty fine.
• penalty
Punishing someone by taking their life is **capital punishment** or **execution**.

puny *ADJECTIVE*
Miles was rather a puny child.
• delicate, weak, feeble, frail, weedy
OPPOSITE strong, sturdy

pupil *NOUN*
There are 33 pupils in our class.
• schoolchild, student, learner, scholar
Someone who follows a great teacher is a **disciple**.

purchase *VERB*
I'm saving my pocket money to purchase a bike.
• buy, pay for, get, obtain, acquire
purchase *NOUN*
❶ *She opened her bag and examined her purchases.*
• acquisition
❷ *The climbers had difficulty getting any purchase on the ice.*
• grasp, hold, leverage

pure *ADJECTIVE*
❶ *The bracelet is made of pure gold.*
• authentic, genuine, real
❷ *He was talking pure nonsense.*
• complete, absolute, utter, sheer, total
❸ *All our dishes are made from pure ingredients.*
• natural, wholesome
❹ *They swam in the pure, clear water of the lake.*
• clean, fresh, unpolluted
OPPOSITE impure

purify *VERB*
You can't drink this water unless you purify it.
• clean, make pure
You destroy germs by **disinfecting** or **sterilizing** things.
You take solid particles out of a liquid by **filtering** it.
To purify water by boiling it and condensing the vapour is to **distil** it.
To purify crude oil is to **refine** it.

purpose *NOUN*
❶ *Have you got a particular purpose in mind?*
• intention, aim, end, goal, target, objective, outcome, result
❷ *What's the purpose of your invention?*
• point, use, usefulness, value

purposeful *ADJECTIVE*
Dekka barged into the room with a purposeful look on her face.
• determined, decisive, positive
OPPOSITE aimless

purse *NOUN*
I always keep some loose change in my purse.
• money bag, pouch
A purse which holds paper money and credit cards is a **wallet**.

pursue *VERB*
❶ *The thief ran off, pursued by two police officers.*
• chase, follow, run after, tail, track, hunt, trail, shadow
❷ *She wants to pursue a career in law.*
• follow, undertake, practise, conduct, carry on, continue, maintain, proceed with

pursuit *NOUN*
❶ *The pursuit of the criminals lasted for months.*
• hunt (for), search (for), tracking, chase, trail
❷ *The family enjoy many outdoor pursuits.*
• activity, pastime, hobby, interest

a
b
c
d
e
f
g
h
i
j
k
l
m
n
o
p
q
r
s
t
u
v
w
x
y
z

A
B
C
D
E
F
G
H
I
J
K
L
M
N
O
P
Q
R
S
T
U
V
W
X
Y
Z

push *VERB*
❶ *We pushed our way through the crowd.*
• shove, thrust, force, propel, barge, elbow, jostle
OPPOSITE pull
❷ *Pete pushed his things into a bag.*
• pack, press, cram, crush, compress, ram, squash, squeeze
❸ *They pushed him to work even harder.*
• pressurize, press, drive, urge, compel, bully
(informal) lean on
❹ *The actors are pushing their latest film.*
• promote, publicize, advertise
(informal) plug

put *VERB* puts, putting, put
❶ *You can put your school bags in the corner.*
• place, set down, leave, deposit, dump, stand
❷ *The dog put its head on my lap.*
• lay, lean, rest
❸ *I'll put some pictures on the wall.*
• attach, fasten, fix, hang
❹ *Where are the builders planning to put the car park?*
• locate, situate
❺ *They put guards outside the bank.*
• position, post, station
❻ *I'm not sure of the best way to put this.*
• express, word, phrase, say, state
➤ **to put someone off**
The colour of the food put me off eating.
• deter, discourage, distract
➤ **to put something off**
We put off our journey because of the fog.
• delay, postpone, defer
➤ **to put something out**
The firefighters quickly put out the blaze.
• extinguish, quench, smother
➤ **to put something up**
It doesn't take long to put up the tent.
• set up, construct, erect
I'm going to buy a new bike before they put up the price.
• increase, raise

➤ **to put up with something**
I don't know how you put up with that noise.
• bear, stand, tolerate, endure

puzzle *NOUN*
Has anyone managed to solve the puzzle?
• question, mystery, riddle, conundrum, problem
(informal) brain-teaser, poser

puzzle *VERB*
❶ *Phil was puzzled by the mysterious message.*
• confuse, baffle, bewilder, bemuse, mystify, perplex, fox
❷ *We puzzled over the problem for hours.*
• ponder, think, meditate, worry, brood

puzzled *ADJECTIVE*
Why are you looking so puzzled?
• confused, baffled, bewildered, mystified, perplexed

puzzling *ADJECTIVE*
There was something puzzling about the signature on the letter.
• confusing, baffling, bewildering, mystifying, perplexing, mysterious, inexplicable
OPPOSITE straightforward

pyramid *NOUN*

WORD WEB

THINGS FOUND INSIDE OR NEAR ANCIENT EGYPTIAN PYRAMIDS:

• burial chamber, Canopic jar, frieze, hieroglyphics, mummy (of a pharaoh), papyrus, sarcophagus, sphinx, tomb
A pyramid which does not have smooth sides is a **stepped** pyramid.

Qq

quaint *ADJECTIVE*
They stayed in a quaint thatched cottage.
• charming, picturesque, sweet,
old-fashioned, old-world

quake *VERB*
*The ground quaked with the thud of the
giant's footsteps.*
• shake, shudder, tremble, quiver, shiver,
vibrate, rock, sway, wobble

qualification *NOUN*
❶ *What kind of qualification do you need to
be a vet?*
• diploma, certificate, degree, knowledge,
training, skill
❷ *The committee approved the plan, but with
some qualifications.*
• condition, reservation

qualified *ADJECTIVE*
❶ *This job needs a qualified electrician.*
• experienced, skilled, trained, professional
OPPOSITE amateur
❷ *He received qualified praise for his efforts.*
• limited, cautious, half-hearted

qualify *VERB*
❶ *The licence qualifies her to work as
a private detective.*
• authorize, permit, allow, entitle
❷ *The first three runners will qualify to take
part in the final.*
• get through, pass, be eligible
❸ *She felt the need to qualify her remarks.*
• limit, modify, restrict, soften, weaken

quality *NOUN*
❶ *We only use ingredients of the highest
quality.*
• grade, class, standard
❷ *The most obvious quality of rubber is that
it stretches.*
• characteristic, feature, property, attribute,
trait

quantity *NOUN*
❶ *She receives a huge quantity of fan mail
every week.*
• amount, mass, volume, bulk, weight
(informal) load
❷ *We recycled a large quantity of empty
bottles.*
• number
When you add up numbers, you get a **sum**
or **total**.

quarrel *NOUN*
*We have quarrels, but really we are good
friends.*
• argument, disagreement, dispute, difference
of opinion, row, squabble, clash, tiff
Continuous quarrelling is **strife**.
A long-lasting quarrel is a **feud** or **vendetta**.
A quarrel in which people become violent is a
brawl or **fight**.

quarrel *VERB*
*The twins quarrelled over who should sit in
the front.*
• disagree, argue, row, squabble, bicker, clash,
fight, fall out
➤ **to quarrel with something**
I can't quarrel with your decision.
• disagree with, object to, take exception to,
oppose

quarrelsome *ADJECTIVE*
Goblins can be very quarrelsome creatures.
• bad-tempered, irritable, aggressive,
argumentative
OPPOSITE placid

quaver *VERB*
The boy's voice quavered with fear.
• shake, tremble, waver, quake, quiver, falter

quay *NOUN*
The ship unloaded its cargo on to the quay.
• dock, harbour, pier, wharf, jetty, landing stage

a
b
c
d
e
f
g
h
i
j
k
l
m
n
o
p
q
r
s
t
u
v
w
x
y
z

A
B
C
D
E
F
G
H
I
J
K
L
M
N
O
P
Q
R
S
T
U
V
W
X
Y
Z

queer *ADJECTIVE*
❶ *The engine made a queer rattling noise.*
• curious, strange, unusual, weird, funny, mysterious, puzzling
❷ *There's something queer going on.*
• odd, peculiar, abnormal, suspicious, shady *(informal)* fishy
OPPOSITES normal, ordinary

quench *VERB*
❶ *The iced lemonade soon quenched her thirst.*
• cool, satisfy
❷ *They dumped sand on the embers to quench the fire.*
• extinguish, put out, smother

query *NOUN*
If you have any queries, please phone this number.
• question, enquiry, problem
query *VERB*
The manager queried the referee's decision.
• question, challenge, dispute, argue over, quarrel with, object to

quest *NOUN*
The knights set out on a quest to find the enchanted tower.
• search, hunt, expedition, mission

question *NOUN*
❶ *Does anyone have any questions?*
• enquiry, query, problem
A question which someone sets as a puzzle is a **brain-teaser**, **conundrum** or **riddle**.
A series of questions asked as a game is a **quiz**.
A set of questions which someone asks to get information is a **questionnaire** or **survey**.
❷ *There's some question over the player's fitness.*
• uncertainty, doubt, argument, debate, dispute
question *VERB*
❶ *The detective decided to question the suspect.*
• ask, examine, interview, quiz, interrogate
To question someone intensively is to **grill** them.

❷ *He questioned the referee's decision.*
• challenge, dispute, argue over, quarrel with, object to, query

queue *NOUN*
There was a queue of people outside the cinema.
• line, file, column, string
A long queue of traffic on a road is a **tailback**.
queue *VERB*
Please queue at the door.
• line up, form a queue

quick *ADJECTIVE*
❶ *You'd better be quick—the bus leaves in 10 minutes.*
• fast, swift, rapid, speedy, hasty *(informal)* nippy
A common simile is **as quick as a flash**.
OPPOSITE slow
❷ *Do you mind if I make a quick phone call?*
• short, brief, momentary, immediate, instant, prompt, snappy
OPPOSITES long, lengthy
❸ *She's very quick at mental arithmetic.*
• bright, clever, sharp, acute, alert *(informal)* on the ball
OPPOSITE slow

quicken *VERB*
The front runners quickened their pace.
• accelerate, speed up, hurry up, hasten

quiet *ADJECTIVE*
❶ *The deserted house was still and quiet.*
• silent, noiseless, soundless
A common simile is **as quiet as a mouse**.
OPPOSITE noisy
❷ *The children spoke in quiet whispers.*
• hushed, low, soft
Something that is so quiet that you can't hear it is **inaudible**.
OPPOSITE loud
❸ *Amy has always been a quiet child.*
• shy, reserved, subdued, placid, uncommunicative, retiring, withdrawn,
OPPOSITE talkative

❹ *We found a quiet place for a picnic.*
• peaceful, secluded, isolated, restful, tranquil, calm, serene
OPPOSITE busy

quieten VERB
❶ *The mother tried to quieten her baby.*
• calm, soothe, hush, pacify
❷ *Turn this dial to quieten the volume.*
• deaden, muffle, mute, soften, suppress

quit VERB quits, quitting, quitted or quit
❶ *She quit her teaching job to travel round the world.*
• leave, give up, resign from
(informal) pack in
❷ *(informal) Quit pushing me!*
• stop, cease, leave off

quite ADVERB
❶ *The two puppies have quite different personalities.*
• completely, totally, utterly, entirely, absolutely, very, wholly
❷ *They played quite well, but far from their best.*
• fairly, reasonably, moderately, rather
WHICH WORD? Note that quite has two different meanings, which are almost opposites, so be sure to choose the correct synonyms!

quiver VERB
The jelly quivered when the table was banged.
• shake, wobble, quake, shiver, quaver, tremble, shudder, vibrate

quiz NOUN
Our class took part in a general knowledge quiz.
• test, competition, questionnaire, exam, examination

quiz VERB
The teacher quizzed us on our times tables.
• question, ask, examine, interrogate

quota NOUN
I've completed my quota of the work.
• ration, share, portion, allowance, helping

quotation NOUN
I copied a short quotation from the book.
• extract, excerpt, passage, piece
A piece taken from a newspaper is a **cutting.**
A piece taken from a film or TV programme is a **clip.**

quote VERB
He quoted some lines from a poem.
• recite, repeat

Rr

race NOUN
❶ *We had a race to see who was the fastest runner.*
• competition, contest, chase
A race to decide who will take part in the final is a **heat.**
❷ *We belong to different races but we're all humans.*
• nation, people, ethnic group

race VERB
❶ *We raced each other to the end of the road.*
• have a race with, run against, compete with
❷ *She had to race home because she was late.*
• run, rush, dash, hurry, sprint, fly, tear, whizz, zoom

rack NOUN
Cooking pots hung from a rack on the wall.
• frame, framework, shelf, support

racket NOUN
❶ *A racket is used to hit the ball in tennis.*
In cricket and some other games you hit the ball with a **bat.**
In golf you hit the ball with a **club.**
❷ *Please stop making that awful racket!*
• noise, row, din, commotion, disturbance, uproar, rumpus

a
b
c
d
e
f
g
h
i
j
k
l
m
n
o
p
q
r
s
t
u
v
w
x
y
z

A B C D E F G H I J K L M N O P Q R S T U V W X Y Z

radiate VERB

❶ *This fire radiates a lot of heat.*
• give off, send out, emit
❷ *The bus routes radiate from the centre of town.*
• spread out

radical ADJECTIVE

❶ *They have made radical changes to school meals.*
• fundamental, drastic, thorough, sweeping
OPPOSITE superficial
❷ *The politician was known for her radical views.*
• extreme, revolutionary
OPPOSITE moderate

rage NOUN

Derek slammed the door in a show of rage.
• anger, fury, indignation, ire
(old use) wrath
A child's rage is a **tantrum** or fit of **temper**.

rage VERB

❶ *He was still raging about the cost of the meal.*
• be angry, be fuming, seethe, rant
❷ *The hurricane raged for three days.*
• blow, storm, rampage

ragged ADJECTIVE

❶ *They met a traveller wearing ragged clothes.*
• tattered, tatty, threadbare, torn, frayed, patched, ripped, shabby, worn-out
❷ *A ragged line of people waited in the rain.*
• irregular, uneven

raid NOUN

The enemy raid caught them by surprise.
• attack, assault, strike, onslaught, invasion, blitz

raid VERB

❶ *Long ago, Vikings raided the towns on the coast.*
• attack, invade, ransack, plunder, loot, pillage
Someone who raids ships at sea is a **pirate**.
Someone who raids and steals cattle is a **rustler**.
❷ *Police raided the house at dawn.*
• descend on, rush, storm, swoop on

rail NOUN

The fence was made of iron rails.
• bar, rod, spar
A fence made of rails is also called **railings**.

railway NOUN

WORD WEB

VARIOUS TYPES OF RAILWAY:

• branch line, cable railway, funicular, main line, metro, monorail, mountain railway, tramway, underground railway

TYPES OF RAILWAY TRAIN:

• diesel, electric train, express, freight train or goods train, intercity, sleeper, steam train, tram, underground train
Vehicles which run on the railway are **locomotives** and **rolling stock**.

PARTS OF A RAILWAY TRAIN:

• buffet car, carriage or coach, dining car, engine, goods van, guard's van, locomotive, sleeping car

THINGS YOU MIGHT SEE ON OR NEAR A RAILWAY:

• buffers, cutting, level crossing, platform, points, signals, signal box, sleepers, station, track, trolley, tunnel, viaduct
The rails which trains run on are the **line** or **track**.
The end of the line is the **terminus**.

PEOPLE WHO WORK ON A TRAIN OR RAILWAY:

• conductor, driver, engineer, guard, porter, signaller, station manager, steward

rain NOUN

A formal word for rain is **precipitation**.
The rainy season in south and south-east Asia is the **monsoon**.

When there is no rain for a long time there is a **drought**.
for ways to describe rain see **weather**

raise *VERB*
❶ *Raise your hand if you need help.*
• hold up, put up, lift
❷ *The box was too heavy for him to* **raise**.
• lift, pick up, elevate, hoist, jack up
❸ *The Post Office is* **raising** *the price of stamps.*
• increase, put up
❹ *The runners hope to* **raise** *£1000 for charity.*
• collect, gather, take in, make
❺ *He* **raised** *some objections to the plan.*
• bring up, mention, put forward, present, introduce
❻ *The doctor didn't want to* **raise** *their hopes.*
• encourage, build up, arouse
❼ *It's hard work trying to* **raise** *a family.*
• bring up, care for, look after, nurture, rear

rally *NOUN*
Some demonstrators held a **rally** *in the town square.*
• demonstration, meeting, march, protest
(informal) demo

ram *VERB*
The car skidded and **rammed** *into a lamp post.*
• bump, hit, strike, crash into, collide with, smash into

ramble *VERB*
❶ *They* **rambled** *round the country park.*
• walk, stroll, wander, roam, rove, range, hike, trek
❷ *The speaker* **rambled** *on for hours.*
• chatter, babble, drift
(informal) rabbit, witter

rampage *VERB*
An angry mob **rampaged** *through the streets.*
• run riot, run amok, go berserk, go wild, race about, rush about

ran *past tense see* **run**

random *ADJECTIVE*
They picked a **random** *selection of pupils.*
• arbitrary, chance, haphazard, casual, unplanned
OPPOSITE deliberate

rang *past tense see* **ring**

range *NOUN*
❶ *There is a* **range** *of mountains to the south.*
• chain, line, row, series, string
❷ *Supermarkets sell a wide* **range** *of goods.*
• variety, assortment, selection, choice, spectrum
❸ *The shop caters for all age* **ranges** *from toddlers to teenagers.*
• span, scope

range *VERB*
❶ *Prices* **range** *from five to twenty euros.*
• vary, differ, extend, fluctuate
❷ *Rows of jam jars were* **ranged** *on the shelf.*
• arrange, order, lay out, set out, line up
❸ *Wild deer* **range** *over the hills.*
• wander, ramble, roam, rove, stray

rank *NOUN*
❶ *The soldiers formed themselves into* **ranks**.
• column, line, file, row
❷ *A black belt is the highest* **rank** *in judo.*
• grade, level, position, status
To raise someone to a higher rank is to **promote** them.
To reduce someone to a lower rank is to **demote** them.

ransack *VERB*
❶ *Mrs Nowak* **ransacked** *the house looking for her keys.*
• search, scour, rummage through, comb
(informal) turn upside down
❷ *Thieves had* **ransacked** *the building.*
• loot, pillage, plunder, wreck

rap *VERB*
Someone **rapped** *urgently on the door.*
• knock, tap

a b c d e f g h i j k l m n o p q r s t u v w x y z

A
B
C
D
E
F
G
H
I
J
K
L
M
N
O
P
Q
R
S
T
U
V
W
X
Y
Z

rapid *ADJECTIVE*
The cyclists set off at a **rapid** pace.
• fast, quick, speedy, swift, brisk
OPPOSITE slow

rare *ADJECTIVE*
❶ These flowers are now very **rare** in the wild.
• uncommon, unusual, infrequent, scarce, sparse
OPPOSITE common
❷ She has a **rare** ability to make people laugh.
• exceptional, remarkable, special

rarely *ADVERB*
Our next-door neighbour **rarely** goes out.
• seldom, infrequently, hardly ever
OPPOSITE often

rash *ADJECTIVE*
Don't make any **rash** promises.
• reckless, foolhardy, hasty, hurried, impulsive, unthinking
OPPOSITE careful

rash *NOUN*
❶ Rory had an itchy red **rash** on his leg.
• spots
❷ There has been a **rash** of break-ins lately.
• outbreak, series, succession, spate

rate *NOUN*
❶ The cyclists were pedalling at a furious **rate**.
• pace, speed
❷ What's the usual **rate** for washing a car?
• charge, cost, fee, payment, price, figure, amount

rate *VERB*
How do you **rate** their chance of winning?
• judge, regard, consider, estimate, evaluate

rather *ADVERB*
❶ It's **rather** chilly today.
• quite, fairly, moderately, slightly, somewhat, a bit, a little
❷ I'd **rather** not go out tonight.
• preferably, sooner

ratio *NOUN*
The **ratio** of boys to girls is about 50-50.
• proportion, balance
You can express a ratio as a **percentage**.

ration *NOUN*
The pirates each had a daily **ration** of rum.
• portion, quota, share, allowance, helping, measure
➤ **rations**
The astronauts took enough **rations** to last a month.
• food, provisions, stores, supplies

ration *VERB*
During the war, the government had to **ration** food.
• limit, restrict, share out, allot

rattle *NOUN, VERB*
for various sounds see **sound**

rave *VERB*
❶ Connie **raved** about the film she saw last week.
• be enthusiastic, talk wildly
❷ The head **raved** on about their bad behaviour.
• shout, rage, storm, yell, roar

ravenous *ADJECTIVE*
The children were **ravenous** after their walk.
• hungry, starved, starving, famished

raw *ADJECTIVE*
❶ **Raw** vegetables are supposed to be good for you.
• uncooked
OPPOSITE cooked
❷ The factory imports a lot of **raw** materials from abroad.
• crude, natural, unprocessed, untreated
OPPOSITES manufactured, processed
❸ Her knee felt **raw** after she fell off her bike.
• red, rough, sore, tender, inflamed
❹ There was a **raw** wind blowing from the east.
• bitter, cold, chilly, biting, freezing, piercing

ray NOUN
A ray of light shone into the dark cave.
• beam, shaft, stream

reach VERB
❶ *They hoped to reach Oxford by lunchtime.*
• arrive at, go as far as, get to, make
❷ *The appeal fund has reached its target.*
• achieve, attain
❸ *I'm not tall enough to reach the top shelf.*
• get hold of, grasp, touch
➤ **to reach out**
Reach out your hands.
• extend, hold out, put out, stick out, stretch out
reach NOUN
❶ *The shelf was just within his reach.*
• grasp
❷ *The shops are within easy reach.*
• distance, range

react VERB
How did he react when he read the letter?
• respond, behave, answer, reply

reaction NOUN
What was her reaction when you said you were sorry?
• response, answer, reply

read VERB reads, reading, read
They couldn't read the doctor's handwriting.
• make out, understand, decipher
To read through something very quickly is to **skim through** it.
To read here and there in a book is to **dip into** it.
To read something intently is to **pore over** it.

readily ADVERB
❶ *My friends readily agreed to help.*
• willingly, gladly, happily, eagerly
❷ *The recipe uses ingredients which are readily available.*
• easily, conveniently, quickly

ready ADJECTIVE
❶ *When will tea be ready?*
• prepared, set, done, available, in place
OPPOSITE not ready

❷ *He's always ready to help.*
• willing, glad, pleased, happy, keen, eager
OPPOSITE reluctant
❸ *She's always got a ready reply.*
• quick, prompt, immediate
OPPOSITE slow

real ADJECTIVE
❶ *History is about real events.*
• actual, true, factual, verifiable
OPPOSITES fictitious, imaginary
❷ *The necklace was made from real rubies.*
• authentic, genuine, bona fide, natural
OPPOSITES artificial, fake
❸ *She doesn't often show her real feelings.*
• true, honest, sincere, genuine, heartfelt
OPPOSITE insincere

realize VERB
It took him a long time to realize what she meant.
• understand, appreciate, grasp, comprehend, recognize, see
(informal) catch on to, tumble to, twig

realistic ADJECTIVE
❶ *The portrait of the artist is very realistic.*
• lifelike, true to life, faithful, convincing, recognizable
❷ *It's not realistic to expect a puppy to be quiet.*
• feasible, practical, sensible, possible, workable
OPPOSITE unrealistic

reality NOUN
Stop daydreaming and face reality.
• the facts, the real world, the truth

really ADVERB
❶ *Are you really going to Peru?*
• actually, definitely, truly, in fact, certainly, genuinely, honestly
❷ *I saw a really good film last night.*
• very, extremely, exceptionally

A B C D E F G H I J K L M N O P Q R S T U V W X Y Z

realm *NOUN*
The king ruled the realm for fifty years.
• country, kingdom, domain, empire

rear *ADJECTIVE*
They found seats in the rear coach of the train.
• back, end, last
The rear legs of an animal are its hind legs.
OPPOSITE front

rear *NOUN*
The buffet car is at the rear of the train.
• back, end, tail end
The rear of a ship is the stern.

rear *VERB*
❶ *The couple have reared three children.*
• bring up, raise, nurture
❷ *The deer reared their heads when they caught his scent.*
• hold up, lift, raise

reason *NOUN*
❶ *What was the reason for the delay?*
• cause, grounds, explanation, motive, justification, excuse
❷ *It was clear that the poor man had lost his reason.*
• mind, sanity, senses, wits
❸ *They tried to make him see reason.*
• sense, common sense, logic

reason *VERB*
➤ to reason with someone
We tried to reason with him, but he wouldn't change his mind.
• argue with, persuade, talk round

reasonable *ADJECTIVE*
❶ *That seems like a reasonable plan.*
• sensible, intelligent, rational, logical, sane, sound
OPPOSITE irrational
❷ *They bought the house for a reasonable price.*
• fair, acceptable, average, moderate, respectable, normal, proper
OPPOSITE excessive

reassure *VERB*
The doctor reassured her that the wound was not serious.
• calm, comfort, encourage, hearten, give confidence to
OPPOSITE threaten

rebel *VERB*
The queen feared that the people would rebel.
• revolt, rise up
To rebel against the captain of a ship is to mutiny and someone who does this is a mutineer.
OPPOSITE obey

rebellion *NOUN*
The protest soon became a widespread rebellion.
• revolt, revolution, uprising, resistance
A rebellion on a ship is a mutiny.

rebound *VERB*
The ball rebounded off the wall.
• bounce back, spring back
If a bullet rebounds off a surface, it ricochets.

recall *VERB*
Try to recall what happened.
• remember, recollect, think back to

recede *VERB*
When the rain stopped, the flood receded.
• go back, retreat, decline, subside, ebb

receive *VERB*
❶ *The captain went up to receive the winners' cup.*
• collect, take, accept, be given
OPPOSITES give, present
❷ *Some passengers received minor injuries.*
• experience, suffer, undergo, sustain
OPPOSITE inflict
❸ *We went to the front door to receive our visitors.*
• greet, meet, welcome

recent ADJECTIVE
We watch the news to keep up with recent events.
• current, up-to-date, contemporary, new, the latest, fresh

reception NOUN
❶ *The home crowd gave the team a friendly reception.*
• greeting, welcome
❷ *Who are they inviting to the wedding reception?*
• party, gathering, celebration, function *(informal)* do

recipe NOUN
I followed my granny's recipe for making apple pie.
• directions, instructions
The items you use for a recipe are the ingredients.

recital NOUN
There will be a short recital of piano music at noon.
• concert, performance

recite VERB
Abigail recited a poem she had written.
• say aloud, read out, narrate

reckless ADJECTIVE
A man has been charged with reckless driving.
• careless, irresponsible, mindless, thoughtless, negligent, foolhardy, rash, wild
OPPOSITE careful

reckon VERB
❶ *I tried to reckon how much she owed me.*
• calculate, work out, add up, figure out, assess, estimate
❷ *Do you reckon it's going to rain?*
• think, believe, guess, imagine, feel

recline VERB
Paula reclined lazily on the sofa.
• lean back, lie, lounge, rest, stretch out, sprawl, loll

recognize VERB
❶ *I didn't recognize her with her new haircut.*
• identify, know, distinguish, make out, recall, recollect, remember
❷ *He refused to recognize that he was to blame.*
• acknowledge, admit, accept, grant, concede, confess, realize

recoil VERB
Joe recoiled as a spider scuttled towards him.
• draw back, flinch, quail, wince, shrink back

recollect VERB
❶ *Do you recollect what happened?*
• remember, recall, have a memory of
❷ *The two friends sat for hours recollecting the past.*
• reminisce about, think back to, cast your mind back to
OPPOSITE forget

recommend VERB
❶ *The doctor recommended complete rest.*
• advise, counsel, propose, suggest, advocate, prescribe, urge
❷ *The restaurant was recommended by a friend of mine.*
• approve of, endorse, praise, commend

record NOUN
The zookeepers keep a record of the animals' diet.
• account, report
A record of daily events is a **diary** or **journal**.
The record of a voyage at sea or in space is the **log**.
The record of what happened at a meeting is the **minutes**.
A record of people's names is a **register**.
Records consisting of historical documents are **archives**.

record VERB
❶ *The concert is being recorded by the BBC.*
• tape, video, film
❷ *She recorded our interview in a notebook.*
• write down, note, set down, put down, enter

a
b
c
d
e
f
g
h
i
j
k
l
m
n
o
p
q
r
s
t
u
v
w
x
y
z

A
B
C
D
E
F
G
H
I
J
K
L
M
N
O
P
Q
R
S
T
U
V
W
X
Y
Z

recover *VERB*
❶ *It took a long time to recover after my illness.*
• get better, heal, improve, recuperate, pick up, mend, come round, pull through, revive, rally
❷ *The police have recovered the stolen vehicles.*
• get back, retrieve, reclaim, repossess, find, trace

recovery *NOUN*
The doctors were surprised at her speedy recovery.
• healing, cure, revival, recuperation, convalescence

recreation *NOUN*
What do you do for recreation around here?
• fun, enjoyment, pleasure, relaxation, leisure, amusement, diversion, entertainment, play
A particular activity you do as recreation is a **hobby** or **pastime.**

recruit *NOUN*
The police recruits were very inexperienced.
• beginner, learner, novice
A recruit learning a trade is an **apprentice** or **trainee.**
A recruit training to be in the armed services is a **cadet.**

recruit *VERB*
The book club has recruited two new members.
• bring in, take on, attract, enrol
To be recruited into the armed services is to **enlist** or **sign up.**

rectangle *NOUN*
• oblong

recur *VERB*
Go to the doctor if the symptoms recur.
• happen again, come again, reappear, return

recycle *VERB*
You can recycle glass by putting it in the bottle bank.
• reuse, reprocess, salvage, use again

red *ADJECTIVE, NOUN*
❶ *I chose a red ribbon for my doll.*
Something which is rather red is **reddish.**
A common simile is **as red as a beetroot.**
❷ *My nose and cheeks were red with cold.*
• flushed, glowing, rosy, ruddy, blushing
❸ *Her eyes were red from lack of sleep.*
• bloodshot, inflamed, red-rimmed
❹ *The fairy queen had flaming red hair.*
• ginger, auburn, coppery
(informal) **carroty**

WORD WEB

SOME SHADES OF RED:

• brick red, cherry, crimson, maroon, pillar-box red, pink, rose, ruby, scarlet, vermilion

reduce *VERB*
We've reduced the amount of sugar in our diet.
• decrease, lessen, lower, cut, cut back, slash
To reduce something by half is to **halve** it.
To reduce the width of something is to **narrow** it.
To reduce the length of something is to **shorten** or **trim** it.
To reduce speed is to **decelerate.**
To reduce the strength of a liquid is to **dilute** it.
OPPOSITE increase

reel *NOUN*
I bought a reel of white cotton thread.
• spool

reel *VERB*
❶ *The blow made his head reel.*
• spin, whirl
❷ *The injured man reeled as if he was drunk.*
• stagger, stumble, sway, rock, totter, lurch, roll
➤ **to reel off**
The chef reeled off a long list of ingredients.
• recite, rattle off, fire off

refer *VERB*
The shop assistant referred me to another department.
• hand over, pass on, direct, send

➤ to refer to
❶ *Please don't refer to this matter again.*
• mention, speak of, make reference to, allude to, bring up
❷ *If you can't spell a word, refer to a dictionary.*
• look up, consult, go to, turn to

referee *NOUN*
The referee blew his whistle.
• umpire, adjudicator
(informal) ref
A person who helps the referee in football is a referee's assistant or touch judge.

refill *VERB*
The waiter refilled our glasses of water.
• top up
To refill a fuel tank is to refuel.

reflect *VERB*
❶ *Catseyes™ reflect the light from car headlights.*
• send back, throw back, shine back
❷ *Their success reflects their hard work.*
• show, indicate, demonstrate, exhibit, reveal
➤ to reflect on
We need time to reflect on what to do next.
• think about, contemplate, consider, ponder, mull over

reflection *NOUN*
❶ *Gus could see his reflection in the pond.*
• image, likeness
❷ *Their success is a reflection of their hard work.*
• indication, demonstration, evidence, result
❸ *We need more time for reflection.*
• thinking, contemplation, meditation

reform *NOUN*
They're making reforms to the school curriculum.
• change, improvement, modification, amendment

refrain *VERB*
➤ to refrain from
Please refrain from talking in the library.
• avoid, abstain from, stop
(informal) leave off, quit

refresh *VERB*
❶ *The players refreshed themselves with a glass of lemonade.*
• cool, freshen, revive, restore, invigorate, stimulate
❷ *Let me refresh your memory.*
• jog, prompt, prod
To reload a website is to refresh the page.

refreshing *ADJECTIVE*
We went for a refreshing dip in the pool.
• reviving, invigorating, restorative, bracing, stimulating

refuge *NOUN*
❶ *The climbers looked for refuge from the blizzard.*
• shelter, cover, protection, safety
❷ *The outlaws hid in their mountain refuge.*
• hideaway, hideout, retreat, haven, sanctuary

refund *VERB*
She asked them to refund her money.
• give back, pay back, repay, return

refuse *VERB*
❶ *Why did you refuse my offer of help?*
• decline, reject, turn down, say no to
OPPOSITE accept
❷ *They were refused permission to enter the building.*
• deny, deprive of
OPPOSITES give, allow

refuse *NOUN*
The refuse was taken to the local tip.
• rubbish, garbage, trash, waste, litter, junk

regain *VERB*
The patient began to regain consciousness.
• get back, get back to, return to

regard *VERB*
❶ *Do you still regard him as your friend?*
• think of, consider, judge, value
❷ *The cat regarded us curiously.*
• look at, gaze at, stare at, eye, view, scrutinize, watch

a b c d e f g h i j k l m n o p q r s t u v w x y z

regarding *PREPOSITION*
I must speak with you regarding a private matter.
• about, concerning, on the subject of, with reference to, with regard to

region *NOUN*
❶ *The Arctic and Antarctic are polar regions.*
• area, place, land, territory, part of the world
❷ *There are two local radio stations serving this region.*
• area, district, neighbourhood, locality, vicinity, zone

register *VERB*
❶ *The parents registered the birth of their child.*
• record, set down, write down
❷ *The thermometer registered a very high temperature.*
• show, indicate, display, read

regret *VERB*
She regretted her decision to leave Ireland.
• be sorry for, repent, feel sad about

regular *ADJECTIVE*
❶ *Signs are placed at regular intervals along the cycle path.*
• evenly spaced, fixed
OPPOSITES irregular, uneven
❷ *The drummer kept up a regular rhythm.*
• constant, consistent, steady, uniform, unvarying
A common simile is as regular as clockwork.
OPPOSITE erratic
❸ *Is this your regular route to school?*
• normal, usual, customary, habitual, ordinary, routine
OPPOSITE unusual
❹ *Craig is a regular customer at the sweet shop.*
• frequent, familiar, persistent
OPPOSITES rare, unusual

regulate *VERB*
❶ *Just turn the knob to regulate the volume.*
• control, set, adjust, alter, change, moderate
❷ *The new roundabout is meant to regulate the traffic.*
• control, manage, direct, govern, monitor

regulation *NOUN*
There are new regulations on school uniform.
• rule, law, order, decree, requirement

rehearsal *NOUN*
The actors had to learn their words before the rehearsal.
• practice, preparation
(informal) try-out
A final rehearsal in which actors wear their costumes is a dress rehearsal.

rehearse *VERB*
We had to rehearse the scene all over again.
• go over, practise, try out

reign *VERB*
Which British monarch reigned the longest?
• be king or queen, be on the throne, govern, rule

reject *VERB*
❶ *At first, she rejected their offer of help.*
• decline, refuse, turn down, say no to
OPPOSITE accept
❷ *As we picked the berries, we rejected any bad ones.*
• discard, get rid of, throw out, scrap

rejoice *VERB*
The people rejoiced when the war finally ended.
• celebrate, delight, be happy, exult
OPPOSITE grieve

relate *VERB*
❶ *Do you think the two crimes are related?*
• connect, link, associate
❷ *The travellers related the story of their adventures.*
• tell, narrate, report, describe

A B C D E F G H I J K L M N O P Q R S T U V W X Y Z

➤ **relate to**
The letter relates to your great-grandfather.
• be about, refer to, have to do with, concern

relation *NOUN*
❶ *The stolen car has no relation to the robbery.*
• connection, link, association, bond
❷ *Are you a relation of hers?*
• relative, member of the family, kinsman or kinswoman
for members of a family see **family**

relationship *NOUN*
❶ *There is a relationship between your diet and health.*
• connection, link, association, bond
The relationship between two numbers is a **ratio.**
❷ *The twins have a close relationship.*
• friendship, attachment, understanding

relative *NOUN*
see **relation**

relax *VERB*
❶ *I like to relax by listening to music.*
• unwind, rest, take it easy
❷ *This exercise will relax your shoulder muscles.*
• loosen, ease
OPPOSITE tighten
❸ *He relaxed his hold on the dog's leash.*
• slacken, loosen, ease, lessen, reduce
OPPOSITE tighten

relaxed *ADJECTIVE*
They liked the relaxed atmosphere of village life.
• informal, casual, carefree, leisurely, easy-going, peaceful, restful, unhurried, calm *(informal)* laid-back
OPPOSITES tense, stressful

release *VERB*
❶ *The prisoners were released early.*
• free, let go, discharge, liberate, set free
To release slaves is to **emancipate** *them.*
OPPOSITE imprison

❷ *The dog was tied up—who released him?*
• let loose, set loose, unfasten, unleash, untie
❸ *The band will release their new album in April.*
• issue, publish, put out

relent *VERB*
Her parents relented and let her stay up late.
• give in, give way, yield, soften, weaken

relentless *ADJECTIVE*
The footballer faced relentless questions from the press.
• constant, continuous, incessant, perpetual, persistent, never-ending, unrelenting, remorseless, ruthless

relevant *ADJECTIVE*
❶ *The detective noted everything that was relevant to the case.*
• applicable, pertinent, appropriate, suitable, significant, related, connected
❷ *Don't interrupt unless your comments are relevant.*
• to the point, pertinent
OPPOSITE irrelevant

reliable *ADJECTIVE*
❶ *The queen summoned her most reliable knights.*
• faithful, dependable, trustworthy, loyal, constant, devoted, staunch, true
❷ *The secret agent always sent reliable information.*
• dependable, valid, trustworthy, safe, sound, steady, sure
OPPOSITE unreliable

relief *NOUN*
❶ *The pills gave some relief from the pain.*
• comfort, ease, help, release
❷ *I watched a film for some light relief after work.*
• relaxation, rest

a b c d e f g h i j k l m n o p q r s t u v w x y z

A **B** **C** **D** **E** **F** **G** **H** **I** **J** **K** **L** **M** **N** **O** **P** **Q** **R** **S** **T** **U** **V** **W** **X** **Y** **Z**

relieve VERB
❶ *The doctor said the pills would relieve the pain.*
• ease, help, lessen, diminish, relax, soothe, comfort
❷ *We played cards to relieve the boredom of waiting.*
• reduce, lighten, dispel, counteract
OPPOSITE intensify

religion NOUN
People from all religions went to the service.
• faith, belief, creed, denomination, sect

WORD WEB

MAJOR WORLD RELIGIONS:

• Buddhism, Christianity, Hinduism, Islam, Judaism, Shintoism, Sikhism, Taoism, Zen

MAJOR RELIGIOUS FESTIVALS:

• Buddhist: Buddha Day, Nirvana Day
• Christian: Lent, Easter, Christmas Day
• Hindu: Holi, Diwali
• Muslim: Ramadan, Eid
• Jewish: Passover, Rosh Hashanah, Yom Kippur, Hanukkah
• Sikh: Baisakhi, Birth of Guru Nanak
The study of religion is **divinity** or **theology**.
for religious leaders see **priest**

religious ADJECTIVE
❶ *The choir sang a selection of religious music.*
• sacred, holy, divine
OPPOSITE secular
❷ *My grandparents were very religious.*
• devout, pious, reverent, spiritual, godly
OPPOSITE ungodly

relish VERB
He would relish the chance to appear on television.
• enjoy, delight in, appreciate

reluctant ADJECTIVE
The old woman was reluctant to open the door.
• unwilling, hesitant, slow, grudging, loth, half-hearted, resistant
OPPOSITE eager

rely VERB
Are you sure that we can rely on their help?
• depend on, count on, have confidence in, trust
(informal) bank on

remain VERB
❶ *The children were told to remain behind after school.*
• stay, wait, linger
(informal) hang about
❷ *It will remain warm and sunny all weekend.*
• continue, persist, keep on, carry on
❸ *Little remained of the house after the fire.*
• be left, survive

remainder NOUN
We played games for the remainder of the afternoon.
• rest, what is left, surplus, remains

remains PLURAL NOUN
They cleared away the remains of the picnic.
• remnants, leftovers, fragments, traces, scraps, debris
The remains at the bottom of a cup are the **dregs**.
Remains still standing after a building has collapsed are **ruins**.
Historic remains are **relics**.

remark VERB
He remarked that it was a nice day.
• say, state, comment, note, declare, mention, observe
see also **say**

remark NOUN
We exchanged a few remarks about the weather.
• comment, observation, word, statement, thought, mention

338

remarkable ADJECTIVE

❶ *He described his remarkable escape from the island.*
• amazing, extraordinary, astonishing, memorable, wonderful, incredible, unforgettable, breathtaking
❷ *The young violinist shows remarkable skill for her age.*
• exceptional, notable, noteworthy, striking, outstanding, impressive, phenomenal
OPPOSITE ordinary

remedy NOUN

❶ *There is no known remedy for his illness.*
• cure, treatment, medicine, therapy, relief
A remedy to act against a poison is an antidote.
❷ *We may have found a remedy for the problem.*
• solution, answer

remember VERB

❶ *Can you remember what she looked like?*
• recall, recollect, recognize, place
❷ *He was trying to remember his lines for the play.*
• learn, memorize, keep in mind
OPPOSITE forget
❸ *My granny likes to remember the old days.*
• reminisce about, think back to

remind VERB

Remind me to buy a newspaper.
• prompt, jog your memory
➤ **to remind you of something**
What does this tune remind you of?
• make you think of, take you back to

reminder NOUN

❶ *They sent him a reminder to pay the bill.*
• prompt, cue, hint, nudge
❷ *The photographs are a reminder of our holiday.*
• souvenir, memento

reminiscent ADJECTIVE

➤ **be reminiscent of something**
The tune is reminiscent of an old folk song.
• remind you of, make you think of, call to mind

remnants PLURAL NOUN

They had to clear up the remnants of the party.
• remains, scraps, traces, fragments, debris, leftovers

remorse NOUN

She showed no remorse for stealing the money.
• regret, repentance, guilt, guilty conscience, sorrow, shame

remote ADJECTIVE

❶ *The tour will explore a remote part of Brazil.*
• distant, faraway, isolated, cut-off, inaccessible, out of the way, unfrequented
OPPOSITE accessible
❷ *The chances of us winning are remote.*
• poor, slender, slight, small, faint, doubtful
OPPOSITE likely

remove VERB

❶ *Please remove your rubbish.*
• clear away, take away
❷ *The rowdy passengers were removed from the bus.*
• throw out, turn out, eject, expel
(informal) kick out
To remove people from a house where they are living is to evict them.
To remove a monarch from the throne is to depose him or her.
❸ *The author decided to remove the last paragraph.*
• cut out, delete, erase, get rid of, do away with, eliminate
❹ *The dentist removed my bad tooth.*
• extract, pull out, take out, withdraw
❺ *The divers slowly removed their wetsuits.*
• take off, peel off, strip off, shed, cast off

a
b
c
d
e
f
g
h
i
j
k
l
m
n
o
p
q
r
s
t
u
v
w
x
y
z

A B C D E F G H I J K L M N O P Q R S T U V W X Y Z

render VERB
❶ *The shock rendered her speechless.*
• make, leave, cause to be
❷ *Many volunteers rendered their assistance.*
• give, provide, offer, furnish, supply

renew VERB
❶ *The church roof has been completely renewed.*
• repair, renovate, restore, replace, rebuild, reconstruct, revamp, refurbish, overhaul
(informal) do up
❷ *We stopped for a cup of tea to renew our energy.*
• refresh, revive, restore, replenish, revitalize
❸ *You must renew your passport before you go abroad.*
• bring up to date, update

rent VERB
We rented a couple of bikes to tour the Lake District.
• hire, charter, lease

repair VERB
It took them a week to repair the damaged car.
• mend, fix, put right, patch up

repay VERB repays, repaying, repaid
❶ *I can repay you the money next week.*
• pay back, refund
❷ *How can we ever repay your kindness?*
• return, reciprocate

repeat VERB
❶ *The parrot repeated everything he said.*
• say again, copy, duplicate, reproduce, echo
❷ *The actors had to repeat the opening scene.*
• do again, redo

repeatedly ADVERB
We warned them repeatedly about the danger.
• again and again, over and over, regularly, time after time, frequently, often

repel VERB
❶ *The humans managed to repel the Martian invasion.*
• drive back, beat back, push back, fend off, resist
❷ *This spray will repel wasps and other insects.*
• keep away, scare off, deter, ward off
❸ *They were repelled by the smell of the dragon's lair.*
• disgust, revolt, sicken, offend
(informal) turn you off

repellent ADJECTIVE
The princess found the ogre quite repellent.
• disgusting, repulsive, revolting, hideous, horrible, loathsome, objectionable, foul, offensive, vile
(OPPOSITE) attractive

replace VERB
❶ *The spy carefully replaced the missing document.*
• put back, return, restore, reinstate
❷ *Who will replace the head teacher when she retires?*
• follow, succeed, take over from, take the place of
❸ *I need to replace one of the tyres on my bike.*
• change, renew

replacement NOUN
They found a replacement for the injured player.
• substitute, standby, stand-in, reserve
Someone who can take the place of an actor is an understudy.

replica NOUN
In the garden, there's a replica of a Roman statue.
• copy, reproduction, duplicate, model, imitation, likeness
An exact copy of a document is a facsimile.

reply NOUN
He has received no replies to his email.
• response, answer, reaction, acknowledgement
An angry reply is a retort.

reply *VERB*
➤ **to reply to**
She took a long time to reply to my letter.
• answer, respond to, give a reply to, react to, acknowledge

report *VERB*
❶ *The newspapers reported what happened.*
• give an account of, record, state, describe, announce, publish
❷ *We were told to report to reception when we arrived.*
• present yourself, make yourself known, check in
❸ *If you cause any damage, I'll report you to the police.*
• complain about, inform on, denounce

report *NOUN*
❶ *There was a report in the paper about the crash.*
• account, record, story, article, description
❷ *The deer were startled by the report of the gun.*
• bang, blast, crack, noise

reporter *NOUN*
The film star was being interviewed by a TV reporter.
• journalist, correspondent

represent *VERB*
❶ *The picture represents an ancient legend.*
• depict, illustrate, portray, picture, show, describe
❷ *A dove is often said to represent peace.*
• stand for, symbolize
❸ *He appointed a lawyer to represent him.*
• speak for

reprimand *VERB*
He reprimanded them for their bad behaviour.
• reproach, scold, criticize
(informal) tell off, tick off
OPPOSITE praise

reproduce *VERB*
❶ *The robot can reproduce a human voice.*
• copy, duplicate, imitate, simulate, mimic

❷ *Mice reproduce very quickly.*
• breed, produce offspring, multiply, procreate
Fish reproduce by **spawning**.
To reproduce plants is to **propagate** them.

reproduction *NOUN*
❶ *Vets have to know about animal reproduction.*
• breeding, procreation
❷ *Is that an original painting or a reproduction?*
• copy, replica, imitation, likeness, duplicate, print
A reproduction of something which is intended to deceive people is a **fake** or **forgery**.
An exact reproduction of a document is a facsimile.

reptile *NOUN*

WORD WEB

SOME ANIMALS WHICH ARE REPTILES:

• alligator, chameleon, crocodile, gecko, iguana, lizard, salamander, slow-worm, snake, terrapin, tortoise, turtle
see also **snake**
A reptile found in myths and legends is a **basilisk**.
for other animals see **animal**

repulsive *ADJECTIVE*
We were put off eating by the repulsive smell.
• disgusting, revolting, offensive, repellent, disagreeable, foul, repugnant, obnoxious, sickening, hateful, hideous, horrible, loathsome, objectionable, vile
OPPOSITE attractive

reputation *NOUN*
The singer's reputation spread throughout the world.
• fame, celebrity, name, renown, eminence, standing, stature

a b c d e f g h i j k l m n o p q r s t u v w x y z

A B C D E F G H I J K L M N O P Q R S T U V W X Y Z

request *VERB*
*She has **requested** a transfer to a different job.*
• ask for, appeal for, apply for, beg for, call for, entreat, implore, invite, pray for, seek

request *NOUN*
*They have ignored our **request** for help.*
• appeal, plea, entreaty, call, cry
A request for a job or membership is an **application**.
A request signed by a lot of people is a **petition**.

require *VERB*
❶ *They **require** a draw to win the championship.*
• need, must have
❷ *Visitors are **required** to sign the register.*
• instruct, oblige, request, direct, order, command

rescue *VERB*
❶ *A helicopter was sent to **rescue** the trapped climbers.*
• free, liberate, release, save, set free
To rescue someone by paying money is to **ransom** them.
❷ *The divers **rescued** some items from the sunken ship.*
• retrieve, recover, salvage

resemblance *NOUN*
*It's easy to see the **resemblance** between the two sisters.*
• likeness, similarity, closeness
OPPOSITE difference

resemble *VERB*
*The twins closely **resemble** their mother.*
• look like, be similar to
(informal) take after

resent *VERB*
*She **resents** having to work such long hours.*
• be annoyed about, take exception to, be resentful about, begrudge, grudge

reservation *NOUN*
❶ *We have a **reservation** for two nights in the hotel.*
• booking

❷ *They saw giraffes on the wildlife **reservation**.*
• reserve, park, preserve, sanctuary
❸ *She had **reservations** about whether the plan would work.*
• doubt, misgiving, hesitation, qualm
If you have reservations about something, you are **sceptical** about it.

reserve *VERB*
❶ *The astronauts had to **reserve** fuel for the return voyage.*
• keep, put aside, set aside, save, preserve, retain, hold back
❷ *Have you **reserved** your seats on the train?*
• book, order, secure

reserve *NOUN*
❶ *The climbers kept a **reserve** of food in their base camp.*
• stock, store, supply, hoard, stockpile
A reserve of money is a **fund** or **savings**.
❷ *The coach put him down as a **reserve** for Saturday's game.*
• substitute, standby, stand-in, replacement
Someone who can take the place of an actor is an **understudy**.
❸ *The wildlife **reserve** has a new baby rhino.*
• reservation, park, preserve, sanctuary

reserved *ADJECTIVE*
❶ *These seats are **reserved**.*
• booked, set aside, ordered
❷ *He is too **reserved** to speak up for himself.*
• shy, timid, quiet, bashful, modest, retiring, reticent
OPPOSITE outgoing

residence *NOUN*
*The palace is the official **residence** of the queen.*
• dwelling, home, house
(formal) abode

resident *NOUN*
*The **residents** of New York are proud of their city.*
• citizen, inhabitant, occupant
A temporary resident in a hotel is a **guest**.
A resident in rented accommodation is a **boarder**, **lodger** or **tenant**.

resign VERB
The manager of the football team was forced to *resign*.
• leave, quit, stand down, step down, give in your notice
When a monarch resigns from the throne, he or she abdicates.

resist VERB
❶ They were too weak to *resist* the sorcerer's magic.
• stand up to, defend yourself against, withstand, defy, oppose, fend off
(OPPOSITES) yield to, surrender to
❷ I couldn't *resist* having another piece of chocolate.
• avoid, hold back from, refuse
(OPPOSITES) give in, accept

resolve VERB
❶ I *resolved* to try harder next time.
• decide, determine, make up your mind
❷ We held a meeting to try to *resolve* the dispute.
• settle, sort out, straighten out, end, overcome

resort NOUN
As a last *resort*, we could always walk.
• option, choice, course of action

resort VERB
He didn't want to *resort* to violence.
• start using, turn to, fall back on, rely on, stoop to

resound VERB
The howling of the wolves *resounded* through the forest.
• echo, boom

resources PLURAL NOUN
❶ The country is rich in natural *resources*.
• materials, raw materials, reserves
❷ The library has limited *resources* for buying new books.
• funds, money, capital, assets, means, wealth

respect NOUN
❶ Her colleagues have the deepest *respect* for her.
• admiration, esteem, regard, reverence, honour
❷ Have some *respect* for other people's feelings.
• consideration, sympathy, thought, concern
❸ In some *respects*, he's a better player than I am.
• way, point, aspect, feature, characteristic, detail, particular

respect VERB
❶ Everyone *respects* her for her courage.
• admire, esteem, revere, honour, look up to, value
(OPPOSITES) scorn, despise
❷ We tried to *respect* the wishes of our families.
• obey, follow, observe, adhere to, comply with
(OPPOSITE) ignore

respectable ADJECTIVE
❶ He came from a very *respectable* family.
• decent, honest, upright, honourable, worthy
❷ I finished the race in a *respectable* time.
• reasonable, satisfactory, acceptable, passable, adequate, fair, tolerable

respective ADJECTIVE
We all returned to our *respective* homes.
• separate, individual, own, particular, personal, specific

respond VERB
➤ to respond to
He didn't *respond to* my question.
• reply to, answer, react to, acknowledge

response NOUN
Did you get a *response* to your letter?
• reply, answer, reaction, acknowledgement
An angry response is a retort.

a
b
c
d
e
f
g
h
i
j
k
l
m
n
o
p
q
r
s
t
u
v
w
x
y
z

A B C D E F G H I J K L M N O P Q R S T U V W X Y Z

responsible *ADJECTIVE*
❶ *Parents are legally responsible for their children.*
• in charge
OPPOSITE not responsible
❷ *He's a very responsible sort of person.*
• reliable, sensible, trustworthy, dependable, conscientious, dutiful, honest
OPPOSITE irresponsible
❸ *Looking after people's money is a responsible job.*
• important, serious
❹ *Who is responsible for all this mess?*
• to blame, guilty (of), at fault

rest *NOUN*
❶ *The actors had a short rest in the middle of the rehearsal.*
• break, breather, breathing space, pause, respite, lie-down, nap
❷ *The doctor said the patient needed complete rest.*
• relaxation, leisure, inactivity, ease, quiet, time off

rest *VERB*
❶ *I think we should stop and rest for a while.*
• have a rest, lie down, relax, lounge, have a nap
❷ *Rest the ladder against the wall.*
• lean, prop, stand, place, support

rest *NOUN*
➤ **the rest**
Take a few sweets now, but leave the rest for later.
• the remainder, the surplus, the others, the remains

restaurant *NOUN*

WORD WEB

SOME TYPES OF RESTAURANT:

• buffet, cafe, cafeteria, canteen, chip shop, coffee shop, diner, grill, snack bar, steakhouse, takeaway, tea room
A French-style restaurant is a **bistro**.
A restaurant which serves pizza is a **pizzeria**.

restful *ADJECTIVE*
We spent a restful Sunday morning reading magazines.
• peaceful, quiet, relaxing, leisurely, calm, tranquil, undisturbed
OPPOSITE stressful

restless *ADJECTIVE*
❶ *The animals became restless during the storm.*
• agitated, nervous, anxious, edgy, fidgety, excitable, jumpy
(informal) jittery
OPPOSITE relaxed
❷ *I'm tired—I had a restless night.*
• sleepless, troubled, disturbed, unsettled, interrupted
OPPOSITE restful

restore *VERB*
❶ *Please restore the book to its proper place on the shelf.*
• put back, replace, return
❷ *The council are going to restore the Sunday bus service.*
• bring back, reinstate
To restore someone to health is to **cure** them.
❸ *Our neighbour loves to restore old cars.*
• renew, repair, renovate, fix, mend, rebuild

restrain *VERB*
❶ *Dogs must be restrained on a lead in the park.*
• hold back, keep back, keep under control, subdue, repress, restrict
❷ *I tried to restrain my anger.*
• control, curb, suppress, stifle

restrict *VERB*
The new law restricts the sale of fireworks.
• control, limit, regulate
➤ **to restrict to**
In a safari park, animals are not restricted to enclosures.
• confine to, enclose in, keep in, shut in, imprison in

result NOUN

❶ *The water shortage is a result of a long drought.*
• consequence, effect, outcome, sequel, upshot
The result of a game is the **score**.
The result of a trial is the **verdict**.
❷ *If you multiply 9 by 12, what is the result?*
• answer, product

result VERB

The bruising on his leg resulted from a bad fall.
• come about, develop, emerge, happen, occur, follow, ensue, take place, turn out
➤ **to result in**
Severe flooding resulted in chaos on the roads.
• cause, bring about, give rise to, lead to, develop into

resume VERB

We'll resume work after lunch.
• restart, start again, recommence, proceed with, continue, carry on

retain VERB

❶ *Please retain your ticket.*
• hold on to, keep, preserve, reserve, save *(informal)* hang on to
OPPOSITE surrender
❷ *This type of soil is good at retaining water.*
• hold in, keep in, hold back
OPPOSITE release

retire VERB

❶ *The manager plans to retire at the end of the season.*
• give up work, stop working
To leave your job voluntarily is to **resign**.
❷ *Mrs Hara retired to her room to rest.*
• withdraw, adjourn

retort VERB

'There's no need to be rude!' retorted Hannah.
• reply, answer, respond, react
for other ways to say something see **say**

retreat VERB

❶ *The army retreated to a safe position.*
• move back, draw back, fall back, withdraw, retire
To retreat in a shameful way is to **run away** or *(informal)* **turn tail**.
❷ *The snail retreated into its shell.*
• shrink back, recoil

retrieve VERB

I had to climb the fence to retrieve our ball.
• get back, bring back, fetch, recover, rescue, salvage

return VERB

❶ *We hope to return to Kenya next summer.*
• go back, revisit
❷ *My husband returns on Friday.*
• get back, come back, come home
❸ *I returned the book to its rightful owner.*
• give back, restore
❹ *Faulty goods may be returned to the shop.*
• send back, take back
❺ *Please return the money I lent you.*
• give back, repay, refund
❻ *We hoped that the fever would not return.*
• happen again, recur

return NOUN

❶ *She looked forward to her friends' return.*
• reappearance, homecoming
❷ *Did you get a good return from your investment?*
• profit, interest, gain

reveal VERB

❶ *The spy refused to reveal his real identity.*
• declare, disclose, make known, confess, admit, announce, proclaim, publish, tell
❷ *She swept aside the curtain to reveal a secret door.*
• uncover, unveil, expose
OPPOSITE hide

A
B
C
D
E
F
G
H
I
J
K
L
M
N
O
P
Q
R
S
T
U
V
W
X
Y
Z

revenge NOUN
*They sought **revenge** for the killing of their leader.*
• reprisal, vengeance
➤ **to take revenge on someone**
*He declared that he would **take revenge on** them all.*
• get even with, repay
(informal) get your own back on

revere VERB
*The painter was greatly **revered** by his fellow artists.*
• admire, respect, honour, esteem, worship, adore
OPPOSITE despise

reverse NOUN
*The letter had a handwritten note on the **reverse**.*
• other side, back

reverse VERB
❶ *You can use tracing paper to **reverse** a drawing.*
• turn round, swap round, transpose, invert
❷ *The driver tried to **reverse** into the parking space.*
• back, drive backwards, go backwards

review NOUN
❶ *They are carrying out a **review** of after-school clubs.*
• study, survey, examination, inspection
❷ *We had to write **reviews** of our favourite books.*
• report, criticism, appraisal, critique

review VERB
❶ *The judge began to **review** the evidence.*
• examine, go over, study, survey, consider, assess, appraise, evaluate, weigh up
❷ *He **reviews** the latest films for the Sunday paper.*
• criticize, write a review of

revise VERB
❶ *We **revised** the work we did last term.*
• go over, review, study

❷ *The new evidence forced me to **revise** my opinion.*
• change, modify, alter, reconsider, re-examine
❸ *The last chapter has been **revised** by the author.*
• correct, amend, edit, rewrite, update

revive VERB
❶ *The patient **revived** slowly after the operation.*
• come round, come to, recover, rally, wake up
❷ *A cold drink will **revive** you.*
• refresh, restore, invigorate, bring back to life, revitalise

revolt VERB
❶ *The people **revolted** against the cruel king.*
• rebel, riot, rise up
To revolt on a ship is to **mutiny**.
❷ *They were **revolted** by the stench in the dungeon.*
• disgust, repel, sicken, nauseate, offend, appal

revolting ADJECTIVE
*What is that **revolting** smell?*
• disgusting, foul, horrible, nasty, loathsome, offensive, obnoxious, repulsive, repugnant, sickening, nauseating, vile, unpleasant
OPPOSITES pleasant, attractive

revolution NOUN
❶ *The **revolution** brought in a new government.*
• rebellion, revolt, uprising
❷ *Computers brought about a **revolution** in the way people work.*
• change, transformation, shift
❸ *One **revolution** of the earth takes 24 hours.*
• rotation, turn, circuit, cycle

revolutionary ADJECTIVE
*The inventor had come up with a **revolutionary** design.*
• new, novel, innovative, radical

revolve *VERB*
The earth **revolves** once every 24 hours.
• rotate, turn
To revolve quickly is to **spin** or **whirl**.
To move round something is to **circle**
or **orbit** it.

reward *NOUN*
There is a **reward** for finding the missing cat.
• prize, bonus, payment, award, decoration
OPPOSITE punishment

reward *VERB*
❶ The firefighters were **rewarded** for their
bravery.
• honour, decorate
❷ She was generously **rewarded** for her work.
• compensate, pay

rewarding *ADJECTIVE*
Being a vet must be a **rewarding** job.
• satisfying, pleasing, gratifying, worthwhile
OPPOSITE thankless

rhyme *NOUN*
The children like listening to nursery **rhymes**.
• poem, verse

rhythm *NOUN*
We tapped our feet to the **rhythm** of the
music.
• beat, pulse
The speed or type of rhythm of a piece of
music is the **tempo**.
The type of rhythm of a piece of poetry is its
metre.

rich *ADJECTIVE*
❶ They must be **rich** to live in a castle.
• wealthy, affluent, prosperous, well-off,
well-to-do
OPPOSITE poor
❷ The palace was full of **rich** furnishings.
• expensive, costly, luxurious, sumptuous,
opulent, lavish, splendid, ornate
❸ The dancer wore a dress of a **rich** red colour.
• deep, strong, vivid, intense
❹ The soil in this area is very **rich**.
• fertile, productive

riches *PLURAL NOUN*
The inventors acquired **riches** beyond their
wildest dreams.
• wealth, money, affluence, prosperity,
fortune, treasure

rickety *ADJECTIVE*
Take care—that ladder looks **rickety**.
• shaky, unsteady, unstable, wobbly, flimsy
OPPOSITE solid

rid *VERB* rids, ridding, rid
The new vaccine may **rid** the world of the
disease.
• clear, free, empty, strip, purge
➤ to get rid of
He decided to **get rid of** his old guitar.
• dispose of, throw away or out, scrap
(informal) dump

riddle *NOUN*
They had to solve the **riddle** to find the treasure.
• puzzle, mystery, question, conundrum,
problem

ride *VERB* rides, riding, rode, ridden
My little sister is learning to **ride** a bike.
• control, handle, manage, steer
ride *NOUN*
They took us for a **ride** in their new car.
• drive, run, journey, trip
(informal) spin

ridicule *VERB*
The inventor was **ridiculed** for his wacky ideas.
• laugh at, make fun of, mock, scoff at,
jeer at, sneer at, taunt, tease, deride

ridiculous *ADJECTIVE*
❶ We looked **ridiculous** in our fancy dress
costumes.
• silly, stupid, foolish, daft, absurd, funny,
laughable
❷ That is a **ridiculous** price for a pair
of trainers!
• ludicrous, senseless, nonsensical,
preposterous, outrageous, absurd,
unreasonable, crazy
OPPOSITE sensible

a
b
c
d
e
f
g
h
i
j
k
l
m
n
o
p
q
r
s
t
u
v
w
x
y
z

right ADJECTIVE

❶ *The entrance is on the the right side of the building.*
The right side of a ship when you face forwards is the **starboard** side.
OPPOSITE left

❷ *Put up your hand if you got the right answer.*
• correct, accurate, true, exact
OPPOSITE wrong

❸ *She was waiting for the right moment to tell him.*
• proper, appropriate, fitting, suitable, ideal
OPPOSITE wrong

❹ *It's not right to steal.*
• fair, honest, decent, just, honourable, lawful, moral, upright, virtuous, ethical
OPPOSITE wrong

right ADVERB

❶ *Turn right at the corner.*
OPPOSITE left

❷ *Turn right round.*
• all the way, completely

❸ *She stood right in the middle.*
• exactly, precisely

❹ *Go right ahead.*
• directly, straight

right NOUN

❶ *The post office is on the right along the High Street.*
OPPOSITE left

❷ *People have the right to walk across the common.*
• freedom, liberty

❸ *You don't have the right to tell me what to do.*
• authority, power

rigid ADJECTIVE

❶ *The tent was supported by a rigid framework.*
• solid, stiff, firm, hard

❷ *The referee was rigid in applying the rules.*
• strict, inflexible, harsh, stern, uncompromising
OPPOSITE flexible

rigorous ADJECTIVE

The detective carried out a rigorous investigation.
• thorough, careful, meticulous, painstaking

rim NOUN

Mrs Sharpe peered at us over the rim of her glasses.
• brim, edge, lip, brink

ring NOUN

❶ *The dancers linked arms in a ring.*
• circle, round, loop, circuit

❷ *The wooden barrel had metal rings round it.*
• band, hoop

ring VERB rings, ringing, ringed

The ancient city is ringed by mountains.
• surround, encircle, enclose, circle

ring VERB rings, ringing, rang, rung

❶ *The doorbell rang.*
• chime, peal, toll, jangle, tinkle, sound, buzz
see also **bell**

❷ *Ring me tomorrow evening.*
• phone, call, telephone, ring up
(informal) give a buzz

rinse VERB

After shampooing your hair, rinse it in clean water.
• wash, clean, bathe, swill
To rinse out a toilet is to **flush** it.

riot NOUN

The police moved in to stop the riot.
• commotion, disorder, disturbance, turmoil, uproar, uprising

riot VERB

The crowds were rioting in the streets.
• run riot, run wild, run amok, rampage, revolt, rise up, rebel

rip VERB

She snatched the letter and ripped it to pieces.
• tear

ripe ADJECTIVE

Some of the plums on the tree are ripe now.
• mature, ready to eat
To become ripe is to **ripen**.

ripple *VERB*
*The wind **rippled** the surface of the pond.*
• ruffle, stir, disturb, make waves on

rise *VERB* rises, rising, rose, risen
❶ *The kite **rose** high into the air.*
• climb, mount, fly up, ascend, soar
When a plane rises into the air, it **takes off.**
When a rocket rises into the air, it **lifts off.**
OPPOSITE descend
❷ *The outer wall of the castle **rose** before us.*
• tower, loom, reach up, stick up
❸ *House prices **rose** again last year.*
• go up, increase
OPPOSITE fall
❹ *The audience **rose** and applauded wildly.*
• stand up, get up
OPPOSITE sit

rise *NOUN*
❶ *There will be a **rise** in temperature over the next few days.*
• increase, jump
OPPOSITE fall
❷ *At the top of the **rise** they paused for a break.*
• hill, slope, ascent, incline, bank, ramp
(Scottish) brae

risk *VERB*
❶ *If you place a bet, you **risk** losing the money.*
• chance, dare, gamble, venture
❷ *The firefighter **risked** her life to save them.*
• endanger, put at risk, jeopardise, hazard

risk *NOUN*
❶ *All outdoor activities carry an element of **risk.***
• danger, hazard, peril
❷ *Starting a business involves **risk.***
• a gamble, uncertainty
❸ *The forecast says there's a **risk** of snow.*
• chance, likelihood, possibility

risky *ADJECTIVE*
*Cycling on icy roads is **risky.***
• dangerous, hazardous, perilous, unsafe
OPPOSITE safe

ritual *NOUN*
*The temple was used for ancient religious **rituals.***
• ceremony, rite, service

rival *NOUN*
*He has no serious **rival** for the championship.*
• competitor, adversary, challenger, opponent, contender, contestant

rival *VERB*
*Few countries can **rival** Scotland for mountainous scenery.*
• compete with, contend with

rivalry *NOUN*
*There was fierce **rivalry** between the two local teams.*
• competition, competitiveness, opposition
OPPOSITE cooperation

river *NOUN*
A small river is a **stream** or **rivulet** or *(Scottish)* **burn.**
A small river which flows into a larger river is a **tributary.**
The place where a river begins is its **source.**
The place where a river goes into the sea is its **mouth.**
A wide river mouth is an **estuary** or *(Scottish)* **firth.**
The place where the mouth of a river splits before going into the sea is a **delta.**
A river of ice is a **glacier.**
This rivulet … broadens out into salt marshes below the village, and loses itself at last in a lake of brackish water.—MOONFLEET, J. Meade Faulkner

---

WRITING TIPS

You can use these words to describe a **river.**

TO DESCRIBE HOW A RIVER FLOWS:

• cascade, eddy, flood, glide, gush, meander, plunge, run, rush, snake, sweep, swirl, twist, wind

TO DESCRIBE HOW A RIVER SOUNDS:

• babble, burble, gurgle, murmur, ripple, roar, splash, thunder

a
b
c
d
e
f
g
h
i
j
k
l
m
n
o
p
q
r
s
t
u
v
w
x
y
z

A B C D E F G H I J K L M N O P Q R S T U V W X Y Z

road *NOUN*

WORD WEB

KINDS OF ROAD:

• bypass, dual carriageway, highway, main road, motorway, one-way street, ring road, trunk road
A road which is closed at one end is a **dead end**.
A private road up to a house is a **drive**.

KINDS OF ROAD IN A TOWN:

• alley, avenue, boulevard, crescent, cul-de-sac, lane, street, terrace
see also **path**

roam *VERB*
❶ *We roamed about town aimlessly.*
• wander, ramble, drift, stroll, amble, meander
❷ *Herds of wild deer roamed over the hills.*
• range, rove, prowl

roar *NOUN, VERB*
The dragon lifted its mighty head and roared.
• bellow, cry, yell, bawl, howl, thunder

rob *VERB*
The thieves planned to rob several banks in the city.
• steal from, break into, burgle, hold up, raid, loot, ransack, rifle

robber *NOUN*
see **thief**

robbery *NOUN*
see **stealing**

robe *NOUN*
A kind of robe you might wear in your bedroom is a **dressing gown** or bathrobe.
Robes worn by a priest are **vestments**.
The robe worn by a monk or nun is a **habit**.
A robe an official might wear at a ceremony is a **gown**.
Robe is also a formal word for a woman's dress.

robot *NOUN*
The robot spoke in a flat, metallic voice.
• automaton, android
A robot which is part-human is a **cyborg**.
A word meaning 'to do with robots' is **robotic**.
The study and design of robots is **robotics**.
A robot that flies is a **drone**.

WORD WEB

PARTS A ROBOT MIGHT HAVE:

• antenna, buttons, computer brain or chip, control panel, flashing lights, arm or limb, gripper, laser, motor, sensor, wheels

SOME WAYS TO DESCRIBE A ROBOT:

• bionic, intelligent, machine-like, mechanical, metallic, superhuman

robust *ADJECTIVE*
❶ *To be an explorer, you must be robust.*
• strong, vigorous, fit, hardy, healthy
OPPOSITE weak
❷ *I bought a robust pair of boots for hiking.*
• sturdy, tough, durable, hard-wearing
OPPOSITE flimsy

rock *NOUN*
We clambered over the rocks on the seashore.
• boulder, stone

WORD WEB

A small rock is a **pebble**.
A steep face of rock is a **cliff** or **crag**.

SOME KINDS OF ROCK:

• basalt, chalk, flint, granite, gypsum, lava, limestone, marble, quartz, sandstone, shale, slate
Rock from which metal or valuable minerals can be extracted is **ore**.
A layer of rock is a **stratum**.
A person who studies rocks is a **geologist**.

rock VERB
❶ *I rocked the baby's cradle to and fro.*
• sway, swing
❷ *The ship rocked in the storm.*
• roll, toss, lurch, pitch, tilt, reel

rocky ADJECTIVE
❶ *Nothing was growing in the rocky ground.*
• barren, stony, pebbly
❷ *Take care—that chair's a bit rocky.*
• rickety, shaky, unsteady, unstable, wobbly

rod NOUN
The framework is held together by steel rods.
• bar, rail, pole, strut, shaft, stick, spoke, staff

rode *past tense see* ride

rodent NOUN
for various kinds of animal see animal

rogue NOUN
Don't trust him—he's a rogue.
• rascal, scoundrel, villain, cheat, fraud, swindler, charlatan

role NOUN
❶ *Who is playing the lead role in the play?*
• character, part
❷ *Each player has an important role in the team.*
• job, task, function, position

roll VERB
❶ *The wheels of the chair began to roll.*
• move round, turn, revolve, rotate, spin, twirl, whirl
❷ *Roll the paper around your finger.*
• curl, wind, wrap, twist, coil
To roll up a sail on a yacht is to furl *it.*
❸ *Roll the pastry into a large circle.*
• flatten, level out, smooth
❹ *The ship rolled about in the storm.*
• pitch, rock, sway, toss, wallow, lurch

romantic ADJECTIVE
❶ *The film had a very romantic ending.*
• sentimental, emotional, tender
(informal) soppy, mushy
❷ *The life of an explorer sounds very romantic.*
• exotic, glamorous, exciting

romp VERB
The children romped around the playground.
• leap about, run about, skip about, caper, frisk, frolic

roof NOUN
The sloping beams in the framework of a roof are rafters.
The overhanging edge of a roof is the eaves.
A building without a roof is an open-air building.
A vehicle without a roof is an open-top vehicle.

room NOUN
❶ *How many rooms are there in your house?*
An old word for room is chamber.
❷ *Is there room in the car for another suitcase?*
• space, capacity

WORD WEB

ROOMS YOU MIGHT FIND IN A HOUSE OR FLAT:

• bathroom, bedroom, box room, conservatory, dining room, drawing room, hall, kitchen or kitchenette, living room, lounge, nursery, pantry, parlour, sitting room, spare room or guest room, study, toilet or lavatory or *(informal)* loo, utility room

ROOMS YOU MIGHT FIND IN A SCHOOL:

• assembly hall, classroom, cloakroom, corridor, drama room, laboratory, library, music room, office, sickroom, staffroom, storeroom, toilets or lavatories or *(informal)* loos

SOME OTHER ROOMS:

A small room in a monastery or prison is a cell.

a b c d e f g h i j k l m n o p q r s t u v w x y z

An underground room is a **basement** or **cellar**. In a church it is a **vault**.

The space in the roof of a house is the **attic** or **loft**.

A room where an artist works is a **studio**.

A room where you wait to see a doctor or dentist is a **waiting room**.

A room in a hospital for patients is a **ward**.

roomy ADJECTIVE
The flat is surprisingly roomy inside.
• big, large, spacious, sizeable

root NOUN
We need to get to the root of the problem.
• origin, source, cause, basis, starting point

rope NOUN
The sailors threw a rope to the men in the water.
• cable, cord, line
The ropes that support a ship's mast and sails are the **rigging**.
A rope with a loop at one end used for catching cattle is a **lasso**.

rose past tense see **rise**

rot VERB
The wooden fence had begun to rot.
• decay, decompose, become rotten, crumble, disintegrate
If metal rots it is said to **corrode**.
If rubber rots it is said to **perish**.
If food rots it is said to **go bad** or **putrefy**.

rotate VERB
The globe rotates on its axis.
• revolve, turn, spin, pivot, wheel, swivel, twirl, twist, whirl

rotten ADJECTIVE
❶ *The window frame is rotten.*
• decayed, decaying, decomposed, crumbling, disintegrating
Rotten metal is **corroded** or **rusty** metal.
OPPOSITE sound

❷ *The fridge smelled of rotten eggs.*
• bad, mouldy, mouldering, foul, putrid, smelly
OPPOSITE fresh
❸ *(informal) The weather has been rotten all week.*
• bad, unpleasant, disagreeable, awful, abysmal, dreadful, nasty
(informal) lousy
OPPOSITE good

rough ADJECTIVE
❶ *A rough track led to the farm.*
• bumpy, uneven, irregular, rocky, stony, rugged, craggy, jagged
OPPOSITES even, smooth
❷ *The sea was rough and the boat lurched from side to side.*
• stormy, turbulent, heaving
If the sea is rough with small waves it is said to be **choppy**.
OPPOSITE calm
❸ *The woman wore a rough woollen cloak.*
• coarse, harsh, scratchy, bristly
OPPOSITE soft
❹ *The prisoners had suffered rough treatment.*
• harsh, severe, cruel, hard, tough, violent
OPPOSITES gentle, mild
❺ *I had only a rough idea of where we were.*
• approximate, vague, inexact, imprecise, hazy
OPPOSITE exact
❻ *Our guide made a rough sketch of the route.*
• quick, hasty, crude, basic
OPPOSITES detailed, careful

roughly ADVERB
The cinema can seat roughly a hundred people.
• approximately, about, around, close to, nearly

round ADJECTIVE
Holly bushes have small round berries.
• rounded, spherical
A flat round shape is **circular**.

round NOUN
Our team got through to the second round of the competition.
• stage, heat, bout, contest, game

round VERB
*The motorbike **rounded** the corner at top speed.*
• go round, travel round, turn
➤ **to round something off**
*They **rounded** the evening **off** with some songs.*
• bring to an end, conclude, end, finish, complete
➤ **to round up people** or **things**
*The captain **rounded up** his players.*
• assemble, gather, bring together, collect, muster, rally

roundabout ADJECTIVE
*We went by a **roundabout** route to avoid the traffic.*
• indirect, circuitous, long, winding, twisting
OPPOSITE direct

rouse VERB
❶ *We were **roused** by the sound of birds singing.*
• arouse, awaken, call, wake up
❷ *He was a quiet man, not easily **roused** to anger.*
• provoke, agitate, excite, stimulate, stir up

route NOUN
*We drove home by the quickest **route**.*
• path, road, way, course, direction, journey

routine NOUN
❶ *Brushing my teeth is part of my morning **routine**.*
• pattern, procedure, way, custom, habit, practice, order
❷ *The ice-skaters practised their new **routine**.*
• act, programme, performance, number

row NOUN (rhymes with go)
*The gardener planted the vegetables in **rows**.*
• column, line, string, series, sequence
A row of people waiting for something is a **queue**.
A row of people walking behind each other is a **file**.
A row of soldiers standing side by side on parade is a **rank**.

row NOUN (rhymes with cow)
❶ *The class next door was making a terrible **row**.*
• noise, racket, din, commotion, disturbance, uproar, rumpus
❷ *One of the pirates had a **row** with the captain.*
• argument, fight, quarrel, squabble, disagreement, dispute

rowdy ADJECTIVE
*Later in the evening, the party became **rowdy**.*
• noisy, unruly, wild, disorderly, boisterous, riotous
OPPOSITE quiet

royalty NOUN

WORD WEB

SOME MEMBERS OF A ROYAL FAMILY:

• king, monarch, prince, princess, queen, sovereign
The husband or wife of a royal person is a **consort**.
The way to address a king or queen is **Your Majesty**.
The way to address a prince or princess is **Your Highness**.
see also **ruler**

rub VERB
❶ *Kathy **rubbed** her sore elbow.*
• stroke, knead, massage
❷ *I **rubbed** some suncream on my arms.*
• spread, smooth, smear, apply (to)
❸ *These boots are **rubbing** against my ankles.*
• graze, scrape, chafe
❹ *He **rubbed** the mirror until it gleamed.*
• polish, wipe, shine, buff
➤ **to rub something out**
*Can you **rub out** those pencil marks?*
• erase, wipe out, delete, remove

a b c d e f g h i j k l m n o p q r s t u v w x y z

rubbish NOUN
❶ *Ramesh took the rubbish out to the bin.*
• refuse, waste, trash, garbage, junk, litter, scrap
❷ *Don't talk rubbish!*
• nonsense, drivel, balderdash, piffle, gibberish, claptrap, gobbledegook
(informal) rot, tripe, twaddle

rude ADJECTIVE
❶ *It's very rude to talk with your mouth full.*
• impolite, discourteous, disrespectful, impertinent, impudent, insolent, offensive, insulting, bad-mannered, ill-bred
To be rude to someone is to **insult** or **snub** them.
To be rude about sacred things is to be **blasphemous** or **irreverent**.
OPPOSITE polite
❷ *Some of the jokes in the film are rather rude.*
• indecent, improper, offensive, coarse, crude
OPPOSITES decent, clean

ruffle VERB
The peacock shook and ruffled its tail feathers.
• stir, ripple, rumple, tousle

ruin VERB
The storm had ruined the farmer's crops.
• damage, destroy, spoil, wreck, devastate, demolish, lay waste, shatter

ruin NOUN
When they lost the match, it was the ruin of their dream.
• collapse, failure, breakdown
Financial ruin is **bankruptcy**.
➤ **ruins**
Archaeologists have discovered the ruins of a Roman fort.
• remains, remnants, fragments

ruined ADJECTIVE
Bats flew in and out of the ruined abbey.
• wrecked, crumbling, derelict, dilapidated, tumbledown, ramshackle

rule NOUN
❶ *Players must stick to the rules of the game.*
• law, regulation, principle
A set of rules is a **code**.
❷ *The country was formerly under a different leader's rule.*
• control, authority, command, power, government, reign

rule VERB
❶ *The Romans ruled a vast empire.*
• command, govern, control, direct, lead, manage, run, administer
❷ *Queen Victoria continued to rule for many years.*
• reign, be ruler
❸ *The umpire ruled that the batsman was out.*
• judge, decree, pronounce, decide, determine, find

ruler NOUN

WORD WEB

SOME KINDS OF RULER:

• emir, emperor, empress, governor, head of state, king, lord, monarch, president, prince, princess, queen, sovereign
A person who rules while a monarch is too young or too ill to rule is a **regent**.

SOME RULERS IN PAST TIMES:

• Caesar, pharaoh, raja or rani, sultan or sultana, tsar or tsarina

rummage VERB
I rummaged through my bag looking for my purse.
• search, hunt, ransack, scour

rumour NOUN
There was a rumour that the thief had struck again.
• gossip, hearsay, talk
(informal) title-tattle

run *VERB* runs, running, ran, run
❶ *We ran as fast as our legs could carry us.*
• race, sprint, dash, tear, bolt, career, speed, hurry, rush, streak, fly, whizz, zoom, scurry, scamper, scoot
To run at a gentle pace is to **jog**.
When a horse runs, it **gallops**, **canters** or **trots**.
❷ *Tears ran down the merman's cheeks.*
• stream, flow, pour, gush, flood, cascade, spill, trickle, dribble, leak
❸ *That old sewing machine still runs well.*
• function, operate, work, go, perform
❹ *My aunt runs a restaurant in Leeds.*
• manage, be in charge of, direct, control, supervise, govern, rule
❺ *The High Street runs through the city centre.*
• pass, go, extend, stretch, reach
➤ **to run away** or **off**
The thieves ran off when they heard footsteps.
• bolt, fly, flee, escape, take off, hurry off *(informal)* make off, clear off, scarper
➤ **to run into**
Guess who I ran into the other day?
• meet, come across, encounter *(informal)* bump into
A cyclist skidded and ran into a tree.
• hit, collide with

run *NOUN*
❶ *She goes for a run in the park every morning.*
A fast run is a **dash**, **gallop**, **race** or **sprint**.
A gentle run is a **jog**.
❷ *We went for a run in the car.*
• drive, journey, ride
❸ *They've had a run of good luck recently.*
• sequence, stretch, series
❹ *The farmer built a new chicken run.*
• enclosure, pen, coop

runaway *NOUN*
A person who has run away from the army is a **deserter**.
A person who is running away from the law is a **fugitive** or **outlaw**.

runner *NOUN*
The runners were ready to start the race.
• athlete, competitor
Someone who runs fast over short distances is a **sprinter**.
Someone who runs to keep fit is a **jogger**.

runny *ADJECTIVE*
This custard is too runny.
• watery, thin, liquid, fluid
OPPOSITE thick

rural *ADJECTIVE*
They live in a peaceful rural area.
• country, rustic, agricultural, pastoral
OPPOSITE urban

rush *VERB*
I rushed home with the good news.
• hurry, hasten, race, run, dash, fly, bolt, charge, shoot, speed, sprint, tear, zoom
When cattle or other animals rush along together they **stampede**.

rush *NOUN*
❶ *We've got plenty of time, so what's the rush?*
• hurry, haste, urgency
❷ *There was a sudden rush of water.*
• flood, gush, spurt, stream, spate

rustic *ADJECTIVE*
The village had a rustic charm.
• country, rural, pastoral, countrified

rut *NOUN*
The tractor left ruts along the track.
• furrow, groove, channel, trough

ruthless *ADJECTIVE*
The pirates launched a ruthless attack.
• cruel, brutal, bloodthirsty, barbaric, heartless, pitiless, merciless, callous, ferocious, fierce, savage, vicious, violent
OPPOSITE merciful

a
b
c
d
e
f
g
h
i
j
k
l
m
n
o
p
q
r
s
t
u
v
w
x
y
z

Ss

A B C D E F G H I J K L M N O P Q R S T U V W X Y Z

sack *NOUN*
The farmer delivered a large **sack** of potatoes.
• bag, pack

sack *VERB*
The manager threatened to **sack** the whole team.
• dismiss, discharge
(informal) fire, give you the sack

sacred *ADJECTIVE*
The Koran is a **sacred** book.
• holy, religious, divine, heavenly

sacrifice *VERB*
❶ I **sacrificed** my lunch break to practise guitar.
• give up, surrender, go without
❷ The ancient Greeks **sacrificed** animals to please the gods.
• offer up, kill, slaughter

sad *ADJECTIVE*

OVERUSED WORD

Try to vary the words you use for **sad**. Here are some other words you could use.

FOR A SAD MOOD OR SAD PERSON:

• unhappy, sorrowful, miserable, depressed, downcast, downhearted, despondent, crestfallen, dismal, gloomy, glum, blue, low, dejected, forlorn, desolate, doleful, wretched, woebegone, tearful, heartbroken, broken-hearted
The Big Friendly Giant looked suddenly so forlorn that Sophie got quite upset. 'I'm sorry,' she said. 'I didn't mean to be rude.'—THE BFG, Roald Dahl
If you are sad because you are away from home, you are **homesick**.
OPPOSITE happy

FOR A SAD STORY OR SAD TUNE:

• depressing, melancholy, mournful, moving, touching, plaintive, wistful, sorrowful, woeful
*The pirate related the **mournful** tale of Billy Bones.*
OPPOSITE cheering

FOR A SAD SITUATION OR SAD NEWS:

• unfortunate, unpleasant, painful, regrettable, lamentable, grim, serious, grave, tragic, grievous
*The letter contained some **painful** news.*
OPPOSITES cheerful, pleasant

FOR SOMETHING THAT MAKES YOU FEEL SAD:

• upsetting, distressing, heartbreaking, heart-rending, pitiful, pathetic
*It was **heartbreaking** to watch the injured bird.*

sadden *VERB*
The news of her friend's illness **saddened** her.
• distress, upset, depress, grieve, disappoint
(informal) break your heart
OPPOSITE cheer up

sadness *NOUN*
see **sorrow**

safe *ADJECTIVE*
❶ The kitten was found **safe** and well in a neighbour's garden.
• unharmed, unhurt, uninjured, undamaged, sound, intact
(informal) in one piece
OPPOSITES hurt, damaged
❷ They felt **safe** indoors as the storm raged outside.
• protected, guarded, defended, secure
OPPOSITE vulnerable

❸ *The secret code is in safe hands.*
• reliable, trustworthy, dependable
❹ *Is the tap water safe to drink?*
• harmless, uncontaminated, innocuous
OPPOSITE dangerous

safety *NOUN*
You must wear a seat belt for your own safety.
• protection, security, well-being
OPPOSITE danger

sag *VERB*
The settee was old and stained and sagged in the middle.
• sink, dip, droop, flop, slump

said *past tense see* say

sail *VERB*
❶ *We sailed to Norway rather than going by air.*
• travel by ship
To have a holiday sailing on a ship is to **cruise** or **go on a cruise**.
To begin a sea voyage is to **put to sea** or **set sail**.
❷ *None of the survivors knew how to sail the ship.*
• pilot, steer, navigate

sailor *NOUN*
The crew comprised three sailors and a cook.
• seaman, seafarer, mariner, boatman
A person who sails a yacht is a **yachtsman** or **yachtswoman**.

sake *NOUN*
➤ **for the sake of**
He put some money aside for the sake of his children.
• for the good of, on behalf of, in the interests of, to help

salary *NOUN*
The job has an annual salary of £30,000.
• income, pay, earnings
If your pay is paid week by week, it is called **wages**.

sale *NOUN*
They made a lot of money from the sale of their house.
• selling, marketing, vending
OPPOSITE purchase

salvage *VERB*
The crew tried to salvage some supplies from the wreck.
• rescue, save, recover, retrieve, reclaim

same *ADJECTIVE*
➤ **the same**
❶ *Each pirate was given the same ration of rum.*
• equal, identical, equivalent
❷ *Everyone in the choir wore the same outfit.*
• matching, similar, alike, uniform
❸ *Her feelings have remained the same.*
• unaltered, unchanged, constant
Words which mean the same are **synonymous** with each other.
OPPOSITE different

sample *NOUN*
The detective asked for a sample of her handwriting.
• specimen, example, instance, illustration, selection

sample *VERB*
Would you like to sample some home-made jam?
• taste, test, try

sand *NOUN*
We built a huge castle out of sand and seashells.
Hills of sand along the coast are **dunes**.
➤ **sands**

We played on the **sands** until the tide came in.
• beach, shore

sane *ADJECTIVE*
No **sane** person would stand out in the pouring rain!
• sensible, rational, reasonable
OPPOSITE insane

sang *past tense see* **sing**

sank *past tense see* **sink**

sarcastic *ADJECTIVE*
He made a **sarcastic** remark about my hat.
• mocking, satirical, ironical, sneering, taunting

sat *past tense see* **sit**

satisfaction *NOUN*
She gets a lot of **satisfaction** from growing vegetables.
• happiness, pleasure, enjoyment, contentment, fulfilment, sense of achievement, pride
OPPOSITE dissatisfaction

satisfactory *ADJECTIVE*
I'm afraid this work is not **satisfactory**.
• acceptable, adequate, passable, good enough, tolerable, competent
(informal) all right, up to scratch
OPPOSITE unsatisfactory

satisfy *VERB*
Nothing **satisfies** him—he's always complaining.
• please, content, make happy
OPPOSITE dissatisfy
To satisfy your thirst is to **quench** or slake it.

savage *ADJECTIVE*
❶ The invaders launched a **savage** attack on the town.
• vicious, cruel, barbaric, brutal, bloodthirsty, pitiless, ruthless, merciless, inhuman
OPPOSITE humane
❷ A **savage** beast is said to live in the cave.
• untamed, wild, ferocious, fierce
OPPOSITE domesticated

save *VERB*
❶ The owners managed to **save** most of the books from the fire.
• rescue, recover, retrieve, salvage
❷ The knight pledged to **save** the prince from the witch's curse.
• protect, defend, guard, shield, preserve
❸ She **saved** him from making a fool of himself.
• stop, prevent, deter
❹ I **saved** you a piece of my birthday cake.
• keep, reserve, set aside, hold on to
❺ If you share a car, then you can **save** petrol.
• be sparing with, conserve, use wisely

savings *PLURAL NOUN*
They used all their **savings** to go on a cruise.
• reserves, funds, resources, investments

saw *past tense see* **see**

saw *NOUN*
for various tools see **tool**

say *VERB* says, saying, said
❶ He found it hard to **say** what he meant.
• express, communicate, put into words, convey
❷ I would like to **say** a few words before we start.
• utter, speak, recite, read

358

OVERUSED WORD

Try to vary the words you use for **say**, especially with direct speech.
Here are some other words you could use.

TO SAY LOUDLY:

• call, cry, exclaim, bellow, bawl, shout, yell, roar
'Land ahoy!' bellowed the cabin boy.

TO SAY QUIETLY:

• whisper, mumble, mutter
'That woman,' I whispered, 'is a secret agent.'

TO SAY STRONGLY:

• state, announce, assert, declare, pronounce, insist, maintain, profess
'You may leave us,' Miss Minchin announced to the servants with a wave of her hand.—A LITTLE PRINCESS, Frances Hodgson Burnett

TO SAY CASUALLY:

• remark, comment, observe, note, mention
'It's very warm for this time of year,' Mr Lewis remarked.

TO SAY ANGRILY:

• snap, snarl, growl, thunder, bark, rasp, rant, rave
'Give me that piece of paper!' snapped Miss Crabbit.

TO SAY SUDDENLY:

• blurt out
'That's just a pretend dinosaur!' Ben blurted out.

TO SAY UNCLEARLY:

• babble, burble, gabble, stammer, stutter
The stranger kept babbling about hidden treasure.

TO SAY IN SURPRISE OR ALARM:

• gasp, cry, squeal
'The tunnel is sealed! There's no way out!' gasped Alex.

TO SAY SOMETHING FUNNY:

• joke, quip, tease
'Were you singing? I thought it was a cat,' teased my big sister.

TO GIVE AN ORDER:

• command, demand, order
A voice outside demanded, 'Open the door at once!'

TO ASK A QUESTION:

• enquire, demand, query
'How do you spell your name?' the judge enquired.

TO GIVE A REPLY:

• answer, reply, respond, retort
'Certainly not!' retorted Lady Dimsley.

TO MAKE A REQUEST OR AN EXCUSE:

• beg, entreat, implore, plead, urge
'I didn't mean it!' pleaded poor Alice. 'But you're so easily offended, you know!'—ALICE'S ADVENTURES IN WONDERLAND, Lewis Carroll

TO MAKE A SUGGESTION:

• suggest, propose
'Let's make them walk the plank,' suggested Captain Hook.

TO SAY AGAIN:

• repeat, reiterate, echo
The Martians repeated, 'Take us to your leader!'

saying NOUN
'Many hands make light work' is a common saying.
• expression, phrase, motto, proverb, catchphrase
An overused saying is a **cliché.**

a b c d e f g h i j k l m n o p q r s t u v w x y z

A B C D E F G H I J K L M N O P Q R S T U V W X Y Z

scamper *VERB*
The rabbits *scampered* away
to safety.
• hurry, dash, run, rush, hasten,
scuttle

scan *VERB*
❶ The lookout *scanned* the horizon, hoping
to see land.
• search, study, survey, examine, scrutinize,
stare at, eye
❷ I *scanned* through some magazines in the
waiting room.
• skim, glance at, flick through

scandal *NOUN*
❶ The waste of food after the party was a
scandal.
• disgrace, embarrassment, shame,
outrage
❷ Some newspapers like to publish the latest
scandal.
• gossip, rumours, dirt

scar *NOUN*
The warrior had a *scar* across his
forehead.
• mark, blemish, wound
scar *VERB*
The injuries he received *scarred* him for
life.
• mark, disfigure, deface

scarce *ADJECTIVE*
Water is very *scarce* in the desert.
• hard to find, in short supply, lacking,
sparse, scanty, rare, uncommon
(informal) thin on the ground
OPPOSITE plentiful

scarcely *ADVERB*
She was so tired that she could *scarcely*
walk.
• barely, hardly, only just

scare *NOUN*
The explosion gave them a nasty *scare*.
• fright, shock, alarm
scare *VERB*
My brother tried to *scare* us by making
ghost noises.
• frighten, terrify, petrify, alarm, startle,
panic
OPPOSITE reassure

scared *ADJECTIVE*
When we heard the footsteps, we were too
scared to move.
• frightened, terrified, petrified, horrified,
alarmed, fearful, panicky
see also **afraid**

scary *ADJECTIVE (informal)*
I had to close my eyes at the *scary* bits in
the film.
• frightening, terrifying, horrifying,
alarming, nightmarish, fearsome, chilling,
spine-chilling, hair-raising, blood-curdling,
chilling, eerie, sinister

scatter *VERB*
❶ She *scattered* the seeds on the
ground.
• spread, sprinkle, sow, strew, throw about,
shower
OPPOSITE collect
❷ The animals *scattered* when the children
ran towards them.
• break up, separate, disperse, disband
OPPOSITE gather

scene *NOUN*
❶ The police arrived quickly at the *scene* of
the crime.
• location, position, site, place, situation,
spot
❷ They were rehearsing a *scene* from the
play.
• episode, part, section, act

❸ *I gazed out of the window at the moonlit scene.*
• landscape, scenery, view, sight, outlook, prospect, spectacle, setting, backdrop
❹ *He didn't want to create a scene in the restaurant.*
• fuss, commotion, disturbance, quarrel, row

scenery NOUN
We admired the scenery from the top of the hill.
• landscape, outlook, prospect, scene, view, panorama

scent NOUN
Aasma loves the scent of roses.
• smell, fragrance, perfume, aroma
see also **smell**

sceptical ADJECTIVE
At first, I was sceptical about the legend of the ghost.
• disbelieving, doubtful, doubting, unconvinced, dubious, incredulous, suspicious, uncertain, unsure
OPPOSITE trustful

schedule NOUN
The athletes had a rigorous training schedule.
• programme, timetable, plan, calendar, diary
A schedule of topics to be discussed at a meeting is an **agenda**.
A schedule of places to be visited on a journey is an **itinerary**.

scheme NOUN
They worked out a scheme to raise some money.
• plan, proposal, project, procedure, method, system
scheme VERB
The smugglers were scheming against each other.
• plot, conspire, intrigue

school NOUN

WORD WEB
VARIOUS KINDS OF SCHOOL:

• academy, boarding school, comprehensive school, faith school, grammar school, high school, independent school, infant school, junior school, kindergarten, nursery school, preparatory or prep school, primary school, private school, public school, secondary school
for rooms in a school see **room**

science NOUN

WORD WEB
SOME BRANCHES OF SCIENCE:

• aeronautics, anatomy, astronomy, biology, botany, chemistry, climatology, computer science, earth sciences, ecology, electronics, engineering, genetics, geology, information technology, mechanics, medicine, meteorology, physics, psychology, veterinary science, zoology

scoff VERB
➤ **to scoff at**
Everyone scoffed at their ideas.
• mock, ridicule, sneer at, jeer at, deride, make fun of, poke fun at

scold VERB
He scolded us for being late.
• reprimand, reproach, tell off
(informal) tick off

scoop VERB
We scooped out a moat for our sandcastle.
• dig, gouge, scrape, excavate, hollow

a b c d e f g h i j k l m n o p q r s t u v w x y z

A
B
C
D
E
F
G
H
I
J
K
L
M
N
O
P
Q
R
S
T
U
V
W
X
Y
Z

scope *NOUN*
❶ *The park offers plenty of scope for children to play.*
• opportunity, room, space, freedom, liberty
❷ *These things are outside the scope of the project.*
• range, extent, limit, reach, span

scorch *VERB*
The dragon's breath scorched the wizard's beard.
• burn, singe, sear, blacken, char

score *NOUN*
We added up each other's scores.
• marks, points, total
The final score is the **result**.

score *VERB*
❶ *How many goals did you score?*
• win, get, make, gain, earn
❷ *Some lines were scored into the bark of the tree.*
• cut, gouge, mark, scrape, scratch

scorn *NOUN*
She dismissed my suggestion with scorn.
• contempt, derision, disrespect, mockery, ridicule
OPPOSITE admiration

scour *VERB*
❶ *He scoured the pan until it shone.*
• scrape, scrub, rub, clean, polish
❷ *Edith scoured the room looking for her glasses.*
• search, hunt through, ransack, comb

scowl *VERB*
The witch scowled under her floppy black hat.
• frown, glower
for other facial expressions see
expression

scramble *VERB*
❶ *The smugglers escaped by scrambling over the rocks.*
• clamber, climb, crawl, scrabble
❷ *The children scrambled to get the best seats.*
• push, jostle, struggle, fight, scuffle

scrap *NOUN*
❶ *They fed the scraps of food to the birds.*
• bit, piece, fragment, morsel, crumb, speck, particle
❷ *We took a pile of scrap to the tip.*
• rubbish, waste, junk, refuse, litter
Scraps of cloth are **rags** or **shreds**.
❸ *(informal) There was a scrap between the two gangs.*
• fight, brawl, scuffle, tussle, squabble

scrap *VERB*
❶ *The author scrapped the last paragraph.*
• discard, throw away, abandon, cancel, drop, give up
(informal) dump
❷ *(informal) The cubs enjoy scrapping with each other.*
• fight, brawl, tussle, scuffle

scrape *VERB*
❶ *She scraped her knee when she fell over.*
• graze, scratch, scuff
❷ *I tried to scrape the mud off my trainers.*
• rub, scour, scrub, clean

scrape *NOUN*
My little brother is always getting into scrapes.
• trouble, mischief
(informal) jam, pickle

scratch *VERB*
❶ *Someone scratched the side of the car.*
• mark, score, scrape, gouge, graze
❷ *The cat tried to scratch me.*
• claw

scratch *NOUN*
Who made this scratch on the side of the car?
• gash, groove, line, mark, scrape

scrawl *VERB*
She scrawled his phone number on a scrap of paper.
• jot down, scribble, write

scream *NOUN, VERB*
We heard a woman's scream in the distance.
A man ran out of the house screaming.
• shriek, screech, shout, yell, cry, bawl, howl, wail, squeal, yelp

screen *NOUN*
The large room was divided into two by a screen.
• curtain, partition, divider

screen *VERB*
❶ *Jumani wore a baseball cap to shield his face from the sun.*
• shield, protect, shelter, shade, cover, hide, mask, veil
❷ *All employees are screened before being appointed.*
• examine, investigate, test, check

scribble *VERB*
He scribbled his phone number on a scrap of paper.
• scrawl, jot down, dash off, write
To scribble a rough drawing, especially when you are bored, is to **doodle**.

script *NOUN*
The script for a film is a **screenplay**.
A handwritten or typed script is a **manuscript**.

scrub *VERB*
He scrubbed the floor clean.
• rub, brush, clean, wash, scour

scruffy *ADJECTIVE*
Magnus wore an old jumper and scruffy jeans.
• untidy, messy, ragged, tatty, tattered, worn-out, shabby
OPPOSITE smart

scrutinize *VERB*
She scrutinized the handwriting on the letter.
• examine, inspect, look at, study, investigate, explore

sculpture *NOUN*
The temple was full of marble sculptures.
• carving, figure, statue

sea *NOUN*

WORD WEB

The very large seas of the world are called **oceans**.
An area of sea partly enclosed by land is a **bay** or **gulf**.
A wide inlet of the sea is a **sound**.
A wide inlet where a river joins the sea is an **estuary**, or *(in Scotland)* a **firth**.
A long narrow sea inlet between cliffs is a **fjord**.
A narrow stretch of water linking two seas is a **strait**.
The bottom of the sea is the **seabed**.
The land near the sea is the **coast** or the **seashore**.
Creatures that live in the sea are **marine** creatures.

THINGS YOU MIGHT SEE ON THE SEA:

• breaker, iceberg, sea spray, surf, swell, waves
• boat, cruise ship, ocean liner, yacht

SOME CREATURES THAT LIVE IN THE SEA:

• cuttlefish, dolphin, eel, fish, jellyfish, killer whale, octopus, porpoise, seahorse, seal, sea lion, shark, squid, stingray, turtle, whale
see also **seashore**

a b c d e f g h i j k l m n o p q r s t u v w x y z

A
B
C
D
E
F
G
H
I
J
K
L
M
N
O
P
Q
R
S
T
U
V
W
X
Y
Z

WRITING TIPS

You can use these words to describe the sea.

TO DESCRIBE A CALM SEA:

• calm, crystal clear, glassy, sparkling, tranquil, unruffled

TO DESCRIBE A ROUGH SEA:

• choppy, raging, rough, stormy, tempestuous, turbulent, wild
The Tankadere started to move fast over the raging sea whose waves were now colliding with those previously produced by the wind.
—AROUND THE WORLD IN EIGHTY DAYS, Jules Verne

WAVES ON THE SEA MIGHT:

• billow, break, crash, heave, pound, roll, surge, swell, tumble, wash

seal *VERB*

The entrance to the burial chamber had been sealed.
• close, fasten, shut, lock, secure
To seal a leak is to **plug** it or **stop** it.

seam *NOUN*

❶ *The seam on his trousers split.*
• join, stitching
❷ *Geologists discovered a seam of coal.*
• layer, stratum

search *VERB*

❶ *He was searching for the book he had lost.*
• hunt, look, seek
To search for gold or some other mineral is to **prospect**.
❷ *The police searched the house but didn't find anything.*
• explore, scour, ransack, rummage through, comb
❸ *Security staff searched all the passengers.*
• check, inspect, examine, scrutinize
(informal) frisk

search *NOUN*

After a long search, she found her keys.
• hunt, look, check
A long journey in search of something is a **quest**.

seashore *NOUN*

We explored the seashore, looking for shells and fossils.
• seaside, beach, shore, coast

WORD WEB

THINGS YOU MIGHT SEE ON THE SEASHORE:

• cave, cliff, coral reef, driftwood, dunes, lighthouse, mudflats, pebbles, rock pool, rocks, sand, seashell, seaweed, shingle
see also **seaside**

CREATURES THAT LIVE ON THE SEASHORE:

• barnacle, clam, cockle, coral, crab, limpet, mussel, oyster, prawn, razor shell, sea anemone, seabird, seagull, sea urchin, shrimp, sponge, starfish, whelk
for names of seabirds see **bird**
for other sea creatures see **sea**

seaside *NOUN*

If it's sunny tomorrow, we might go to the seaside.
• beach, sands, seashore

WORD WEB

THINGS YOU MIGHT SEE AT THE SEASIDE:

• beach huts, funfair, harbour, ice cream van, jetty, lifeguard, pier, promenade
A town where you go to have fun by the sea is a **seaside resort**.

THINGS YOU MIGHT TAKE TO THE SEASIDE:

• beach ball, bucket and spade, deckchair, fishing net, snorkel, sunglasses, sunhat, sunshade, suncream, surfboard, wetsuit, swimming costume, towel, windbreak

THINGS YOU MIGHT DO AT THE SEASIDE:

• ball games, beachcombing, building sandcastles, collecting shells, fishing, paddling, scuba diving, snorkelling, sunbathing, surfing, swimming, waterskiing, windsurfing

season *NOUN*
The hotels are full during the holiday season.
• period, time

seat *NOUN*
We found two empty seats at the back of the cinema.
• chair, place
A long seat for more than one person is a **bench**.
A long wooden seat in a church is a **pew**.
A seat on a bicycle or horse is a **saddle**.
A special seat for a king or queen is a **throne**.

seat *VERB*
❶ *The guests seated themselves around the table.*
• place, position, sit down, settle
❷ *The theatre can seat two hundred people.*
• have seats for, accommodate, hold, take

second *ADJECTIVE*
Would anyone like a second helping of pudding?
• another, additional, extra, further

second *NOUN*
❶ *The magic potion only takes a second to work.*
• instant, moment, flash
(informal) jiffy, tick
❷ *Inga was second in the cross-country race.*
• runner-up

second *VERB*
We need someone to second the proposal.
• back, support

secondary *ADJECTIVE*
She loves to run and winning is of secondary importance to her.
• lesser, lower, minor, inferior, subordinate

second-hand *ADJECTIVE*
The shop sells second-hand computers.
• used, pre-owned
OPPOSITE new

secret *ADJECTIVE*
❶ *The spy managed to get hold of a secret document.*
• confidential, classified, restricted
(informal) hush-hush
❷ *The detectives are part of a secret operation.*
• undercover, covert
❸ *The things I write in my diary are secret.*
• private, confidential, personal, intimate
❹ *The cook showed us a secret passageway into the castle.*
• hidden, concealed, disguised
for secret agents see **spy**

secretive *ADJECTIVE*
Why is she being so secretive about her past?
• uncommunicative, tight-lipped, reticent, reserved, mysterious, quiet
(informal) cagey
OPPOSITES communicative, open

section *NOUN*
The website has a special section aimed at children.
• part, division, sector, portion, segment, bit, fragment
A section of a book is a **chapter**.
A section from a piece of classical music is a **movement**.
A section taken from a book or long piece of music is a **passage**.
A section of a journey is a **stage**.

a b c d e f g h i j k l m n o p q r s t u v w x y z

A
B
C
D
E
F
G
H
I
J
K
L
M
N
O
P
Q
R
S
T
U
V
W
X
Y
Z

secure *ADJECTIVE*
❶ *The ladder was not very secure.*
• steady, firm, solid, fixed, fast, immovable
OPPOSITES insecure, unsafe
❷ *She is still trying to find a secure job.*
• permanent, regular, steady
❸ *They bolted the doors to make the castle secure.*
• safe, guarded, protected, defended
secure *VERB*
❶ *The door wasn't properly secured.*
• fasten, lock, seal, bolt
❷ *He managed to secure two tickets for the match.*
• get hold of, acquire, obtain

security *NOUN*
You must wear a seat belt for your own security.
• protection, safety

see *VERB* sees, seeing, saw, seen
❶ *If you look closely, you might see a dragonfly.*
• catch sight of, spot, notice, observe, make out, distinguish, note, perceive, recognize, sight, spy
(old use) behold
To see something briefly is to **glimpse** it.
To see an accident or an unusual event is to **witness** it.
❷ *Did you see the news yesterday?*
• watch, look at, view
❸ *See me in my office after school.*
• go to, report to
❹ *I didn't expect to see you here!*
• meet, run into, encounter
(informal) bump into
❺ *Will we have time to see them on the way home?*
• visit, call on, drop in on
❻ *I see what you mean.*
• understand, appreciate, comprehend, follow, grasp, realize, take in
❼ *I find it hard to see him in the role of Peter Pan.*
• imagine, picture, visualize

❽ *Please see that the windows are shut.*
• make sure, make certain, ensure
❾ *I'll see what I can do.*
• think about, consider, ponder, reflect on, weigh up
❿ *I'll see you to the door.*
• conduct, escort, accompany, guide, lead, take
➤ **to see to something**
Who's going to see to the refreshments?
• deal with, attend to, take care of, sort out

seed *NOUN*
The seeds in an orange, lemon, etc., are the **pips.**
The seed in a date, plum, etc., is the **stone.**

seek *VERB* seeks, seeking, sought
❶ *For many years he sought his long-lost brother.*
• search for, hunt for, look for
❷ *The king sought only to make his daughter happy.*
• try, attempt, strive, want, wish, desire

seem *VERB*
Everything seems to be all right.
She is far more friendly than she seems.
• appear, look, give the impression of being

seep *VERB*
Oil began to seep through the crack.
• leak, ooze, escape, flow, dribble, trickle, soak

seethe *VERB*
The mixture in the cauldron began to seethe.
• boil, bubble, foam, froth up
➤ **to be seething**
Greg was seething when I crashed his bike.
• be angry, be furious, rage, storm

segment NOUN
Divide the orange into segments.
• section, portion, piece, part, bit, wedge, slice

seize VERB
❶ *The climber stretched out to seize the rope.*
• grab, catch, snatch, take hold of, grasp, grip, clutch
❷ *The police seized the robbers as they left the bank.*
• arrest, capture
(informal) collar, nab
To seize someone's property as a punishment is to **confiscate** it.
To seize someone's power or position is to **usurp** it.
To seize an aircraft or vehicle during a journey is to **hijack** it.

seldom ADVERB
It seldom rains in the desert.
• rarely, infrequently
OPPOSITE often

select VERB
They had to select a new captain.
• choose, pick, decide on, opt for, settle on, appoint, elect

select ADJECTIVE
Only a select few were invited to the party.
• privileged, chosen, special, hand-picked

selection NOUN
The shop has a wide selection of roller skates.
• choice, range, variety, assortment

selfish ADJECTIVE
He's so selfish that he kept all the chocolate to himself.
• greedy, mean, miserly, grasping, self-centred, thoughtless
OPPOSITES unselfish, generous

sell VERB sells, selling, sold
The corner shop sells newspapers and sweets.
• deal in, trade in, stock, retail
Uncomplimentary synonyms are **peddle** and **hawk**.
for people who sell things see **shop**
OPPOSITE buy

send VERB sends, sending, sent
❶ *I sent each of my friends a postcard.*
• post, mail, dispatch
❷ *They plan to send a rocket to Mars.*
• launch, propel, direct, fire, shoot
➤ **to send for someone**
I think we should send for a doctor.
• call, summon, fetch
➤ **to send something out**
The device was sending out weird noises.
• emit, issue, give off, discharge

senior ADJECTIVE
❶ *She's one of the senior players in the squad.*
• older, long-standing, principal
❷ *She is a senior officer in the navy.*
• high-ranking, superior
OPPOSITE junior

sensation NOUN
❶ *He had a tingling sensation in his fingers.*
• feeling, sense
❷ *The unexpected news caused a sensation.*
• excitement, thrill
A sensation caused by something bad is an **outrage** or a **scandal**.

sensational ADJECTIVE
❶ *The newspaper printed a sensational account of the murder.*
• shocking, horrifying, startling, lurid
❷ *(informal) Did you hear the sensational result of yesterday's match?*
• amazing, extraordinary, remarkable, fantastic, spectacular, stupendous

a b c d e f g h i j k l m n o p q r s t u v w x y z

A
B
C
D
E
F
G
H
I
J
K
L
M
N
O
P
Q
R
S
T
U
V
W
X
Y
Z

sense *NOUN*
❶ *A baby learns about the world through its senses.*
Your five senses are **hearing, sight, smell, taste** and **touch.**
❷ *A drummer needs to have a good sense of rhythm.*
• awareness, consciousness, perception, feeling (for)
❸ *If you had any sense you'd stay at home.*
• common sense, intelligence, wisdom, wit, brains
❹ *The sense of the word is not clear.*
• meaning, significance, import
➤ **to make sense of something**
They couldn't make sense of the garbled message.
• understand, make out, interpret, follow

sense *VERB*
❶ *He sensed that she didn't like him.*
• be aware, realize, perceive, feel, guess, notice, suspect
❷ *The device senses any change of temperature.*
• detect, respond to

senseless *ADJECTIVE*
❶ *Smashing the window was a senseless act.*
• foolish, stupid, crazy, daft, irrational, mad, illogical, pointless, futile
OPPOSITE sensible
❷ *The blow on the head left the ogre senseless.*
• unconscious, knocked out
OPPOSITE conscious

sensible *ADJECTIVE*
❶ *It would be sensible to wait until the weather improves.*
• wise, intelligent, shrewd, rational, reasonable, careful, prudent, logical, sane, sound
OPPOSITE stupid
❷ *You will need sensible shoes for the hiking trip.*
• comfortable, practical
OPPOSITE impractical

sensitive *ADJECTIVE*
❶ *She has sensitive skin which gets sunburnt.*
• delicate, tender, fine, soft
❷ *Take care what you say—he's very sensitive.*
• easily offended, easily upset, touchy
❸ *He's very sensitive towards other people.*
• tactful, considerate, thoughtful, sympathetic, understanding
OPPOSITE insensitive

sentence *VERB*
The judge sentenced them to five years in prison.
• pass judgement on, pronounce sentence on, condemn

sentimental *ADJECTIVE*
❶ *He gets sentimental looking at old photographs.*
• emotional, nostalgic, tearful
❷ *I hate sentimental messages on birthday cards.*
• romantic, tender
(informal) soppy, mushy

sentry *NOUN*
A sentry was on duty at the gate.
• guard, lookout, sentinel, watchman

separate *ADJECTIVE*
❶ *The zoo kept the male lions separate from the cubs.*
• apart, separated, distinct, independent
OPPOSITE together
❷ *They slept in separate rooms.*
• different, detached, unattached
OPPOSITES attached, joined

separate *VERB*
❶ *The sheepdog separated the sheep from the lambs.*
• cut off, divide, fence off, isolate, keep apart, remove, segregate, set apart, take away
OPPOSITES combine, mix

To separate something which is connected to something else is to **detach** or **disconnect** it.
To separate things which are tangled together is to **disentangle** them.
❷ *They walked along together until their paths separated.*
• split, branch, fork
OPPOSITE merge
❸ *Her friend's parents have separated.*
• split up, break up, part company
To end a marriage legally is to **divorce**.

sequence *NOUN*
The detective tried to piece together the **sequence** *of events.*
• order, progression, series, succession, string, chain, train

serene *ADJECTIVE*
The woman in the painting had a **serene** *smile on her face.*
• calm, contented, untroubled, peaceful, quiet, placid, tranquil
OPPOSITE agitated

series *NOUN*
❶ *We had to answer a* **series** *of questions in our exam.*
• succession, sequence, string, set, chain, train
❷ *Are you watching the new* **series** *on TV?*
• serial

serious *ADJECTIVE*
❶ *His* **serious** *expression told them something was wrong.*
• solemn, sombre, unsmiling, grave, grim
OPPOSITE cheerful
❷ *She is writing a* **serious** *book about global warming.*
• learned, intellectual, scholarly
(informal) heavy
OPPOSITE light
❸ *Are you* **serious** *about wanting to learn to ski?*
• sincere, genuine, in earnest

❹ *This hospital ward is for people with* **serious** *injuries.*
• severe, acute, critical, bad, terrible, appalling, dreadful, major, grave
OPPOSITES minor, trivial

servant *NOUN*
This part of the house was where the **servants** *lived.*
• attendant, retainer, helper, domestic, manservant, maid
The chief manservant in a private house is a **butler**.
The servant of a medieval knight was a **page** or **squire**.

serve *VERB*
❶ *The shopkeeper was busy* **serving** *customers.*
• help, assist, aid
❷ *When everyone had sat down they* **served** *the first course.*
• give out, dish up, pass round, distribute
❸ *This room will* **serve** *as a study.*
• be suitable, be useful, function

service *NOUN*
❶ *The genie bowed and said he was glad to be of* **service**.
• help, assistance, aid, use, usefulness, benefit
❷ *Their marriage* **service** *was held in the local church.*
• ceremony, ritual, rite
A service in church is a meeting for worship.
❸ *Mum says her car needs a* **service**.
• check-over, maintenance, servicing

service *VERB*
The garage **serviced** *her car.*
• maintain, check, repair, mend, overhaul

session *NOUN*
❶ *We have a training* **session** *on Saturday mornings.*
• period, time

a b c d e f g h i j k l m n o p q r **s** t u v w x y z

A
B
C
D
E
F
G
H
I
J
K
L
M
N
O
P
Q
R
S
T
U
V
W
X
Y
Z

❷ *The Queen will open the next **session** of Parliament.*
• meeting, sitting

set *VERB* sets, setting, set
❶ *The removal team **set** the piano on the floor.*
• place, put, stand, position
❷ *I helped Dad to **set** the table.*
• arrange, lay, set out
❸ *Have they **set** a date for the wedding yet?*
• appoint, specify, name, decide, determine, choose, fix, establish, settle
❹ *The jelly will **set** quicker in the fridge.*
• become firm, solidify, harden, stiffen
❺ *The sun was just beginning to **set**.*
• do down, sink

➤ **to set about something**
*We **set about** clearing the table immediately.*
• begin, start, commence

➤ **to set off**
❶ *The knights **set off** on their quest.*
• depart, get going, leave, set out, start out
❷ *The burnt toast **set off** the smoke alarm.*
• activate, start, trigger

➤ **to set something out**
*The information is clearly **set out** on the page.*
• lay out, arrange, display, present

➤ **to set something up**
*They're trying to **set up** an after-school club.*
• establish, create, start, begin, introduce, organize

set *NOUN*
❶ *There is a **set** of measuring spoons in the drawer.*
• collection, batch, kit
❷ *Is there something wrong with the TV **set**?*
• apparatus, receiver
❸ *Our class painted the **set** for the play.*
• scenery, setting

setting *NOUN*
*The house stood in a rural **setting**.*
• surroundings, location, place, position, site, background
for ways to describe the setting of a story
see **writing**

settle *VERB*
❶ *The brothers tried to **settle** their differences.*
• resolve, sort out, deal with, end
❷ *The cat had just **settled** on the sofa.*
• sit down, relax, rest
❸ *A robin **settled** on a nearby branch.*
• land, alight
❹ *The family is planning to **settle** in Canada.*
• emigrate (to), move (to), set up home
❺ *You can see lots of fish when the mud **settles**.*
• sink to the bottom, clear, subside
❻ *We'll **settle** the hotel bill in the morning.*
• pay, clear, square

➤ **to settle on**
*Have you **settled on** a date for the wedding?*
• agree on, decide on, choose, name, fix

settlement *NOUN*
*There was once a Viking **settlement** in this area.*
• community, colony, encampment, village

sever *VERB*
*The couple decided to **sever** their relationship.*
• break off, end, terminate
To sever a branch of a tree is to **cut it off** or **remove** it.
To sever a limb is to **amputate** it.

several *DETERMINER*
*The spy was able to adopt **several** disguises.*
• a number of, some, a few, various

severe *ADJECTIVE*
❶ *The jailer was very **severe** with the prisoners.*
• harsh, strict, hard, stern
OPPOSITE lenient

❷ *The traffic warden gave him a severe look.*
• unkind, unsympathetic, disapproving, grim
OPPOSITE kind
❸ *Ruby has a severe case of chickenpox.*
• bad, serious, acute, grave
OPPOSITE mild
❹ *The Arctic has a severe climate.*
• extreme, tough, harsh, hostile
A severe frost is a **sharp** frost.
Severe cold is **intense** cold.
A severe storm is a **violent** storm.

sew VERB sews, sewing, sewed, sewn or sewed
Mum sewed a name tag on to my coat.
• stitch, tack
To sew a picture or design is to **embroider** it.
see also **needlework**

sex NOUN
What sex is the hamster?
• gender

shabby ADJECTIVE
❶ *The witch disguised herself in a shabby cloak.*
• ragged, scruffy, tattered, worn, worn–out, threadbare, frayed, tatty, seedy, dingy
OPPOSITE smart
❷ *That was a shabby trick!*
• mean, nasty, unfair, unkind, dishonest, shameful, low, cheap

shade NOUN
❶ *They sat in the shade of a chestnut tree.*
• shadow
❷ *The porch had a shade to keep out the sun.*
• screen, blind, canopy
A type of umbrella used as a sunshade is a **parasol**.
❸ *The bathroom walls are a pale shade of blue.*
• hue, tinge, tint, tone, colour

shade VERB
❶ *Wearing a cap will shade your eyes from the sun.*
• shield, screen, protect, hide, mask
❷ *He shaded the background of the picture with a pencil.*
• fill in, make darker, darken

shadow NOUN
Her face was deep in shadow.
• shade, darkness, gloom
shadow VERB
The detective was shadowing the suspect.
• follow, pursue, tail, stalk, track, trail

shady ADJECTIVE
❶ *They found a shady spot under a tree.*
• shaded, shadowy, sheltered, dark, sunless
OPPOSITE sunny
❷ *They took part in some shady business deals.*
• dishonest, disreputable, suspicious, dubious, suspect, untrustworthy
(informal) fishy, dodgy
OPPOSITE honest

shaft NOUN
❶ *Modern arrow shafts are made of wood.*
• spine, stick, pole, rod, staff
❷ *He nearly fell into an old mine shaft.*
• pit, tunnel, hole
❸ *A shaft of moonlight shone through the window.*
• beam, ray

shaggy ADJECTIVE
Llamas have long shaggy coats.
• bushy, woolly, fleecy, hairy, thick

shake VERB shakes, shaking, shook, shaken
❶ *The hurricane made the whole house shake.*
• quake, shudder, shiver, rock, sway, totter, wobble, quiver, vibrate, rattle
❷ *He was so upset that his voice was shaking.*
• tremble, quaver

a b c d e f g h i j k l m n o p q r s t u v w x y z

A B C D E F G H I J K L M N O P Q R S T U V W X Y Z

❸ *The giant shook his fist and growled angrily.*
• wave, brandish, flourish, wag, waggle, joggle
❹ *They were shaken by the terrible news.*
• shock, startle, distress, upset, disturb, alarm, frighten

shaky *ADJECTIVE*
❶ *Be careful—the table is rather shaky.*
• unsteady, wobbly, insecure, rickety, flimsy, weak
❷ *He was so nervous that his hands were shaky.*
• shaking, trembling, quivering
❸ *She spoke in a shaky voice.*
• quavering, faltering, nervous, tremulous
OPPOSITE steady

shallow *ADJECTIVE*
The children paddled about in the shallow water.
OPPOSITE deep

sham *NOUN*
I discovered that the story was a sham.
• pretence, deception, lie

shame *NOUN*
The guilty children hung their heads in shame.
• disgrace, dishonour, humiliation, embarrassment, guilt
➤ a shame
It's a shame that you can't stay for longer.
• a pity, unfortunate

shameful *ADJECTIVE*
The player was sent off for his shameful conduct on the pitch.
• disgraceful, outrageous, scandalous, contemptible, despicable, wicked
OPPOSITE honourable

shape *NOUN*
The Halloween cake was in the shape of a bat.
• form, figure

A line showing the shape of a thing is the **outline**.
A dark outline seen against a light background is a **silhouette**.
A container for making things in a special shape is a **mould**.

WORD WEB

FLAT SHAPES:

• circle, diamond, ellipse, heptagon, hexagon, oblong, octagon, oval, parallelogram, pentagon, polygon, quadrilateral, rectangle, rhombus, ring, semicircle, square, trapezium, triangle

THREE-DIMENSIONAL SHAPES:

• cone, cube, cylinder, hemisphere, polyhedron, prism, pyramid, sphere

shape *VERB*
The potter shaped the clay into a tall vase.
• form, mould, fashion
To shape something in a mould is to **cast** it.

share *NOUN*
Each of the pirates got a share of rum.
• ration, allowance, portion, quota, helping, division, part
(informal) cut

share *VERB*
The children shared the cake between them.
• divide, split, distribute, allot, allocate, deal out, ration out

sharp *ADJECTIVE*
❶ *Use a pair of sharp scissors.*
• keen, sharpened, razor-sharp
OPPOSITE blunt
❷ *Barbed wire has sharp points all along it.*
• pointed, spiky, jagged
OPPOSITE smooth
❸ *She felt a sharp pain in her side.*
• acute, piercing, stabbing
OPPOSITE dull

❹ *Eagles have sharp eyes to see far in the distance.*
• keen, keen-sighted, observant, perceptive
OPPOSITE unobservant
❺ *You need to focus the camera to get a sharp picture.*
• clear, distinct, well defined, crisp
OPPOSITE blurred
❻ *Sherlock Holmes had a very sharp intelligence.*
• clever, quick, shrewd, perceptive
OPPOSITES dull, slow
❼ *The bus slowed down before a sharp bend in the road.*
• abrupt, sudden, steep
A bend that doubles back on itself is a **hairpin** bend.
OPPOSITE gradual
❽ *The sharp frost killed our geraniums.*
• severe, extreme, intense, serious
OPPOSITES slight, mild
❾ *This salad dressing is a bit sharp.*
• sour, tart, bitter
OPPOSITES mild, sweet

sharpen VERB
I need to sharpen these crayons.
• make sharp, grind, whet, hone

shatter VERB
❶ *The ball shattered a window.*
• break, smash, destroy, wreck
❷ *The windscreen shattered when a stone hit it.*
• break, splinter, disintegrate

sheaf NOUN
She had a sheaf of papers in her hand.
• bunch, bundle

sheath NOUN
The knight put her sword back in its sheath.
• casing, covering, sleeve
A sheath for a sword or dagger is a **scabbard**.

shed NOUN
They kept their lawnmower in the garden shed.
• hut, shack, outhouse

shed VERB sheds, shedding, shed
A lorry shed its load on the motorway.
• drop, let fall, spill, scatter

sheen NOUN
He waxed the table to give it a nice sheen.
• shine, polish, gloss, gleam, lustre

sheep NOUN
A male sheep is a **ram**.
A female sheep is a **ewe**.
A young sheep is a **lamb**.
Meat from sheep is **mutton** or **lamb**.
The woolly coat of a sheep is its **fleece**.

sheer ADJECTIVE
❶ *The story he told was sheer nonsense.*
• complete, total, utter, absolute, pure
❷ *Don't try to climb that sheer cliff.*
• vertical, perpendicular
❸ *The ballgown was made of sheer silk.*
• fine, thin, transparent, see-through

sheet NOUN
❶ *He started his diary on a fresh sheet of paper.*
• page, leaf, piece
❷ *The pond was covered with a thin sheet of ice.*
• layer, film, covering, surface
❸ *The glazier came to fit a new sheet of glass.*
• panel, pane, plate

shelf NOUN
She put the books back on the shelf.
• ledge, rack
A shelf above a fireplace is a **mantelpiece**.

shell NOUN
Tortoises have hard shells.
• covering, case, casing, outside, exterior

a b c d e f g h i j k l m n o p q r s t u v w x y z

A B C D E F G H I J K L M N O P Q R S T U V W X Y Z

shellfish NOUN

WORD WEB

SOME TYPES OF SHELLFISH:

• barnacle, clam, cockle, conch, crab, crayfish, cuttlefish, limpet, lobster, mussel, oyster, prawn, razor shell, scallop, shrimp, whelk, winkle

Shellfish with legs, such as crabs, lobsters and shrimps are **crustaceans**.

shelter NOUN

*The hikers reached **shelter** just before the storm broke.*

• cover, protection, safety, refuge, sanctuary

shelter VERB

❶ *The hedge **shelters** the garden from the wind.*

• protect, screen, shield, guard, defend, safeguard

❷ *We **sheltered** from the rain under the trees.*

• hide, take refuge

shelve VERB

*They had to **shelve** their plans for a summer holiday.*

• postpone, put off, defer, suspend

(informal) put on ice

shield NOUN

*The trees act as an effective wind **shield**.*

• screen, barrier, defence, guard, protection

The part of a helmet that shields your face is the **visor**.

shield VERB

*The mother bear **shielded** her cubs from danger.*

• protect, defend, guard, safeguard, keep safe, shelter

shift VERB

❶ *I need some help to **shift** the furniture.*

• move, rearrange, reposition

❷ *It was hard work **shifting** the mud off the tyres.*

• remove, dislodge, budge

shine VERB shines, shining, shone or (in sense 2) shined

❶ *A light **shone** from an upstairs window.*

• beam, glow, blaze, glare, gleam

for other ways to describe light see **light**

❷ *He **shines** his shoes every morning.*

• polish, rub, brush

❸ *She's good at all sports, but she **shines** at tennis.*

• be outstanding, excel, stand out

shiny ADJECTIVE

*She polished the mirror until it was **shiny**.*

• shining, bright, gleaming, glistening, glossy, polished, burnished, lustrous

OPPOSITE dull

ship NOUN

Ships that travel long distances at sea are **ocean-going** or **seagoing** ships.

People who work on ships at sea are **nautical** or **seafaring** people.

for types of boat or ship see **boat**

ship VERB

*The firm **ships** goods all over the world.*

• transport, send, post, mail

shirk VERB

*He always **shirks** the unpleasant tasks.*

• avoid, evade, get out of, dodge, duck

shiver VERB

*Ali waited outside, **shivering** with cold.*

• tremble, quiver, shake, shudder, quake

shock NOUN

❶ *The news of his death came as a great **shock**.*

• blow, surprise, fright, upset

❷ *People felt the **shock** of the explosion miles away.*

• bang, impact, jolt

❸ *The driver involved in the accident was in a state of **shock**.*

• distress, trauma

shock *VERB*
*The whole town was **shocked** by the news.*
• horrify, appal, startle, alarm, stun, stagger, shake, astonish, astound, surprise, dismay, upset
A formal synonym is **traumatize**.

shoe *NOUN*

WORD WEB

SOME TYPES OF SHOE OR BOOT:

• ankle boot, ballet shoe, baseball boot, boot, brogue, clog, court shoe, espadrille, flat shoe, flip-flop, football boot, gym shoe, high-heel shoe, moccasin, mule, plimsoll, pump, sandal, slipper, sneaker, stiletto, tap shoe, tennis shoe, trainer, wedge, wellington or *(informal)* wellie

shone *past tense see* shine

shook *past tense see* shake

shoot *VERB* shoots, shooting, shot
❶ *Robin Hood **shot** an arrow into the air.*
• fire, discharge, launch, aim
❷ *It is now illegal to hunt and **shoot** tigers.*
• fire at, hit, open fire on, gun down
❸ *They watched the racing cars **shoot** past.*
• race, speed, dash, rush, streak, hurtle, fly, whizz, zoom
❹ *Part of the film was **shot** in Canada.*
• film, photograph

shoot *NOUN*
*Young **shoots** grow in the spring.*
• bud, sprout

shop *NOUN*

WORD WEB

VARIOUS TYPES OF SHOP:

• boutique, corner shop, department store, market, online store, shopping centre, supermarket

SPECIALIST SHOPS:

• antique shop, baker, bookshop, butcher, charity shop, cheesemonger, chemist, clothes shop, delicatessen, DIY or do-it-yourself store, fishmonger, florist, garden centre, gift shop, greengrocer, grocer, health-food shop, ironmonger, jeweller, music shop, newsagent, pharmacy, post office, shoe shop, sweet shop, toy shop

PEOPLE WHO WORK IN SHOPS:

• cashier, sales assistant, shopkeeper or storekeeper

shopping *NOUN*
*Just put the **shopping** in the boot of the car.*
• goods, purchases

shore *NOUN*
see **seashore**

short *ADJECTIVE*
❶ *They live a **short** distance from the shops.*
• little, small
OPPOSITE long
❷ *It was a very **short** visit.*
• brief, quick, fleeting, hasty, temporary
OPPOSITE long
❸ *The troll was very **short**.*
• small, tiny, little, squat, dumpy, diminutive, petite
OPPOSITE tall
❹ *The supply of water was getting **short**.*
• low, meagre, scant, limited, inadequate, insufficient
OPPOSITE plentiful
❺ *There is no need to be **short** with me!*
• abrupt, rude, sharp, curt, impolite, snappy
OPPOSITES patient, polite

shortage *NOUN*
*The **shortage** of water is worrying.*
• scarcity, deficiency, lack, want, dearth
A shortage of water is a **drought**.
A shortage of food is a **famine**.

a b c d e f g h i j k l m n o p q r s t u v w x y z

A B C D E F G H I J K L M N O P Q R S T U V W X Y Z

shortcoming NOUN
As an actor, he has some shortcomings.
• defect, failing, fault, weakness, limitation, drawback

shorten VERB
She had to shorten the essay because it was too long.
• cut down, reduce, cut, trim, abbreviate, abridge, condense, compress, curtail
(OPPOSITE) lengthen

shortly ADVERB
The post should arrive shortly.
• soon, before long, presently

shot past tense see **shoot**

shot NOUN
❶ *I heard a noise like the shot of a pistol.*
• bang, blast, crack
❷ *The archer was an excellent shot.*
A person who is good at shooting with a gun is a **marksman**.
❸ *The striker had an easy shot at the goal.*
• hit, strike, kick
❹ *The photographer took some unusual shots.*
• photograph, picture, snap, snapshot
❺ *(informal) We each had a shot at solving the riddle.*
• try, go, attempt
(informal) bash

shout VERB
The ogre was shouting and stamping with rage.
• call, cry out, bawl, yell, bellow, roar, howl, yelp, scream, screech, shriek
(OPPOSITE) whisper

shout NOUN
We heard a shout from far away.
• call, cry, yell, yelp, bellow, roar, howl

shove VERB
A man ran past and shoved me to the side.
• push, thrust, force, barge, elbow, jostle, shoulder

shovel VERB
We shovelled the snow into a huge heap.
• dig, scoop, shift, clear, move

show VERB shows, showing, showed, shown
❶ *My uncle showed us his coin collection.*
• present, reveal, display, exhibit
❷ *The photo shows my grandparents on holiday.*
• portray, picture, depict, illustrate, represent
❸ *The dance tutor showed them what to do.*
• explain to, make clear to, instruct, teach, tell
❹ *The evidence shows that he was right.*
• prove, demonstrate
❺ *A nurse showed them into the waiting room.*
• direct, guide, conduct, escort, usher
❻ *The signpost shows the way.*
• indicate, point out
❼ *His vest showed through his shirt.*
• be seen, be visible, appear
➤ **to show off**
Walter is always showing off.
• boast, brag, crow, gloat, swagger
(informal) blow your own trumpet
A person who shows off is a **show-off**.

show NOUN
❶ *There is a show of artwork at the end of term.*
• display, exhibition, presentation
❷ *There's a good show on at the theatre.*
• performance, production, entertainment

shower NOUN
for various types of rain see **weather**
shower VERB
A passing bus showered mud over them.
• spray, splash, spatter, sprinkle

showy ADJECTIVE
She was wearing very showy earrings.
• gaudy, flashy, bright, loud, garish, conspicuous
(OPPOSITE) plain

shred NOUN
The police couldn't find a **shred** of evidence.
• bit, piece, scrap, trace
➤ **shreds**
The gale ripped the tent to **shreds**.
• tatters, ribbons, rags, strips

shrewd ADJECTIVE
The spy was too **shrewd** to be caught.
• clever, quick-witted, intelligent, sharp, cunning, crafty, artful, ingenious, wily, canny
OPPOSITE stupid

shriek NOUN, VERB
'Quick!' **shrieked** Alice. 'Open the door!'
• cry, scream, screech, shout, howl, bawl, squeal, wail, yell

shrill ADJECTIVE
They heard the **shrill** sound of a whistle.
• high, high-pitched, piercing, sharp, screechy
OPPOSITES low, soft

shrink VERB
My jeans have **shrunk** in the wash.
• become smaller, contract
OPPOSITE expand

shrivel VERB
The plants **shrivelled** in the heat.
• wilt, wither, droop, dry up, wrinkle, shrink

shroud VERB
The mountain was **shrouded** in mist.
• cover, envelop, wrap, blanket, hide, conceal, mask, screen, veil

shrub NOUN
She bought some **shrubs** at the garden centre.
• bush

shudder VERB
They **shuddered** with fear when they heard the creature roar.
• tremble, quake, quiver, shake, shiver

shuffle VERB
❶ He **shuffled** along the corridor in his slippers.
• shamble, scuffle, hobble, scrape
❷ Did you remember to **shuffle** the cards?
• mix, mix up, jumble

shut VERB shuts, shutting, shut
Please **shut** the door behind you.
• close, fasten, seal, secure, lock, bolt, latch
To shut a door with a bang is to **slam** it.
➤ **to shut down**
The restaurant may have to **shut down**.
• close down
➤ **to shut someone up**
They had been **shut up** in a dungeon for five years.
• imprison, confine, detain
➤ **to shut up** (informal)
I wish those people behind us would **shut up**!
• be quiet, be silent, stop talking, hold your tongue

shy ADJECTIVE
The child was too **shy** to say anything.
• bashful, timid, coy, reserved, hesitant, self-conscious, inhibited, modest
OPPOSITE bold

sick ADJECTIVE
❶ Katie is off school because she's **sick**.
• ill, unwell, poorly, sickly, ailing, indisposed, off colour, peaky
OPPOSITE healthy
❷ The sea was rough and the cabin boy felt **sick**.
• nauseous, queasy
➤ **to be sick of**
I'm **sick of** this miserable weather!
• be fed up with, be tired of, have had enough of

sicken VERB
They were **sickened** by the smell in the dungeon.
• disgust, revolt, repel, offend
(informal) turn your stomach

a b c d e f g h i j k l m n o p q r s t u v w x y z

sickly *ADJECTIVE*
*He has always been a **sickly** child.*
• unhealthy, weak, delicate, frail
(OPPOSITES) healthy, strong

sickness *NOUN*
see **illness**

side *NOUN*
❶ *A cube has six **sides**.*
• face, surface
❷ *The path runs along the **side** of the field.*
• edge, border, boundary, fringe, perimeter
The side of a page is the **margin**.
The side of a road is the **verge**.
❸ *I could see both **sides** of the argument.*
• point of view, view, angle, aspect
❹ *The football club has a strong **side** this year.*
• team

side *VERB*
➤ **to side with someone**
*Some of the townspeople **sided with** the enemy.*
• support, favour, take the side of, agree with, back

siege *NOUN*
*The town held out against the **siege** for months.*
• blockade

sift *VERB*
Sift the flour to get rid of any lumps.
• sieve, strain, filter
➤ **to sift through something**
*The detective began to **sift through** the evidence.*
• examine, inspect, sort out, analyse, scrutinize, review

sigh *NOUN, VERB*
*'I'll never be good at tennis,' **sighed** Libby.*
• moan, lament, grumble, complain

sight *NOUN*
❶ *Weasels have sharp **sight** and excellent hearing.*
• eyesight, vision
❷ *The woods in autumn are a lovely **sight**.*
• spectacle, display, show, scene
❸ *By the third day, the ship was in **sight** of land.*
• view, range
❹ *We went to London to see the **sights**.*
• attraction, landmark

sight *VERB*
*The lookout **sighted** a ship on the horizon.*
• see, spot, spy, make out, observe, notice, distinguish, recognize, glimpse

sign *NOUN*
❶ *A **sign** pointed to the exit.*
• notice, placard, poster, signpost
The sign belonging to a particular business or organization is its **logo**.
The sign on a particular brand of goods is a **trademark**.
❷ *The manager gave no **sign** that she was angry.*
• indication, clue, hint, warning, signal, portent
❸ *The guard gave us a **sign** to pass through the gates.*
• signal, gesture, cue, reminder

sign *VERB*
❶ *Please **sign** your name on the form.*
• write, inscribe
❷ *The club **signed** a new player last week.*
• take on, engage, recruit, enrol

signal *NOUN*
*The spy waited for the **signal** that all was clear.*
• sign, indication, prompt, cue
A signal that tells you not to do something is a **warning**.

signal *VERB*
*The pilot **signalled** that he was going to descend.*
• give a sign or signal, gesture, indicate, motion

significance NOUN
What's the significance of that symbol?
• importance, meaning, message, point, relevance

significant ADJECTIVE
❶ *The book describes the significant events of last century.*
• important, major, noteworthy, influential
❷ *Global warming is having a significant effect on wildlife.*
• noticeable, considerable, perceptible, striking
OPPOSITE insignificant

signify VERB
❶ *A red light signifies danger.*
• represent, stand for, symbolize, indicate, denote, mean
❷ *The crew signified their agreement by raising their hands.*
• show, express, communicate, convey

silence NOUN
There was silence while we sat the exam.
• quiet, quietness, hush, stillness, calm, peace
OPPOSITE noise

silence VERB
He silenced the audience by ringing a bell.
• deaden, muffle, quieten, suppress
To silence someone by putting something over their mouth is to **gag** them.

silent ADJECTIVE
❶ *At night, the desert was cold and silent.*
• quiet, noiseless, soundless, still, hushed
Something you can't hear is **inaudible**.
A common simile is **as silent as the grave**.
OPPOSITE noisy
❷ *Morris kept silent throughout the meeting.*
• quiet, speechless, mute
(informal) mum
To be too shy to speak is to be **tongue-tied**.
OPPOSITE talkative

silky ADJECTIVE
Some types of rabbit have long, silky fur.
• smooth, soft, fine, sleek, velvety

silly ADJECTIVE
It was silly of me to lock myself out of the house.
• foolish, stupid, idiotic, senseless, thoughtless, brainless, unwise, unintelligent, half-witted, hare-brained, scatterbrained
(informal) daft
OPPOSITE sensible

similar ADJECTIVE
The puppies are similar in appearance.
• alike, identical, indistinguishable, matching, the same
OPPOSITES dissimilar, different
➤ **similar to**
The new book is similar to the previous one.
• like, close to, comparable to, unlike, different from

similarity NOUN
It's easy to see the similarity between the twins.
• likeness, resemblance
OPPOSITE difference

simple ADJECTIVE
❶ *Can you answer this simple question?*
• easy, elementary, straightforward
OPPOSITE difficult
❷ *The help file is written in simple language.*
• clear, plain, uncomplicated, understandable, intelligible
OPPOSITE complicated
❸ *The girl wore a simple cotton dress.*
• plain, undecorated
OPPOSITE elaborate
❹ *He enjoys simple pleasures like walking and gardening.*
• ordinary, unsophisticated, humble, modest, homely
OPPOSITE sophisticated

simply ADVERB
❶ *I found his story simply unbelievable.*
• absolutely, wholly, completely, totally, utterly
❷ *He won't eat peas simply because they're green!*
• just, merely, purely, only, solely

a b c d e f g h i j k l m n o p q r **s** t u v w x y z

A
B
C
D
E
F
G
H
I
J
K
L
M
N
O
P
Q
R
S
T
U
V
W
X
Y
Z

sin *NOUN*
Some people believe that lying is a sin.
• wrong, evil, wickedness, wrongdoing

sincere *ADJECTIVE*
Please accept my sincere apologies.
• genuine, honest, true, truthful, real, earnest, wholehearted, frank
OPPOSITE insincere

sing *VERB* sings, singing, sang, sung

WORD WEB

SOME WAYS TO SING:

• chant, chirp, croon, hum, trill, warble, yodel

TYPES OF SINGING VOICE:

• alto, baritone, bass, contralto, soprano, tenor, treble
for kinds of music for singing see **song**

singe *VERB*
The iron was too hot and singed my T-shirt.
• burn, scorch, sear, blacken, char

singer *NOUN*
The band comprises two guitarists and a singer.
• vocalist
A group of singers is a **choir** or **chorus**.
A member of a choir is a **chorister**.

single *ADJECTIVE*
❶ *We saw a single house high on the moors.*
• solitary, isolated
When only a single example of something exists, it is **unique**.
❷ *We are content with our decision to stay single.*
• unmarried
An unmarried man is a **bachelor**.
An old word for an unmarried woman is a **spinster**.

single *VERB*
➤ **to single someone out**
They singled her out as the best player in the team.
• pick out, select, choose, identify

sinister *ADJECTIVE*
He looked up with a sinister smile on his face.
• menacing, threatening, malevolent, evil, disturbing, unsettling, eerie
(informal) creepy

sink *VERB* sinks, sinking, sank, sunk
❶ *The ship hit the rocks and sank.*
• go down, become submerged, founder, capsize
To let water into a ship to sink it deliberately is to **scuttle** it.
❷ *The sun began to sink below the horizon.*
• drop, fall, descend, subside, dip
When the sun sinks to the horizon it **sets**.

sit *VERB* sits, sitting, sat
❶ *Rachel sat on the sofa reading a magazine.*
• have a seat, settle down, rest, perch
To sit on your heels is to **squat**.
To sit to have your portrait painted is to **pose**.
❷ *My brother is sitting his driving test next week.*
• take
(informal) go in for

site *NOUN*
This is the site of an ancient burial ground.
• location, place, position, situation, setting, plot
site *VERB*
The new cinema will be sited in the middle of the town.
• locate, place, position, situate

situation *NOUN*
❶ *The house is in a pleasant situation.*
• location, locality, place, position, setting, site, spot
❷ *I found myself in an awkward situation.*
• position, circumstances, condition, state of affairs

A bad situation is a **plight** or **predicament**.
❸ *She applied for a situation in the bank.*
• job, post, position, appointment

size NOUN
❶ *What size is the garden?*
• dimensions, proportions, area, extent
❷ *The tourists were amazed by the sheer size of the pyramids.*
• scale, magnitude, immensity

skeleton NOUN
❶ *Inside the crypt, they found several human skeletons.*
• bones
❷ *So far they've only put up the skeleton of the building.*
• frame, framework, shell

sketch NOUN
❶ *She drew a quick sketch of her cat.*
• drawing, picture, outline
A sketch you do while you think of other things is a **doodle**.
❷ *The actors performed a comic sketch.*
• scene, turn, routine

sketch VERB
He sketched a rough design for the poster.
• draw, draft, outline, rough out

skid VERB
The van skidded on the icy road.
• slide, slip

skilful ADJECTIVE
Dickens was a skilful writer.
• expert, skilled, accomplished, able, capable, talented, brilliant, clever, masterly, deft
If you are skilful at a lot of things, you are **versatile**.
OPPOSITE incompetent

skill NOUN
It takes a lot of skill to build a boat.
• expertise, ability, aptitude, capability, competence, accomplishment, talent, proficiency, deftness

skim VERB
The stone skimmed across the surface of the pond.
• glide, slide, skid, slip
➤ **to skim through**
Luke skimmed through the newspaper.
• scan, look through, skip through, flick through

skin NOUN
The cave people were dressed in animal skins.
• coat, fur, hide, pelt
The type of skin you have on your face is your **complexion**.
Skin on fruit or vegetables is **peel** or **rind**.
Skin that might form on top of a liquid is a coating, film or **membrane**.

skinny ADJECTIVE
A skinny girl in bare feet answered the door.
• thin, lean, bony, gaunt, lanky, scrawny, scraggy
OPPOSITE plump

skip VERB
❶ *The children skipped along the pavement.*
• hop, jump, leap, bound, caper, dance, prance
❷ *I skipped the boring bits in the book.*
• pass over, miss out, ignore, omit, leave out

skirt VERB
The path skirts the playing field.
• circle, go round, pass round

sky NOUN
Clouds drifted slowly across the sky.
• air, heavens

WRITING TIPS
You can use these words to describe **the sky**.

TO DESCRIBE THE SKY BY DAY:
• blue, clear, cloudless, cloudy, grey, overcast, stormy, sunless, sunny, thundery
see also **weather**
The sky was overcast and still. Thin wisps of mist clung to the tops of the pine trees, and the oak and wild cherry were bare-leaved, waiting for spring.—SKY HAWK, Gill Lewis

A B C D E F G H I J K L M N O P Q R S T U V W X Y Z

TO DESCRIBE THE SKY AT NIGHT:

• moonless, moonlit, pitch-black, starless, starlit, starry, star-studded

slab NOUN
The words were engraved on a **slab** of marble.
• block, piece, tablet, slice, chunk, hunk, lump

slack ADJECTIVE
❶ One of the ropes on the tent was **slack**.
• loose, limp
OPPOSITE tight
❷ The team looked very **slack** in defence.
• lazy, lax, negligent, casual, relaxed, easy-going
OPPOSITE alert

slacken VERB
❶ The climber **slackened** the rope around her waist.
• loosen, relax, release, ease off
OPPOSITE tighten
❷ The pace of the game **slackened** after half-time.
• lessen, reduce, decrease, slow down
OPPOSITE increase

slam VERB
Don't **slam** the door!
• bang, shut loudly

slant VERB
❶ Her handwriting **slants** backwards.
• lean, slope, tilt, incline, be at an angle
❷ He **slanted** his story to make it more dramatic.
• distort, twist, warp

slant NOUN
❶ The floor of the caravan was at a **slant**.
• slope, angle, tilt, incline, gradient
A slant on a damaged ship is a **list**.
A slanting line joining opposite corners of a square, etc., is a **diagonal**.

A surface slanting up to a higher level is a **ramp**.
❷ The film brings a new **slant** to an old story.
• point of view, angle, emphasis, bias

slap VERB
He **slapped** his hand against his thigh and laughed.
• smack, strike, spank, hit, clout
(informal) whack

slash VERB
for various ways to cut things see **cut**

slaughter VERB
They had to **slaughter** the diseased cattle.
• kill, butcher, massacre

slaughter NOUN
The battle ended in terrible **slaughter**.
• bloodshed, killing, massacre, butchery

slave VERB
They **slaved** all day to get the job done.
• work hard, labour, toil, grind, sweat

slavery NOUN
The prisoners were sold into **slavery**.
• captivity, bondage
OPPOSITE freedom

sledge NOUN
We dragged our **sledges** up the snowy slope.
• toboggan
(North American) sled
A large sledge pulled by horses is a **sleigh**.
A sledge used in winter sports is a **bobsleigh**.

sleek ADJECTIVE
Otters have **sleek** coats.
• smooth, glossy, shiny, silky, soft, velvety
OPPOSITE coarse

sleep VERB sleeps, sleeping, slept
The baby is **sleeping** in the next room.
• be asleep, take a nap, doze
(informal) snooze
To go to sleep is to **drop off** or **nod off**.

sleep NOUN
Mr Khan had a short sleep after lunch.
• nap, rest, doze, catnap
(informal) snooze, forty winks, shut-eye
An afternoon sleep is a **siesta**.
The long sleep some animals have through the winter is **hibernation**.

sleepless ADJECTIVE
The wanderers spent a sleepless night.
• restless, wide awake
The formal name for sleeplessness is **insomnia**.

sleepy ADJECTIVE
The giant was usually sleepy after dinner.
• drowsy, tired, weary, heavy-eyed, lethargic, ready to sleep
(informal) dopey
OPPOSITE wide awake

slender ADJECTIVE
❶ *A slender figure stepped off the train.*
• slim, lean, slight, graceful, trim, svelte
OPPOSITE fat
❷ *The spider dangled on a slender thread.*
• thin, fine, fragile, delicate
OPPOSITE thick
❸ *They only had a slender chance of winning.*
• poor, slight, slim, faint, negligible, remote
OPPOSITE good
❹ *The team won by a slender margin.*
• narrow, small, slim
OPPOSITE wide

slice VERB
To slice meat is to **carve** it.
see also **cut**

slick ADJECTIVE
He was very slick at shuffling cards.
• skilful, artful, clever, cunning, deft, quick
OPPOSITE clumsy

slide VERB
I like sliding down the chute in the playground.
• glide, skid, slip, slither

slight ADJECTIVE
❶ *There's a slight problem with the computer.*
• minor, unimportant, insignificant, negligible, superficial, trifling, trivial
OPPOSITE important
❷ *A slight elderly lady met us at the door.*
• delicate, fragile, frail, slender, slim, small, spare, thin, tiny
OPPOSITES stout, tall

slightly ADVERB
She was slightly hurt in the accident.
• a little, a bit, somewhat, rather
OPPOSITES very, seriously

slim ADJECTIVE
❶ *A tall, slim figure appeared out of the fog.*
• graceful, lean, slender, spare, thin, trim
OPPOSITE fat
❷ *Their chances of winning are slim.*
• faint, poor, slight, slender, negligible, remote
OPPOSITE good
❸ *Our team won by a slim margin.*
• narrow, small, slender
OPPOSITE wide

slimy ADJECTIVE
The floor of the tunnel was covered with slimy mud.
• slippery, slithery, sticky, oozy
(informal) gooey

sling VERB slings, slinging, slung
Robin Hood slung his quiver over his shoulder.
• throw, cast, fling, hurl, pitch, heave, toss, lob
(informal) chuck

slink VERB slinks, slinking, slunk
The spy slunk away without being seen.
• slip, sneak, steal, creep, edge, sidle

a
b
c
d
e
f
g
h
i
j
k
l
m
n
o
p
q
r
s
t
u
v
w
x
y
z

A
B
C
D
E
F
G
H
I
J
K
L
M
N
O
P
Q
R
S
T
U
V
W
X
Y
Z

slip VERB

❶ *The runners **slipped** on the ice.*
• skid, slither, skate
❷ *The lifeboat **slipped** into the water.*
• glide, slide
❸ *Marion **slipped** out while everyone was talking.*
• sneak, steal, slink, tiptoe, creep, edge, sidle

slip NOUN

❶ *She wrote her phone number on a **slip** of paper.*
• piece, scrap
❷ *The pianist made a tiny **slip** at the start of the concert.*
• mistake, error, fault, blunder, gaffe, lapse
➤ **to give someone the slip**
The robber gave them all the slip.
• escape, get away, run away

slippery ADJECTIVE

*Take care—the floor is **slippery**.*
• slithery, slippy, smooth, glassy
A surface slippery with frost is **icy**.
A surface slippery with grease is **greasy** or **oily**.
A common simile is **as slippery as an eel**.

slit NOUN

*The archers shot arrows through the **slits** in the castle wall.*
• opening, chink, gap, slot, split, tear, cut

slit VERB

for various ways to cut things see **cut**

slither VERB

*The rattlesnake **slithered** through the long grass.*
• slide, slip, glide, slink, snake

slope VERB

*The beach **slopes** gently down to the sea.*
• fall or rise, incline, bank, shelve

slope NOUN

❶ *It was hard work pushing my bike up the **slope**.*
• hill, rise, bank, ramp
An upward slope is an **ascent**.

A downward slope is a **descent**.
❷ *Rain runs down the roof because of the **slope**.*
• incline, slant, tilt, gradient

sloppy ADJECTIVE

❶ *For breakfast, there was a bowl of steaming, **sloppy** porridge.*
• runny, slushy, watery, liquid, wet
(informal) gloopy
❷ *His handwriting is very **sloppy**.*
• untidy, messy, careless, slovenly, slapdash, slipshod

slot NOUN

❶ *To use the locker, put a pound coin into the **slot**.*
• slit, chink, hole, opening
❷ *The programme has been moved from its usual **slot**.*
• time, spot, space, place

slouch VERB

*Sue sat at her desk, **slouched** over the computer.*
• hunch, stoop, slump, droop, flop

slow ADJECTIVE

❶ *Tortoises move at a **slow** but steady pace.*
• unhurried, leisurely, gradual, plodding, dawdling, sluggish
❷ *They took the train to London, followed by a **slow** bus journey.*
• lengthy, prolonged, drawn-out, tedious
❸ *The prisoner was **slow** to answer.*
• hesitant, reluctant, tardy
(OPPOSITE) quick

slow VERB

➤ **to slow down**
Slow down—you're driving too fast!
• go slower, brake, reduce speed, decelerate
(OPPOSITE) accelerate

sludge NOUN

*They cleared a lot of **sludge** out of the pond.*
• muck, mud, ooze, slime
(informal) gunk

slump VERB

❶ *Sales of new cars have **slumped** recently.*
• decline, fall, drop, plummet, plunge, crash, collapse
❷ *The professor **slumped** into an armchair.*
• flop, collapse, sink, sag, slouch

slump NOUN

*There was a **slump** in trade after Christmas.*
• collapse, drop, fall, decline
A general slump in trade is a **depression** or **recession**.
OPPOSITE boom

sly ADJECTIVE

*The chess player knew several **sly** moves.*
• crafty, cunning, artful, clever, wily, tricky, sneaky, devious, furtive, secretive, stealthy, underhand
A common simile is **as sly as a fox**.
OPPOSITE straightforward

smack VERB

*He **smacked** the other player on the head by accident.*
• slap, strike, hit, cuff
(informal) whack
for other ways of hitting see **hit**

small ADJECTIVE

OVERUSED WORD

Try to vary the words you use for **small**. Here are some other words you could use.

FOR A SMALL OBJECT:

• little, tiny, minute, compact, miniature, microscopic, minuscule, mini, baby
(informal) teeny, titchy
(Scottish) wee
OPPOSITES big, large
'Put vun drop, just vun titchy droplet, of this liqvid into a chocolate or a sveet, and at nine o'clock the next morning the child who ate it vill turn into a mouse in tventy-six seconds!'
–THE WITCHES, Roald Dahl

FOR A SMALL PERSON OR CREATURE:

• little, short, petite, slight, dainty, diminutive, undersized
(informal) pint-sized
*Although **slight** in stature, Ellie was remarkably strong.*
OPPOSITES big, tall, large

FOR A SMALL HELPING OR PORTION:

• meagre, inadequate, insufficient, paltry, scanty, stingy, skimpy
(informal) measly
OPPOSITES large, generous, ample
Interesting smells rose from the camp-kitchens, and Snibril thought sadly of the meagre rations he carried in his pack.–DRAGONS AT CRUMBLING CASTLE, Terry Pratchett

FOR A SMALL PROBLEM OR CHANGE:

• minor, slight, unimportant, insignificant, trivial, trifling, negligible
OPPOSITES major, substantial
*Don't worry about the **trivial** details.*

smart ADJECTIVE

❶ *Everyone looked **smart** at the wedding.*
• elegant, well-dressed, well-groomed, stylish, spruce, fashionable, chic, neat, trim
To make yourself smart is to **smarten up**.
OPPOSITE scruffy
❷ *They booked a table in a very **smart** restaurant.*
• fashionable, high-class, exclusive, fancy
(informal) posh
❸ *The detective made a very **smart** move.*
• clever, ingenious, intelligent, shrewd, crafty
OPPOSITE stupid
❹ *The cyclists set off at a **smart** pace.*
• fast, quick, rapid, speedy, swift, brisk
OPPOSITE slow

smart VERB

*The smoke from the barbecue made our eyes **smart**.*
• hurt, sting, prick, prickle, tingle

a b c d e f g h i j k l m n o p q r **s** t u v w x y z

A
B
C
D
E
F
G
H
I
J
K
L
M
N
O
P
Q
R
S
T
U
V
W
X
Y
Z

smash *VERB*
The vase rolled off the table and smashed to pieces on the floor.
• break, crush, shatter, crack
When wood smashes it **splinters**.
To smash something completely is to **demolish**, **destroy** or **wreck** it.
➤ **to smash into**
A lorry had smashed into the side of a bus.
• crash into, collide with, bang into, bump into

smear *VERB*
First smear the dish with butter.
• spread, wipe, plaster, rub, dab, smudge, daub
smear *NOUN*
There were smears of paint all over the carpet.
• streak, smudge, blotch, splodge, splotch, daub, mark

smell *VERB* smells, smelling, smelt or smelled
❶ *I could smell something baking in the oven.*
• scent, sniff
(informal) get a whiff of
❷ *After walking all day, my feet were beginning to smell.*
• stink, reek
(informal) pong
smell *NOUN*
❶ *The air was filled with the smell of roses.*
• scent, aroma, perfume, fragrance
❷ *The smell of mouldy cheese was unbearable.*
• odour, stench, stink, reek, whiff
(informal) pong, niff

WRITING TIPS

You can use these words to describe a **smell**.

TO DESCRIBE A GOOD SMELL:

• aromatic, fragrant, perfumed, scented, sweet, sweet-smelling
In the garden below were lilac-trees purple with flowers, and their dizzily sweet fragrance drifted up to the window on the morning wind.—ANNE OF GREEN GABLES, L. M. Montgomery

TO DESCRIBE A BAD SMELL:

• evil-smelling, fetid, foul, musty, odorous, rancid, reeking, rotten, smelly, stinking
(informal) pongy, whiffy
There was the same musty smell about the place that I had noticed in the Ballroom. It was the stench of witches.—THE WITCHES, Roald Dahl

TO DESCRIBE A STRONG SMELL:

• heady, overpowering, pungent
The heady scent of spices hung in the air.

smile *VERB, NOUN*
The stranger smiled and introduced himself.
• grin, beam
To smile in a silly way is to **simper**.
To smile in a self-satisfied way is to **smirk**.
To smile in an insulting way is to **sneer**.

smoke *NOUN*
Puffs of green smoke came from the dragon's nostrils.
• fumes, gas, steam, vapour
The smoke given out by a car is **exhaust**.
A mixture of smoke and fog is **smog**.
smoke *VERB*
❶ *The bonfire was still smoking next morning.*
• smoulder
❷ *A man stood silently smoking a cigar.*
• puff at

smooth *ADJECTIVE*
❶ *This part of the road is smooth and good for cycling.*
• flat, even, level
OPPOSITE uneven
❷ *In the early morning, the lake was perfectly smooth.*
• calm, still, unruffled, undisturbed, glassy
OPPOSITE rough
❸ *Otters have smooth and shiny coats.*
• silky, sleek, velvety
OPPOSITE coarse

❹ *The journey by train is very quick and* **smooth**.
• comfortable, steady
OPPOSITE **bumpy**
❺ *Stir the cake mixture until it is* **smooth**.
• creamy, flowing, runny
OPPOSITE **lumpy**

smooth VERB
Mia stood up and **smoothed** *her dress.*
• flatten, level, even out
To smooth cloth you can **iron** or **press** it.
To smooth wood you can **plane** or **sand** it.

smother VERB
❶ *Pythons* **smother** *their prey to death.*
• suffocate, choke, stifle
❷ *The pudding was* **smothered** *with cream.*
• cover, coat

smoulder VERB
see **burn**

smudge NOUN
There were **smudges** *of ink all over the page.*
• smear, blot, streak, stain, mark

smudge VERB
Don't **smudge** *the icing on the cake!*
• smear, blur, streak

snack NOUN
I usually bring an apple or banana for a **snack**.
• bite, refreshments
(informal) nibble

snag NOUN
We've hit a **snag** *with our holiday plans.*
• problem, difficulty, obstacle, hitch, complication, setback

snake NOUN
The **snake** *coiled itself around a branch.*
• serpent

WORD WEB

SOME KINDS OF SNAKE:

• adder, asp, anaconda, boa constrictor, cobra, coral snake, grass snake, mamba, puff adder, python, rattlesnake, sand snake, sea snake, sidewinder, tree snake, viper

PARTS OF A SNAKE:

• fangs, hood, scales, skin, venom
A snake **sheds** or **sloughs off** its old skin.
Snakes are **oviparous**, meaning that they lay eggs.
A route or river that twists like a snake is **serpentine**.

snap VERB
❶ *A twig* **snapped** *under one of my boots.*
• break, crack
❷ *The dog* **snapped** *at the postman's ankles.*
• bite, nip
❸ *Mr Doyle was in a bad mood and* **snapped** *at everyone.*
• snarl, bark

snare NOUN
A bird had got caught in the **snare**.
• trap

snarl VERB
❶ *The guard dog* **snarled** *as we approached.*
• growl, bare its teeth
❷ *'Go away!'* **snarled** *a voice inside the cave.*
• snap, growl, thunder, bark

snatch VERB
The thief **snatched** *the jewels and ran off.*
• grab, seize, grasp, pluck, wrench away, wrest away

a b c d e f g h i j k l m n o p q r s t u v w x y z

sneak VERB sneaks, sneaking, sneaked or
(North American) snuck
I managed to sneak in without anyone seeing.
• slip, steal, creep, slink, tiptoe, sidle, skulk

sneaky ADJECTIVE
That was a really sneaky trick.
• sly, underhand, cunning, crafty, devious,
furtive, untrustworthy
OPPOSITE honest

sneer VERB
➤ to sneer at
He sneered at my attempt to write a poem.
• make fun of, mock, ridicule, scoff at,
jeer at, deride

sniff NOUN, VERB
for various sounds see **sound**

snigger VERB
*Please stop sniggering at the back of the
room.*
• laugh, giggle, titter, chuckle

snip VERB
Remember to snip off any loose threads.
• cut, chop, clip, trim

snippet NOUN
*We could hear snippets of their
conversation.*
• piece, fragment, bit, scrap, morsel, snatch

snivel VERB
For goodness' sake, stop snivelling!
• cry, sob, weep, sniff, whimper, whine

snobbish ADJECTIVE
She's too snobbish to mix with us.
• arrogant, pompous, superior, haughty
(informal) stuck-up, snooty, toffee-nosed
OPPOSITE humble

snoop VERB
*They caught an intruder snooping round the
building.*
• sneak, pry, poke, rummage, spy

snort NOUN, VERB
for various sounds see **sound**

snout NOUN
Aardvarks have long, narrow snouts.
• muzzle, nose

snub VERB
*They snubbed the neighbours by not inviting
them to the party.*
• insult, offend, be rude to, brush off
(informal) put down

snuck (North American)
past tense see **sneak**

snug ADJECTIVE
The girls were tucked up snug in bed.
• cosy, comfortable, warm, relaxed
(informal) comfy
A common simile is as snug as a bug in a rug.
OPPOSITE uncomfortable

soak VERB
❶ *Days of rain had soaked the cricket pitch.*
• wet thoroughly, drench, saturate
❷ *Leave the beans to soak in water
overnight.*
• steep, immerse, submerge

soaking ADJECTIVE
My socks are absolutely soaking!
• wet through, drenched, dripping, wringing,
saturated, sodden, sopping, soggy
*Ground that has been soaked by rain is
waterlogged.*

soar VERB
❶ *The seagull spread its wings and soared
upwards.*
• climb, rise, ascend, fly, wing
❷ *Prices have continued to soar.*
• go up, rise, increase, shoot up

sob VERB
*Temi threw himself on the bed, sobbing
loudly.*
• cry, weep, bawl, blubber, shed tears, snivel

sober *ADJECTIVE*
❶ *He drank a little wine, but he stayed sober.*
• clear-headed
OPPOSITE drunk
❷ *The funeral was a sober occasion.*
• serious, solemn, sombre, grave, dignified, sedate
OPPOSITES light-hearted, frivolous

sociable *ADJECTIVE*
Our new neighbours are very sociable.
• friendly, outgoing, amiable, hospitable, neighbourly
OPPOSITE unfriendly

social *ADJECTIVE*
❶ *Elephants are social animals.*
People and creatures that like to be in groups or communities are **gregarious**.
OPPOSITE solitary
❷ *The club organized several social activities.*
• communal, community, public, group

society *NOUN*
❶ *Ancient Egypt was a society ruled by pharaohs.*
• community, civilization
❷ *Mrs Byrd is head of the local music society.*
• association, group, organization, club
❸ *She enjoys the society of her friends.*
• companionship, company, fellowship, friendship

soft *ADJECTIVE*
❶ *The kittens can only eat soft food.*
• pulpy, spongy, squashy
(informal) squidgy
OPPOSITES hard, dry
❷ *My head sank into the soft pillow.*
• supple, pliable, springy, yielding, flexible
OPPOSITES firm, rigid
❸ *The rabbit's fur felt very soft.*
• smooth, silky, sleek, velvety, downy, feathery
OPPOSITE coarse

❹ *A soft breeze stirred the leaves.*
• gentle, light, mild, delicate
OPPOSITES rough, strong
❺ *The smugglers spoke in soft whispers.*
• quiet, low, faint
OPPOSITE loud
❻ *It was hard to see clearly in the soft light.*
• subdued, muted, pale, dim, low
OPPOSITES bright, dazzling
❼ *You are being too soft with that puppy.*
• lenient, easy-going, tolerant, indulgent
OPPOSITES strict, tough

soggy *ADJECTIVE*
❶ *The pitch was soggy after all the rain.*
• wet, drenched, soaked, saturated, sodden, waterlogged
❷ *The bread had started to go soggy.*
• moist, soft, mushy, pulpy, squelchy
(informal) squidgy
OPPOSITE dry

soil *NOUN*
The plants grow best in well-drained soil.
• earth, ground, land
Good fertile soil is **loam**.
The fertile top layer of soil is **topsoil**.
Rich soil made by decaying leaves and plants is **humus**.

soil *VERB*
My trainers were soiled with mud and grass.
• dirty, make dirty, stain, muddy, tarnish

sold *past tense see* **sell**

soldier *NOUN*
Three soldiers stood guard outside the building.
• serviceman or servicewoman
A soldier paid to fight for a foreign country is a **mercenary**.
An old word for a soldier is **warrior**.
Soldiers who use heavy guns are the **artillery**.
Soldiers who fight on horseback are the **cavalry**.
Soldiers who fight on foot are the **infantry**.
see also **armed forces**

a b c d e f g h i j k l m n o p q r s t u v w x y z

sole *ADJECTIVE*
The castaway was the **sole** inhabitant of the island.
• only, single, one, solitary, lone, unique

solemn *ADJECTIVE*
❶ Inspector Fry always wore a **solemn** expression.
• serious, grave, sober, sombre, unsmiling, glum
OPPOSITE cheerful
❷ The funeral was a **solemn** occasion.
• formal, dignified, grand, stately, majestic, pompous
OPPOSITE frivolous

solid *ADJECTIVE*
❶ A cricket ball is **solid**.
OPPOSITE hollow
❷ The water turned into **solid** ice.
• hard, firm, dense, compact, rigid, unyielding
A common simile is **as solid as a rock**.
OPPOSITE soft
❸ The bars of the climbing frame are quite **solid**.
• firm, robust, sound, strong, stable, sturdy
OPPOSITES weak, unstable
❹ The crown was made of **solid** gold.
• pure, genuine
❺ She got **solid** support from her teammates.
• firm, reliable, dependable, united, unanimous
OPPOSITES weak, divided

solidify *VERB*
The lava **solidifies** as it cools.
• harden, become solid, set, stiffen
OPPOSITES soften, liquify

solitary *ADJECTIVE*
❶ He was a **solitary** man and rarely spoke to others.
• isolated, secluded, lonely, unsociable
To be solitary is to be **alone**.
OPPOSITE sociable.
❷ There was a **solitary** tree in the middle of the field.
• single, sole, one, only

solitude *NOUN*
On the island, there was total peace and **solitude**.
• privacy, seclusion, isolation, loneliness

solve *VERB*
No one has been able to **solve** this ancient riddle.
• interpret, explain, answer, work out, find the solution to, unravel, decipher

sombre *ADJECTIVE*
❶ The hall was decorated in **sombre** hues.
• dark, dull, dim, dismal, dingy, drab, cheerless
OPPOSITE bright
❷ A messenger arrived with a **sombre** look on his face.
• gloomy, serious, grave, sober, sad, melancholy, mournful
OPPOSITE cheerful

song *NOUN*

WORD WEB

SOME KINDS OF SONG:

• anthem, aria, ballad, calypso, carol, chant, ditty, folk song, hymn, jingle, lament, lay, love song, lullaby, madrigal, nursery rhyme, pop song, psalm, rap, round, shanty, spiritual
A play or film that includes many songs is a **musical**.
A song from a musical is a **number**.
The words for a song are the **lyrics**.
for other musical terms see **music**

soon *ADVERB*
Dinner will be ready **soon**.
• before long, in a minute, shortly, presently, quickly

soothe *VERB*
❶ The quiet music **soothed** her nerves.
• calm, comfort, relax, pacify
❷ This cream will **soothe** the pain.
• ease, lessen, relieve

soothing *ADJECTIVE*
*They played **soothing** music.*
• calming, relaxing, restful, peaceful, gentle, pleasant

sophisticated *ADJECTIVE*
❶ *Frida looked very **sophisticated** with her hair up.*
• grown-up, mature, cultivated, cultured, refined
OPPOSITE naive
❷ *This is our most **sophisticated** camera.*
• advanced, complex, complicated, intricate, elaborate
OPPOSITES primitive, simple

sorcerer and **sorceress** *NOUN*
see **magic**

sore *ADJECTIVE*
*My feet are still **sore** from the walk.*
• painful, aching, hurting, smarting, tender, sensitive, inflamed, raw, red
sore *NOUN*
*A nurse put a dressing on the **sore**.*
• wound, inflammation, swelling

sorrow *NOUN*
❶ *Those were years of **sorrow** for the family.*
• sadness, unhappiness, misery, woe, grief, anguish, despair, distress, heartache, heartbreak, melancholy, gloom, depression, desolation, wretchedness
Sorrow because of someone's death is mourning.
Sorrow at being away from home is homesickness.
OPPOSITE happiness
❷ *Jo felt no **sorrow** for what she had done.*
• regret, remorse, repentance, apologies

sorry *ADJECTIVE*
❶ *I am so **sorry** I forgot your birthday!*
• apologetic, regretful, remorseful, ashamed (of), repentant
OPPOSITE unapologetic

❷ *Everyone felt **sorry** for the losers.*
• sympathetic, pitying, understanding, compassionate
OPPOSITE unsympathetic

sort *NOUN*
*What **sort** of music do you like?*
• kind, type, variety, form, nature, style, genre, category, order, class
A sort of animal is a **breed** or **species**.
sort *VERB*
*The books are **sorted** according to size.*
• arrange, organize, class, group, categorize, classify, divide
OPPOSITE mix
➤ **to sort something out**
*Did you manage to **sort out** the problem?*
• settle, resolve, clear up, cope with, deal with

sought *past tense see* **seek**

sound *NOUN*
*We heard the **sound** of footsteps approaching.*
• noise, tone
A loud, harsh sound is a **din** or **racket**.
A harsh mixture of sounds is a **cacophony**.

WORD WEB

SOUNDS MADE BY PEOPLE:

• achoo, bawl, bellow, boo, boom, cackle, clap, croak, cry, gasp, giggle, groan, gurgle, hiccup, hiss, howl, hum, laugh, moan, murmur, puff, scream, shout, shriek, sigh, sing, sniff, snore, snort, sob, splutter, stammer, stutter, wail, wheeze, whimper, whine, whisper, whistle, whoop, yell
see also **say**
*for sounds made by animals and birds
see* **animal, bird**

SOUNDS MADE BY THINGS:

• bang, blare, beep, bleep, boing, bong, boom, burble, buzz, chime, chink, chug, clang, clank, clash, clatter, click, clink, clunk, crack, crackle, crash, creak, crunch, ding, drone, drum, fizz, grate, gurgle, hum,

a b c d e f g h i j k l m n o p q r s t u v w x y z

jangle, jingle, kaboom, patter, peal, ping, plink, plop, pop, purr, putter, rattle, ring, rumble, rustle, scrunch, sizzle, slam, snap, splash, squeak, squelch, swish, throb, thud, thunder, tick, ting, tinkle, twang, wham, whirr, whoosh, whistle, whizz, zap, zoom

Great whooshes of sound filled the air as the beam engine started to move, then generators started to hum, and power surged through the sizing machine.–HERE BE MONSTERS!, Alan Snow

WRITING TIPS

You can use these words to describe a sound.

TO DESCRIBE A PLEASANT SOUND:

• sweet, harmonious, melodious, mellifluous, dulcet
It sounded like the sweet singing of a mermaid.

TO DESCRIBE AN UNPLEASANT SOUND:

• grating, harsh, jarring, piercing, rasping, raucous, shrill, thin, tinny
A startled raven burst upward uttering its harsh, grating alarm cry, and flew off northward with slow, indignant wing-beats, caaking as it went.–THE EAGLE OF THE NINTH, Rosemary Sutcliff

TO DESCRIBE A LOUD SOUND:

• blaring, deafening, noisy, thunderous

TO DESCRIBE A QUIET SOUND:

• low, muffled, muted, soft
In the distance they could hear the muted sound of traffic going round Hyde Park Corner.–THE BFG, Roald Dahl

sound *VERB*
A trumpet sounded in the distance.
• make a noise, resound, be heard

sound *ADJECTIVE*
❶ *The walls of the fortress seemed sound.*
• firm, solid, stable, safe, secure, intact, undamaged
OPPOSITES unsound, unstable
❷ *She gave us some sound advice.*
• good, sensible, wise, reasonable, trustworthy
OPPOSITE unwise
❸ *The travellers returned safe and sound.*
• strong, well, fit, healthy
OPPOSITES weak, unfit

sour *ADJECTIVE*
❶ *These apples are a bit sour.*
• tart, bitter, sharp, acid
OPPOSITE sweet
❷ *The guard opened the door with a sour look on his face.*
• cross, bad-tempered, grumpy, disagreeable, peevish

source *NOUN*
The vet has found the source of the infection.
• origin, start, starting point, head, root, cause
The source of a river or stream is usually a spring.

south *NOUN, ADJECTIVE, ADVERB*
The parts of a continent or country in the south are the **southern** parts.
To travel towards the south is to travel **southward** or **southwards** or **in a southerly direction**.
A wind from the south is a **southerly** wind.
A person who lives in the south of a country is a **southerner**.

sow *VERB* sows, sowing, sowed, sown or sowed
To sow seeds in the ground is to **plant** them.
To sow an area of ground with seeds is to **seed** it.

space *NOUN*
❶ *There wasn't much space to move about.*
• room, freedom, scope
❷ *He peered through the tiny space in the curtains.*
• gap, hole, opening, break

A space without any air in it is a **vacuum**.
A space of time is an **interval** or **period**.
❸ *The astronauts will spend ten days in space.*
• outer space

Everything that exists in space is the **universe** or **cosmos**.
Distances in space stretch to **infinity**.
Travel to other planets is **interplanetary** travel.
Travel to other stars is **interstellar** travel.
Travel to other galaxies is **intergalactic** travel.
A traveller in space is an **astronaut**.
A Russian astronaut is a **cosmonaut**.
In stories, beings from other planets are **aliens** or **extraterrestrials**.
see also **alien, astronaut**

NATURAL OBJECTS FOUND IN SPACE:

• asteroid, black hole, comet, constellation, galaxy, meteor, meteorite, Milky Way, moon, nebula, nova, planet, red dwarf, red giant, shooting star, solar system, star, sun, supernova
see also **moon, planet**

WORDS TO DO WITH TRAVEL IN SPACE:

• blast-off, countdown, launch, mission, orbit, re-entry, rocket, satellite, spacecraft, spaceship, space station, spacesuit, spacewalk
A robot spacecraft is a **probe**.
A vehicle which can travel on the surface of a planet is a **buggy** or **rover**.

THINGS YOU MIGHT FIND ON A SPACECRAFT:

• airlock, booster rocket, bridge, cargo bay, capsule, computer, docking bay, fuel tank, heat shield, instrument panel, life support system, module, pod, solar panel, thruster

THINGS A SPACECRAFT MIGHT DO:

• blast off, burn up, drift off-course, jettison parts, land, lift off, malfunction, orbit, re-enter the earth's atmosphere, splash down, touch down

spacious ADJECTIVE
The living room is spacious and bright.
• big, large, roomy, sizeable
OPPOSITES small, cramped

span NOUN
The bridge has a span of 200 metres.
• breadth, extent, length, width, distance, reach
A span of time is a **period** or **stretch**.

span VERB
A rickety footbridge spanned the river.
• cross, stretch over, extend across, straddle, bridge, traverse

spare VERB
❶ *Can you spare any money for a good cause?*
• afford, part with, give, provide, do without
❷ *Gretel begged the witch to spare her brother.*
• show mercy to, pardon, reprieve, let off, release, free

spare ADJECTIVE
❶ *The spare tyre is in the boot.*
• additional, extra, reserve, standby
❷ *Have you any spare change?*
• leftover, surplus, odd, remaining, unused, unwanted
❸ *The ghostly figure was tall and spare.*
• lean, thin, slender, slim, trim

spark NOUN
There was a spark of light as she struck the match.
• flash, gleam, glint, flicker, sparkle

sparkle VERB
The diamond ring sparkled in the sunlight.
• glitter, glisten, glint, twinkle

sparse ADJECTIVE
In the desert, vegetation is very sparse.

• scarce, scanty, scattered, inadequate, infrequent
OPPOSITE plentiful

spatter *VERB*
The bus **spattered** mud all over us.
• splash, spray, sprinkle, scatter, shower

speak *VERB* speaks, speaking, spoke, spoken
The robot opened its mouth and began to **speak**.
• communicate, express yourself, say something, talk, utter

speaker *NOUN*
A person who gives a talk is a **lecturer**.
A person who makes formal speeches is an **orator**.
A person who speaks on behalf of an organization is a **spokesperson**.

spear *NOUN*
A spear used in whaling is a **harpoon**.
A spear thrown as a sport is a **javelin**.
A spear carried by a medieval knight on horseback was a **lance**.

special *ADJECTIVE*
❶ Are you keeping the champagne for a **special** occasion?
• important, significant, memorable, noteworthy, momentous, exceptional, extraordinary, out of the ordinary
OPPOSITE ordinary
❷ My grandpa has his own **special** way of making porridge.
• unique, individual, characteristic, distinctive, different, peculiar
❸ You need a **special** camera to film underwater.
• particular, specific, proper, specialized

speciality *NOUN*
The chef's **speciality** is sticky toffee pudding.
• strength, strong point, expertise, forte

specific *ADJECTIVE*
The treasure map gave **specific** directions.
• detailed, precise, exact, definite, particular, clear-cut
OPPOSITES general, vague

specify *VERB*
Please **specify** your shoe size.
• be specific about, identify, name, define

specimen *NOUN*
The police asked for a **specimen** of his handwriting.
• sample, example, illustration, instance

speck *NOUN*
She brushed a **speck** of dust from her shoes.
• bit, dot, spot, fleck, grain, particle, trace, mark
see also **bit**

speckled *ADJECTIVE*
A brown, **speckled** egg lay on the nest.
• flecked, spotted, spotty, mottled
If you have a lot of brown spots on your skin you are **freckled**.
Something with patches of colour is **dappled** or **patchy**.

spectacle *NOUN*
The fireworks for Diwali will be a great **spectacle**.
• display, show, performance, exhibition, extravaganza

spectacles *PLURAL NOUN*
see **glasses**

spectacular *ADJECTIVE*
❶ The acrobats gave a **spectacular** performance.
• dramatic, exciting, impressive, thrilling, magnificent, sensational
❷ The tulips are **spectacular** at this time of year.
• eye-catching, showy, splendid, breathtaking, colourful

A B C D E F G H I J K L M N O P Q R S T U V W X Y Z

spectator NOUN
The spectators at a show are the **audience**.
The spectators at a football match are the **crowd**.
A person watching TV is a **viewer**.
If you see an accident or a crime you are an **eyewitness** or **witness**.
If you just happen to see something going on you are a **bystander** or **onlooker**.

speech NOUN
❶ *His speech was slurred and he looked tired.*
• speaking, talking, articulation, pronunciation
❷ *She was invited to give an after-dinner speech.*
• talk, address, lecture, oration
A talk in church is a **sermon**.
Speech between actors in a play is **dialogue**.
A speech delivered by a single actor is a **monologue**.

speechless ADJECTIVE
She was speechless with surprise.
• dumbstruck, dumbfounded, tongue-tied

speed NOUN
❶ *Could a spacecraft travel faster than the speed of light?*
• pace, rate
A formal synonym is **velocity**.
The speed of a piece of music is its **tempo**.
To increase speed is to **accelerate**.
To reduce speed is to **decelerate**.
❷ *They finished clearing up with amazing speed.*
• quickness, rapidity, swiftness
OPPOSITE slowness

speed VERB speeds, speeding, sped
The skiers sped down the mountain.
• race, rush, dash, dart, hurry, hurtle, career, fly, streak, tear, shoot, zoom, zip

speedy ADJECTIVE
They sent their best wishes for a speedy recovery.
• fast, quick, swift, rapid, prompt, brisk
OPPOSITE slow

spell NOUN
❶ *We're hoping for a spell of dry weather.*
• period, interval, time, stretch, run
❷ *A magic spell had turned the knight into a toad.*
• charm, incantation
Making magic spells is **sorcery**, **witchcraft** or **wizardry**.
for other words to do with magic see **magic**

spend VERB spends, spending, spent
❶ *Have you spent all your pocket money already?*
• pay out, use up, get through, exhaust
(informal) fork out, shell out
To spend money unwisely is to **fritter** or **squander** it.
❷ *She spends a lot of time working in the garden.*
• pass, occupy, fill
To spend time doing something useless is to **waste** it.

sphere NOUN
❶ *The earth has the shape of a sphere.*
• ball, globe, orb
❷ *He's an expert in the sphere of photography.*
• subject, area, field

spherical ADJECTIVE
The earth is spherical.
• round, ball-shaped

spice NOUN

> ### WORD WEB
>
> SOME SPICES USED IN COOKING:
>
> • allspice, aniseed, bay leaf, capsicum, cardamom, cayenne, chilli, cinnamon, cloves, coriander, cumin, curry powder, ginger, juniper, mace, nutmeg, paprika, pepper, pimento, saffron, sesame, turmeric

spicy ADJECTIVE
The meat was cooked in a spicy chilli sauce.
• hot, peppery, fiery

a b c d e f g h i j k l m n o p q r s t u v w x y z

A
B
C
D
E
F
G
H
I
J
K
L
M
N
O
P
Q
R
S
T
U
V
W
X
Y
Z

spike *NOUN*
His shirt got caught on a metal spike.
• point, prong, spear, stake, barb

spill *VERB*
❶ *Katie spilled her juice all over the table.*
• overturn, upset, tip over
❷ *Milk spilled on to the floor.*
• overflow, pour, slop, slosh, splash
❸ *The treasure chest fell open, spilling gold coins everywhere.*
• shed, tip, scatter, drop

spin *VERB* spins, spinning, spun
The rear wheels of the jeep spun round.
• turn, rotate, revolve, whirl, twirl

spine *NOUN*
❶ *Your spine runs down the middle of your back.*
• backbone, spinal column
The bones in your spine are your **vertebrae**.
❷ *A porcupine has sharp spines.*
• needle, quill, point, spike, bristle

spiral *NOUN*
The staircase wound upwards in a long spiral.
• coil, twist, corkscrew, whorl
A tight spiral of swirling air or water is a **vortex**.

spirit *NOUN*
❶ *He carried a charm to keep evil spirits away.*
• ghost, ghoul, phantom, spectre, demon
see also **ghost**
❷ *The orchestra played the piece with great spirit.*
• energy, liveliness, enthusiasm, vigour, zest, zeal, fire
❸ *There is a real spirit of cooperation in the team.*
• feeling, mood, atmosphere

spiritual *ADJECTIVE*
The Dalai Lama is the spiritual leader of Tibet.
• religious, holy, sacred
OPPOSITE worldly

spite *NOUN*
I believe that she ripped my book out of spite.
• malice, spitefulness, ill will, ill feeling, hostility, bitterness, resentment, venom

spiteful *ADJECTIVE*
He made some really spiteful comments.
• malicious, malevolent, ill-natured, hostile, venomous, vicious, nasty, unkind
OPPOSITE kind

splash *VERB*
❶ *The bus splashed water over us.*
• shower, spray, spatter, sprinkle, squirt, slop, slosh, spill, splatter
(informal) splosh
❷ *The children splashed about in the playing pool.*
• paddle, wade, dabble, bathe

splendid *ADJECTIVE*
❶ *There was a splendid banquet on the eve of the wedding.*
• magnificent, lavish, luxurious, impressive, imposing, grand, great, dazzling, glorious, gorgeous, elegant, rich, stately, majestic
❷ *That's a splendid idea!*
• excellent, first-class, admirable, superb, wonderful, marvellous

splendour *NOUN*
They admired the splendour of the cathedral.
• magnificence, glory, grandeur, majesty, richness, brilliance, spectacle

splinter *NOUN*
There were splinters of glass all over the floor.
• fragment, sliver, chip, flake
splinter *VERB*
The glass splintered into pieces.
• shatter, smash, fracture, chip, crack, split

split *VERB*
❶ *She split the log in two.*
• chop, cut up, crack open, splinter
❷ *He split his trousers climbing over the fence.*
• rip open, tear

❸ *The pirates split the gold between them.*
• distribute, share out
❹ *The path splits here.*
• branch, fork, separate
➤ **to split up**
The search party decided to split up.
• break up, part, separate, divide
If a married couple splits up, they may divorce.

split *NOUN*
She had a split in her trousers.
• rip, tear, slash, slit

spoil *VERB*
❶ *Bad weather spoiled the holiday.*
• ruin, wreck, upset, mess up, mar, scupper
❷ *The graffiti spoils the look of the new building.*
• damage, harm, hurt, disfigure, deface
❸ *His parents have spoiled him since he was a baby.*
• indulge, pamper, make a fuss of

spoke *past tense see* **speak**

spoken *ADJECTIVE*
Her spoken Spanish is excellent.
• oral, spoken
OPPOSITE written

spongy *ADJECTIVE*
The mossy ground felt spongy to walk on.
• soft, springy, squashy, absorbent, porous

spoon *NOUN*
see **cutlery**

sport *NOUN*
I enjoy playing sport at the weekend.
• exercise, games

WORD WEB

TEAM SPORTS INCLUDE:

• American football, baseball, basketball, bowls, cricket, football or soccer, hockey, kabaddi, lacrosse, netball, polo, rounders, rugby, volleyball, water polo

INDIVIDUAL SPORTS INCLUDE:

• angling, archery, athletics, badminton, billiards, boxing, bowling, canoeing, climbing, croquet, cross-country running, cycling, darts, diving, fencing, golf, gymnastics, horse racing, jogging, judo, karate, motor racing, mountaineering, orienteering, pool, rowing, sailing, showjumping, snooker, squash, surfing, swimming, table tennis, taekwondo, tennis, waterskiing, weightlifting, windsurfing, wrestling
for individual athletic events see **athletics**

WINTER SPORTS INCLUDE:

• bobsleigh, cross-country skiing, curling, downhill skiing, ice hockey, ice skating, luge, skeleton, ski jumping, slalom, snowboarding, speed skating, tobogganing

PEOPLE WHO TAKE PART IN SPORT:

• athlete, coach, competitor, Olympian, Paralympian, player, sportsman or sportswoman

PLACES WHERE SPORT TAKES PLACE:

• arena, field, ground, park, pitch, pool, ring, rink, run, slope, stadium, track

sporting *ADJECTIVE*
It was sporting of her to admit the ball was out.
• sportsmanlike, fair, generous, honourable
OPPOSITE unsporting

spot *NOUN*
❶ *There were several spots of paint on the carpet.*
• mark, stain, blot, blotch, smudge, dot, fleck, speck
Small brown spots on your skin are freckles.

a b c d e f g h i j k l m n o p q r s t u v w x y z

A small dark spot on your skin is a **mole**.
A mark you have had on your skin since you were born is a **birthmark**.
A small round swelling on your skin is a **pimple**.
A lot of spots is a **rash**.
❷ *We felt a few* ***spots*** *of rain.*
• drop, blob, bead
❸ *Here's a nice* ***spot*** *for a picnic.*
• place, position, location, site, situation, locality

spot *VERB*
❶ *Nina* ***spotted*** *her friend in the crowd.*
• see, sight, spy, catch sight of, notice, observe, make out, recognize, detect
❷ *The tyres were* ***spotted*** *with mud.*
• mark, stain, blot, spatter, fleck, speckle, mottle

spotless *ADJECTIVE*
Mr Travis washed his car until it was ***spotless***.
• clean, unmarked, immaculate, gleaming
OPPOSITE dirty

spout *VERB*
Molten lava and ash ***spouted*** *from the volcano.*
• gush, spew, pour, stream, spurt, squirt, jet

sprawl *VERB*
❶ *We* ***sprawled*** *on the lawn.*
• flop, lean back, lie, loll, lounge, recline, relax, slouch, slump, spread out, stretch out
❷ *New houses have started to* ***sprawl*** *across the countryside.*
• spread, stretch

spray *VERB*
A passing bus ***sprayed*** *mud over us.*
• shower, spatter, splash, sprinkle, scatter

spray *NOUN*
❶ *We gave the plants a* ***spray*** *of water with the hose.*
• shower, sprinkling, fountain, mist
❷ *She picked a* ***spray*** *of snowdrops from the garden.*
• bunch, posy

spread *VERB*
❶ *I* ***spread*** *the map on the table.*
• lay out, open out, fan out, unfold, unfurl, unroll
❷ *The milk spilled and* ***spread*** *all over the floor.*
• expand, extend, stretch, broaden, enlarge, swell
❸ *The school website is a good way of* ***spreading*** *news.*
• communicate, circulate, distribute, transmit, make known, pass on, pass round
❹ *She* ***spread*** *jam on a piece of toast.*
• smear
❺ *He* ***spread*** *the seeds evenly over the ground.*
• scatter, strew

sprightly *ADJECTIVE*
My granny is quite ***sprightly*** *for her age.*
• lively, energetic, active, agile, nimble, frisky, spry
OPPOSITE inactive

spring *VERB* springs, springing, sprang, sprung
Suddenly a rabbit ***sprang*** *over the fence.*
• jump, leap, bound, hop, vault
When a cat springs at a mouse, it **pounces**.
➤ **to spring up**
Weeds ***spring up*** *quickly in damp weather.*
• appear, develop, emerge, shoot up, sprout

springy *ADJECTIVE*
The bed felt soft and ***springy***.
• bouncy, elastic, stretchy, flexible, pliable
OPPOSITE rigid

sprinkle *VERB*
She ***sprinkled*** *flakes of chocolate over the cake.*
• scatter, shower, spray, dust, powder

sprout *VERB*
The seeds will ***sprout*** *if they are warm and damp.*
• grow, germinate, shoot up, spring up, develop, emerge

spruce *ADJECTIVE*
He looked very **spruce** in a clean white shirt.
• smart, well-dressed, well-groomed, elegant, neat, trim
OPPOSITE scruffy

spun *past tense see* **spin**

spur *VERB*
➤ **to spur someone on**
The cheers of the crowd **spurred on** the athletes.
• egg on, encourage, inspire, prompt, stimulate, urge, empower

spurt *VERB*
Water **spurted** from the hole in the pipe.
• gush, spout, shoot out, stream, squirt, jet

spy *NOUN*
The **spy** was on a top secret mission.
• agent, secret agent
The work of a spy is **spying** or espionage.
A spy who works for two rival countries or organizations is a **double agent**.
An informal name for a spy who works undercover is a **mole**.

WORD WEB

THINGS A SPY MIGHT DO:

• adopt a disguise or cover, assume a secret identity, carry out a secret mission, crack or decipher a code, gather intelligence, keep someone under surveillance, report to headquarters, uncover an enemy agent, work undercover
see also **code**

THINGS A SPY MIGHT USE OR CARRY:

• coded message, false passport, hidden camera or microphone, listening device, motion detector, night-vision goggles, password, torch, walkie-talkie

A SPY'S MISSION MIGHT BE:

• clandestine, covert, secret, stealthy, surreptitious, top secret, undercover, *(informal)* cloak-and-dagger, hush-hush

spy *VERB*
The lookout **spied** a ship on the horizon.
• see, sight, spot, catch sight of, notice, observe, make out, detect

squabble *VERB*
We are always **squabbling** in the car.
• argue, fight, quarrel, bicker, wrangle

squalid *ADJECTIVE*
The prisoners were kept in a **squalid** underground cell.
• degrading, dingy, dirty, filthy, foul, mucky, nasty, unpleasant
OPPOSITE clean

squander *VERB*
He **squandered** his money on an expensive watch.
• waste, fritter away, misuse
(informal) blow
OPPOSITE save

square *ADJECTIVE*
All the tiles have **square** corners.
• right-angled
A pattern of squares is a **chequered** pattern.

squarely *ADVERB*
The ball hit her **squarely** in the face.
• directly, straight, head-on
OPPOSITE obliquely

squash *VERB*
❶ My sandwich got **squashed** at the bottom of my school bag.
• crush, flatten, press, compress, mangle
To squash food deliberately is to **mash** or **pulp** or **purée** it.
❷ We **squashed** our sleeping bags into our rucksacks.
• squeeze, stuff, force, cram, pack, ram

squat *VERB*
We **squatted** on the ground to watch the puppet show.
• crouch, sit

a b c d e f g h i j k l m n o p q r **s** t u v w x y z

squat *ADJECTIVE*
The alien had a *squat* little body on three short legs.
• dumpy, stocky, plump, podgy, portly

squeak and **squeal** *NOUN, VERB*
for various sounds see **sound**

squeeze *VERB*
❶ She *squeezed* the water out of the sponge.
• press, wring, compress, crush
❷ Five of us *squeezed* into the back of the car.
• squash, cram, crowd, stuff, push, ram, shove, wedge
❸ Holly *squeezed* her sister affectionately.
• clasp, hug, embrace, cuddle
To squeeze something between your thumb and finger is to **pinch** it.

squirm *VERB*
The guinea pig *squirmed* out of the vet's grasp.
• wriggle, writhe, twist

squirt *VERB*
My little brother made the tap water *squirt* all over me.
• spurt, spray, gush, spout, shoot, jet

stab *VERB*
❶ He *stabbed* the sausage with his fork.
• spear, jab, pierce, impale
❷ She *stabbed* a finger at him.
• stick, thrust, push, jab
stab *NOUN*
Jake felt a sudden *stab* of pain in his chest.
• pang, prick, sting

stable *ADJECTIVE*
❶ The ladder doesn't look very *stable*.
• steady, secure, firm, fixed, solid, balanced
OPPOSITES wobbly, shaky
❷ They've been in a *stable* relationship for years.
• steady, established, lasting, durable, strong
OPPOSITE temporary

stack *NOUN*
There were *stacks* of books all over the floor.
• pile, heap, mound, tower
Another word for a stack of hay is a **rick** or **hayrick**.
stack *VERB*
Stack the papers on the desk.
• gather, assemble, collect, heap up, pile up

staff *NOUN*
There was a party at the hospital for all the *staff*.
• workers, employees, personnel, workforce, team
The staff on a ship or aircraft are the **crew**.

stage *NOUN*
❶ They went up on the *stage* to collect their prizes.
• platform
❷ The final *stage* of the journey was made by coach.
• leg, step, phase, portion, stretch
❸ At this *stage* in her life, she wants to try something new.
• period, point, time, juncture

stagger *VERB*
❶ The wounded deer *staggered* and fell.
• reel, stumble, lurch, totter, sway, falter, waver, wobble
❷ We were *staggered* at the size of the pyramid.
• amaze, astonish, astound, surprise, flabbergast, stupefy, startle, stun

stagnant *ADJECTIVE*
Mosquitoes swarmed around the pool of *stagnant* water.
• still, motionless, static
OPPOSITES flowing, fresh

stain *NOUN*
There were several coffee *stains* on the tablecloth.
• mark, spot, blot, blotch, blemish, smear, smudge

400

stain VERB
❶ *Her trainers were stained with mud.*
• discolour, mark, soil, dirty, blacken, tarnish
❷ *The wood can be stained a darker shade.*
• dye, colour, paint, tint, tinge

stairs PLURAL NOUN
The stairs up to the front door were worn with age.
• steps
A set of stairs taking you from one floor to another is a **flight** of stairs, or a **staircase** or **stairway**.
A moving staircase is an **escalator**.
A handrail at the side of a staircase is a **banister**.

stake NOUN
The fence was made from sharp wooden stakes.
• pole, post, stick, spike, stave, pile

stale ADJECTIVE
The bread had gone stale.
• dry, hard, old, mouldy, musty
(OPPOSITE) fresh

stalk NOUN
The recipe requires half a stalk of celery.
• stem, shoot, twig

stalk VERB
❶ *The cheetah stalked its prey.*
• hunt, pursue, track, trail, follow, shadow, tail
❷ *The customer turned and stalked out of the room.*
• stride, strut
for other ways to walk see **walk**

stall VERB
The man was stalling to give his friends time to escape.
• play for time, delay, hesitate, hedge

stammer VERB
Angela went red and started stammering.
• stutter, falter, stumble, splutter

stamp VERB
❶ *He stamped on the flower by mistake.*
• step, tread, trample

❷ *The librarian stamped my library book.*
• mark, print
To stamp a postmark on a letter is to **frank** it.
To stamp a mark on cattle with a hot iron is to **brand** them.

stamp NOUN
I put a first-class stamp on the letter.
A person who studies or collects stamps is a **philatelist**.

stand VERB stands, standing, stood
❶ *The newborn pup was too weak to stand.*
• get to your feet, get up, rise
❷ *They stood the ladder against the wall.*
• put, place, set, position, station, erect
❸ *The offer still stands.*
• remain valid, be unchanged, continue
❹ *I can't stand the smell any longer.*
• bear, abide, endure, put up with, tolerate, suffer
➤ **to stand for something**
She won't stand for any nonsense.
• put up with, tolerate, accept, allow, permit
What do these initials stand for?
• mean, indicate, signify, represent
➤ **to stand out**
Among all the photographs, this one really stood out.
• catch your eye, stick out, be prominent
➤ **to stand up for someone**
He always stands up for his friends.
• support, defend, side with, speak up for
(informal) stick up for

stand NOUN
A three-legged stand for a camera or telescope is a **tripod**.
A stand for a Bible or other large book is a **lectern**.
A stand to put a statue on is a **pedestal** or **plinth**.

standard NOUN
❶ *Their writing is of a very high standard.*
• grade, level, quality
❷ *He considered the book good by any standard.*
• guidelines, ideal, measurement, model

a
b
c
d
e
f
g
h
i
j
k
l
m
n
o
p
q
r
s
t
u
v
w
x
y
z

401

A
B
C
D
E
F
G
H
I
J
K
L
M
N
O
P
Q
R
S
T
U
V
W
X
Y
Z

❸ *The soldiers carried their* **standard** *proudly.*
• colours, flag, banner

standard *ADJECTIVE*
The teacher showed us the **standard** *way to write a letter.*
• normal, usual, common, conventional, typical, customary, accepted, approved, established, orthodox, regular, traditional
OPPOSITE abnormal

standby *NOUN*
We need a **standby** *in case someone drops out.*
• reserve, substitute, replacement

standstill *NOUN*
➤ **to come to a standstill**
The traffic had **come to a standstill.**
• stop moving, draw up, halt, stop

staple *ADJECTIVE*
Rice is the **staple** *food in many countries.*
• chief, main, principal, standard, basic

star *NOUN*
❶ *Astronomers study the* **stars.**
for objects found in space see **space**
for signs of the zodiac see **zodiac**
Words meaning 'to do with stars' are **astral** and **stellar.**
A night sky in which you can see stars is **starry** or **star-studded.**
A mark in the shape of a star in a piece of writing is an **asterisk.**
❷ *Several Hollywood* **stars** *attended the premiere of the film.*
• celebrity, idol, superstar

stare *VERB*
The guard **stared** *straight ahead, not blinking.*
• gaze, gape, peer, look
➤ **to stare at someone**
The wolf was **staring** *hungrily* **at** *us.*
• gaze at, gawp at, goggle at, eye, ogle, scrutinize, watch

To stare angrily at someone is to **glare** at them.

start *VERB*
❶ *The new course will* **start** *in the autumn.*
• begin, commence
(informal) get going, get cracking, kick off
OPPOSITES finish, end
❷ *We are planning to* **start** *a book club.*
• create, set up, establish, found, institute, originate, introduce, initiate, open, launch
OPPOSITE close
❸ *The horses* **started** *when the gun went off.*
• jump, flinch, jerk, twitch, recoil, wince

start *NOUN*
❶ *Try not to miss the* **start** *of the film.*
• beginning, opening, introduction, commencement
OPPOSITES end, close, finish
❷ *She has been with the theatre company right from the* **start.**
• beginning, outset, creation, inception, birth, dawn, launch
❸ *The explosion gave us all a nasty* **start.**
• jump, jolt, shock, surprise

startle *VERB*
The sudden noise **startled** *the deer.*
• alarm, panic, frighten, scare, make you start, make you jump, surprise, take you by surprise

starve *VERB*
Many animals will **starve** *if the drought continues.*
• die of starvation, go hungry
To choose to go without food is to **fast.**

starving *ADJECTIVE (informal)*
What's for dinner? I'm **starving!**
• hungry, famished, ravenous
To be slightly hungry is to be **peckish.**

state *NOUN*
❶ *The roof of the cottage is in a bad* **state.**
• condition, shape

The state of a person or animal is their **fitness** or **health.**
❷ *He gets into a terrible state before an exam.*
• panic, fluster
(informal) flap
❸ *The Queen is the head of state.*
• country, nation

state *VERB*
Her passport states that she is an Australian citizen.
• declare, announce, report, say, proclaim, pronounce, communicate

stately *ADJECTIVE*
The royal banquet will be a stately occasion.
• grand, dignified, formal, imposing, majestic, noble, splendid

statement *NOUN*
The prime minister made a statement to the press.
• announcement, declaration, communication, report, testimony

station *NOUN*
❶ *Does the train stop at the next station?*
The station at the end of a line is the **terminus.**
for other words to do with trains see **railway.**
❷ *She was taken to the police station for questioning.*
• depot, headquarters
❸ *There are two local radio stations.*
• channel

station *VERB*
A lookout was stationed on the roof of the building.
• place, position, put, stand, situate, locate

stationary *ADJECTIVE*
The bus was stuck behind a stationary vehicle.
• still, static, unmoving, immobile, motionless, standing, at rest
OPPOSITE moving

statue *NOUN*
There is a statue of Millicent Fawcett in Parliament Square.

• figure, sculpture, carving
A small statue is a **statuette.**

status *NOUN*
Peasants had a very low status in medieval England.
• rank, level, position, grade, importance, prestige

staunch *ADJECTIVE*
The Green Knight was a staunch ally of the prince.
• firm, strong, faithful, loyal, true, reliable, dependable, steadfast, trusty
OPPOSITE unreliable

stay *VERB*
❶ *Can you stay there while I park the car?*
• wait, hang about, remain
OPPOSITES leave, depart
❷ *We tried to stay warm by stamping our feet.*
• keep, carry on being, continue
❸ *Do you plan to stay in Scotland for long?*
• live, reside, dwell, lodge, settle, stop

stay *NOUN*
Our friends came for a short stay.
• visit, stopover, holiday, break

steady *ADJECTIVE*
❶ *You need a steady hand to be a surgeon.*
• stable, balanced, settled, secure, fixed, firm, fast, solid
A common simile is as **steady as a rock.**
OPPOSITES unsteady, shaky
❷ *The plants need a steady supply of water.*
• continuous, uninterrupted, non-stop, consistent
OPPOSITE intermittent
❸ *The runners kept up a steady pace.*
• regular, constant, even, smooth, rhythmic, unvarying
OPPOSITE irregular

steady *VERB*
The crew managed to steady the yacht.
• balance, stabilize

a
b
c
d
e
f
g
h
i
j
k
l
m
n
o
p
q
r
s
t
u
v
w
x
y
z

A
B
C
D
E
F
G
H
I
J
K
L
M
N
O
P
Q
R
S
T
U
V
W
X
Y
Z

steal *VERB* steals, stealing, stole, stolen
❶ *The thieves* ***stole*** *several valuable paintings.*
• rob, thieve, take, lift, make off with
(*informal*) pinch, nick, swipe, snaffle
❷ *The children* ***stole*** *quietly upstairs.*
• creep, sneak, tiptoe, slip, slink

stealing *NOUN*
The police have accused them of ***stealing***.
• robbery, theft
Stealing from someone's home is **burglary** or **housebreaking**.
Stealing from a shop is **shoplifting**.
Stealing small things is **pilfering**.

stealthy *ADJECTIVE*
We heard ***stealthy*** *footsteps going upstairs.*
• furtive, secretive, surreptitious, sly, sneaky, underhand
OPPOSITES conspicuous, open

steam *NOUN*
Clouds of ***steam*** *were coming from the cauldron.*
• vapour, mist, haze
Steam on a cold window is **condensation**.

steamy *ADJECTIVE*
❶ *The climate in a rainforest is hot and* ***steamy***.
• humid, muggy, close, damp, moist
❷ *She wiped the* ***steamy*** *mirror.*
• misty, hazy, cloudy

steep *ADJECTIVE*
The bus inched its way slowly up the ***steep*** *slope.*
• abrupt, sudden, sharp
A cliff or drop which is straight up and down is **sheer** or **vertical**.
OPPOSITES gradual, gentle

steer *VERB*
She ***steered*** *the car into the parking space.*
• direct, guide
To steer a vehicle is to **drive** it.
To steer a boat is to **navigate** or pilot it.

stem *NOUN*
The gardener pulled out the dead ***stems***.
• stalk, shoot, twig, branch
The main stem of a tree is its **trunk**.
stem *VERB*
Chloe blinked, trying to ***stem*** *the flow of her tears.*
• stop, check, hold back, restrain, curb

step *NOUN*
❶ *The baby took her first* ***steps*** *yesterday.*
• footstep, pace, stride
❷ *Be careful not to trip on the* ***step***.
• doorstep, stair
A set of steps going from one floor of a building to another is a **staircase**.
A folding set of steps is a **stepladder**.
The steps of a ladder are the **rungs**.
❸ *The first* ***step*** *in making a cake is to weigh the ingredients.*
• stage, phase, action
step *VERB*
Don't ***step*** *in the puddle!*
• put your foot, tread, walk, stamp, trample
➤ **to step something up**
They have ***stepped up*** *security at the airport.*
• increase, intensify, strengthen, boost

sterile *ADJECTIVE*
❶ *Very little grows in the* ***sterile*** *soil of the desert.*
• barren, dry, arid, infertile, lifeless
OPPOSITE fertile
❷ *The nurse put a* ***sterile*** *bandage on the wound.*
• sterilized, disinfected, germ-free, antiseptic, hygienic, clean,
OPPOSITE infected

stern *ADJECTIVE*
The coach gave each of the players a ***stern*** *look.*
• disapproving, unsmiling, severe, strict, hard, harsh, grim
OPPOSITE lenient

stew *VERB*
for ways to cook food see **cook**

stick NOUN
❶ The campers collected *sticks* to make a fire.
• twig, branch, stalk
❷ The old man walked with a *stick*.
• cane, rod, staff, pole
A stick used by a conductor is a **baton**.
A stick carried by a police officer is a **truncheon**.
A magic stick used by a fairy, witch or wizard is a **wand**.

stick VERB sticks, sticking, stuck
❶ He *stuck* his fork into the potato.
• poke, prod, stab, thrust, dig, jab
❷ She tried to *stick* the broken pieces of china together.
• glue, paste, cement, bond, join, fasten
❸ The stamp wouldn't *stick* to the envelope.
• adhere, attach, cling
❹ The wheels of the caravan *stuck* fast in the mud.
• jam, wedge, become trapped
❺ (informal) I can't *stick* people who're always complaining.
• put up with, stand, tolerate, bear, abide, endure
➤ **to stick out**
The shelf *sticks out* too far.
• jut out, poke out, project, protrude
➤ **to stick up for someone** (informal)
She *stuck up for* him when he was in trouble.
• support, defend, side with, stand up for, speak up for

sticky ADJECTIVE
❶ Someone had left a blob of *sticky* toffee on the chair.
• tacky, gummy, gluey
(informal) gooey
❷ I don't like hot *sticky* weather.
• humid, muggy, clammy, close, steamy, sultry
OPPOSITE dry
❸ (informal) The pirates came to a *sticky* end.
• grisly, gruesome, horrible, nasty, unpleasant

stiff ADJECTIVE
❶ Stir the flour and water to a *stiff* paste.
• firm, hard, solid
A common simile is as *stiff* as a poker.
OPPOSITE soft

❷ He mounted the picture on *stiff* card.
• rigid, inflexible, thick
OPPOSITE pliable
❸ Her muscles were *stiff* after the long walk.
• aching, achy, painful, taut, tight
OPPOSITE supple
❹ The team will face *stiff* competition in the final.
• strong, powerful, tough, difficult
OPPOSITE easy
❺ His *stiff* manner made him hard to talk to.
• unfriendly, cold, formal, awkward, wooden
OPPOSITE relaxed
❻ The judge imposed a *stiff* penalty.
• harsh, severe, strict, hard
OPPOSITE lenient
❼ A *stiff* breeze was blowing.
• strong, brisk, fresh
OPPOSITE gentle

stifle VERB
❶ We were almost *stifled* by the fumes from the exhaust pipe.
• choke, suffocate, smother
To kill someone by stopping their breathing is to **strangle** or **throttle** them.
❷ She tried to *stifle* a yawn.
• suppress, muffle, hold back, repress, restrain

still ADJECTIVE
❶ The prisoner sat *still* and said nothing.
• motionless, unmoving, stationary, static, inert
❷ It was a beautiful *still* evening.
• calm, peaceful, quiet, tranquil, serene, hushed, silent, noiseless, windless

still VERB
I breathed deeply to try to *still* my nerves.
• calm, quieten, soothe, lull
OPPOSITE agitate

stimulate VERB
❶ Her travels *stimulated* her to write a book.
• encourage, inspire, spur
❷ The exhibition *stimulated* my interest in painting.
• arouse, rouse, stir up, kindle, excite, provoke, trigger
OPPOSITE discourage

a
b
c
d
e
f
g
h
i
j
k
l
m
n
o
p
q
r
s
t
u
v
w
x
y
z

A B C D E F G H I J K L M N O P Q R S T U V W X Y Z

sting VERB stings, stinging, stung
❶ One of the campers was **stung** by a wasp.
• bite, nip
❷ The smoke made our eyes **sting**.
• smart, hurt, prick, prickle, tingle

stingy ADJECTIVE (informal)
He's too **stingy** to give anyone a birthday card.
• mean, miserly, selfish, uncharitable
(informal) tight-fisted, penny-pinching
OPPOSITE generous

stink VERB
The dungeon **stank** of unwashed bodies.
• reek, smell
see also **smell**
stink NOUN
The mouldy cheese gave off a dreadful **stink**.
• odour, stench, reek, bad smell

stir VERB
❶ **Stir** the mixture until it is smooth.
• mix, beat, blend, whisk
❷ The giant **stirred** in his sleep.
• move slightly, shift, toss, turn
➤ to stir something up
The bandits were always **stirring up** trouble.
• arouse, encourage, provoke, set off, trigger, whip up
stir NOUN
The news caused quite a **stir**.
• fuss, commotion, excitement, hullabaloo

stock NOUN
❶ **Stocks** of food were running low.
• supply, store, reserve, hoard, stockpile
❷ The shopkeeper arranged her new **stock**.
• goods, merchandise, wares
❸ The duke is descended from royal **stock**.
• descent, ancestry, family, line

stock VERB
Most supermarkets now **stock** organic food.
• sell, carry, trade in, deal in, keep in stock

stocky ADJECTIVE
The wrestler had a strong **stocky** body.
• dumpy, squat, thickset, solid, sturdy
OPPOSITE thin

stodgy ADJECTIVE
❶ The pudding was rich and **stodgy**.
• heavy, solid, starchy, filling
OPPOSITE light
❷ I'm finding the book a bit **stodgy**.
• boring, dull, uninteresting, slow, tedious
OPPOSITE lively

stole VERB past tense see **steal**

stomach NOUN
He rolled over and lay on his **stomach**.
• belly, gut, paunch
(informal) tummy
The part of the body that contains the stomach is the **abdomen**.
stomach VERB
I can't **stomach** watching horror films.
• stand, bear, put up with, tolerate, take

stone NOUN
The columns of the temple were carved from **stone**.
A large lump of stone is a **rock**.
A large rounded stone is a **boulder**.
Small rounded stones are **pebbles**.
A mixture of sand and small stones is **gravel**.
Pebbles on the beach are **shingle**.
Round stones used to pave a path are **cobbles**.
for precious stones see **jewel**

stony *ADJECTIVE*
❶ *The waves broke over the **stony** beach.*
• pebbly, rocky, shingly
OPPOSITE sandy
❷ *There was a **stony** silence in the room.*
• unfriendly, cold, hostile, frosty, icy
OPPOSITES warm, friendly

stood *past tense see* **stand**

stoop *VERB*
*We had to **stoop** to go through the tunnel.*
• bend, duck, bow, crouch

stop *VERB*
❶ *I'll go into town when the rain **stops**.*
• end, finish, cease, conclude, terminate
OPPOSITE start
❷ *Can you **stop** talking for a minute?*
• give up, cease, suspend, quit, leave off,
break off
(informal) knock off, pack in
OPPOSITES continue, resume
❸ *Guards, **stop** that man!*
• hold, detain, seize, catch, capture,
restrain
❹ *You can't **stop** me from going.*
• prevent, obstruct, bar, hinder
❺ *How do you **stop** this machine?*
• turn off, immobilize
❻ *The bus will **stop** at the school gates.*
• come to a stop, halt, pull up, draw up
❼ *If you tighten the valve, it will **stop** the
leak.*
• close, plug, seal, block up, bung up

stop *NOUN*
❶ *Everything suddenly came to a **stop**.*
• end, finish, conclusion, halt, standstill
❷ *They drove down through France, with a
short **stop** in Paris.*
• break, pause, stopover, rest

store *VERB*
*Squirrels need to **store** food for the winter.*
• save, set aside, stow away, hoard, reserve,
stockpile
(informal) stash

store *NOUN*
❶ *The building is now used as a grain **store**.*
• storeroom, storehouse, repository, vault
A store for food is a **larder** or **pantry**.
A store for weapons is an **armoury** or
arsenal.
❷ *She kept a large **store** of wine in the cellar.*
• hoard, supply, quantity, stock, stockpile,
reserve
❸ *He's the manager of the local grocery
store.*
see also **shop**

storey *NOUN*
*The new building has six **storeys**.*
• floor, level, tier

storm *NOUN*
❶ *Crops were damaged in the heavy **storms**.*
• squall, blizzard, gale, thunderstorm,
hurricane, typhoon
An old word for storm is **tempest**.
When a storm begins to develop it is
brewing.
see also **weather**
❷ *Plans to close the library caused a **storm** of
protest.*
• outburst, outcry, uproar, clamour

storm *VERB*
*The soldiers **stormed** the castle.*
• charge at, rush at, attack

stormy *ADJECTIVE*
❶ *It was a dark, **stormy** night.*
• blustery, squally, tempestuous, wild, windy,
rough, choppy, gusty, raging
OPPOSITE calm
❷ *Fighting broke out at the end of a **stormy**
meeting.*
• bad-tempered, quarrelsome, turbulent,
violent

story *NOUN*
*Peter Pan is a **story** about a boy who never
grew up.*
• tale
(informal) yarn

a
b
c
d
e
f
g
h
i
j
k
l
m
n
o
p
q
r
s
t
u
v
w
x
y
z

A
B
C
D
E
F
G
H
I
J
K
L
M
N
O
P
Q
R
S
T
U
V
W
X
Y
Z

WORD WEB

VARIOUS KINDS OF STORY:

• adventure story, bedtime story, crime story, detective story, fable, fairy tale, fantasy, folk tale, ghost story, horror story, legend, love story, mystery, myth, narrative poem, novel, parable, romance, saga, science fiction or *(informal)* sci-fi, short story, spy story, thriller
Invented stories are **fiction.**
for other types of writing see **writing**
❶ *The book tells the **story** of her childhood growing up in Thailand.*
• account, history, narrative
A story of a person's life is a **biography.**
The story of your life, told by you, is your **autobiography.**
❷ *It was the front-page **story** in all the papers.*
• article, item, feature, report, piece
❸ *(informal) Have you been telling **stories** again?*
• lie, fib

stout ADJECTIVE
❶ *The doctor was **stout** with grey hair.*
• fat, plump, chubby, dumpy, tubby, portly, stocky, beefy, burly
OPPOSITE thin
❷ *You will need a pair of **stout** walking boots.*
• strong, sturdy, tough, robust, sound, substantial
OPPOSITE weak
❸ *The enemy put up a **stout** resistance.*
• brave, courageous, spirited, plucky, determined, staunch, resolute, firm
OPPOSITE cowardly

stow VERB
*They **stowed** the boxes in the attic.*
• store, put away, pack, pile, load

straight ADJECTIVE
❶ *They walked in a **straight** line.*
• direct, unswerving
A common simile is **as straight as an arrow.**
OPPOSITE crooked
❷ *It took a long time to get the room **straight**.*
• neat, orderly, tidy
OPPOSITE untidy
❸ *She found it difficult to get a **straight** answer from him.*
• honest, plain, frank, straightforward
OPPOSITES indirect, evasive

straightforward ADJECTIVE
*The cake recipe is fairly **straightforward**.*
• simple, plain, uncomplicated, easy, clear, direct
OPPOSITE complicated

strain VERB
❶ *The dog was **straining** at its lead.*
• pull, tug, stretch, haul
❷ *People were **straining** to see what was going on.*
• struggle, strive, make an effort, try, attempt
❸ *Take it easy and don't **strain** yourself.*
• weaken, exhaust, wear out, tire out, tax

strain NOUN
*The **strain** of her job was making her ill.*
• stress, tension, worry, anxiety, pressure

strand NOUN
*The **strands** of the wool began to unravel.*
• fibre, filament, thread

stranded ADJECTIVE
❶ *A whale lay **stranded** on the beach.*
• run aground, beached, marooned
❷ *He was **stranded** in London without any money.*
• abandoned, deserted, helpless, lost, stuck
(informal) **high and dry**

strange ADJECTIVE

❶ *A strange thing happened this morning.*
• funny, odd, peculiar, unusual, abnormal, curious, extraordinary, remarkable, singular, uncommon
OPPOSITES ordinary, everyday
❷ *Did you hear strange noises in the night?*
• mysterious, puzzling, baffling, mystifying, perplexing, bewildering, inexplicable
❸ *The professor showed us his strange inventions.*
• weird, eccentric, peculiar, bizarre
(informal) oddball, wacky
❹ *I find it hard to get to sleep in a strange bed.*
• unfamiliar, unknown, new, alien
OPPOSITE familiar

stranger NOUN

A stranger stopped us and asked for directions to the castle.
• newcomer, outsider, visitor, foreigner

strangle VERB

The victim had been strangled.
• throttle

strap NOUN

The trunk was fastened with a leather strap.
• belt, band

strategy NOUN

The school has a strategy to deal with bullying.
• plan, policy, procedure, approach, scheme, programme

stray VERB

Some sheep had strayed on to the road.
• wander, drift, roam, rove, straggle, meander, ramble

streak NOUN

❶ *The horse had a white streak on his muzzle.*
• band, line, stripe, strip, smear, stain
❷ *There is a streak of meanness in his character.*
• element, trace

streak VERB

❶ *Rain had begun to streak the window.*
• smear, smudge, stain, line
❷ *A group of motorbikes streaked past.*
• rush, speed, dash, fly, hurtle, flash, tear, zoom

stream NOUN

❶ *The climbers dipped their feet in the cool mountain stream.*
• brook, rivulet
(Scottish) burn
❷ *The raft was carried along with the stream.*
• current, flow, tide
❸ *A stream of water poured through the hole.*
• cataract, flood, gush, jet, rush, torrent
❹ *The museum had a steady stream of visitors.*
• series, string, line, succession

stream VERB

Warm sunlight streamed through the window.
• pour, flow, flood, issue, gush, spill

street NOUN

see **road**

strength NOUN

❶ *Hercules was said to have enormous strength.*
• power, might, muscle, brawn, toughness, force, vigour
❷ *The main strength of the team is in scoring goals.*
• strong point, asset, advantage
OPPOSITE weakness

strengthen VERB

❶ *Regular exercise strengthens your muscles.*
• make stronger, build up, toughen, harden
❷ *Concrete was used to strengthen the tunnel.*
• fortify, reinforce, bolster, prop up
OPPOSITE weaken

a b c d e f g h i j k l m n o p q r s t u v w x y z

A
B
C
D
E
F
G
H
I
J
K
L
M
N
O
P
Q
R
S
T
U
V
W
X
Y
Z

strenuous *ADJECTIVE*
❶ *We are making* **strenuous** *efforts to recycle our rubbish.*
• determined, strong, vigorous, energetic, resolute
OPPOSITE feeble
❷ *The doctor told him to avoid* **strenuous** *exercise.*
• hard, tough, difficult, demanding, tiring, exhausting
OPPOSITE easy

stress *NOUN*
❶ *The hospital staff were working under a lot of* **stress**.
• strain, pressure, tension, worry, anxiety
❷ *My piano teacher puts great* **stress** *on the need to practise.*
• emphasis, importance, weight

stress *VERB*
She **stressed** *the need for absolute secrecy.*
• emphasize, draw attention to, highlight, underline

stretch *VERB*
❶ *He* **stretched** *the rubber band until it snapped.*
• expand, extend, draw out, pull out, elongate, lengthen
❷ *She* **stretched** *her arms wide.*
• extend, open out, spread out
❸ *The road* **stretched** *into the distance.*
• continue, extend

stretch *NOUN*
❶ *He had a two-year* **stretch** *in the army.*
• spell, period, time, stint
❷ *There are often accidents on this* **stretch** *of road.*
• section, length, piece
❸ *It's a beautiful* **stretch** *of countryside.*
• area, tract, expanse, sweep

strict *ADJECTIVE*
❶ *The club has* **strict** *rules about who can join.*
• rigid, inflexible

(informal) hard and fast
OPPOSITE flexible
❷ *The sergeant was known for being* **strict** *with new recruits.*
• harsh, severe, stern, firm
OPPOSITE lenient
❸ *She used the word in its* **strict** *scientific sense.*
• exact, precise, correct
OPPOSITE loose

stride *NOUN*
The robot took two **strides** *forward.*
• pace, step

strike *VERB* strikes, striking, struck
❶ *Roy* **struck** *his head on the low ceiling.*
• bang, bump, hit, knock, thump, collide with
(informal) wallop, whack
❷ *The enemy could* **strike** *again at any time.*
• attack
❸ *The clock* **struck** *one.*
• chime, ring

striking *ADJECTIVE*
The most **striking** *feature of the merman was his iridescent tail.*
• conspicuous, noticeable, prominent, remarkable, memorable, extraordinary, outstanding, impressive
OPPOSITE inconspicuous

string *NOUN*
❶ *She tied some* **string** *round the parcel.*
• rope, cord, twine
for musical instruments with strings
see **music**
❷ *They have received a* **string** *of complaints.*
• series, succession, chain, sequence

string *VERB* strings, stringing, strung
We **strung** *the fairy lights on the Christmas tree.*
• hang, arrange, thread

stringy *ADJECTIVE*
This meat is very stringy.
• chewy, fibrous, tough
OPPOSITE tender

strip *VERB*
❶ *Lottie stripped the paper off her present.*
• peel, remove
OPPOSITES cover, wrap
❷ *He stripped and got into the bath.*
• get undressed, undress
OPPOSITE dress

strip *NOUN*
In front of the house was a narrow strip of grass.
• band, length, ribbon, piece, bit

stripe *NOUN*
The tablecloth was white with blue stripes.
• line, strip, band, bar

strive *VERB* strives, striving, strove, striven
Each athlete strives to do his or her best.
• try hard, aim, attempt, endeavour

stroke *NOUN*
❶ *He split the log with a single stroke.*
• blow, hit, action, movement, effort
❷ *She added a few quick pencil strokes to her drawing.*
• line, mark

stroke *VERB*
Jess was curled up on the sofa, stroking the cat.
• pat, caress, rub, touch, fondle, pet

stroll *VERB*
The children strolled quietly home.
• walk slowly, amble, saunter
see also **walk**

strong *ADJECTIVE*

OVERUSED WORD

Try to vary the words you use for **strong**. Here are some other words you could use.

FOR A STRONG PERSON OR STRONG BODY:

• powerful, muscular, mighty, well-built, beefy, brawny, burly, strapping
Crocodiles have powerful jaws.
A common simile is as **strong** as an ox.
OPPOSITES weak, puny

FOR STRONG MATERIAL:

• robust, sturdy, tough, hard-wearing, durable, stout, substantial, resilient
The tent is made from hard-wearing material.
OPPOSITES thin, flimsy

FOR A STRONG LIGHT OR STRONG COLOUR:

• bright, brilliant, dazzling, glaring
The glaring noonday sunlight was streaming in at our door, outside of which some kind of a band appeared to be playing.—THE VOYAGES OF DOCTOR DOLITTLE, Hugh Lofting
OPPOSITES weak, pale

FOR A STRONG FLAVOUR OR STRONG SMELL:

• overpowering, pronounced, pungent, piquant
I smelt the pungent aroma of burnt toast.
OPPOSITES faint, slight

FOR A STRONG ARGUMENT OR STRONG CASE:

• convincing, persuasive, effective, sound, solid, valid
The police have solid evidence of his guilt.
OPPOSITES weak, feeble, flimsy

FOR A STRONG INTEREST OR STRONG SUPPORTER:

• enthusiastic, keen, passionate, fervent, avid, zealous
Viv takes a keen interest in fashion.
OPPOSITE slight

a b c d e f g h i j k l m n o p q r **s** t u v w x y z

struck *past tense see* **strike**

structure *NOUN*
❶ *The pagoda is a magnificent* **structure**.
• building, construction, framework
❷ *Can you explain the* **structure** *of the poem?*
• design, plan, shape, arrangement, organization

struggle *VERB*
❶ *The captives* **struggled** *to get free.*
• strain, strive, wrestle, writhe about, tussle, fight, battle
❷ *The expedition had to* **struggle** *through a snowstorm.*
• stagger, stumble, flounder, labour

struggle *NOUN*
❶ *The rebels surrendered without a* **struggle**.
• fight, battle, combat, clash, contest
❷ *It was a* **struggle** *to keep going in the blazing heat.*
• effort, exertion, problem, difficulty

stubborn *ADJECTIVE*
She's too **stubborn** *to admit that she was wrong.*
• obstinate, pig-headed, strong-willed, uncooperative, inflexible, wilful
A common simile is as stubborn as a mule.
(OPPOSITE) compliant

stuck *past tense see* **stick**

stud *VERB*
➤ **studded with**
The lid of the chest was **studded with** *jewels.*
• inlaid with, encrusted with

student *NOUN*
A student at school is a **pupil**.
An old word for a pupil is **scholar**.

studious *ADJECTIVE*
Sadiq is a quiet, **studious** *boy.*
• hard-working, diligent, scholarly, academic, bookish

study *VERB*
❶ *He went to university to* **study** *medicine.*
• learn about, read, research into
❷ *The spy* **studied** *the document carefully.*
• examine, inspect, analyse, investigate, look closely at, scrutinize, survey
❸ *She has to* **study** *for her exams.*
• revise, cram
(informal) swot

stuff *NOUN*
❶ *What's that sticky* **stuff** *on the carpet?*
• matter, substance
❷ *You can put your* **stuff** *in one of the lockers.*
• belongings, possessions, things, gear

stuff *VERB*
❶ *We managed to* **stuff** *everything into the boot of the car.*
• pack, push, shove, squeeze, ram, compress, force, cram, jam
❷ *The cushions are* **stuffed** *with foam rubber.*
• fill, pad

stuffy *ADJECTIVE*
❶ *Open a window—it's* **stuffy** *in here.*
• airless, close, muggy, humid, stifling, musty, unventilated
(OPPOSITE) airy
❷ *I found the book a bit* **stuffy**.
• boring, dull, dreary, pompous, stodgy
(OPPOSITE) lively

stumble *VERB*
❶ *He* **stumbled** *on a tree root and twisted his ankle.*
• trip, stagger, totter, flounder, lurch
❷ *The actress* **stumbled** *over her words.*
• stammer, stutter, falter, hesitate
➤ **to stumble across something**
I **stumbled across** *some old photos.*
• come across, encounter, find, unearth, discover

stump *VERB*
The detective was **stumped** *by the case.*
• baffle, bewilder, perplex, puzzle, fox, mystify, outwit, defeat
(informal) flummox

stun VERB
❶ *The pilot was alive but **stunned**.*
• daze, knock out, knock senseless, make unconscious
❷ *The whole town was **stunned** by the news.*
• amaze, astonish, astound, shock, stagger, stupefy, bewilder, dumbfound

stunt NOUN
*The acrobats performed breathtaking **stunts**.*
• feat, exploit, act, deed, trick

stupid ADJECTIVE
❶ *Trolls are often very **stupid**.*
• foolish, unintelligent, dense, dim, dim-witted, brainless, dumb, slow, thick, feeble-minded, half-witted, simple, simple-minded, dopey, dull
❷ *It would be **stupid** to go snowboarding without a helmet.*
• senseless, mindless, idiotic, unwise, foolhardy, silly, daft, crazy, mad
OPPOSITE intelligent

sturdy ADJECTIVE
❶ *Shetland ponies are short and **sturdy**.*
• stocky, strong, robust, athletic, brawny, burly, healthy, hefty, husky, muscular, powerful, vigorous, well-built
OPPOSITE weak
❷ *She bought some **sturdy** walking boots.*
• durable, solid, sound, substantial, tough, well-made
OPPOSITE flimsy

stutter VERB
*He tends to **stutter** when he's nervous.*
• stammer, stumble, falter

style NOUN
❶ *I don't like that **style** of jeans.*
• design, pattern, fashion
❷ *The book is written in an informal **style**.*
• manner, tone, way, wording
❸ *The actor always dresses with great **style**.*
• elegance, stylishness, taste, sophistication

stylish ADJECTIVE
*Jacqueline always wears **stylish** clothes.*
• fashionable, elegant, chic, smart, sophisticated, tasteful
(informal) trendy, snazzy
OPPOSITE unfashionable

subdue VERB
❶ *The army managed to **subdue** the rebels.*
• beat, conquer, defeat, overcome, overpower, crush, vanquish
❷ *Jason tried hard to **subdue** his anger.*
• suppress, restrain, repress, check, hold back, curb, control

subject NOUN
❶ *Do you have any strong views on the **subject**?*
• matter, issue, question, point, theme, topic
❷ *Her passport shows that she is a British **subject**.*
• citizen, national

subject VERB
*The press **subjected** him to a string of questions.*
• expose, submit, lay open

submerge VERB
❶ *The submarine **submerged** slowly.*
• dive, go down, go under
OPPOSITE surface
❷ *The tsunami **submerged** several coastal villages.*
• engulf, flood, drown, immerse, inundate, swallow up

submit VERB
❶ *He was finally forced to **submit** to his opponent.*
• give in, surrender, yield
❷ *You need to **submit** a membership form to join the club.*
• give in, hand in, present

subordinate ADJECTIVE
*She began as a police officer of **subordinate** rank.*
• junior, lesser, lower, inferior
OPPOSITES superior, higher

a b c d e f g h i j k l m n o p q r s t u v w x y z

subscribe *VERB*
➤ **to subscribe to**
She subscribes to several good causes.
• contribute to, donate to, give to, support

subsequent *ADJECTIVE*
I missed the first episode and two subsequent ones.
• later, succeeding, following, ensuing, next
OPPOSITE previous

subside *VERB*
❶ *One side of the old cottage has started to subside.*
• sink, settle
❷ *After three days, the flood waters began to subside.*
• go down, fall, recede, decline, ebb
❸ *The pain will eventually subside.*
• decrease, diminish, lessen, die down, dwindle

substance *NOUN*
❶ *The spacecraft was made from an alien substance.*
• material, matter, stuff
❷ *What was the substance of the book?*
• theme, essence, gist, subject matter

substantial *ADJECTIVE*
❶ *They have made substantial improvements to the city.*
• considerable, significant, sizeable, worthwhile, big, large, generous
OPPOSITE small
❷ *There is a substantial fence to keep out wild animals.*
• strong, sturdy, solid, robust, hefty, durable, sound, well-built
OPPOSITE flimsy

substitute *VERB*
You can substitute margarine for butter in the recipe.
• exchange, swap, switch
You can also say: Margarine can **take the place of** butter, or You can **replace** butter with margarine.

➤ **to substitute for someone**
He substituted for the injured goalkeeper.
• stand in for, take the place of, deputise for

substitute *NOUN*
The manager brought on a substitute during extra time.
• replacement, reserve, standby, stand-in
A substitute for a sick actor is an **understudy**.

subtle *ADJECTIVE*
❶ *There was a subtle smell of roses in the air.*
• faint, slight, mild, delicate
❷ *His jokes are too subtle for most people.*
• ingenious, sophisticated
❸ *I tried to give her a subtle hint.*
• gentle, tactful, indirect
OPPOSITE obvious

subtract *VERB*
If you subtract 5 from 20, you will have 15 left.
• take away, deduct, remove
OPPOSITE add

succeed *VERB*
❶ *You have to work hard if you want to succeed.*
• be successful, do well, prosper, flourish, thrive
(informal) make it
❷ *Everyone hoped that the plan would succeed.*
• be effective, produce results, work
(informal) catch on
OPPOSITE fail
❸ *Edward VII succeeded Queen Victoria.*
• come after, follow, take over from, replace

success *NOUN*
❶ *She talked about her success as a performer.*
• achievement, attainment, fame
❷ *They congratulated the team on their success.*
• victory, win, triumph

A B C D E F G H I J K L M N O P Q R S T U V W X Y Z

❸ *The group's last tour was a great success.*
• hit, bestseller
(informal) winner
❹ *The success of the mission depends on the astronauts.*
• effectiveness, successfulness, successful outcome, completion
OPPOSITE failure

successful *ADJECTIVE*
❶ *She owns a very successful chain of restaurants.*
• thriving, flourishing, booming, prosperous, profitable, popular
❷ *The supporters cheered the successful team.*
• winning, victorious, triumphant
OPPOSITE unsuccessful

succession *NOUN*
Arthur received a succession of mysterious emails.
• series, sequence, run, string, chain

successive *ADJECTIVE*
It rained on seven successive days.
• consecutive, uninterrupted
You can also say: It rained on several days in succession.

suck *VERB*
➤ **to suck something up**
A sponge will suck up water.
• soak up, draw up, absorb

sudden *ADJECTIVE*
❶ *Maria felt a sudden urge to burst into song.*
• unexpected, unforeseen, impulsive, rash, quick
OPPOSITE expected
❷ *The bus came to a sudden halt.*
• abrupt, sharp, swift
OPPOSITE gradual

suffer *VERB*
❶ *He suffers terribly with his back.*
• feel pain, hurt
❷ *They will suffer for their crimes.*
• be punished, pay
❸ *The home team suffered a humiliating defeat.*
• experience, undergo, go through, endure, withstand, bear, tolerate

suffering *NOUN*
The people endured great suffering during the war.
• hardship, deprivation, misery, anguish, pain, distress

sufficient *ADJECTIVE*
The castaways had sufficient food for few days.
• enough, adequate, satisfactory
OPPOSITE insufficient

suffix *NOUN*
OPPOSITE prefix

suffocate *VERB*
The firefighters were nearly suffocated by the fumes.
• choke, stifle
To stop someone's breathing by squeezing their throat is to **strangle** or **throttle** them. To stop someone's breathing by covering their nose and mouth is to **smother** them.

suggest *VERB*
❶ *Mum suggested going to the zoo.*
• propose, advise, advocate, recommend
❷ *Her comments suggest that she's not happy.*
• imply, hint, indicate, signal

suggestion *NOUN*
They didn't like his suggestion.
• proposal, plan, idea, proposition, recommendation

a
b
c
d
e
f
g
h
i
j
k
l
m
n
o
p
q
r
s
t
u
v
w
x
y
z

A
B
C
D
E
F
G
H
I
J
K
L
M
N
O
P
Q
R
S
T
U
V
W
X
Y
Z

suit VERB
❶ *Would it suit you to stay here overnight?*
• be convenient for, be suitable for, please, satisfy
OPPOSITE displease
❷ *His new haircut doesn't suit him.*
• look good on, become, flatter

suitable ADJECTIVE
❶ *Please wear clothes suitable for wet weather.*
• appropriate, apt, fitting, suited (to), proper, right
OPPOSITE unsuitable
❷ *Is this a suitable time to have a chat?*
• convenient, acceptable, satisfactory
OPPOSITE inconvenient

sulk VERB
I was sulking because I wasn't allowed to play outside.
• be sullen, mope, brood, pout

sulky ADJECTIVE
Ron had turned into a sulky teenager.
• moody, sullen, brooding, moping, mopey

sullen ADJECTIVE
Beth slouched on the sofa, looking sullen.
• sulky, moody, bad-tempered, mopey, morose, surly, sour
OPPOSITES cheerful, good-tempered

sum NOUN
❶ *The sum of 2 and 2 is 4.*
• total, result
❷ *They lost a large sum of money.*
• amount, quantity
➤ **sums**
Desmond is good at doing sums.
• adding up, arithmetic
(informal) maths
for other mathematical terms see **mathematics**
sum VERB
➤ **to sum up**
• summarize

summarize VERB
Can you summarize the main points of the story?
• sum up, outline, review
(informal) recap

summary NOUN
We each wrote a summary of the poem.
• synopsis, precis, outline, overview

summit NOUN
The summit of the mountain was shrouded in mist.
• top, cap, peak, tip
OPPOSITE base

summon VERB
The king summoned his knights from far and wide.
• call, send for, order to come, bid to come
To ask someone politely to come is to **invite** them.

sun NOUN
They went out into the garden to sit in the sun.
• sunshine, sunlight
To sit or lie in the sun is to **sunbathe**.

sunlight NOUN
Most plants can only grow in sunlight.
• daylight, sun, sunshine
Rays of light from the sun are **sunbeams**.

sunny ADJECTIVE
❶ *It was a beautiful sunny day.*
• fine, clear, cloudless
OPPOSITE cloudy
❷ *The flat has a large, sunny living room.*
• bright, sunlit, cheerful
OPPOSITE gloomy
A place that gets a lot of sunshine is **sunbaked**.
see *also* **weather**

sunrise NOUN
The magic spell wears off at sunrise.
• dawn, daybreak
OPPOSITE sunset

sunset NOUN
The group arranged to meet in the churchyard at sunset.
• sundown, dusk, twilight, evening, nightfall
OPPOSITE sunrise

superb ADJECTIVE
Brazil scored another superb goal.
• excellent, outstanding, exceptional, remarkable, impressive, magnificent, marvellous, splendid, tremendous, wonderful
(informal) brilliant, fantastic, terrific, fabulous, sensational, super
for other ways to describe something good see **good**

superficial ADJECTIVE
❶ *The scratch on his leg was only superficial.*
• on the surface, shallow, slight
OPPOSITE deep
❷ *The book gives a very superficial view of history.*
• simple, trivial, lightweight, shallow, frivolous, casual
OPPOSITES thorough, profound

superhero NOUN

WORD WEB

The arch-enemy of a superhero is a **super-villain** or **nemesis**.
A story with drawings featuring a superhero is a **comic book** or **comic strip**.

THINGS A SUPERHERO MIGHT WEAR OR USE:

• belt, bodysuit, cape, costume, force field, laser beam, logo, mask, gadget, invisibility, superhuman strength, superpower, X-ray vision
Zack had a force field and we had to know how powerful it was. Clearly the easiest way to find out was to throw things at him.—MY BROTHER IS A SUPERHERO, David Solomons

SOUNDS MADE BY SUPERHEROES:

• pow, whoosh, zap, zoom

superior ADJECTIVE
❶ *A colonel is superior in rank to a captain.*
• senior, higher, greater
❷ *They only sell chocolate of superior quality.*
• first-class, first-rate, top, top-notch, choice, select, better
❸ *I don't like her superior attitude.*
• arrogant, haughty, snobbish, stuck-up, self-important
(informal) snooty
OPPOSITE inferior

supernatural ADJECTIVE
The fortune-teller claimed to have supernatural powers.
• magic, magical, miraculous
OPPOSITE natural

supervise VERB
Children must be supervised by an adult in the park.
• oversee, superintend, watch over, be in charge of, be responsible for, direct, manage
To supervise candidates in an exam is to invigilate.

supple ADJECTIVE
The moccasins are made of supple leather.
• flexible, pliable, soft
OPPOSITES stiff, rigid

supplementary ADJECTIVE
There is a supplementary charge for postage.
• additional, extra

supply VERB
The art shop can supply you with brushes and paints.
• provide, equip, furnish

supply NOUN
They had a good supply of fuel for the winter.
• quantity, stock, store, reserve
➤ **supplies**
We bought supplies for the camping trip.
• provisions, stores, rations, food, necessities

a b c d e f g h i j k l m n o p q r **s** t u v w x y z

A B C D E F G H I J K L M N O P Q R S T U V W X Y Z

support *NOUN*
❶ *She thanked them for their support.*
• assistance, backing, aid, cooperation, encouragement, help
❷ *The cinema was reopened with support from local businesses.*
• donations, contributions, sponsorship
❸ *The supports prevented the wall from collapsing.*
• prop, brace
A support for a shelf is a **bracket**.
A support built against a wall is a **buttress**.
A support for someone with an injured leg is a **crutch**.
A bar of wood or metal supporting a framework is a **strut**.
A support put under a board to make a table is a **trestle**.

support *VERB*
❶ *The rope couldn't support his weight.*
• bear, carry, stand, hold up
❷ *The beams support the roof.*
• prop up, strengthen, reinforce
❸ *His friends supported him when he was in trouble.*
• aid, assist, help, back, encourage, stand by, stand up for, rally round
❹ *She had to work to support her family.*
• maintain, keep, provide for
❺ *He supports several local charities.*
• donate to, contribute to, give to
❻ *Which team did you support in the World Cup?*
• be a supporter of, follow

supporter *NOUN*
❶ *The home supporters cheered their team.*
• fan, follower
❷ *She is a well-known supporter of animal rights.*
• champion, advocate, backer, defender

suppose *VERB*
❶ *I suppose you want to borrow some money.*
• expect, presume, assume, guess, believe, think
❷ *Suppose a spacecraft landed in your garden!*
• imagine, pretend, fancy

➤ **to be supposed to do something**
The bus is supposed to leave at 9 o'clock.
• be meant to, be due to, be expected to, ought to

suppress *VERB*
❶ *He managed to suppress his anger.*
• check, hold back, contain, control, repress, restrain, curb, bottle up, stifle
To suppress ideas for political or moral reasons is to **censor** them.
❷ *The army suppressed the rebellion.*
• crush, quash, quell, put down, stamp out, stop, subdue

supreme *ADJECTIVE*
Her supreme achievement was winning a gold medal.
• greatest, highest, best, outstanding, top

sure *ADJECTIVE*
❶ *I'm sure that I'm right.*
• certain, convinced, confident, definite, positive
OPPOSITES unsure, uncertain
❷ *He's sure to phone tonight.*
• bound, certain
OPPOSITE unlikely
❸ *A high temperature is a sure sign of illness.*
• clear, definite, true, undoubted, undeniable
OPPOSITES unclear, doubtful

surface *NOUN*
❶ *The surface of Mars is barren and rocky.*
• exterior, outside
The surface of something may be covered with a **crust** or **shell** or **skin**.
A thin surface of expensive wood on furniture is a **veneer**.
OPPOSITE centre
❷ *A dice has dots on each surface.*
• face, side
OPPOSITE inside

❸ *Oil floated on the **surface** of the water.*
• top
OPPOSITE bottom

surface VERB
❶ *The road is **surfaced** with cobbles.*
• cover, coat
❷ *The head of an alligator **surfaced** in the river.*
• rise to the surface, come up, emerge, appear
(informal) pop up

surge VERB
❶ *Massive waves **surged** around the tiny raft.*
• rise, roll, swirl, heave, billow
❷ *The crowd **surged** forward.*
• rush, push, sweep

surpass VERB
*It will be hard to **surpass** last year's performance.*
• beat, exceed, do better than, outdo

surplus NOUN
*Farmers have produced a **surplus** of apples this year.*
• excess, glut, surfeit, oversupply
OPPOSITES shortage, lack

surprise NOUN
*The news that Sara was married came as a **surprise**.*
• shock, revelation
(informal) bombshell

surprise VERB
❶ *I was **surprised** by how well she could sing.*
• amaze, astonish, astound, stagger, startle, stun, take aback, take by surprise, dumbfound
(informal) bowl over, flabbergast
❷ *He **surprised** the burglars as they came through the window.*
• discover, come upon, catch unawares, catch off guard, catch red-handed

surprised ADJECTIVE

WRITING TIPS

SOMEONE WHO FEELS SURPRISED MIGHT:

• have eyes bulging out of their head, have eyes on the end of stalks, jump out of their skin, stare wide-eyed
The Queen… simply sat there staring wide-eyed and white-faced at the small girl who was perched on her window-sill in a nightie.
—THE BFG, Roald Dahl

SOMETHING WHICH SURPRISES YOU MIGHT:

(informal) knock you for six, knock your socks off, knock you sideways, make your eyes pop
for things you might say when surprised
see **exclamation**

surprising ADJECTIVE
*There are a **surprising** number of errors in the book.*
• amazing, astonishing, astounding, extraordinary, remarkable, incredible, staggering, startling, stunning, unexpected
OPPOSITE predictable

surrender VERB
❶ *The band of outlaws refused to surrender.*
• admit defeat, give in, yield, submit, capitulate
❷ *Please **surrender** your ticket to the driver.*
• give, hand over

surround VERB
❶ *The garden was **surrounded** by a stone wall.*
• enclose, fence in, wall in
❷ *The pack of wolves **surrounded** its prey.*
• encircle, ring, hem in, besiege

surroundings PLURAL NOUN
The hotel is set in very pleasant surroundings.
• setting, location, environment

a
b
c
d
e
f
g
h
i
j
k
l
m
n
o
p
q
r
s
t
u
v
w
x
y
z

survey NOUN
❶ *They did a* **survey** *of local leisure facilities.*
• review, investigation, study
A survey to count the population of an area is
a census.
❷ *The builders did a* **survey** *of the house.*
• inspection, examination

survey VERB
❶ *You can* **survey** *the whole valley from the
top of the tower.*
• view, look over, look at, observe
❷ *The farmer* **surveyed** *the damage done by
the storm.*
• inspect, examine, scrutinize, study
❸ *The builders will need to* **survey** *the area.*
• map out, plan out, measure

survive VERB
❶ *He managed to* **survive** *alone on the island
for six months.*
• stay alive, last, live, keep going, carry on,
continue
OPPOSITE die
❷ *Ada* **survived** *her husband by twenty years.*
• outlast
❸ *Will the birds* **survive** *this cold weather?*
• endure, withstand, live through, weather

suspect VERB
❶ *The police* **suspected** *his motives.*
• doubt, mistrust, have suspicions about
❷ *I* **suspect** *that the shop will be closed on
Sundays.*
• expect, imagine, presume, guess, sense, fancy

suspend VERB
❶ *The meeting was* **suspended** *until the next
day.*
• adjourn, break off, discontinue, interrupt
❷ *For the party, we* **suspended** *balloons from
the ceiling.*
• hang, dangle, swing

suspense NOUN
*The film was a thriller, full of action and
suspense.*
• tension, uncertainty, anticipation,
expectancy, drama, excitement

suspicion NOUN
I have a **suspicion** *that he is lying.*
• feeling, hunch, inkling, intuition,
impression

suspicious ADJECTIVE
❶ *There is something about him which makes
me* **suspicious**.
• doubtful, distrustful, mistrustful, unsure,
uneasy, wary
OPPOSITE trusting
❷ *What do you make of her* **suspicious**
behaviour?
• questionable, suspect, dubious, shady
(informal) fishy

sustain VERB
❶ *Squirrels store nuts to* **sustain** *them
through the winter.*
• keep going, nurture, provide for
❷ *The runners couldn't* **sustain** *the high
speed.*
• keep up, maintain
❸ *Will the bridge* **sustain** *our weight?*
• support, bear, carry, stand

swagger VERB
The lead actor **swaggered** *about on
stage.*
• strut, parade

swallow VERB
*The bread was so dry that it was hard to
swallow.*
• gulp down
for other ways to eat and drink
see **eat, drink**
➤ **to swallow something up**
*As it climbed higher, the rocket was
swallowed up by the clouds.*
• envelop, engulf, cover over, absorb

swam *past tense see* **swim**

swamp VERB
A huge wave threatened to **swamp** *the ship.*
• overwhelm, engulf, inundate, flood,
submerge

swamp *NOUN*
Much of the land near the coast is swamp.
• marsh, bog, mire, fen, quicksand, quagmire

swan *NOUN*
A female swan is a **pen**.
A male swan is a **cob**.
A young swan is a **cygnet**.

swap or **swop** *VERB*
We swapped seats so I could sit in the aisle.
• change, exchange, switch, substitute

swarm *VERB*
Hundreds of people swarmed around the film star.
• crowd, flock
➤ **to swarm with**
The garden is swarming with ants.
• be overrun by, be crawling with, be infested with, teem with

sway *VERB*
The tall grass swayed in the breeze.
• wave, swing, rock, bend, lean

swear *VERB* swears, swearing, swore, sworn
❶ *The knight swore that she would protect the unicorn.*
• pledge, promise, vow, give your word, take an oath
❷ *The player swore when he bashed his knee.*
• curse

sweat *VERB*
He sweats a lot in hot weather.
• perspire

sweaty *ADJECTIVE*
When I'm nervous, my palms get sweaty.
• sweating, perspiring, clammy, sticky, moist

sweep *VERB*
❶ *He swept the floor with an old broom.*
• brush, clean, dust

❷ *The bus swept past.*
• shoot, speed, zoom
➤ **to sweep something away**
He tried to sweep away the rubbish.
• clear away, get rid of, remove
The flood swept away several houses.
• destroy, flatten, level

sweet *ADJECTIVE*
❶ *The pudding is too sweet for me.*
• sickly, sugary, sweetened, syrupy
OPPOSITES acid, bitter, savoury
❷ *The sweet smell of roses filled the room.*
• fragrant, pleasant
OPPOSITE foul
❸ *We heard the sweet sound of a harp.*
• melodious, pleasant, soothing, tuneful
OPPOSITE ugly
❹ *What a sweet little cottage!*
• attractive, charming, dear, lovely, pretty, quaint
OPPOSITE unattractive

sweet *NOUN*
❶ *The bag contained a mixture of sweets.*
A North American word is **candy**.
A formal word for sweets is **confectionery**.
❷ *We had rhubarb crumble as our sweet.*
• dessert, pudding

sweet *NOUN*

WORD WEB

SOME KINDS OF SWEET:

• barley sugar, boiled sweet, bubblegum, butterscotch, candyfloss, caramel, chewing gum, chocolate, fruit pastille, fudge, jelly baby, liquorice, lollipop, marshmallow, marzipan, mint or peppermint, nougat, rock, tablet, toffee, Turkish delight

a b c d e f g h i j k l m n o p q r s t u v w x y z

swell VERB swells, swelling, swelled, swollen or swelled
The balloon swelled as it filled with hot air.
• expand, inflate, bulge, grow, enlarge, puff up, billow
OPPOSITE shrink

swelling NOUN
He had a painful swelling on his foot.
• inflammation, lump, bump, growth
A **tumour** is a serious swelling on the body.

swerve VERB
The car swerved to avoid a hedgehog.
• turn aside, veer, dodge, swing

swift ADJECTIVE
❶ *The runners set off at a swift pace.*
• fast, quick, rapid, speedy, brisk, lively
❷ *She received a swift reply to her email.*
• quick, fast, immediate, instant, prompt, speedy, snappy
OPPOSITE slow

swim VERB swims, swimming, swam, swum
We swam in the sea on our holiday.
• go swimming, bathe, take a dip

WORD WEB

VARIOUS SWIMMING STROKES:

• backstroke, breaststroke, butterfly, crawl, doggy-paddle

PLACES WHERE YOU CAN SWIM:

• baths, leisure pool, lido, paddling pool, swimming baths or swimming pool

CLOTHING FOR SWIMMING:

• bathing costume, bathing suit, bikini, swimming cap, swimming costume, swimming dress, swimsuit, trunks

OTHER EQUIPMENT FOR SWIMMING:

• armbands, flippers, float, goggles, nose-clip, rubber ring, snorkel

swindle VERB
They swindled the firm out of a lot of money.
• cheat, trick, dupe, fleece
(informal) con, diddle

swing VERB swings, swinging, swung
❶ *A glass chandelier swung from the ceiling.*
• hang, dangle, sway, flap, wave about
❷ *She swung round when I called her name.*
• turn, twist, veer, swerve

swipe VERB
The polar bear swiped the seal with its paw.
• swing at, hit, strike, slash
for other ways to hit things see **hit**

swirl VERB
Clouds of dust swirled up in the desert wind.
• spin, twirl, whirl, churn

switch VERB
❶ *Please remember to switch off the light.*
• turn
❷ *The teams will switch ends at half-time.*
• change, swap, exchange, shift

swivel VERB
The dentist swivelled round in her chair.
• spin, turn, twirl, pivot, revolve, rotate

swollen ADJECTIVE
My feet were swollen from walking all day.
• inflamed, bloated, puffed up, puffy

swoop VERB
The owl swooped and caught the mouse.
• dive, drop, plunge, plummet, descend, pounce

swop VERB
see **swap**

sword NOUN
Athena raised her shield and drew her sword.
• blade

WORD WEB

SOME TYPES OF SWORD:

• broadsword, claymore, cutlass, foil, rapier, sabre, scimitar
Fighting with swords is **fencing** or swordsmanship.
for other weapons see **weapon**

swore *past tense see* **swear**

symbol *NOUN*
The dove is a symbol of peace.
• sign, emblem, image, motif
The symbols we use in writing are **characters** or **letters**.
The symbols used in ancient Egyptian writing were **hieroglyphics**.
The symbol of a club or school is their **badge**.
The symbol of a firm or organization is their **logo**.

symbolize *VERB*
The dove symbolizes peace.
• represent, stand for, signify, indicate, mean, denote

sympathetic *ADJECTIVE*
My boss was sympathetic when my mother was ill.
• understanding, compassionate, concerned, caring, comforting, kind, supportive
OPPOSITE unsympathetic

sympathize *VERB*
➤ **to sympathize with**
We sympathized with those who had lost their homes.
• be sympathetic towards, be sorry for, feel for, commiserate with

sympathy *NOUN*
Did you feel any sympathy for the characters in the story?
• understanding, compassion, pity, fellow-feeling, tenderness

synonym *NOUN*
'Cheerful' is a synonym of 'happy'.
OPPOSITE antonym

synthetic *ADJECTIVE*
Nylon is a synthetic material.
• artificial, man-made, manufactured, imitation
OPPOSITE natural

system *NOUN*
❶ *The city has an archaic transport system.*
• organization, structure, network, framework
(informal) set-up
❷ *Do you understand the new cataloguing system?*
• procedure, process, scheme, arrangement, method, routine

systematic *ADJECTIVE*
Inspector Giles works in a systematic way.
• methodical, logical, orderly, organized, scientific
OPPOSITE unsystematic

a
b
c
d
e
f
g
h
i
j
k
l
m
n
o
p
q
r
s
t
u
v
w
x
y
z

Tt

table *NOUN*
for items of furniture see **furniture**

tablet *NOUN*
❶ *The doctor prescribed some tablets for the pain.*
• pill, capsule, pellet
❷ *There was a stone tablet above the entrance to the tomb.*
• slab, plaque
❸ *He put a tablet of powder in the washing machine.*
• block, piece, bar, chunk

tack *VERB*
❶ *The carpet needs to be tacked down.*
• nail, pin
❷ *She tacked up the hem of her skirt.*
• sew, stitch

tackle *VERB*
❶ *They left him to tackle the washing-up.*
• cope with, deal with, attend to, handle, manage, grapple with
❷ *Another player tackled her and got the ball.*
• challenge, intercept, take on
tackle *NOUN*
❶ *The referee said it was a fair tackle.*
• challenge, interception
❷ *He kept his fishing tackle in a special case.*
• gear, equipment, apparatus, kit

tactful *ADJECTIVE*
I tried to think of a tactful way to let them know the outcome.
• subtle, discreet, diplomatic, sensitive, thoughtful
OPPOSITE tactless

tactics *PLURAL NOUN*
The players discussed their tactics for the next game.
• moves, manoeuvres, plan of action
An overall plan for a game or battle is a strategy.

tag *NOUN*
The price is marked on the tag.
• label, sticker, ticket
tag *VERB*
Every item is tagged with a price label.
• identify, label, mark
➤ **to tag along with someone**
She tagged along with them when they left.
• accompany, follow, go with, join
➤ **to tag something on**
He tagged on a PS at the end of his letter.
• add, attach, tack on

tail *NOUN*
He joined the tail of the queue.
• end, back, rear
tail *VERB*
The detective tailed the suspect to this address.
• follow, pursue, track, trail, shadow, stalk
➤ **to tail off**
The number of tourists tails off in October.
• decrease, decline, lessen, diminish, dwindle, wane

take *VERB* takes, taking, took, taken
❶ *Naomi took her sister's hand.*
• clutch, clasp, take hold of, grasp, grip, seize, snatch, grab
❷ *The soldiers took many prisoners.*
• catch, capture, seize, detain
❸ *Someone has taken my pen.*
• steal, remove, make off with
(informal) swipe, pinch
❹ *The guide will take you to the edge of the forest.*
• conduct, escort, lead, accompany
❺ *The bus took us right to the station.*
• bring, carry, convey, transport
❻ *It'll take two people to lift that table.*
• need, require

❼ *The caravan can take six people.*
• hold, contain, accommodate, have room for
❽ *He couldn't take the heat of the midday sun.*
• bear, put up with, stand, endure, tolerate, suffer, stomach
❾ *She took their names and addresses.*
• make a note of, record, write down
❿ *The magician asked me to take a card.*
• pick, choose, select
⓫ *Take 2 from 8 and you get 6.*
• subtract, take away, deduct

➤ to take someone in
Everyone was taken in by his disguise.
• fool, deceive, trick, cheat, dupe, hoodwink

➤ to take off
Our flight took off on time.
• depart, lift off

➤ to take something off
Please take off your coat.
• remove, strip off, peel off

➤ to take part in something
Would you like to take part in the show?
• participate in, be involved in, join in

➤ to take place
When did the accident take place?
• happen, occur, come about

➤ to take something up
She has recently taken up tap-dancing.
• begin to do, start learning

tale NOUN
Pinocchio is a tale about a boy made of wood.
• story, narrative, account
(informal) yarn
for various kinds of story see story

talent NOUN
She has a great talent for music.
• gift, ability, aptitude, skill, flair, knack
Unusually great talent is genius.

talented ADJECTIVE
He's a very talented dancer.
• gifted, able, accomplished, capable, skilled, skilful, clever, brilliant
If you are talented in several ways, you are versatile.

talk VERB
❶ *Doug was trying to teach his parrot to talk.*
• speak, say things, communicate, express yourself
❷ *The two old friends had a lot to talk about.*
• discuss, converse, chat, chatter, gossip
(informal) natter
❸ *The prisoner refused to talk.*
• give information, confess
for other ways to say things see say

talk NOUN
❶ *I need to have a talk with you soon.*
• conversation, discussion, chat
The talk between characters in a story is the dialogue.
❷ *There is a talk about Japanese art at lunchtime.*
• lecture, presentation, speech, address
A talk in church is a sermon.

talkative ADJECTIVE
You're not very talkative this morning.
• chatty, communicative, vocal, forthcoming, articulate
An informal name for a talkative person is a chatterbox.

tall ADJECTIVE
❶ *Jasmine is tall for her age.*
• big
OPPOSITE short
❷ *Singapore has many tall buildings.*
• high, lofty, towering, soaring, giant
Buildings with many floors are high-rise or multi-storey buildings.
OPPOSITE low

tally VERB
➤ to tally with
Their story didn't tally with ours.
• agree with, correspond with, match

tame ADJECTIVE
❶ *The guinea pigs are tame and used to people.*
• domesticated, broken in, docile, gentle, obedient, manageable
OPPOSITE wild

a b c d e f g h i j k l m n o p q r s t u v w x y z

❷ *The film seems very tame nowadays.*
• dull, boring, tedious, bland, unexciting, uninteresting
OPPOSITE exciting

tame *VERB*
They were trying to tame a wild horse.
• break in, subdue, master, control

tamper *VERB*
➤ **to tamper with something**
Someone has been tampering with the lock.
• meddle with, tinker with, fiddle about with, interfere with

tan *VERB*
Do you tan easily in the sun?
• get a tan, go brown
If your skin goes red in the sun, you get **sunburn**.

tang *NOUN*
You can taste the tang of oranges in the soup.
• sharpness, zest, zing

tangle *VERB*
❶ *Her sewing threads were all tangled together.*
• entangle, twist, knot, jumble, muddle
Tangled hair is **dishevelled** or **matted** hair.
❷ *Dolphins can get tangled in fishing nets.*
• catch, trap, ensnare, entangle

tangle *NOUN*
The computer cables have got into a tangle.
• muddle, jumble, knot, twist, confusion

tap *VERB*
Someone tapped three times on the door.
• knock, rap, strike

tape *NOUN*
The stack of old letters was tied up with tape.
• ribbon, braid, binding

target *NOUN*
❶ *Her target was to swim thirty lengths.*
• goal, aim, objective, intention, purpose, hope, ambition
❷ *She was the target of his jokes.*
• object, victim, butt

tarnish *VERB*
❶ *The bronze sculptures had tarnished with age.*
• discolour, corrode
When iron corrodes it **rusts**.
❷ *The scandal tarnished his reputation.*
• stain, taint, blot, spoil, mar

tart *ADJECTIVE*
Lemons have a tart taste.
• sharp, sour, acid, tangy
OPPOSITE sweet

task *NOUN*
❶ *The robot was given a number of tasks to do.*
• job, chore, exercise, errand
❷ *The soldiers' task was to capture the hill.*
• assignment, mission, duty, undertaking

taste *VERB*
❶ *Taste the soup to see if it needs salt.*
• sample, try, test, sip
❷ *The curry tastes quite mild.*
for ways to describe how food tastes see **food**

taste *NOUN*
❶ *I love the taste of ginger.*
• flavour
❷ *May I have a taste of the cheese?*
• mouthful, bite, morsel, nibble, bit, piece, sample
❸ *His taste in clothes is a bit odd.*
• choice, preference, discrimination, judgement

tasteful *ADJECTIVE*
The room was decorated in tasteful colours.
• refined, cultivated, smart, stylish, artistic, elegant, attractive
OPPOSITE tasteless

tasteless *ADJECTIVE*
❶ *He apologized for making a tasteless remark.*
• crude, tactless, indelicate, inappropriate
OPPOSITE tasteful
❷ *The sprouts were overcooked and tasteless.*
• flavourless, bland, insipid
OPPOSITE flavourful

tasty *ADJECTIVE*
That pie was very tasty.
• delicious, appetizing
see also **food**
OPPOSITE unappetizing

tattered *ADJECTIVE*
Some of the blankets were worn and tattered.
• ragged, ripped, torn, frayed, tatty, threadbare
OPPOSITE smart

taught *past tense see* **teach**

taunt *VERB*
The gladiator taunted his opponent.
• barrack, insult, jeer at, laugh at, make fun of, mock, ridicule, sneer at

taut *ADJECTIVE*
Make sure the rope is taut.
• tight, tense, stretched
OPPOSITE slack

teach *VERB* **teaches, teaching, taught**
My mum is teaching me to play the guitar.
• educate, inform, instruct
To teach people to play a sport is to **coach** or train them.
To teach one person at a time or a small group is to **tutor** them.

teacher *NOUN*
We have a new ballet teacher.
• tutor, instructor, trainer
Someone who teaches you to play a sport is a **coach**.
In the past, a woman who taught children in a private household was a **governess**.

team *NOUN*
She's been picked for the junior hockey team.
• side

tear *VERB* **tears, tearing, tore, torn**
❶ *The tree branch tore a hole in our kite.*
• rip, snag, gash, shred, split, slit

❷ *He tore home to watch his favourite TV programme.*
• run, rush, dash, hurry, race, sprint, speed
see also **run**

tear *NOUN*
There was a tear in one of the sails.
• cut, rip, rent, split, gash, hole, opening, slit, gap

tease *VERB*
They teased him about his new haircut.
• taunt, make fun of, poke fun at, mock, ridicule, laugh at

technical *ADJECTIVE*
The computer manual uses technical language.
• specialized, scientific, advanced

technique *NOUN*
❶ *The archaeologists use modern techniques.*
• method, procedure, approach
❷ *The pianist's technique was flawless.*
• skill, expertise, art, craft

tedious *ADJECTIVE*
It was a tedious journey by bus.
• boring, dreary, dull, tiresome, monotonous, unexciting, uninteresting
OPPOSITE exciting

teem *VERB*
➤ **to teem with**
The pond teemed with tadpoles.
• be overrun by, be crawling with, be infested with, swarm with

teenager *NOUN*
The film is designed to appeal to teenagers.
• adolescent, youth

telephone *NOUN, VERB*
see **phone**

tell *VERB* **tells, telling, told**
❶ *Tell us what you can see.*
• describe, explain, reveal, report, say, state

a
b
c
d
e
f
g
h
i
j
k
l
m
n
o
p
q
r
s
t
u
v
w
x
y
z

A

❷ *Tell me when you are ready.*
• let you know, inform, notify, announce, communicate

B

❸ *He told them to stop making so much noise.*

C

• order, command, direct, instruct
❹ *We told each other scary ghost stories.*

D

• narrate, relate

E

❺ *He told me he would buy the tickets.*
• assure, promise

F

❻ *She couldn't tell where she was in the dark.*

G

• make out, recognize, identify, perceive

H

❼ *Can you tell one twin from the other?*
• distinguish, separate

I

➤ **to tell someone off**
She told them off for being late.

J

• scold, reprimand, reproach
(informal) tick off

K

L

temper NOUN
❶ *Mr Black had been in a bad temper all morning.*

M

• mood, humour, state of mind
❷ *The chef is always flying into a temper.*

N

• rage, fury, fit of anger, tantrum
➤ **to lose your temper**

O

When she loses her temper, her cheeks go red.
• get angry, get annoyed, fly into a rage

P

see also **angry**

Q

R

temperature NOUN
for units for measuring temperature
see **measurement**

S

T

tempestuous ADJECTIVE
There was a tempestuous storm at sea.
• stormy, squally, rough, raging, turbulent, wild

U

OPPOSITE calm

V

temple NOUN
for places where people worship see **building**

W

X

temporary ADJECTIVE
They made a temporary shelter for the night.

Y

• makeshift, provisional

Z

OPPOSITE permanent

---

tempt VERB
Can I tempt you to have more pudding?
• coax, entice, persuade, attract
To tempt someone by offering them money is to **bribe** them.
To tempt an animal into a trap is to **lure** it.

tend VERB
❶ *She tends to worry too much.*
• be inclined to, be liable to, be apt to
❷ *One of the campers was left to tend the fire.*
• mind, watch over, maintain
❸ *Ned spends a lot of time tending his garden.*
• take care of, cultivate, manage
❹ *Nurses tended those who were injured.*
• care for, attend to, look after, nurse, treat

tendency NOUN
He has a tendency to be lazy.
• inclination, leaning, predisposition

tender ADJECTIVE
❶ *Frost may damage tender plants.*
• delicate, fragile
OPPOSITES hardy, strong
❷ *Cook the meat slowly until it is tender.*
• soft, succulent, juicy
OPPOSITE tough
❸ *The bruise is still tender.*
• painful, sensitive, sore
❹ *She gave him a tender smile.*
• affectionate, kind, loving, caring, warm-hearted, compassionate, sympathetic, fond
OPPOSITE uncaring

tennis NOUN

WORD WEB

WAYS TO HIT A TENNIS BALL:

• lob, serve, slice, smash, volley
drop shot, backhand, forehand

tense ADJECTIVE
❶ *The muscles in her shoulders were tense.*
• taut, tight, strained, stretched
❷ *The crowd were tense as they waited to hear the results.*
• anxious, nervous, apprehensive, edgy, on edge, fidgety, jumpy
(informal) uptight, jittery
❸ *It was a tense moment for all of us.*
• nerve-racking, stressful, worrying
OPPOSITE relaxed

tension NOUN
❶ *Can you check the tension on the guy ropes?*
• tightness, tautness
❷ *The tension of waiting was almost unbearable.*
• stress, strain, anxiety, nervousness, suspense, worry

tent NOUN

WORD WEB

SOME KINDS OF TENT:

• dome tent, frame tent, marquee, pop-up tent, tepee, tunnel tent, yurt
The ropes which hold down a tent are the guy ropes.

term NOUN
❶ *She was sentenced to a term in prison.*
• period, time, spell, stretch, session
❷ *The book has a glossary of technical terms.*
• word, name, expression

terrible ADJECTIVE
We heard there had been a terrible accident.
• awful, dreadful, horrible, appalling, shocking, ghastly, horrific, frightful
for other ways to describe something bad
see **bad**

terrific ADJECTIVE *(informal)*
❶ *The footprint of the yeti was a terrific size.*
• big, huge, immense, enormous, giant, gigantic, colossal, massive
see also **big**
❷ *He's a terrific tennis player.*
• excellent, first-class, first-rate, superb, marvellous, wonderful
(informal) brilliant, fantastic, fabulous

terrify VERB
The dogs were terrified by the thunder.
• frighten, scare, startle, alarm, panic, horrify, petrify

territory NOUN
We had now entered uncharted territory.
• land, area, ground, terrain, country, district, region, sector, zone
A territory which is part of a country is a **province**.

terror NOUN
They described the terror they felt when the plane crash-landed.
• fear, fright, horror, panic, alarm, dread

test NOUN
How did you do in the maths test?
• exam, examination, assessment, appraisal, evaluation
A set of questions you answer for fun is a **quiz**.
A test for a job as an actor or singer is an **audition**.
A test to find the truth about something is an **experiment** or **trial**.

A
B
C
D
E
F
G
H
I
J
K
L
M
N
O
P
Q
R
S
T
U
V
W
X
Y
Z

test VERB
❶ *I made an appointment to have my eyes tested.*
• examine, check, evaluate, assess, screen
❷ *He is testing a new formula for invisible ink.*
• experiment with, try out, trial

text NOUN
❶ *The lawyer studied the text of the document.*
• wording, words, content
❷ *She quoted a text from Shakespeare.*
• passage, extract, quotation

textiles PLURAL NOUN
see **fabric**

texture NOUN
Silk has a smooth texture.
• feel, touch, quality, consistency
for ways to describe texture see **feel**

thankful ADJECTIVE
➤ **to be thankful for something**
The travellers were thankful for our help.
• grateful for, appreciative of, pleased about, relieved about
OPPOSITE ungrateful

thanks PLURAL NOUN
She sent them a card to show her thanks.
• gratitude, appreciation

thaw VERB
❶ *The snowman gradually began to thaw.*
• melt, dissolve
❷ *Leave frozen food to thaw before cooking it.*
• defrost, unfreeze
OPPOSITE freeze

theatre NOUN

WORD WEB

PARTS OF A THEATRE:
• auditorium, balcony, bar, boxes, box office, circle, dress circle, dressing rooms, foyer, gallery, orchestra pit, stage, stalls

PEOPLE WHO PERFORM OR WORK IN A THEATRE:
• actor, actress, ballet dancer, dancer, director, dresser, make-up artist, musician, producer, prompter, scene shifter, stage manager, understudy, usher or usherette
A person who writes plays for the theatre is a **dramatist** or **playwright**.

PERFORMANCES YOU MIGHT SEE AT A THEATRE:
• ballet, comedy, dance, drama, farce, mime, musical, opera, pantomime, play, puppet show

theft NOUN
They were found guilty of theft.
• robbery, stealing
for various kinds of theft see **stealing**

theme NOUN
What is the theme of the poem?
• subject, topic, idea, gist, argument

theory NOUN
❶ *The detective has a theory about the case.*
• explanation, hypothesis, view, belief, idea, notion, suggestion
❷ *She bought a book about musical theory.*
• laws, principles, rules

therapy NOUN
He tried several therapies to cure his headaches.
• treatment, remedy

thick *ADJECTIVE*
❶ *The Roman wall was about 2 metres thick.*
• wide, broad
❷ *The cabin was made from thick logs of wood.*
• stout, chunky, heavy, solid, substantial
OPPOSITES thin, slender
❸ *We had to hack our way through the thick undergrowth.*
• dense, close, compact
❹ *His boots got stuck in a thick layer of mud.*
• deep, heavy
OPPOSITES thin, shallow
❺ *The guide spoke with a thick Polish accent.*
• heavy, noticeable
OPPOSITE slight
❻ *(informal) Fortunately, the giant was rather thick.*
• stupid, brainless, foolish
OPPOSITE intelligent

thief *NOUN*
The police managed to catch the thief.
• robber
Someone who steals from people's homes is a **burglar** or **housebreaker**.
Someone who steals from people in the street is a **pickpocket**.
Someone who steals from shops is a **shoplifter**.
Someone who used to steal from travellers was a **highwayman**.

thin *ADJECTIVE*
❶ *The animal looked dreadfully thin.*
• lean, skinny, bony, gaunt, spare, slight, underweight
Someone who is thin and tall is **lanky**.
Someone who is thin but strong is **wiry**.
Someone who is thin can also be **slim** or **slender**.
Thin arms or legs are **spindly**.
A common simile is **as thin as a rake**.
OPPOSITE fat
❷ *The fairy wore a thin cloak of spider's silk.*
• fine, light, delicate, flimsy, sheer, wispy
A thin line is a **fine** or **narrow** line.
A thin book is a **slim** book.
OPPOSITE thick

❸ *The icing should be thin enough to spread.*
• runny, watery
OPPOSITE thick

thin *VERB*
You can thin the paint with a little water.
• dilute, water down, weaken
➤ **to thin out**
The crowd thinned out later in the day.
• diminish, disperse

thing *NOUN*
❶ *What's that green thing on the floor?*
• item, object, article
❷ *We had a lot of things to talk about.*
• matter, affair, detail, point, factor
❸ *Some strange things have been happening.*
• event, happening, occurrence, incident
❹ *I have only one thing left to do.*
• job, task, act, action
❺ *Put your things in one of the lockers.*
• belongings, possessions, stuff, equipment, gear

think *VERB* thinks, thinking, thought
❶ *Think before you do anything rash.*
• consider, contemplate, reflect, deliberate, reason
To think hard about something is to **concentrate** on it.
To think quietly and deeply about something is to **meditate**.
To keep thinking anxiously about something is to **brood** on it.
❷ *Do you think this is a good idea?*
• believe, feel, consider, judge, conclude
❸ *What do you think this ring is worth?*
• reckon, suppose, imagine, estimate, guess, expect
➤ **to think about something**
I need some more time to think about it.
• consider, reflect on, ponder, muse on, mull over
➤ **to think something up**
They thought up a good plan.
• invent, make up, conceive, concoct, devise

a b c d e f g h i j k l m n o p q r s t u v w x y z

thirsty *ADJECTIVE*
They were **thirsty** after their long walk.
• dry, parched
If someone is ill through lack of fluids, they are dehydrated.

thorn *NOUN*
The florist cut the **thorns** off the rose stems.
• prickle, spike, needle, barb

thorny *ADJECTIVE*
❶ He scratched his arm on a **thorny** rose bush.
• prickly, spiky, spiny, sharp, bristly, scratchy
❷ They discussed the **thorny** problem for hours.
• tricky, difficult, complicated, hard, perplexing, ticklish

thorough *ADJECTIVE*
❶ The doctor gave him a **thorough** examination.
• comprehensive, full, rigorous, careful, methodical, systematic, meticulous, painstaking, conscientious
OPPOSITE superficial
❷ He's made a **thorough** mess of things!
• complete, total, utter, absolute, downright

thought *past tense see* **think**

thought *NOUN*
❶ She gave a lot of **thought** to the problem.
• consideration, deliberation, study
❷ The detective was lost in **thought**.
• thinking, contemplation, reflection, meditation
❸ What are your **thoughts** on modern art?
• opinion, belief, idea, notion, conclusion

thoughtful *ADJECTIVE*
❶ Mr Levi had a **thoughtful** expression on his face.
• pensive, reflective, absorbed, preoccupied
OPPOSITES blank, vacant
❷ She added some **thoughtful** comments in the margin.
• well-thought-out, careful, conscientious, thorough
OPPOSITE careless

❸ It was very **thoughtful** of you to visit me in hospital.
• caring, considerate, kind, friendly, good-natured, unselfish
OPPOSITE thoughtless

thoughtless *ADJECTIVE*
It was **thoughtless** of him to mention her dead husband.
• inconsiderate, insensitive, uncaring, unthinking, negligent, ill-considered, rash
OPPOSITE thoughtful

thrash *VERB*
❶ The rider **thrashed** and spurred his horse to go faster.
• hit, beat, whip, flog
(informal) whack, wallop
❷ The crocodile **thrashed** its tail in the mud.
• swish, flail, jerk, toss
❸ (informal) The visitors **thrashed** the home side 6–0.
• beat, defeat, trounce

thread *NOUN*
❶ There was a loose **thread** hanging from the hem of the dress.
• strand, fibre
❷ Do you sell embroidery **thread**?
• cotton, yarn, wool, silk
Sewing thread is wound on to a **reel** or **spool**.

threat *NOUN*
❶ She made a **threat** about phoning the police.
• warning
❷ Earthquakes are a constant **threat** in California.
• danger, menace, hazard, risk

threaten *VERB*
❶ The bandits **threatened** him when he tried to escape.
• make threats against, menace, intimidate, terrorize, bully, browbeat
❷ The forecast **threatened** rain.
• warn of
❸ Wild tigers are **threatened** with extinction.
• endanger, put at risk

A B C D E F G H I J K L M N O P Q R S T U V W X Y Z

three *NOUN*
A group of three musicians is a **trio**.
Three babies born at the same time are **triplets**.
A shape with three sides is a **triangle**.
To multiply a number by three is to **triple** it.

threw *past tense see* **throw**

thrifty *ADJECTIVE*
Isla had been **thrifty** and saved her pocket money.
• careful, economical, frugal, prudent, sparing
OPPOSITE extravagant

thrill *NOUN*
Kim loves the **thrill** of rock climbing.
• adventure, excitement, sensation, tingle
(informal) buzz, kick

thrill *VERB*
The thought of seeing a real shark **thrilled** him no end.
• excite, exhilarate, electrify, rouse, stir, stimulate
OPPOSITE bore

thrilled *ADJECTIVE*
I was **thrilled** to be invited to the wedding.
• delighted, pleased, excited, overjoyed, ecstatic

thrive *VERB* thrives, thriving, thrived or throve, thrived or thriven
Tomato plants **thrive** in greenhouses.
• do well, flourish, grow, prosper, succeed

throb *VERB*
She could feel the blood **throbbing** through her veins.
• beat, pound, pulse, pulsate

throng *NOUN*
There were **throngs** of people on the street.
• crowd, swarm, horde

throttle *VERB*
My tie was so tight that it nearly **throttled** me!
• strangle, choke

throw *VERB* throws, throwing, threw, thrown
❶ I **threw** some bread into the pond for the ducks.
• fling, cast, pitch, sling, toss
(informal) bung, chuck
To deliver the ball in cricket or rounders is to **bowl**.
To throw the shot in athletics is to **put** the shot.
To throw something high in the air is to **lob** it.
To throw something heavy is to **heave** it.
To throw something with great force is to **hurl** it.
If someone throws a lot of things at you, they **pelt** you.
❷ The horse **threw** its rider.
• throw off, shake off, dislodge
➤ **to throw away**
We **threw away** a pile of old junk.
• get rid of, dispose of, discard, scrap
(informal) dump, ditch

thrust *VERB*
❶ Drew **thrust** his hands into his pockets.
• push, force, shove
❷ The bandit **thrust** at him with a dagger.
• lunge, jab, prod, stab, poke

thump *VERB*
'Silence!' he rasped, **thumping** his fist on the table.
• bang, bash, pound, hit, strike, knock, rap
(informal) whack, wham

thunder *NOUN, VERB*
We could hear **thunder** in the distance.
A burst of thunder is a **clap**, **crack**, **peal** or **roll** of thunder.
see also **weather**

tick *VERB*
A clock was **ticking** in the background.
for various ways to make sounds see **sound**

a b c d e f g h i j k l m n o p q r s t u v w x y z

➤ **to tick someone off** *(informal)*
*She **ticked him off** for talking in class.*
• tell off, reprimand, reproach, scold

ticket *NOUN*
❶ *They got free **tickets** for the concert.*
• pass, permit, token, voucher, coupon
❷ *What does it say on the price **ticket**?*
• label, tag, tab

tide *NOUN*
*The beach is completely covered at high **tide**.*
When the tide is coming in it is **flowing**
or **incoming**.
When the tide is going out it is **ebbing**
or **outgoing**.
The tide is fully in at **high tide** and fully out at
low tide.

tidy *ADJECTIVE*
*Mrs Akinwole likes to keep her office **tidy**.*
• neat, orderly, uncluttered, trim, smart,
spruce, straight
OPPOSITE **untidy**

tie *VERB*
❶ *Frankie **tied** a pink ribbon round the parcel.*
• bind, fasten, hitch, knot, loop, secure
To tie up a boat is to **moor** it.
To tie up an animal is to **tether** it.
OPPOSITE **untie**
❷ *The two teams are still **tied**.*
• be equal, be level, draw

tight *ADJECTIVE*
❶ *The lid was too **tight** for him to unscrew.*
• firm, fast, secure
If something is so tight that air cannot get
through, it is **airtight**.
If something is so tight that water cannot get
through, it is **watertight**.
OPPOSITE **loose**
❷ *They squeezed into the **tight** space.*
• cramped, compact, small, narrow, poky,
snug
OPPOSITE **spacious**

❸ *Make sure that the ropes are **tight**.*
• taut, tense, stretched, rigid
A common simile is **as tight as a drum**.
OPPOSITE **slack**
❹ *He can be very **tight** with his money.*
• mean, miserly, stingy
OPPOSITE **generous**

tighten *VERB*
❶ *She **tightened** her grip on his hand.*
• increase, strengthen, tense, stiffen
❷ *You need to **tighten** the guy ropes.*
• make taut, pull tighter, stretch
❸ *He tried to **tighten** the screw.*
• make tighter, screw up
OPPOSITE **loosen**

till *VERB*
*Farmers use tractors to **till** the land.*
• cultivate, farm, plough, dig

tilt *VERB*
*The caravan **tilted** to one side.*
• lean, incline, tip, slant, slope, angle
When a ship tilts to one side, it **lists**.

timber *NOUN*
*She bought some **timber** to build a shed.*
• wood, lumber, logs, planks

time *NOUN*
❶ *Is this a convenient **time** to talk?*
• moment, occasion, opportunity
❷ *Autumn is my favourite **time** of the year.*
• phase, season
❸ *He spent a short **time** living in Seoul.*
• period, while, term, spell, stretch
❹ *Shakespeare lived in the **time** of Elizabeth I.*
• era, age, days, epoch, period
❺ *Please try to keep **time** with the music.*
• tempo, beat, rhythm

WORD WEB
UNITS FOR MEASURING TIME:
• second, minute, hour, day, week, fortnight, month, year, decade, century, millennium

---

INSTRUMENTS USED TO MEASURE TIME:

• clock, egg timer, hourglass, pocket watch, stopwatch, sundial, timer, watch, wristwatch

➤ **on time**

Please try to be on time.

• punctual, prompt

---

timid *ADJECTIVE*

At first, the mermaid was too timid to say anything.

• shy, bashful, modest, nervous, fearful, shrinking, retiring, sheepish

A common simile is as timid as a mouse.

OPPOSITES brave, confident

tingle *VERB*

My ears were tingling with the cold.

• prickle, sting, tickle

tingle *NOUN*

❶ *She felt a tingle in her foot.*

• prickling, stinging, tickle, tickling, pins and needles

❷ *He felt a tingle of excitement.*

• thrill, sensation, quiver, shiver

tinker *VERB*

She tinkered with the computer to get it to work.

• fiddle, play about, dabble, meddle, tamper

tint *NOUN*

The paint was white with a faint tint of blue.

• colour, hue, shade, tone

for names of colours see **colour**

tiny *ADJECTIVE*

The ladybird was so tiny that you could hardly see it.

• little, minute, miniature, microscopic, minuscule

(informal) teeny, titchy

OPPOSITES big, large

tip *NOUN*

❶ *The tip of his nose felt cold.*

• end, point

The tip of an ink pen is the **nib**.

❷ *The tip of the mountain was covered in snow.*

• cap, peak, top, summit, pinnacle, crown

❸ *He gave them some useful tips on first aid.*

• hint, piece of advice, suggestion, clue, pointer

❹ *They took a load of rubbish to the tip.*

• dump, rubbish heap

tip *VERB*

❶ *The wheelchair tipped backwards.*

• lean, tilt, incline, slope, slant

When a ship tips slightly to one side, it **lists**.

When a ship tips right over, it **capsizes**.

❷ *Jiya tipped the box of crayons on to the table.*

• empty, turn out, dump, unload

❸ *Have you tipped the waiter?*

• give a tip to, reward

➤ **to tip over**

He tipped the milk jug over by accident.

• knock over, overturn, topple, upset

tiptoe *VERB*

for various ways to walk see **walk**

tire *VERB*

➤ **to tire someone out**

Running in the playground had tired us all out.

• exhaust, wear out

OPPOSITES refresh, invigorate

tired *ADJECTIVE*

Have a lie-down if you're tired.

• exhausted, fatigued, weary, worn out, listless, sleepy, drowsy

(informal) all in

➤ **to be tired of something**

I'm tired of watching TV.

• bored with, fed up with, sick of

If you are not interested in anything, you are apathetic.

tiring *ADJECTIVE*

Digging the garden is tiring work.

• exhausting, fatiguing, demanding, difficult, hard, laborious, tough

OPPOSITE refreshing

a
b
c
d
e
f
g
h
i
j
k
l
m
n
o
p
q
r
s
t
u
v
w
x
y
z

title NOUN

❶ *She couldn't think of a title for the story.*
• name, heading
The title above a newspaper story is a **headline**.
A title or brief description next to a picture is a **caption**.
❷ *The form asks you to fill in your name and title.*
• form of address, designation, rank
The ordinary title used before a man's name is **Mr**.
The ordinary title used before a woman's name is **Miss** or **Mrs** or **Ms**.
A polite way to address someone whose name you don't know is **sir** or **madam**.
for royal titles see **royalty**

together ADVERB

❶ *They walked to school together.*
• side by side, hand in hand
❷ *The choir sang the first verse together.*
• all at once, at the same time, simultaneously, in chorus, in unison
OPPOSITES independently, separately

toil VERB

They had been toiling all day in the fields.
• work hard, labour, sweat, slave
(informal) grind, slog

toilet NOUN

Can you tell me where the toilet is?
• lavatory, WC, bathroom
(informal) loo

token NOUN

❶ *You can exchange this token for a free drink.*
• voucher, coupon, ticket, counter
❷ *They gave her a card as a token of their thanks.*
• sign, symbol, mark, expression, indication, proof, reminder

told *past tense see* tell

tolerant ADJECTIVE

Mohammed was very tolerant towards other people.
• understanding, easy-going, open-minded, sympathetic, charitable, forgiving, lenient, indulgent, long-suffering
OPPOSITE intolerant

tolerate VERB

❶ *He won't tolerate sloppy writing.*
• accept, permit, put up with
❷ *Cactus plants can tolerate extreme heat.*
• bear, endure, stand, abide, suffer, stomach
(informal) stick

tomb NOUN

Inside the tomb were several ancient skeletons.
• burial chamber, crypt, grave, mausoleum, sepulchre, vault
An underground passage containing several tombs is a **catacomb**.
A tomb is often marked by a **tombstone**, **gravestone** or **headstone**.
see also **pyramid**

tone NOUN

❶ *There was an angry tone to her voice.*
• note, sound, quality, intonation, manner
❷ *The room is painted in subtle tones.*
• colour, hue, shade, tint
❸ *Eerie music created the right tone for the film.*
• feeling, mood, atmosphere, spirit, effect

took *past tense see* take

tool NOUN

There's a box of tools in the garage.
• implement, utensil, device, gadget, instrument

WORD WEB

TOOLS THAT ARE USED FOR WOODWORK:

• awl, chisel, clamp, drill, gimlet, hammer, jigsaw, plane, rasp, sander, saw, set square, T-square, vice

TOOLS THAT ARE USED IN THE HOME:

• broom, brush, ladder, mop, needle, pliers, scissors, screwdriver, tape measure, tweezers
for cooking utensils see **cook**

TOOLS THAT ARE USED FOR GARDENING OR FARMING:

• dibber or dibble, fork, hoe, lawnmower, pitchfork, rake, roller, scythe, secateurs, shears, shovel, sickle, spade, *(trademark)* strimmer, trowel

TOOLS YOU MIGHT USE ON A BIKE OR CAR:

(trademark) Allen key, jack, lever, pump, spanner, wrench

OTHER TOOLS:

• axe, chainsaw, crowbar, file, hacksaw, hatchet, mallet, paintbrush, palette knife, penknife, pick, pickaxe, punch, sledgehammer, stapler

tooth NOUN

WORD WEB

TEETH IN A PERSON'S MOUTH:

• canine tooth, eye tooth, incisor, molar, wisdom tooth
A dog's or wolf's canine tooth is a **fang**.
A long tooth that sticks out of an animal's mouth is a **tusk**.

THINGS A DENTIST MIGHT FIT TO YOUR TEETH:

• braces, bridge or bridgework, crown, dentures, plate

SOME PROBLEMS PEOPLE HAVE WITH THEIR TEETH:

• cavity, decay, plaque, tartar, toothache
see also **dentist**

WRITING TIPS

You can use these words to describe **teeth** or **jaws**:
• jagged, needle-sharp, pincer-like, razor-sharp, serrated
I knew of the Hydra … A monstrous dragon creature of the marshes, with nine great heads, each one full of razor-sharp teeth.—MEASLE AND THE DOOMPIT, Ian Ogilvy

TEETH MAY:

• bite, chew, chomp, clench, gnash, grind, munch, puncture, rip, snap, tear; chatter (with cold), flash, gleam
A fierce animal or creature might **bare its teeth** or **bare its fangs**.

top NOUN

❶ *They climbed to the **top** of the hill.*
• peak, summit, tip, crown, crest, head
OPPOSITES bottom, base
❷ *The **top** of the cabinet was covered with dust.*
• surface
❸ *The **top** of the jar was screwed on tightly.*
• lid, cap, cover, covering

top ADJECTIVE

❶ *Their office is on the **top** floor.*
• highest, topmost, uppermost, upper
OPPOSITES bottom, lowest
❷ *She got **top** marks in her exam.*
• most, best, highest
❸ *The skiers set off at **top** speed.*
• greatest, maximum
❹ *He is one of Europe's **top** chefs.*
• best, leading, finest, foremost, principal, superior
OPPOSITE junior

a
b
c
d
e
f
g
h
i
j
k
l
m
n
o
p
q
r
s
t
u
v
w
x
y
z

A
B
C
D
E
F
G
H
I
J
K
L
M
N
O
P
Q
R
S
T
U
V
W
X
Y
Z

top VERB
❶ *Dad topped the cake with fudge icing.*
• cover, decorate, garnish, crown
❷ *The athlete is hoping to top her personal best.*
• beat, better, exceed, outdo, surpass

topic NOUN
What was the topic of the conversation?
• subject, talking point, issue, matter, question

topical ADJECTIVE
The website often discusses topical issues.
• current, recent, up-to-date

topple VERB
❶ *The books were piled too high and toppled over.*
• fall, tumble, overbalance, collapse
❷ *The gale toppled their TV aerial.*
• knock down, overturn, upset
❸ *The rebels plotted to topple the ruler.*
• overthrow, bring down, remove from office

tore *past tense see* tear

torment VERB
❶ *He was tormented by bad dreams.*
• afflict, torture, plague, distress
❷ *He told them to stop tormenting the other children.*
• annoy, bother, harass, pester, tease, bully
To torment someone continually is to persecute or victimize them.

torrent NOUN
A torrent of water flowed down the hill.
• flood, gush, rush, stream, cascade

toss VERB
❶ *He tossed a coin into the wishing well.*
• throw, cast, hurl, fling, pitch, sling
(informal) chuck
❷ *Let's toss a coin to see who'll go first.*
• flip, spin

❸ *The little boat tossed about in the storm.*
• lurch, pitch, roll, heave, rock, bob
❹ *She tossed and turned, unable to get to sleep.*
• thrash about, flail, writhe, wriggle

total NOUN
You need a total of fifty points to win.
• sum, whole, entirety, amount
total ADJECTIVE
❶ *The bill shows the total amount due.*
• full, complete, whole, entire
❷ *The party was a total disaster.*
• complete, utter, absolute, thorough, downright, sheer

total VERB
The donations total almost 300 euros.
• add up to, amount to, come to, make

totter VERB
The child tottered across the floor.
• stagger, stumble, reel, wobble
for various ways to walk see walk

touch VERB
❶ *Some animals don't like to be touched.*
• feel, handle, stroke, fondle, caress, pat, pet
❷ *The car just touched the gatepost.*
• brush, graze, contact
❸ *The speed of the racing car touched 200 miles per hour.*
• reach, rise to
❹ *I was touched by the poem that she wrote.*
• move, affect, stir
➤ **to touch on something**
Your letter touched on the issue of payment.
• refer to, mention, raise
touch NOUN
❶ *I felt a light touch on my arm.*
• pat, stroke, tap, caress, contact
❷ *Working with animals requires a special touch.*
• sensitivity, understanding, feel, knack, manner
❸ *There's a touch of frost in the air.*
• hint, trace, suggestion

touchy *ADJECTIVE*
Be careful what you say—he's very touchy.
• easily offended, sensitive, irritable, quick-tempered

tough *ADJECTIVE*
❶ *You'll need tough shoes for hiking.*
• strong, sturdy, robust, durable, stout, hard-wearing, substantial
Common similes are as tough as nails and as tough as old boots.
OPPOSITE flimsy
❷ *The meat was very tough.*
• chewy, leathery, rubbery
OPPOSITE tender
❸ *They played against tough opposition.*
• strong, stiff, powerful, resistant, determined, stubborn
OPPOSITES weak, feeble
❹ *The police deal with some tough criminals.*
• rough, violent, vicious, hardened
❺ *It was a tough job to clean the oven.*
• demanding, laborious, strenuous, gruelling, tiring, exhausting
OPPOSITE easy
❻ *The crossword puzzle was too tough for him.*
• difficult, hard, puzzling, baffling, knotty, thorny
OPPOSITE easy

tour *NOUN*
They went on a sightseeing tour.
• journey, trip, excursion, expedition, outing, drive, ride

tourist *NOUN*
The cathedral was full of tourists.
• sightseer, holidaymaker, traveller, visitor

tournament *NOUN*
She reached the semi-final of the chess tournament.
• championship, competition, contest, series

tow *VERB*
Horses used to tow barges up and down the river.
• pull, tug along, drag, haul, draw

tower *NOUN*
A small tower on a castle or other building is a **turret**.
A church tower is a **steeple**.
The pointed structure on a steeple is a **spire**.
The part of a tower with a bell is a **belfry**.
The tall tower of a mosque is a **minaret**.

tower *VERB*
➤ **to tower above something**
The castle towers above the village.
• rise above, stand above, dominate, loom over

town *NOUN*
A town with its own local council is a **borough**.
A large and important town is a **city**.
Several towns that merge into each other are a **conurbation**.
A word meaning 'to do with a town or city' is **urban**.
The people who live in a town are the **townspeople**.
see also **city**

toxic *ADJECTIVE*
The flask contained a toxic gas.
• poisonous, deadly, lethal, harmful
OPPOSITE harmless

toy *NOUN*

WORD WEB

SOME TOYS YOU MIGHT PLAY WITH:

• ball, balloon, bicycle, board game, boomerang, building bricks, computer or video game, doll, doll's house, frisbee, go-kart, hoop, jigsaw, kaleidoscope, kite, *(trademark)* Lego, marbles, model, playing cards, puppet, puzzle, rattle, rocking horse, *(trademark)* Rollerblades, roller skates, scooter, skateboard, skipping rope, teddy bear, top, train set, trampoline, water pistol, yo-yo
see also **game**

a b c d e f g h i j k l m n o p q r s t u v w x y z

A
B
C
D
E
F
G
H
I
J
K
L
M
N
O
P
Q
R
S
T
U
V
W
X
Y
Z

trace *NOUN*
❶ *The burglars left no trace of their presence.*
• evidence, sign, mark, indication, hint, clue, track, trail
A trace left by an animal might be its **footprint** or **scent** or **spoor**.
❷ *They found traces of blood on the carpet.*
• tiny amount, drop, spot
trace *VERB*
She is trying to trace her distant ancestors.
• track down, discover, find, uncover, unearth

track *NOUN*
❶ *A rough track leads past the farm.*
• path, pathway, footpath, trail
❷ *The hunters followed the deer's tracks for miles.*
• footprint, footmark, trail, scent
❸ *They are laying the track for a new railway.*
• line, rails
❹ *The athletes are warming up on the track.*
• racetrack, circuit, course
track *VERB*
Astronomers are tracking the path of the comet.
• follow, trace, pursue, chase, tail, trail, hunt, stalk
➤ **to track someone** or **something down**
They tracked down the owner of the car.
• find, discover, trace, hunt down, sniff out, run to ground

tract *NOUN*
They had to cross a tract of desert.
• area, expanse, stretch

trade *NOUN*
❶ *The trade in antiques has been booming recently.*
• business, dealing, buying and selling, commerce, market
❷ *He is still learning his trade as a plumber.*
• craft, skill, occupation, profession, business

trade *VERB*
➤ **to trade in something**
The company trades in second-hand computers.
• deal in, do business in, buy and sell
for people who sell things see **shop**

tradition *NOUN*
It's a tradition to sing 'Auld Lang Syne' on New Year's Eve.
• custom, convention, habit, routine

traditional *ADJECTIVE*
❶ *The drummers wore traditional costumes.*
• national, regional, historical
❷ *They chose to have a traditional wedding.*
• conventional, customary, established, time-honoured, habitual, typical, usual

traffic *NOUN*
for types of traffic see **vehicle**

tragedy *NOUN*
❶ *'Romeo and Juliet' is a tragedy.*
OPPOSITE comedy
❷ *The accident at sea was a terrible tragedy.*
• disaster, catastrophe, calamity, misfortune

tragic *ADJECTIVE*
❶ *He died in a tragic accident.*
• catastrophic, disastrous, calamitous, terrible, appalling, dreadful, unfortunate, unlucky
❷ *She had a tragic expression on her face.*
• sad, sorrowful, mournful, grief-stricken, pitiful, woeful, wretched, pathetic
OPPOSITES comic, happy

trail *NOUN*
❶ *We walked along a trail through the woods.*
• path, pathway, track, route
❷ *The police were on the trail of the bank robbers.*
• track, chase, hunt, pursuit
The trail left in the water by a ship is its **wake**.

trail VERB

❶ *The detective trailed the suspect all day.*
• follow, chase, tail, track, pursue, shadow, stalk, hunt
❷ *She trailed her suitcase behind her.*
• pull, tow, drag, draw, haul
❸ *He is already trailing behind the front runners.*
• fall behind, lag, straggle, dawdle

train NOUN

❶ *They travelled to Johannesburg by train.*
for words to do with trains see **railway**
❷ *It was a strange train of events.*
• sequence, series, string, chain, succession

train VERB

❶ *She trains the football team every Saturday.*
• coach, instruct, teach, tutor
❷ *The athletes are training hard for the Paralympics.*
• practise, exercise, prepare yourself
(informal) work out
❸ *The archer trained his arrow on the target.*
• aim (at), point (at), level (at)

trainer NOUN

❶ *Their trainer makes them work hard.*
• coach, instructor, teacher, tutor
❷ *These trainers are for indoor use.*
for types of shoe or boot see **shoe**

tramp VERB

They tramped across the muddy fields.
• march, hike, trek, trudge, plod, stride
for other ways to walk see **walk**

trample VERB

Don't trample the flowers!
• crush, flatten, squash, tread on, walk over, stamp on

trance NOUN

The fortune-teller was lost in a trance.
• daydream, daze, dream
One way to be in a trance is to be **hypnotized**.
Unconsciousness caused by an illness or accident is a **coma**.

tranquil ADJECTIVE

❶ *They led a tranquil life in the country.*
• calm, peaceful, quiet, restful, serene, sedate
(informal) laid-back
OPPOSITES eventful, busy
❷ *The sea was tranquil after the storm had passed.*
• calm, placid, still, undisturbed, unruffled

transfer VERB

Some paintings have been transferred to the new gallery.
• move, remove, shift, relocate, convey, hand over

transform VERB

They transformed the attic into an office.
• change, alter, turn, convert, adapt, modify

translate VERB

She translates Russian poetry into English.
• interpret, convert
A person who translates a foreign language is an **interpreter** or **translator**.
An expert in languages is a **linguist**.

transmit VERB

❶ *The spy transmitted her messages in code.*
• send, communicate, relay, emit
To transmit a programme on radio or TV is to **broadcast** it.
OPPOSITE receive
❷ *Can the disease be transmitted to humans?*
• pass on, spread, carry

transparent ADJECTIVE

The box had a transparent lid.
• clear
(informal) see-through
Something which is not fully transparent, but allows light to shine through, is **translucent**.

transport VERB

The goods are transported to Europe by sea.
• take, carry, convey, ship, transfer, move, bring, fetch, haul, shift

a
b
c
d
e
f
g
h
i
j
k
l
m
n
o
p
q
r
s
t
u
v
w
x
y
z

A
B
C
D
E
F
G
H
I
J
K
L
M
N
O
P
Q
R
S
T
U
V
W
X
Y
Z

transport NOUN

WORD WEB

TRANSPORT BY AIR:

• aeroplane, airship, helicopter, hot-air balloon
see also **aircraft**

TRANSPORT BY ROAD:

• bicycle, bus, car, coach, horse, jeep, lorry, minibus, taxi, van
see also **vehicle**

TRANSPORT BY RAIL:

• monorail, train, tram, underground
see also **railway**

TRANSPORT BY WATER:

• barge, boat, canoe, dhow, ferry, junk, punt, raft, ship, yacht
see also **boat**
for various ways to travel see **travel**

trap NOUN

❶ The animal was caught in a **trap**.
• snare, net, noose, booby trap
❷ The police set up a **trap** to catch the robbers.
• ambush

trap VERB

They tried to **trap** the mouse.
• capture, catch, snare, corner

trash NOUN

❶ He put the **trash** into the bin.
• rubbish, waste, garbage, junk, litter, refuse
❷ Don't listen to that **trash**!
• nonsense

travel VERB

She prefers to **travel** to work by bus.
• go, journey, move along, proceed, progress

WORD WEB

VARIOUS WAYS TO TRAVEL:

• cruise, cycle, drive, fly, go by rail, hike, hitch-hike, motor, pedal, ramble, ride, roam, row, sail, tour, trek, voyage, walk, wander
When birds travel from one country to another they **migrate**.
When people travel to another country to live there they **emigrate**.
for methods of transport see **transport**

PEOPLE WHO TRAVEL AS A WAY OF LIFE:

• itinerant, nomad, traveller

OTHER PEOPLE WHO TRAVEL:

• astronaut, commuter, cyclist, driver or motorist, explorer, hitch-hiker, holidaymaker, motorcyclist, passenger, pedestrian, pilot or aviator, rambler or walker, sailor, tourist
A person who travels to a religious place is a **pilgrim**.
A person who travels illegally on a ship or plane is a **stowaway**.
A person who likes travelling round the world is a **globetrotter**.

treacherous ADJECTIVE

❶ His **treacherous** plan was to ambush them as they escaped.
• disloyal, traitorous, deceitful, double-crossing, faithless, false, unfaithful, untrustworthy
A treacherous person is a **traitor**.
OPPOSITE loyal
❷ The roads are often **treacherous** in winter.
• dangerous, hazardous, perilous, unsafe, risky
OPPOSITE safe

tread VERB

Please **tread** carefully.
• step, walk, proceed

➤ to tread on

Don't tread on the wet cement!
• walk on, step on, stamp on, trample, crush, squash

treasure *NOUN*

The treasure was buried somewhere on the island.
• hoard, riches, wealth, fortune
A hidden store of treasure is a **cache**.
for things you might find as treasure
see **coin, jewel**

treasure *VERB*

She treasures the photograph of her grandmother.
• cherish, prize, value

treat *VERB*

❶ *The old woman had always treated him kindly.*
• behave towards, deal with
❷ *She is being treated for minor injuries.*
• give treatment to
To treat a wound is to **dress** it.
To treat an illness or wound successfully is to **cure** or **heal** it.
❸ *Let me treat you by buying you dinner.*
• give you a treat, pay for

treatment *NOUN*

❶ *The hospital is for the treatment of sick animals.*
• care, nursing, healing
❷ *He is trying a new treatment for back pain.*
• remedy, therapy, medication
Emergency treatment at the scene of an accident is **first aid**.
for kinds of medical treatment
see **medicine**
❸ *The sculpture has been damaged by careless treatment.*
• handling, use, care, management

treaty *NOUN*

The two sides signed a peace treaty.
• agreement, pact, contract

tree *NOUN*

WORD WEB

Trees which lose their leaves in winter are **deciduous**.
Trees which have leaves all year round are **evergreen**.
Trees which grow cones are **conifers**.
A young tree is a **sapling**.
Small, low trees are **bushes** or **shrubs**.
Miniature trees grown in very small containers are **bonsai** trees.

SOME VARIETIES OF TREE:

• alder, ash, aspen, baobab, banyan, bay, beech, birch, cedar, chestnut, cypress, elder, elm, eucalyptus, fir, flame tree, hawthorn, hazel, holly, juniper, larch, lime, maple, monkey puzzle, oak, olive, palm, pine, plane, poplar, redwood, rowan, spruce, sycamore, tamarind, willow, yew
for names of fruit trees see **fruit**

PLACES WHERE TREES GROW:

• forest, grove, plantation, rainforest, spinney, thicket, wood, woodland
An area covered with trees is a **wooded** area.
A small group of trees is a **copse** or **coppice**.
An area planted with fruit trees is an **orchard**.

tremble *VERB*

The little fairy was trembling with cold.
• shake, shiver, quake, quiver, shudder

tremendous *ADJECTIVE*

❶ *They heard a tremendous roar issuing from the cave.*
• big, enormous, great, huge, immense, massive, mighty, fearful
❷ *Winning the cup was a tremendous achievement.*
• marvellous, magnificent, wonderful, superb, terrific, sensational, spectacular, stupendous, extraordinary, outstanding

a b c d e f g h i j k l m n o p q r s **t** u v w x y z

tremor NOUN
A tremor in her voice showed she was nervous.
• trembling, shaking, quavering, quivering, vibration, wobble

trend NOUN
❶ *There is a general trend towards healthier eating.*
• tendency, movement, shift, leaning
❷ *This type of computer game is the latest trend.*
• fashion, style, craze, fad, vogue

trial NOUN
❶ *Scientists are conducting trials on a new space probe.*
• test, experiment
❷ *The trial will be heard in a crown court.*
• case, hearing
A military trial is a **court martial**.

triangular ADJECTIVE
A triangular shape is **three-cornered** or **three-sided**.

tribe NOUN
see **family**

trick NOUN
❶ *Stephie played a trick on her brother.*
• joke, practical joke, prank
Tricks which a magician performs are **conjuring tricks**.
❷ *The Trojans never guessed that the wooden horse was a trick.*
• deception, pretence, fraud, cheat, hoax
(informal) con

trick VERB
He tricked them into believing he was a police officer.
• deceive, dupe, fool, hoodwink, cheat, swindle
(informal) con

trickle VERB
Water trickled from the tap.
• dribble, drip, leak, seep, ooze
OPPOSITE gush

tricky ADJECTIVE
❶ *There were a couple of tricky questions in the exam.*
• difficult, complicated, awkward, intricate, involved, ticklish
OPPOSITES straightforward, easy
❷ *Redbeard is a tricky person to deal with.*
• crafty, cunning, sly, wily

trigger VERB
The burnt toast triggered the smoke alarm.
• activate, set off, switch on, start

trim ADJECTIVE
Mr Abid always keeps his garden trim.
• neat, orderly, tidy, well-kept, smart, spruce
OPPOSITE untidy
trim VERB
❶ *He asked the barber to trim his beard.*
• cut, clip, shorten, crop, neaten, tidy
❷ *The cuffs of the blouse are trimmed with lace.*
• edge, decorate, adorn

trip NOUN
We went on a trip to the seaside.
• journey, visit, outing, excursion, jaunt, expedition
trip VERB
❶ *I nearly tripped on the stairs.*
• catch your foot, stumble, fall, slip, stagger
❷ *We heard her tripping along the corridor.*
• run, skip

triumph NOUN
The team celebrated their triumph at the Olympic Games.
• victory, win, success, conquest

triumphant ADJECTIVE
❶ *They cheered the triumphant team.*
• winning, victorious, conquering, successful
OPPOSITE unsuccessful
❷ *'I've solved the riddle!' said Nat with a triumphant smile.*
• elated, exultant, joyful, gleeful, jubilant

A
B
C
D
E
F
G
H
I
J
K
L
M
N
O
P
Q
R
S
T
U
V
W
X
Y
Z

trivial *ADJECTIVE*
*Don't bother me with **trivial** details.*
• unimportant, minor, insignificant, trifling, negligible, petty, silly, slight, frivolous
OPPOSITE important

troop *NOUN*
*A **troop** of horse riders crossed the river.*
• group, band, party, body, company
troop *VERB*
*The children **trooped** along the road.*
• march, parade, walk, proceed
To walk one behind the other
is to **file** along.

troops *PLURAL NOUN*
see **armed forces**

trophy *NOUN*
*My friend Mason won a **trophy** for gymnastics.*
• award, prize, cup, medal

trouble *NOUN*
❶ *The family has had a lot of **trouble** recently.*
• difficulty, hardship, suffering, unhappiness, distress, misfortune, pain, sadness, sorrow, worry
❷ *The police dealt with **trouble** in the crowd.*
• disorder, unrest, disturbance, commotion, fighting, violence
❸ *The **trouble** with this computer is that it's very slow.*
• problem, difficulty, disadvantage, drawback
➤ **to take trouble**
*He **took trouble** to remember all our names.*
• bother, make an effort, take pains
trouble *VERB*
❶ *What's **troubling** you?*
• distress, upset, bother, worry, concern, pain, torment, vex
❷ *I don't want to **trouble** her if she's busy.*
• disturb, interrupt, bother, pester
❸ *Nobody **troubled** to tidy up the room.*
• bother, make an effort, take trouble

troublesome *ADJECTIVE*
❶ *Do you find the heat **troublesome**?*
• annoying, irritating, trying, tiresome, bothersome, distressing, inconvenient, upsetting
❷ *There are two **troublesome** teenagers in the family.*
• badly behaved, disorderly, rowdy, unruly, disobedient

trousers *PLURAL NOUN*
for items of clothing see **clothes**

truce *NOUN*
*The two sides agreed on a **truce**.*
• ceasefire, armistice, peace

true *ADJECTIVE*
❶ *Do you think the newspaper report is **true**?*
• accurate, correct, right, factual, authentic, undeniable
OPPOSITES untrue, false
❷ *This is a **true** copy of my birth certificate.*
• genuine, real, actual, faithful, exact
OPPOSITE false
❸ *Jia has always been a **true** friend.*
• faithful, loyal, constant, devoted, sincere, steady, trustworthy, dependable, reliable
OPPOSITE unreliable

trunk *NOUN*
❶ *The **trunk** of a palm tree can bend in the wind.*
• stem, stock
❷ *Push up from the ground, keeping your **trunk** straight.*
• torso, body, frame
❸ *The magician kept her things in a huge travelling **trunk**.*
• chest, case, box, crate, suitcase, coffer

trust *VERB*
❶ *I **trusted** her to keep my identity a secret.*
• rely on, depend on, count on, bank on, believe in, be sure of, have confidence in, have faith in
❷ *I **trust** you are well.*
• hope

a
b
c
d
e
f
g
h
i
j
k
l
m
n
o
p
q
r
s
t
u
v
w
x
y
z

trust *NOUN*
❶ *The director has **trust** in her acting ability.*
• belief, confidence, faith
❷ *They put their lives in the **trust** of the pilot.*
• responsibility, safekeeping, hands

trustworthy *ADJECTIVE*
*Sir Boldwood was a **trustworthy** ally of the king.*
• reliable, dependable, loyal, trusty, true, honourable, responsible
OPPOSITE untrustworthy

truth *NOUN*
❶ *The detective doubted the **truth** of her story.*
• accuracy, authenticity, correctness, genuineness, reliability, truthfulness, validity
OPPOSITE inaccuracy, falseness
❷ *Are you sure you're telling the **truth**?*
• facts
OPPOSITE lies

truthful *ADJECTIVE*
❶ *She is normally a **truthful** person.*
• honest, frank, sincere, straight, straightforward, reliable, trustworthy
❷ *He gave a **truthful** answer.*
• accurate, correct, proper, right, true, valid
OPPOSITE dishonest

try *VERB*
❶ *I'm going to **try** to beat my dad at chess.*
• aim, attempt, endeavour, make an effort, strive, struggle
❷ *Would you like to **try** a larger size?*
• test, try out, evaluate, experiment with
try *NOUN*
❶ *We may not succeed, but it's worth a **try**!*
• attempt, effort, go, shot
❷ *Would you like a **try** of my mango smoothie?*
• trial, test, taste

trying *ADJECTIVE*
*The way he keeps asking questions is very **trying**.*
• tiresome, irritating, annoying, wearing, wearisome

tub *NOUN*
*We shared a large **tub** of popcorn between us.*
• pot, drum, barrel, cask, vat

tube *NOUN*
*Roll the paper into a **tube**.*
• cylinder, pipe
A flexible tube is a **hose**.
A tube which liquid pours out of is a **spout**.

tuck *VERB*
*She **tucked** her t-shirt into her jeans.*
• push, insert, stuff

tuft *NOUN*
*The goat stood munching on a **tuft** of grass.*
• clump, bunch

tug *VERB*
❶ *It annoys me when my brother **tugs** my hair.*
• pull, yank, jerk, pluck, wrench
❷ *We **tugged** the sledge up the hill.*
• drag, pull, tow, haul, lug, draw, heave

tumble *VERB*
*The child slipped and **tumbled** into the water.*
• topple, drop, fall, pitch, flop, stumble, plummet

tumult *NOUN*
*He had to shout to be heard above the **tumult**.*
• noise, uproar, commotion, clamour, din, racket, rumpus, hubbub, cacophony

tune *NOUN*
*Can you play the **tune** to 'Happy Birthday'?*
• melody, song, air, theme

tunnel *NOUN*
A tunnel dug by rabbits is a **burrow**.
A system of burrows is a **warren**.
A tunnel in a mine is a **gallery**.
A tunnel beneath a road is a **subway** or **underpass**.

tunnel VERB
Badgers use their strong front paws to tunnel for food.
• burrow, dig, excavate

turmoil NOUN
The whole country was in turmoil.
• chaos, upheaval, uproar, disorder, unrest, commotion, disturbance, pandemonium
OPPOSITES calm, peace

turn VERB
❶ *A wheel turns on its axle.*
• go round, revolve, rotate, roll, spin, swivel, pivot, twirl, whirl
❷ *The van turned into a side street.*
• change direction, corner
To turn unexpectedly is to **swerve** or **veer** off course.
If you turn to go back in the direction you came from, you **do a U-turn.**
If marching soldiers change direction, they **wheel.**
❸ *He turned a curious shade of green.*
• become, go, grow
❹ *They turned the attic into a spare bedroom.*
• convert, adapt, change, alter, modify, transform, develop
➤ **to turn something down**
She turned down the offer of a part in the play.
• decline, refuse, reject
➤ **to turn something on** or **off**
He turned on the radio.
• switch on or off
➤ **to turn out**
Everything turned out well in the end.
• end up, come out, happen, result
➤ **to turn over**
The boat turned over.
• capsize, overturn, turn upside down, flip over, keel over
➤ **to turn up**
A friend turned up unexpectedly.
• arrive, appear, drop in

turn NOUN
❶ *She gave the handle a turn.*
• twist, spin, whirl, twirl
A single turn of a wheel is a **revolution.**
The process of turning is **rotation.**
❷ *The house is just past the next turn in the road.*
• bend, corner, curve, angle, junction
A sharp turn in a country road is a **hairpin bend.**
❸ *It's your turn to do the washing up.*
• chance, opportunity, occasion, time, slot, go
❹ *Everyone had to do a turn in the show.*
• act, performance, scene, sketch
❺ *(informal) Seeing the skeleton gave her quite a turn.*
• fright, scare, shock, start, surprise

turret NOUN
see **tower**

twig NOUN
The campers gathered twigs to make a fire.
• stick, branch, stalk, stem, shoot

twin NOUN
This vase is a twin of the one in the museum.
• double, duplicate, lookalike, match, clone

twinkle VERB
The stars twinkled in the sky.
• sparkle, shine, glitter, glisten, glimmer, glint

twirl VERB
❶ *The dancers twirled faster and faster.*
• spin, turn, whirl, revolve, rotate, pirouette
❷ *He paced up and down, twirling his umbrella.*
• twiddle, twist

twist VERB
❶ *She twisted a bandage round her wrist.*
• wind, loop, coil, curl, entwine
❷ *Twist the handle to open the door.*
• turn, rotate, revolve, swivel

a
b
c
d
e
f
g
h
i
j
k
l
m
n
o
p
q
r
s
t
u
v
w
x
y
z

A
B
C
D
E
F
G
H
I
J
K
L
M
N
O
P
Q
R
S
T
U
V
W
X
Y
Z

❸ *The road twists through the hills.*
• wind, weave, curve, zigzag
❹ *He twisted and turned in his sleep.*
• toss, writhe, wriggle
❺ *I tried to twist the cap off the bottle.*
• unscrew
❻ *Heat can twist metal out of shape.*
• bend, buckle, warp, crumple, distort

twisted *ADJECTIVE*
The trunk of the olive tree was twisted with age.
• warped, gnarled, buckled, misshapen, deformed

twitch *VERB*
The cat twitched in his sleep.
• jerk, jump, start, tremble

two *NOUN*
Two musicians playing or singing together are a **duet** or a **duo**.
Two people or things which belong together are a **couple** or a **pair**.
To multiply a number by two is to **double** it.

type *NOUN*
❶ *What type of films do you like to watch?*
• kind, sort, variety, category, class, genre
❷ *The book was printed in large type.*
• print, lettering, letters, characters

typical *ADJECTIVE*
❶ *The weather is typical for this time of year.*
• normal, usual, standard, ordinary, average, predictable, unsurprising
OPPOSITE unusual
❷ *The pointed arch is typical of Gothic architecture.*
• characteristic, representative
OPPOSITE uncharacteristic

Uu

ugly *ADJECTIVE*
❶ *The view is ruined by an ugly tower.*
• grotesque, hideous, unattractive, repulsive, revolting, monstrous
OPPOSITE beautiful
❷ *The room was filled with ugly furniture.*
• unattractive, unsightly, displeasing, tasteless, horrid, nasty
OPPOSITE beautiful
❸ *The crowd was in an ugly mood.*
• unfriendly, hostile, menacing, threatening, angry, dangerous
OPPOSITE friendly

ultimate *ADJECTIVE*
Her ultimate goal is to be a writer.
• eventual, final
OPPOSITE initial

umpire *NOUN*
see **referee**

un– *PREFIX*

WRITING TIPS

There are so many words which begin with **un-** that there is not enough space to include them all below, but you can still find synonyms for them using your thesaurus. First, take away the prefix **un-** to find the positive word (e.g. **able** from **unable**), then add **un-** or **not** to the synonyms listed in that entry to make their opposites (for example, **not allowed** or **unwilling**).

unanimous *ADJECTIVE*
It was a unanimous decision.
• collective, joint, united
A decision where most, but not all, people agree is a **majority** decision.

unattractive ADJECTIVE
see **ugly**

unavoidable ADJECTIVE
The accident was unavoidable.
• inevitable, bound to happen, certain, destined

unaware ADJECTIVE
➤ **unaware of**
They were unaware of the dangers that lay ahead.
• ignorant of, oblivious to, unconscious of

unbearable ADJECTIVE
The stench in the cave was unbearable.
• unendurable, intolerable, impossible to bear

unbelievable ADJECTIVE
❶ *The account of the UFO sighting was unbelievable.*
• unconvincing, unlikely, far-fetched, improbable, incredible
❷ *She scored an unbelievable goal.*
• amazing, astonishing, extraordinary, remarkable, sensational, phenomenal

uncertain ADJECTIVE
❶ *I was uncertain what to do next.*
• unsure, doubtful, in two minds, unclear
❷ *They are facing an uncertain future.*
• indefinite, unknown, undecided, unpredictable

unclean ADJECTIVE
see **dirty**

unclear ADJECTIVE
see **uncertain**

uncomfortable ADJECTIVE
❶ *She complained that her shoes were uncomfortable.*
• restrictive, cramped, hard, stiff, tight, tight-fitting
❷ *He spent an uncomfortable night sleeping on the floor.*
• restless, troubled, disagreeable, uneasy
OPPOSITE comfortable

uncommon ADJECTIVE
see **unusual**

unconscious ADJECTIVE
❶ *The patient had been unconscious for two days.*
If you are unconscious because of a hit on the head, you are **knocked out**.
If you are unconscious for an operation, you are **anaesthetized**.
If you are unconscious because of an accident or illness, you are **in a coma**.
❷ *She's unconscious of the effect she has on other people.*
• ignorant, unaware
❸ *They laughed at her unconscious slip of the tongue.*
• accidental, unintended, unintentional
OPPOSITE conscious
➤ **unconscious of**
He's unconscious of all the trouble he's caused.
• unaware of, ignorant of, oblivious to

uncover VERB
❶ *Archaeologists have uncovered two more skeletons.*
• dig up, unearth, expose, reveal, show, disclose
To uncover your body is to **strip** or **undress**.
❷ *He uncovered the truth about his family's past.*
• detect, discover, come across
OPPOSITES cover up, hide

undergo VERB
Wizards have to undergo rigorous training.
• go through, be subjected to, experience, put up with, endure

undermine VERB
Losing the race could undermine her confidence.
• weaken, lessen, reduce, destroy, ruin
OPPOSITES support, boost

a b c d e f g h i j k l m n o p q r s t u v w x y z

understand _VERB_ understands, understanding, understood
❶ _I don't **understand** what you mean._
• comprehend, grasp, follow, see, take in, realize, appreciate, recognize, work out, fathom
❷ _Can you **understand** this writing?_
• read, interpret, make out, make sense of
To understand something in code is to **decode** or **decipher** it.
❸ _I **understand** they're moving to Sydney._
• believe, hear

understanding _NOUN_
❶ _The robot has limited powers of understanding._
• intelligence, intellect, sense, judgement
❷ _The book will increase your understanding of science._
• appreciation, awareness, knowledge, comprehension, grasp
❸ _The two sides reached an understanding._
• agreement, deal, settlement, arrangement, accord
❹ _She treats her patients with understanding._
• sympathy, compassion, consideration

understanding _ADJECTIVE_
Martha is an **understanding** person.
• sympathetic, caring, friendly, kind, helpful, open-minded, tolerant

undertake _VERB_
❶ _She was asked to **undertake** a secret mission._
• take on, accept, tackle, handle
❷ _He **undertook** to pay all the costs._
• agree, consent, promise, guarantee, commit yourself

underwear _NOUN_
• underclothes, underclothing, undergarments
(informal) undies
Women's underclothes are **lingerie**.
for items of underwear see **clothes**

undo _VERB_ undoes, undoing, undid, undone
❶ _I'll have to **undo** this row of knitting._
• unfasten, untie, unravel, loosen, release
To undo stitching is to **unpick** it.
❷ _Eliza **undid** the wrapping on the parcel._
• open, unwrap, unfold, unwind, unroll, unfurl
❸ _Click **undo** to reverse a mistake on a computer._
• reverse, cancel out, wipe out

undoubtedly _ADVERB_
She is **undoubtedly** our best player.
• definitely, certainly, surely, doubtless, of course

undress _VERB_
He **undressed** quickly and got into bed.
• get undressed, take off your clothes, strip
OPPOSITE dress

unearth _VERB_
❶ _The dog **unearthed** an old bone._
• dig up, uncover
❷ _She **unearthed** some old diaries in the attic._
• find, discover, come across, stumble upon, track down

uneasy _ADJECTIVE_
❶ _I had an **uneasy** feeling that something was wrong._
• anxious, nervous, apprehensive, tense, troubling, upsetting, worrying
OPPOSITE confident
❷ _Our guest passed an **uneasy** night._
• restless, unsettled, uncomfortable, disturbed
OPPOSITE comfortable

unemployed _ADJECTIVE_
Since the factory closed, he has been unemployed.
• out of work, jobless
(informal) on the dole
To be unemployed because there is not enough work to do is to be **redundant**.
OPPOSITES employed, working

uneven *ADJECTIVE*
❶ *The ground was very **uneven** in places.*
• rough, bumpy, rutted
OPPOSITE smooth
❷ *Their performance has been **uneven** this season.*
• erratic, inconsistent, irregular, variable, unpredictable
OPPOSITE consistent
❸ *It was a very **uneven** contest.*
• one-sided, unbalanced, unequal, unfair
OPPOSITE balanced

unexpected *ADJECTIVE*
*Her reaction was totally **unexpected**.*
• surprising, unforeseen, unpredictable, unplanned
OPPOSITE expected

unfair *ADJECTIVE*
❶ *Do you think that the umpire's decision was **unfair**?*
• unjust, unreasonable, wrong, one-sided, unbalanced, impartial, biased
OPPOSITES fair, just
❷ *I felt that her criticism of my work was **unfair**.*
• undeserved, unmerited, uncalled for, unjustified
OPPOSITES fair, deserved

unfaithful *ADJECTIVE*
see **disloyal**

unfamiliar *ADJECTIVE*
*The astronauts looked on an **unfamiliar** landscape.*
• strange, unusual, curious, novel, alien
➤ **unfamiliar with**
*They were **unfamiliar with** the local customs.*
• unaccustomed to, unused to, unaware of

unfit *ADJECTIVE*
❶ *He used to be **unfit** before he took up swimming.*
• out of condition, unhealthy
OPPOSITE fit

❷ *He is **unfit** to be left in charge of the house.*
• unsatisfactory, unsuitable, incompetent, inadequate

unfortunate *ADJECTIVE*
❶ *The **unfortunate** couple had lost all their possessions.*
• unlucky, poor, unhappy, hapless, wretched, ill-fated
❷ *The goalkeeper made one **unfortunate** error.*
• disastrous, calamitous, unwelcome
OPPOSITES fortunate, lucky
❸ *Sorry, that was an **unfortunate** choice of words.*
• regrettable, inappropriate, tactless, unsuitable, untimely

unfriendly *ADJECTIVE*
*The housekeeper greeted us with an **unfriendly** glare.*
• unwelcoming, inhospitable, unsympathetic, unkind, impolite, uncivil, unhelpful, hostile, cold, cool, distant, stand-offish, aloof, unsociable, unneighbourly
OPPOSITES friendly, amiable

ungrateful *ADJECTIVE*
*Don't be so **ungrateful**.*
• unappreciative, unthankful
OPPOSITE grateful

unhappy *ADJECTIVE*
❶ *You look **unhappy**—what's the matter?*
• sad, miserable, depressed, downhearted, despondent, gloomy, glum, downcast, dejected, forlorn, woeful, crestfallen *(informal)* down in the dumps, down in the mouth
OPPOSITES happy, cheerful
❷ *I'm still **unhappy** with my score.*
• dissatisfied, disappointed, displeased, discontented
OPPOSITES satisfied, pleased

a
b
c
d
e
f
g
h
i
j
k
l
m
n
o
p
q
r
s
t
u
v
w
x
y
z

unhealthy *ADJECTIVE*
❶ *One of the calves has been **unhealthy** since birth.*
• unwell, ill, sick, diseased, infirm, sickly, poorly, weak, delicate, feeble, frail
OPPOSITES healthy, strong
❷ *He eats an **unhealthy** diet of junk food.*
• unwholesome, unnatural, harmful, unhygienic
OPPOSITES healthy, wholesome

unhelpful *ADJECTIVE*
*The shop assistant was most **unhelpful**.*
• uncooperative, unfriendly, inconsiderate, reluctant to help
OPPOSITE helpful

unidentified *ADJECTIVE*
*An **unidentified** aircraft was spotted at night.*
• unknown, unrecognized, unspecified, unnamed, anonymous, nameless
OPPOSITE named

uniform *NOUN*
*The guards at the Tower of London wear fancy **uniforms**.*
• costume, outfit, regalia, livery

uniform *ADJECTIVE*
*The greenhouse is kept at a **uniform** temperature.*
• consistent, regular, even, unvarying, identical, similar, the same
OPPOSITES different, varying

unify *VERB*
*The new president tried to **unify** the country.*
• unite, bring together, harmonize, combine, integrate, join, merge, amalgamate
OPPOSITE separate

unimportant *ADJECTIVE*
*Don't worry about **unimportant** details.*
• insignificant, minor, trivial, trifling, irrelevant, secondary, slight, small, negligible, worthless, petty
OPPOSITE important

uninhabited *ADJECTIVE*
*The island had been **uninhabited** for centuries.*
• unoccupied, empty, deserted, abandoned
OPPOSITES inhabited, populated

uninteresting *ADJECTIVE*
see **boring**

union *NOUN*
*The city was formed by the **union** of two neighbouring towns.*
• uniting, joining, integration, combination, merger, amalgamation, fusion
A union of two rivers is a **confluence**.
A union of two countries is their **unification**.
A union of two people is a **marriage** or **partnership**.

unique *ADJECTIVE*
*Each person's fingerprints are **unique**.*
• distinctive, different, individual, special, peculiar
(informal) one-off

unit *NOUN*
*The bookcase is built up from separate **units**.*
• piece, part, bit, section, segment, element, component, module
for units of measurement see **measurement**

unite *VERB*
❶ *King Bluetooth **united** the kingdoms of Denmark and Norway.*
• combine, join, merge, link, integrate, unify, amalgamate, bring together
OPPOSITE separate
❷ *People of all ages **united** to celebrate Diwali.*
• collaborate, cooperate, join forces
OPPOSITE compete
To unite to do something bad is to **conspire**.

universal *ADJECTIVE*
*Scientists have made a discovery of **universal** importance.*
• general, widespread, global, worldwide

unjust ADJECTIVE
see **unfair**

unkind ADJECTIVE
*It was a thoughtless and **unkind** remark.*
• callous, hard-hearted, cruel, thoughtless, heartless, uncaring, unfeeling, inconsiderate, unsympathetic, unfriendly, uncharitable, harsh, mean, nasty, selfish, spiteful, vicious, malicious
OPPOSITE kind

unknown ADJECTIVE
❶ *The letter was in an **unknown** hand.*
• unidentified, unrecognized
OPPOSITE known
❷ *The author of the story is **unknown**.*
• anonymous, nameless, unnamed, unspecified
OPPOSITE named
❸ *The explorers entered **unknown** territory.*
• unfamiliar, alien, foreign, undiscovered, unexplored, uncharted
OPPOSITE familiar
❹ *The part was played by an **unknown** actor.*
• little known, unheard of, obscure
OPPOSITE famous

unlike ADJECTIVE
*The food was **unlike** anything I had tasted before.*
• different from, distinct from
OPPOSITE similar (to)

unlikely ADJECTIVE
*No-one believed her **unlikely** excuse.*
• unbelievable, unconvincing, improbable, implausible, incredible, far-fetched
OPPOSITE likely

unlucky ADJECTIVE
❶ *Some people think that 13 is an **unlucky** number.*
• unfavourable, ill-omened, ill-starred, jinxed
❷ *By an **unlucky** chance, their plan was discovered.*
• unfortunate, unwelcome, untimely
OPPOSITE lucky

unmarried ADJECTIVE
If you are unmarried, you are **single**.
If your marriage has been legally ended, you are **divorced**.
An unmarried man is a **bachelor**.
An old word for an unmarried woman is a **spinster**.

unmistakable ADJECTIVE
*There was an **unmistakable** smell of burnt toast.*
• distinct, distinctive, clear, obvious, plain, telltale

unnatural ADJECTIVE
❶ *It's **unnatural** for it to snow in April.*
• unusual, abnormal, odd, strange, weird, bizarre
❷ *Some of the acting in the film was a bit **unnatural**.*
• stiff, stilted, unrealistic, forced, self-conscious
❸ *Her hair was an **unnatural** orange colour.*
• artificial, synthetic, man-made, manufactured
OPPOSITE natural

unnecessary ADJECTIVE
*I'm deleting any **unnecessary** files from my computer.*
• inessential, non-essential, uncalled for, unwanted, excessive, superfluous, surplus, extra, redundant
OPPOSITE necessary

unoccupied ADJECTIVE
❶ *Since the fire, the flats have been unoccupied.*
• empty, uninhabited, deserted, unused, vacant
OPPOSITE occupied
❷ *The bathroom is **unoccupied**.*
• available, vacant
OPPOSITE engaged

a
b
c
d
e
f
g
h
i
j
k
l
m
n
o
p
q
r
s
t
u
v
w
x
y
z

A
B
C
D
E
F
G
H
I
J
K
L
M
N
O
P
Q
R
S
T
U
V
W
X
Y
Z

unpleasant *ADJECTIVE*
❶ *Mr Smallweed was a thoroughly **unpleasant** man.*
• disagreeable, unfriendly, unkind, bad-tempered, nasty, malicious, spiteful, hateful
❷ *Being on the boat in the storm had been an **unpleasant** experience.*
• uncomfortable, disagreeable, awful
❸ *The smell from the drain was very **unpleasant**.*
• disgusting, foul, repulsive, revolting, horrible, horrid, repellent, offensive, objectionable
see also **bad**
OPPOSITE pleasant

unpopular *ADJECTIVE*
*The new manager was **unpopular** at first.*
• disliked, hated, despised, unloved
OPPOSITE popular

unreal *ADJECTIVE*
*Everything seemed **unreal**, as if in a dream.*
• imaginary, made-up, fictitious, false, pretend
OPPOSITE real

unsafe *ADJECTIVE*
see **dangerous**

unsatisfactory *ADJECTIVE*
*The repairs to the roof were **unsatisfactory**.*
• unacceptable, inadequate, disappointing, displeasing, poor, incompetent, insufficient
OPPOSITE satisfactory

unseen *ADJECTIVE*
see **invisible**

unsteady *ADJECTIVE*
*The table was a bit **unsteady**.*
• unstable, shaky, wobbly, insecure, unbalanced, rickety
OPPOSITES stable, steady

unsure *ADJECTIVE*
see **uncertain**

untidy *ADJECTIVE*
❶ *Our house is the one with the **untidy** garden.*
• messy, disorderly, cluttered, jumbled, tangled, littered, chaotic
(informal) higgledy-piggledy, topsy-turvy
❷ *His work was **untidy** and full of mistakes.*
• careless, disorganized, slapdash
(informal) sloppy
❸ *She arrived looking **untidy** and flustered.*
• dishevelled, bedraggled, rumpled, unkempt, scruffy, slovenly

untrue *ADJECTIVE*
see **false**

unusual *ADJECTIVE*
❶ *The weather was **unusual** for the time of year.*
• abnormal, out of the ordinary, exceptional, remarkable, extraordinary, odd, peculiar, singular, strange, unexpected, irregular, unconventional, unheard of
OPPOSITE ordinary
❷ *Ebenezer is an **unusual** name.*
• uncommon, rare, unfamiliar
OPPOSITE common

unwell *ADJECTIVE*
see **ill**

unwilling *ADJECTIVE*
see **reluctant**

unwise *ADJECTIVE*
see **foolish**

upheaval *NOUN*
*Moving to a new house causes such an **upheaval**.*
• disruption, disturbance, upset, commotion, fuss

uphill ADJECTIVE
❶ *The last part of the road is uphill.*
• upward, ascending, rising
❷ *Finding a job proved to be an uphill struggle.*
• hard, difficult, tough, strenuous, laborious, arduous, exhausting, gruelling, taxing

upkeep NOUN
The upkeep of a car can be expensive.
• care, maintenance, running

upper ADJECTIVE
My bedroom is on the upper floor.
• higher, upstairs
OPPOSITE lower

upright ADJECTIVE
❶ *The car seat should be in an upright position.*
• erect, perpendicular, vertical
OPPOSITE horizontal
❷ *He is an upright member of the local community.*
• honest, honourable, respectable, reputable, moral, virtuous, upstanding, principled, trustworthy
OPPOSITE corrupt

uproar NOUN
The meeting ended in uproar.
• chaos, confusion, disorder, commotion, turmoil, pandemonium, mayhem, rumpus, furore

upset VERB
❶ *Something in the letter had upset her.*
• distress, trouble, disturb, displease, unsettle, offend, dismay, grieve, fluster, perturb
❷ *Bad weather upset the train timetable.*
• disrupt, interfere with, interrupt, affect, throw out
❸ *The baby upset a whole bowl of cereal.*
• knock over, spill, tip over, topple
❹ *A fallen tree branch upset the canoe.*
• overturn, capsize

upset NOUN
❶ *He is off school with a stomach upset.*
• illness, ailment
(informal) bug
❷ *They caused a major upset by winning 7–0.*
• shock, surprise, upheaval

upside down ADJECTIVE
❶ *I can't read the writing if it's upside down.*
• wrong way up, inverted
(informal) topsy-turvy
❷ *(informal) Everything in her life seemed to be upside down.*
• in a mess, chaotic, disorderly, jumbled
(informal) higgledy-piggledy
OPPOSITE orderly

up-to-date ADJECTIVE
❶ *The spacecraft uses up-to-date technology.*
• new, modern, present-day, recent, current, the latest, advanced, cutting-edge
OPPOSITE out of date
❷ *Her clothes are always up to date.*
• fashionable, stylish, contemporary
(informal) trendy, hip
OPPOSITE old-fashioned

upward ADJECTIVE
He started on the steep, upward climb.
• uphill, ascending, rising
OPPOSITE downward

urban ADJECTIVE
Most of the population live in urban areas.
• built-up, densely populated
OPPOSITE rural

urge VERB
He urged her to reconsider her decision.
• advise, counsel, appeal to, beg, implore, plead with, press
To urge someone to do something is to advocate or recommend it.
➤ **to urge someone on**
The fans tried to urge on their team.
• encourage, spur on, egg on discourage

a b c d e f g h i j k l m n o p q r s t u v w x y z

A B C

urge NOUN
*I had a sudden **urge** to burst into song.*
• impulse, compulsion, longing, wish,
yearning, desire, itch
(informal) yen

D E F G

urgent ADJECTIVE
❶ *She had **urgent** business in New York.*
• pressing, immediate, essential, important,
top-priority
OPPOSITE unimportant
❷ *He spoke in an **urgent** whisper.*
• anxious, insistent, earnest

H I J

usable ADJECTIVE
❶ *The lift is not **usable** today.*
• operating, working, functioning,
functional
OPPOSITE unusable
❷ *This ticket is **usable** only on certain trains.*
• valid, acceptable
OPPOSITE invalid

K L M N O P Q R S T

use VERB
❶ *She **used** a calculator to add up
the figures.*
• make use of, employ, utilize
To use your knowledge is to **apply** it.
To use your muscles is to **exercise** them.
To use a musical instrument is to **play** it.
To use an axe or sword is to **wield** it.
To use people or things selfishly is to
exploit them.
❷ *Can you show me how to **use** the
photocopier?*
• operate, work, handle, manage
❸ *You've **used** all the hot water.*
• use up, go through, consume, exhaust,
spend

use NOUN
❶ *Would these books be any **use** to you?*
• help, benefit, advantage, profit, value
❷ *A sonic screwdriver has many **uses**.*
• function, purpose, point

U V W X Y Z

useful ADJECTIVE
❶ *A flask is **useful** for keeping food warm.*
• convenient, handy, effective, efficient,
practical

❷ *The website offers some **useful** advice.*
• good, helpful, valuable, worthwhile,
constructive, invaluable
OPPOSITE useless

useless ADJECTIVE
❶ *This old vacuum cleaner is **useless**.*
• ineffective, inefficient, impractical,
unusable
OPPOSITES useful, effective
❷ *Her advice was completely **useless**.*
• worthless, unhelpful, pointless, futile,
unprofitable, fruitless
OPPOSITE useful
❸ *(informal) I'm **useless** at drawing.*
• bad, poor, incompetent
(informal) rubbish, hopeless
OPPOSITE good

user-friendly ADJECTIVE
*The computer manual isn't very **user-friendly**.*
• easy to use, straightforward, uncomplicated,
understandable

usual ADJECTIVE
❶ *I'll meet you at the **usual** time.*
• normal, customary, familiar, habitual,
regular, standard
❷ *It's **usual** to knock before entering.*
• common, accepted, conventional, traditional
OPPOSITE unusual

utensil NOUN
*A row of cooking **utensils** hung on the wall.*
• tool, implement, device, gadget, instrument,
appliance
for various tools see **tool**

utter VERB
*The robot could only **utter** a few phrases.*
• say, speak, express, pronounce,
put into words

utter ADJECTIVE
*They stared at the unicorn in **utter**
amazement.*
• complete, total, absolute, sheer,
downright, out and out

Vv

vacancy NOUN
*They have a **vacancy** for a trainee journalist.*
• job, opening, post, position, situation

vacant ADJECTIVE
❶ *The house over the road is still **vacant**.*
• unoccupied, uninhabited, deserted, empty
OPPOSITE occupied
❷ *The receptionist gave me a **vacant** stare.*
• blank, expressionless, mindless, absent-minded, deadpan
OPPOSITE alert

vague ADJECTIVE
❶ *The directions she gave me were rather **vague**.*
• indefinite, imprecise, broad, general, ill-defined, unclear, woolly
OPPOSITES exact, detailed
❷ *A **vague** shape could be seen through the mist.*
• blurred, indistinct, obscure, dim, hazy, shadowy
OPPOSITE definite

vain ADJECTIVE
❶ *The duke was **vain** about his appearance.*
• arrogant, proud, conceited, haughty, self-satisfied
OPPOSITE modest
❷ *He made a **vain** attempt to tidy the room.*
• unsuccessful, ineffective, useless, worthless, fruitless, futile, pointless
OPPOSITE successful

valid ADJECTIVE
❶ *The ticket is **valid** for three months.*
• current, legal, approved, authorized, official, permitted, suitable, usable
❷ *She made several **valid** points.*
• acceptable, reasonable, sound, convincing, genuine, legitimate
OPPOSITE invalid

valley NOUN
*A rocky path meandered through the **valley**.*
• vale, dale, dell, gorge, gully, hollow, pass, ravine, canyon
(Scottish) glen

valuable ADJECTIVE
❶ *Apparently the painting is very **valuable**.*
• expensive, costly, dear, precious, priceless
❷ *He gave her some **valuable** advice.*
• useful, helpful, constructive, good, worthwhile, invaluable
OPPOSITE worthless
WHICH WORD? Note that **invaluable** is not the opposite of **valuable**. A piece of invaluable advice is very good, but a piece of bad advice is worthless.

value NOUN
❶ *The house has recently increased in **value**.*
• price, cost, worth
❷ *She stressed the **value** of taking regular exercise.*
• advantage, benefit, merit, use, usefulness, importance

value VERB
❶ *He had always **valued** her advice.*
• appreciate, respect, esteem, have a high opinion of, set great store by
To value something highly is to **prize** or **treasure** it.
❷ *A surveyor was sent to **value** the house.*
• price, cost, rate, evaluate, assess

van NOUN
*for various vehicles see **vehicle***

vanish VERB
*With a flick of his wand, the wizard **vanished** into thin air.*
• disappear, go away, fade, dissolve, disperse
OPPOSITE appear

vanity NOUN
*His **vanity** is such that he never admits he's wrong.*
• arrogance, pride, conceit, self-esteem, self-importance

a b c d e f g h i j k l m n o p q r s t u v w x y z

A
B
C
D
E
F
G
H
I
J
K
L
M
N
O
P
Q
R
S
T
U
V
W
X
Y
Z

vapour *NOUN*
Thick clouds of vapour poured from the volcano.
• smoke, fumes, steam, gas
Vapour hanging in the air is haze, fog, mist or smog.
When something turns to vapour it **vaporizes**.

variable *ADJECTIVE*
The temperature is variable at this time of year.
• changeable, varying, fluctuating, erratic, inconsistent, uncertain, unpredictable, unsteady, unstable
If your loyalty to friends is variable, you are **fickle**.
OPPOSITE constant

variation *NOUN*
There are huge variations in age within the group.
• difference, alteration, change, fluctuation, shift

variety *NOUN*
❶ *The centre offers a variety of leisure activities.*
• assortment, mixture, array
❷ *The supermarket has over thirty varieties of pasta.*
• kind, sort, type, make, brand
A variety of animal is a **breed** or **species**.
❸ *There is not much variety in her choice of words.*
• variation, change, difference, diversity

various *ADJECTIVE*
The hats are available in various colours.
• different, assorted, several, varying, differing, a variety of, diverse

vary *VERB*
❶ *The length of daylight varies with the seasons.*
• change, alter, differ, fluctuate
❷ *They vary the menu from week to week.*
• change, modify, adjust, alter

vast *ADJECTIVE*
❶ *The miser accumulated a vast fortune.*
• large, huge, enormous, great, immense, massive
❷ *A vast stretch of water lay between them and dry land.*
• broad, wide, extensive, sweeping
OPPOSITES small, tiny

vault *VERB*
➤ **to vault over something**
He vaulted over the fence.
• jump over, leap over, bound over, spring over, clear, hurdle

vault *NOUN*
The gold was stored in the vaults of the bank.
• strongroom, treasury
An underground part of a house is a **cellar**.
A room underneath a church is a **crypt**.

veer *VERB*
The car suddenly veered to the left.
• change direction, swerve, turn

vegetable *NOUN*

WORD WEB

GREEN VEGETABLES:
• broccoli, Brussels sprout, cabbage, cauliflower, Chinese cabbage, kale, spinach

ROOT VEGETABLES:
• beetroot, carrot, parsnip, radish, swede, sweet potato, turnip, yam

LEGUMES OR PULSES:
• broad bean, butter bean, chickpea, French bean, kidney bean, lentil, mangetout, sugar-snap, pea, runner bean, soya bean

OTHER VEGETABLES:

• artichoke, asparagus, aubergine, celeriac, celery, courgette, garlic, leek, marrow, mushroom, okra, onion, pepper, potato, pumpkin, shallot, squash, sweetcorn, water chestnut, yam

vegetarian *NOUN*

A person who doesn't eat any animal products is a **vegan**.
The opposite—a person or animal that eats flesh—is a **carnivore**.
An animal that feeds only on plants is a **herbivore**.

vegetation *NOUN*

The rainforest is filled with lush vegetation.
• foliage, greenery, growth, plants, undergrowth

vehicle *NOUN*

WORD WEB

VEHICLES WHICH CARRY PEOPLE:

• buggy, bus, cab, car or motor car, caravan, coach, hovercraft, jeep, minibus, minicab, motorcycle or motorbike, taxi, train, tram
see also **aircraft, bicycle, boat, car, railway**
for space travel see **space**

VEHICLES USED FOR WORK:

• ambulance, bin lorry, bulldozer, fire engine, hearse, horsebox, lorry, removal van, pick-up truck, police car, steamroller, tank, tanker, tractor, truck, van

VEHICLES WHICH TRAVEL ON SNOW OR ICE:

• sled, sledge, sleigh, snowmobile, snowplough, toboggan

OLD HORSE-DRAWN VEHICLES:

• carriage, cart, chariot, coach, gig, stagecoach, trap, wagon

veil *VERB*

Her face was partly veiled by a scarf.
• cover, conceal, hide, mask, shroud

vein *NOUN*

A tube in the body that carries blood away from the heart is an **artery**.
Veins and arteries are **blood vessels**.
Delicate hair-like blood vessels are **capillaries**.

vengeance *NOUN*

The knight swore vengeance on his enemies.
• revenge, retribution, retaliation
OPPOSITE forgiveness

venomous *ADJECTIVE*

The adder is Britain's only venomous snake.
• poisonous
OPPOSITE harmless

vent *NOUN*

A vent in the roof lets the smoke out.
• gap, hole, opening, outlet, slit
➤ **to give vent to**
She gave vent to her anger.
• express, let go, release

venture *NOUN*

His first business venture was a disaster.
• enterprise, undertaking, project, scheme

venture *VERB*

They ventured out into the snow.
• journey, set forth, dare to go

verdict *NOUN*

What was the jury's verdict?
• conclusion, decision, judgement, opinion

verge *NOUN*

Don't park on the verge of the road.
• side, edge, margin
A stone or concrete edging beside a road is a **kerb**.
The flat strip of road beside a motorway is the **hard shoulder**.

a b c d e f g h i j k l m n o p q r s t u **v** w x y z

verify *VERB*
Several witnesses verified his statement.
• confirm, prove, support
(informal) check out

versatile *ADJECTIVE*
He's a very versatile musician.
• adaptable, resourceful, many-sided, all-round, flexible

verse *NOUN*
❶ *Most of the play is written in verse.*
• rhyme
The rhythm of a line of verse is its **metre**.
Something written in verse is **poetry** or a **poem**.
see also **poem**
❷ *We need to learn the first two verses of the poem by heart.*
• stanza

version *NOUN*
❶ *The two newspapers gave different versions of the accident.*
• account, description, story, report
❷ *It's an English version of a French play.*
• adaptation, interpretation
A version of something which was originally in another language is a **translation**.
❸ *A new version of the computer game will be released in May.*
• design, model, form, variation

vertical *ADJECTIVE*
The fence posts must be vertical.
• erect, perpendicular, upright
A vertical drop is a **sheer** drop.
OPPOSITE horizontal

very *ADVERB*
Carl is a very talented juggler.
• extremely, highly, enormously, exceedingly, truly, intensely, especially, particularly, remarkably, unusually, uncommonly, outstandingly, really
(informal) terribly
OPPOSITE slightly

vessel *NOUN*
❶ *A fishing vessel has gone missing in the North Sea.*
• boat, ship, craft
for types of boat or ship see **boat**
❷ *Archaeologists found clay vessels at the site.*
• pot, dish, bowl, jar, bottle, container
➤ **blood vessels**
Blood vessels are your **arteries**, **capillaries** and **veins**.

vex *VERB*
Their behaviour vexed me.
• annoy, irritate, make you cross, upset, anger, exasperate

vibrate *VERB*
I pulled a lever and the whole engine began to vibrate.
• shake, shudder, tremble, throb, judder, quake, quiver, rattle

vicious *ADJECTIVE*
❶ *This was once the scene of a vicious murder.*
• brutal, barbaric, violent, bloodthirsty, cruel, merciless, pitiless, ruthless, callous, inhuman, malicious, sadistic, atrocious, barbarous, murderous, villainous, wicked
❷ *Male baboons can be vicious if provoked.*
• fierce, ferocious, violent, savage, wild

victim *NOUN*
❶ *Ambulances took the victims to hospital.*
• casualty
Victims of an accident are also **the injured** or **the wounded**.
A person who dies in an accident is a **fatality**.
❷ *The hawk carried its victim in its talons.*
• prey

victor *NOUN*
Who were the victors in the battle?
• winner, conqueror, champion

victorious *ADJECTIVE*
A trophy was presented to the victorious team.
• winning, triumphant, conquering, successful, top, first
OPPOSITE defeated

victory NOUN
*Hannibal won several **victories** over the Romans.*
• win, success, triumph
OPPOSITE defeat

view NOUN
❶ *There's a good **view** from the top of the hill.*
• outlook, prospect, scene, panorama, scenery
❷ *What are your **views** on animal testing?*
• opinion, thought, attitude, belief, conviction, idea, notion
➤ **in view of something**
In view of the circumstances, they gave her a refund.
• because of, as a result of, considering, taking account of

view VERB
❶ *Thousand of tourists come to **view** Niagara Falls each year.*
• look at, see, watch, observe, regard, contemplate, gaze at, inspect, survey, examine, eye
❷ *Mila **viewed** her cousin with extreme dislike.*
• think of, consider, regard

viewer NOUN
People who view a performance are the **audience** or **spectators**.
People who view something as they happen to pass by are **bystanders, onlookers** or **witnesses**.

vigilant ADJECTIVE
*A lookout has to be **vigilant** at all times.*
• alert, watchful, attentive, wary, careful, observant, on the lookout, on your guard
OPPOSITE negligent

vigorous ADJECTIVE
❶ *She does an hour of **vigorous** exercise every week.*
• active, brisk, energetic, enthusiastic, lively, strenuous
❷ *I gave the door a **vigorous** push.*
• forceful, powerful, mighty

❸ *He was a **vigorous** man in the prime of life.*
• healthy, strong
OPPOSITE feeble

vigour NOUN
*When they sighted land, they began to row with **vigour**.*
• energy, force, spirit, vitality, gusto, verve, enthusiasm, liveliness, zeal, zest

vile ADJECTIVE
❶ *The professor gave us a **vile** concoction to drink.*
• disgusting, repulsive, revolting, foul, horrible, loathsome, offensive, repellent, sickening, nauseating
OPPOSITE pleasant
❷ *Murder is a **vile** crime.*
• dreadful, despicable, appalling, contemptible, wicked, evil

villain NOUN
*Detectives are on the trail of an infamous **villain**.*
• criminal, offender, rogue, wrongdoer
An informal word for the villain in a story is **baddy**.
OPPOSITE hero
see also **criminal**

violate VERB
*The player was penalized for **violating** the rules.*
• break, disobey, infringe, flout, disregard, ignore

violation NOUN
*They're guilty of a **violation** of the rules.*
• breach, breaking, offence (against)
A violation of the rules of a game is a **foul** or an **infringement**.

violence NOUN
❶ *The marchers protested against the use of **violence**.*
• fighting, might, war, brute force, barbarity, brutality, cruelty, savagery
OPPOSITES non-violence, pacifism

a b c d e f g h i j k l m n o p q r s t u **v** w x y z

A B C D E F G H I J K L M N O P Q R S T U V W X Y Z

❷ *The violence of the storm uprooted trees.*
• force, power, strength, severity, intensity, ferocity, fierceness, fury, rage
OPPOSITES gentleness, mildness

violent *ADJECTIVE*
❶ *There were violent clashes in the streets.*
• aggressive, forceful, rough, fierce, frenzied, vicious, brutal
OPPOSITES gentle, mild
❷ *The bridge was washed away in a violent storm.*
• severe, strong, powerful, forceful, raging, tempestuous, turbulent, wild
OPPOSITES weak, feeble

virtually *ADVERB*
It's virtually impossible to tell if the letter is genuine.
• almost, nearly, practically, as good as, in effect

virtue *NOUN*
❶ *She has the virtue of a saint!*
• goodness, decency, honesty, integrity, righteousness, uprightness, worthiness, morality
OPPOSITE vice
❷ *One virtue of living in the country is that it's quiet.*
• advantage, benefit, asset, good point, merit, strength

virtuous *ADJECTIVE*
He had always tried to lead a virtuous life.
• good, honest, honourable, innocent, just, law-abiding, moral, praiseworthy, pure, righteous, trustworthy, upright, worthy
OPPOSITE wicked

visible *ADJECTIVE*
There were no visible signs that the door had been forced.
• noticeable, obvious, conspicuous, clear, distinct, evident, apparent, perceptible, recognizable, detectable
OPPOSITE invisible

vision *NOUN*
❶ *He began to have problems with his vision.*
• eyesight, sight
❷ *In the story they keep having nightmarish visions.*
• apparition, dream, hallucination
Something travellers in the desert think they see is a **mirage**.
❸ *As an artist, she has great vision.*
• foresight, imagination, insight

visit *VERB*
They're visiting friends in Toronto for a few days.
• call on, come to see, drop in on, go to see, pay a call on, stay with

visit *NOUN*
❶ *My grandmother is coming for a visit.*
• call, stay
❷ *We are planning a short visit to Paris.*
• trip, excursion, outing

visitor *NOUN*
❶ *They've got some Polish visitors staying with them.*
• guest, caller
❷ *Rome welcomes millions of visitors every year.*
• tourist, holidaymaker, sightseer, traveller

visualize *VERB*
I can't visualize him with curly hair.
• imagine, picture, envisage, see

vital *ADJECTIVE*
It is vital that you remember the secret password.
• essential, crucial, imperative, important, necessary, indispensable
OPPOSITE unimportant

vitality *NOUN*
That painting of sunflowers bursts with vitality.
• energy, life, liveliness, spirit, animation, exuberance, vigour, zest

vivid ADJECTIVE
❶ *Gauguin often painted in* **vivid** *colours.*
• bright, colourful, strong, intense, vibrant, dazzling, brilliant, glowing, striking, showy
❷ *He gave a* **vivid** *description of his travels in Mexico.*
• lively, clear, powerful, evocative, imaginative, dramatic, lifelike, realistic, graphic
OPPOSITE dull

voice NOUN
The robot spoke with a slow, metallic **voice.**
• speech, tone, way of speaking
for types of singing voice see **sing**

WRITING TIPS

You can use these words to describe a voice:
• croaky, deep, droning, gruff, high-pitched, husky, low, shrill, soft-spoken, squeaky, throaty
It was a low, soft voice, plush as velvet, with sibilants as swashing as the sea.—PETER PAN IN SCARLET, Geraldine McCaughrean

voice VERB
We **voiced** *several objections to the plan.*
• express, communicate, put into words, speak

volcano NOUN
Molten rock that builds up inside a volcano is **magma.**
Molten rock that pours from a volcano is **lava.**
Lava and ash pouring from a volcano is an **eruption.**
A volcano that often erupts is an **active volcano.**
A volcano that can no longer erupt is an **extinct volcano.**
A volcano that is neither active nor extinct is a **dormant volcano.**
A scientist who studies volcanoes is a **volcanologist.**

volume NOUN
❶ *We had to measure the* **volume** *of the jug.*
• capacity, size, dimensions
❷ *They struggle to cope with the* **volume** *of fan mail they receive.*
• amount, quantity, bulk, mass
❸ *The full encyclopedia consists of twenty* **volumes.**
• book, tome

voluntary ADJECTIVE
She does **voluntary** *work for a charity.*
• optional, unpaid
OPPOSITE compulsory

volunteer VERB
No-one **volunteered** *to do the washing-up.*
• offer, put yourself forward, be willing

vomit VERB
The seasickness made him want to **vomit.**
• be sick, heave, retch
(informal) throw up

vortex NOUN
see **spiral**

vote VERB
Everyone has a right to **vote** *in the election.*
• cast your vote
➤ **to vote for someone** or **something**
I haven't decided who to **vote** *for.*
• choose, opt for, nominate, elect

vote NOUN
The results of the **vote** *will be known tomorrow.*
• ballot, election, poll, referendum

voucher NOUN
You can exchange this **voucher** *for a free drink.*
• coupon, ticket, token

vow VERB
He **vowed** *never to reveal the genie's name.*
• pledge, promise, guarantee, swear, give your word, take an oath

a b c d e f g h i j k l m n o p q r s t u v w x y z

A B C D E F G H I J K L M N O P Q R S T U V W X Y Z

vow *NOUN*
The mermaid took a vow to leave the sea forever.
• pledge, promise, oath, word

voyage *NOUN*
A holiday voyage is a cruise.
A voyage across a channel or sea is a crossing.
A long voyage is a sea passage.
for other ways to travel see travel

vulgar *ADJECTIVE*
❶ *The new colour scheme just looks vulgar to me.*
• tasteless, unsophisticated, cheap, tawdry
(informal) tacky
(OPPOSITE) tasteful
❷ *The book sometimes uses vulgar language.*
• indecent, offensive, rude, coarse
(OPPOSITE) decent

vulnerable *ADJECTIVE*
As night fell, the outlaws were in a vulnerable position.
• defenceless, exposed, unguarded, unprotected, at risk
(OPPOSITE) safe

Ww

waddle *VERB*
A pair of geese waddled along the path.
• toddle, totter, shuffle, shamble, wobble

wade *VERB*
❶ *Is it safe to wade in the river?*
• paddle, wallow
❷ *She had piles of paperwork to wade through.*
• toil, labour, work, plough

wag *VERB*
The dog was eagerly wagging its tail.
• move to and fro, shake, swing, wave, waggle, wiggle

wage *NOUN*
Our weekly wage was barely enough to live on.
• earnings, income, pay, pay packet
A fixed amount someone is paid per year for work is a salary.

wage *VERB*
The Greeks waged a long war against Troy.
• carry on, conduct, fight

wail *VERB*
Upstairs, the baby began to wail.
• cry, howl, bawl, cry, moan, shriek

wait *VERB*
Please wait here until I get back.
• remain where you are, stay, stop, rest, pause, linger
(informal) hang about or around, hold on

wait *NOUN*
There was a long wait before the show began.
• interval, pause, delay, hold-up

wake or **waken** *VERB*
❶ *Hagor the giant woke from a deep sleep.*
• awake, awaken, become conscious, come round, rise, arise, stir, wake up
❷ *The alarm clock woke me at 6 a.m.*
• rouse, arouse, awaken, disturb

walk *VERB*

OVERUSED WORD

Try to vary the words you use for **walk**. Here are some other words you could use.

TO WALK SLOWLY:

• amble, saunter, stroll, crawl, creep, pace, plod, step, wander
I sauntered down the lane, humming a tune.

---

stagger, stumble, totter, hobble, limp, lope, lurch, shamble, shuffle, toddle, waddle
Sleeping people are not fast. They stumble, they stagger; they move like children wading through rivers of treacle, like old people whose feet are weighed down by thick, wet mud.
—THE SLEEPER AND THE SPINDLE, Neil Gaiman

TO WALK HEAVILY OR LOUDLY:

• stamp, tramp, clump, pound, traipse, trudge, wade
*The robot **clumped** its way along the corridor.*

TO WALK QUIETLY:

• pad, patter, tiptoe, slink, steal, prowl, stalk
*The burglar **slunk** away into the shadows.*

TO WALK SMARTLY OR PROUDLY:

• march, stride, strut, parade, swagger, trot
*Captain Flint **swaggered** on board the ship.*

TO WALK A LONG DISTANCE:

• hike, trek, ramble
*They are planning to **trek** across the Himalayas.*

TO WALK IN A GROUP:

• file, troop
*The children **trooped** into the classroom.*

walk NOUN
❶ *We went for a **walk** in the country.*
• stroll, ramble, hike, trek, tramp, trudge
❷ *There are some lovely **walks** through the forest.*
• path, route

walker NOUN
When you walk along the street, you are a **pedestrian**.
If you go for long walks, you are a **hiker** or **rambler**.

wall NOUN
*A crumbling stone **wall** surrounded the cottage.*
• barricade, barrier, fortification, embankment
A wall to hold back water is a **dam** or **dyke**.
A low wall along the edge of a roof is a **parapet**.
A wall built on top of a bank of earth is a **rampart**.
A wall or fence made of sticks is a **stockade**.

wallow VERB
❶ *Hippos like to **wallow** in mud.*
• roll about, flounder, wade, lie, loll
❷ *He is **wallowing** in all the attention.*
• revel, take delight, bask

wand NOUN
*The fairy gave a flick of her magic **wand**.*
• stick, rod, baton, staff
*for other words to do with magic see **magic***

wander VERB
❶ *Sheep **wandered** about the hills.*
• stray, roam, rove, range, ramble, meander, travel, walk
❷ *We must have **wandered** off the path.*
• stray, turn, veer, swerve

wane VERB
❶ *At sunset, the light began to **wane**.*
• fade, fail, dim
OPPOSITE brighten
❷ *Her enthusiasm **waned** after a while.*
• decline, decrease, lessen, diminish, subside, weaken, dwindle
OPPOSITE strengthen

want VERB
❶ *He desperately **wants** to win a medal.*
• wish, desire, long, hope
❷ *Gayle had always **wanted** a pony of her own.*
• wish for, desire, fancy, crave, long for, yearn for, hanker after, pine for, set your heart on, hunger for, thirst for
❸ *That floor **wants** a good scrub.*
• need, require

a
b
c
d
e
f
g
h
i
j
k
l
m
n
o
p
q
r
s
t
u
v
w
x
y
z

A B C D E F G H I J K L M N O P Q R S T U V W X Y Z

want NOUN
❶ *The hotel staff saw to all their wants.*
• demand, desire, wish, need, requirement
❷ *The plants died for want of water.*
• lack, need, absence

war NOUN
The war between the two countries lasted many years.
• fighting, warfare, conflict, strife, hostilities
see also **fight**

ward VERB
➤ **to ward off someone** or **something**
❶ *He put up his shield to ward off the blow.*
• avert, block, check, deflect, turn aside, parry
❷ *The charm was intended to ward off bad luck.*
• fend off, drive away, repel, keep away, push away

wares PLURAL NOUN
The market traders displayed their wares.
• goods, merchandise, produce, stock, commodities

warlike ADJECTIVE
The Picts were said to be a warlike people.
• aggressive, fierce, violent, hostile, quarrelsome, militant
OPPOSITE peaceful

warm ADJECTIVE
❶ *It was a warm September evening.*
Weather which is unpleasantly warm is **close** or **sultry**.
Water or food which is only just warm is **lukewarm** or **tepid**.
A common simile is **as warm as toast**.
OPPOSITE cold
❷ *Sandy put on a warm jumper.*
• cosy, thick, woolly, snuggly
OPPOSITE thin
❸ *The fans gave the singer a warm welcome.*
• friendly, warm-hearted, welcoming, kind, affectionate, genial, amiable, loving, sympathetic
OPPOSITE unfriendly

warm VERB
She sat by the fire, warming her hands and feet.
• heat, make warmer, thaw out
OPPOSITE chill

warn VERB
The guide warned us to keep to the path.
• advise, caution, alert, remind
To warn people of danger is to **raise the alarm**.

warning NOUN
❶ *There was no warning of the danger ahead.*
• sign, signal, portent, indication, advance notice
❷ *The traffic warden let him off with a warning.*
• caution, reprimand

warp VERB
The wheel had slightly warped with age.
• bend, buckle, twist, curl, bend out of shape, distort

warrior NOUN
see **fighter**

wary ADJECTIVE
The cat is always wary when strangers are around.
• cautious, distrustful, suspicious, careful, watchful, attentive, vigilant, on your guard
OPPOSITE reckless

wash VERB
❶ *It took Rapunzel a long time to wash her hair.*
• clean
To wash something with a cloth is to **mop**, **sponge** or **wipe** it.
To wash something with a brush is to **scrub** it.
To wash something in clean water is to **rinse**, **sluice** or **swill** it.
To wash yourself all over is to **bath** or **shower**.
❷ *Waves washed over the beach.*
• flow, splash

waste VERB
Let's not waste any more time.
• squander, misuse, throw away, fritter away
OPPOSITE save

waste NOUN
A lot of household waste can be recycled.
• rubbish, refuse, trash, garbage, junk, litter
Waste food is **leftovers**.
Waste metal is **scrap**.

wasteful ADJECTIVE
It's wasteful to cook more food than you need.
• extravagant, uneconomical, prodigal, lavish, spendthrift
OPPOSITES economical, thrifty

watch VERB
❶ *I could sit and watch the sea for hours.*
• gaze at, look at, stare at, view, contemplate
❷ *Watch how the batsman holds the bat.*
• observe, take notice of, keep your eyes on, pay attention to, attend to, heed, note
❸ *Could you watch my bag for a few minutes?*
• keep an eye on, keep watch over, guard, mind, look after, safeguard, supervise, tend
➤ **to watch out**
Watch out—there's a car coming!
• be careful, pay attention, beware, take care, take heed

watch NOUN
for instruments used to measure time
see **time**

watchful ADJECTIVE
He kept a watchful eye on the baby.
• alert, attentive, observant, vigilant, careful, sharp-eyed, keen

water NOUN

WORD WEB

SOME AREAS OF WATER:

• brook, *(Scottish)* burn, canal, lake, lido, *(Scottish)* loch, ocean, pond, pool, reservoir, river, rivulet, sea, stream
Animals and plants which live in water are **aquatic**.

SPORTS PLAYED IN OR NEAR WATER:

• angling, canoeing, deep-sea diving, diving, kayaking, rafting, rowing, sailing, snorkelling, swimming, surfing, water polo, waterskiing, windsurfing

WRITING TIPS

You can use these words to describe **how water moves**:
• bubble, cascade, dribble, drip, flood, flow, froth, gurgle, gush, jet, ooze, overflow, ripple, roll, run, seep, shower, spill, spatter, splash, spout, spray, sprinkle, spurt, squirt, stream, surge, sweep, swirl, swish, trickle, well up
see also **flow**
The water cascaded over the lip of the basin and dropped, in a miniature Niagara Falls, onto the kitchen floor.—MEASLE AND THE SLITHERGHOUL, Ian Ogilvy

water VERB
Please remember to water the plants.
• wet, irrigate, sprinkle, dampen, moisten, soak, drench

watery ADJECTIVE
❶ *The soup was watery and tasteless.*
• weak, thin, runny, diluted, watered down
❷ *Chopping onions makes my eyes watery.*
• tearful, wet, damp, moist

wave VERB
❶ *The tall grass waved in the breeze.*
• move to and fro, sway, swing, flap, flutter
❷ *I tried to get their attention by waving a newspaper.*
• shake, brandish, flourish, twirl, wag, waggle, wiggle

wave NOUN
❶ *We watched the waves break on the shore.*
• breaker, roller, billow
A very small wave is a **ripple**.
A huge wave caused by an earthquake is a **tidal wave** or **tsunami**.

a
b
c
d
e
f
g
h
i
j
k
l
m
n
o
p
q
r
s
t
u
v
w
x
y
z

A
B
C

A number of white waves following each other is **surf.**
The top of a wave is the **crest** or **ridge.**
❷ *A wave of anger spread through the crowd.*
• surge, outbreak

D
E
F
G

waver VERB
❶ *She wavered about whether to send the letter.*
• hesitate, dither, falter, be uncertain, think twice
❷ *The candle flame wavered in the draught.*
• flicker, quiver, tremble, shake, shiver

H
I
J

wavy ADJECTIVE
The mermaid combed her long wavy hair.
• curly, curling, rippling, winding, zigzag
OPPOSITE straight

K
L
M
N
O
P
Q
R
S

way NOUN
❶ *Can you show me the way to the bus station?*
• direction, route, road, path
❷ *Is your house a long way from here?*
• distance, journey
❸ *This is the best way to make porridge.*
• method, procedure, process, system, technique
❹ *What a childish way to behave!*
• manner, fashion, style
❺ *In some ways, the brothers are very alike.*
• respect, particular, feature, detail, aspect
❻ *Things are in a bad way.*
• state, condition

T
U
V

weak ADJECTIVE
❶ *The footbridge was old and weak in places.*
• fragile, flimsy, rickety, shaky, unsound, unsteady, unsafe, decrepit
❷ *The patient was too weak to walk very far.*
• feeble, frail, ill, sickly, infirm, delicate, puny
❸ *The nobles plotted against the weak king.*
• timid, spineless, ineffective, powerless, useless

W
X
Y
Z

❹ *The film was fun, but the plot was a bit weak.*
• feeble, lame, unsatisfactory, unconvincing
❺ *He asked for a mug of weak tea.*
• watery, diluted, tasteless, thin
(informal) wishy-washy
OPPOSITE strong

weaken VERB
❶ *Too much water will weaken the flavour.*
• reduce, lessen, diminish, sap, undermine
❷ *The storm had weakened overnight.*
• decrease, decline, die down, fade, dwindle, ebb away, wane
OPPOSITE strengthen

weakness NOUN
❶ *He pointed out the weakness in their plan.*
• fault, flaw, defect, imperfection, weak point
❷ *Eve has a weakness for toffee apples.*
• liking, fondness
(informal) soft spot

wealth NOUN
The family had acquired its wealth from coal.
• fortune, money, riches, affluence, prosperity
OPPOSITE poverty
➤ **a wealth of**
There's a wealth of information on the Internet.
• lots of, plenty of, an abundance of, a profusion of

wealthy ADJECTIVE
They say that he comes from a very wealthy family.
• rich, well-off, affluent, prosperous, moneyed, well-to-do
(informal) flush, loaded
OPPOSITE poor

weapon NOUN

WORD WEB

Weapons in general are **weaponry** or **arms.**
A collection or store of weapons is an **armoury** or **arsenal.**

VARIOUS WEAPONS:

• bayonet, blowpipe, bomb, dagger, gun, hand grenade, harpoon, machine gun, missile, mortar, pistol, revolver, rifle, shell, sword, torpedo, truncheon
see also **sword**

SOME WEAPONS USED IN THE PAST:

• battering ram, battleaxe, blunderbuss, bow and arrow, cannon, catapult, crossbow, javelin, lance, longbow, musket, pike, spear, staff, tomahawk, trident

wear *VERB* wears, wearing, wore, worn
❶ *Can I wear my new dress to the party?*
• dress in, be dressed in, have on
❷ *The rug in the hallway is starting to wear.*
• fray, wear away, wear out
❸ *Those tyres have worn well.*
• last, endure, survive
➤ **to wear off**
The pain will wear off soon.
• die down, disappear, ease, fade, lessen, subside, weaken

weary *ADJECTIVE*
The children were weary after the long walk.
• tired, worn out, exhausted, fatigued, flagging
(informal) all in

weather *NOUN*

WORD WEB

The typical weather in a particular area is the **climate**.
A person who studies and forecasts the weather is a **meteorologist**.

SOME TYPES OF WEATHER:

• fog: mist, *(Scottish)* haar, haze, smog
• ice and snow: blizzard, frost, hail, ice, sleet, snowstorm

• light rain: drizzle, shower
• heavy rain: cloudburst, deluge, downpour, monsoon, torrent
• sun: drought, heatwave, sunshine
• storm: squall, tempest
• light wind: breeze, gust
• strong wind: cyclone, gale, hurricane, tornado, typhoon, whirlwind
see also **sky, wind**

WRITING TIPS

You can use these words to describe weather.

TO DESCRIBE CLOUDY WEATHER:

• dull, grey, overcast, sunless

TO DESCRIBE COLD WEATHER:

• arctic, bitter, chilly, frosty, icy, raw, snowy, wintry
(informal) nippy, perishing
It was one January morning, very early—a pinching, frosty morning—the cove all grey with hoar-frost.—TREASURE ISLAND, Robert Louis Stevenson

TO DESCRIBE SNOW:

• crisp, powdery, slushy

TO DESCRIBE HOT WEATHER:

• baking, humid, melting, roasting, sizzling, sticky, sultry, sweltering

TO DESCRIBE STORMY WEATHER:

• rough, squally, tempestuous, turbulent, violent, wild

THUNDER MAY:

• boom, crash, resound, roar, rumble

TO DESCRIBE SUNNY WEATHER:

• bright, cloudless, fair, fine, springlike, summery, sunny, sunshiny

a b c d e f g h i j k l m n o p q r s t u v w x y z

A B C D E F G H I J K L M N O P Q R S T U V W X Y Z

TO DESCRIBE WET WEATHER:

• damp, drizzly, raining cats and dogs, showery, spitting, torrential

RAIN MAY:

• lash or pelt down, pour, pour down, teem (*informal*) bucket, tip down
The sky rumbled loudly above them and the rain continued to pour down, bouncing on the lane and running into little streams.
—GOODNIGHT MISTER TOM, Michelle Magorian

TO DESCRIBE WINDY WEATHER:

• biting, blowy, blustery, breezy, gusty

WIND MAY:

• batter, blast, buffet, howl, moan, wail

weather VERB
Somehow, the tiny ship weathered the storm.
• survive, withstand, endure, come through

weave VERB
A messenger weaved his way through the crowd.
• wind, zigzag, twist and turn

web NOUN
A web of tunnels lay under the castle.
• net, network, mesh

wedding NOUN
She was a bridesmaid at her cousin's wedding.
• marriage
A formal word for a wedding is **nuptials**.

WORD WEB

PEOPLE WHO MAY BE INVOLVED IN A WEDDING:

• best man, bride, bridegroom, bridesmaid, groom, maid or matron of honour, minister, page, registrar, usher, wedding guests
see also **marry**

---

wedge VERB
The door was wedged open with an old shoe.
• jam, stick

weep VERB weeps, weeping, wept
Oisin buried his face in his hands and began to weep.
• cry, sob, shed tears
To weep noisily is to **bawl** or **blubber**.
To weep in an annoying way is to **snivel** or **whimper**.

weigh VERB
➤ **to weigh someone down**
❶ *Many troubles weighed him down.*
• bother, worry, trouble, distress, burden
❷ *He was weighed down with shopping.*
• load, burden, lumber
➤ **to weigh something up**
The detective weighed up the evidence.
• consider, assess, evaluate, examine, study, ponder

weight NOUN
Take care when lifting heavy weights.
• load, mass, burden
for units for measuring weight see **measurement**

weighty ADJECTIVE
❶ *She lifted a weighty volume off the shelf.*
• heavy, bulky, cumbersome
OPPOSITE **light**
❷ *They had weighty matters to discuss.*
• important, serious, grave, significant
OPPOSITES **unimportant, trivial**

weird ADJECTIVE
❶ *Weird noises have been heard in the tower at midnight.*
• eerie, ghostly, unearthly, mysterious, uncanny, unnatural
(*informal*) spooky, creepy
OPPOSITES **ordinary, natural**

470

❷ *My big sister has a **weird** taste in music.*
• strange, odd, peculiar, bizarre, curious, quirky, eccentric, outlandish, unconventional, unusual
(informal) wacky, way-out
OPPOSITE conventional

welcome *NOUN*
*The landlady gave us a friendly **welcome**.*
• greeting, reception

welcome *ADJECTIVE*
❶ *A cup of tea would be very **welcome**.*
• pleasant, pleasing, agreeable, appreciated, desirable, acceptable
OPPOSITES unwelcome, unacceptable
❷ *You're **welcome** to use my bike.*
• allowed, permitted, free
OPPOSITE forbidden

welcome *VERB*
❶ *An elderly butler **welcomed** us at the door.*
• greet, receive, meet, hail
❷ *We **welcome** suggestions from the public.*
• appreciate, accept, like, want

welfare *NOUN*
*Her only concern was the **welfare** of her children.*
• well-being, good, benefit, interests

well *ADVERB*
❶ *The whole team played **well** on Saturday.*
• ably, skilfully, expertly, effectively, efficiently, admirably, marvellously, wonderfully
OPPOSITE badly
❷ *It's cold outside, so you'd better wrap up **well**.*
• properly, suitably, correctly, thoroughly, carefully
❸ *I know her brother **well**.*
• closely, intimately, personally

well *ADJECTIVE*
*We felt really **well** after our holiday.*
• healthy, fit, strong, sound, robust, vigorous, lively, hearty
OPPOSITE ill

well-known *ADJECTIVE*
*A **well-known** athlete will open the new sports shop.*
• famous, celebrated, prominent, notable, renowned, distinguished, eminent
OPPOSITES unknown, obscure

went *past tense see* **go**

west *NOUN, ADJECTIVE, ADVERB*
The parts of a continent or country in the west are the **western** parts.
To travel towards the west is to travel **westward** or **westwards**.
A wind from the west is a **westerly** wind.

wet *ADJECTIVE*
❶ *Archie took off his **wet** clothes and had a hot bath.*
• damp, soaked, soaking, drenched, dripping, sopping, wringing wet
❷ *The pitch was too **wet** to play on.*
• waterlogged, saturated, sodden, soggy, dewy, muddy, boggy
❸ *Take care—the paint is still **wet**.*
• runny, sticky, tacky
❹ *It was cold and **wet** all afternoon.*
• rainy, showery, pouring, drizzly, misty
see also **weather**
OPPOSITE dry

wet *VERB* wets, wetting, wet or wetted
Wet the clay before you start to mould it.
• dampen, moisten, soak, water
OPPOSITE dry

wheel *NOUN*
A small wheel under a piece of furniture is a **caster**.

a
b
c
d
e
f
g
h
i
j
k
l
m
n
o
p
q
r
s
t
u
v
w
x
y
z

A
B
C
D
E
F
G
H
I
J
K
L
M
N
O
P
Q
R
S
T
U
V
W
X
Y
Z

The centre of a wheel is the **hub**.
The outer edge of a wheel is the rim.

wheel *VERB*
❶ *A pair of seagulls **wheeled** overhead.*
• circle, orbit
❷ *The column of soldiers **wheeled** to the right.*
• swing round, turn, veer, swerve

whiff *NOUN*
*I caught a **whiff** of coffee as I walked past the cafe.*
• smell, scent, aroma

while *NOUN*
*You may need to wait a **while** for the next train.*
• period, time, spell

whimper or **whine** *VERB*
*A dog **whimpered** in the corner of the room.*
• cry, moan

whip *VERB*
❶ *The jockey **whipped** his horse to make it go faster.*
• beat, hit, lash, flog, thrash
❷ ***Whip** the cream until it is thick.*
• beat, whisk

whirl *VERB*
*The snowflakes **whirled** in the icy wind.*
• turn, twirl, spin, twist, circle, spiral, reel, pirouette, revolve, rotate

whisk *VERB*
***Whisk** the egg yolks together in a bowl.*
• beat, whip, mix, stir

whisper *VERB*
*What are you two **whispering** about?*
• murmur, mutter, mumble
OPPOSITE shout

whistle *NOUN, VERB*
*for various sounds see **sound***

white *ADJECTIVE, NOUN*

WORD WEB

SOME SHADES OF WHITE:

• cream, ivory, off-white, platinum, silvery, snow-white
When coloured things become whiter they become **bleached** or **faded**.
When someone turns white with fear they **blanch** or **turn pale**.
Hair that is **hoary** is white with age.
Something which is rather white is **whitish**.
Common similes are as **white as a sheet**, as **white as chalk** and as **white as snow**.

whole *ADJECTIVE*
❶ *I haven't read the **whole** book yet.*
• complete, entire, full, total, unabbreviated
OPPOSITE incomplete
❷ *The dinosaur skeleton appears to be **whole**.*
• in one piece, intact, unbroken, undamaged, perfect
OPPOSITES broken, in pieces

wholesome *ADJECTIVE*
*Pets should be fed a **wholesome** diet.*
• healthy, nutritious, nourishing
OPPOSITE unhealthy

wholly *ADVERB*
*I'm not **wholly** convinced by this story.*
• completely, totally, fully, entirely, utterly, thoroughly
OPPOSITE partly

wicked *ADJECTIVE*
❶ *Snow White had a **wicked** stepmother.*
• evil, cruel, vicious, villainous, detestable, mean, corrupt, immoral, sinful, foul, vile
OPPOSITES good, virtuous
❷ *They hatched a **wicked** scheme to take over the world.*

• evil, fiendish, malicious, malevolent, diabolical, monstrous, deplorable, dreadful, shameful
❸ *The goblin had a wicked grin on his face.*
• mischievous, playful, impish, naughty

wide *ADJECTIVE*
❶ *The hotel is close to a wide sandy beach.*
• broad, expansive, extensive, large, spacious
OPPOSITE narrow
❷ *She has a wide knowledge of classical music.*
• comprehensive, vast, wide-ranging, encyclopedic
OPPOSITE limited

widely *ADVERB*
The legend of King Arthur is widely known.
• commonly, everywhere, far and wide

widespread *ADJECTIVE*
There is widespread interest in the new engine design.
• general, extensive, universal, wholesale
Something which spreads over the whole world is global or worldwide.
OPPOSITE uncommon

width *NOUN*
The room is about eight feet in width.
• breadth
The distance across a circle is its diameter.

wield *VERB*
The lumberjack was wielding his axe.
• brandish, flourish, hold, use

wife *NOUN*
Katherine is Mr Gray's second wife.
Another word for a person's wife or husband is spouse.

wild *ADJECTIVE*
❶ *I don't like seeing wild animals in captivity.*
• undomesticated, untamed
OPPOSITE tame
❷ *The hedgerow was full of wild flowers.*
• natural, uncultivated
OPPOSITE cultivated
❸ *To the west is a wild and mountainous region.*
• rough, rugged, uncultivated, uninhabited, desolate
OPPOSITE cultivated
❹ *The crowd was wild with excitement.*
• riotous, rowdy, disorderly, unruly, boisterous, excited, noisy, uncontrollable, hysterical
OPPOSITES calm, restrained
❺ *The weather looked wild outside.*
• blustery, windy, gusty, stormy, turbulent, tempestuous
OPPOSITE calm

wilful *ADJECTIVE*
❶ *He was very wilful as a child.*
• obstinate, stubborn, strong-willed, pig-headed
❷ *There is a fine for wilful damage to trees.*
• deliberate, intentional, planned, conscious

will *NOUN*
They seem to have lost the will to win.
• desire, wish, determination, resolution, willpower, resolve, purpose

willing *ADJECTIVE*
❶ *She is always willing to help.*
• eager, happy, pleased, ready, prepared
OPPOSITE unwilling
❷ *I need a couple of willing volunteers.*
• enthusiastic, helpful, cooperative, obliging

wilt *VERB*
The flowers wilted in the heat.
• become limp, droop, flop, sag, fade, shrivel, wither
OPPOSITE flourish

a b c d e f g h i j k l m n o p q r s t u v w x y z

wily *ADJECTIVE*
The player was outwitted by his wily opponent.
• clever, crafty, cunning, shrewd, scheming, artful, sly, devious

win *VERB* wins, winning, won
❶ *Who do you think will win?*
• come first, be victorious, succeed, triumph, prevail
To win against someone is also to **beat, conquer, defeat** or **overcome** them.
OPPOSITE lose
❷ *She won first prize in the poetry competition.*
• get, receive, gain, obtain, secure
(informal) pick up, walk away with

wind *NOUN (rhymes with tinned)*
A gentle wind is a **breath, breeze** or **draught**.
A violent wind is a **cyclone, gale, hurricane** or **tornado**.
A sudden unexpected wind is a **blast, gust, puff** or **squall**.
see also **weather**
for wind instruments see **music**

wind *VERB (rhymes with find)* winds, winding, wound
❶ *He wound the wool into a ball.*
• coil, loop, roll, turn, curl
❷ *The road winds up the hill.*
• bend, curve, twist and turn, zigzag, meander

window *NOUN*
The glass in a window is a **pane**.
A semicircular window above a door is a **fanlight**.
A window in a roof is a **skylight**.
A decorative window with panels of coloured glass is a **stained-glass window**.
A person whose job is to fit glass in windows is a **glazier**.

windy *ADJECTIVE*
❶ *It was a cold, windy day.*
• breezy, blustery, gusty, squally, stormy
OPPOSITE calm
❷ *This spot is too windy for a picnic.*
• windswept, exposed, draughty
OPPOSITE sheltered

wink *VERB*
❶ *My friend winked at me and smiled.*
To shut and open both eyes quickly is to **blink**.
❷ *The lights winked on and off.*
• flash, flicker, sparkle, twinkle

winner *NOUN*
The winner was presented with a silver cup.
• victor, prizewinner, champion, conqueror
OPPOSITE loser

winning *ADJECTIVE*
The winning team went up to receive their medals.
• victorious, triumphant, conquering, successful, top-scoring, champion
OPPOSITE losing

wintry *ADJECTIVE*
It was a grey, wintry day.
• cold, frosty, freezing, bitter, icy, snowy

wipe *VERB*
I wiped the table with a cloth.
• rub, clean, polish, mop, swab, sponge
➤ **to wipe something out**
Pompeii was wiped out by the eruption of Mount Vesuvius.
• destroy, annihilate, exterminate, get rid of

wire *NOUN*
Several wires protruded from the robot's head.
• cable, lead, flex
A system of wires is **wiring**.

wisdom *NOUN*
She's a woman of great wisdom.
• sense, judgement, understanding, intelligence, common sense, good sense, insight, reason

A B C D E F G H I J K L M N O P Q R S T U V W X Y Z

wise *ADJECTIVE*
❶ *The soothsayer was very old and wise.*
• sensible, reasonable, intelligent, perceptive, knowledgeable, rational, thoughtful
❷ *I think you made a wise decision.*
• good, right, proper, sound, fair, just, appropriate
OPPOSITE foolish

wish *NOUN*
Her dearest wish was to travel to the Amazon.
• desire, want, longing, yearning, hankering, craving, urge, fancy, hope, ambition
(informal) yen

wish *VERB*
I wish that everyone would sit still for a minute!
If you wish something would happen, you can say that you **want** or **would like** it to happen.

➤ **to wish for**
If you had three wishes, what would you wish for?
• desire, want, crave, fancy, long for, yearn for, hanker after

wisp *NOUN*
She blew a wisp of hair away from her face.
• shred, strand

wistful *ADJECTIVE*
He gave a wistful sigh as he read the letter.
• sad, melancholy, thoughtful, pensive

wit *NOUN*
❶ *Ogres are creatures with very little wit.*
• intelligence, cleverness, brains, sharpness, understanding
❷ *The film script sparkled with wit.*
• humour, comedy, jokes
❸ *Charlie is regarded as the class wit.*
• joker, comedian, comic

witch and **witchcraft** *NOUN*
see **magic**

withdraw *VERB* withdraws, withdrawing, withdrew, withdrawn
❶ *The general withdrew his troops.*
• call back, recall
OPPOSITE send in
❷ *She withdrew her offer of help.*
• take back, cancel, retract
OPPOSITES make, present
❸ *The wolves withdrew into the forest.*
• retire, retreat, draw back, fall back, back away
OPPOSITE advance
❹ *He withdrew his hands from his pockets.*
• draw back, pull back, take away, remove
OPPOSITES put out, extend
❺ *Some competitors withdrew at the last minute.*
• pull out, back out, drop out
OPPOSITE enter

wither *VERB*
The flowers had withered and died.
• shrivel, dry up, shrink, wilt, droop, sag, flop
OPPOSITE flourish

withhold *VERB* withholds, withholding, withheld
The police believe they are withholding information.
• hold back, keep back, refuse
OPPOSITE grant

withstand *VERB* withstands, withstanding, withstood
Penguins can withstand extreme cold.
• bear, endure, stand up to, tolerate, cope with, survive, resist, weather

witness *NOUN*
A witness said that the car was going too fast.
• bystander, observer, onlooker, eyewitness, spectator

a b c d e f g h i j k l m n o p q r s t u v **w** x y z

witty *ADJECTIVE*
He gave a witty account of his schooldays.
• humorous, amusing, comic, funny
OPPOSITE dull

wizard *NOUN*
❶ *The wizard cast a spell over the whole palace.*
• magician, sorcerer, enchanter
see also **magic**
❷ *My sister is a wizard with computers.*
• expert, specialist, genius
(informal) **whizz**

wobble *VERB*
❶ *The cyclist wobbled all over the road.*
• sway, totter, teeter, waver, rock
❷ *The jelly wobbled as I carried the plate.*
• shake, tremble, quake, quiver, vibrate

wobbly *ADJECTIVE*
❶ *The baby giraffe was a bit wobbly on its legs.*
• shaky, tottering, unsteady
❷ *This chair is a bit wobbly.*
• loose, rickety, rocky, unstable, unsafe
OPPOSITE steady

woman *NOUN*
A polite word for a woman is **lady**.
A married woman is a **wife**.
A woman who has children is a **mother**.
An old word for an unmarried woman is a **spinster**.
A woman whose husband has died is a **widow**.
A woman on her wedding day is a **bride**.
A woman who is engaged to be married is a **fiancée**.
Words for a young woman are **girl** and **lass**.
Old words for a young woman are **maid** and **maiden**.

won *past tense see* **win**

wonder *NOUN*
❶ *The sight of the Taj Mahal filled them with wonder.*
• admiration, awe, reverence, amazement, astonishment

❷ *It's a wonder that he is still alive.*
• marvel, miracle

wonder *VERB*
I wonder why she left in such a hurry.
• be curious about, ask yourself, ponder, think about
➤ **to wonder at**
People wondered at the skill of the acrobats.
• marvel at, admire, be amazed by, be astonished by

wonderful *ADJECTIVE*
❶ *It's wonderful what computers can do these days.*
• amazing, astonishing, astounding, incredible, remarkable, extraordinary, marvellous, miraculous, phenomenal
❷ *We had a wonderful time at the party.*
• excellent, splendid, superb, delightful
(informal) brilliant, fantastic, terrific, fabulous, super, great
OPPOSITE ordinary

wood *NOUN*
❶ *All the furniture in the room was made of wood.*
• timber, lumber, planks, logs
❷ *We followed a nature trail through the wood.*
• woodland, woods, forest, trees
see also **tree**

wood *NOUN*

WORD WEB
KINDS OF WOOD USED TO MAKE THINGS:

• ash, balsa, beech, cedar, chestnut, ebony, elm, lime, mahogany, oak, pine, rosewood, sandalwood, spruce, teak, walnut
A person who makes things from wood is a **carpenter** or **woodcarver**.
A person whose job is to cut down trees for wood is a **lumberjack**.

wooden *ADJECTIVE*
❶ *They sat down on a wooden bench.*
• wood, timber
❷ *The acting was a bit wooden at times.*
• stiff, lifeless, awkward, unnatural, unemotional, expressionless

woolly *ADJECTIVE*
❶ *He wore a woolly hat with a bobble on top.*
• wool, woollen
Clothes made of wool, such as hats and scarves, are woollens.
❷ *Mammoths were like elephants with woolly coats.*
• thick, fleecy, furry, downy, fuzzy, hairy, shaggy, soft, cuddly
❸ *Some parts of the plot were rather woolly.*
• vague, confused, unclear, unfocused, hazy, indefinite, uncertain

word *NOUN*
❶ *What's the French word for 'birthday'?*
• expression, term
All the words you know are your vocabulary.
❷ *You gave me your word.*
• promise, assurance, guarantee, pledge, vow
❸ *There has been no word from him for several weeks.*
• news, message, information

word *VERB*
I spent ages trying to word the letter correctly.
• express, phrase, put into words
The way that you word something is the wording or phrasing.

wore *past tense see* **wear**

work *NOUN*
❶ *Digging the garden involves a lot of hard work.*
• effort, labour, toil, exertion
❷ *Do you have any work to do this weekend?*
• task, assignment, chore, job, homework, housework
❸ *What kind of work does she do?*

• occupation, employment, job, profession, business, trade, vocation
for various kinds of work see **job**

work *VERB*
❶ *She's been working in the garden all day.*
• be busy, exert yourself, labour, toil, slave
❷ *He works in the bookshop on Saturdays.*
• be employed, have a job, go to work
❸ *My watch isn't working.*
• function, go, operate
❹ *Is your new phone easy to work?*
• operate, run, use, control, handle
➤ **to work out**
Things didn't quite work out as planned.
• turn out, happen, emerge, develop
➤ **to work something out**
Can anyone work out this sum?
• answer, calculate, solve, explain, figure out

worker *NOUN*
The biscuit factory employs around 200 workers.
• employee
All the workers in a business or factory are the staff or workforce.
for people who do specific jobs see **job**

world *NOUN*
❶ *Antarctica is a remote part of the world.*
• earth, globe
❷ *Scientists are searching for life on other worlds.*
• planet

worried *ADJECTIVE*
You look worried. Is something the matter?
• anxious, troubled, uneasy, distressed, disturbed, upset, apprehensive, concerned, bothered, tense, strained, nervous
OPPOSITE relaxed

worry *VERB*
❶ *There's no need to worry.*
• be anxious, be troubled, be disturbed, brood, fret

a
b
c
d
e
f
g
h
i
j
k
l
m
n
o
p
q
r
s
t
u
v
w
x
y
z

❷ *It worried her that he hadn't replied to her letter.*
• trouble, distress, upset, concern, disturb
❸ *Don't worry her now—she's busy.*
• bother, annoy, disturb, pester, harass
(informal) badger, bug

worry NOUN
❶ *He's been a constant source of worry to her.*
• anxiety, distress, uneasiness, vexation
❷ *I don't want to add to your worries.*
• trouble, concern, burden, care, problem

worsen VERB
❶ *Moving the patient may worsen the pain.*
• make worse, aggravate
❷ *The weather had worsened overnight.*
• get worse, deteriorate, degenerate
OPPOSITE improve

worship VERB
❶ *Ancient Egyptians worshipped the sun god, Ra.*
• pray to, glorify, praise
for places where people worship see **building**
❷ *She adores her sons and they worship her.*
• adore, be devoted to, look up to, love, revere, idolize

worth NOUN
This ring was once an object of great worth.
• value, merit, quality, significance, importance

worthless ADJECTIVE
It's nothing but a worthless piece of junk.
• useless, unusable, valueless
(informal) trashy
OPPOSITE valuable

worthwhile ADJECTIVE
It may be worthwhile to get a second opinion.
• helpful, useful, valuable, beneficial, profitable
OPPOSITE useless

worthy ADJECTIVE
They gave the money to a worthy cause.
• good, worthwhile, deserving, praiseworthy, admirable, commendable, respectable
OPPOSITE unworthy

wound *(rhymes with* **sound***) past tense see* **wind** VERB

wound NOUN *(say* woond*)*
He is being treated in hospital for a head wound.
• injury, cut, gash, graze, scratch, sore
for other types of wound see **injury**
wound VERB *(say* woond*)*
The fox was wounded in the leg and bleeding.
• injure, hurt, harm

wrap VERB
❶ *She wrapped the presents in shiny gold paper.*
• cover, pack, enclose, enfold, swathe
To wrap water pipes is to **insulate** or **lag** them.
❷ *The mountain was wrapped in mist.*
• cloak, envelop, shroud, surround, hide, conceal, wreathe

wreathe VERB
The tree was wreathed in fairy lights.
• encircle, festoon, surround, adorn, decorate

wreck VERB
❶ *His bicycle was wrecked in the accident.*
• demolish, destroy, crush, smash, shatter, crumple
❷ *The injury wrecked her chances of becoming a professional skier.*
• ruin, spoil

wreckage NOUN
Divers have discovered the wreckage of an old ship.
• debris, fragments, pieces, remains
The wreckage of a building is **rubble** or **ruins**.

wrench VERB
The giant wrenched the door off its hinges.
• pull, tug, prise, jerk, twist, force
(informal) yank

wrestle VERB
He wrestled with the thief as he tried to escape.
• struggle, tussle, grapple

wretched ADJECTIVE
❶ *I lay in bed with flu feeling wretched.*
• miserable, unhappy, woeful, pitiful, unfortunate
❷ *The wretched computer has frozen again!*
• annoying, maddening, exasperating, useless

wriggle VERB
The prisoner managed to wriggle out of his bonds.
• twist, writhe, squirm, worm your way

wring VERB wrings, wringing, wrung
❶ *She wrung the water out of her skirt.*
• press, squeeze, twist
❷ *He wrung her hand enthusiastically.*
• shake, clasp, grip, wrench
➤ **wringing wet**
Your socks are wringing wet!
• soaked, drenched, dripping, sopping, saturated

wrinkle NOUN
The old hag's face was covered in wrinkles.
• crease, fold, furrow, line, ridge, crinkle, pucker, pleat
A small hollow on someone's skin is a **dimple**.

wrinkle VERB
The creature wrinkled its nose and sniffed.
• pucker up, crease, crinkle, crumple, fold
OPPOSITE smooth

write VERB writes, writing, wrote, written
❶ *My granny wrote a diary when she was a girl.*
• compile, compose, draw up, set down, pen

To write letters or emails to people is to **correspond** with them.
To write a rough version of a story is to **draft** it.
❷ *He wrote his address on the back of an envelope.*
• jot down, note, print, scrawl, scribble
To write on a document or surface is to **inscribe** it.
To write your signature on something is to **autograph** it.

writer NOUN
A person who writes books is an **author**.
A person who writes novels is a **novelist**.
A person who writes plays is a **dramatist** or **playwright**.
A person who writes scripts for films or television is a **scriptwriter** or **screenwriter**.
A person who writes poetry is a **poet**.
A person who writes about someone else's life is a **biographer**.
A person who writes for newspapers is a **correspondent**, **journalist** or **reporter**.
A person who writes music is a **composer**.
A person who writes a blog is a **blogger**.

writhe VERB
The wounded man was writhing in agony.
• thrash about, twist, squirm, wriggle

writing NOUN
❶ *Can you read the writing on the envelope?*
• handwriting
Untidy writing is a **scrawl** or **scribble**.
The art of beautiful handwriting is **calligraphy**.
❷ *The writing on the stone was very faint.*
• inscription
❸ *(often plural) She introduced me to the writings of Roald Dahl.*
• literature, works

a b c d e f g h i j k l m n o p q r s t u v **w** x y z

A
B
C
D
E
F
G
H
I
J
K
L
M
N
O
P
Q
R
S
T
U
V
W
X
Y
Z

WORD WEB

VARIOUS FORMS OF WRITING AND LITERATURE:

• autobiography, biography, blog, children's literature, classic, comedy, crime or detective story, diary, drama or play, essay, fable, fairy story or fairy tale, fantasy, fiction, film or TV script, folk tale, ghost story, historical fiction, history, journalism, legend, letters or correspondence, lyrics, myth, newspaper article, non-fiction, novel, parody, philosophy, poetry or verse, prose, romance, saga, satire, science fiction or (informal) sci-fi, script, screenplay, spy story, thriller, tragedy, travel writing, western

I'm not really sure what makes a book a 'classic' to begin with, but I think it has to be at least fifty years old and some person or animal has to die at the end.—DIARY OF A WIMPY KID: DOG DAYS, Jeff Kinney

WRITING TIPS

You can use these words to describe a piece of writing.

TO DESCRIBE THE LANGUAGE OR STYLE IN A POSITIVE WAY:

• elegant, literary, ornate, poetic; colloquial, informal, slangy; formal, old-fashioned; hard-boiled, sparse
The author uses poetic words, like 'cornucopia'.

TO DESCRIBE THE LANGUAGE OR STYLE IN A NEGATIVE WAY:

• banal, dry, insipid, lacklustre, monotonous, plodding, prosaic

TO DESCRIBE A CHARACTER:

• hero, heroine, protagonist, narrator, villain; believable, convincing, lifelike, realistic, strong, well-drawn; feeble, thin, unbelievable, unconvincing, weak

Mr Scruggs is a thoroughly convincing villain.

TO DESCRIBE THE SETTING:

• atmospheric, moody; alien, exotic, fanciful, fantastic, fictitious, made-up, imaginary, strange, unfamiliar; eerie, spooky, weird; accurate, authentic, familiar, recognizable, true to life
The story is set on an imaginary planet.

TO DESCRIBE THE STORYLINE OR PLOT IN A POSITIVE WAY:

• action-packed, dramatic, dynamic, engrossing, entertaining, eventful, fast-paced, gripping, hair-raising, intriguing, mind-boggling, page-turning, rip-roaring, spellbinding, thrilling; creative, imaginative, moving, thought-provoking, well-crafted; amusing, diverting, entertaining, hilarious, humorous; romantic, sentimental
Finn's adventures are dramatic and at times moving.

TO DESCRIBE THE STORYLINE OR PLOT IN A NEGATIVE WAY:

• dull, insipid, uneventful, unimaginative; absurd, far-fetched, ludicrous, ridiculous, unbelievable, unlikely

TO DESCRIBE THE ENDING IN A POSITIVE WAY:

• cliffhanger, climax, conclusion, finale; electrifying, nail-biting, sensational, spectacular, surprising, unexpected
The book keeps you guessing until the sensational finale.

TO DESCRIBE THE ENDING IN A NEGATIVE WAY:

• abrupt, banal, clichéd, predicable, trite, unsatisfying

wrong *ADJECTIVE*
❶ *It was **wrong** to take the book without asking.*
• bad, dishonest, irresponsible, immoral, sinful, wicked, criminal, unfair, unjust
❷ *His calculations were all **wrong**.*
• incorrect, mistaken, inaccurate
❸ *Did I say the **wrong** thing?*
• inappropriate, unsuitable, improper
❹ *There's something **wrong** with the TV.*
• faulty, defective, not working, out of order
OPPOSITE right

➤ **to go wrong**
*The professor's plan began to **go wrong**.*
• fail, backfire
(informal) flop, go pear-shaped
succeed

wrote *past tense see* **write**

yacht *NOUN*
for types of boat or ship see **boat**

yard *NOUN*
*A solitary tree stood in the middle of the **yard**.*
• court, courtyard, enclosure

yearly *ADJECTIVE*
*I'm due for my **yearly** dental check-up.*
• annual

yearn *VERB*
➤ **to yearn for something**
*She **yearned for** some peace and quiet.*
• want, wish for, desire, long for, pine for
(informal) be dying for

yell *VERB*
*I **yelled** to attract their attention.*
• call out, cry out, shout, roar, bawl, bellow
yell *NOUN*
*The pirates gave a bloodcurdling **yell**.*
• cry, roar, bellow

yellow *ADJECTIVE, NOUN*

WORD WEB

SOME SHADES OF YELLOW:

• amber, chrome yellow, cream, gold, golden, lemon, sandy, tawny
Something which is rather yellow is yellowish.

yelp *VERB*
for sounds made by animals see **animal**

yield *VERB*
❶ *In the end, her parents **yielded** and let her go out.*
• give in, give way, concede, surrender, admit defeat, submit, comply

a
b
c
d
e
f
g
h
i
j
k
l
m
n
o
p
q
r
s
t
u
v
w
x
y
z

A
B
C
D
E
F
G
H
I
J
K
L
M
N
O
P
Q
R
S
T
U
V
W
X
Y
Z

❷ *The apple trees yielded a good crop of fruit.*
• bear, grow, produce, supply, generate

yield NOUN
The farmers got a good yield from the orchard this year.
• crop, harvest, produce, return

young ADJECTIVE
❶ *A lot of young people went to the concert.*
• youthful, juvenile
(OPPOSITES) older, mature
❷ *I think this book is a bit young for you.*
• childish, babyish, immature, infantile
(OPPOSITES) adult, grown-up
A young person is a **child** or **youngster**.
A young adult is an **adolescent** or **youth**.
A very young child is a **baby** or **infant**.
A young bird is a **chick, fledgling** or **nestling**.
Young fish are **fry**.
A young plant is a **cutting** or **seedling**.
A young tree is a **sapling**.
for other young animals and birds see **animal, bird**

young PLURAL NOUN
The mother bird returned to feed her young.
• offspring, children, young ones, family
A family of young birds is a **brood**.
A family of young cats or dogs is a **litter**.

youth NOUN
❶ *In his youth, he had been a keen hockey player.*
• childhood, boyhood or girlhood, adolescence, teens
❷ *The fight was started by a group of youths.*
• adolescent, youngster, juvenile, teenager, young adult

youthful ADJECTIVE
The magic potion will keep you eternally youthful.
• young, youngish, vigorous, sprightly, young-looking

Zz

zero NOUN
Four minus four makes zero.
• nothing, nought
A score of zero in football is **nil**; in cricket it is a **duck**, and in tennis it is **love**.

zest NOUN
Our family has a great zest for life.
• enthusiasm, eagerness, enjoyment

zigzag VERB
The road zigzags up the hill.
• wind, twist, meander

zodiac NOUN

WORD WEB

THE SIGNS OF THE ZODIAC ARE:

• **Aquarius** (or the Water Carrier), **Aries** (or the Ram), **Cancer** (or the Crab), **Capricorn** (or the Goat), **Gemini** (or the Twins), **Leo** (or the Lion), **Libra** (or the Scales), **Pisces** (or the Fish), **Sagittarius** (or the Archer), **Scorpio** (or the Scorpion), **Taurus** (or the Bull), **Virgo** (or the Virgin)

---

zone NOUN
No-one may enter the forbidden zone.
• area, district, region, sector, locality, neighbourhood, territory, vicinity

zoo NOUN
Which is your favourite animal in the zoo?
• menagerie, safari park, wildlife reserve, nature reserve, zoological gardens
for animals you might see in a zoo see **animal**

Become a
Word Explorer

Contents

Explore your thesaurus

You don't need a map and a compass to be an explorer. You can explore the world of **words** equipped with your thesaurus.

You can:

explore the differences between **synonyms**

explore effects like **simile** and **alliteration**

explore ways to **build words**

explore ideas to improve your **stories**

explore **overused words** and how to choose a better word

learn how to be a **writer**

explore other types of writing such as **non-fiction** and **writing letters**

and *even* explore some **punctuation**

Use the following pages to help you **explore** your creative adventure.

Synonyms

The main job of a thesaurus is to list **synonyms**. Synonyms are words which mean the same—or nearly the same—as each other, such as *big* and *huge*, or *horrible* and *nasty*.

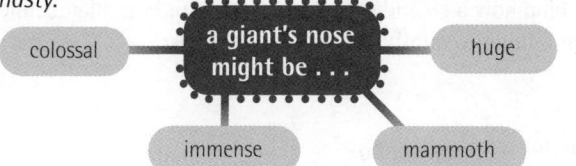

◄ You can swap these words around and it makes little difference to the meaning.

However, some synonyms are more limited and only fit certain contexts, for example:

- formal or informal synonyms (*yummy* is an informal synonym of *delicious*)
- synonyms which are special cases (*trunk* and *casket* are special types of box)

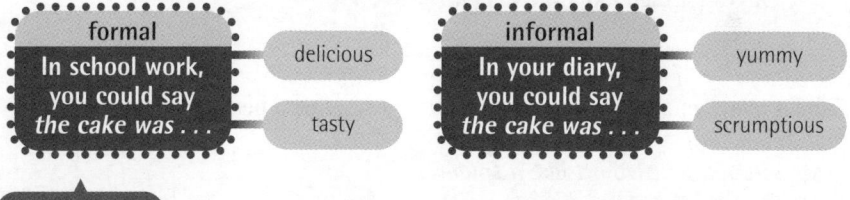

EXPLORER TIP

You can easily spot **special synonyms**, look for the labels *formal, informal* or *old use*. They are listed and defined in a separate paragraph.

Overused words

Words like *bad, big* and *nice* are very useful, but they can make your writing boring if you use them too often, we call these **overused words**.

TOP TIP You don't need to avoid overused words completely! If you choose a synonym which is more unusual and detailed, it will make your writing more interesting.

For example:

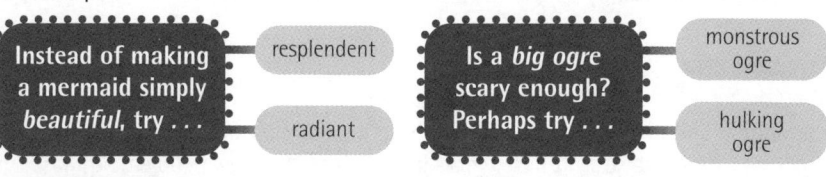

EXPLORER TIP

You can easily spot **OVERUSED WORDS** in the thesaurus, as they have their own panels. There is a complete list of **OVERUSED WORDS** at the front of the thesaurus.

Similes

This thesaurus notes common **similes** like *as fit as a fiddle*.
But you can also make up your own, using your thesaurus for ideas.

Similes are useful for describing how a character looks or sounds, or how a landscape appears. Similes compare one thing to another using the words 'like' or 'as'.

For example:

*Miss Mullins had a face **like a soggy sponge**.*

*The dragon's eyes were **as dark as a moonless night**.*

*The waves crashed **like cymbals** on the shore.*

Similes allow you to mix and match. You can describe a person like an animal:

*Mr Scruggs scuttled off **like a spider**.*

Or an animal can be described like a thing:

*The snake sprang up **like a jack-in-the-box**.*

Similes can also make your writing individual and create wonderful pictures in the reader's mind. Lots of people may describe the road as *bumpy*, but you might be the only person to say:

The road is *as bumpy as the back of a crocodile*.

EXPLORER TIP

The **animal** and **bird** panels list ways to describe animals and birds.
However, you can also use these words in similes to describe people or things.

For example:

He was *as spiky as a stegosaur*.

The dress was *as fluffy as a puffling*.

Idioms

An **idiom** is a phrase that doesn't mean exactly the same as the words in it. For example, *to be in hot water* is an idiom which means 'to be in trouble' (not to be in actual hot water).

Idioms can make your writing more lively. But be careful: your writing can look clichéd if you use too many!

For example, a character in your story has just seen a ghost. How do you describe their reaction?

> *Anita **blanched** and stood **rooted to the spot**.*

> *She **had goosebumps** all over and began to **tremble like a leaf**.*

EXPLORER TIP

You will find suggestions for idioms and other words to use in the **WRITING TIPS** panels for **afraid, angry** and **surprised**.

Special names

A thesaurus can help you find the **special names** for certain things, such as the special names for young animals or birds, or for animal homes. Using these words can make your writing more accurate and interesting.

Special names for groups of people, animals or things are called **collective nouns**. Instead of simply *a group of elephants* or *a group of whales*, you can say *a herd of elephants* or *a pod of whales*.

Here are some more:

> *There was a **vixen** and three fox **cubs** in the **earth**.*

> *We saw a **colony** of puffins perched on the cliffs.*

You can also make up your own collective nouns. You could say *a flutter of butterflies* or *a rumble of rhinoceroses*!

EXPLORER TIP

You will find special names and collective nouns listed in the **WORD WEB** panels for **animal, bird** and **group**.

Sound effects

Some words come with their own sound effects. These are called **onomatopoeic** words, and they sound like the thing they are describing. Using a sound-effect word can give an extra *zing* to your writing.

For example, you are describing footsteps on a path:

- On a dry, stony path, the footsteps might *crunch*, but on a muddy path, they would *squelch*.

- A dog's paws might *patter* on the path, whereas a giant's feet would *thud*.

EXPLORER TIP

You will find lots of sound-effect words in the **WORD WEB** panel for **sound**.

Another sound effect that you can create yourself is **alliteration**, which means using two or more words which start with the same sound. This is especially useful in poetry, but can also be effective in story writing.

They went to sea in a Sieve, they did,
In a Sieve they went to sea.
—THE JUMBLIES, Edward Lear

For example, if you are writing a poem about food, you could use alliteration to describe it as:

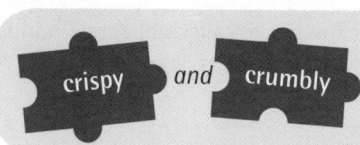

However, if the food is disgusting, you might describe it as:

EXPLORER TIP

You will find words to describe both delicious and disgusting food in the **WRITING TIPS** panel for **food**.

Word building

You can build up words by adding **suffixes** to the end of root words. Look at how the suffixes below can be added to root words to create interesting descriptions.

Try building a new word by starting with a word you know, or a word you have found in the thesaurus, and adding one of these suffixes (endings) to it:

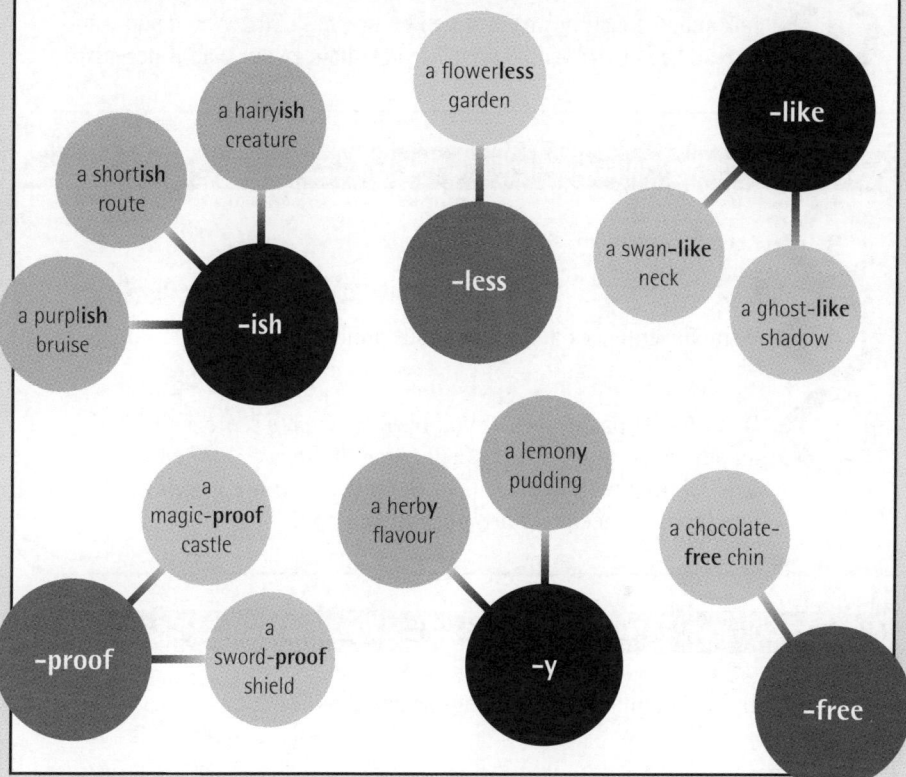

You can also build **compound words** by joining two whole words together. Here are a few suggestions for words to use, but you can also try out your own:

-feeling *rough-feeling* skin
-looking *scary-looking* teeth
-smelling a *musty-smelling* room
-sounding an *eerie-sounding* wail

For example, if you are describing a dragon, you could give it:

lidless eyes, *bat-like* wings, **sour-smelling** breath and **fire-emitting** nostrils.

Writing stories

1 Plan your story. Think about the setting, the characters and the action (what happens).

2 Talk about the story with a friend before you write. Would you want to read this story? Would your friend? Change your plan if necessary.

While you are writing:

3 Keep to your plan.

4 Write in sentences and think about punctuation.

5 Don't forget paragraphs. If you need to begin a sentence with an adverbial clause of time (e.g. *Later that day . . . When it was all over . . .*) or place (e.g. *Outside . . . In the woods . . .*) you probably need to start a new paragraph.

After you have written the first draft:

6 Use a dictionary to check your spelling.

7 Use a thesaurus to make sure you have chosen the best words.

8 If you have included overused words (see the list on page vii), try to replace them with other words.

9 Can you add more details about your characters to increase your reader's interest in them?

10 Can you add more information about your setting to help your reader 'see' it in their mind?

Creating a setting—**Place**

The first thing to decide is **where** your story takes place.

- Does the action happen *at sea* or *on a desert island*?
- Is it set in an *ancient castle* or in *outer space*?

Once you have a general setting, you can draw attention to details such as trees or buildings, animals or birds, or even mythological creatures.

EXPLORER TIP

Look up these entries and panels to help you describe your setting:
cave desert island jungle landscape mountain planet polar river sea seashore seaside pace

To describe features of your setting, look up words such as **boat, castle, ice** and **tree**.

Creating a setting—**Time**

You also need to tell your readers **when** your story takes place.

- Does it take place in *late spring* or in *early autumn*?
- Does it begin at *dusk* or at *dawn*?
- Is it set in the *present* day, in *ancient* times, or even in the *future*?

EXPLORER TIP

Try looking up the entries for **day, night, season** and **time** for ideas.

Creating a setting—**Atmosphere and weather**

Now you can start to think about the **atmosphere** and mood. This is often created through descriptions of **weather**.

- Is the sky *cloudy* or *cloudless*?
- Is the wind *blustery* or *breezy*?
- Is a storm *brewing*?

EXPLORER TIP

Look up the entries for **ice, rain, sky, snow, sun** and **wind** to help you.

You can also look up **hot** and **cold** for more ways to describe temperature.

Describing a character

Describing how your **characters** look, sound (and even smell!) will make them more believable and vivid. Think about the details which make people different from each other.

- Are your characters *lean* and *lanky*, or *short* and *squat*?
- Is their hair *straight* and *stringy*, or *fine* and *frizzy*?
- Are they more likely to *scowl* and *grimace*, or to *beam*?

EXPLORER TIP

Look up the entries for **body, expression, eye, face, hair, nose** and **voice** to help you describe your characters.

You can also look up the **clothes** panel for things that your characters might wear.

Typical characters

Some types of story require certain **characters**. For example, a detective story needs a detective, and a pirate story needs at least one pirate. A number of the **WORD WEB** panels focus on typical story characters such as these. They are rather like dressing-up boxes with words (rather than costumes) with which to dress up your characters.

- **detective** lists things a detective might look for (*fingerprints, suspect*)
- **astronaut** lists places an astronaut might visit (*moonbase, spacelab*)

These **WORD WEB** panels don't list everything a detective or astronaut might do, but they do list typical things and can give you ideas for writing your own mystery story or space story.

EXPLORER TIP

Look up the entries for **astronaut, criminal, detective, explorer, fairy, ghost, knight, pirate, robot, spy** and **superhero** to help you create those characters.

The **magic** panel also has suggestions for **witches** and **wizards**.

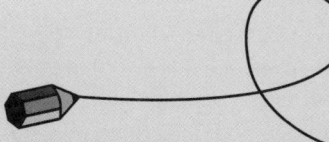

Imaginary creatures

If your **characters** are not human, it is even more important to let your readers know how they look and sound. Not all aliens and ogres are alike, so be sure to describe your imaginary creatures in detail.

You can make an imaginary monster vivid by giving it body parts of real animals, for example the head of a snake, the wings of a bat and the legs of a beetle.

If you are writing a space story, how might you describe your alien creatures?

*The aliens had **insect-like bodies**, with **spindly legs** and **spiky antennae**.*

*Their **scaly backs** were patterned with **purple blotches**.*

*They spoke to each other in **high-pitched screeches**.*

Describing action

When you describe what your characters do and how they **act**, try to be specific.

- How do they move? Do they *scurry* quickly, *glide* gracefully, or *slink* stealthily?
- Do they *tap* gently on a door, or *pound* it insistently?
- Do they *nibble* their food politely, or *gobble* it greedily?

There is nothing wrong with using simple words like *move, hit* and *eat*. But your writing will be more interesting if you sometimes use more specific verbs.

If you are writing a detective story, how might your main character act?

*Inspector Giles **paced** slowly round the room, **twitching** his moustache. He **inspected** the broken window and **peered** closely at the stains on the carpet.*

EXPLORER TIP

Look up the entries for **eat, drink, look, move** and **walk** to help you describe action.

You will find even more action words in the entries for **hit** and **run**.

Look up the **animal** or **bird** panels for ways that creatures might move.

Writing dialogue

The words that your characters say in the story is the **dialogue**.

When you are writing dialogue, try not to use the verb **say** each time.

Your story will be more interesting if you vary the words which report what each character says. For example:

> *'Stop that racket!'* **snapped** *Miss Grump.*

> *'Don't look now, but there's a ghost behind us,'* **whispered** *Evie.*

These sound far more interesting than simply *said Miss Grump* and *said Evie*.

Exclamations

Lively dialogue can bring the characters in your story to life. Try using **exclamations** at exciting moments in your story.

If a character in your story suddenly gets angry or annoyed, what might they say?

> *'**Blast** that parrot!' said Captain Cutlass with an evil leer.*

> *'**Bother**! The magic potion is wearing off!' said Megan, frowning.*

EXPLORER TIP

The panels for **say** and **exclamation** have ideas that you can use to write dialogue.

Writing non–fiction

Your thesaurus can help you with **non-fiction** writing, too. There are lots of different types of non-fiction writing. In fact, it's everywhere, from food packaging to board game instructions, reports in newspapers and on websites, diary entries, explanations about how things work, brochures that give you advice and texts that try to sell you things.

Unlike fiction, non-fiction is based on fact, things that are true or have happened. You write non-fiction when you are describing something that happened to you, something you did or saw or something else that you believe to be true.

- How can you describe a *book* you have read, or a *place* you have visited?

- What words can you use to report a *sports match*?

- What words can you use in a *recipe* for cooking?

If you are writing a book review, how might you describe the way that the book ends?

> *'Smugglers Cove' hurtles towards a* **gripping finale***. The final chapter is a* **nail-biting** *description of a sea chase.*

If you are writing a report of a football match, how might you describe the winning goal?

> *Martinez* **dribbled** *the ball past two* **defenders***, then* **chipped** *it across to the* **captain** *who* **blasted** *it into the back of the net.*

EXPLORER TIP

You will find useful words and phrases to describe a book in the **WRITING TIPS** panel for **writing**.

EXPLORER TIP

You will find words that are used in various sports in the **WORD WEB** panels for **football, tennis**, etc. You can also get ideas for how a player might hit or throw a ball in the **WRITING TIPS** panel for **ball**.

Word webs for non-fiction writing

In the thesaurus the **WORD WEB** panels include lists of related words which can give you ideas or information on that topic.

For example, if you are writing a project on animals, look up the **animal** panel to find:

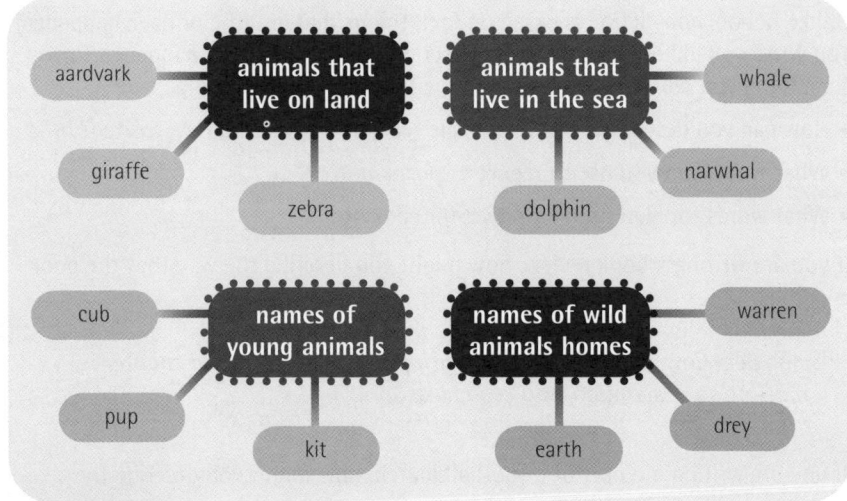

aardvark · **animals that live on land** · giraffe · zebra

animals that live in the sea · whale · narwhal · dolphin

cub · **names of young animals** · pup · kit

names of wild animals homes · warren · earth · drey

EXPLORER TIP

You can easily spot **WORD WEBS** in the thesaurus.
They are treated in special panels and have this symbol next to them:

There is a complete list of **WORD WEB** panels at the front of the thesaurus.

Explore further . . .

Like a good explorer, be prepared to follow a trail. The *see also* sections in the **WORD WEBS** will help you to find other panels with related information. For example, the panel for **dinosaur** points you also to **prehistoric**, where you will find a list of other prehistoric animals.

You may want to explore your topic further by looking up the listed words in a dictionary or an encyclopedia.

The Five Ws

To help you make sure your writing is clear for your reader, especially if you are writing a report or retelling an event, think about the **FIVE Ws**:

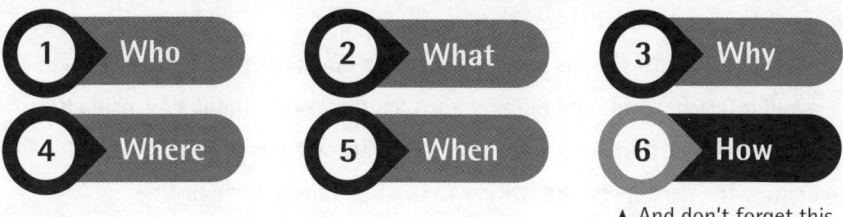

1 Who   **2** What   **3** Why

4 Where   **5** When   **6** How

▲ And don't forget this extra one!

Ask yourself:

- **Who** are you talking about or to?
- **What** are you trying to say? **What** happened?
- **Why** are you wanting to tell your reader this? **Why** did it happen?

- **Where** did this take place?
- **When** did this take place?
- **How** did it happen?

You don't need to answer these questions directly within your writing, but keep them in mind to help make sure your writing is clear.

Writing letters

When you are writing a **letter** or email, think about who you are writing to and why. This will help you decide what type of letter to write.

> You might write a formal letter to a teacher, but an informal email to a friend.

> You might send informal invitations to your birthday party, but receive a formal invitation to a wedding.

If a character in your story writes a letter, it should also fit with the person and situation you are describing.

> A medieval knight would write an elaborate, formal letter to a king.

> A spy might send a hasty, informal email to headquarters.

TOP TIPS When writing letters it's important to remember to use paragraphs so the reader can clearly follow what you are saying.

Paragraphs divide up your thoughts and make it easier for the reader to understand different points you are making. This is important, whether it's a letter to your friend or a letter in a story where your warrior is describing all the adventures they have been on!

See page 498 for some tips on writing formal and informal letters.

Formal letters:

In a **formal letter**, you should:

- write in complete sentences
- avoid short forms such as *don't* and *I'm* (use *do not* and *I am*)
- avoid informal words and phrases, such as *thanks* (use *thank you* instead)
- begin with *Dear*, and end with *Yours sincerely* or *Yours faithfully*
- address the person you are writing to by their family name or title (if you don't know their name, call them *Sir* or *Madam*)

> *Dear Prince Charming,*
>
> *Thank you for your invitation to the Palace Ball on Saturday. Unfortunately I am unable to come, as I must stay at home all evening to sweep the floors. Please accept my apologies.*
>
> *Yours sincerely,*
> *Cinderella*

Informal letters:

Informal letters and emails are often chatty in tone, as if you were speaking rather than writing the words.

- use incomplete sentences
- use short forms such as *don't* and *I'm*
- use informal words and phrases, such as *terrific* or *thanks*
- use exclamation marks when you (or your characters) are excited
- begin with *Dear* or *Hello* or *Hi* (or just a name), and end with *Yours* or *Best wishes*
- call the person you are writing to by their first or given name, or by a nickname

> *Dear Cinders*
>
> *Just had a terrific idea! Meet me at the kitchen door at 6pm on Sat. Bring a pumpkin and a few mice.*
>
> *Yours*
> *Fairy Godmother*

EXPLORER TIP

Use the **WORD WEB** panel at **communication** to help you look for ways to address people you are speaking to or writing to.

Types of writing

There are four main types of writing, these are:

Descriptive writing

Explanatory writing

Narrative writing

Persuasive writing

Descriptive writing

Descriptive writing gives your reader detailed descriptions, about a place or a character, to help create a vivid picture in their mind.

Instead of a sunset being *pretty*, perhaps it is *extraordinarily beautiful, with colours of amber, rose, fiery red and dashes of purple the shade of lavender.*

Explanatory writing

This type of writing is all about informing your reader of something. It is a factual piece of writing that aims to be as truthful as possible.

Cheetah's are the fastest animal on earth, they can run speeds of up to 75mph. Their spotty tan-coloured coat helps them to be camouflaged in their natural habitat.

TOP TIP To remember what it means, think *explain*, you are trying to explain some information.

Narrative writing

Narrative writing tells a sequence of events, such as in a fiction story or a recount of something that has happened in real life. You will find more tips on writing story narratives on pages 490-494.

Persuasive writing

This type of writing aims to persuade or convince the reader of something. Maybe you want them to buy something you're selling. Or perhaps you would like them to believe something you are telling them.

TOP TIP You can use **emotive language, alliteration, repetition,** and **questions** to help persuade them. This will make your writing stick in your reader's mind. If it sticks in their mind, they are more likely to do what you want, or at least remember what you said!

Punctuation

Punctuation makes writing easier to read and understand. Explore the punctuation that you can use in your writing on these pages.

full stop
.

A **full stop** comes at the end of a sentence. It marks the end of a clause or several related clauses, and creates a pause in your writing.

The journey to the castle was very long.

comma
,

A **comma** separates items in a list, or parts of a sentence:
Hedgehogs eat slugs, snails and worms.

After four days at sea, we sighted land.

apostrophe
'

An **apostrophe** shows that a letter is missing, or tells you who something belongs to:
Don't enter the dragon's lair! = Do not enter the lair of the dragon!

These punctuation marks are especially useful for writing dialogue in a story:

quotation marks
' ' *or* **" "**

Quotation marks come before and after words that a character says:
'My name,' said the knight, 'is Sir Joustalot.'

TOP TIP You can use single or double quotation marks. Remember to be consistent.

question mark
?

A **question mark** comes at the end of a question:
'How old are you?'
I asked the wizard.

TOP TIP You don't need a question mark if the question is reported, not spoken:
I asked the wizard how old he was.

exclamation mark
!

An **exclamation mark** comes after a shout, or can be used to show that a character has a strong emotion, such as excitement, shock, surprise, anger.
'Wow! Look at the size of that crater!'

: colon

A **colon** can be used to introduce a list, an idea, an example or an explanation.

TOP TIP You don't need a capital letter after a colon unless the word is a proper noun.

; semi colon

A **semi colon**:

1 Connects two independent clauses: *It was cold outside; they wanted to leave.*

2 Divides up longer phrases in a list.

3 Shows a longer break in a sentence than a comma.

( ) *or* [ ] brackets

Brackets are used to include extra information within a sentence.

My friend is coming over after school to have tea (I am very excited!).

- hyphen

A **hyphen** can be used to join words to make one word, called a compound word. A hyphen in a compound word can be very helpful. *A man eating tiger* is different to *a man-eating tiger.*

Can you see the difference?

— dash

A **dash** is a short line. It can be used to emphasize a phrase, introduce additional information and separate or connect separate clauses in a sentence: *I enjoy running—I can run faster than my brother.*

... ellipsis

An **ellipsis** is a punctuation mark of three dots. It shows that something is missing or indicates a long pause: *They opened the chest and discovered ... hidden treasure!*

EXPLORER TIP

The **WORD WEB** panel for **punctuation** lists various punctuation marks that you might use or come across. You will find more tips on writing **dialogue** and using **exclamations** in the **Writing stories** section on pages 490-494.

Confusable words

Take extra care when you use any of these **confusable words** in your writing. Although the words in each group sound alike, they each have a different spelling (some with an apostrophe) and a different meaning. If you choose the wrong one, your writing will not make sense.

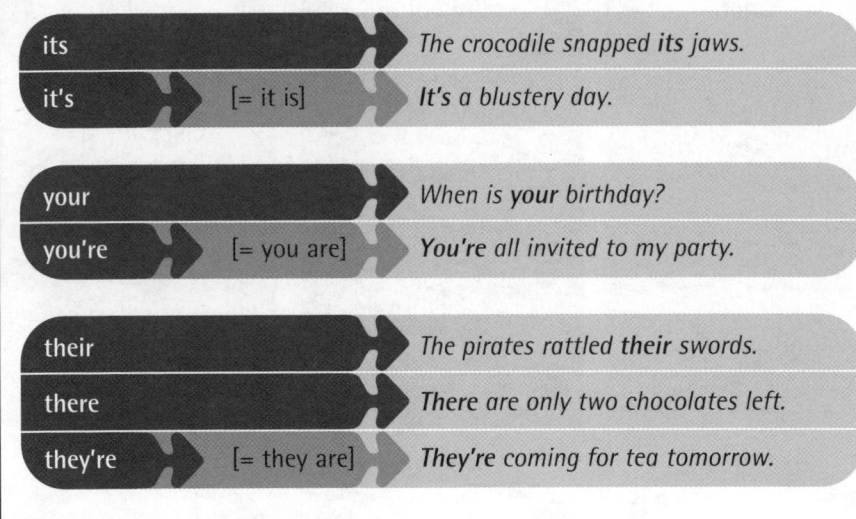

| its | *The crocodile snapped its jaws.* |
| it's [= it is] | *It's a blustery day.* |

| your | *When is your birthday?* |
| you're [= you are] | *You're all invited to my party.* |

their	*The pirates rattled their swords.*
there	*There are only two chocolates left.*
they're [= they are]	*They're coming for tea tomorrow.*

Note the three different spellings in this example:

'Where are the penguins?'
*'**They're** over **there**, feeding **their** chicks.'*

Have fun on your **creative adventure!**